Families
Changing Trends in Canada

FIFTH EDITION

Maureen Baker
General Editor
University of Auckland

Patrizia Albanese
Ryerson University

Bettina Bradbury
York University

Walter S. DeKeseredy
University of Ontario Institute of Technology

Margrit Eichler
OISE and University of Toronto

Meg Luxton
York University

Susan A. McDaniel
University of Windsor

Gillian Ranson
University of Calgary

Glenda Wall
Wilfrid Laurier University

Sue Wilson
Ryerson University

Zheng Wu and Christoph M. Schimmele
University of Victoria

 **McGraw-Hill
Ryerson**

Toronto Montréal Boston Burr Ridge, IL Dubuque, IA Madison, WI New York San Francisco
St. Louis Bangkok Bogotá Caracas Kuala Lumpur Lisbon London Madrid
Mexico City Milan New Delhi Santiago Seoul Singapore Sydney Taipei

McGraw-Hill Ryerson

FAMILIES
Changing Trends in Canada
Fifth Edition

Statistics Canada information is used with the permission of the Minister of Industry, as Minister responsible for Statistics Canada. Information on the availability of the wide range of data from Statistics Canada can be obtained from Statistics Canada's Regional Offices, its World Wide Web site at http://www.statcan.ca, and its toll-free access number 1-800-263-1136.

ISBN: 0-07-091685-3

1 2 3 4 5 6 7 8 9 10 TCP 0 9 8 7 6 5

Care has been taken to trace ownership of copyright material contained in this text; however, the publisher will welcome any information that enables them to rectify any reference or credit for subsequent editions.

Vice President and Editorial Director: Pat Ferrier
Senior Sponsoring Editor: James Buchanan
Developmental Editor: Christine Gilbert
Sales Manager: Tim McCleary
Senior Marketing Manager: Sharon Loeb
Editorial Coordinator: Carole Harfst
Manager, Editorial Services: Kelly Dickson
Supervising Editor: Joanne Limebeer
Copy Editor: Jim Zimmerman
Senior Production Coordinator: Jennifer Wilkie
Composition: Dianna Little
Cover Design: Dianna Little
Cover Image: © Rick Fischer/Masterfile
Printer: Transcontinental Printing Group

National Library of Canada Cataloguing in Publication Data

Families : changing trends in Canada / Maureen Baker, general editor ; Patrizia Albanese ... [et al.]. -- 5th ed.

First ed. published under title: The family : changing trends in Canada.
Includes bibliographical references and index.
ISBN 0-07-091685-3

1. Family--Canada. I. Baker, Maureen II. Albanese, Patricia

HQ560.F34 2004   306.85'0971   C2004-904580-6

Printed in Canada

Brief Contents

PART ONE: **CONCEPTUALIZING FAMILIES**   **1**

Chapter One: Definitions, Cultural Variations, and Demographic Trends
Maureen Baker   3

Chapter Two: Conceptualizing "Families": Theoretical Frameworks
and Family Research   *Meg Luxton*   29

Chapter Three: Biases in Family Literature   *Margrit Eichler*   52

PART TWO: **INDUSTRIALIZATION, IMMIGRATION,
WORK, AND FAMILIES**   **69**

Chapter Four: Social, Economic, and Cultural Origins of
Contemporary Families   *Bettina Bradbury*   71

Chapter Five: Paid and Unpaid Work: How Do Families
Divide Their Labour?   *Gillian Ranson*   99

Chapter Six: Ethnic Families   *Patrizia Albanese*   121

PART THREE: **THE DYNAMICS OF FAMILY LIFE**   **143**

Chapter Seven: Partnering, Cohabitation, and Marriage
Sue J. Wilson   145

Chapter Eight: Childhood and Child Rearing   *Glenda Wall*   163

Chapter Nine: The Family Lives of the Middle-Aged and Elderly in Canada
Susan A. McDaniel   181

PART FOUR: **FAMILIES, LAWS, AND POLICIES**   **201**

Chapter Ten: Divorce and Repartnering
Zheng Wu and Christoph Schimmele   202

Chapter Eleven: Patterns of Family Violence
Walter S. DeKeseredy   229

Chapter Twelve: Families, the State, and Family Policies
Maureen Baker   258

PART FIVE: **THE FUTURE OF FAMILY LIFE**   **277**

Chapter Thirteen: The Future of Family Life
Maureen Baker   279

Table of Contents

List of Tables and Figures   xii
Preface   xiv

PART ONE: **CONCEPTUALIZING FAMILIES**   **1**

Chapter One: **Definitions, Cultural Variations, and Demographic Trends**
                                 Maureen Baker   3

Introduction   3
Defining Families   4
Cultural Variations in Families   6
Nuclear vs. Extended Families   6
    Monogamy vs. Polygamy   7
    Free-Choice and Arranged Marriage   8
    Patterns of Authority, Descent, and Inheritance   11
Family Trends   12
    The Decline of Legal (Heterosexual) Marriage   13
    Fertility Trends: Declining and Delayed   14
    More Mothers in Paid Work   17
    Rise in Births outside Marriage   18
    Low Adoption Rates   19
    The Increasing Use of Medically Assisted Conception   20
    Rising Rates of Separation and Divorce   21
    The Increase in Lone-Parent Families   23
    More Blended Families   25
    Changing Canadian Families   26
    Suggested Readings   28
    Web Resources   28

Chapter Two: **Conceptualizing "Families": Theoretical Frameworks**
                     and Family Research   *Meg Luxton*   29

Introduction   29
Conceptualizing the Problem   31
    Common-Sense Assumptions   31
    The Meanings of "Family"   31
    Shifting Patterns of Family   32
The History and Development of Sociological Theories   34
Contemporary Sociological Theories   37
    Liberal Theories   37
    Marxist and Feminist Theories   42
    Postmodernity and Postmodernism or Poststructuralist Theory   47

Conclusion   49
    Suggested Readings   49
    Web Resources   50
    Endnotes   50

Chapter Three: Biases in Family Literature   52
                    Margrit Eichler

Introduction   52
Definitions of the Family   53
Biases   55
    Monolithic Bias   55
    Conservative Bias   56
    Ageist Bias   58
    Sexist Bias   58
    Microstructural Bias   59
    Racist Bias   60
    Heterosexist Bias   60
Example of the Application of the Biases   61
Conclusion   63
Appendix   64
    Parenthood after the New Reproductive Technologies   64
    Fatherhood after the New Reproductive Technologies   64
    Motherhood with the New Reproductive Technologies   65
    Suggested Readings   66
    Web Resources   67
    Endnotes   67

PART TWO: INDUSTRIALIZATION, IMMIGRATION,
                 WORK, AND FAMILIES   69

Chapter Four: Social, Economic, and Cultural Origins of
                   Contemporary Families   *Bettina Bradbury*   **71**

Introduction   71
Ongoing Cultural Confrontations   72
    First Nations and Europeans   72
    Competing Visions of Family among French Canadians and the English
        before and after the Conquest   76
    Canadians and Immigrants: Four Centuries of Family Confrontations 80
Class and Family Economies   83
    Farming and Artisanal Families   83
    Industrialization, Urbanization, and the Expansion of the Working Classes 84
    Changing Middle-Class Families, Changing Society   89
Continuities and Changes   92

Love, Abuse, and Family Breakup 92
The Particularities of the 1950s and 1960s 93
Conclusion 96
Suggested Readings 97
Web Resources 98

Chapter Five: Paid and Unpaid Work: How Do Families Divide Their Labour? *Gillian Ranson* **99**

Introduction: Work, Income, and Families 99
The Economy and Paid Work 100
Economic Change 100
Changes in the Labour Force, Changes in Work 101
Gender at Work 103
Families and Earning 104
The Division of Caring Work 105
Childcare 105
Unpaid Work in the Home 109
Connecting Paid Work and Family Work 113
Unionization 114
Organizations and "Work-Life Balance" 115
Gender, Ideology, and the Division of Labour 116
"Doing Gender" 117
Conclusion 119
Suggested Readings 120
Web Resources 120

Chapter Six: Ethnic Families *Patrizia Albanese* **121**

Introduction 121
Defining Ethnicity and Race 122
Ethnicity 122
Race 122
Canada—A Land of Immigrants? 123
Immigration Policies and Family Life 125
The Early Years 126
White Families Wanted—Settling the Prairies (1896–1914) 127
Chinese and East Indian Bachelor Communities 128
Industrialization/Urbanization and Post-War Immigrant Families 130
Post-1967—Merit Point System 130
Ethnicity through the Life Course: Family Demography of Immigrants 131
Mate Selection and Rates of Ethnic Exogamy 132
Cohabitation 133
Work and Economic Life of Immigrant Families 134
Fertility, Family Size, and Parenting 136
Stress and Conflict—A Focus on Domestic Violence 138

Immigrant Household Structure   139
Aging and Ethnicity   140
Conclusion   141
Suggested Readings   141
Web Resources   142

PART THREE: THE DYNAMICS OF FAMILY LIFE   **143**

Chapter Seven: Partnering, Cohabitation, and Marriage
Sue J. Wilson   **145**

Introduction   145
The Development of Intimate Relationships   146
Sexuality and Intimacy   147
Theories: Similarities and Differences between Partners   150
Exchange Theory   152
Cohabitation and Marriage   154
Marriage   155
Children   158
Gay and Lesbian Partnering   159
Predicting Marital Happiness and Stability   160
Conclusion   161
Suggested Readings   162
Web Resources   162

Chapter Eight: Childhood and Child Rearing
Glenda Wall   **163**

Introduction   163
Child-Rearing Advice throughout the 20th Century   164
Advice in the Early 20th Century   164
Child-Rearing Advice in the Latter Half of the 20th Century   165
The Role of Developmental Psychology   166
Maternal Deprivation   166
Attachment   167
Children's Needs and Child Rearing Today   168
Intensive Parenting   168
Child-Rearing Advice and New Brain Science   172
The Child in the Womb   173
Childhood in Canada Today and in the Future   175
Conclusion   179
Suggested Readings   180
Web Resources   180
Endnotes   180

Chapter Nine: **The Family Lives of the Middle-Aged and Elderly in Canada**
Susan A. McDaniel   **181**

Introduction   181
What is Middle Age and When Does It Begin?   182
The Historical Emergence and Diversity of Mid-Life Families   183
Families as They Age   185
Canadian Families in Middle and Old Age: Demographics   187
Caregiving Families: The Mid-Life Family Crunch   189
Social Policies, Entitlement, and Gender in Mid-Life Families   193
Work, Work-Leaving, and Retirement for Mid-Life and Older Families   194
Conclusion   197
    Suggested Readings   198
    Web Resources   198
    Endnotes   199

PART FOUR: **FAMILIES, LAWS, AND POLICIES**   **201**

Chapter Ten: **Divorce and Repartnering**
Zheng Wu and Christoph Schimmele   **202**

Introduction   202
Historical Perspective   203
The Divorce Revolution   204
Micro-Level Differences in Divorce   207
Canadian Divorce Law   209
Interpreting Divorce   212
Divorce Outcomes   215
    Economic Consequences   215
    Child Custody and Access   217
Repartnering   221
    Cohabitation   224
    Stepfamilies   225
Conclusion   226
    Suggested Readings   227
    Web Resources   228

Chapter Eleven: **Patterns of Family Violence**
Walter S. DeKeseredy   **229**

Introduction   229
Definition of Violence in the Family   229
    The Breadth of Definitions   230
    Narrow Definitions   231
    Broad Definitions   234

Language   236
Summary   238
"Living in a House of Horrors": Wife Abuse   239
    The Extent of Wife Abuse   239
    Theories of Wife Abuse   240
"Spare the Rod and Spoil the Child": Child Abuse   242
    The Extent of Child Abuse   244
    Theories of Child Abuse   246
"A Normal Part of Growing Up": Sibling Violence   247
    Definition of Sibling Violence   248
    Why Is Sibling Violence Overlooked?   248
    The Extent of Sibling Violence   250
    Theories of Sibling Violence   251
The Dark Side of the Golden Years: Elder Abuse   252
    The Extent of Elder Abuse   252
    Theories of Elder Abuse   253
Conclusion   254
    Suggested Readings   256
    Web Resources   256
    Endnotes   257

Chapter Twelve: Families, the State, and Family Policies
                    Maureen Baker   **258**

State Intervention and Family Discourse   258
Gendered Practices in the Patriarchal Family   260
Provincial Social Assistance and Social Service Programs   263
Maternity/Paternity Leave and Benefits   265
Federal Child and Family Benefits   266
Comparing the Generosity of Family Policies   271
Advocacy for Family Reform   272
Conclusion   275
    Suggested Readings   276
    Web Resources   276
    Endnotes   276

PART FIVE: THE FUTURE OF FAMILY LIFE   **277**

Chapter Thirteen: The Future of Family Life
                    Maureen Baker   **279**

The Changing Focus of Family Research   279
The Future of Family Life   283
    Dating, Cohabitation, and Marriage   283
    Gendered Households in the Future   286
    Child-Bearing and Adoption in the Future   289

The Future of Families in Mid-Life and Later Life 291
The Impact of Immigration and Cultural Differences on Family Life 295
Conclusion 296
  Suggested Readings 297
  Web Resources 297

Glossary 299

References 309

Credits 345

Index 347

List of Tables and Figures

Chapter 1

Table 1.1   Crude Birth Rates in Canada, 1851–2001
Table 1.2   Labour Force Participation Rates of Canadian Parents, by Marital Status and Age of Child, 1978, 1988, and 1998
Table 1.3   Divorce Rates in Selected Countries (per 1,000 population), 1973 and 1998
Table 1.4   Summary Statistics of Canadian Families

Chapter 2

Figure 2.1   Turn-of-the-Century Theories

Chapter 3

Figure 3.1   Dimensions of Familial Interaction

Chapter 5

Figure 5.1   Proportion of Fathers Claiming Parental Leave
Figure 5.2   Parents Aged 25 to 44, with Children under 25

Chapter 6

Table 6.1   Toronto's Immigrants: Top Ten Source Countries (Principal Applicants and Dependants)
Table 6.2   Major Occupation Groups of Immigrants before and after Arriving in Canada, 2001

Chapter 7

Table 7.1   Proportion of Mixed-Race Unions
Figure 7.1   Probability for Women of Experiencing a Marriage or a Common-Law Union as a First Union, Canada, 2001
Figure 7.2   Marriages per 1,000 Population, Canada, 1921–2001

Chapter 8

Table 8.1   Percentage Employment of Mothers by Family Status and Age of Youngest Child, 1976–2003
Figure 8.1   Percentage of Children with Delayed Vocabulary, by Household Income
Figure 8.2   Percentage of Children with Basic Health Problems Related to Daily Functioning, by Household Income

Chapter 9

Table 9.1   Providing Unpaid Care to Seniors by Hours Spent per Week,
                 1996 and 2001 Censuses of Canada, Men and Women (100,000)
Table 9.2   The Quandaries of Those in Mid-Life in Canada in 2002

Chapter 10

Table 10.1   Cumulative Percentage of Marital Disruption by Marriage Cohort
Figure 10.1   Total Divorce Rate: Canada, 1969–2000
Table 10.2   Cumulative Percentage of Repartnering after Marital Disruption
Figure 10.2   Remarriage Rate: Canada, 1955–1989

Chapter 11

Table 11.1   North American Wife Abuse Surveys
Figure 11.1   The Economic Exclusion/Male Peer Support Model

Chapter 12

Table 12.1   The Establishment and Reform of Social Benefits in Canada
Table 12.2   Child Poverty Rates by Household Type in Selected Countries

Preface

The 5th edition of *Families: Changing Trends in Canada* features five new contributors and incorporates recent family research, legal reforms, and updated statistics about family demography and paid/unpaid work. Generally, this new edition shows that family life in Canada, as elsewhere, is always changing, influenced by patterns of work and migration, by cultural and technological transformations, by laws and social policies, and by personal choice.

Since the first edition was published in 1984, research on family life has burgeoned, including the analysis of four censuses and numerous demographic surveys, new studies in social history, extensive legal debates, and a growing focus on cultural difference in families. In addition, theoretical approaches that incorporate poststructuralist and feminist theory have been further developed. In all five editions, I have attempted to design a Canadian post-secondary textbook that caters to students interested in the sociology of families, but one that also is interdisciplinary, historical, and comparative. This book deliberately uses and critiques various theoretical perspectives, but most chapters favour a feminist and structuralist approach.

Acknowledgements

Preparing a book like this involves the work of many people. All the contributors were carefully selected for their expertise in an aspect of family research. I appreciate the fact that all these busy academics were able to prepare their chapters within the company's time frame. All the contributors were involved in other writing, research, teaching, and administrative projects, as well as family activities, and several were changing jobs and moving house.

Numerous reviewers also helped to make this edition possible. McGraw-Hill Ryerson engaged several to read the 4th edition and to suggest changes for the new version; several other reviewers were engaged to read the first draft of the 5th edition manuscript and suggest further revisions. I would like to thank all these people for their time and useful suggestions:

Dr. Alison Thomas, *University of Victoria*
Karen Wightman, *Saskatchewan Institute of Applied Science and Technology (SIAST)*
Mary E. Morton, *Queen's University*
Michelle K. Owen, *University of Winnipeg*
Dr. Elaine Porter, *Laurentian University*
Stephen H. Riggins, *Memorial University*
Jane Gordon, *Mount St. Vincent University*
Helene Cummins, *Brescia College – University of Western Ontario*
Debra Clarke, *Trent University*
Robert Biezenski, *University of Regina*

Linda Parsons, *Memorial University*
Michelle Webber, *Brock University*
Scott Kline, *St. Jerome's University – University of Waterloo*
Barbara A. Mitchell, *Simon Fraser University*
Joan E. Norris, *University of Guelph*
Dr. Don Swenson, *Mount Royal College*

At McGraw-Hill Ryerson, I want to thank James Buchanan, who first persuaded me to begin the 5th edition, Joanne Limebeer for her work as the supervising editor, and Jim Zimmerman who completed the copy editing. Most of all, I want to express my appreciation for the efforts of Christine Gilbert, our developmental editor, who clearly understood the tasks involved in preparing this book from the other side of the world.

Professor Maureen Baker
Department of Sociology
University of Auckland
Auckland, New Zealand
July 2004

What's New and Updated in the Fifth Edition?

Chapter 1 – Definitions, Cultural Variations, and Demographic Trends

- Updated statistics and legal sections
- Demographic trends revised to focus more on family trends

Chapter 2 – Conceptualizing "Families": Theoretical Frameworks and Family Research

- Updated statistics, using the data from the 2001 census
- Updated and new suggested readings

Chapter 3 – Biases in Family Literature

- Passage on heterosexist bias has been completely rewritten and updated
- Dimensions of familial interaction have been updated to include the Quebec civil union
- New Web resources added

Chapter 4 – Social, Economic, and Cultural Origins of Contemporary Families

- Updated and new suggested readings and Web sources
- New key terms added to glossary at end of the book

New Contributor! Chapter 5 – Paid and Unpaid Work: How Do Families Divide Their Labour?

- Chapter has been completely rewritten, with more in-depth discussion of the linkages between paid work and family work
- More information about childcare and parental benefits in Canada
- Attention to a greater diversity of family forms, notably the inclusion of same-sex couples
- A more nuanced discussion of family work as "caring"
- More theoretical discussion of gender and the division of labour
- Statistics using the data from the 2001 census are included
- New Web resources, suggested readings, and key terms

New Contributor! Chapter 6 – Ethnic Families

- Chapter has been completely revised from the previous edition to include a more complete general background on the history of Canadian immigration, with personal vignettes by the contributor about growing up as an Italian immigrant
- Chapter provides a more general overview of patterns, trends, and experiences
- Statistics using the data from the 2001 census are included
- New Web resources, suggested readings, and key terms

Chapter 7 – Partnering, Cohabitation, and Marriage

- Revised chapter title to reflect the recent trends in same-sex partners and marriage
- Updated and revised content on same-sex marriage and relations
- Updated statistics using the data from the 2001 census
- New section on exchange theory included
- Revised Web resources, suggested readings, and key terms

New Contributor! Chapter 8 – Childhood and Child Rearing

- Chapter has been completely rewritten from the previous edition, including current trends on child-rearing advice and childcare
- New sections on attachment theory and research
- Statistics using the data from the 2001 census are included
- New Web resources, suggested readings, and key terms

Chapter 9 – The Family Lives of the Middle-Aged and Elderly in Canada

- Updated statistics and tables using the data from the 2001 census
- Updated and new suggested readings
- Revised Web resources

New Contributors! Chapter 10 – Divorce and Repartnering

- Chapter title revised from previous edition to reflect current trends in same-sex marriage and relationships
- Chapter has been completely revised and updated from previous edition, using more up-to-date references and data
- Focus of chapter revised to emphasize how gender ideologies structured historical patterns of divorce and divorce legislation, and to illustrate that gender influences every major aspect of the divorce and repartnering process

- Historical perspectives section has been reformulated to address the ways social ideologies influence patterns of divorce and how modern divorce legislation must be understood in historical context
- New section on "Divorce Revolution" illustrates basic social, economic, and ideational changes behind revision of divorce legislation in Canada and how these changes triggered the rapid growth in the divorce rate
- Section on divorce law in Canada has also been revised
- New section on major sociological interpretations of divorce, replacing the Perspective on Divorce section
- Sections on divorce outcomes and remarriage have been completely rewritten

Chapter 11 – Patterns of Family Violence

- Updated statistics on the four variations of violence in the family
- Chapter revised to include new theoretical perspectives
- More concrete examples of abuse experienced by family members
- New Web resources and suggested readings

Chapter 12 – Families, the State, and Family Policies

- Updated statistics and legal sections
- Updated content on maternal/parental leave and benefits
- Revised and new Web resources and suggested readings

Chapter 13 – The Future of Family Life

- Updated statistics
- Chapter revised to provide more linkages to the other chapters
- Updated content on various topics such as adoption and the household
- Revised and new Web resources and suggested readings

Supplements

A full range of supplements is available to complement *Families: Changing Trends in Canada*, Fifth Edition.

For the Instructor:

i-Learning Sales Specialist:

Your **Integrated Learning Sales Specialist** is a McGraw-Hill Ryerson representative who has the experience, product knowledge, training, and support to help you assess and integrate any of the below-noted products, technology, and services into your course for optimum teaching and learning performance. Whether it's using our test bank software, helping your students improve their grades, or putting your entire course online, your *i*-Learning Sales Specialist is there to help you do it. Contact your local *i*-Learning Sales Specialist today to learn how to maximize all of McGraw-Hill Ryerson's resources!

i-Learning Services Program

McGraw-Hill Ryerson offers a unique *i*-Services package designed for Canadian faculty. Our mission is to equip providers of higher education with the superior tools and resources required for excellence in teaching. For additional information visit www.mcgrawhill.ca/highereducation/eservices.

Instructor's CD-Rom

This CD-ROM includes the Computerized Test Bank as well as the Instructor's Manual. The **Computerized Test Bank**, compiled by Maureen Baker, allows instructors to select, edit, and/or write their own questions, print exams, administer network-based tests, compile curve averages, generate reports, and more. The **Instructor's Manual** includes chapter summaries and discussion questions.

Online Learning Centre (www.mcgrawhill.ca/college/baker)

This text-specific Web site provides vital support for learning and teaching online. For students, it includes interactive quizzes and Web resources. For instructors, it includes downloadable supplements.

PageOut

PageOut (Online Course Management System)

With PageOut, an exclusive product of the McGraw-Hill Companies, you can create a professionally designed Web site in less than an hour. No knowledge of HTML coding is required. Simply fill in your course information and click on one of 16 designs. PageOut is free with an adoption of any McGraw-Hill Ryerson text.

For the Student:

Online Learning Centre (www.mcgrawhill.ca/college/baker)

This Web site includes a searchable online version of the text's Glossary, hyperlinks to all end-of-chapter Web Resources, Suggested Readings, and interactive multiple choice and true/false questions for student review. (Note to instructors: The quiz questions do *not* reproduce Test Bank questions.)

S-STAT Σ-STAT

Σ-Stat is Statistics Canada's education resource that allows socioeconomic and demographic data to be viewed in charts, graphs, and maps. Access to Σ-Stat and the CANSIM II database is made available to purchasers of the book, via the Baker Website, by special agreement between McGraw-Hill Ryerson and Statistics Canada. The Online Learning Centre provides additional information.

About the Contributors

Maureen Baker, General Editor, is Professor of Sociology at the University of Auckland in New Zealand. She received her doctorate in Sociology from the University of Alberta in 1975. Since then, she has taught in Canada, Australia, and New Zealand. From 1984 to 1990, she worked as a senior researcher for Canada's Parliament, specializing in policy issues relating to families, women, and children. From 1990 to 1997, Professor Baker taught at McGill University. She is the author or editor of 13 books and over 70 articles on family trends, cross-national family policies, women and work, and comparative restructuring. She has lived in New Zealand since January 1998.

Patrizia Albanese is Assistant Professor of Sociology at Ryerson University. She received her undergraduate degree from the University of Western Ontario (Sociology and History), and her M.A. and Ph.D from the University of Toronto (Sociology) in 2003. She has published on the impact of the rise of nationalism on gender and family policies. Her most recent publication examined women's reproductive rights under nationalist regimes in selected European nations. Professor Albanese currently is researching housework and lifelong learning (with Margrit Eichler, OISE/UT), and assessing the impact of $7/day childcare on an economically disadvantaged region of Quebec.

Bettina Bradbury teaches women's studies and gender history at York University, and is the author of many articles on the history of families and widowhood. Her book, *Working Families: Age, Gender and Daily Survival in Industrializing Montreal* (McClelland and Stewart, 1993), received both the John A. Macdonald prize for the best book in Canadian history published in 1993, and the Harold A. Innis prize for the most outstanding book published with an Aid to Scholarly Publications Grant in English that year. Professor Bradbury is currently completing a manuscript entitled *Wife to Widow: 19th Century Lives, Laws and Politics* which explores legal, political, and personal aspects of marriage and widowhood in Montreal. Current research projects involve comparative studies of marriage in the British Empire.

Walter S. DeKeseredy is Professor of Criminology at The University of Ontario Institute of Technology. He has published nearly 50 referenced journal articles and numerous book chapters on woman abuse, crime in public housing, and criminological theory. In 1995, Professor DeKeseredy received the Critical Criminologist of the Year Award from the American Society of Criminology's Division on Critical Criminology. In 1993, he received Carleton University's Research Achievement Award. Currently, he serves on the editorial boards of *Criminal Justice, Women & Criminal Justice, Violence Against Women: An International and Interdisciplinary Journal*, and *Crime and Delinquency*. Professor DeKeseredy currently is conducting an exploratory study, funded by the National Institute of Justice, of sexual assault during and after separation/divorce in three rural Ohio communities.

Margrit Eichler is Professor of Sociology and Equity Studies in Education at the Ontario Institute for Studies in Education at the University of Toronto. She has published numerous books, chapters, and articles on family policy, Women's Studies, feminist methodology, reproductive technologies, feminist eco-sociology, and other areas. She is currently working on an empirical study of housework and on further developing a bias-free approach to research to avoid biases based on gender, race, disability, or any other social hierarchy. Professor Eichler is a fellow of the Royal Society of Canada and the European Academy of Sciences, and a former President of the Canadian Research Institute for the Advancement of Women and the Canadian Sociology and Anthropology Association.

Meg Luxton is a Professor and Graduate Programme Director in the School of Women's Studies, York University, Toronto. She has published extensively on women's work, paid and unpaid, families, social policy, and the women's movement in Canada.

Susan A. McDaniel is Vice-President, Research, of the University of Windsor and Professor of Sociology. She was, for 15 years, Professor of Sociology at the University of Alberta. Her research interests include generational relations and shifts, the restructuring of the welfare state, family change and demographic aging, social contexts of innovation, and the social impacts of technology. Professor McDaniel is the author of many books, research articles, and book chapters, a frequent keynote speaker at national and international conferences, and a frequent advisor on social policies and official data collection to governments in Canada, the UK, and the EU. Professor McDaniel serves as the ISA representative to the United Nations for 2002-2006, and chairs a national Task Force on Enhancing Social Science Research Capacity in Canada. She is a Fellow of the Royal Society of Canada and recipient of many research and other awards, including the University Cup (2002).

Gillian Ranson is Associate Professor of Sociology at the University of Calgary. Her research interests are in the interwoven fields of gender, families, and work, and she has published numerous articles and book chapters on these topics. Currently, she is working on a book about couples who confound gender stereotypes in the ways they organize and share paid work and family responsibilities. Professor Ranson also is co-investigator in an international, multi-disciplinary study of employment relations in information technology workplaces.

Christoph M. Schimmele is a full-time research assistant in the Department of Sociology at the University of Victoria. His current research focuses on various aspects of family demography and population health. He has an M.A. in political science from the University of Victoria, with a specialization in economic development.

Glenda Wall is Associate Professor and Chair of Sociology at Wilfrid Laurier University, where she teaches family sociology. Her research centres on historical and cultural representations of motherhood and childhood, with a particular focus on media representations and expert advice. Professor Wall is currently engaged in a study examining the impact on the lives and experiences of mothers of a recent development in child-rearing advice which emphasizes the importance of enhancing child brain potential.

Sue Wilson holds a PhD in Sociology and teaches at the School of Nutrition at Ryerson University, where she is Associate Dean of the Faculty of Community Services. Professor Wilson has written sociology textbooks as well as chapters in texts in the areas of family and women's work. Currently, she is co-authoring a book about mid-life women in Canada and is involved in research in the areas of breast cancer and spirituality.

Zheng Wu is Professor of Sociology at the University of Victoria. He is affiliated with the Population Research Group and the Centre on Aging at the University of Victoria, and the Centre for Studies in Demography and Ecology at the University of Washington. He researches family demography, social gerontology, and population health, and teaches demography, survey research methods, and statistics.

PART ONE

Conceptualizing Families

CHAPTER ONE

Definitions, Cultural Variations, and Demographic Trends

Maureen Baker

INTRODUCTION

Most of us were raised within a family and have visited the homes of friends, which provide a certain amount of knowledge of different dimensions of family life. Yet, if we generalize from our own experiences and those of our friends, we have a poor basis for understanding the sociology of family life. It is tempting to assume that others behave the way we do and share our beliefs, family patterns, and lifestyles. Furthermore, when we discover that some cultures prefer arranged marriages, allow more than one spouse, offer men the best food, or practise female circumcision, it is easy to become moralistic and judgmental. We need a broader approach to family life that focuses on social research and theory.

Sixty years ago, social scientists talked about "maternal instincts" and "natural sex differences." Now, they are more likely to argue that, although personality and aptitudes *may* be affected by physiology and genetic inheritance, they are also influenced by gendered and cultural practices within families and the larger society, as well as socio-economic constraints. Earlier biological theories of instincts and current theories of the genetic basis of human behaviour suggest that altering behaviour would be very difficult. In contrast, sociological theories argue that behaviour is largely learned and therefore can be modified. Valuable insights about the relativity of behaviour can be gained from an understanding of variations in family practices by culture and throughout history. These variations illustrate the importance of socialization and culturally based learning in the development of personal identity.

The fact that families are ancient institutions with many structural variations provides sociologists, anthropologists, and historians an opportunity to note patterns and trends over time and to uncover the socio-economic factors leading to change. Social scientists have tried to understand how behaviour inside families has been influenced by economic trends, such factors as the separation of home and men's work during industrialization, the expansion of the service sector of the economy in the 1960s to include more women in the labour force, and the trend toward non-family childcare in the 1980s. Furthermore, researchers and theorists have studied how these changes have led to the development of public discourse about "proper" behaviour for men and women within families. The analysis of relations between families and the economy encompasses a variety of topics, including changing perceptions of childhood and adolescence, the importance of domestic work to the larger society, variations in birth rates by social class, and the development of state policies affecting families.

Studying variations in family life may provide us with important but disturbing insights. If change is possible and family patterns are culturally specific, then our own way of life could be challenged. If monogamy is not universal, for example, maybe it is not intrinsically "wrong" to have more than one spouse at a time, despite the fact that our laws prohibit it. It is difficult not to take the study of family sociology personally, not to think of our own lifestyle and moral values while reading about others'. Furthermore, our own beliefs may interfere with attempts to study personal relationships and family life as objectively as possible. We also may be pressured to rethink the biological limitations of human behaviour as well as the strength of cultural prescriptions and social control.

In this chapter, we will define *family* and *household*, discuss some cultural variations, and then outline several trends occurring in family life in Canada and other industrialized countries.

DEFINING FAMILIES

Different definitions of "family" have been used in academic research, census taking, social policy, and social program delivery. All of these include parents and their children sharing a home, including single parents and heterosexual couples. Legal marriage is no longer a requirement for being a family, although cohabiting heterosexual couples are expected to share a home for a specified length of time, which varies by jurisdiction. Most definitions of family involve couples with children as well as those who have never reproduced or no longer live with their children. Lone parents, however, are expected to live with their children to be considered a family. Academic definitions of family also extend to three generations sharing a household or several siblings and their spouses and children, called an **extended family**. Some academics even broaden the definition to include those *considered* related, whether or not they really are.

Most definitions of family focus on its structure and legality, as well the functions the unit is assumed to provide for individual members and for the larger society. For example, anthropologists and sociologists from the 1940s to the 1970s provided definitions that sounded overly idealistic and conservative by today's standards. They stated that "the family" was both an economic and social unit, and was the basic institution of society. According to these early definitions, the family consisted of at least two adults of the opposite sex who shared economic resources, sexual intimacy, labour, accommodation, reproduction, and child rearing, and provided each other with companionship, assistance, love and respect, heirs and social status (Murdock, 1949; Goode, 1964). However, most sociologists have focused on the **nuclear family**, consisting of parents and their children sharing a residence. As family life has changed over the years, this definition has been challenged as ideological and less representative of today's reality. As Beck and Beck-Gernsheim argued in *The Normal Chaos of Love* (1995: 147): "Family research is only gradually waking up from its drowsy fixation on the nucleus of the family."

The most prevalent definition used in Canadian research and policy making is Statistics Canada's **census family**. This unit includes a married couple with or without never-married children or a single parent living together with never-married children. These "children" may be any age as long as they have never been married. According to the government, cohabiting couples living together for longer than one year are considered to be married, although separate statistics are kept for legally married and cohabiting couples. Until recently, only heterosexual couples could legally marry in this country. Since 2003, British Columbia, Ontario, and Quebec have passed legislation to permit gay and lesbian couples to enter civil unions, as in the Netherlands and Belgium (Moore, 2003). As Margrit Eichler notes in Chapter Three, Canadian public opinion is divided on this issue.

Government definitions may not encompass the group that most people consider as their family, either through blood relationships, legal adoption, marriage, or feelings of closeness. Many have questioned why the government includes in their definition of family adult children who have never married, but excludes divorced children who have returned to their parents' home. Cultural groups who prefer to live in extended families argue that the definition of census family creates problems when they want to sponsor relatives as immigrants and misrepresents sources of caring and social support. Gays and lesbians in some provinces claim that these definitions assume that their family relationships are different and less valid, and consequently deprive them of family benefits. Yet definitions of this sort are always contentious, and a clear definition is necessary when taking a national census, designing a research project, or establishing eligibility for family benefits.

Statistics Canada also uses the term **economic family** to refer to people who are related by blood ties, marriage, or legal adoption, and are sharing a dwelling. The Canadian government also uses the term **household** in gathering statistics relating to family and personal life. A household is defined as the people sharing a dwelling, whether or not they are related by blood ties, legal adoption, or marriage. For example, a boarder might be part of the household, but not necessarily part of the family. Similarly, in some parts of the country, a same-sex couple would be considered as a household rather than a family.

Increasingly, researchers and advocacy groups are arguing that definitions of family should be broadened to encompass caring and enduring intimate relationships regardless of legal or blood ties (Eichler, 1997a; Jamieson, 1998; Smart and Neale, 1999). In other words, they suggest that the structure of the unit or its legality is less important in defining family than the shared feelings among participants or the services they provide for each other. In certain kinds of research such as comparative policy analysis, however, it may not be possible to define family in such a subjective way. Certainly, governments would not be willing to allow us to use our own definitions when they decide who is eligible for family benefits or other forms of state income support.

Despite varying definitions, it is necessary to clarify the meaning of family in this book. We will use the term "families" in the plural to indicate that there are many structures and acceptable definitions. We will also use qualifying words such as remarried families, commuter families, extended families, lone-parent families, and same-sex families to clarify our meaning. Without these qualifying words, family will refer to cohabiting or legally married couples (both heterosexual and same-sex) with or without dependent children, who share a home and are assumed to be sexually intimate, as well as lone parents or related adults raising children.

CULTURAL VARIATIONS IN FAMILIES

Nuclear vs. Extended Families

Most Canadians who live in families create households comprised only of couples or   parents and their children, which academics call nuclear families. Sociologists in the 1950s lamented the isolation of the modern nuclear family, implying that households used to contain more relatives prior to industrialization (Parsons and Bales, 1955). Historians, however, have argued that nuclear families were always the most typical living arrangements both Europe and among the European settlers to North America (Laslett, 1971; Goldthorpe, 1987). Nett (1981) contended that it had never been a widespread practice for married   couples to live with their parents at any time in Canadian history. Nevertheless, extended families have become slightly more prevalent in Canada with more immigration from southern Europe, Africa, and south Asia, and these extended families serve both as living arrangements and support groups. Different cultural groups tend to organize their living arrangements depending on traditions, religious beliefs, socio-economic background, immigrant or indigenous status, and historical experiences.

An extended family household may contain several siblings with their spouses and children, but often involves parents, children, and grandparents. Widowed parents may be invited to live with one of their children. In some cultures, brides are brought to the groom's family home to live with his parents and unmarried siblings. Even when they do not share a residence, many people maintain close ties with siblings and parents after marriage. Relatives may live next door or in the neighbourhood, visit regularly, telephone daily, assist with childcare, provide economic and emotional support, and help find employment and accommodation for one another (Paletta, 1992; Thomas, 2001). When relatives do not share a household but still maintain close contact, this has been called the **modified extended family**.

Extended family living was prevalent among certain cultural groups such as some First Nations People, and continues to be practised by many immigrants, such as some from Southern Europe, the Middle East, and south Asia. As well, extended family households are sometimes used in times of difficulty to provide assistance to family members. For example, mature-aged couples often provide short-term accommodation to their children in marital or financial crises, or a home for a widowed and frail parent in need of company or care.

Statistics Canada has collected data on the percentage of "multi-family households," which somewhat approximates the concept of extended family. From 1951 to 1986, the percentage of such households actually declined from 6.7 percent to only 1.1 percent despite the fact that many immigrants came from countries where people live in extended families, and widowed parents sometimes live with their married children (Ram 1990:44). The numbers remain low because most Canadians consider living alone more acceptable and feasible both for single persons and elderly widow(er)s. Also, many immigrant groups alter their traditional practices after coming to Canada.

Over the last decade the percentage of three-generation households increased by 39 percent, mainly as a result of increased Asian immigration. Yet only 3 percent of Canadian households included three generations in 1996 (Che-Alford and Hamm, 1999). Statistics

Canada data also show that 13% of Canadian-born people lived with relatives in 1996 compared to 26% of a sample of immigrants who came to Canada in 1985 (Thomas, 2001: 18). However, living with relatives is more prevalent among female immigrants, those with lower education and income, and recent arrivals (ibid: 21).

Monogamy vs. Polygamy

Monogamy, or having one legal spouse at a time, is the custom in Canada and most industrialized countries, and bigamy, or marrying two partners at once, is a criminal offence. Yet many Canadians marry more than once over their lifetime, referred to as **serial monogamy**. In the 19th and early 20th centuries, anthropologists and sociologists collected considerable information about comparative family and marriage structures. George Murdock (1949) concluded that the nuclear family was the basic family unit, although several nuclear families often lived together in larger households. Murdock also noted that only about 20 percent of the 554 societies he studied were strictly monogamous and 75 percent permitted **polygyny**, or having more than one wife at a time, and were characterized by a mixture of polygyny and monogamy. Since then, however, there has been a rise in monogamy with westernization.

Today, polygyny continues to be legal in some African countries as well as some in southern and western Asia, especially those using Moslem law. In sub-Saharan Africa throughout the 1990s, about half of married women aged 15-49 were in polygynous unions in Benin, Burkino Faso, and Guinea, and over 40 percent in Mali, Senegal, and Togo (United Nations, 2000: 28). These unions are far more common among rural and less-educated women in these countries, as well as those who do not work for pay, and tend to be associated with wider age gaps between husbands and wives and with patriarchal authority. Multiple wives are sometimes sisters, but they could also be unrelated women. Wives in polygynous marriages may resent their husband taking a new wife, but they may also welcome her companionship and help with household duties, childcare, and horticulture (Leslie and Korman, 1989: 27). Furthermore, when the husband marries a second wife, the rank of the first wife is elevated (United Nations, 2000: 28).

The term **polygamy** refers to the practice of having more than one spouse at a time, but polygyny is much more prevalent than **polyandry**, or the marriage of one woman to several husbands. More children can be born into marriages with several wives, and this could be important if children are a source of labour for the family or community. Paternity could be questioned in marriages with more than one husband, and identifying the father could be important. Obligations and rights flow from lineage, or to whom a child is related, and most societies make men responsible for supporting their children, especially within marriage.

In recent years, laws in all westernized countries have prohibited polygamy. This is due, in part, to the assumed difficulties of providing adequate financial and emotional support for more than one partner, but also relates to Christian ideas of sexual exclusivity. Some cultural communities in 19th century North America practised polygamy, including Mormons in Utah and Alberta, and the Oneida Community in New York State. Now, this is against the law, although polygyny continues to exist clandestinely in some communities, where a man may have one legal wife but in fact lives with other women.

In the Middle East and parts of Africa, polygamy may be permitted if a man can support all his wives.

Free-Choice and Arranged Marriage

In Canada and western countries, most of us choose our own marriage partner. Our laws require the consent of both bride and groom, so no one can be coerced into marriage. We are most likely to meet future partners in the classroom, at work, at community functions, or somewhere in our neighbourhood. Our friends and relatives may offer a little assistance by introducing us to potential mates, but we make our own final choices based on compatibility, physical attraction, and love. Yet there are definite cultural and gendered ideas about who is a "good catch." In Canada, heterosexual men are not encouraged to fall in love with a female partner who is taller, heavier, older, more educated, or with higher earning capacity than themselves. Partners are expected to have similar values, interests, and cultural backgrounds.

These prevalent ideas about suitability mean that older, taller, and highly educated women may find it more difficult to find a partner, as would younger, smaller, and less educated men with poor earning potential. For this reason, researchers sometimes talk about **marriage markets** and suggest that some people, such as beautiful women and rich men, have a higher value placed on them when looking for a partner. However, high divorce rates in North America suggest that we may be choosing our mates unwisely, perhaps emphasizing superficial characteristics such as physical appearance or sex appeal, rather than sound knowledge of the person's background and personality, or mutual respect, shared values, and companionship.

In many parts of the world, marriages are arranged because parents and older relatives feel that they are more qualified than young people to make such decisions, and in order to enhance family resources, reputation, and alliances. Some marriages are arranged in Middle Eastern and Moslem African countries, and in parts of Indonesia and Pakistan. The family of either bride or groom may make initial arrangements, but marriage brokers or intermediaries are often used to help the family find a suitable spouse for their offspring. This intermediary may be a family friend or relative, an acquaintance with an extensive network of contacts, or a professional marriage broker charging a fee for service.

Immigrants living in Canada sometimes participate in arranged or semi-arranged marriages. For example, relatives may identify several potential partners (which involves considerable networking among families), arrange initial meetings with potential partners and their relatives, and expect their young people to select one of the candidates for marriage. Other immigrants encourage their young people to return to their home country to marry a partner selected by marriage brokers or family members still living there. Increasingly, however, young people expect to have some choice from among several potential spouses or the right to veto all of them. However, considerable pressure may remain to abide by the judgment of elders, especially back in their home country (Nanda, 1991: 238).

In arranged marriages, a dowry is sometimes used to attract a marriage partner for a family's daughter, to cement an alliance between families, and to set up a new household, especially in rural areas. It may also provide a bride with some measure of financial security in case of partner abuse, divorce, or widowhood, depending on how much control

---

Exhibit 1.1   *Arranging a Marriage in India*

In India, almost all marriages are arranged. So customary is the practice of arranged marriage that there is a special name for a marriage that is not arranged: It is called a "love match."

As a young woman anthropologist in India for the first time, I found this custom of arranged marriage oppressive. It was contrary to everything I had been taught to believe about the importance of romantic love and individual choice as the only basis of a happy marriage.

At the first opportunity, I questioned young people I met about how they felt about the practice of arranged marriage. One of my first informants was Sita, a college graduate who had been waiting over a year while her parents were arranging a match for her.

"How can you go along with this?" I asked her. "Don't you care who you marry?"

"Of course I care," she answered. "That is why I must have my parents choose a boy for me. My marriage is too important to be arranged by such an inexperienced person as myself."

"But how can you marry the first man you meet? You will miss the fun of meeting a lot of different people and you will not give yourself the chance to know who is the right man for you," I countered.

"Meeting a lot of different men doesn't sound like any fun at all," Sita answered. "One hears that in America the girls spend all their time worrying whether they will meet a man and get married. Here we have the chance to enjoy our life and let our parents do this work and worry for us."

"I still can't imagine it," I said. "How can you agree to marry a man you hardly know?"

"But of course he will be known," she replied. "My parents would never arrange a marriage for me without knowing all about the boy and his family background. Naturally we will not rely on what the family tells us. We will check the particulars ourselves and through our friends and relatives. No one will want to marry their daughter into a family that is not good."

"But Sita," I protested, "I don't mean know the family, I mean know the man. How can you think of spending your whole life with someone you don't love or may not even like?"

"If he is a good man, why should I not like him?" she replied. "With you Americans, you know the boy so well before you marry, where is the fun to get married? There is no mystery and no romance. Here we have the whole of our married life to get to know and love our husband. This way is better, is it not?"*

* An Addendum to this article can be found in the References on page 332

From Serena Nanda, "Arranging a Marriage in India." In Philip R. DeVita, ed. *Stumbling Toward Truth: Anthropologists* (Waveland Press, Prospect Heights, Il., 2000) pp.196–204

---

she has of the money or property (Barker, 2003). A dowry involves a payment of money or gift of property that accompanies a bride into marriage and becomes part of the marriage agreement. Although the types of payment vary considerably, dowries might include household possessions, jewels, money, servants, or land. If a woman has a large dowry, she can find a "better" husband, which usually means one who is wealthier, healthier, highly educated, and from a more respected family.

The dowry system places a great financial burden on poorer families, especially if they must provide money or property for several daughters but have no or few sons to attract dowries. This system also encourages families to prefer sons to daughters. Males

Canadian society today encompasses both free-choice and arranged marriages. This couple met for the first time on the day of their wedding in Montreal.

perpetuate the family name and can more easily find jobs, support themselves, and acquire property through marriage. In some cases, female infants, children, and adults are neglected or mistreated because of this preference for males and the economics perpetuating it. For this reason, the dowry system has been outlawed in some countries such as India, although it continues to operate clandestinely in rural areas (Nanda, 1991).

In other societies practising arranged marriages (such as sub-Saharan Africa), the groom's family group is expected to pay the bride's family group a bride price as permission to marry this woman, as a way of establishing and securing alliances, and to compensate for the bride's lost labour or child-bearing potential in her community (Fleishing 2003). It is more prevalent in subsistent horticultural economies, patrilineal societies, and where the bride customarily moves to the groom's community. Dowries and bride prices are disappearing as both men and women become more educated and westernized, as women gain more opportunities to enter the labour force and become self-supporting, and as more people live in urban areas. Yet, traditional free-choice marriages have retained some symbolic remnants of dowries and bride prices in the trousseau or the clothing and household items collected for the wedding, the bride's family paying for portions of the wedding festivities, and the groom providing an engagement ring and gold wedding band.

In arranged marriages, more importance is placed on financial security, potential heirs, and extended family solidarity than on sexual attraction, love between the young people, or personal gratification (Nanda, 1991: 237-239). Potential marital partners are urged to respect each other, as well as their family's wishes, and it is hoped that love will develop after partners marry and share a home. Since both families have a stake in marital stability, arranged marriages are often more stable than free-choice unions. In addition, divorce is often legally restricted and women cannot always support themselves outside marriage. Nevertheless, urbanization, westernization (including the prevalence of foreign films, popular music, CDs, the Internet, and advertising), as well as university education and international travel have encouraged young people to anticipate "falling in love" and to seek a more intensive marital relationship (Nanda, 1991).

Patterns of Authority, Descent, and Inheritance

All societies develop practices and rules guiding behaviour within and between families. Most family systems designate a "head" to make major decisions and to represent the family to the community and government. In both western and eastern societies, the oldest male is typically the family head, a system referred to as **patriarchy**. An example of extreme patriarchy could be found in ancient Roman families before the Punic Wars, in which the father had the power of life and death over his children and held all legal and political authority on behalf of his wife (Leslie and Korman, 1989: 160).

An authority system in which women are granted more authority than men is called **matriarchy**. Matriarchal systems are rare, although American anthropologist Margaret Mead referred to the Tchambuli people of New Guinea as matriarchal (Mead, 1935) and some Black families in the Caribbean and the United States have also been referred to as matriarchal or at least **matrifocal** (Queen et al., 1985; Smith, 1996). In both these examples, women hold considerable control over the economy as well as decision-making power within their families. Canadian families used to be legally patriarchal, but men and women have acquired equal legal rights and men no longer are considered by government to be heads of families. In practice, however, remnants of patriarchy linger within many aspects of Canadian family life. One example is the practice of fathers "giving away" their daughters during a traditional marriage ceremony.

Patterns of descent may determine where newly married couples live, how they address family members, what surname their children will receive, and from whom they inherit. When Canadians marry, they usually consider their primary relationship to be with each other rather than with either set of parents or siblings. In most cases, the newly married couple is still considered to be a part of both kin groups, called a **bilateral descent** pattern. The couple is expected to maintain contact with both sides of the family and to participate in family gatherings. They are permitted to inherit from either side of the family.

The bride and groom are considered to be members of only one kin group in some cultures. If they belong to the groom's kin group, we call this **patrilineal descent**, which is the most prevalent and has a long history in both eastern and western civilizations (Leslie and Korman, 1989: 48). The important kinship ties are passed from father to son to grandson. A wife would marry into her husband's family, and their children would become members of his kin group. With **matrilineal descent**, relationships are traced through females and the female line, downplaying the importance of the father's relatives. Matrilineal descent as well as matrilocality, or living with the bride's kin group, were typical of the peoples of the Iroquois Confederacy in North America at the time of European contact (Brown, 1988).

In Canada, both kin membership and inheritance are based on bilateral descent, but patrilineal descent has been used for surnames. Until recently, the bride and the couple's subsequent children took the groom's family name. Canadian brides were expected (but not always legally required) to take their husband's name because he was considered to be the head of the household and because having one family name was a symbol of their legal and social union. In Quebec, married women are now legally required to keep their birth names but may add their husband's surname to it. In Ontario, brides may choose either their (father's) surname or the groom's without going through a legal name change.

If the newly married couple moves to the bride's community or household, the marriage system is called **matrilocal**. If the couple moves into the husband's community or household, the marriage system is **patrilocal**. Often, matrilineal family systems are also matrilocal, but this does not mean that women have more authority than men within the community or the family. More often, it means that the maternal uncle or the wife's brother is the authority figure.

Most North American marriages are **neolocal**, which means that the newly married couple establishes a new place of residence separate from both kin groups. Most young couples prefer to establish a separate residence and lifestyle from their family of origin even if it means accepting a lower living standard and later forgoing live-in childcare services. Although the couple may reside with either set of in-laws at some point during their marriage, especially if they are in financial difficulty, it is often defined as temporary and a hardship, except among certain cultural groups.

In the past century, family life has changed considerably, reflecting transformations in the larger society. Economic, demographic, legal, technological, and social changes have influenced labour markets and earnings, the structure of households, the nature of intimate relationships and individual aspirations. In the next section, nine major trends in Canadian families are discussed in comparison to other industrialized countries.

FAMILY TRENDS

Governments generally collect statistics about family life, and the media usually report family trends, sometimes without placing them in a comparative or historical context. In order to understand family trends, we need to know both what they were in the past and what they are in other places. With that information, family demography can help us understand how families differ by jurisdiction, ethnicity, income, and life cycle over the past decades. However, we need to understand that these trends are based on official statistics, gathered by governments during the census, and for special studies. They cannot tell us about issues neglected by the census takers or patterns not reported to the state. Nor can they explain family trends or tell us what they mean to different people. Therefore, we will need to draw on more detailed research from social history and sociology in order to explain the trends and to understand their implications for family and personal life. We will begin by discussing changes in marriage.

The Decline of Legal (Heterosexual) Marriage

First, more Canadians are avoiding or delaying legal marriage than in previous decades. Among people aged 30 to 39 in 2001, about 73% of men and 78% of women are predicted to marry at some point in their life, compared to 90% of men and women aged 50 to 69 (Statistics Canada, 2002c). Younger Canadians are now more likely to start their conjugal life through cohabitation (also called a **common-law relationship**), although most people eventually marry. Cohabitation is more prevalent in Quebec, where it is   estimated that 70% of all women start their conjugal lives through cohabitation, compared to 34% in the rest of Canada (ibid). As more people cohabit, a smaller percentage of the population is getting married.

The Canadian marriage rate has declined from 5.5 marriages per 1,000 population in 1994 to 5.0 in 2000 (Statistics Canada, 2003b: 27). In addition, the average age of first marriage has increased from about 22 for women and 25 for men in the 1960s to 28 for women and 30 for men in 2000 (McDaniel and Tepperman, 2004: 109; Statistics Canada, 2003c). Added together with remarriages, the average age of marriage in Canada is now 31.7 for brides and 34.3 for grooms (Statistics Canada, 2003c).

For younger generations, cohabitation serves mostly as a prelude or alternative to marriage, while for older people it is a prelude or alternative to remarriage (Le Bourdais et al., 2000). When people use cohabitation as an alternative to marriage, they often feel that their intimate relationships are their own business and the state or church has no right to intervene. Others feel that legal marriage involves gendered practices and expectations of behaviour that they would like to avoid (Elizabeth, 2000).

Common-law relationships used to be considered as temporary arrangements, but they are now becoming more like legal marriages. Statistically, however, they still differ from legal marriage, as their duration is shorter and their fertility rates are lower. Furthermore, researchers still find that legal marriages preceded by cohabitation have slightly higher rates of dissolution (Beaujot, 2000; Wu, 2000), perhaps because people who cohabit are less traditional and more likely to see divorce as an alternative to an unhappy marriage.

The distinction between legal marriage and cohabitation is becoming blurred both legally and socially in many industrialized countries. Several nations (including Canada) now consider women to be married for social security purposes if they have cohabited in a heterosexual relationship for at least one year or produced a child within that relationship within a year. If cohabiting partners do not want to divide their property equally (or the same as married couples) in the event of separation, they must sign a legal contract within a time limit. However, parents must always support their children whether or not they are married or living with them.

The rise in cohabitation also includes an increase in gay and lesbian people living as couples and families. In many countries, these couples have been fighting for legislative recognition of partnership rights, same-sex marriage, and equal rights to assisted reproduction services, fostering, and adoption (McNair et al., 2002; Weeks, 2002). Some jurisdictions have recently changed their laws, regulations, or practices about these issues. For example, several Canadian provinces have passed legislation to legally recognize gay marriages, but these laws have been referred to the Supreme Court, while Belgium and the Netherlands have legally recognized gay marriages since 2001 (Moore 2003).

Researchers are also beginning to discuss a new kind of relationship, called "living apart together" (LAT). Although figures are unavailable for Canada, about 6% of 35-44-year-old women in France and over 10% of 25–34-year-old women in Austria report being in such a relationship (González-López, 2002). Some of these couples work in different cities or countries but live together on the weekends or at regular intervals. This indicates that living arrangements are becoming more varied, but also suggests that employment opportunities continue to influence family formation.

Although legal marriage rates are declining and the age of marriage is rising, most people continue to live in couple relationships. Over three-quarters of Canadian women aged 35-44 years live as a couple, either legally married or cohabiting (Statistics Canada, 2002c). This suggests that "marriage"— broadly defined—is still very popular.

Fertility Trends: Declining and Delayed

Birth rates have been declining rapidly since the 1960s in most industrialized countries, but they have actually been declining in Canada since the late 1800s (Beaujot, 2000). In the 1850s, the crude birth rate in Canada was 45 live births per 1,000 population, but this rate fell to about 22 during the 1930s' Depression and 10.8 in 2001, as Table 1.1 indicates (Bélanger, 1999: 20; Statistics Canada, 2002b: 29). After the Second World War, there was a twenty-year increase in Canadian and American birth rates, called the Post-War Baby Boom (1945-65), which was not experienced to the same extent in Europe. Crude birth

TABLE 1.1 Crude Birth Rates in Canada, 1851-2001

Year	Live Births per 1,000 population
1851–61*	45
1861–7	40
1871–8	37
1881–91	34
1891–1901	30
1901–1911	31
1911–1921	29
1921	29.3
1931	23.2
1941	22.4
1951	27.2
1961	26.1
1971	16.8
1981	15.0
1991	14.4
2001	10.8

* birth rates from 1851 to 1921 are estimates
Source: Adapted from the Statistics Canada publication, "Births and deaths, vital statistics, volume I," Catalogue no. 84-204 April 1, 1989, and from the Statistics Canada CANSIM database http://cansim2.statcan.ca, Table 051-0004.

rates, as their name suggests, are not very accurate measures of fertility because they fluctuate annually with economic conditions and are influenced by the average age of the population and the sex ratio.

A more accurate measure is the total fertility rate, which is the average number of children produced by women aged 15 and 49 years. Yet the same declining trend is apparent for this measure as well. In 1921, each woman in Canada bore an average of 3.5 children (Ram, 1990: 82) compared to 1.49 in 2002 (Statistics Canada, 2002a). Fertility rates are also calculated for different age categories, called "age-specific fertility rates." These statistics allow us to say that women in Canada are delaying childbearing, and more are having their first child after the age of 30 (Beaujot, 2000). More women postpone both legal marriage and childbearing to complete their education and secure a job, but there is also less pressure to marry before experimenting with sex. Furthermore, about 20 percent of Canadians are not producing any children, either because of lifestyle choice or infertility problems.

Canada is similar to other industrialized countries in experiencing declining fertility rates, although ours did not decline as early or as severely as in some European countries (except in Quebec). There are many reasons why fertility declines with industrialization and urbanization. New jobs in manufacturing and services are created in towns and cities. People migrate to these towns to find work but then discover that the cost of housing and food is higher than in rural areas and that they cannot afford to have as many children as they want. Industrialization also creates the need for new technical skills and literacy, requiring a more educated and skilled labour force. Young people need more formal education in order to find work, and compulsory education laws keep children in school longer and out of the labour force (Gaffield, 1990). Wage labour tends to generate higher incomes than agricultural work or domestic service, and employed parents can better afford to educate their children. Eventually, children become economic liabilities to parents rather than assets.

As the cost of living rises and one wage is no longer sufficient to support a family, both husbands and wives need a regular paycheque. Childcare becomes problematic and expensive unless parents work in different shifts, or relatives or neighbours are available to care for young children. Consequently, couples tend to limit their family size, regardless of how many children they actually want. Producing fewer children is one way that couples reduce the conflict between earning a living and raising a family in urban conditions (Beck-Gernsheim, 2002). The public demand for birth control then increases, family planning becomes more widespread and socially acceptable, and public discourse supports a more public role for women. Although this pattern has been prevalent in many industrialized countries, there are cultural variations within countries as well as between them in fertility, the use of contraception, and the encouragement of paid work for mothers.

Contrary to popular myth, immigrant women produce fewer children than women born in Canada. Many immigrants leave their homelands in order to improve their living standard, which often requires two incomes, and women's labour force participation historically has been associated with lower birth rates and smaller family size. In addition, immigrants tend to adjust to the lifestyle of the majority (Beaujot, 2000). Birth rates used to vary by religion, language, and culture in Canada. Catholics, some fundamentalist Protestant groups, and some orthodox Jewish groups historically had high fertility, while mainstream Protestants and reform Jewish groups tended to reduce their family size. In addition, French Canadians (who were mainly Catholic) and rural dwellers used to have larger families (Kalbach and McVey, 1979: 107). Now, more similarities than differences exist between religious and cultural groups, as well as between rural and urban dwellers, as Patrizia Albanese reports in Chapter Six. However, fertility rates continue to be higher in Canada's north and among First Nations people than among non-aboriginal people living in the south. In addition, these rates vary by province, and were lowest in New-foundland at 1.21 children per woman (Bélanger et al., 2001: 16), since younger people of childbearing age migrate elsewhere to find work.

In the past thirty years, Quebec birth rates have declined considerably despite the Catholic background of most French Quebeckers. Only two generations ago, Quebec women were still having large families in comparison to all Canadians. In 1959, for example, the total fertility rate in Quebec was 4.0 children per woman, but it fell to 1.47 in 1998 (ibid). This decline originally was attributed to the sweeping cultural changes in the 1960s and 1970s known as the **Quiet Revolution**. The Catholic Church lost much of its control over Quebec society, the education system became more secularized, young people placed more emphasis on occupational success, and young women played down their traditional role as mothers (Lachapelle and Henripin, 1982: 116ff). Another reason for declining fertility in Quebec relates to women's low marriage rates and high employ-ment rates, and perhaps their personal reaction against previous generations' experience in childbearing and child rearing, which many young women perceived to be emotionally and physically draining.

From 1988 to 1997, the Quebec government offered cash payments to parents at child-birth, which reached a maximum of $8,000 for the third and subsequent child. After a small rise in the birth rate at the beginning of the 1990s, the rate continued to decline in Quebec as well as most of the rest of Canada, and the birth incentives were abolished (Bélanger et al., 2001:16). Since the 1970s, fertility has declined in most industrialized countries, which are now experiencing rates below replacement level (OECD, 2001: 24). Canada's fertility rates remain moderate compared to some European countries such as Spain and Italy, whose fertility rates are even lower than Canada's.

The consequences of declining fertility are not necessarily the same for women, families, and governments. For women, fewer children may mean greater opportunities to accept paid work and engage in self-development activities, more time to devote to each existing child, and a higher standard of living (Eichler, 1988: 312). Therefore, feminists tend to see declining fertility in a positive light. For both parents, fewer children could mean more time to earn a living, a higher per capita income, easier residential mobility, and less time devoted to childcare. For these reasons, social workers and welfare administrators have encouraged low-income families to produce fewer children.

From the government's viewpoint, families with high birth rates and low incomes are a problem because these parents require higher levels of income support and social services. At the same time, falling birth rates lead to an aging population, which could require higher social expenditures on medical care and pensions. Furthermore, rapidly declining birth rates among cultural minorities could have political implications, as with concern about the declining francophone population in Canada (Baker, 1994b). In addition, some economists have warned that declining fertility will reduce economic productivity and prosperity, although this has not occurred in Germany or Sweden. In other words, various groups interpret the significance of declining birth rates according to their own political agendas.

More Mothers in Paid Work

Before the Second World War, Canadian women usually left paid work when they announced their engagement to be married. They were given parties by their co-workers and expected to retire from paid employment and become full-time homemakers. During the Second World War, some married women were needed to work in the munitions factories and other jobs vacated by men serving in the armed forces. Nevertheless, only 4.5 percent of married women were in the paid labour force in 1941 (Baker, 1990a: 8), compared to 62.3 percent in 1998 (Chaykowski and Powell, 1999).

By the 1960s, more married women were employed, but the income of husbands and the presence of children continued to influence their paid work. Married women were less likely than single women to be working outside the home, unless their husband was unemployed, underemployed, or a low earner. Similarly, the presence of preschool children and the absence of non-family childcare also kept mothers out of the labour force. Now, younger women are more likely than older women to be in the Canadian labour force regardless of marriage or motherhood (ibid). Canadian government statistics indicate that about three-quarters of mothers with children under 15 are now working for pay. In addition, married women are almost as likely to be working for pay as single or divorced women, and much more likely than widowed women. In 1998, 74 percent of mothers in two-parent families were in the labour force compared to 67 percent of lone mothers (ibid), as Table 1.2 indicates. In Chapter Five, Gillian Ranson discusses in more detail how labour force participation varies by family status.

TABLE 1.2 Labour Force Participation Rates of Canadian Parents, by Marital Status and Age of Child, 1978, 1988, and 1998.

Marital Status and Age of Child	Females			Males		
	1978	1988	1998	1978	1988	1998
Spouse Present						
Child 0–2	37.7	60.0	67.2	Na	Na	Na
Child 0–5	40.9	62.3	69.0	Na	Na	Na
Child 0–15	47.4	67.6	73.9	Na	Na	Na
Lone Parent						
Child 0–2	40.3	41.3	44.4	90.0	85.2	81.1
Child 0–5	45.7	51.0	53.9	89.5	86.6	86.3
Child 0–15	56.6	63.7	67.0	89.4	87.5	88.0

Source: Adapted from the Statistics Canada publication "Labour force historical review," 1999, Catalogue no. 71F0004, February 18, 2000.

There are numerous reasons for the increasing presence of Canadian mothers in the paid workforce:

1. The expansion of the service sector of the labour force in the 1960s created a new demand for workers, and married women and mothers were enticed into these "clean" indoor jobs that were considered suitable for "feminine skills."
2. The rising cost of living throughout the 1960s and 1970s encouraged married women and mothers to enter paid work to help pay for housing and daily expenses at a time when male wages alone were no longer keeping pace with inflation.
3. Private firms created more part-time jobs, enabling mothers to earn money without relinquishing their family responsibilities.
4. Divorce rates soared in the 1970s and 1980s, encouraging women to enter full-time work if they became family heads or foresaw the possibility of divorce.
5. Laws relating to maternity and parental leave and benefits were amended to require employers to protect women's jobs while they give birth. This allowed women to keep their jobs rather than quit and seek new ones later.
6. Improvements in birth control since the 1960s enabled couples to plan conception to fit in with educational and work requirements.
7. As women gained more formal education, they raised their expectations about using this education to support themselves, contribute to the family income, or make some public contribution to society.

These labour market trends had many implications for family life. Historically, men's authority as family heads began to erode when they left the home and farm to find wage work in the 19th century. When more wives began to contribute their wages to the household, the gendered division of labour, with men deriving additional authority from breadwinning, was further challenged. At the beginning of the 21st century, earning is typically shared, and patterns of family authority are becoming more equitable. Nevertheless, government statistics still indicate that most husbands work longer hours for pay and earn more money than their wives, and that wives accept much more responsibility for family caring and housework (Davies and Carrière, 1999; Statistics Canada, 2003b). Laws, social policies, and public attitudes are starting to acknowledge new earning patterns in families but do not always recognize that gendered patterns of caring and housework have remained remarkably stable.

Rise in Births outside Marriage

More babies are now born outside marriage in most industrialized countries, with the rise in cohabitation and decline of legal marriage. In Canada, 31 percent of live births in 1996 were to women who were not legally married, compared to 9 percent in 1975 (VIF, 2000: 55) and 4 percent in 1960 (VIF, 1994: 58). There are notable provincial differences in these statistics, with a high of 64 percent of births outside marriage in the Northwest Territories and a low of 17 percent in Ontario (VIF, 2000: 55). Most of these children are born to couples in their 20s and 30s who are living in permanent but non-legal relationships. Le Bourdais and Marcil-Gratton (1994) noted that 48 percent of first births in Quebec were classified as "out-of-wedlock," but 90 percent were actually born to cohabiting couples.

Canada's extramarital birth rate, at 31 percent of all live births, is moderate compared to Sweden's rate of 55 percent and Italy's of 9 percent (Lewis, 2003). Countries with higher rates of cohabitation usually have higher rates of extramarital births. As societies become more secularized, attitudes change about the state's right to be involved in personal life or moral issues. Sexual attitudes and practices have certainly become more liberal in Canada since the 1950s, especially within committed relationships (McDaniel and Tepperman, 2004). In addition, Canadian laws tend to treat children equally, regardless of the marital status of their parents.

Fewer children are born outside marriage to adolescent women in Canada compared to the United States, where fertility rates are higher. Of all births outside marriage in Canada, only 20 percent are to women under twenty, while 60 percent are to women between 20 and 30 (Vanier Institute of the Family, 1994: 58). Teenage birth rates have declined considerably in Canada since the 1950s because of improved contraception, legalized abortion, public health insurance, and social assistance benefits which have enabled poorer women to receive medical attention and prescription drugs.

Low Adoption Rates

Some women always have become pregnant outside marriage, but prior to the 1960s this event was considered to be very detrimental to the woman's reputation and the reputation of her family. Unmarried pregnant women used to be sent away to have their babies secretly with distant relatives or in maternity homes run by charitable organizations. Middle class couples adopted these babies, and the birth mothers were not always permitted to see their babies after birth. Some pregnant women obtained illegal abortions, while others gave birth and suffered social disgrace, struggling to raise their child with minimal public assistance. A few were fortunate enough to receive emotional support, money, a home, or childcare assistance from their parents or other relatives. Occasionally, fathers provided financial assistance, but it was often surreptitious. The law did not require unmarried fathers to support their children unless they publicly declared their paternity or it was proven in court.

In 1968, about 70 percent of unmarried mothers in Ontario had their children placed for adoption, but by 1977, this figure had already declined to about 12 percent (Eichler 1983: 281). Since that time, the percentage of unmarried mothers across North America who allow their children to be adopted has dwindled. In Canada, 3,399 infants were involved in domestic, non-relative, and non-native adoptions in 1981, but this figure fell to 1,688 by 1990 (Daly and Sobol, 1993). In recent years, only 1.2 percent of children in Canada are adopted (VIF 2000: 64).

Over the decades, adoption rates have declined because fewer babies are born to women of all ages and marital statuses due to more effective birth control and the legalization of abortion since 1969. Each year, about 10 pregnancies are terminated for every 1,000 women aged 15 to 44, and this rate remained stable from 1981 to 1995 (Bélanger and Dumas, 1998: 16). Also, social workers and psychologists consider that giving up a child for adoption can be psychologically damaging for both mother and child. Consequently, they often advocate social assistance and special services to enable lone mothers to raise their own children. If the child is adopted, social workers usually advocate pre-adoption counselling, open adoptions, and state assistance for post-adoption reunions. Changing morality, improved social benefits, and better employment opportunities have permitted lone mothers to raise their own infants.

About five percent of children born outside marriage are born to women without partners, but most "unmarried" mothers are cohabiting with the baby's father and are not parenting alone (VIF, 2000: 54). The social trend to raise children outside legal marriage has decreased the availability of children for adoption. Although most adopted children in the 1950s were born to unmarried mothers, most now are part of stepfamilies. Daly and Sobol, (1993) found that 60 percent of Canadian adoptions were by relatives or stepfamilies and the rest arose from parental death, abuse, neglect, or shortage of parental resources.

International adoption remains one of the few alternatives for prospective parents, and the main sources of adoptive infants are war-torn or less-developed countries. Other couples are adopting young children rather than infants, partly out of humanitarian concerns, but also because too few infants are available. The shortage of infants may have led to a more child-focused attitude in adoption processes rather than emphasizing parental needs. However, the trend toward international adoptions, which is predominant in Europe and subject to fewer regulations in many countries, may reverse this focus (Speirs and Baker, 1994). With problems finding infants to adopt, more couples are turning to medically assisted conception to help them to become parents (Donchin, 1996; Daniels and Haime,s 1998).

The Increasing Use of Medically Assisted Conception

Married or cohabiting couples often view the creation of a child as a joint project that will "complete" their relationship. They say that having children will enable them to pass on their knowledge and values, to expand their social networks, to relive the discoveries of childhood, to receive unconditional love, and to pass on their name, genes, or family line (Veevers, 1980; Ramu and Tavuchis, 1986; Cameron, 1990). Some also believe that their children will care for them in their old age. Consequently, the inability to conceive can disrupt the normal life expectations of both men and women (Daniluk, 2001; Exley and Letherby, 2001) and often is viewed as a major life crisis (Bergart, 2000).

The causes of low fertility and infertility are numerous and include exposure to sexually transmitted diseases, long-term use of certain contraceptives, workplace hazards, environmental pollutants, hormonal imbalances, and lifestyle factors such as tobacco smoking, excessive exercise, a large consumption of caffeine or other drugs, and prolonged stress. (Adair and Rogan, 1998). As women's average age at marriage and first birth rises, more women are trying to conceive in their later 30s or early 40s, sometimes with little success.

Since the first "test-tube" baby was born in Britain in 1978, reproductive technologies have become more widespread and many different procedures have become routine, such as egg retrieval, in vitro fertilization, and re-implantation into a woman's womb (Coney and Else, 1999: 1). Frozen sperm and embryos make conception possible after their donor's death, postmenopausal women can bear children, and potential parents can contract "surrogates" to bear children for them. These interventions could radicalize family life, but could also be used to help create ordinary nuclear families.

Sociologists have been ambivalent about medically assisted conception. On the one hand, they concede that it offers the opportunity for more women and couples to become parents, and permits lesbian couples to become parents without heterosexual intercourse (Michaels, 1996). At the same time, these interventions still are somewhat experimental and have a relatively low success rate, although it is gradually rising. Only 50% to 60% of couples are able to conceive after four cycles of treatment, but most couples do not continue that long (Pearn, 1997; Bergert, 2000). Medically assisted conception is also intrusive, tends to reinforce the social pressure for all women to reproduce, medicalizes the natural act of childbearing, and offers costly services unavailable to the poor (Albury, 1999; Eichler, 1996). These interventions could also promote the use of sex selection to reinforce the cultural preference for sons rather than daughters. They permit the financial and emotional exploitation of working class women through surrogacy arrangements (Baird, 1997). Because reproductive and genetic technologies could fundamentally transform and reshape family life, many social activists have called for full public debate about their legality, ethics, and potential impact on society (Coney and Else, 1999).

Eichler (1996) argues that reproductive technologies complicate "parenthood" so significantly that they represent a quantum leap in complexity by blurring the role designations of mother, father, and child. Potentially, medically assisted reproduction could reshape families, separate biological and social parenthood, change generational lines, and create the possibility of sex selection. Yet the social circumstances and relationships of couples using these technologies have not been widely studied. This situation may relate to the difficulty of finding participants for such research, but is also due to the small but growing percentage of the population that uses these technologies. Nevertheless, these interventions are becoming more prevalent.

Although some patients using fertility clinics may believe they have the "right" to reproduce, controversies remain about who should be entitled to fertility services (married heterosexual couples or all couples) and who should pay for the treatments. Public health insurance sometimes pays for part of the treatment for some patients, but most people must pay additional fees, which means that higher income couples gain more opportunities to become parents. Even privately funded treatments sometimes have public costs, especially when things go wrong, such as ectopic pregnancies and miscarriages (Baird, 1997). In countries with a public health system, such as Canada, issues of access and cost have become important policy questions.

Rising Rates of Separation and Divorce

Separation and divorce rates have increased in many industrialized countries, especially since the late 1960s. The Canadian divorce rate rose from .06 divorces per 1,000 population in 1921 to 3.5 in 1987, before falling gradually to 2.3 in 2000 (Bélanger, 1999: 38; Statistics Canada, 2003b: 27). After the Canadian divorce law reforms in 1968 and 1985, the rate rapidly increased. The 1968 change added "marriage breakdown" to the existing grounds for divorce based on **matrimonial fault**, and the 1985 law redefined marriage breakdown as only one year of separation. The decrease in divorce rates at the end of the

TABLE 1.3 Divorce Rates in Selected Countries (per 1,000 population), 1973 and 1998

Country	1973	1998
Ireland	—	—
Italy	0.3	0.6
Spain	—	0.9
France	1.0	2.0
Germany	1.5	2.3
Canada	1.7	2.3
Sweden	2.0	2.3
Denmark	2.5	2.5
Australia	1.2	2.7
Finland	1.9	2.7
United Kingdom	2.1	2.7
United States	4.4	4.2

Source: Lewis 2003: 25.

1980s reflected a declining marriage rate and a slower economy in which legal divorce was considered to be too expensive for many couples.

Despite the rise in divorce throughout the 1970s and 1980s, Canada's divorce rate remains moderate compared to many industrialized countries, as Table 1.3 indicates. It is much lower than the American rate, for example. The divorce rate in the United States was 4.2 divorces per 1,000 population in 1998 (Lewis, 2003: 25), which may reflect many years of more liberal divorce laws and continuing high rates of legal marriage. At the same time, Canada's divorce rate is higher than some European countries such as Italy and Spain. Canada's population is younger than some European countries, and divorces tend to occur at younger ages. Also, the higher Canadian rate may reflect a higher marriage rate than in some European countries as well as the liberalization of Canadian laws in 1985. Ireland legalized divorce in 1996 and Spain in 1981 (ibid).

As Zheng Wu and Christoph Schimmele note in Chapter Ten, there are many reasons for rising separation and divorce rates. The growing secularization of society has encouraged more people to view marriage as they would a business contract that can be broken under certain circumstances. In addition, growing individualism, including the idea that people deserve happiness in their personal relationships, has discouraged couples from staying together out of duty or concern for family reputation. Furthermore, the decline in fertility has made divorce more prevalent as the logistics become easier with fewer children per family. Now that more women are working for pay and government income support is available, divorce is more economically feasible for both men and women wanting to leave unhappy marriages. Consequently, many individuals and advocacy groups lobbied governments, resulting in legal reform in 1968 and 1985. These legal reforms further contributed to rising Canadian divorce rates. As with declining fertility, rising divorce rates upset many conservatives, who saw them as an example of "the death of the family." At the same time, others viewed this trend as an exemplification of greater choice and personal freedom, and an opportunity to create a better life after an unfortunate marriage.

Societal changes may encourage the prevalence of divorce, but certain social and psychological conditions also tend to increase conflict within marriage. If unresolved, this conflict could lead to separation and divorce. Researchers have found, for example, that those who marry well below the average age, especially if the bride is pregnant, have greater chances of marital discord and divorce (McDaniel and Tepperman, 2004: 395). This suggests that emotional and social immaturity, an incomplete education, inability to be self-supporting, and lack of opportunity to adjust to marriage before the strains of pregnancy tend to jeopardize the stability of marriage.

Studies have also found that the previously divorced and those with divorced parents also are more likely to terminate unsatisfactory marriages (Pryor and Rodgers, 2001). This may simply suggest that people with previous family experience of marriage dissolution see divorce as a viable alternative to an unhappy marriage. They know from personal experience that there is "life after marriage," or that a smooth transition from marriage to a single life is possible. They may also be familiar with the legal procedures involved. On the other hand, this correlation may indicate that people learn unhealthy ways of resolving marital conflict from their parents or from previous relationships. Since more Canadian young people have parents whose marriages and partnerships dissolved, this will likely contribute to higher rates of partnership dissolution in the future.

Large age discrepancies, differences in cultural, religious, or socio-economic background of spouses, as well as the absence of religious affiliation have also been correlated with high divorce rates. More marriages now take place between people from different social and cultural backgrounds, as a result of urbanization, high rates of immigration, greater geographic mobility, and more people attending colleges and universities away from their home communities. In addition, religious attendance has declined throughout North American society. Rates of childlessness appear to be rising in Canada, and couples without children have a higher probability of divorce (Baker, 2001). This does not imply that childless couples are more dissatisfied with their marriages, but rather that it is easier to obtain a legal divorce and survive economically afterwards if couples do not have to agree on the custody and financial support of their children. All these trends may influence future divorce rates.

These and other studies suggest that although all marriages experience conflict, some may experience more conflict than others. Furthermore, the way in which this conflict is resolved relates to conflict resolution skills, parental role models, social circumstances, and opportunities to leave the marriage. Whether or not separation is legalized in the form of a divorce, however, further depends on laws, social values, and economic circumstances.

Most divorced people remarry, but lone parents have higher remarriage rates than those without children. Furthermore, never-married parents have higher marriage rates than previously married parents. The high marriage rates of never-married lone mothers may reflect their youthfulness, but also indicate the financial and emotional difficulties of lone parenting (Pryor and Rodgers, 2001).

The Increase in Lone-Parent Families

Lone-parent families were prevalent in the last century when parental death rates were higher, but declined throughout the first part of the twentieth century. As divorce

Juggling work and family can be challenging for lone mothers.

increased in the 1970s, lone-parent families increased as a percentage of all families, from 11.3 percent in 1981 to 16.1 percent in 2001 (Statistics Canada, 1998a: 188; Statistics Canada, 2003b: 27). We should keep in mind that lone-parent families may have been just as prevalent in the 1930s' Depression as in recent years, but reliable historical statistics are not readily available (Ram, 1990). Although the most prevalent path to lone parenthood used to be the death of a partner, it now is separation and divorce.

The increase in lone-parent families has occurred in most countries since the early 1970s, and 90 percent are led by mothers (OECD, 2001: 34). The majority of countries in the Organisation of Economic Co-operation and Development (OECD) have experienced an increase of between 30 percent and 50 percent, and lone parents typically constitute between 10 percent and 20 percent of all families with children (Bradshaw et al., 1996: 12). The percentage in the United States is closer to 29 percent (ibid). Many policy makers and researchers have focused on one-parent households led by mothers because of their rising numbers, high poverty rates, and heavy reliance on social assistance.

Lone parents are not a homogeneous group, but rather differ in economic and demographic characteristics as well as in the circumstances that led them to lone parenthood. The major reason for the rise in lone-parent families in all countries is the dissolution of couple relationships. Never-married lone parents constitute a growing percentage of the lone-parent population, but some of these parents were cohabiting when their child was born. Although 30 percent of Canadian children are born outside marriage, only about 9 percent live with only one parent at the time of birth (Marcil-Gratton, 1999). The rest live with both parents, even though their parents are not legally married.

Poverty rates for lone-parent families with children differ dramatically among industrialized countries for several reasons. First, jurisdictions vary in the percentage of lone mothers who are in the labour market and working full-time, and employed lone mothers are less likely to be poor than those relying on government benefits (Bradshaw, et al. 1996). Second, countries vary in the availability and generosity of family benefits or social welfare programs, as well as in the stigma attached to receiving these benefits. Some provide income support for lone mothers or for all mothers with young children, while others do not. Some nations encourage married mothers but not lone mothers to care for their children at home. In addition, some welfare programs provide a strong disincentive for mothers to look for paid work while receiving social benefits. A third reason for variations in child and family poverty rates relates to both male and female unemployment rates, which vary dramatically. Other aspects of the structure of the labour market vary as well, including the availability of part-time jobs, minimum and average wages, employment equity for women, and job training programs (Baker and Tippin, 1999; Millar and Rowlingson, 2001).

Of all reasons for becoming a single parent (separation, divorce, widowhood, or premarital pregnancy), women who have a child outside a couple relationship are most vulnerable to poverty. This is especially true if the mother is an adolescent or has not completed her education (Dooley, 1995). Higher unemployment rates are associated with lower levels of education and less job experience in most countries. Low poverty rates among lone-parent families result from a combination of factors. These include generous packages of state income support for families with children, direct services such as childcare to enable mothers to enter the labour force during child-rearing years, high wages for employed mothers, and child support payments guaranteed by the state for the children of parents who live apart (Millar and Rowlingson, 2001).

More Blended Families

More marriages now involve at least one partner who has been previously married. In 1967, only 12.3 percent of marriages involved one spouse who had been previously married, but by 2000 it was 32.6 percent (Dumas, 1994: 29; Statistics Canada, 2003c). Men have always been more likely than women to remarry after divorce, but remarriage rates have declined for both men and women as cohabitation becomes more prevalent.

Remarried parents bring their children into their new families, but often find that they are different from families created from first marriages. Stepfamilies tend to involve a greater complexity of relationships, more permeable boundaries, and people living in different households. Adjustment may be complicated by the presence of the ex-spouse, by lingering hostility between formerly married people, and unresolved conflicts surrounding child custody and support (Pryor and Rogers, 2001; Boyd, 2003). In popular mythology, the stepmother has been portrayed as unloving and punitive, while the stepfather is seen as somewhat more benign. Not surprisingly, some studies indicate that relations between children and their stepmother are more often contentious than with the natural parent of the same sex or with the stepfather (Cheal, 1996). This is probably because mothers spend more time in the home with responsibility for child supervision, but may also be affected by negative stereotypes. The portrayal of both divorce and remarriage in social science research also tends to be negative, especially when studying the effects on children (Sev'er, 1992: 243-245). This is exacerbated by research results generalized from clinical samples, or samples comprised of clients seeking marriage therapy and assistance with children's behavioural problems.

Lone parents often justify their remarriage decisions by saying that they are providing their children with a father or mother. Compared to children in lone-parent families, however, children in stepfamilies have been found to have higher rates of accidents, higher levels of bedwetting, more contact with the police, lower self-esteem, and to leave school earlier without qualifications (Ferri, 1984; Elliott et al., 1993). Pryor and Rodgers (2001) argue that these experiences can be explained by friction within these households as well as by the lower family aspirations and expectations that step-parents have for their stepchildren compared to their own biological children. They also indicate that young children fare better than older children in stepfamilies because adaptation is easier at an earlier age before allegiances are developed with the absent parent. A few studies have noted that remarriage provides a stabilizing influence for children and their parents. Furthermore, living in a blended family is much better for children than remaining in an intact family with conflicting parents or living in a one-parent household in which the parent is lonely and poor.

In second and subsequent marriages, the age gap between spouses tends to be larger than in first marriages, and men typically remarry women younger than their first wife. Although the age gap averages about two years in first marriages, it is nearly five years for the remarriage of divorced people and seven years for widowed people (Beaujot, 2000: 105). With rising rates of remarriage, age-discrepant marriages will become more prevalent, which could have implications for spousal equality and for parenting.

Changing Canadian Families

Family life is never static, reflecting trends in the economy, social values, laws, and social policies. In this chapter, I have shown that legal marriage and birth rates have been declining, but the percentage of people living as couples has been relatively stable over the decades, with higher rates of cohabitation. Both families and households are becoming smaller, and two-income families are now in the distinct majority in Canada. Many middle-class women are delaying first births until after their education is completed and their finances more secure. In addition, families are becoming less permanent units, with moderate rates of separation and divorce, but high rates of repartnering. Most people eventually live in an intimate relationship and produce children and grandchildren. In addition, most people maintain close contact with their parents and siblings even when they move away or marry. Table 1.4 provides some current statistics on the issues discussed in this chapter.

Raising children while earning a living has always been difficult for women, but now couples produce fewer children than they actually want because of the high cost of raising them in terms of time, money, and emotional investment. Furthermore, a greater

TABLE 1.4 Summary Statistics of Canadian Families

Life Expectancy at Birth (2000)	Male: 76.7 years Female: 82.0 years
Crude Birth Rate (2001)	10.8 births per 1,000 population
Immigration Rate (2001)	8.0 per 1,000 population
Marriage Rate (2001)	4.9 per 1,000 population
Total Fertility Rate (2000)	1.49 births per woman aged 15-49
Couple Living "Common-Law" (2001)	14% of all couple families in Canada 30% of couple families in Quebec
Rate of Pregnancies Terminated (1998)	19.8 per 100 births
Births outside Marriage (1996)	31 per 100 births
Husband/Wife Families with children (2001)	49.4% of all families
Mother-Led Households (2001)	83.6% of lone-parent households
Employed Mothers (2001)	63% of women with children under 3 were employed
Women's Earnings as % of Men's (2000)	71.7% for full-time, full-year workers
Lone Parents in Labour Force (with children aged 0-15) (1997)	67.0 % of mothers 88.0 % of fathers
Lone-Parent Families	16.1% of all families (2001) 20% of all families with children
Divorce Rate (2000)	2.3 divorces per 1,000 population
Mean Duration of Marriage for Persons Divorcing in that Year (1998)	10.8 years
Remarriages (2000)	32.6 % of marriages involve at least one spouse who was previously married

Source: New table comprised of individual statistics from various publications by Statistics Canada, UN, and OECD.

percentage of children are experiencing parental separation and are living in blended families. At the same time, marriage to one person for life is becoming less feasible, with the necessity to change jobs several times throughout one's working life, retrain, and perhaps move to a new location. Finding two new careers in the same place remains challenging, and maintaining long-distance relationships throughout these transitions is difficult, though it is more feasible than it used to be, with e-mail and text messaging.

Stress and conflict were always present in marriage and family life. The stress involved in modern relationships should not be seen as new or necessarily unfortunate. The two-earner family is in the process of encouraging less gendered practices in families, and more options are now available for adults who do not see themselves as living within a heterosexual marriage or raising children. Children's lives in North America appear to be less stable than in the 1950s, but children now have many advantages not available to them in earlier eras or in other countries. Family and personal life are clearly changing, allowing more flexibility and choice for adults. How we evaluate these changes may vary with our age, gender, and cultural background, but certainly with our personal values.

In the following two chapters of Part 1, we delve more deeply into conceptualizations of family before discussing the implications of historical changes in industrialization, migration, and work on family life in Part 2. We examine empirical research and theories relating to family dynamics, sexuality, socialization, marital satisfaction, and caring for the elderly in Part 3. Legal and policy changes, divorce, violence, and relations between families and the state are the topics of Part 4. The final section deals with research trends and the future of family life. In the next chapter, Meg Luxton examines the various ways that social theorists have viewed and explained changing family life.

Suggested Readings

Bélanger, Alain, et al. (2001). *Report of the Demographic Situation in Canada 2000*. Catalogue no. 91-209-XPE. Ottawa: Ministry of Industry. This annual report from Statistics Canada includes a variety of statistics about families and population trends in Canada.

Canadian Social Trends (Catalogue no. 11-008-XPE). Ottawa. This journal from Statistics Canada includes articles about social trends written in everyday language.

Jamieson, Lynn (1998). *Intimacy: Personal Relationships in Modern Societies*. Cambridge: Polity Press. Jamieson examines the research on families to question the thesis that relationships in "post-modern" society now involve more sharing of our innermost selves. She concludes that intimate relationships are still fundamentally shaped by power, gender, and economic considerations.

McDaniel, Susan A. and Lorne Tepperman (2004). *Close Relations: An Introduction to the Sociology of Families*. 2nd edition. Scarborough Ontario: Pearson/Prentice Hall. An introductory textbook to family studies, designed for a Canadian audience.

Vanier Institute of the Family (VIF) (2000). *Profiling Canadian Families II*. Ottawa: VIF. This monograph provides numerous tables of family trends in Canada.

Web Resources

Statistics Canada in Ottawa provides a wide range of census documents and statistics relating to families and households: **www.statcan.ca**

Vanier Institute of the Family in Ottawa is a privately funded organization providing educational material, news items, and research on Canadian families. They also publish a magazine called *Transition*: **www.vifamily.ca**

CHAPTER TWO

Conceptualizing "Families": Theoretical Frameworks and Family Research[1]

Meg Luxton

INTRODUCTION

On 10 June 2003, the Ontario Court of Appeal upheld a lower court ruling allowing same-sex marriage. A few hours later, two men were legally married in Toronto. That same day, 24 same-sex couples applied for marriage licences in Toronto. That same month, the federal government drafted legislation to include unions of same-sex couples and asked the Supreme Court of Canada to assess its legality. That report is expected in the Fall of 2004. On 8 July 2003 the British Columbia courts redefined marriage as between two persons, and on 19 March 2004, the Quebec Court of Appeal followed suit. Since three-quarters of all people in Canada live in these three jurisdictions, the legal right of gays and lesbians to marry is now a practical reality.[2] Those supporting such rulings celebrated these changes, noting they were only fair as a way of ending discrimination.

In contrast, in July 2003, the Vatican launched a global campaign against gay unions, and Pope John Paul affirmed the Catholic church's position that marriage is a sacred union between a man and a woman, that is human and divine, and should be defended by society.[3] On 25 February 2004, President Bush of the United States called for an amendment to the American Constitution banning same-sex marriage (McFetters, 2004). Opponents argue that same-sex marriages threaten to destroy "the traditional family." At stake in this dispute are competing conceptualizations of families. This example is just one of many similar debates in various federal, provincial, and territorial legislatures and courts, as people struggle to win legal recognition and support for their way of viewing "families."

Underlying these different positions or ways of conceptualizing families are contending theories of family which rest on different starting assumptions about human nature, the relevance of biology in social life, the significance of masculinity and femininity, the importance of childhood socialization, and the nature of sexuality. In 1983, sociologists

John Fisher (centre), executive director of the gay rights organization EGALE, and Svend Robinson (right), Canada's first openly gay MP, address reporters following the tabling of Bill C-23.

Peter Berger and Brigitte Berger published a book called *The War Over the Family*, which claimed that a battle was taking place in the United States between feminists and the Christian New Right over the definition of "the family." In 1992, a right wing polemicist, William Gairdner, applied their argument to Canada in a journalistic book called *The War Against the Family*, which claimed that the "natural family" (p. 55), which he defined as "that immemorial unit of a married man and woman and their dependent children living together in the same house," (p. 3) was under attack from all sides. In particular, he argued, feminists were destroying the traditional family and thus threatening to destroy the whole society. In contrast, in 1980, sociologists Michele Barrett and Mary McIntosh published *The Anti-Social Family* in which they argued that the nuclear family was anti-social and that the way it was privileged over other kinds of relationships was dangerous. Writing about Canada in 1997, sociologist Margrit Eichler, in *Family Shifts: Families, Policies, and Gender Equality*, showed that when social policy assumed that the nuclear family was the normative or best family form, it just didn't work. These different opinions show that contestations over how to conceptualize family in the social and political realm are at work in the theoretical debates as well. In order to assess any theoretical work on the family, it is necessary to understand its starting assumptions.

CONCEPTUALIZING THE PROBLEM

Common-Sense Assumptions

When people use the term "family" they usually assume that what they mean by it is clear.[4] And yet, depending on the context, the term has a variety of different meanings. An adult man who talks about working to support his family probably means his wife and young children. The adult woman who plans to stop work to have a family is referring to children. The university student going home to spend the holidays with her family likely means her parents. Someone who explains that his family was killed in the Holocaust probably means an extended kin group, while someone else who describes a group of friends as "my real family" is identifying those who give significant emotional and personal support. At the same time, when a play or film is advertised as "family entertainment," the implication is that few people will find anything offensive in it. When politicians claim to support "family values" they usually mean something quite different from gays and lesbians who claim "we are family too." These diverse usages show how slippery the term is. The complexities, contradictions, and confusions surrounding the way the term "family" is used in everyday talk derive from several, often poorly understood, issues.

The Meanings of "Family"

The term "family" contains several different meanings. The word comes from the Latin "famulus," meaning servant, which became "familia," meaning the servants of a house or the household—that is, the group of people who live in one house or under one male head, including parents, children, and servants (*The Oxford Dictionary*, 1967: 673). By implication, the term encompassed the dual meaning of those who lived in the same household and those whose collective work maintained that household (Flandrin, 1979). This was its original (late fourteenth-century) meaning in English.[5]

By the late fifteenth century, the meaning of "family" was extended to describe a lineage or kin group that shared descent from a common ancestor, rather than a household (Flandrin, 1979). Between the seventeenth and nineteenth centuries, the term increasingly came to be used differently by the aristocracy and the newly emerging bourgeois class. The aristocracy continued to use the term to mean kinship lineage, a practice that continues today among the upper class, as in the British use of the phrase "the Royal family." A similar usage is sometimes applied to wealthy capitalists where a kin group has extensive corporate holdings, such as "the Bronfman or Reichman families."[6] In contrast, the bourgeois class increasingly used "family" to refer to the married couple and their children as distinct from other household members who were (usually) servants.

Through the nineteenth century, as capitalism developed, "family" was increasingly distinguished from "work," and for men the idea developed of working to support a family (Hall and Davidoff, 1987). In this meaning, family referred primarily to the small kin group with whom one had close personal ties and intimacy, usually those who have at some time lived together in one house (parents, siblings, spouse, children). In the twentieth century, the terms "nuclear family" and "extended family" emerged to express the distinction between the now-dominant notion of small kin group involving the married couple and their children and the increasingly subordinate meaning of a large kin group. In the various everyday usages of the word "family" we hear echoes of all the earlier meanings.

Shifting Patterns of Family

The term "family" now encompasses a number of overlapping though distinctly different types of relationships and conveys multiple meanings of kinship, co-residence, and emotional intimacy. Some of these are legally constituted. "Family" is a legal term that carries particular definitions and entails specific legal rights and obligations for certain legally designated people. Those who are not specifically included in the definition of family are excluded. Parents are required to provide material support and emotional nurturing for their children, and in return, are normally entitled to custody of, or access to, those children. Other people who may have deep emotional relations with the children are not recognized in law. Thus, a divorced father's lover, who may have lived with the children on a daily basis and cared for them, has no legal claim, while the father's parents do—even though they may never have met the children. Similarly, because workers' families are entitled to certain benefits, a wife of only weeks may be entitled to a widows' pension, while a same-sex lover of twenty years may not be. As well, state-regulated institutions such as schools or hospitals use marriage and family relations to determine which people will be informed and consulted about the experiences of someone in the institution. Thus, critically ill patients may find that family members with whom they have little contact are admitted to their rooms and entitled to make significant medical decisions, while the friends who actually provide daily support, and who know best the patient's wishes, are excluded. Finally, even when someone designates an heir in a will, the "immediate family" have some legal grounds to challenge that will and claim a right to the inheritance.

Other aspects of family relationships are normatively regulated. That is, social conventions and notions of respectability adhere to certain types of sexual relations, some child-rearing and socialization practices, and some cohabitation arrangements. For the vast majority of people, "family," however defined, constitutes the social relationships within which basic **socialization** occurs, at least during the formative infant and early childhood years. Thus, family relations are among the most fundamental emotional and social relations within which intersubjectivity develops. As a result, at the most basic level, the "self" is formed in relation to family. Thus, norms about family are deeply instilled in us all (Miller, 1983, 1984).

Complicating formulations on the meaning of "family" is the way in which the various relationships involved in family are changing. Although there have always been dominant norms and practices embedded in law and reinforced in a myriad of ways such as religion, there have always been as well those who did not conform, either by deliberately flouting convention or by simply doing something else. However, throughout the twentieth century, the numbers of people actively and openly challenging prevailing family conventions dramatically increased. And many of their challenges have altered formal legal and social policies by legitimating a greater diversity of practices.

One of the central relationships encompassed by the concept of families is marriage. As recent court rulings indicate, marriage historically has been a relatively precise term referring to a heterosexual relationship between a woman and a man that is socially and legally recognized and privileged. In the early part of the twentieth century, social norms and conventions around marriage were so strong that almost anyone violating them was subject to severe social pressure. Changing social practices and shifting ideologies produced, by the end of the century, a climate in which a greater diversity of practices was tolerated. This loosening up allows some people greater choice in how they live: More gays, lesbians, and transgendered people are "out"; women who have children without being married are no longer socially ostracized, and increasing numbers of women deliberately opt to be single parents; people who are single are less likely to be regarded with suspicion. As gay and lesbian couples fight for the right to marry, they argue that they want to have their relationships recognized and validated in the same way that heterosexual couples do. So, even as the definitions of who can marry are extended, the importance of marriage is reaffirmed. Marriage remains one of the most significant and privileged of interpersonal relations. And it is central to ideas about family. Precisely because it is so privileged, it also carries enormous emotional weight, so that getting married and staying married remain for many people vitally important commitments so taken for granted they seem a natural part of life.

Other practices embedded in law have been challenged. One of the most significant is the legal and social subordination of women to men. For example, in the nineteenth century, married women were subordinate to their husbands in law. Their property became their husbands', their children were subject only to the father's authority, they could be beaten by their husbands or committed to institutions by them, and they could make no decisions without their husbands' approval. All of these male powers have been removed from law. Until recently, however, men had the legal right to sex with their wives regardless of their consent, and marriage could be terminated if either partner (especially the woman) had sex with anyone other than his or her legal spouse. Government welfare provisions vary about whether or not a woman is entitled to welfare benefits if the authorities suspect she has a male lover, who is, in some regulations, automatically assumed to be obligated to support her.

Another social practice embedded in law concerned legitimate sexuality, conception, and childbirth. Although male privilege meant that men could engage in a variety of sexual relations with little fear of sanction, there were strong conventions about what kind of sexual behaviour was acceptable. Homosexuality was illegal until 1969 in Canada, and heterosexual, monogamous sex between a married couple was the only publicly acceptable practice. The sanctions for women who violated these norms were often severe, and children born "out of wedlock" were legally illegitimate and subject to financial and social penalties.

As former practices are challenged, and legal regulation and social norms change, a situation develops in which there are extensive and widespread disagreements about what is appropriate. Behaviours that previously remained hidden and a source of embarrassment or shame, become increasingly tolerated, although many people still find them problematic or offensive. Increasing numbers of women are now having children without being married. Teenage girls increasingly keep their children rather than give them up for adoption. Women and men increasingly are open about having sexual relationships outside of marriage. Gays and lesbians are fighting against discrimination on the basis of sexual orientation, and once homosexuality was no longer illegal, homosexuals organized and fought for various legal rights such as benefits for same-sex partners, custody rights, access to medically assisted insemination, and the right to adopt. Divorce is increasingly easier to obtain, and is no longer a major social shame. Women are increasingly entitled to welfare benefits, even if they have a male lover. All children are now legitimate.

This greater diversity in actual practices and in what is socially acceptable has generated considerable confusion. For example, the previous legal assumption that a man was obligated to support his wife and their children became increasingly problematic as married woman took paid jobs. Family law no longer holds the man automatically responsible for supporting his wife and children, but women's relatively poor position in the labour market means that with divorce many women still need the continuing support for which often they are technically ineligible. Legal rights to custody of children have always been disputed. In the nineteenth century fathers had sole rights. Woman challenged that, and in the early twentieth century, in conjunction with prevailing notions that mothers provided the ideal care for children, women tended to get custody. More recently, in conjunction with increasing demands that fathers be more actively involved in childcare, men have reasserted their demands for custody. In response, the courts have implemented policies revolving around a notion of the child's best interests, but this policy change in no way has reduced disputes over custody (Smart and Neale, 1999). As same-sex couples marry and divorce, they too have struggled over support and custody arrangements. The courts increasingly are dealing with individual situations, rather than assuming that widespread norms prevail.

Another confusing situation is that, although it has become increasingly acceptable for people not to marry, to divorce, and to live common law, there is still a powerful norm that restricts people to either being single or in a couple. Multiple intimate sexual groups (known in some societies as polygamous relations) are taboo. Housing stock, hotel rooms, and spousal benefits all are structured around single people or couples. For example, houses are simply not built with four or five "master bedrooms," and most hotels could not accommodate and would not tolerate a request for a room for five adults. Although increasing numbers of workplaces have acknowledged same-sex partners for spousal benefits, none would recognize two or more spouses. Similarly, the lovers or partners of a parent often have great difficulty getting formal recognition from schools, doctors, and other authorities that they are, in practice, parents of the child. Likewise, friends of a parent who are intimately involved in childcare have no recognized claim to parenting. Thus, although acceptable family practices have widened considerably, especially in the last thirty years, there are still deeply embedded legal, social, political, and economic conventions that constrain people's behaviour and shape the possibilities available to them.

THE HISTORY AND DEVELOPMENT OF SOCIOLOGICAL THEORIES

Debates among sociologists about the best ways to conceptualize families have their origins in mid-nineteenth-century European and North American intellectual debates about the nature of social organization, about the bases of authority, social order, power, human nature, and the relation between the individual and the ruling authorities. At the heart of these debates were contending assumptions about families.[7]

Prior to the 1850s, the prevailing assumptions were expressed in what was called at the time "the patriarchal theory." This perspective assumed that the "primary family," that is, a married man and woman and their children, was the natural condition of humanity. In this family form the husband/father, as patriarch, held authority over and provided protection for his wife and children. This primary family was based on the sexual division of labour, marriage patterns, sexual practices, and kinship organization, which were the ideal, and to some extent the practice of the time in bourgeois or middle-class European society. According to patriarchal theory, this family form was the basis of all social organization, since the original husband and wife had children who, in turn, married and had children. All these extended kin groups remained under the authority and protection of the original husband/father until his death, when his descendants divided into as many families as he had sons. Each of these groups resembled the original group and continued to recognize the social authority derived from their common ancestor. As each generation "begat" the next, the system expanded until it became so large that central government became necessary. That central government, whether headed by a monarch or president, was considered by these theorists to be an extension of the husband/father, and the primary family was thought to be the basic unit of society.

This patriarchal theory assumed that the primary family was the natural condition of humanity. Rooted in Judeo-Christian ideas about creation, it assumed that the primary family was God-given and had existed since the beginning of human life. Because it was universal and necessary, it was impervious to change. When these theorists confronted examples of people who did not conform to the primary family, for example, the newly emerging urban **working classes** or the indigenous peoples living in other parts of the world, they dismissed them as immoral, deviant, or degenerate.

In the 1850s a debate emerged which sharply challenged patriarchal theory and which established the theoretical and conceptual foundations of modern sociology. The impetus for the debate lay in contemporary political, economic, and social developments, as capitalism emerged as the dominant economic and socio-political organization of society. The white, middle-class male scholars of the time confronted a society undergoing rapid transformation and widespread social unrest in the world, which increasingly proved the enormous diversity of human social organization. In Europe, there were widespread social movements which challenged these prevailing values, arguing, for example, that women should not be subordinate to their husbands—indeed, that marriage was often oppressive and harmful to women. Some social movements proposed, instead of capitalist economic arrangements, intentional communities based on communal living arrangements in which children would be raised collectively by the community and adults would pool their economic resources. In the colonized world, anti-imperialist struggles contested the idea that the way of life of imperial Europe was superior.

The idea of a universal, unchanging patriarchal family form was also undermined by the discovery of a wide range of different social forms in different parts of the world. Darwin's theories of evolution were influential in the study of the human sciences, since they challenged creationist ideas and paved the way for an historical and comparative approach to studying social development.[8] This context led to major debates about how to understand family.

The dominant position was held by those seeking to defend or promote the capitalist liberal democracies. Within this pro-capitalist position, two tendencies emerged. One, represented by scholars such as E. Westermark or E. B. Tylor, retained the essential arguments of the earlier patriarchal theory. For them what they called the "procreative family," which had previously been known as the primary family and is now identified as the nuclear family, was a universal biological form. They explained away the existence of alternative forms and practices, saying that they must have developed for specific political reasons, but insisting that they would inevitably fail because of the necessity for the procreative family. This line of argument continues to the present, represented, for example, by the formal positions of the Roman Catholic Church, or by writers such as William Gairdner (1992), but it was (and continues to be) seriously challenged by theorists who dispute the universality of the patriarchal family.

Deeply influenced by theories of evolution, and recognizing the importance of an historical appreciation, late-nineteenth-century theorists such as John Lubbock and Herbert Spencer (recognized as one of the "fathers" of sociology) developed within a pro-capitalist framework, viewpoints that opposed patriarchal theory. These theorists rejected any notion that the patriarchal primary family was a natural, unchanging human form. Instead, they hypothesized that in the course of human history, societies had evolved through various stages of development. For most of them, the key criteria for distinguishing these various stages were the different prevailing family forms. Although there was extensive debate about what the various stages were like, most agreed that the earliest stage was one in which marriage was unknown, and men and women engaged in unregulated "sexual mingling." All agreed that such societies must have been unsuccessful and that a new stage in which there was some form of marriage practice and sexual regulation emerged, gradually followed by a stage of patriarchal family. The culmination of social evolution was considered to be patriarchal marriage and family forms.

Because these theorists saw the family forms idealized by their own class as the end result of the evolution of society from primitive anarchy to civilized regulation, they considered the family forms of their own society, and specifically their own class, as the pinnacle of human achievement. In contrast, a minority position was put forward by political activists such as the socialist and feminist movements and writers who, although agreeing that nineteenth-century capitalist society was a result of social evolution, disagreed that it represented the highest achievement of human social organization. Political activists such as the Owentites (Taylor, 1983) and writers such as Lewis Henry Morgan, Frederick Engels, and Karl Marx documented changes in family organization, functions, and authority relations over time, noting that there was a close correlation between changes in economic, political, and social organization and changes in the sexual divisions of labour, marital practices, and the status of women relative to men and of children relative to adults. Furthermore, they argued, society would continue to develop and change, and they envisioned a future society in which there would be equality among all people, and family forms and relations would be very different from what existed at the time.

By the 1880s sociology was established as a formally recognized academic discipline. The intellectual tradition inherited by this new discipline shaped its approaches to the study of family. Thus, at the beginning of the century, there were three distinct schools of thought. The main one, derived from the historical revision of patriarchal theory, maintained that the nuclear family—a married man and woman and their children—was the best and most appropriate family form and that, compared to the wide variety of other family forms throughout history and in various societies, it represented the best achievement of hundreds of years of social development. A more conservative school of thought maintained that the nuclear family was the only family form and that it had existed in all societies throughout history. A third school of thought maintained that the nuclear family form was just one of many, that it was not necessarily the best or most natural form, and that other forms could and would emerge in changing social conditions.

At the same time that sociology was becoming established as a discipline, Sigmund Freud was developing psychoanalysis, and his theories strongly influenced many sociological theorists, especially those working in the area of family. Freud argued that the early experiences of children, particularly their pre-verbal experiences, were central in shaping their adult personalities and behaviours. He paid particular attention to childhood sexuality, and to the processes whereby masculinity and femininity were distinguished and developed in the child. He argued that the incest taboo (which prohibited sex between parents and children) was universal. His theories took for granted a nuclear family form and assumed that the sexual division of labour between the adults, and the child-rearing practices they engaged in, were essential features in psychic development. Because Freud tended to focus on individuals rather than on the organization of social groups, his work had greater impact on psychology than on sociology, but his ideas were, and continue to be, profoundly influential in sociology. Some writers in each of the three schools of thought took up aspects of psychoanalytic theory and engaged them in their works.

CONTEMPORARY SOCIOLOGICAL THEORIES

Liberal Theories

Structural-Functionalism

Within the general framework of liberal theories, one of the most popular in the first half of the twentieth century was **structural-functionalism**, which represented a shift away from historical and comparative studies to analytic studies, which concentrated on the

FIGURE 2.1 Turn-of-the-Century Theories

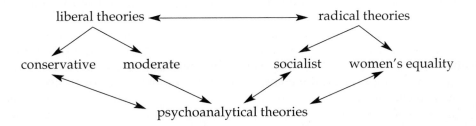

internal features of the society. This way of thinking about social organization combined two ideas: structure and function.

The concept of structure assumed that every society has an underlying structure, which is often not recognized by the people who live in it. This structure could be understood by examining "the mutual relations of constituent parts or elements of a whole as defining its particular nature" (Williams, 1976: 301). This structure could be revealed by studying different aspects of the social whole such as the religious, political, and legal systems, or the workings of the economy. The organization of kinship, marriage, and families was an obvious aspect of social structure.

In contrast to structure, which was about organization, the concept of function was about performance—how something worked. Structural-functionalists generally assumed that particular social arrangements existed because they were functional or worked to keep the social structure intact. They assumed that if something were dysfunctional, it would be disruptive and either the social structure would be reorganized so that its various parts were in harmony and functional, or great social crisis and upheaval would occur. Thus, functional arguments assumed that if a particular social form had existed for any length of time, it must be functional, and the task for researchers was to find out what those functions were.

In 1913 Bronislav Malinowski published *The Family Among the Australian Aboriginees*, which drew on nineteenth century debates about families and crystalized the prevailing intellectual ideas of his time (Malinowski, 1913). His book used a structural-functionalist approach and laid out the argument which became the basis for most sociological theories of family in the first half of the twentieth century. He argued that "the family" consisted of a man and a woman and their children, and that this family form—the nuclear family—was universal, appearing in all societies, even those that appeared to be very different from European societies, such as the Aboriginal societies of Australia.

Malinowski's theory of the family made several assumptions that became taken for granted in much sociological theory. First, he argued, the nuclear family is universal because it is rooted in biological sex differences. Second, he assumed that those biological sex differences resulted in different social and psychological characteristics in men and women. These differences meant that there should be a division of labour in which men and women do different things. Third, he claimed that the male-female couple and their children always exist as a bounded social group distinct from any other social groupings. The function of this group is to provide a geographical place (the home), to organize sexual reproduction, and to provide affection, love, and nurturance. Fourth, he assumed that all members of a family share the same interest and goals. Finally, he insisted that this family form was necessary for the smooth functioning of society as a whole.

During the first half of the twentieth century, most of the leading scholars who studied families accepted the various assumptions laid out by Malinowski. George P. Murdock, for example, asserted that the nuclear family, based on harmonious co-operation between men and women, is a "universal human grouping" which fulfils a number of functions necessary for social survival. His definition of family has been widely accepted: "A social group characterized by common residence, economic co-operation, and reproduction. It includes adults of both sexes, at least two of whom maintain a socially approved sexual relationship, and one or more children, own or adopted, of the sexually cohabiting adults." (Murdock, 1949: 2). Thus structural-functionalism assumed that "the family" was an essential institution of society because one of its main functions was to raise children to become properly socialized members of their society, that is, people willing and able to behave in socially appropriate ways. It also assumed that "the family" was essential to maintaining social order because it was the most socially efficient or functional way of ensuring people received emotional support, organizing both sexual relations and the production and raising of children, and arranging economic co-operation (Goode, 1963, 1964).

Talcott Parsons applied these theories to the mid-twentieth-century society of the U.S. Like Malinowski and Murdock, he considered the family a small social group distinct from other social units. Parsons became well known as the leading structural-functionalist theorist of families (Parsons and Bales, 1955). In Canada, the most important structural-functionalists to write about families were Seeley, Sim, and Loosely in their 1950s study of middle-class families in a Toronto neighbourhood they called Crestwood Heights (1956) and Benjamin Schlesinger (1979). Their work replicated the theoretical assumptions articulated by Parsons in his general theories of families.

Parsons argued that, in pre-industrial societies, families combined productive work such as farming with domestic life so that the family household was a site both of productive economic labour and of affective caregiving. With the development of modern industrialized society, productive functions were taken out of the family into specialized paid worksites, leaving the family as a residential consumption unit whose primary function is to satisfy emotional needs. According to Parsons, men and women within the family assumed certain specialized modern functions: Men had the instrumental role of relating to the larger society, of providing rationality, and earning the money necessary to support the family; women had the affective role of mediating emotional relationships, providing nurturing sensitivity, and taking care of the home. This organization of family life with its particular sexual division of labour was, according the Parsons, functional because all small groups need a "task leader" and "emotional leader" if they are going to work smoothly. Parsons also affirmed the idea that there was a functional fit between the family and other spheres of social life. More importantly, it was functional for the needs of capitalist labour markets dependent on a mobile workforce of male breadwinners.

Parsons's work, influential though it was, has been criticized and dismissed by some (see Morgan, 1975). Although it was astounding to label the provision of childcare, socialization of children, and maintenance and management of the household "emotional" and not "instrumental," Parsons's work was even more offensive in its blatant rationalization of the gender inequality inherent in the division of labour to which he referred. Although Parsons's analysis of family was benign in intent, it had unintended consequences. By asserting that the family form predominant among white middle-class Americans was functional and natural, he paved the way for those who insisted that other family forms—especially Native, Black, and working-class families—were "deviant" or inadequate. Because his theme of functional fit could not predict the changes that are now so evident in families, because he assumed that what was functional (or good) for society was good for the individual, and most importantly, because his work confused a description and approbation of normative values with an analysis of social life, Parsons's conceptualization has been disputed by many.

Because structural-functionalism viewed change as inevitably disruptive and negative, few of its theorists were able to develop useful analyses of social change.[9] Many, in fact, were openly hostile to change. More significantly, their commitment to notions of social harmony led them to deny conflict. This was particularly true in their studies of families, where men's power and women's subordination, and the sexual antagonism that resulted, were hidden by the concept of separate, complementary roles. For example, Parsons and others insisted that the nuclear family in which the man, as the husband/father, was the breadwinner and the woman was the homemaker whose major preoccupation was her roles as wife and mother, was functional for society. When some women protested the constraints of this role, they were told that it was their problem that they were unable to adjust or adapt to their proper social position. Other women who violated the role by taking on paid employment were criticized, labelled deviant, and blamed for any dysfunctions in family life. As subsequent historians and theorists have shown, the family form described so positively by the structural-functionalists reflected not the actual family forms and familial relations of the time, but the normative ideals of the period. That family form was actually based on inequalities and coercion (Coontz, 1992; Barrett and McIntosh, 1980).

As a result, structural-functionalism is now generally recognized either as inadequate or worse, as defending the status quo rather than analyzing it. Nevertheless, many researchers focusing on limited and specific topics still make structural-functionalist assumptions in their work, and many contemporary approaches to studying families are strongly influenced by structural-functionalism.

Symbolic Interactionism

Because structural-functionalism focused on social structures and the ways in which individual personality and behaviour are shaped by the particular society they live in, most of its theorists did not investigate the ways in which individuals act. Some theorists such as George Herbert Mead (1934), although rarely disputing the structural-functionalist assumptions of social organization, assumed that people are not passive recipients but active agents who negotiate meaning through their interactions with other people. These symbolic interactionists turned their attention to studying the ways in which individuals interpret social organization and then interact with others based on that interpretation. They concentrated on the ways in which people modify or change their behaviour depending on how others react to them. Thus, symbolic interactionism examines the ways in which individuals construct the meaning of what they are doing in their interactions with others. The strength of this approach is that it starts from everyday and face-to-face relations. Merrill and Eldridge (1952: 486) defined symbolic interactionism as the

> reciprocal influencing of the acts of persons and groups mediated through communication which includes the interaction of the person with self.

Inevitably, such studies had to concentrate on small groups and family behaviours, and interactions were one of the preferred subjects for research. Investigators have observed interactions between mothers and children, looking at the process of socialization and the expression of affection and love, and between husbands and wives, looking at decision-making, divisions of labour, and relative marital satisfaction. The concept of "**roles**" has been a useful tool for symbolic interactionism. Taken from the theatre, where "role" is the part or character an actor assumes or has to play, sociologists investigate the different roles social actors assume in the course of their lives. Someone may be a daughter in the morning over breakfast, a student during the day at university, a friend during break, a worker in the evening, and a lover later that night. Symbolic interactionists assume that in each of those roles, the individual's behaviour and reactions will vary with the type of interaction and the expectations of the others around him or her.

However, the idea of families as co-operating groups with shared interests prevails in most symbolic interactionist research. For example, in Rosenthal's study of ritual occasions when several generations get together, she assumed that such events strengthened family ties, and argued that families are viewed as organizations in which people assume responsibility for specialized tasks in order to maintain familial solidarity (1986). Symbolic interactionist research also tends to accept uncritically the ideas of family harmony, assuming that conflict and interpersonal tensions and disputes or violence are the results of individual quirks. **Family violence**, for example, is typically understood as a problem arising from the personal biographies of the individuals involved. The abusive practices of men are often attributed to the fact that, as children, they witnessed their fathers abusing their mothers or were themselves victims of men's violence. Little in the framework of symbolic interactionism invites researchers to move beyond such individualistic perspectives to explore the impact of people's political, economic, or cultural circumstances in order to investigate, for example, to what extent domestic violence reflects either the social subordination of women and children or the glorification of violence in film, computer games, or war.

In general, symbolic interactionism has produced an extensive literature describing how people interact, but its focus on specific interpersonal relationships means that it typically overlooks or downplays the larger contexts that shape people's interactions. It is particularly unable to explain why some people do not conform to typically accepted norms and values (Mackie, 1987).[10]

Systems Theory

In the 1950s, researchers developed what they called a systems approach to studying families. Influenced by the ideas of symbolic interactionism and by the experiences of family therapists such as R. D. Laing (Laing and Esterson, 1964), this approach assumed that families were "relatively closed, **boundary maintaining**" groups (Hill, 1971: 12). This theory focuses on the ways that families must maintain their boundaries and assumes that they are systems of relationships and interactions in which what happens to one member affects all the others.

This approach was most popular among therapists or social workers who found that many illnesses or socially disruptive behaviours in an individual could best be understood by looking at the family as a group. For example, systems theorists examined wife abuse and argued that in cases of recurring abuse, women must contribute to the problem which is really not the abuse per se but the dysfunctional marital relationship: "If abuse is an integral part of spousal interaction, then, in a sense, she supports the continuation of the abuse" (Montgomery and Fewer, 1988: 41).

They also used the idea of a family system to explain how abusive behaviours (or other dysfunctional patterns) are repeated in families in "cycles of violence." If a child grows up in a family in which abuse occurs, the child learns to tolerate abuse and is likely either to become abusive or to become a victim of abuse.

The notion of a family as a bounded system encouraged researchers to focus on what happens when the boundaries are broken. Many systems theorists studied the ways in which families redefine themselves when divorce and remarriage create "boundary confusion."

Developmental Approaches

The **developmental approach**, informed by structural-functionalist assumptions that stable family life is desirable and shaped by the external social structures, by systems theory's notion of families as closed groups, and by symbolic interactionist ideas about the ways in which family relationships are interactive and develop over time, uses the concept of a family life cycle to study the ways in which families go through different stages. Each stage—marriage, the birth of the first and then subsequent children, when the children leave, death—is understood as generating specific tasks and challenges which the family has to respond to.

Like the theories it is derived from, the developmental approach is good at describing family life. Its focus on the ever-changing nature of family life allows a dynamic analysis of the ways in which family structure and practices change as individual members develop personally, as relationships change, new members arrive, and others go.

Exchange Theory

Inspired by symbolic interactionism, some researchers have applied the notions of exchange and cost-benefit as a way of understanding family relationships. Many family interactions are assumed to be exchanges based on bargaining and negotiation. It is assumed that people make cost-benefit analyses in deciding how to behave toward one another. Many researchers have used this approach to study the divisions of labour between women and men. A woman's decision to work at home full-time is presumed to be based on an exchange with her husband who will support her economically in return for her domestic labour. These theorists assume that such a woman assesses her loss of employment status and income as "worth it" because of the benefits accruing from being at home. Although exchange theory is useful in situations in which people are making actual decisions, it does not easily take account of the ways in which people, especially in families, often adapt and adjust to accommodate one another.

Marxist and Feminist Theories

In contrast to the various liberal theories of social organization, two critical nineteenth-century currents continued throughout the twentieth century to offer critiques of the various liberal theories and to provide alternative analysis. Although various Marxist theories of family have been developed, they have always been a minority perspective in the sociology of Western Europe and North America. With the revival of Marxist theories in the 1970s, however, they have provided some innovative analyses. Various feminist theories have profoundly transformed the terrain of family sociology.

Marxism

Nineteenth-century Marxist theories of family were explicitly argued in Frederick Engels's *Origin of the Family, Private Property and the State* which "offered the first systematic theory of the way sex and class structures combine in the economy and the state to determine women's oppression" (Maroney and Luxton, 1987: 13). Engels argued that "the determining factor in history is, in the final instance, the production and reproduction of immediate life. This, again, is of a two-fold character: on the one side, the production of the means of existence, of food, clothing, and shelter, and the tools necessary for that production; on the other side, the production of human beings themselves, the propagation of the species" ([1884] 1972: 71).

Like other theorists of his time, Engels argued that there were a number of stages of development in human history. Unlike most of his contemporaries who assumed the different stages were distinguished by different family forms, Engels developed the concept he and Marx had employed. He argued that the different stages of human society were distinguished by the prevailing types and relations of labour by which social wealth was produced—the mode of production. Each mode—for example, feudalism or capitalism—had a specific family form associated with it, and those family forms varied in the ways they organized economic co-operation, sexual relations, child rearing, and the division of labour. Engels showed how, with the development of class and state societies, the position of women relative to men deteriorated.

In their studies of capitalist societies, Engels and Marx showed how the oppressive and exploitative situation of working people was particularly dreadful for women. They did not, however, theorize families. Most subsequent Marxist theorists similarly assumed that the historically specific family forms of capitalism were oppressive to women and that when capitalism ended, new forms could emerge in which women and men would be equal. They did not move beyond that position until the intervention of the women's liberation movement in the late 1960s produced feminist theories, some of which engaged and reworked Marxist theories.

Feminist Theories

There is no single, coherent feminist theory; rather, there are several distinct theoretical currents, each of which provides a different perspective on family theory. Feminist theories have emerged in part from critiques of pre-existing, non-feminist theoretical and political perspectives, and thus share the theoretical frameworks of those traditions, reworked to take account of sex/gender and whether it is useful to think about "women" as a social category distinct from men.[11] Although each theoretical perspective is quite different and approaches studies of families differently, they engage with and influence one another, and they all share certain general assumptions.

What feminist theories have in common is their recognition that sexism privileges men and discriminates against women, their commitment to exposing the way sexism and misogyny operate in society, and their goal of eliminating this inequality. As a result, there are certain themes that most feminist theories share in common. In general, feminist theories of family argue that no particular family form, especially the widespread heterosexual nuclear family, is God-given, biologically determined, or functional to society. Instead, family forms are historically specific, and even such apparently biological aspects as conception and childbirth are socially constructed and vary with time and place. Some have pointed out that popular conservative assumptions about the "natural-ness" of particular family forms are inherently racist and Eurocentric, and that they fail to appreciate the diversity of household, kinship, and community networks that exists in other parts of the world. Feminists also recognize that most family forms and divisions of labour discriminate against women while relatively privileging men, although the ways in which this occurs vary significantly by class, race, and ethnicity.

Feminist politics addressed a wide array of topics related to family, ranging from reproductive rights (such as freedom from forced sterilization, access to abortion and med-ically assisted fertility) to employment rights (such as paid maternity, parental, and family leaves). Aboriginal women have fought for their land and rights to self-determination, especially their rights to keep their children in the face of state policies of assimilation and child protection. Immigrant women have fought for full citizenship rights, including the right to bring their children to Canada. As they engaged in political struggles over these issues, they developed a range of theoretical positions that influenced family theory (Rebick 2000).

One of the most important contributions of feminist theory to studies of families is the analysis of familial **ideology**. Theorists such as Barrett and McIntosh (1980), Eichler (1988), and Finch (1989) have shown that the idea that the nuclear family is the preferred family form is political and ideological, with negative consequences for women. It is from

Filipina nanny, Leticia Cables, is greeted by supporters after being allowed to return to Canada. She sought refuge in a church for five months when she faced deportation for working an extra job.

that understanding that feminist theorists, rather than analyzing families, have developed extensive critiques of most non-feminist theories, arguing that they tend to justify women's inequality and men's privilege. Critiques of state policies in Canada reveal how thoroughly they are shaped by, and reinforce, familial ideology, rather than responding to the actual needs of people (Ursel, 1992; Eichler, 1997a; Dua, 1999). Similarly, many socialist, anti-imperialist, and anti-racist theorists have argued that a narrow focus on "women" and "men" masks the significant differences between people, especially those of race, ethnicity, and class (Davis, 1981; Weedon, 1999).

Feminist theorists criticized structural-functionalist arguments that the heterosexual nuclear family was functional to capitalism. Instead, they argued, capitalist economic practices are incompatible with childcare; most paid workplaces are organized on the assumption that workers do not have any other conflicting responsibilities. This "male model" does not work for most women, who typically have childcare and other domestic responsibilities to juggle as well.[12] Feminists have documented extensively the ways in which women's primary responsibility for domestic labour, and particularly childcare and other caregiving responsibilities, is central to women's economic dependency on men and their unequal access to paid employment and to income, as Baker indicates in Chapter Five. They have shown that the nuclear family form results in women doing vast amounts of socially necessary labour for free and in ways that are not recognized or validated socially (Luxton, 1980; Luxton and Corman, 2001).

Women of colour and anti-racist feminists took this argument further, pointing out that in racialized and immigrant communities, families are important sources of support in the face of, and defence against, systemic racism and overt racist attacks. As the primary caregivers, women are often actively responsible for coping with the devastating impact of racism on the lives of family members (Campbell, 1973; Das Gupta, 1995). A study that focused on racism and immigration investigated the ways in which the Canadian state's development depended on its preferential treatment of white Anglo and Quebecois families in contrast to the discrimination faced by immigrants of colour from other parts of the world (Dua, 1999). Another studies the role of immigrant labour as a source of paid domestic labour (Bakan and Stasiulis, 1994). As more and more women in Canada entered the paid labour force, they confronted the ways in which paid employment and domestic labour are incompatible. Although this crisis of domestic labour increased demands on employers and the state for better maternity, parental, and family leaves, childcare services, and support for caregiving, it also increased the demands of middle-class Canadians for paid domestic workers, a demand that governments responded to by importing foreign workers who are low-paid and subject to a range of oppressive working conditions (Silvera, 1989; Arat-Koc, 1989).

The recognition that domestic labour was not just a private emotional service promoted socialist feminist efforts to theorize its relationship to the larger society.[13] Drawing on Engels's theory of the two-sided character of production, Wally Seccombe (1991) reconceptualized a history of economic development, arguing that changes in economic relations could only be fully understood if family patterns were included. He documented the way "the production of life itself" had an influential effect on the transition from feudalism to capitalism and on the transition to industrial production. Marriage, family, and household forms in feudalism controlled access to land, lifetime birth rates, and gender hierarchies. Along with inheritance patterns, they influenced the development of a pool of labourers necessary for capitalist production and the rate of capital accumulation.

Using the same concept of a mode of production, several studies of the impact of imperialism on Aboriginal peoples in Canada showed how colonization depended on restructuring gender and family relations among colonized peoples. Colonizers disrupted kin-based patterns of work and landholding, promoted men's control over women's sexuality, and imposed European marriage practices to women's disadvantage, and so were able to undermine earlier communal modes of production (Bourgeault, 1983; Anderson, 1991).

Socialist feminists, focusing on analyzing the relationship between the processes of capital accumulation (patterns of capital investment and organization of paid employment) and "the reproduction of labour power," argue that capitalism depends on the existence of workers who are ready and able to labour to produce both their own wages and profits for the employers.[14] They have analyzed working-class family households as sites where labour power is reproduced, both daily and generationally (Seccombe, 1993). To ensure an income, one or more family members sell their capacity to work, or their labour power, to an employer. On the job, their labour power is consumed, and they earn its monetary recompense, a wage or salary. In consumer markets and in their homes, people use those earnings and their unpaid labour to obtain and produce the goods and services that make up the means of subsistence for themselves and their families. Each day, the means of subsistence are prepared and consumed, and family subsistence, including the capacity to work again, is produced. This labour of social reproduction ensures the survival of both individuals and the society as a whole (Luxton, 1980; Fox, 1980; Hamilton and Barrett, 1986; Picchio, 1992; Fox and Luxton, 2000).

The recognition that unpaid domestic labour is work that contributes not only to the well-being of individual family members, but to the society as a whole, inspired feminists to argue that this unpaid work should be measured and valued, to ensure that the women who do it receive appropriate compensation and social recognition (Waring, 1990). In 1985 the International Wages for Housework Campaign presented a motion to the Third United Nations World Conference on Women in Nairobi, Kenya, that led to a United Nations resolution that directed countries to:

> recognize the remunerated and unremunerated contributions of women in national economic statistics and the gross domestic product, especially those contributions of women in agriculture, food production, reproduction, and household activities (Status of Women Canada 1990: 120).[15]

As international agencies and federal governments began to respond to this directive, their findings confirmed feminist claims. The United Nations (1991) estimated that women's unpaid work internationally was worth about $4 trillion annually. In Canada, the 1992 General Social Survey indicated that people performed at least 25 billion hours of unpaid work, 95 percent of which was domestic labour—looking after children and caring for the home. Statistics Canada estimated that this labour was equivalent to about 13 million full-time jobs, was worth about $234 billion, and equalled about 40 percent of Canada's gross domestic product, and that women did two-thirds of it (Statistics Canada, 1992; Chandler, 1994; Statistics Canada, 1995).[16] Statistics Canada demonstrates that, since 1960, women have continued to do about two-thirds of all unpaid work in Canada; women do more domestic labour than men, even as teenagers (Statistics Canada, 2000: 97). Women who are employed do more than their male partners; in fact, men living with employed women do less than men whose wives are not employed (Statistics Canada, 2000:111). The 2001 census reported that women were 2.5 times more likely than men to spend more than 30 hours a week looking after children without pay, 2.9 times more likely to spend more than 30 hours a week on unpaid housework, and 2 times more likely to spend 10 or more hours on unpaid caregiving to seniors (Statistics Canada, 2003). These figures lent weight to feminist demands for social policies that recognized the importance of women's work to their families and provided support for that work (Eichler, 1997; Baker, 2001, this text).[17]

Radical feminist theory tends to focus on differences between women and men and on the ways in which men's power controls and oppresses women. Many researchers influenced by this perspective have revealed the ways in which families are all too often unsafe places for women and children who are subject to men's violence and sexual assaults. They have noted that "compulsory heterosexuality"— that is, the belief that people are naturally sexually attracted to the opposite sex and that homosexual and lesbian relations are either unnatural or not as good—acts to reinforce the nuclear family. Instead they have called for a plurality of personal relations, both sexual and domestic. From that perspective they have asked what social arrangements provide the best environments for raising children, and for ensuring that both women and men get affection, caring, and opportunities for self-development. Some feminists have argued that families as they now exist are anti-social, and that people would be better off if communities and collectivities of people co-operated to live together, sharing resources and caring for one another.

As David Cheal has pointed out, the revival of feminism since the 1970s has resulted in a "basis for new sociological theorizing" which has challenged the earlier non-feminist approaches, which tended to be "descriptive and problem focused" (1991: 18). Similarly, the lesbian and gay liberation movements and anti-imperialist and anti-racist movements challenge sociological theories of families to investigate the impact of compulsory heterosexuality and of racism on the ways in which theories have developed.

Postmodernity and Postmodernism or Poststructuralist Theory

In the latter part of the twentieth century, new forms of business organization such as multinationals and transnationals, relying significantly on computers and automation, developed a world capitalist system based on new international divisions of labour, international banking systems, and stock exchanges, and, consequently, a penetration of capitalist relations into almost all areas of human life (including biological conception and genetic manipulation). With the defeats and collapse of the communist states, this restructured capitalism gained global ascendency. Simultaneously, new cultural forms and practices in areas such as architecture, art, literature and poetry, advertising, dance, and film—all based on new information technologies—combined with the challenges to social, political, and economic life posed by a range of related political movements demanding equality and liberation for workers, women, people of colour, immigrants, peoples of the Third World and its diasporas, disabled people, gays, lesbians, intersexed and transgendered peoples, and children, as well as environmental protection and animal rights. The new social, economic, and political relations generated by these changes have been identified as either "late capitalism" or "postmodernity."[18]

Academic attempts to develop ways of interrogating contemporary life and capturing these new perspectives drew on a variety of approaches such as critiques of structuralism, semiotics, studies of language and arts, cultural studies, marketing studies, and new therapies. They generated a new theoretical orientation identified, particularly in the humanities, as postmodernism. As Frederick Jameson (1991: x) notes: "a range of different analyses have coalesced into a new discursive genre, which we might as well call 'postmodernism theory.'" This postmodern theory is closely related to poststructuralism, a loosely knit intellectual movement, based largely in a social sciences' critique of structuralism, in which "language, meaning, social institutions, and the self are destabilized" (Palmer, 1997: 145). Although there are important differences between the two currents, they share many approaches and are often treated as if they were the same (Segal, 1999: 29).

Many researchers find the concept of postmodern society useful without adopting postmodernism or poststructuralism as a theoretical framework, making a distinction between discussions of family in postmodern society and poststructuralist or postmodernist analyses of families. Sociologist Judith Stacey (1990: 17), for example, argues: "Americans today have crafted a multiplicity of family and household arrangements that we inhabit uneasily and reconstitute frequently in response to changing personal and occupational circumstances." She describes "the contested, ambivalent, and undecided character of contemporary gender and kinship arrangements" in the U.S., identifying them as "the postmodern family."

To date, few researchers have used either postmodernism or poststructuralism to study topics directly related to the sociology of family, but many topics of interest, such as body image, sexuality, and representation, are indirectly related. Based on deconstructing prevailing beliefs, especially those that claim to know the "truth" about the social world, postmodernism and poststructuralism pay close attention to meaning, refusing to accept any categories as "real," but rather insisting that all categories are produced by discourse. Applied to studies of family, these approaches argue that the use of images and language in legislation, social policy, political discourses, and popular culture produce particular understandings about gender and family life that influence the way people think of themselves and understand their relationships. Baker and Tippin, (1999), for example, reveal the implicit assumptions in social policies about what constitutes "good enough mothering."

Postmodernism and poststructuralism both recognize a multiplicity of different experiences and perspectives and focus on decentring power relations (Yeatman, 1994). One of their central preoccupations is the recognition of difference (Weedon, 1999:,100). Because they include many themes that have been central feminist ideas—that knowledge is contextual and situated, that language is important in constructing difference, questioning the notions of truth or self as unitary and consistent—a current identified as postmodern feminism has developed which questions whether it is even useful to think about "women" (Riley, 1988; Gatens, 1991; Yeatman, 1994; Phoca and Wright, 1999). Poststructuralist or postmodern approaches to the study of families could begin with their appreciation of diversity or pluralism and a strong scepticism about the capacity of any overarching theory to adequately explain contemporary family forms and practices. Poststructuralism and postmodernism explore that multiplicity while trying to identify the ways in which changing circumstances affect family and household arrangements (Dehli, 1996).

This focus on deconstructive critiques and difference invites new kinds of research questions, but raises a number of important questions. Writing about the importance of critical thought for the struggles of Black women in the U.S., Patricia Hill Collins (1998: 124) identifies the strengths of postmodernism, noting that it rejects discourses that have been used to justify Black women's oppression: "Postmodernism can foster a powerful critique of existing knowledges and the hierarchical power relations they defend. For example, postmodernism questions the taken-for-granted nature of categories such as race, gender, and heterosexuality." She also argues that postmodernism is problematic because, in disclaiming truth claims, it rejects ethical positions and eschews social policy recommendations and so "fails to provide direction for constructing alternatives" (1998: 125).

CONCLUSION

What this survey of different theories of families shows is that the starting assumptions and organizing concepts of different perspectives lead to different questions, different research methods, and different "takes" on families. It also shows how the perspectives each of us have on families are shaped by the particular theoretical orientation we hold and that there are competing and contradictory theoretical perspectives. Describing the instabilities of post-modern social theory, David Cheal (1991: 162) argues: "The leading sociologists of the family today are engaged in a search for the future, in order to discover who will occupy it, and which claims made in the present will prevail."

As the debates about whether or not gay and lesbian couples should have the same legal rights to marry as opposite-sex couples show, the stakes are high. The challenge for sociologists is to develop theoretical approaches which constantly examine their own assumptions and concepts, and which recognize that there is no "truth," but rather different and often competing ways of understanding the world.

Suggested Readings

Beaujot, Rod (2000). *Earning and Caring in Canadian Families*. Peterborough, Ontario: Broadview Press. Winner of the Porter Prize for the best sociology book of the year, this offers an impressive summary of the Canadian literature relating to income-generating work and caring labour.

Cheal, David (ed.) (2003). *Family: critical concepts in sociology*. London and New York: Routledge (4 volumes). This collection includes 81 of the most important articles published on family from a sociological perspective. Its emphasis is on the USA, Europe, Canada, Australia, and Asia.

Leeder, Elaine (2004). *The Family in Global Perspective: A Gendered Journey*. Thousand Oaks, California: Sage. This book examines a variety of topics related to families and draws on material from North America (mainly the USA), Africa, Asia, and Latin America.

David, Miriam (2003). *Personal and Political: feminisms, sociology and family lives* Stoke-on-Trent: Trentham. This book examines sociological approaches to family with an emphasis on theory, education, and biography.

Web Resources

At the date of publication there were no Web resources that provided particularly helpful insights into the subject matter of this chapter.

Endnotes

1   I want to acknowledge the contribution Bonnie Fox has made to my thinking about families in general and specifically about the topic of this chapter. More than twenty years of important collaboration has deeply shaped my thinking. In particular, for this chapter I have drawn heavily from a report she and I co-authored for the Demographic Review Secretariate in July 1991 called "Conceptualizing Families" (Fox and Luxton, 1991).

2   For a review of the various legal decisions and the actions taken in response to them, see www.cbc.ca/news/background/samesexrights/timeline_canada.html.

3   For the Vatican campaign, see Winfield, Nicole "Vatican campaign" *Montreal Gazette*, Monday 29 December 2003:A1

4   The material in these two subsections is drawn from the report submitted by Bonnie Fox and Meg Luxton to the Demographic Review Secretariate, "Conceptualizing Families" (Fox and Luxton, 1991).

5   This section on etymology of "family" is derived from Raymond Williams, *Keywords: A Vocabulary of Culture and Society*. London: Flamingo, Fontana Paperbacks, 1983.

6   See, for example, Newman (1978) and Foster (1986).

7   This section is drawn from an early paper published by CRIAW, which includes a review of the literature of the period. See Luxton (1983).

8   Charles Darwin published *The Origin of Species* in 1859. He argued that all living things are related and have descended from a common origin which emerged as the simplest form of life from inanimate materials.

9   Talcott Parsons was a notable exception. Although he was a leading structural-functionalist, he was also a complex and subtle thinker. His works include careful discussions about the ways social change occurs, and his theory of "the family" included a recognition that with the change from agriculture to industrial capitalism, "the family" changed significantly in its functions. (Parsons, 1960).

10 The University of Chicago during the 1950s and 1960s was a centre for symbolic interactionism. Many early Canadian sociologists studied at that university, were familiar with, and often took up that approach. As a result, there has been a strong current of symbolic interationism in Canadian sociology since its founding in the 1950s and 1960s.

11 For a discussion of the different theories, see Jagger (1983), Tong (1989), and Segal (1999). Typically, contemporary feminist theories are divided into liberal, radical, and socialist feminism, psychoanalytical feminism, anti-imperialist, or anti-racist feminism, and, most recently, postmodern or poststructuralist feminism.

12 Although this topic is the main focus of liberal feminists, most feminists investigating family pay attention to this. For an excellent review of the literature and of the issues, see Armstrong and Armstrong (1994).

13 This discussion is based on a more detailed analysis in Maroney and Luxton (1997) and Luxton (2004).

[14] The concept of "labour power" is based on the recognition that, unlike slavery, in which bosses own slaves and can force them to work, or petty commodity production in which small-scale producers produce goods they then sell in the market place, in capitalist economies, the majority of people make their living by selling their labour power, or capacity to work, to an employer in exchange for wages. They use these wages to purchase the goods and services that enable them to sustain themselves and their families, thus reproducing their labour power on both a daily, and often generational, basis.

[15] This resolution is contained in paragraphs 58, 64, 20, 130, and 179 of the *Forward Looking Strategies for the Advancement of Women*. It is reproduced in *Status of Women Canada* (1990: 120). Note that the term "reproduction" in the U.N. text refers to childbearing, child rearing, and other caregiving work typically done by women for ill, disabled, and elderly people as well as for   family, friends, and neighbours.

[16] There are several different ways of calculating the economic value of unpaid work: replacement costs (what it costs to pay someone to do the work), opportunity costs (what the worker would earn if she or he were employed instead of doing domestic labour), or input/output costs (calculating the market equivalents to determine the price of household output) (Goldschmidt-Clermont 1993; INSTRAW 1995).

[17] Unfortunately, official interest in pursuing such issues has waned, and neither the United Nations nor Statistics Canada has collected more recent figures.

[18] For analyses of postmodernity, see Mandel (1978), Harvey (1990), Jameson (1991), and Anderson (1998). A good introduction to poststructuralism is Palmer (1997).

CHAPTER THREE

Biases in Family Literature

Margrit Eichler

INTRODUCTION

Families are contested political ground. "**Family values**" is a political rallying cry, and people are split according to how they view certain issues related to family life, for instance, **gay and lesbian marriage**, or who should be able to sponsor whom for immigration purposes, to name just two.

This split also manifests itself in the academic literature, although it is usually not expressed quite so starkly, and hence is somewhat more difficult to identify. An example is a highly critical review of US textbooks by an American sociologist (Glenn, 1997a) that resulted in a storm of counter-critiques (Cherlin, 1997; Glenn, 1997b; Responses to Special Section on Family Textbooks, 1998; Scanzoni, 1997; Skolnik, 1997). It is difficult to do justice to a debate in a few sentences, but at the core of the argument was that Glenn felt that the textbooks he surveyed were not sufficiently positive towards marriages and families, and that we need to recreate a marriage culture that is restricted to heterosexual couples. His critics suggest that the nuclear family, as envisioned by Glenn, is based on the subordination of women, and that the task of scholarship is not to regain the old structures, but instead "to invent workable structural arrangements that, among other things, enhance the aspirations for autonomy and equity that live at the core of Western society" (Scanzoni, 1997: 216).

It is obvious, then, that both popular writings as well as scholarly writings are informed by different ideological positions. One of the ways in which the divide can be described is by whether families are defined by "who" or "what." People who think of families in terms of "who" typically describe desirable families in terms of their makeup; for instance, a "good family" is one made up of a heterosexual married couple and their dependent children. These, then, are the families that are identified as worthy of public support. People who think in terms of "what" point out that such families may harbour dark secrets, such as abuse or neglect (see Sev'er, 2002), and that a more meaningful way to describe desirable families consists of looking at their relationships: Is there mutual respect, support, and love between family members? Are all dependants well cared for? If so, this would be a family worthy of public support, regardless of its specific makeup or the legality of the relationships.

The literature on families thus presents discrepant versions, both in terms of what is typical of modern families and what is desirable. In order to be able to understand some of the biases that underlie such discrepant versions, it is helpful to identify a series of biases that are typical of some parts of the family literature.

This chapter will present seven such biases: the monolithic, conservative, sexist, ageist, microstructural, racist, and heterosexist biases. First, we will look at some definitions of families; second, identify salient dimensions of familial interaction; third, look in some detail at all seven biases; and fourth, apply the biases to an example.

DEFINITIONS OF THE FAMILY

As we have seen in the first two chapters of this book, considerable discussion is focused on how families are defined, since definitions both enclose and exclude. Since there is general agreement that the family is a social institution that is basic to our society and hence deserves social support, who is included in the definition of a family is an issue of great importance as well as great consequence. For instance, who is eligible to claim certain tax benefits, to sponsor family members for immigration, to inherit from a deceased person who died intestate, to claim insurance benefits in case of an accident, or to transmit Indian status to descendants are all direct consequences of how we define families.
One example of a **"who" definition** is the following:

> "the essence of a family group is that the persons who constitute it and who interact with each other in a meaningful context are considered to be related to each other. That is to say, they are related by blood (parent/child, siblings, grandparent/grandchild) or by marriage (wife/husband, in-laws, step-parent/step-child)" (Nett, 1988: 20).

The wording "considered to be" includes "quasi-family members" such as adopted children or common-law marriages.

An example of a **"what" definition** would be the following:

> "Family is defined as any combination of two or more persons who are bound together over time by ties of mutual consent, birth and/or adoption/placement and who, together, assume responsibilities for variant combinations of some of the following:
> *   physical maintenance and care of group members;
> *   addition of new members through procreation or adoption;
> *   socialization of children;
> *   social control of members;
> *   production, consumption, and distribution of goods and services; and
> *   affective nurturance-love" (Vanier Institute of the Family 1994: 10).

There are, of course, many other definitions, many of which refer to particular types of families and serve useful purposes in specifying which type of family is under consideration at a given point in time.

One helpful way to understand familial relations is to look at various dimensions of familial interaction. Each of the following dimensions describes the range of interactions that can be found in different types of families. These dimensions represent important aspects of familial interaction. Today, we find a great variation in the way different families structure their interactions. The ideal of many people is that all interactions be at the highest level within each dimension; i.e., the couple is legally married, they have children together whom they both parent, they live together in the same household, the couple have sexual relations only with one another, the family functions as a social and economic

FIGURE 3.1   Dimensions of Familial Interaction1

Marital Dimension	• legally married • common-law union • separated • divorced • ex-partners of common-law union • no personal contact (e.g., sperm or egg donor)
Procreative Dimension	• the couple have child(ren) together only • one spouse has child(ren) by other partner and couple have child(ren) together • both spouses have child(ren) by other partners and couple have child(ren) together • both spouses have child(ren) by other partner, no joint child(ren) • one spouse has child(ren) by other partner only • both childless
Socialization Dimension	• both spouses involved in parenting • one spouse only involved in parenting • neither spouse involved in parenting or irrelevant
Social Dimension	• all members represented as a social unit all of the time • some members represented as a social unit all of the time • some members represented as a social unit part of the time • no representation as a social unit
Sexual Dimension	• couple have sex together only • couple have sex together and one of them has sex with other(s) • couple have sex together and both of them have sex with other(s) • one is celibate, the other has sex with other(s) • both have sex with other(s) only • both are celibate
Residential Dimension	• all family members live in the same residence only • all family members live in the same residence, but one of them has an additional separate residence • all family members live in the same residence, but more than one have additional separate residences • one family member lives in a separate residence only • all family members live in separate residences only or are homeless
Economic Dimension	• complete economic interdependence between all family members via mutual or one-sided support • partial economic interdependence between family members • each family member is responsible for own support
Emotional Dimension	• symmetrical positive affective involvement • asymmetrical positive affective involvement • asymmetrical negative affective involvement • symmetrical negative affective involvement • lack of any affective involvement

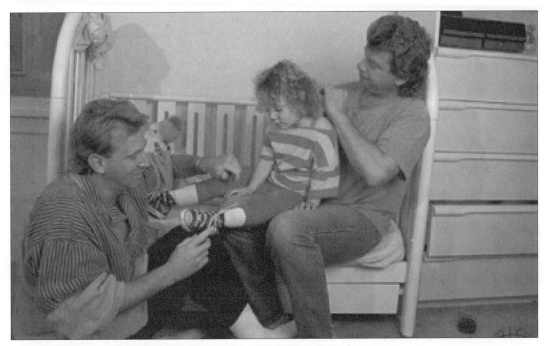

Does the definition of family include a gay couple with children?

unit, the members are mutually economically interdependent, and all family members love each other. However, we find that in reality families may be at a different level of interaction in one or more of the dimensions. The couple may not be legally married to each other; they may not have children together, but may either be childless or one or both partners have a child or children from previous unions; one partner may have a separate residence, for instance, live in a nursing home or hospital, or have a job that takes him or her regularly to a different city; the couple may not have a social life together; or there may be abuse or neglect within the family. The importance of the dimensions is that it allows us to actually describe the nature of the interactions rather than just assume what they are on the basis of one criterion—for instance, that a couple is legally married. Making such assumptions without empirically checking their accuracy is a source of bias, specifically, the monolithic bias.

BIASES[2]

Monolithic Bias

The **monolithic bias** consists of a tendency to treat the family as a social institution that is characterized by uniformity of experience and universality of structure rather than by diversity of experiences and structures. It assumes, rather than examines, that there is congruence between the various dimensions of familial interaction.

For instance, if there is an assumption that the nuclear family is the norm, and that all other family forms are regrettable deviations from this norm, this would be an indication of a monolithic bias, since throughout history different family forms have co-existed, including one-parent households, and other family constellations.

Statistics Canada continues, to this day, to treat husband-wife families with dependent children as if they were **two-parent families**, and uses these terms interchangeably. This involves an assumption of congruence between the marital, procreative, socialization, and residential dimensions, which hides the fact that many husband-wife families, in fact, involve the biological or adopted children of only one partner. It also leads to a lack of recognition of family relationships across different households. For instance, in the case of union dissolution of two people who had children together, the parent with whom the children do not live most of the time is likely not to be counted as a parent—regardless of whether or not this parent continues to be an important socializing influence in the life of his or her child(ren).

Another manifestation of the monolithic bias consists of the presentation of a simple life cycle of the family which assumes that all couples go through the same series of stages (e.g., newly married couple, birth of first child, parenting of young children and adolescents, launching young adults, and empty nest).

In fact, this is only one possible way in which a **family life cycle** may evolve. Many families are formed in different ways. For instance, an unmarried woman may have a child and some time later marry a man who is not the father of the child. Or a divorced person with children from the first union may marry again, and there may or may not be children generated within the second union. Alternatively, the family may consist of two lesbian mothers who decide to have a child via artificial insemination. Recently, we have seen some dramatic changes concerning the age at which young adults leave the parental home. In 1981, 27.5% of persons aged 20–29 lived with their parents; by 2001 the figure had risen to 41.1%—a tremendous increase in a rather short time (Beaujot, 2004: 15) For some parents, this means that the "empty nest" has become a "cluttered nest."

Finally, a monolithic approach tends to lead to an identification of problems in terms of structural characteristics, such as when one-parent households are seen as intrinsically "worse" for the children than a husband-wife family (which is correctly or incorrectly identified with a two-parent family). An alternative, non-biased approach would be to ask: What is the nature of the familial interactions, and are these interactions positive for all family members? Is there mutual support, a healthy economic basis, adequate living quarters, etc.? The latter approach leads us to identify problems within families, such as neglect, physical violence, sexual abuse, etc., rather than to label particular families as "problem families."

Conservative Bias[3]

The conservative bias consists of two tendencies:
- to regard fundamental recent changes as ephemeral
- to either ignore or represent as very rare, atypical deviations, the ugly aspects of familial interactions, such as intrafamilial violence, which are, in fact, widespread

These are two quite different manifestations of a conservative bias, and we shall look at them in sequence.

In order to be able to argue that a particular approach fails to recognize fundamental recent changes, we need to be able to demonstrate convincingly that a) a particular set of changes has occurred, and b) that it is, in fact, of fundamental importance to families. This means, of course, that such an argument must always be specific to a particular time and place. When this bias was first discussed in the early 1980s, one of the forms it took was to either ignore (among other things) the high incidence of divorce and consequent remarriages or to treat remarriages involving one or two divorced people as either similar to remarriages involving widowed people or to first marriages. The difference between a divorced parent and a widowed parent who remarries is that, in the first case, the other parent is still alive, and in the latter, the other parent is dead. These two situations may result in very different interaction patterns. When one of the parents is dead, the new marital partner will be a step-parent, with its attendant complications, but there is no third parent in the picture. When everyone is still alive, the dynamics of interaction obviously become more complex. Today, almost twenty-five years later, this would be well accepted by most sociologists.

I would argue that today's fundamental change involves the generation of children via technologically assisted conception. Here is not the place to discuss this issue at the length it deserves. Although only a very small number of people are affected by the more radical technological interventions in the processes of conception or insemination (such as *in vitro* **fertilization, IVF**), almost every pregnant woman in Canada today will undergo a series of prenatal diagnostic tests, which were either not available or not routinely administered a generation ago. This has fundamentally changed how some women experience their pregnancy, and has raised the question of whether or not to carry a pregnancy to term, not because the woman is not able or willing, for whatever reasons, to do so, but because the fetus is categorized as "sub-optimal." By having to make such a decision, women or couples have become the eugenic gatekeepers of today.

Furthermore, the new reproductive technologies, with their bewildering array of interventions, have changed the processes involved in generating a child, both legally and socially. For example, we have had to adjust our understanding of who exactly is a mother, when there may be a split between whose egg is being fertilized, who has gestated the child, and who is rearing the child. Taking all these factors into account, we can distinguish between twenty-five different types of mothers and nine types of fathers that exist at present (Eichler, 1997a: 72, 80-82). (See the Appendix to this chapter for a listing of the various types.) These new technological developments raise questions that it has not been necessary to contemplate before. Biological motherhood is no longer defined only by giving birth to a child. Death is no longer a barrier—for both women and men—to becoming a biological parent (Eichler, 1996).

The second manifestation of a conservative bias, namely completely ignoring the ugly aspects of familial interactions such as physical, sexual and/or emotional abuse, neglect, etc. is much less prevalent today than it used to be in the 1970s and even the 1980s. Today, most students of the family will admit that such interactions happen with depressing frequency. The difference lies often in the reasons that are cited for this—whether this is due to the structure of the family (the who) or other factors (the what). We also encounter this bias in a rosy conception of families of the past, some reputedly golden time when such ugly things were considered to be not present or highly aberrant (e.g., Popenoe, 1993, 1994). In fact, families have always been complex structures with many problems, although the nature of the problems tends to shift over time (Coontz, 1992).

Ageist Bias

The **ageist bias** takes two forms:
- to regard children only as passive members of families
- to regard the aged only as passive members of families

This is a difficult bias to deal with, since the literature is more limited on this issue than on some others. Basically, we are dealing with a bias in favour of adopting the perspective of middle-aged adults. Where this bias is present, children are seen only in so far as parents (sometimes grandparents) experience joy or grief, fulfilment or work, financial cost or emotional gain through their children. Of course, parents do experience all these factors, and they do socialize their children, but children also experience family matters in a way that may diverge from the way their parents do. Children and parents influence one another, and socialization is not a one-way street from adults to children, but a two-way street in which children also socialize their parents (Ambert, 1997).

With respect to the aged, a similar situation exists: The aged are not just recipients of care from their adult children, they are also care providers of material and emotional support to their children. The aged have their own needs and desires—for instance sexual desires—that may not be seen as legitimate by their adult children.

Avoidance of the ageist bias, then, involves seeing children, middle-aged adults, and the aged as actors as well as acted upon, as having agency as well as being (inter-) dependent (Connidis, 1989b).

The sexual needs of older people are often dismissed by their adult children.

Sexist Bias

The sexist bias involves exhibiting any of the following gender biases:

- **Androcentricity** - adopting an overall male perspective

- **Paradoxical Gynocentricity** - ignoring men in issues having to do with family, household, or procreation

- **Gender Insensitivity** - ignoring sex or gender as a socially important variable in contexts within which it is important

- **Householdism** - treating the family as the smallest unit of analysis in cases when it is, in fact, individuals within families or households that engage in certain actions, have certain experiences, and suffer or profit from particular costs or benefits, etc.

- **Double Standards** - differentially evaluating identical situations, behaviours, or traits on the basis of sex

Our understanding of sexism in research has mushroomed in the past twenty years due to the effect of feminist scholarship (Eichler, 1997b). The literature on this topic is vast and the above is by no means an exhaustive list. We can only touch here on a few selected ways in which the sexist bias manifests itself specifically in family studies.

Family studies is one of very few areas in which we find paradoxical gynocentricity—the tendency to ignore men in situations in which they are vitally involved. It is a subform of androcentricity, since it is an offspring of the notion of "separate spheres"—the idea that men belong in the public realm and women in the private realm, in this context understood as everything having to do with family, procreation, socialization of children, or care of the aged.

For instance, fertility is conventionally defined in terms of the number of children a woman bears—few studies deal with male fertility. The literature tends to look at a potential role conflict between paid work and family work for women, but rarely examines the same issue with respect to men. When we talk about parenting, often this is used as a code word for mothering, rather than looking at the role both parents play. (An exception is Hobson, 2002.)

When householdism is present, the family is considered as a unit, although it would be more illuminating to look at the individuals within a family before talking about the unit as a whole. For instance, when a family has a severely disabled child, who gives up his or her job? Who does most of the caring work? It is not "the family" as a whole, since the consequences tend to be dramatically different for mothers and fathers and, potentially, for siblings as well. Since the 1990s, some provincial governments in Canada as well as some at the federal level have increasingly assigned responsibility for the well-being of people to "their families." We need to ask ourselves, "Who in the family is supposed to deliver this service? To pay for this program? To do without?"

Double standards are frequently encountered when people try to find fault with particular outcomes—for instance, a mother who is represented as failing to look after the family properly, without considering the role of the father.

Microstructural Bias

This bias consists of a disproportionate emphasis on psychological variables and the concomitant relative neglect of macrostructural variables. Identifying this bias in no way negates the utility of psychological studies which may provide crucial insights into the internal workings of families, but it posits that intrafamilial dynamics cannot be fully explained by intrafamilial or interpersonal variables alone. For instance, when we look at how families function, it is not enough to look at personality and family systems variables. We also need to acknowledge that the presence or absence of social services, the adequacy of our public health-care system and of our public housing programs, and the absence or presence of well-paying jobs with good fringe benefits exert an important effect on how families manage to survive (or fail to survive) as social units.

Racist Bias

This bias consists in an explicit or implicit assumption of the superiority of the family form seen as typical for a dominant group, as well as ignoring race and/or racism as a social variable in instances in which it is relevant.

Like the other biases, this one is not always easy to see. For instance, in Canada the conventional wisdom of students of the family is that, until fairly recently, the Canadian state has supported the patriarchal family. Although this is an appropriate description for the majority of policies and families, it does not apply to First Nations' families and many families of colour. Canada has a shameful history with respect to the destruction of First Nations' families, which were torn apart through the **residential school system** in which native children were removed from their families, forbidden to speak their own language, and often were physically and sexually abused. When the children returned to their families during the summers, often they were no longer able to communicate with their parents and members of their community (Report of the Royal Commission on Aboriginal Peoples, 1996). (For a moving fictionalized account see Highway, 1999.)

For decades, many First Nations' children were removed from their families and given up for adoption to white families, either in Canada or the US—a practice which has been identified as cultural genocide (Johnston, 1983: 61).

Similarly, at a time when the Canadian government strongly supported patriarchal families among its white population, there is a simultaneous history of actively preventing family formation or unification for various non-white immigrant groups. Chinese male labourers who were prohibited from bringing their wives to Canada present one example (Man, 1996). The history of immigration policies affecting domestic workers of colour contains many more examples. Policies that actively discourage the same type of family for people of colour that is encouraged for white people must be recognized as part of Canada's racist legacy when discussing family history or policy in general (Daenzer, 1993; Dua, 1999; Thobani, 1999).

Heterosexist Bias

Heterosexist bias comes in two forms. Historically, the more prevalent version entails:
* ignoring the existence of lesbian and gay families

The stronger version involves active **homophobia**, and manifests in
* treating homosexuality as abnormal or pathological, and hence treating lesbian and gay families as a deviant and problematic family form

This is the area in which we have witnessed truly dramatic changes in the past decades. In 1967, George Klippert was the last Canadian to be jailed for the simple fact of being a homosexual. In 2002, Quebec amended its Code civil to create a new form of union, a "**civil union**," that entails the same rights and obligations as marriage and is available to opposite-sex as well as same-sex partners. In 2003, gay and lesbian marriages were legalized in two Canadian provinces, British Columbia and Ontario, and since that time thousands of gay and lesbian couples have married in Canada (Hurley, 2003). A year later, in the spring of 2004, same-sex marriages also were performed in San Francisco. In May 2004, Massachusetts became the first US state to legalize same-sex marriages. However, at this writing, both Canadian and American courts are still pondering the question of same-sex marriage.

Although the first form of this bias is still found in older materials or in non-Canadian writing, I would expect this to be much less frequent in the future with the arrival of gay and lesbian marriages. There is a growing body of studies on lesbian mothers, gay fathers, and lesbian and gay couples (Bailey, 2000; Cossman, 1997; Lewin, 1999; McCarthy, 1999; Weston, 1991).

Due to rapid changes in the law and policies with respect to same-sex relationships, the debate in Canada centres around same-sex marriage. Although it is now a *fait accompli* in parts of Canada, popular opinion remains almost evenly divided, making it a difficult political issue for governments, since they are certain to displease half the population whatever they do. An opinion poll conducted in January 2004 found that 47% of respondents agreed with the statement that Prime Minister Martin "should change Canada's marriage laws to include same sex couples," 48% disagreed, and 5% expressed no opinion (Lunman, 2004).

Until about 2000, arguments against **same-sex marriage** centred on their presumed incapacity to generate and socialize children. This was so notwithstanding the fact that there is no possibility of joint procreation among many heterosexual couples, either because one or both partners are sterile, or because the woman is too old to bear children—increasingly the case when older people remarry after divorce or (less frequently), after widowhood. Some heterosexual couples adopt children. Step-adoptions, in particular, are quite common. Same-sex couples, too, may have children. They may either be brought by one or both partners into the union, in which case the other partner functions as a step-parent, or the couple may plan for the birth of one or more children using artificial insemination, or they may adopt a child together. Today, both parents are recognized as legal parents when this happens.

Those who oppose same-sex marriage argue that we must defend the sanctity of marriage by restricting it to heterosexual couples. Those who support same-sex marriage see the matter as a human rights issue. Human rights are strengthened, not diminished, by being extended to groups that previously had not been included. Denying the legitimacy, viability, and desirability of families that involve lesbian or gay members is a classic example of looking at the "Who?" rather than the "What?" in family interactions.

EXAMPLE OF THE APPLICATION OF THE BIASES

The biases, as defined, may be found in scholarship and in the political arena, for instance, in speeches delivered by politicians, in party platforms, or in policies which are inevitably premised on particular views as to what families are as well as should be.

There is no such thing as a neutral policy that impacts on families. For instance, our policies either do or do not include same-sex couples, support or fail to support sole responsibility parents, allow or fail to allow the immigration of adoptive children on the same basis as biological children.

We will briefly examine here one publication by the Council of Families in America, an organization that has been identified by one of its members as "centrist" in orientation (Glenn, 1997a: 198)[4]. This booklet of twenty-one pages presents a manifesto about what type of families should be supported in the US. For the main ideas and thrust of this document, consider the complete executive Summary:

> The divorce revolution—the steady displacement of a marriage culture by a culture of divorce and unwed parenthood—has failed. It has created terrible hardships for children, incurred unsupportable social costs, and failed to deliver on its promise of greater adult happiness. The time has come to shift the focus of national attention from divorce to marriage and to rebuild a family culture based on enduring marital relationships.
>
> Making marriage in America stronger will require a fundamental shift in cultural values and public policy. No one sector of society is responsible for the decline of marriage. We are all part of the problem, and therefore we all must be part of the solution. We must reclaim the ideal of marital permanence and recognize that out-of-wedlock childbearing does harm. Our goal for the next generation should be to increase the proportion of children who grow up with their two married parents and decrease the proportion who do not. Possible strategies for regaining a marriage culture are addressed to each major sector in society. (Council of Families in America, New York, n.d.: 1).

Space prohibits a detailed treatment of every bias. Although the pamphlet makes some positive policy suggestions, it also contains some problematic ones. Rather than addressing all the issues, our focus is on how to recognize some of the biases discussed above.

The monolithic bias is strongly evident in this document. The heterosexual married couple is seen as offering unquestionably the best environment in which to raise children. This is the single most important message in the booklet. "The loving two-married-parent family is the best environment for children" (p. 4). Our "most important goal" must be to "strengthen the institution of marriage" (p. 4). We must recreate "a marriage culture" (p. 5). In other words, the ideal family is constructed in terms of the "who," not the "what," although there is the qualifier "loving," which at least hints at the possibility that there may be non-loving relationships. On the other hand, the booklet deplores that "today, divorce may simply occur because one partner is unhappy..." (p. 8).

Problems are identified in terms of the structure of the family (something other than two married parents) rather than in terms of the nature of the relationships. The "steady break-up of the married, mother-father childrearing unit is the principle [sic] cause of declining child well-being in our society" (p. 4).

These statements also incorporate a strong heterosexist bias. "As a foundation for family life and raising children, marriage is better than its fast-growing alternatives" (p. 13). Given that same-sex unions are clearly one of these alternatives, and given the constantly repeated message that the aim is to have children raised by a married heterosexual couple, it follows that families with lesbian co-mothers or gay co-fathers are understood as part of the problem rather than part of the solution.

Likewise, there is a strong microstructural bias. Although there is some acknowledgement that other factors contribute to declining child well-being, "the most important causal factor...is the remarkable collapse of marriage..." (highlighted insert, p. 5; part of the text, p. 7).

There is also a strong sexist bias. This is obvious in several places. Given that there is a strong emphasis on tying biological fathers to their children and the mother of their children, there is an explicit recommendation to discourage unwed motherhood through a variety of policies, for instance, by creating "a bias in favour of marriages-with-children in the allocation of subsidized housing loans and public loans" (p. 17). So, who is to be left out in the cold—sole responsibility mothers and their children.

As stated, a major concern is to tie fathers to their children, since "for men, married fatherhood is a civilizing force of no mean proportions. Conversely, having a large number of men disconnected from the patterns and satisfactions of family life—and thus much more prone to unhappiness, deviance, and crime—has always, and properly, been one of society's worst fears" (p. 10). Given that mere unhappiness is no reason for divorce, the proposed policies would tie women and children into unhappy marriages by reducing the capacities of unmarried or divorced mothers to raise their children. This is not considered an issue worthy of discussion.

There is also an admonition to "develop economic strategies aimed at providing more job opportunities for young males, especially poorly educated minority males..." (p. 14). Although this is certainly laudable, clearly poorly educated minority females should also have access to more job opportunities.

With respect to the ageist bias, there is no consideration of how children themselves perceive living in various types of families. Strong statements merely repeat that the best environment for children is the two-heterosexual-married-parents family.

With respect to the conservative bias, although the stipulation is that the best environment is the loving two-heterosexual-married-parents family, there is also a clear statement that "affective ties between men and women...are notoriously fragile and breakable" (p. 11), which is one of the reasons that policies need to shore up marriage, at the expense of all other alternatives. The issue of child abuse and wife abuse within two-married-parents families is not dealt with.

Finally, with respect to the racist bias, there is one paragraph deploring the particularly high incidence of unmarried motherhood within the African-American community. The solution to the very real problem that "only 15 percent of black children living with their married parents are in poverty, compared to 57 percent of those living with their mother only" (p. 6) is to increase the employment opportunities for males, in order to make them more attractive as husbands. The mother-led African-American family is seen as a deficit, rather than as a potential source of strength.

CONCLUSION

It should be obvious by now that, when it comes to the family, opinions diverge strongly as to what is right and what is wrong. That is to be expected in a democracy—there are other issues on which Canadians disagree strongly (consider, for instance, Quebec separatism or the issue of abortion). However, it is important to state the basis of one's disagreements without distorting facts or failing to take into consideration important relevant factors. It is also important to recognize that people may choose to reject particular forms of behaviours for themselves without denying these possibilities to other people, who may find themselves in very different circumstances.

A lot of discussion, both popular and scholarly, deals with "the family" as if it were a stable institution that remains basically unchanged. It should be clear, by now, that this is a profound misperception. Families have changed significantly in past decades (and in the decades and centuries before) and are likely to continue to do so.

When reading materials, it is helpful to keep the biases discussed above in mind. This should help chart a path through the muddied waters of "family values" and policies for families.

APPENDIX

Parenthood after the New Reproductive Technologies

The typology here presented complicates the picture that we derive from census data. Census data tell us how many couples live together with dependent children—they do not tell us whether these children are, for instance, living with their biological mother, a step-father, or maintain contact with their biological father through visitations. Nor do census data tell us about how children are generated—and, as we can see in the typology of mothers, the situation today is very complicated indeed.

Definitions
1. A full parent has unrestricted access to the children and lives with them.
2. A partial parent has restricted access to the children (such as a non-custodial parent who sees the children during visits).
3. An exclusive parent is the only father or mother of the child.
4. A parent is non-exclusive if there is another parent (such as a step-parent of the same sex who is also involved with the child).

Fatherhood after the New Reproductive Technologies

The new reproductive technologies have a very minor impact on fatherhood in terms of creating new types: If a wife uses artificial insemination by donor, her husband is simply a type 2 father—there is no significant new factor added. The only truly new phenomenon is that of a man who becomes a father after his death or, more accurately, whose sperm is used to impregnate a woman after he is dead. (There have always been instances in which a man became a father after his death if he impregnated a woman, but died before she gave birth.) We thus have to add a ninth type of father: the post-mortem biological father. Our category system now looks like this:

Typology of Fathers after the New Reproductive Technologies
1. Biological, social, exclusive, full fathers
2. Non-biological but social, exclusive, full fathers
3. Biological but not social fathers

4. Biological, social, exclusive, partial fathers
5. Biological, social, non-exclusive, partial fathers
6. Non-biological but social, exclusive, partial fathers
7. Non-biological but social, non-exclusive, partial fathers
8. Gay co-fathers, non-biological, social, non-exclusive fathers
9. Post-mortem biological fathers

Motherhood with the New Reproductive Technologies

For fathers, the new reproductive technologies added one new category—a post-mortem father. For mothers, we enter a complex labyrinth. Fathers make only one biological contribution to a child: They provide the sperm. Mothers make two biological contributions: They provide the egg and they gestate the fetus. The new technologies have split this unity, and thus created many types of mothers with which current laws and policies are ill-equipped to cope. In order to list the new types of mothers, we must now distinguish between partial biological mothers—genetic but not gestational, or gestational but not genetic—in addition to the other types previously in existence.

Typology of Mothers with the New Reproductive Technologies

1. Genetic, gestational, social, exclusive, full mothers (what we think of as the norm)
2. Non-genetic, non-gestational but social, exclusive, full mothers (adoptive or step-mothers)
3. Genetic and gestational but not social mothers (birth mothers who have given up their child)
4. Genetic, gestational, social, exclusive, partial mothers (like type 1 mothers but without custody)
5. Genetic, gestational, social, non-exclusive partial mothers (non-custodial mothers like type 4, but only if the father has formed a new union with a woman who plays a partial mother role)
6. Non-genetic, non-gestational but social, exclusive, partial mothers (e.g., non-custodial adoptive mother in cases where the father does not have a partner who acts as a substitute mother)
7. Non-genetic, and non-gestational but social, non-exclusive, partial mothers (like type 6, but the father has formed a new union with a woman who plays some parental role)
8. Lesbian co-mothers, non-genetic and non-gestational, social, non-exclusive mothers
9. Genetic but non-gestational, social, exclusive, full mothers (women who use another woman as a gestator of their own egg in a preconception agreement)
10. Non-genetic but gestational, social, exclusive, full mothers (recipients of a donor egg)
11. Genetic, non-gestational, non-social mothers (provider of a donor egg)
12. Non-genetic but gestational, non-social mothers (gestational carrier for type 8 mother)
13. Genetic but non-gestational, social, exclusive, partial mothers (like type 8, but without sole custody)
14. Non-genetic but gestational, social, exclusive, partial mothers (like type 9, but without sole custody)

15. Genetic but non-gestational, social, non-exclusive, partial mothers (like type 8, but with a second and potentially third partial mother—the gestational mother and/or the father's new partner)

16. Non-genetic but gestational, social, non-exclusive, partial mothers (like type 9 and 13, but with a second and potential third partial mother)

So far, all these types of mothers are alive at the moment of conception and birth. If the genetic and/or gestational mother is dead at these two crucial times, this adds seven more types of mothers. They are, in a categorical sense, only particular subforms of the preceding types, but because of the extraordinary importance of breaking the barrier of death, it is warranted to list them separately here. At this stage, the already complicated format previously adopted no longer suffices. We must now use an identifier to distinguish the various sequences of mothers with respect to the same child in order to keep track. The mother who is mentioned last is the one being categorized.

17. Dead genetic mother # 1; gestational mother # 2; social, exclusive, full mother #3 (preconception agreement in which the egg of a dead woman is fertilized, implanted in a carrier, and the child is handed over to a third woman)

18. Dead genetic mother #1; gestational but not social mother #2 (the carrier from the previous preconception agreement)

19. Dead genetic mother #1; gestational mother #2; social, exclusive, partial mother #3 (the type 16 mother is now divorced, and her husband has custody of the child, while she has liberal access)

20. Dead genetic mother #1; gestational mother #2; social, non-exclusive, partial mother #3 (same as the type 18 mother, but her former husband has remarried)

21. Dead genetic mother #1 but gestational and social, exclusive, full mother #2 (recipient of donor egg from a dead donor)

22. Dead genetic mother #1; gestational, non-social mother #2 (carrier using dead donor egg in a preconception agreement)

23. Dead genetic mother #1; gestational, social, exclusive, partial mother #2 (type 20 is now divorced and her husband has custody)

24. Dead genetic mother #1 but gestational and social, non-exclusive, partial mother #2 (the former husband of type 22 is now remarried)

25. Dead genetic and gestational mother #1, a woman kept on life support beyond her death so that her fetus will mature and be delivered by Caesarean section

Source: Eichler, M. 1997. *Family Shifts: Families, Policies, and Gender Equality.* Toronto: Oxford University Press.

Suggested Readings

Hurley, Mary C. (2003). *Sexual Orientation and Legal Rights.* Ottawa: Library of Parliament, Parliamentary Research Branch, 92-1E, rev. 2. Available on the Web at http://www.parl.gc.ca/information/library/PRBpubs/921-e.htm This paper presents a legal history concerning sexual orientation, including same-sex marriages.

Dua, Enakshi (1999). "Beyond Diversity: Exploring the Ways in Which the Discourse of Race has Shaped the Institution of the Nuclear Family." In *Scratching the Surface: Canadian Anti-racist Feminist Thought*, edited by Enakshi Dua. Toronto: Women's Press: 237-260. An article documenting a racist bias in family policy and literature.

Eichler, Margrit (1997b). "Feminist Methodology." *Current Sociology* 45(2): 9-36. A discussion of the sexist bias and ways to address it.

Report of the Royal Commission on Aboriginal Peoples (1996). Vol. 3, "Gathering Strength." Ottawa: Minister of Supply and Services: 9-106. A documentation of the stresses experienced by Aboriginal families in the past and present.

Vanier Institute of the Family (2000). Profiling Canadian Families II. Ottawa: Vanier Institute of the Family. An overview of the variety of families in Canada today.

Web Resources

www.Egale.ca
This is the Web site of Egale Canada, an organization founded in 1986 to advance equality for Canadian lesbian, gay, bisexual, and transgendered people and their families, across Canada.

http://www.fotf.ca/familyfacts
This is the Web site of Focus on the Family, a group that opposes same-sex marriage and provides arguments why marriage in a Christian sense must always be between a woman and a man. They use a "who" definition of the family.

For an alternative Christian viewpoint, see **http://www.uccan.org/moderator/.**

This a message from the Moderator of the United Church of Canada stating the United Church of Canada position in favour of same-sex marriages.

Endnotes

[1] This is an extended and revised version of the dimensions of familial interactions in Eichler 1988, pp. 8-9.

[2] An earlier version of five of these biases can be found in Eichler 1988, chapters 1-4. The new formulation of the biases profited greatly from discussions with Rosanne Brown, Allison Conroy, Mirriam Edelson, Georgia Graham, Anne Leishman, Nancy McTavish, and Tammy Siegel.

[3] The earlier discussion of this bias included what is now discussed under the heading of an ageist bias.

[4] There are Canadian organizations and published statements that could have been used instead, for instance, the newsletters of REALWomen of Canada. The advantage of using the publication chosen is that a) it represents the views of some important American scholars of the family, and b) it is compressed, and hence lends itself to be analyzed without the danger of taking things out of context.

PART TWO

Industrialization, Immigration, Work, and Families

CHAPTER FOUR

Social, Economic, and Cultural Origins of Contemporary Families

Bettina Bradbury

INTRODUCTION

Journeys back in time do not reveal the "traditional family" that some observers portray as endangered today. The information that scholars have been able to unearth about family life in the past exposes great diversity in the ways families lived, in their structures, in the work their members performed, the roles of men and women, and in the cultural meanings attached to the concept of the family.

This chapter is divided into three parts. The first investigates the different understandings of family and gender at the heart of three major and ongoing cultural encounters: relations between Aboriginal peoples and the Europeans who took over their lands; between the Canadians of French origin and the English who conquered them in 1760; and between Canadian residents and successive waves of immigrants. The second section examines some of the major changes in the ways Canadians historically have organized their family and working lives. It starts with the characteristics of farm and artisanal families, then looks at working-class families, and finally at middle-class families. The final section of the chapter summarizes some of the major continuities and changes in family lives across the nineteenth and twentieth centuries, focusing especially on the particularities of the period between the end of the Second World War and the early 1960s.

Family has always had many meanings as a word, a concept, and a lived reality. Family can refer to people related biologically—children, grandparents, cousins; to people who recognize each other socially or are recognized legally as related—spouses, stepchildren, same-sex couples; and to a group of people who live together, sharing food and care. Family, as used here, usually refers to men, women, and children sharing both a dwelling and the work and social interactions that make up their daily life. Such families might be headed by grandparents, a married couple, a lone parent, or unrelated adults. They might include one or more generations. In each of these cases the diverse kinds of work of some family members support others—the dependent children and the elderly or sick. The nature of this work has varied with changes in the economy and changing ideas, but a **sexual division of labour** usually has distinguished the work of men and women and girls and boys.

In all historical periods, families have comprised individuals whose power has varied with their age and their sex. Custom and law defined the boundaries of families and historically kept women subordinate to their husbands, and children to their parents. Inequality, combined with the intense physical and emotional challenges involved in childcare, sexual relations, making a living, performing domestic labour, and living together has meant that families always have been places of intense emotion. Love and hate, nurture and violence, anger and joy intermingle in varying proportions. Yet, ideas about the importance of love and the ways of expressing it or the degree of violence allowable between spouses or partners, or parents and children have varied historically.

Historically, families have been the main social unit responsible for the task of raising future generations of citizens through the labour, economic and emotional support, socialization and education they provided themselves or delegated to institutions such as schools. This work is so important that in all historical periods different experts and agents of the state or church have attempted to intervene in some families to ensure that they functioned as these specialists saw best. All cultural groups have their own concepts of family. Many are very similar. Yet, when groups of people from different cultures and classes come into close contact with one another, whether through colonialism, conquest, reform work, or migration, they tend to notice differences most. In Canadian history, specific groups have attempted to use their power and privilege to impose their under-standings of appropriate gender roles, child raising, and meanings of family on those that seemed different. Less powerful groups struggled to retain their own cultural under-standings. Frequently, their own families were as critical to their sense of identity and to resisting change as they were to their economic survival.

ONGOING CULTURAL CONFRONTATIONS

First Nations and Europeans

The cultural history of Canadian families may be approached by considering three sets of confrontations between groups with different understandings of the meanings of family and gender roles. This section starts with the devastating results of contact between indigenous peoples throughout Canada and Europeans, turns to that between French and English Canadians, then briefly examines the ongoing encounters between Canadians and immigrants. Each of these long-term encounters pitted one group with superior economic and political power (as well as faith in the virtue of their forms of family) against another. Although we can roughly date the beginning of each of these sets of confrontations, all are ongoing. They continue to shape the lives and outlook of Canadian families today.

The earliest meetings between most Aboriginal peoples of Canada and Europeans were with European men rather than women. First came explorers, beginning in the late fifteenth century on the East Coast, in the eighteenth and nineteenth centuries in the West, and continuing on into the twentieth century in the Northern Arctic. In most regions, male traders followed. They relied on the expertise and skills of indigenous men and women for the products of their trade. They encouraged the men of different bands and nations to engage in hunting for them at the expense of other subsistence activities, and created new kinds of dependency on European trade goods. Fur traders, whalers, and men searching for gold sometimes officially married First Nations and Inuit women. Others exploited different understandings of sexuality and marriage, and became involved in both short-term and lifelong liaisons with native women (Van Kirk, 1980; Brown, 1980; Brody, 1975; Perry, 2000).

In most regions of the country male missionaries followed the traders. Invariably they were shocked at such interracial intimacies. They sought to convert First Nations men and women to their religion. In their project of "civilization" and Christianization their ideals of family played a key role. Whether they were Catholic Jesuits attempting to convert the Huron in seventeenth century New France, Anglican men and women in the North-West, Methodist missionaries working among the Tsimshian of Northern British Columbia during the nineteenth century, or Moravian missionaries among the Inuit of the North in the 1930s, there were similarities in their goals. Missionaries sought to encourage settlement in one location, utterly changing patterns of survival already disrupted by trade. They sought to impose Christian ideas about marriage, sexuality, and divorce, and to elevate the status of husbands at the expense of their wives. Shocked at parents' apparent unwillingness to discipline their children, they taught new forms of punishment. In the nineteenth and twentieth centuries, government agents on First Nations reserves and settlement managers among the Inuit and other northern groups pursued similar goals. Policemen in the West and the North aided the state in administering policies that restricted Aboriginal peoples' rights of movement and inculcated western understandings of property and crime.

Inuit children in Chesterfield Inlet residential school run by the Oblate Mission.

From the arrival of the first settlers from France, educating native children to Euro-pean ways was a key element of missionary civilizing strategies. Boarding schools were used to keep the children away from the influence of their parents. This policy continued into the twentieth century, when government policy allowed First Nations and Inuit chil-dren to be forcibly taken from their families and sent to residential schools, or pushed to attend local schools where all instruction was in English. From east to west, south to north, this ongoing assault on Canada's indigenous peoples resulted in a devastating restructuring of the bases of economic support and of the meaning of family, kin, and gender relations, the results of which are only too clear on and off the reserves and in northern settlements today.

First Nations peoples and early European explorers, exploiters and expropriators eventually came to see each other as homogeneous—as "Indians," "Eskimos," or as "White," though in early encounters each was aware of vast tribal and national differences. Natives and newcomers alike came from cultures that were not static and unchanging, but that had been developing new and different family values over previous centuries. The ear-liest missionaries, settlers, and fur traders came from European nations in which the mean-ings of gender and family were being contested and reformulated in the wake of the Reformation and the spread of capitalism. The native people they met came from hundreds of different tribes and nations with widely divergent and shifting practices regarding kin-ship, descent, family, and gender roles. The Europeans who ended up in what would become Canada had more in common with one another in their ideas and practices regard-ing gender and the family than they did with the native groups they encountered. Yet there were major differences, for example, between family laws and traditions among the French who settled in the Saint Lawrence Valley and the Maritimes from the early seventeenth cen-tury, the English and Irish in Newfoundland, the Scots and English merchants who migrated to Quebec after the French were defeated by the English in 1760, and the loyalists who came into what is now Canada in the wake of the American Revolution of 1776.

In these encounters across cultures and time, there were always some Europeans who were attracted to life among First Nations and ended up living their lives among them, sometimes refusing all entreaties to return to a "civilized" life (Demos, 1995). Similarly, many First Nations men and women embraced some aspects of European culture, religion, and material goods, incorporating new practices into their cultures. There also were aspects of family life that natives and newcomers shared. First Nations families, like European families, were based on a relatively rigid division of labour by sex. Specific details of the labour performed by each sex varied among different Aboriginal groups and different classes of Europeans, yet there were similarities at the broadest level. War was men's work; so usually was hunting. Politics was largely men's realm among Euro-peans, although formal power was limited to very few of them in France during the period of absolutist monarchs and to propertied men among the English. Women could, however, be queens, and could exercise influence informally as wives, mistresses, and daughters (Noel, 1991; Anderson and Zinsser, 1988). In most Aboriginal societies women appear to have been able to exercise greater influence than their European counterparts in a context in which power was much more diffuse and shared than in Europe. Huron women, for example, spoke at public assemblies and could appoint and depose the male leaders of their matrilineage (Anderson, 1991). In some West Coast societies women could be chiefs. Yet, among most First Nations, women were generally excluded from more public, formal, and symbolic areas of power—from tribal councils and positions as chief or clan leader (Prentice, 1988; Anderson, 1991). Their exclusion became starker as first the French and then the English invested native institutions and their male heads with responsibility for trade deals, selling land, and negotiating treaties.

Both European and Aboriginal women were generally responsible for the immediate tasks of reproduction and mothering. But their methods of childcare diverged. The earliest French settlers and later English fur traders and merchants came from societies in which parents used physical punishment and emphasized teaching children to internalize discipline. Child-rearing practices among First Nations and the Inuit appeared dangerously permissive. In the seventeenth century, the French Jesuits criticized the "excessive love the Savages" bore their children. Natives, in turn, were shocked at the punishment meted out to European children and sometimes intervened to protect them (Anderson, 1991). "Your French people love only your own children," one Naskapi commented, "but we love all the children of the tribe" (Coontz, 1988: 56). Observers of Inuit child-rearing practices misunderstood their permissive attitudes toward young children: In Inuit culture little children were understood not to have achieved the level of rationality that would make them accountable for their behaviour (Brody, 1975).

Most Canadian indigenous peoples survived originally by a combination of hunting or fishing and gathering, combined sometimes with crop cultivation. Sexual divisions of labour were not completely rigid, but generally the women and children gathered roots, berries, and wild rice, and caught fish and small animals, while the men hunted the larger game (Trigger, 1976; Anderson, 1991; Brody, 1987; Carter, 1999). Among the agricultural Huron, women fished, tilled the soil, and sowed the corn. European observers frequently commented negatively on how hard these women worked, sometimes referring to them as drudges or beasts of burden. Such observations bolstered their claims to be part of a more civilized society in which women were protected from physical labour. Yet most ordinary European women during the sixteenth, seventeenth, and eighteenth centuries performed similar tasks, though in different contexts. Childcare, cultivation of the garden plot, raising chickens or a cow, either for cash or food, and seeking other ways to make money kept their families alive on agricultural plots that by the eighteenth century would not provide a living in much of Europe (Hufton, 1975).

First Nations and Inuit people had their own distinct customs and rituals to celebrate and recognize marriages. After a marriage, the conjugal unit of husband, wife, and children did not usually live separately or have great importance. Husbands, wives, and children were embedded in a much wider kinship network and in lineage systems that determined where the couple would live and who would receive the fruits of their labours. The European families who arrived in New France also came from areas where households were seldom made up only of nuclear families. Servants, apprentices, unmarried brothers or sisters, or an elderly parent might all live together at some point in the life cycle of the family. Yet most conjugal units were more separate from wider kin than among Aboriginal peoples. Many cut extended family ties in migrating. This distancing from kin was also greater on the relatively isolated farms of New France, or later on the large, spread-out farms of the Prairies than in the more densely populated European countryside or in the cities.

Traders, missionaries, police, and government agents prepared the path for farmers, railroads, and full-scale occupation of native lands. Native people died of European diseases, were killed in wars fought between European nations, and in some areas were purposely exterminated by Europeans. European diseases such as smallpox swept through Aboriginal communities. Native populations declined dramatically in all occupied areas. In the early twentieth century tuberculosis and childhood diseases killed up to a quarter of the boys and girls in residential schools and continued to decimate reserve populations. Influenza combined with starvation had similar effects in Inuit communities.

During the eighteenth and nineteenth centuries, the numbers of settlers of European origin in the colonies that would become Canada after 1867 increased dramatically. "Scientific" and popular ideas about racial difference hardened. Intermarriage diminished. Governments enacted **Indian Acts** and signed treaties to contain Aboriginal peoples and assimilate them. First Nations families were pushed back to the geographical and social margins of the emerging society. Many resisted by retreating to hunting and gathering territories in the North and West where they attempted to retain their own family patterns and seek subsistence from the land into the twentieth century. Others carved out an existence on reserves, watched by Indian agents, and increasingly curtailed by policies that pushed them further into dependence and poverty. The Indian Acts, enacted for a century starting in the 1850s, set out to assimilate First Nations' people by imposing European notions of landholding and of family. The husband was considered the head of the family and the source of children's status in the band and as Indians. When women married Europeans, they and their children lost their status and any claim to government compensation. Canada's first prime minister, John A Macdonald, was explicit about the aim of the Indian Acts. In 1887 he stated that "the great aim of our legislation has been to do away with the tribal system and assimilate the Indian people in all respects with the inhabitants of the Dominion, as speedily as they are fit for change." First Nations' peoples refused that vision (cited in Dickason, 1992: 257). They struggle today with its legacy.

Competing Visions of Family among French Canadians and the English before and after the Conquest

Colonizers' attempts to change the customs of Aboriginal peoples derived from their belief in the superiority of European civilization and Christianity. Whether they were English or French, they interpreted the conflict as one between savage and civilized peoples. The conquest of the French in North America by the English in 1760, in contrast, pitted two groups of European origin against each other. Each prided itself on its particular form of civilization and religious beliefs. Divergent visions of family have been one thread in conflicts between some Francophones and other Canadians ever since.

Most of the immigrants who came to New France from France from the early seventeenth century on were men, and most were single. A few settled in Acadia—partly in what is now Nova Scotia. More slowly trickled into the Saint Lawrence River Valley. Over time the settlers who stayed in these areas would refer to themselves as Acadiens and Canadiens respectively. As long as fur trading, exploration, and missionary work were the main interests of the French, women and families were not very important to France's plans for these colonies. Some intermarriage between newcomers and Aboriginal women was seen as acceptable, and was even encouraged. By the middle of the seventeenth century, however, France's goal shifted to occupying the land, establishing tighter controls, and increasing the French population. At that point men outnumbered women six to one. Since few women were immigrating, either on their own or as part of families, the Royal government in France decided to send shiploads of young women. Between 1663 and 1673 some 700 *filles du roi*, or daughters of the king, were sent from Paris to Quebec. Largely poor and orphaned and frequently illiterate, most came from Paris institutions for the poor. Once in the colonial outpost of New France, almost all married, though often not without rejecting one or two betrothed before the wedding ceremony. Their marriages and those of the children they bore helped fuel the population growth that made French Canadians famous for their fertility and enabled them to occupy and farm much of the Saint Lawrence Valley over the following two centuries (Landry, 1992). By the time of the British conquest there were some 60,000 French settlers. Without families, there would have been few Europeans in New France. Men who did not marry did not stay. Farmers, artisans, and merchants alike needed wives to work in their homes and to help run their businesses. Women's domestic and productive labour was essential for all but the colonial elites. They were among the families who used both Aboriginal people and Blacks as slaves, mostly to work in their homes.

The family was the most important institution in New France. Settlers were isolated from one another, and social and political structures were minimal. Yet the characteristics of family life in that period fit uneasily with notions of a traditional family. In this new colony where men outnumbered women so dramatically during the seventeenth century, the first Canadian-born girls were snatched up as wives even before they reached puberty—some were under twelve, the minimum marriage age dictated by church law. In more than two-thirds of the earliest marriages in Quebec City the husbands were ten or more years older than their wives. Even as the average age at marriage for women increased, the age gap between husbands and wives remained an average of about five years. In the eighteenth century, men married at an average age of nearly 27, women at around 22. Marriages were frequently brief because death rates were high. Both men and women remarried rapidly (Dechene, 1992).

The formal rules about marriage and family in New France were set out in the **Custom of Paris**—the legal code used in Northern France at the time of settlement. It was egalitarian in its principles, dictating for all but the noble class that family property should be shared equally by all offspring, and that much of husbands' and wives' property should form a community of goods belonging to both partners, but controlled completely by the husband. If wives outlived their husbands, which was usual given the large age-differences, they could take control of their half (Bradbury et. al., 1993; Gérin-Lajoie, 1902). Widows also had the right to a dower—to use one-half of their husbands' land or the revenues from it until their death. Similar legal codes creating community property within marriages were common in much of Europe but not Britain. They were exported to various Spanish, Dutch, and French colonies by the colonists who settled there.

In the early years after the conquest, the British government attempted to impose their laws on the colony. By 1774, it was clear that this would not work, especially as the English needed the support of their new French subjects against the Americans, on the

---

Exhibit 4.1   Wives and Marriage outside Quebec

In all common-law jurisdictions, marriage, for women, represented civil death. Nineteenth-century married women's property law reform provided the first tentative legal recognition of the wife as a being separate from her husband, and remedial legislation …was part of a much wider international phenomenon. Before these reforms were enacted, the wife's legal identity was obliterated at marriage and she was entirely under the power and control of her husband. At law, the wife could not hold, use, or dispose of property, whether land, money, chattels, or wages earned by her own labour. Without the right to own property, wives could not support themselves independently of their husbands, a fact that greatly constrained their options in abusive relationships. Although the physical and economic power differential between spouses could not be abolished by legislative fiat, the possibility of property ownership began to mitigate some of the practical problems faced by abused and unhappy wives. In a more symbolic sense, by recognizing the separate personality and interests of the wife, the married women's property acts represented a crucial turning-point in the theory of married women and the law…Reform was enacted slowly and incrementally in Ontario, beginning with the introduction of the Court of Chancery in 1837 and culminating in formal legal equality for wives under the Married Women's Property Act, 1884.

Source: Chambers, Lori (1997). *Married Women and Property Law in Victorian Ontario*. Toronto: The Osgoode Society for Legal History: pp. 1–2.

---

verge of revolution to the south. In the Quebec Act of 1774, the British Parliament agreed that Québécois should keep their own distinct civil law to regulate family and commercial questions, but follow English rules for criminal matters. The growing number of merchants of English and American origin who were making money in the fur trade and in importing and exporting were not impressed with either the commercial or the family property rules in this law. English merchants expressed horror at the generosity of the Custom of Paris toward wives and widows. The new colonial elite, some of whom were intent on creating an aristocracy similar to England's, were equally horrified at the egalitarian provisions for children. They succeeded in modifying these provisions by legislating freedom of willing for men and women in the hope that wives would give all to their husbands, and that husbands would privilege one son over the other children.

Elites and merchants of English and American origin drew many of their understandings of family, inheritance, marriage, and property from the Common Law of England which concentrated power and property in the hands of husbands and fathers much more than the Custom of Paris. Upon marriage all but a woman's land became the property of her husband, unless very careful and expensive arrangements were made to ensure otherwise. Under this law marriage meant the "suspension of the independent existence of the wife, and an absorption by the husband of the women's person and . . .her belongings," as Clara Brett Martin, Canada's first female lawyer, explained (Backhouse, 1992: 321). Married women could not make a contract, sue or be sued. Their legal status was equivalent to that of lunatics and children. These rules governed marriage in all the Canadian colonies and provinces except Quebec until the later part of the nineteenth century.

There were many areas of tension between the new English colonizers and the conquered French. And, as in the case of Europeans and Aboriginal peoples, assimilation was promoted by the conquerors, who believed fervently that their parliamentary institutions and their notions of family and property were more advanced. The English attempted to use schools as instruments of assimilation and failed within Quebec, but were more successful in other provinces where French-speaking Canadians eventually settled. More recently, successive Quebec governments also have tried to make schools the key focus for assimilation of immigrants, with varying degrees of success. During the 1830s tensions increased between the conservative, Tory, and largely English-speaking colonial elite and reformers, the majority of whom were francophone Quebeckers seeking a greater say in government. These tensions ultimately flared into open rebellion in 1837 and 1838. In the immediate aftermath of the failure of the rebellions, the English elite pushed through key legislation in 1841 that drastically limited widows' claims on their husband's estates. Yet, even with these changes, the law remained somewhat fairer to wives and widows than in the English colonies that came together in 1867 to create Canada, where Common Law rules determined the property rights of husbands and wives. From the 1840s until the 1960s some of Quebec's prominent French-speaking Catholic leaders promoted the family as a major site of resistance to the English. French-Canadian women's capacity to bear many children was central to the idea of "the revenge of the cradle"—to Québéçois maintaining their relative strength in the country's population as more and more immigrants arrived from elsewhere.

This new, more conservative vision of family was promoted by a powerful faction of the elite who sought to confine women in the home under the watchful eye of clergy and the firm hand of the head of the family. Well into the twentieth century, the power of the Catholic church to promote childbirth and cut off access to information about birth control contributed to a woeful ignorance among ordinary women about sex and family planning, as well as to English-Canadian stereotypes about French-Canadian women (Baillargeon 1999). During the 1930s, growing numbers of Protestant Canadians began to accept birth control, if only to control what was seen as overbreeding among poor, working-class, and immigrant families. One nurse, Dorothea Palmer, who was distributing information about family planning among poor, francophone women outside Ottawa was arrested. Her 1936–7 trial made front page headlines. Evidence of French-Canadian Catholic obstetricians opposing birth control was pitted against **eugenicist** and feminist promoters of birth control and the horrific stories told by francophone women. They described repeated miscarriages, abortions, and pregnancies, explaining why they wanted birth control and smaller families. It was illegal to distribute or use birth control information or devices until 1969. Yet the judge found that Dorothea Palmer had acted in the public good because of the costs of raising large families during a time of severe economic depression (Dodd 1983).

Having many children to feed aggravated the levels of poverty that shaped many Quebec families' lives on farms as well as in cities and towns. Throughout the nineteenth century many families fled poverty-stricken rural areas of Quebec and the Maritimes to seek work south of the border in the mills of New England, in Canadian mill towns such as Cornwall, Magog, or Sherbrooke, or in the industrializing city of Montreal. In the cities, francophone men were disproportionately involved in crafts and jobs that were poorly

---

Exhibit 4.2   Sleep in Separate Rooms: Advice to Young Wives

Note: This quotation reminds us that abstinence was seen as a form of birth control and a question of self control and morality. The possibility of husbands and wives having separate bedrooms would have been out of the question for all working-class families and for many farming and middle-class families. In many nineteenth- and early twentieth-century families, parents were lucky if they did not share a bedroom with some of their children.

The custom in many English homes of each (husband and wife) having a room, which is peculiarly one's own, may seem to our freedom-loving natures, a cold custom; but is not this better when a proper self-control seems difficult, than a freedom which degenerates into license? True, the door between these two rooms should seldom be shut; but the fact that there are two rooms relieves of many temptations, and prevents the familiarity, which even in married life, breeds contempt.

Source: Excerpt from *What a Young Wife Ought to Know (Thousand Dollar Prize Book)* by Mrs. Emma F. Angell Drake, M.D. Toronto: VIR Publishing Company, The Ryerson Press, 1908, p. 85.

---

paid. In Montreal until well into the twentieth century, children in francophone families were much more likely to die before they reached school age than the children of any other group, including the Irish, who frequently earned less. Historians suggest that part of the reason may lie in their particularly low levels of breast-feeding (Thornton and Olson, 1991). Poverty and lack of access to information about family planning surely also contributed.

Demographic research shows that only a small proportion of Quebec families in each cohort were very large. Many women never accepted their prescribed role in the revenge of the cradle. And, nowhere in Canada has the revolution in family size and importance been as great or as rapid as in Quebec. Since the Quiet Revolution of the 1960s, government policies and individual choices have transformed French-Canadian families. Fertility and family size have fallen more dramatically and further among French-Canadian women than among most other groups. Fewer francophone men and women are choosing to marry than in the past or than in other provinces. At the same time—indeed, partially in reaction to these choices—government policies regarding daycare and other aspects of family support are more generous in Quebec than in other provinces. Family and children remain key elements of contested visions between Quebec and the rest of the country.

Canadians and Immigrants: Four Centuries of Family Confrontations

There are many parallels between the divergent visions of family, gender, and sexuality that marked relations between Europeans and Aboriginals or French and English and those that have occurred between successive generations of Canadians and immigrants. Canada has been transformed by immigration. Some immigrants came as individuals, most as part of a family migration. Most came voluntarily, a few as slaves. Many were fleeing political, economic, and ethnic discrimination. Some came from legal systems and religious groups with widely divergent traditions of marriage and family. They brought with them multiple family customs and values and diverse understandings of gender, authority, and power.

Until 1962 Canadian immigration policy gave explicit preference to immigrants from the British Isles and Northern Europe. But not even these immigrants were always well received. When the Irish began to arrive in large numbers from the early nineteenth century on, and especially after the terrible Irish famine of 1847, they were widely viewed as unruly, prone to violence, and as particularly uncivilized. Migrants of African origin experienced racism, whether they came as slaves with loyalist masters after the American Revolution, as runaways or free African-Americans in the eighteenth and nineteenth centuries, or as domestics or nurses from the Caribbean after the Second World War. British Columbians were virulent in their expression of hatred toward the Chinese, Japanese, and Sikhs who sought to make British Columbia their home. Their racism fuelled the passage of immigration laws that from 1884 on placed higher and higher head taxes on Chinese immigrants, making family formation or reunification impossible for most. Few Chinese men wishing to bring their wives could afford the head tax, especially after it was raised to $500 in 1904. As a result, in 1921 there was only one Chinese female for every sixteen men. It was only after the most racist elements of immigration law were modified following the Second World War that Chinese and other Asians could enter Canada more readily. Immigration laws and Canadians' reactions to newcomers continue to influence family life for new Canadians.

Conditions in their countries of origin combined with Canadian immigration policies to shape the place of families in migration patterns. English and Irish migrants who had been small landowners before coming to Canada in the early decades of the nineteenth century usually came in family groups, sometimes along with other members of their parishes (Conrad 1993). Later that century more Irish women came alone as single women, initially finding work as domestics. Children came as orphans, shipped out from British cities to work on the farms of Canadians. African-Americans came to the Maritimes and Ontario as slaves and free men and women. They came alone and in families. For some, promises of land in exchange for loyalism during war led to disappointment. Others sought freedom, work, or land and an escape from racism. By mid-century there was a sizeable Black community around Halifax. And there were at least 20,000 men, women, and children of African origin living in families in over 300 of Ontario's townships and cities. A minority lived in all-Black settlements such as Elgin, or communities with sizeable black populations such as Chatham or Buxton. Especially for those families torn apart under slavery or separated during escapes, family reunification was a major long-term goal that was effected only slowly by painfully piecing together information about their partner's or children's whereabouts (Conrad, 1993; Bristow, 1994; Wayne, 1995).

By the end of the nineteenth century, Aboriginal peoples and Métis in the West had been contained in reserves through treaties and laws that controlled their movements. Their former hunting grounds were parcelled out and taken up by families from Ontario, Great Britain, the United States, and parts of Northern and Eastern Europe who hoped to make a living farming. Families of Mennonites, Doukhobours, and Jews came from Russia. Others arrived from Germany, Holland, Scandinavia, and the Austrian-Hungarian Empire. Some groups, such as a minority of Ontario's African population, set up their own ethnic settlements where they could retain family customs as well as their language. In the first two decades of the twentieth century migrants flocked to "The last best west," making the three prairie provinces the most ethnically diverse region of Canada (Finkel 1993).

Other immigrants sought work in the growing cities, in railroad construction, or in the growing numbers of settlements based on mining, lumbering, or wood processing. Men often lived in bunkhouses. Women were scarce. Italian men established a pattern of sojourning in which they worked to earn money which they sent home. Some eventually brought their wives and children, sometimes after years apart. Jewish men and women fleeing persecution in Russia and other parts of Europe shaped the garment industries of major cities, working as both owners and employees.

In all historical periods, some established Anglo-Canadians responded negatively to immigrants. Others were more paternalistic, working with them as volunteers, missionaries, social workers, and nurses. Canadians set up charities and settlement houses as well as welfare agencies where they sought to teach Canadian family ways. In the early parts of the twentieth century, as in the period after World War Two, most Anglo-Canadians who took on such reception work confronted immigrants convinced of the superiority of their own customs, understandings of gender roles, and notions of child rearing and family. Ignoring economic realities, they criticized the way families shared housing or lived in crowded quarters. Many misunderstood why parents took their children out of school early to work or distrusted the patriarchal power of men in Southern European families (Comacchio, 1993, 1999).

For immigrants who faced hostility and criticism of their customs as well as the challenges of daily survival in a new and different country, families were crucial. They could speak to each other in their own language, and work to save money to bring more kin to Canada or to purchase a house. Most embraced Canadian schooling for their children and valued education. Many were able to take what they needed from those offering help, learning some Canadian ways, but retaining what they wished of their language and culture. Family members encountered Canadian society in different ways, depending on their gender, age, and education. Husbands were more likely than their wives to seek and find waged labour, and hence were more likely to learn the English or French needed to negotiate daily life outside the limits of their community. After World War Two, growing numbers of immigrant wives sought waged labour. The work they found was often in poorly paid sectors such as piece work and cleaning where learning English was not necessary. Mothers who worked at home raising children and cooking were even more isolated. The children of immigrants frequently were torn between their parents' understandings of authority, family relationships, and appropriate leisure activities and those they learned in the schoolyard (Iacovetta, 1992).

Since World War Two, Canadian governments have gradually eliminated the most blatant ethnic preferences that marked earlier immigration policy and made family reunification a more important component. Yet the resulting diversity of the Canadian population continues to worry many established Canadians, and many immigrant families continue to face the challenge of making a living in an economy and society that from afar seemed to promise so much, yet frequently proved disappointing on arrival.

When Canadians of all origins and backgrounds married, organized the work of family members, or tried to shape the size and composition of their family and household, they combined cultural norms with the pragmatic demands of daily life. The contours of peoples' daily lives and family economies were shaped within the broad shift from an economy based on agriculture, small production, and trade prior to the nineteenth century to one increasingly based on the extraction and processing of primary materials, factory production, and an expanding service economy in the nineteenth and early twentieth centuries. Most recently, people have had to seek new kinds of work in what some refer to as a post-industrial economy. The following section looks first at changes in the work of different family members. It starts with the **family economy** of farmers and craftspeople, then examines the **family wage economy** that characterized the life of working-class families dependent on wages, and then explores the characteristics of work and gender in middle-class families.

CLASS AND FAMILY ECONOMIES

Farming and Artisanal Families

From seventeenth century New France through to the settling of the Canadian Prairies in the late nineteenth and early twentieth centuries, the major work unit in Canadian society and on farms, in particular, was the family. Clearing the land, working it, and raising food as well as future generations of children required the co-operation of men, women, and children. The work of wives among such petty commodity producers was so vital that officials generally acknowledged the importance of farmers having a wife. "Whatever qualification the farmer should have, mental or physical, all are agreed on this point—that a good wife is indispensable," wrote an agricultural expert during the 1860s (cited in Light, 1980: 160).

Farming was a family enterprise in which all members were expected to work, although the tasks they performed varied. The particular nature of men and women's tasks varied depending on the period, the recency of settlement, the type of agriculture, and the skills of individuals. At the broadest level, men tended to do the field work and to be responsible for any specialized crops or animals that were sold for cash, while women cultivated a kitchen garden, cared for chickens, pigs, milked the cow, and made butter. Women also prepared meals, looked after children, made candles, soap, spun, wove, and made clothing for family members. Young children of both sexes helped their mothers, but as they aged, boys usually worked alongside their fathers, girls their mothers. At times of peak demand for labour—especially planting and harvesting—this sexual division of labour broke down, and women helped in the fields. On more prosperous farms where extra labourers were hired, these times of year were especially busy for the wives who fed and usually sheltered the labourers employed.

Mothers, fathers, and children found a variety of ways to raise extra money. Women might weave, sew, or sell eggs, milk, butter, or extra produce. The extra cash a woman could earn making and selling butter, for example, could be crucial during times of crop failure, low prices, or before crops were harvested (Cohen, 1988; Collective Clio, 1987; Silverman, 1984). In many areas men routinely combined farming with fishing or work in lumber shanties during the winter, or with periodic hunting and trapping, leaving their wives and children to run the farm. Few farms were self-sufficient during the nineteenth century. Few produced only for the market. In the years following the First World War, the families who had settled the Prairies were encouraged to specialize in wheat production for the world market at the expense of the more diversified farming practised earlier. This left farm families exposed to the dangers of world trade fluctuations. In the late 1920s other countries stopped purchasing Canadian wheat. Combined with drought and invasions of locusts, this had a devastating effect on farm families. Many abandoned their farms, seeking work in the cities, just as the worlds' greatest depression hit Canada.

The family economy of craftsmen and women in cities, small towns, or rural areas prior to industrialization was similar in many ways to that of farmers. It was a family effort, characterized by a sexual division of labour in which men were most likely to be responsible for the major revenue-generating activities, while women and children provided supplementary sources of support, and women took charge of daily and generational reproduction. Production took place within the same building as the family resided. Home and workplace were one. With the exception of women involved in making clothes and hats, most recognized artisans were men. When they had no sons to help produce the shoes, furniture, or farm implements that were their specialty, they took in apprentices. Usually they promised both to teach them the trade and to feed, clothe, shelter, and educate them. Generally, the master craftsman taught the apprentices his trade. Wives might help with some tasks around the workshop, keep the books (if they were literate), and provide the domestic labour—meals, clothing, and daily care, required not just for her husband and children, but for the apprentices (Hufton, 1975; Burgess, 1986; Moogk, 1983).

Although apprenticeship was not nearly as widespread as a stage in the life cycle in pre-industrial Canada as it appears to have been in Europe, this period of semi-autonomy, in which young people lived away from their own parents in the homes of others for one to seven years, was the experience of many colonial youths (Katz, 1975). Boy apprentices generally learned a trade, emerging as journeymen shoemakers, bakers, or tinsmiths. Girls, in contrast, were much more likely to be hired out as domestic servants. Although they did learn some skills, they were ones that trained them to be wives rather than   offering a craft they might use later to support themselves.

Although much artisanal production of this type was eliminated with the growth of factories, such family-based work also characterized small family-run shops in the past as it does today. Children remain integral to family-run businesses. It was in such families that youngsters were most likely to be kept home from school to help, after school attendance laws were introduced into the different Canadian provinces from the 1840s on. In Quebec, and probably elsewhere, children in family-run shops and small businesses were still being kept out of school to help in the 1950s (Marshall, 1998).

Industrialization, Urbanization, and the Expansion of the Working Classes

By the 1860s **industrialization** was beginning to transform the family economy of craftsmen and women in the cities of the Maritimes, Quebec, and Ontario. The process would continue slowly and unevenly over the next century throughout the country, as artisans, merchants, and industrial capitalists built factories which replaced much of the artisanal production in cities and small towns. Cities expanded, as sons, daughters, and whole families rejected rural life and immigrants sought work and homes. By the 1880s cities such as Montreal, Toronto, or Halifax boasted a variety of different factories that impressed contemporaries with their use of steam-driven machinery and their hundreds of workers; a few had thousands of employees. Smaller towns in the Maritimes, Ontario, and Quebec were created or transformed when entrepreneurs set up textile mills on local streams, harnessing the waterpower to run their factories. In Paris, Ontario, the Penman Company recruited the skilled female hosiery weavers it needed from as far away as the east midlands of England. Paris was unusual in offering stabler employment opportunities for women than men, making it "a women's town" (Parr, 1990). In contrast, in most of Canada's growing number of single-industry towns built first around mines, logging, or railroad work, and from the later nineteenth century on around pulp mills and hydro-electrical plants, most wage labour was considered suitable only for men. Wives' work was mostly housework, and single women had few wage-earning opportunities (Luxton, 1980; Rosenfeld, 1988; Forestell, 1999).

With industrialization, the proportion of families in cities and towns who depended largely on earning wages increased dramatically. Unlike artisans, family members who earned wages did not usually work in their own homes. They sought employment in the growing number of factories, or on construction sites owned by others. Home and paid labour were usually separate. Furthermore, although payment for farmers or artisans was attached to a product—the wheat grown, or the table that was manufactured—wages were paid to individuals for the amount of time they worked. Wages appeared individualized, the property of the person who had done the work. In the case of wives, the law made them their husbands' property until the 1880s in most provinces. When wage earners had families, those wages were necessary to sustain the earner as well as dependent children, their wives, and sometimes elderly parents or other relatives.

Only the most skilled of working-class men could earn enough by their wages alone to support a wife and more than one or two young children. Day labourers' wages were often half those of a skilled worker such as a machinist or printer. This working-class family economy, or the family wage economy, as historians Joan Scott and Louise Tilly have called it, required the wages of several workers. One study of six Canadian cities, based on the 1901 census, shows that for every dollar earned by the head of a working-class family, a further 30 cents were earned by someone else, usually the head's offspring. Low wages and the lack of government support in times of unemployment and sickness continued to make the contributions of either children or wives necessary to many families well into the twentieth century (Baskerville and Sager, 1998).

In the early phase of industrialization, between the 1860s and the 1890s, children as young as ten and eleven were employed in factories and workshops, though never in the proportions found in the early industrial revolution in Great Britain or in the mill towns of the eastern United States. The dangers and exploitation that such young workers could face were revealed in several investigations and commissions during the 1880s. Commissioners uncovered horrible evidence in 1888 about the abuse of children. In Montreal, workers revealed that one cigar manufacturer disciplined young children by locking them up for hours in a small dark room. Other employers beat young children and imposed heavy fines as they attempted to control their youthful and unruly workforce and to teach them the discipline necessary for factory work. The revelations of the commission encouraged the application of **Factory Acts** that had recently been passed but seldom enforced. By the mid-1880s most provinces had passed legislation to curtail the employment of girls under fourteen or boys under twelve in factories. These acts also placed restrictions on the kinds of work and times of day women could be employed. Early legislation was limited. It did not cover small workshops, such as the sweatshops where so many girls were employed sewing. Nor, initially, did it cover shops or even mines.

The Factory Acts were perhaps more influential in the way they explicitly distinguished between male and female labour. Women's work time was officially limited to ten hours a day or sixty hours a week. Girls could not be employed in factories until they were fourteen, compared to twelve for boys. And the employment of females in specific kinds of workplaces, such as mines, was made illegal. The impulse behind such legislation was protective. Reformers were genuinely and understandably worried about the outrageous exploitation of women and children that was occurring. They sought to curtail it. Most of all, they wanted to protect women from conditions that would inhibit their ability to have babies. Yet no laws attacked women's inferior wages. No laws limited the number of hours of domestic labour at home. So, although some women benefited from such legislation by working shorter days, few derived better remuneration. Overall, the major thrust and long-term consequence of such legislation were to differentiate male and female labour. This served to justify rather than challenge women's lower wages. The legacy of this distinction continues today.

Older offspring continued to be the most usual second and third family earners until after the Second World War, when growing numbers of married women took up full-time wage labour. They were expected to give most of their wages to their parents. Here was a new point of potential conflict and tension in family life. In the early phases of industrialization, boys were more likely to find employment in most areas than girls, in part because there was a greater variety of work available to them, in part because they could earn more, but also because mothers and widowed fathers needed daughters to help with work at home (Bradbury, 1993). In the twentieth century, as running water and electricity helped make housework less physically demanding, mothers had less need of their daughters' help. New jobs in the service sector and especially in offices increased girls' chances of finding a job. These factors combined to mean that by the First World War, a growing number of young working-class girls worked for wages prior to marriage.

When there were no children old enough to earn extra money, families were especially vulnerable to poverty. Unemployment, illness, or desertion by the father left families dependent on kin, neighbours, and on a growing number of charitable institutions. In times of major economic depression, as in the years of the first great depression which hit Canada in 1874 and the Depression of the 1930s, poverty and hunger were widespread. Children stopped going to school because they were without shoes and clothing. Local charities were overwhelmed with requests for food. Women's work-stretching wages intensified. During the 1930s they joined their husbands seeking relief from municipal governments and worked even harder to find ways to scrounge, save, and make money to feed the family (Baillargeon, 1999). They frequently had to nurture men whose senses of identity as fathers and men were bruised by their inability to find work.

"You complain, my poor husband, of your ten hours of labour. Yet I have been working for fourteen hours, and I have not yet finished my day." This 1870s image, produced at a time when unionized men were fighting for a nine-hour day, captures the sexual division of labour between husband and wife, as well as the never-ending nature of women's domestic labour.

In the early phases of industrialization married women in Canada seldom worked full-time for wages, except in towns such as Paris, where the company went out of its way to make combining wage labour and mothering possible (Parr, 1990). This does not mean women were not working: The variety of tasks that they performed to feed, clothe, and shelter the rest of the family constituted more than a full-time job. Their workplaces frequently had no running water, minimal lighting, and lacked storage facilities for food. Washing and making meals were time-consuming and physically demanding chores. Women combined these tasks with caring for babies and young children, whether they were well, pregnant, or sick. Some kept their daughters at home from school to help. Shopping was usually a daily task, at times involving the delicate negotiation of credit with local merchants. Working-class wives did anything they could to make extra money or save cash. They took in extra washing and sewing; cleaned other people's houses; raised pigs, poultry, or vegetables and fruit; or supervised while their children scavenged and sometimes stole food, clothing, and fuel. Among the working classes, a woman's love for her children was as likely to be measured out in meals on the table as in kisses and hugs.

One of the results of industrialization and the spread of wage labour was the growing invisibility and lack of acknowledgement of this domestic labour performed largely by wives and mothers. Well into the twentieth century, wage-earning family members were away from home for ten hours or more a day, when they had employment. As a result much of the housewife's work went unnoticed. This tendency to disregard housework as work accelerated in the twentieth century with the growing availability of running water, electricity, or gas and new appliances which lightened the physical demands of housework.

Between the 1860s and the early decades of the twentieth century, those workers who were organized in unions (mostly men), claimed the right to what came to be called a **family wage**—enough income to support their families on their own. Few were successful, but as the trade union movement came to equate work with wages paid to a family head, this added to the idea that other kinds of work, including domestic labour in the home, barter, or home production, were different. As skilled workers struggled with the degradation of the conditions of their work, with their gradual loss of control over the timing and nature of what they did, they articulated new ways to measure their manliness and to assert their claims on employers. Wages and the ability to support a family became a new yardstick of masculinity.

Industrialization provoked changes in childhood other than work in factories. Increasingly, educators and politicians came to believe that some education was necessary if working-class children and the offspring of the poor and immigrants were to fit into the changing society and acquire the discipline necessary for industrial work and modern society. Parents also sought education for their offspring, hoping that learning would provide the key to a better life. From the mid-nineteenth century on, the various colonies set up education systems that provided minimal instruction, usually with some option of separate schools for those of different religious beliefs. Whereas previously some children were educated at home and others in small local schools run by women in their homes or in religiously run institutions, growing numbers of boys and girls between the ages of four and twelve or thirteen now spent some time in local public schools. There they were taught from standardized textbooks, by teachers trained and hired to teach specific curricula.

Though most provinces made some school attendance compulsory, many children did not spend much time in school. Initially, children were only obliged to attend for around four months a year. Aboriginal children ran away from the industrial and residential schools that were at the heart of education policy from the 1880s on (Carter, 1999). Well into the twentieth century, urban youngsters, like those on farms, continued to spend long periods away from school when their parents needed them to earn wages, run errands, care for sick family members, or babysit (Bullen, 1992; Hamel, 1984; Marshall, 1998; Jean, 1992). Schooling promised some children possibilities of learning that seemed to offer them better opportunities in life than their parents. Generations of immigrants, First Nations, and Inuit children learned English or French along with views of the world that distanced many of them from their parents. Schools in poorer and immigrant neighbourhoods and on reserves were frequently underfunded. Many children spent so little time in school that the skills they acquired were minimal. Parents who needed their children's assistance had to face truant officers and later government workers or social workers who insisted their offspring attend school. Many Inuit and First Nations' parents were forced to place their children in residential schools far from home.

Industrialization was not an economic process separate from family life or daily existence. It was part of a much wider process that reshaped Canadian society and the lives of men, women, and children within all Canadian families in the years between the 1860s and the Second World War. The working class, largely dependent on both wage earning and the housework necessary to transform those wages into nourishment and shelter, expanded in Canadian cities. So too did the middle classes—those who built factories, ran them, and created and ran a growing number of other kinds of professions, businesses, and services.

Changing Middle-Class Families, Changing Society

The industrial capitalists who built factories and mills, and the bankers and financiers who organized major mergers of industries and businesses between the 1880s and the Depression of the 30s were part of a new Canadian elite. They controlled much of the wealth and real estate of their towns and cities and influenced governments' economic policies. They and their wives and daughters played a key role in shaping much charity and welfare work in conjunction with other middle-class Canadians. "Middle class" is a term that is used very loosely, usually to apply to almost everyone who was neither poor nor working class. There was a middle class long before the Industrial Revolution. It was made up of lawyers, doctors, architects, and other professionals who were self-employed, making a living by receiving fees for the services they provided. This group expanded over the nineteenth and twentieth centuries to include major industrialists, financiers, and corporate leaders as well as growing numbers of men and women working in what we would now call white-collar jobs in commerce, trade, or for some level of government on a salary (Noel, 2003; Young, 1981; Burley, 1995).

Although there were significant differences between the industrial and financial elite and less privileged middle-class families, historians do suggest some shared features of middle-class family life that broadly differentiate these families from those of the working classes. Middle-class couples, especially in cities, appear to have been the first group to successfully limit the number of children they bore. They controlled conception through abstinence or careful co-operation between husbands and wives. Doctors shared illegal information about contraception more readily with middle-class families. Having fewer children made sense, since growing numbers of middle-class families sought to finance prolonged education for their children, especially their sons. Historians have also argued that it was among this group that the idea of romance and companionship as the basis of marriage took hold with most force in the nineteenth century (Ward, 1990).

The relative economic security of a successful business or salary secured respectable housing for most middle-class families. Many hired a servant. In the nineteenth and early twentieth century, women working as domestic servants normally lived in the homes of their employers. They worked long hours, had little free time, and moved frequently from mistress to mistress. The demand for servants always outweighed the numbers available. Although most middle-class wives continued to do some housework themselves, and certainly had to oversee their servants' work, the labour of their servants liberated them to put more time into visiting other women of their class, taking part in charitable or reform work outside the home, or working to expand women's rights to education and a say in society.

From the early nineteenth century on, the lives of middle-class wives were increasingly viewed as separate from the changing and public world of politics. Ministers and advice literature stressed that middle-class women's work was to make the home comfortable for men, a refuge from the troubles of the economy. In 1856, the Reverend Robert Sedgewick explained that wives' main task was "to see that the fireside is the place of attraction—the home is the crystal spot on earth." He stressed that in middle-class homes where men were not labouring with their "hands to provide food and raiment," wives should try to be understanding about their husbands' "duty of maintaining a family," even when they did not understand the details of their businesses. Middle-class families began to move away from the centre of cities and to build homes in homogeneous suburbs some distance from the industry and commerce that was the basis of their livelihoods. Thus wives in these families increasingly were cut off from their husbands' work lives.

By the 1850s this idea of separate spheres was widely disseminated by ministers and in advice literature. In this new kind of home, cut off from business and the wider world, women were expected to use their moral superiority to see to the emotional and spiritual well-being of husbands and children. Yet, ironically, the generalized acceptance of women's moral superiority justified excursions out of the increasingly private world of their homes and families and into work in the public sphere of charity and reform (Hall and Davidoff, 1987; Riley, 1988; Prentice et al., 1988). The idea of separate spheres was always more of an ideal than a reality, asserted with perhaps growing vehemence as middle-class women began to spend more time in school, to stay single, or have fewer children, or campaign for the right to a university education, a career, or fuller citizenship rights.

Middle-class men and women were key players in the diverse **social reform movements** that proliferated in late nineteenth and early twentieth century Canada. They formed a range of groups that sought to counteract the impact of industry and urban growth by improving the physical environment of the cities with parks, playgrounds, better water and sewage systems, and healthier dwellings. Middle-class women created institutions to help widows, orphans, and the poor. They sought to reform the morals of immigrants, the poor, and the working classes by promoting temperance, preventing prostitution, and protecting women and children in factories, in their homes, and on the streets. The middle classes were claiming greater privacy in their own family lives at the same time that visitors intervened in the lives of the poor and immigrants in ways that often involved dictating standards and morals that were required in order to receive assistance (Mitchinson, 1991; Valverde, 1991). Few recognized that for so many working class and immigrant families, as increasingly among First Nations' peoples, the most pressing needs were for steady, reasonable wages, and shorter hours.

By the 1870s middle-class women were forming groups that aimed explicitly to deal with women's rights and women's issues. At the time these were labelled the "woman movement." Looking back from the 1960s and 1970s, a new generation of feminists placed this range of groups together as part of what they called first wave feminism, to distinguish it from their second wave feminism. The women involved had many different goals, and like feminists today, different interpretations of the reasons for women's problems. Some, usually referred to by historians as maternalists, based their claims to authority on women's roles as mothers and focused on issues broadly related to mothering and family. Other women as well as some of the maternalists were increasingly frustrated by the social, legal, and political limitations placed on their lives as women, workers, wives, and mothers. In the 1870s a few Canadian women began to follow the lead of women in England and the United States who were seeking equal rights for women in access to higher education, the professions, and the vote. In the following decades more and more middle-class women from across the country became involved in seeking both kinds of changes. They came together as the National Council of Women in 1893. Francophone Quebec women created their umbrella association, the Fédération nationale Saint Jean-Baptiste in 1907 (Prentice, 1988). Changes were slow. By the 1880s **Married Women's Property Acts** were passed in most of the provinces. These modified the common law regarding marriage to allow wives to keep their own property separate from that of their husbands. For the first time wives were recognized as the legal owners of their own wages, earnings, and savings. This was an important gain, but only for those with any property or wages to keep separate. By the end of the First World War women had won the right to vote federally and in most provinces (Backhouse, 1992; Chambers, 1997).

Opponents of the Married Women's Property Acts, like adversaries of the women seeking the vote, argued that allowing women to control their own wages or other property or to take part in elections would destroy marriage and the family. This was not the goal of most early feminists or other middle-class reformers. Although some avoided the problems of marriage by remaining single, the overall thrust of first wave feminism was to improve marriage, not to eliminate it. In the following decades women helped push for legislative changes at the provincial and federal levels that aimed to strengthen the family and to chart appropriate behaviour for husbands, wives, and children. Much legislation targeted working class and immigrant families, perceived to be most in need of reform. Men's obligation to provide for their wives was reinforced in a series of acts starting around the 1850s that aimed to locate husbands who deserted their wives and force them to provide support (Backhouse, 1992). Drunken husbands were a key symbol of the temperance movements that Canadian women were very involved in during the 1840s and again in the early decades of the 20th century.

Growing numbers of middle-class women took advantage of the opening up of universities to women after the 1880s. Some began to train in professions such as medicine from which they had been excluded, or in new ones such as Social Work which by the 1920s had transformed older charity work into a career that attracted large numbers of women. More and more took up jobs in professions, services, and offices before they married. Until the 1960s, however, most professionals and businesswomen felt that they had to choose between a career and marriage. One of Canada's first female doctors, Elizabeth Smith Shortt, for example, agonized over continuing her medical practice after her marriage. She continued for a while, then committed herself full-time to fighting for social reform and women's rights (Smith, 1980). Charlotte Whitton, Canada's first female mayor, was one of many career women who did not marry. Some established lifelong relationships with other women, others managed alone, or lived with parents or siblings. They established associations of professional women and were active in a variety of groups promoting change for families and for women.

CONTINUITIES AND CHANGES

Love, Abuse, and Family Breakup

This section sketches out some further changes and continuities in the history of Canadian families. It starts with changes in the reasons people marry, the continuity of abuse, and the options couples have faced when their relationship no longer worked. It then turns to examine the set of changes that marked as unique the period between the end of the Second World War and the 1960s.

Love and romance have not always been considered the best basis for a successful marriage. Unions in New France and the early colonial period were frequently economic partnerships. By the nineteenth century the idea that love should be the basis of marriage was spreading, though among the wealthy and working-classes alike, unions were frequently undertaken for more pragmatic reasons. Once married, couples were expected to remain together no matter how difficult or abusive the relationship. Spouses were expected to be good companions, rather than ardent lovers. Sexual restraint was idealized both before and during marriage. In the early decades of the twentieth century a new, more commercialized culture of romance was widely diffused through novels, newspapers, films, radio, and magazines. Rituals such as marrying in white and taking a honeymoon became more firmly entrenched. And experts began to argue in the 1910s and 1920s that good sex was crucial to a good marriage. By the Second World War popular images and advice literature placed even greater stress on sexual attractiveness as an ongoing requirement in marriage. In the post-War culture that placed new emphasis on heterosexuality, wives were to greet their husbands at the end of the day not only with the meal ready and the children cared for, but also ready for sex.

The dominant ideals of historical periods and cultural groups stressed   status, economics, love, or sexual attraction as reasons for marriage; but there were always some families whose lives were marked more by violence than by love and affection. Abusive husbands beat their wives and murdered them in every period as they do today. Violence, drunkenness, and incest made family life intolerable for many women and children, as well as for some men. Some men simply failed to provide for their wives and children as the law required. Nineteenth and early twentieth century advocates of temperance blamed non-support and family violence on drink. Alcohol was one cause of these and many other family problems, though the period of prohibition that lasted from the First World War through the twenties in most provinces did little to solve the problem. Poverty and unemployment as well as the power the law gave men to punish their wives with relative impunity also contributed to family problems. When nineteenth-century women were brave enough to complain about abusive husbands, judges frequently sent them back to their proper place—at home with their husbands (Backhouse, 1991). In 1913 a federal law made not supporting a wife, including a common-law wife, a criminal offense. A few years earlier more stringent legislation was passed against wife beating. Women with abusive husbands were offered similar support to that available for deserted wives, who could obtain a court order to protect any property they had from their husbands. Such acts gave those married women in bad marriages who were brave enough to go to court some economic and legal recourse. However, they offered women no independent means of support. Husbands frequently evaded alimony and support payments. Laws reinforced the idea that men should provide and women be dependent (Snell, 1992).

After the First World War the numbers of couples seeking a divorce began to increase very slowly. Until 1925, the double standard embedded in the conditions of divorce made it much easier for men to divorce their wives. And, until 1968, divorce for most Canadians involved the lengthy, expensive, and public process of passing a private statute through the federal Parliament. Canadian politicians resisted relaxing the federal divorce law, arguing it would contribute to the breakdown of the family which they portrayed as rampant in the United States, where divorce was more accessible. Of course, many marriages did not work. Men deserted their wives, some wives walked out on their husbands, and many more couples agreed informally to separate than sought a divorce. Others divorced in the United States, perhaps mistakenly thinking this was legal in Canada. In Quebec, Catholic couples sought a separation of bed and board. Rates of formal and informal separation increased steadily from the 1920s and 1930s on, as men and women came to believe that continued affection was required in marriage (Snell, 1992). Divorce rates only increased significantly after 1968, when new legislation made divorce much simpler. The dramatic increase in divorce rates was largely because so many couples had already separated, or were awaiting a cheaper and simpler process. Thus, family breakup was not a new phenomenon in the twentieth century. Divorce as a way to deal with abuse or disappointment was.

The Particuliarities of the 1950s and 1960s

When Canadians talk about the traditional family, some have in mind the working father and loving, housebound wife and children that were captured in television shows such as *Leave It to Beaver* in the period following the end of the Second World War. Yet, looking back, the time between war's end and the 1960s stands out as anything but traditional. It was a distinctive time in the reversal of some trends, the beginning of new ones, and the initiation of new policies. Seven interrelated features of family life mark the post-War 1940s, 1950s, and early 1960s as special. First, there was the baby boom. The large numbers of babies born after the Second World War and throughout the 1950s temporarily reversed the long-term decline in fertility that had begun among the middle class in urban areas in the middle to late nineteenth century and accelerated over ensuing decades. The average number of children in Canadian families had fallen from about six throughout much of the nineteenth century to closer to two and a half children during the Depression of the thirties. After the War, family size increased suddenly to an average of over three children. In earlier periods family sizes varied dramatically. After the War most families conformed to the average size of three. The baby boom was caused by record proportions of women marrying, by their marrying younger, and because more of them had babies and had slightly more than in the previous decades. An unusually buoyant post-War economy in which the state offered unprecedented new programs to ensure stability of family revenues also made it possible to imagine supporting more children. By 1961, the boom was over. Fertility rates returned to their previous pattern of decline, aided by new forms of contraception. The pill, which was introduced in the

1960s, allowed for predictable family planning for the first time. Selling contraceptives and distributing information were made legal in 1969.

The second atypical characteristic of the 1940s and 1950s was the historically high proportion of women who married and the low proportion who did not. Some of these were marriages that had been delayed because of the Depression or the War. Government policy and popular culture placed significant emphasis on marriage and family as key elements of a return to post-War normalcy. During the nineteenth century some 15 percent of women had remained single throughout their lives. Their reasons were multiple. Some cared for elderly parents or orphaned siblings. Some had decided to avoid men, sex, and marriage. A minority of Catholic women became nuns. Some women dedicated themselves to a career. An unknowable percentage of single men and women may have chosen to live in a same-sex partnership, though evidence of such relationships is hard to uncover. Few gays and lesbians dared live openly, especially after the Second World War when heterosexual marriages and family were aggressively promoted as essential to the return to normalcy, and when gays and lesbians were being expelled from the military and the Civil Service, and faced police harassment in city bars and hotels. With the soaring post-War marriage rate, the proportion of women remaining single dropped to about one woman in ten (Prentice 1988, 413). This too was a temporary and new phenomenon that reversed rapidly during the1970s.

Early marriage was the third anomaly of the 1940s, 1950s, and 1960s. Historical demographers have demonstrated that peoples' decisions about when to marry are closely linked to the economy. Fluctuations rather than long-term trends thus characterize average ages at marriage. After the War the average age of women at the time of their first marriage dropped from over 25 in 1941 to 22 in the 1960s. It then started to rise again (Prentice, 1988: 311).

A fourth, atypical aspect of family life after the Second World War was the particularly low proportion of families with children that were headed by one parent. Despite the toll of war, single-parent-headed families made up only about 10 percent of all families with children during the 1950s and 1960s. In all earlier periods of Canadian history, high death rates left wives as widows, husbands as widowers, and children as orphans. From the eighteenth century on, men remarried more frequently than women, so children were more likely to be raised by stepmothers than stepfathers. Widows raising their children faced challenges similar to many women-headed families today. Throughout the nineteenth century and up to as recently as 1931, some 13 to 15 percent of all families with children were headed by a single parent, usually a widow, though sometimes a widower, or a separated or deserted wife or husband. By the 1950s and 1960s adult death rates had reached an all-time low (Bradbury, 2000). The major cause of single-parenthood began to shift from death to separation and divorce. The proportion of Canadian families with children that were headed by a **lone parent** returned to around 15 percent of all families in the 1980s. It has since increased to some 20 percent, as a result both of divorce and women's decisions to raise children on their own. Most lone-parent families are still headed by women, and many continue to live close to the poverty line (Vanier, 2002).

The problems that widows and other single mothers faced supporting their families when a husband died attracted the attention of first wave feminists and reformers who lobbied for government support for deserving mothers. They succeeded in convincing most provinces to pass acts giving needy mothers pensions—first in Manitoba in 1916, and subsequently in other provinces. Like most early welfare legislation, this help was means-tested and available only to certain groups. Residency and citizenship require-ments made immigrant mothers in most provinces ineligible. In British Columbia, Aboriginal women could not receive mothers' pensions. Aid came with strings attached. The acts sought to assist worthy mothers to stay at home and look after their children. Working full time was discouraged. Applicants had to furnish a letter of reference from a minister. Initially, only widows were eligible in most provinces, and they had to have more than one child. This cut off potential help to deserted wives and unwed mothers. These pensions offered women important economic support for which many were grateful. They came with liberal doses of advice, appreciated by some, but not by others. Pensions could be cut off if the mothers were deemed amoral or unworthy (Strong-Boag, 1979; Little, 1998).

A fifth new element of family life in the period between the 1940s and 1960s was the creation of new programs that, unlike such Mothers' Allowances, made support in times of unemployment, illness, and old age a right for most Canadians. Until then, family members and charity were the major sources of social assistance in such difficult times. Kin provided material help and housing. Wives and mothers nursed sick children, husbands, and relatives themselves. Elderly men and women, who had been unable to save during a life of scrimping, faced destitution or dependence on their kin. The massive unemployment and suffering of the 1930s revealed the inadequacies of family support networks and of relief provision through municipalities and charities. Fear of recession in the aftermath of the Second World War fuelled the implementation of new welfare policies. So did a new sense of citizen rights and the distaste of workers and minorities for the demeaning characteristics of earlier welfare measures such as Mothers' Allowances that gave the state the right to intervene in family life, offering economic support but dictating standards of behaviour and definitions of sexuality and gender that were not always shared. The tension between the social control built into state policies and the real support that social legislation offered continued in the laws passed during and after the Second World War that moved Canada toward a welfare state. So too did the ways in which legislation reinforced gender roles and bolstered heterosexual families at the expense of other living arrangements (Comacchio, 1993; Pierson, 1990; Porter, 1993).

Four major pieces of federal legislation passed between the Second World War and the 1960s heralded the beginning of a welfare state, offering support to families as a uni-versal right rather than something available only to the needy. Unemployment Insurance legislation in 1940 offered families new financial stability in times of unemployment. Reg-ulations that made it much easier for male family heads to be eligible than for their wives or other women continued to reinforce the identification of husbands with family bread-winner. Family Allowances were sent to all Canadian families with children in 1944. The government issued monthly cheques to mothers, with the amount determined by the number of children. Wives were thus given new recognition of their responsibility for daily purchases. In some families these relatively small but regular payments were suffi-cient to keep children in school, provide more nutritious food, and get closer to balancing their budgets (Marshall, 1998). Old Age Pensions enacted in 1951 provided support for the elderly. Subsequent legislation, especially health insurance in the 1960s, helped provide families with sufficient money to deal with the crises that in earlier decades had placed so much strain on family budgets. In the last two decades of the twentieth century, these programs came under attack, as all levels of government cut back on spending and made balancing budgets their primary goal. Canadian families now confront new challenges as they raise children, care for aging parents, and face a changing labour market with less government support in times of poverty, unemployment, and old age.

The sixth special feature of family life between the War and the 1960s resulted from the prosperity of the period and the success of unions in bargaining for better wages and work conditions. If ever there was a time when a large proportion of Canadian families was able to manage on the earnings of one wage-earner—the father—it was this period. Children stayed in school longer, less frequently leaving school early to contribute to family finances. Many wives, who might have worked in munitions plants or the forces during the War, had babies and stayed home. As advertising pushed middle- and working-class families to purchase an unprecedented number of home appliances, men took on second jobs to finance purchases and mortgages. This too was a temporary trend. From the 1960s on growing numbers of wives of all class and ethnic backgrounds began seeking paid work, some for financial reasons, others to relieve their sense of frustration and loneliness as wives and mothers. Initially, most were mothers whose children were already in school. By the 1980s growing numbers had preschool-age children. Wealthier families were able to pay for live-in nannies, who increasingly were women migrating for this purpose from areas such as the Caribbean and later the Philippines. Immigrant women turned to their extended kin networks for childcare. More daycare centres were built, but they were never sufficient for the growing level of demand from both middle- and working-class wives, and have been cut back drastically in recent years. In two-parent families, wives replaced children as the second wage-earners, though husbands took on little extra housework. More recently, growing numbers of youth, have again joined the labour market—some to contribute to family revenues, some to finance further education, and many to fulfil the desires fuelled by advertising and the consumer economy.

The seventh trend of the post-War years continues. Immigration laws changed as a growing number of Canadians embraced a more inclusive approach to peopling the country. Since the end of the War, families from Southern Italy, Eastern Europe, and more recently from parts of Africa, Asia, and the Middle East have transformed the ethnic and cultural map of Canada. The processes of cultural conflict and cultural accommodation around issues of child rearing, marital relations, gender, and family values continues.

CONCLUSION

When people talk about the traditional family they often have in mind either an extended family of three generations or the working father and devoted wife and children associated with the period after the Second World War. Yet these are only two of the many types of families that have nurtured as well as bruised past generations of Canadians. Families in the past were frequently broken by death, so single-parent families were common. So were step-parents. Love has not always been seen as crucial, either to relations between spouses or between parents and children. For most of Canadian history, the most important family task has been the work involved in procuring food and raising and educating the next generation adequately and with decency.

In all periods of Canadian history the idea of the family has been invested with rhetorical power that links particular family structures or characteristics to the strength of the nation or to a particular group or regions' identity. Yet Canadians have always had a range of divergent and frequently conflicting understandings of family, gender, and sexuality. Those with most power have attempted to reshape the families of others. Families have been places of refuge and places of danger for the powerful and powerless alike. The idea of what constitutes a marriage, a family, or proper emotional and power relations between family members has been renegotiated at the public level in times of cultural contact, conquest, and economic and social transformation. Debates about same-sex marriage are the latest area of conflict. In private, men and women have negotiated amicably, aggressively, and violently about whom to live with, whether to have children, and who should do what kinds of work. A combination of private choices, public policies, and historical circumstances has forged a diversity of experiences and forms of family in all periods, as is true today.

Suggested Readings

Baillargeon, Denyse (1999). *Making Do: Women, Family and Home in Montreal during the Great Depression*. Waterloo: Wilfred Laurier University Press.

Bradbury, Bettina (1993). *Working Families: Age, Gender and Daily Survival in Industrializing Montreal*. Toronto: McClelland and Stewart.

Bradbury, Bettina (2000). "Single Parenthood in the Past: Canadian Census Categories, 1891-1951 and the 'Normal' Family" *Historical Methods*, 33(4).

Comacchio, Cynthia (1999). *The Intimate Bonds of Family: Domesticity in Canada, 1850-1940*. Toronto: University of Toronto Press.

Dubinsky, Karen (1993). *Improper Advances. Rape and Heterosexual Conflict in Ontario, 1880-1929*. Chicago: University of Chicago Press.

Iacovetta, Franca (1992). *Such Hardworking People. Italian Immigrants in Post-War Toronto*. Montreal and Kingston: McGill-Queen's Press.

Korinek, Valerie J. (2000). *Roughing it in the Suburbs: Reading Chatelaine Magazine in the Fifties and Sixties*. Toronto, University of Toronto Press.

Mitchinson, Wendy (2002). *Giving Birth in Canada, 1900-1950*. Toronto: University of Toronto Press.

Noel, Françoise (2003). *Family Life and Sociability in Upper and Lower Canada, 1780-1870*. Montreal and Kingston: McGill-Queen's University Press.

Parr, Joy (1990). *The Gender of Breadwinners: Women, Men and Change in Two Industrial Towns, 1880-1950*. Toronto: University of Toronto Press.

Perry, Adele (2000). *On the Edge of Empire: Gender, Race, and the Making of British Columbia, 1849-1971*. Toronto, University of Toronto Press.

Sangster, Joan (2000). *Regulating Girls and Women: Sexuality, Family and the Law, Ontario, 1920-1960*. Oxford University Press.

Web Resources

The *Global Gazette. Canada's Family History Magazine.* This is particularly helpful for students seeking to learn how to explore their own family roots: **www.globalgazette.net**

Canada. Confederation to the Present. This site is a bit hard to use. It offers timelines on women's history that are also useful for Canadian family history. Choose Timelines for women's history and you can consult important events and legal changes that are listed by year: **www.canadianhistory.ca**

Images Canada. This site offers a range of visual images of Canada, past and present. The general site is: http://www.imagescanada.ca/ By following the links to photo essays, you can find a good collection of images of First Nations People taken by surveyors and other government workers. **www.nrcan.gc.ca/ess/esic/photoessay/encounters_e.html**

The popular CBC history series provides background to the study of Canadian families. See **http://history.cbc.ca**

CHAPTER FIVE

Paid and Unpaid Work: How Do Families Divide Their Labour?

Gillian Ranson

INTRODUCTION: WORK, INCOME, AND FAMILIES

It takes both paid and unpaid work to sustain a family. Paid work provides money to pay the rent or the mortgage, and to buy food, clothing, and other necessities of life. Unpaid work is the work involved in cooking dinner, changing diapers, doing laundry, reading bedtime stories, and ensuring that all family members are cared for. Canadian sociologist Roderic Beaujot summarizes these two categories of work as "earning and caring." He calls them "the very basis for family" (Beaujot, 2000: 24).

Many factors contribute to decisions about how earning and caring work is divided. First, the constitution of the family affects not only how much financial support is needed, but the specific nature of the caring work involved as well. So the number of adults available to share the work, and the presence or absence of young children, make a difference. According to the 2001 census, married or common-law couples with children aged 24 and under living at home represented 44 percent of all families; childless couples represented 41 percent; and 16 percent were lone-parent families (Statistics Canada, 2003b). These figures indicate the range of caring activities likely to be needed in the majority of Canadian families. But issues such as the health status of family members also need to be considered. Different caring work will be needed for family members living with chronic ill-health or disability, for example. **Multi-generational households** including elders present different caring needs, as well as different ways of sharing the work. The proportion of three-generation households, though less than 3 percent of all family households in Canada, increased rapidly in the decade to 1996. This increase was related to patterns of immigration, with immigrants from Asia accounting for much of it (Che-Alford and Hamm, 1999).

Another important factor is the availability of paid work in the community where the family lives. What is available, and who might best be suited to do it, also affects decisions about how the work gets divided. In most urban centres, for example, there are diverse employment opportunities for most adults. But in some communities, particularly those built around a single resource or industry, the available employment opportunities may be much more limited, and constructed around a particular kind of worker.

Decisions about how earning and caring should be divided are also influenced by **ideologies of gender**. Many people have strong views about the appropriateness of particular kinds of work for women and for men, both at home and in paid employment. These views link to enduring stereotypes about who, in any family, should be ultimately responsible for earning and for caring, even if other family members "help out."

But external pressures, expectations, and opportunities are not all that is involved in the way family members decide how work is to be divided. Family members are engaged in relationships with one another. Decisions are made, or struggled over, or changed, in the context of these ongoing relationships. *How* family decisions are made is also interesting and important.

This chapter will consider the division of paid and unpaid earning and caring work in the light of these factors. It begins with a broad discussion of the economy and paid work, showing how shifts over time in the way people make their living affect the way family life is organized. Of particular importance here are the implications of women's increased participation in the paid labour force. The discussion then moves to a consideration of caring work—what it consists of, and how it is allocated in families. How people share family work, however, is inextricably linked to their relationship to paid work, the kind of jobs they have, and the obligations and constraints those jobs might entail. These issues are covered in a section linking paid work and family work. The chapter then moves to a more theoretical discussion of gender and ideology, since people's deeply held views about gender help account for the way families divide their labour. It concludes by questioning the equity of this division in many families, and makes some suggestions for change.

THE ECONOMY AND PAID WORK

Economic Change

Family life has always been inextricably linked to the opportunities available to people to make a living. In pre-industrial times, survival depended on the labour of family members working collaboratively to produce the food and other goods needed to sustain life. **Industrialization** in Canada and elsewhere saw the development of different kinds of work and a new form of economic organization. The widespread establishment of workplaces separate from homes, and devoted to the manufacture of goods for sale, also ushered in the phenomenon of working for wages in a paid labour force, in order to buy what family members needed to live.

The latter decades of the 20th century saw another economic shift, with the manufacture of goods losing ground to the **service sector**. This sector of the economy covers everything from fast-food sales to landscape gardening to business consulting—a range that clearly indicates some important differences in the kinds of work involved. Jobs at the low end were unskilled, low-paying, offering little in the way of benefits or job security. Jobs at the high end were often highly skilled, requiring considerable training and educational credentials, and offering high salaries and benefits.

More recent changes are associated with the increasing **globalization** of the economy. This globalization is made possible in part by the rapid diffusion of information technology, which not only introduces a huge array of new jobs, but also links organizations, markets, and production processes in global networks, revolutionizing the scale of economic activity. The thinking about these shifts is sharply divergent. Proponents of this "New Economy"—among them many economists, and global economic organizations such as the Organization for Economic Co-operation and Development (OECD, 2001)—point to the economic growth made possible by the efficient use of new technology on a global scale. But critics point out that a focus on economic growth divorced from any consideration of people ignores the "social embeddedness of economic practices" (Watson, 2001: 505). Economic talk about how organizations need to **"restructure"** in order to become "global competitors" glosses over what this might mean at the level of the individual workplace. One of the most prominent social critics of the "New Economy" is sociologist Manuel Castells, who writes with concern about the effects of globalization and the transformation of work. In particular, he points out that, in the interests of efficiency, employers are moving to make work more **"flexible."** But this often translates into jobs that are part-time, temporary, or available only on a contract basis—in other words, jobs that are much less secure (Castells, 2000).

Changes in the Labour Force, Changes in Work

Changes in the constitution of the labour force have accompanied the economic shifts noted above. Industrialization introduced increasing numbers of paying jobs, as distinct from home-based **subsistence labour**. But, for many decades, most jobs in the formal paid labour force were held by men. In 1901, 87.8 percent of all men older than 15 were in the labour force, compared to 16.1 percent of women (Beaujot, 2000: 136) Women historically contributed to the financial support of their families, but until the last half of the 20th century, that support tended to be informal and home-based. An important barrier to labour force participation for women was marriage. The expectation was that a married woman would be supported by her husband. In 1931, for example, only 3.5 percent of married women had paying jobs, and even by mid-century the proportion was only about 10 percent (Duffy, Mandell, and Pupo, 1989: 10).

Women's labour force participation increased gradually in the early decades of the 20th century, but the most significant shifts occurred in the 1960s and 1970s. In 1961, women's labour force participation rate was 29.1 percent. By 1971 it had reached 39.9 percent, and by 1981, it was 51.8 percent (Beaujot, 2000: 136). By 2002 it was 56 percent (Statistics Canada, 2003c).

Many reasons are cited for this powerful demographic shift. Economic growth in the post-War decades saw an increase in available jobs. The growth of the service sector and the public service invited women to take on paid work (such as nursing, teaching, and "supportive" clerical and secretarial work) that conformed to the work and the roles with which they had historically been associated at home.

Baker (1995, 2001) cites four other reasons. First, she notes the cost of living increases of the 1960s, and the need for two incomes per family. In part, this was because economic growth was accompanied by the availability of new products and an increase in consumerism as people's perceptions of their wants and needs changed. But it was also a consequence of changes in thinking about how people should be rewarded for their work. Baker points out that, before World War II, men's wages were often based on their family status, with increases awarded with marriage and the birth of children. This practice was based on the assumption that men, not women, were the family breadwinners, and needed a "family wage" to support all their dependants. But, through the 1960s and 1970s, as a result of challenges from unions, professional associations, and feminist groups, pay scales came to be based on individual merit. The "family wage" thus, in many cases, needed to be earned by more than one person. With the growing gap between good jobs and bad jobs noted above, and the loss of job security thought by many to be a consequence of the new global economy, a second income continues to be a requirement in most families.

The second reason Baker cites relates to changing ideas about women's roles in society. In the early decades of the 20th century, women in Canada and elsewhere gained political rights (including the right to vote). From the 1960s on women's access to post-secondary education increased enormously. The 1960s also saw the emergence of the second wave of the women's movement, which helped entrench feminist ideals about women's rights to education, access to paid work, and employment equity.

Third, Baker notes that women's participation rates have continued to increase because more women are remaining in paid employment after they have children. Where once childbirth signalled the end of paid employment and a turn to child rearing, at least temporarily, women now are more likely to take temporary maternity leaves and then return to paid work. Finally, Baker notes that women's labour force participation has been significantly shaped by improvements in birth control technology. McLaren and McLaren (1997) point out that the birth control pill was available in Canada by 1961. They further note that although Canada lagged behind countries such as Britain and the U.S. in promoting family planning (the advertisement and sale of contraceptives was technically illegal until 1969), reforms introduced in that year by the Trudeau government as part of the overhaul of the Criminal Code decriminalized birth control and also allowed hospitals to carry out therapeutic abortions. These changes reduced the chance that women would be forced to curtail or forego educational and employment opportunities because of unplanned pregnancies.

These trends can be clearly seen in the shifting age patterns of female labour force participants. In 1971, women's rates were much higher (over 60 percent) at ages 20-24, declining to around 40 percent during the late 20s and 30s, with a slight increase in the 40-54 age range. By 1996, however, women's participation much more closely resembled men's, with both showing relatively stable rates over the ages from 25 to 49 (Beaujot, 2000). The participation of women in the paid labour force during their prime child-bearing years signals another shift—the increased participation of mothers of young children. In 2002, 72 percent of all women with children under age 16 living at home were part of the paid workforce. Of women with children under three, 62 percent were employed. There are differences, however, between women who are lone parents and those who are mothers in dual-parent families. Among single mothers, 67 percent of those with children under 16 were in paid work. This represents a shift from the 1970s, when single mothers were more likely than mothers in two-parent familes to be in the labour force (Statistics Canada, 2003c).

Another significant change in the labour force, noted briefly above, is the increase in part-time, **contract work** or other non-permanent work, and self-employment—collectively known as **non-standard employment**. Marshall (2000) notes that part-time employment increased from 12.6 percent in 1976 to 18.5 percent in 1999. She points out one reason for this increase is the development of a globalized, service-based economy, with employers moving to create a more "flexible" **contingent workforce** in order to save money. A second reason Marshall suggests is that more workers are themselves seeking flexibility and ways to balance their home and family lives. There are corresponding increases in other kinds of non-standard work. About one-third of workers aged 15 and over are in this kind of work. Vosko, Zukewich, and Cranford (2003) point out that, though workers in full-time permanent jobs are still in the majority, there has been a small but steady decrease in their numbers—from 67 percent of all workers in 1989 to 64 percent in 1994 to 63 percent in 2002. This means a shift away from work that is secure, regulated in some way in terms of working conditions, and that provides a stable and adequate income. These writers suggest that "precarious employment" is a better way to describe work that deviates from the "standard" model.

Through the 1990s, technological change and the pressures of global competition also meant more time on the job for many workers (Drolet and Morisette, 2002; Duxbury and Higgins, 2002). According to the 1998 General Social Survey, about a quarter of adult Canadians, and about a third of those with school-aged children, were self-described "workaholics" (Kemeny, 2002).

Gender at Work

Women's labour force participation, as noted above, has increased to such an extent that their numbers, and the stability of their participation, are approaching parity with men's. But participation rates alone mask important differences in the kinds of work women and men do, their distribution in standard compared to non-standard employment, and the money they earn.

One enduring feature of the labour force in industrialized countries, including Canada, is **occupational segregation by gender**. Women in particular tend to cluster in certain sectors of the economy, and in certain kinds of work. In 2002, some 70 percent of all employed women (compared to only 30 percent of employed men) were working in teaching, nursing and related health occupations, clerical or other administrative positions, or sales and service occupations. At the same time, there have been increases in women's participation in a range of other fields. For example, women in 2002 comprised 54 percent of all doctors and dentists, and 34 percent of all managers. In other fields, though, women continue to be significantly underrepresented. In 2002 they made up only 21 percent of professionals in the natural sciences, engineering, and mathematics (Statistics Canada, 2003b).

Another aspect of women's entry into previously male-dominated occupations is their location within the occupation. In an extensive U.S. study of occupations which seemed to be becoming more gender-integrated, Reskin and Roos (1991) found that women tended to occupy the lower ranks, or less prestigious and lower-paying specialties. Beaujot (2000) notes that even as women join the ranks of managers and professionals, they may not be joining on equal terms. For example, though the proportion of women managers is increasing, most were lower-level managers; only about 25 percent were senior managers (Statistics Canada, 2003c).

Differences in the kinds of work done by women and men link to differences in **employment status**. Women, as noted above, tend to cluster in the service sector of the economy. In this sector, too, there is a clustering of part-time work, with as many as nine out of 10 service-sector workers estimated to be working part-time (Crompton and Vickers, 2000). Part-time workers are also typically either young (in the 15-24 years age range) or women aged 25 to 54. Among the younger group, school attendance is the main reason for part-time work. Among the women aged 25-54, family responsibilities tend to dominate (Marshall, 2001). But as noted earlier, the part-time/full-time distinction is only one way in which work may be "non-standard." Women and men are differently affected by the shift to "precarious employment" more generally. Though the overall loss of full-time permanent jobs affected more men than women, men in 2002 were still more likely than women (66 percent compared to 59 percent) to have standard employment. Self-employment is also different for women and men. Men who are self-employed are more likely to have employees working for them, and much more likely to be working full-time (Vosko, Zukewich, and Cranford, 2003).

All the differences along gender lines noted so far have consequences for income as well. A "gender gap" in the relative earnings of women and men continues to exist, even though it has narrowed over the past three decades. Among full-year, full-time earnings, the proportion of women's to men's earnings in 1998 was 72 percent, compared to 58 percent in 1967. Women also tend to have reduced access to benefits, because of their greater representation in part-time jobs (Johnson, Lero, and Rooney, 2001).

Families and Earning

The foregoing discussion of issues related to the economy, the labour force, and gender differences in work and income makes clear that people are not always free to choose the terms of their participation in paid work. Employers responding to global economic trends make changes which affect people's jobs, and some people are affected more adversely than others. When dependants, particularly young children, are involved, differences in people's capacity to weather workplace changes translates into differences in families' economic fortunes. In 1999, about 19 percent of families had no financial assets (apart from the family home and its contents, or assets related to a business) they could draw on in times of crisis. About one in four of these families also had low income. Certain categories of families are considered especially vulnerable: female lone-parent families, families with very young children, and families who are recent immigrants (Morissette, 2002).

In this context, the need for more than one earner in a family becomes clear. Between 1989 and 1998, dual-earner couples with children experienced a 6.3 percent increase in average after-tax income, compared to a 3.2 percent increase among single-earner families. Women's earnings have become increasingly significant, accounting for about a third of income earned in dual-earner heterosexual families, compared to 29 percent in 1989 and 26 percent in 1967. Johnson, Lero, and Rooney (2001) note that during the 1990s, two incomes appeared necessary to maintain a family's standard of living, and to protect many families from poverty. (It may be, however, that rising aspirations are also contributing to the increase in dual-earner couples. The "standard of living" which many families want to maintain is a middle-class standard, not a working-class one. As a result of women's increased access to post-secondary education, the career aspirations of well-educated professional women must also be taken into account.)

THE DIVISION OF CARING WORK

The amount of caring work varies with household constitution. In families where there are no dependent children, the caring work within the home may be less intensive. Time freed up from childcare responsibilities may be expended on community activities, or involvement with non-resident family members. But it is reasonable to assume that much the greatest amount of caring work, and therefore the greatest need to negotiate its division, occurs in families where there are young children—still the majority of Canadian families.

In the days when women were expected to leave their paid employment when children first arrived, and in families where one income—the "family wage"—really could support a family, the division of labour in the home was unproblematic. In general, the expectation was that the person who was in the home, or in the home most, did the family work. In the 1950s, the sociologist Talcott Parsons theorized a division of labour that saw the father as the "instrumental" leader, solely responsible for the family's financial support, while the mother was the "expressive" leader, responsible for the care and emotional nurture of family members (Parsons, 1955). Always a partial, racially and class-biased view, it is now even more removed from the material realities of most families, few of which have a Parsons-style homemaker constantly on duty. Yet childcare and housework still have to be done.

Childcare

Many of the studies to be discussed in the next section concern the unpaid work that women and men do in the home. Much of that work, when parents are at home, either directly or indirectly involves childcare. But an increasing proportion of childcare is now not done by parents, but is contracted out to other individuals, or to organizations such as daycare centres. In this sense, for working parents of young children, most childcare has been converted from unpaid work they do themselves to paid work performed by someone else. The need for non-parental childcare is not restricted to a particular segment of the population. The majority of young Canadian families in all regions, as well as in all economic, ethnic, and language groups, have both parents either in the paid labour force or in education or training programs (Friendly, 2003). Yet, in spite of this widespread need, the public provision of quality childcare is minimal. The one exception is the province of Quebec (see Exhibit 5.1).

A major concern of researchers in the area of early childhood education and care in Canada is the absence of a national childcare policy. The most direct federal government involvement in organized childcare came during World War II, with an agreement

---

Exhibit 5.1   Childcare in Quebec

In 1997, Quebec's Parti Quebecois government instituted an Early Childhood and Childcare Strategy which differentiated it from all other jurisdictions in Canada in terms of childcare provision.

Under the terms of the strategy, regulated childcare was available at the rate of $5 a day to all children from infancy to 12 years. Childcare was available through centres or by licensed family providers. An educational program was available in both centre-based and family agencies, adapted to the age of the children and the amount of time they spend in care. Five-year-olds had access to full-day kindergarten. Refundable tax credits and a financial assistance program were available to parents who were unable to make use of spaces at the $5 rate (Tougas, 2001a, b). In 2001, roughly 40 percent of Canada's regulated childcare spaces were in Quebec (Friendly, Beach, and Turiano, 2001).

What is even more remarkable is that this progressive approach had widespread support. How did this come about? Tougas (2001a) cites several possible reasons: the ability of the Parti Quebecois to articulate values shared by many Quebecers; the infrastructure in place before 1997 which provided funding and a voice in policy making to non-profit childcare associations; the responsibility taken for the childcare portfolio over several years by strong and highly respected women cabinet ministers.

A change of government in Quebec has meant some scaling back of the original $5-a-day strategy. In the face of considerable opposition, the Liberal government increased the daily fee to $7, effective January 1, 2004. But, even taking this change into account, Quebec still remains the most progressive Canadian jurisdiction in terms of childcare policy.

Cleveland and Krashinsky (2001) differentiate the childcare policies prevailing in the rest of Canada and other countries with predominantly Anglo-Saxon heritage (such as the United States, Britain, and Australia) from those operating in many European countries, where universal and low-cost quality childcare is typically available. Quebec's policies are thus much more "European."

---

offering 50 percent cost sharing to help provinces provide childcare for mothers working in essential war industries. But only Ontario and Quebec participated in the scheme. Federal support was withdrawn when the war ended, and most of the childcare centres closed down. In the 1960s, the federal government contributed directly to childcare funding through the Canada Assistance Plan. Though this plan targeted mainly disadvantaged families, it did serve to spur the development of childcare services through the 1970s and 1980s. Another federal initiative, starting in 1971, was the recognition of childcare costs as an employment expense eligible for tax deduction. More recent developments have been less well received by social critics, however. In 1996 the Canada Assistance Plan was abolished, and federal support for childcare was subsumed into a block fund, the Canada Health and Social Transfer. This gave greater discretion to the provinces over social spending, including spending on childcare (Friendly, Beach, and Turiano, 2002). And provincial childcare provision is, in the words of one expert, a "crazy quilt" (Krashinsky, 2001).

Optimally, parents would like children to be in childcare which is regulated; in other words, which is monitored by provincial government regulators, and which must meet certain minimum standards. But such childcare is expensive. Better childcare centres in Ontario, for example, may charge $7-8,000 a year and more for older pre-schoolers, and considerably more for infants (Krashinsky, 2001). For this reason, many parents—one estimate suggests one-third of working parents—avoid formal, paid childcare arrangements, and use other strategies such as working fewer hours, or balancing family work schedules (including shift work) so that one parent is available, or recruiting relatives (Cleveland and Krashinsky, 2001). The number of regulated spaces is also inadequate to meet the demand. The 1994-95 cycle of Statistics Canada's National Longitudinal Survey of Children and Youth indicated that there were then 2.5 million children who were aged 0-5 years. Of those, about 1.4 million had a mother who was either employed or a student. Not counting those who were in kindergarten, about 900,000 used non-parental care. Some 250,000 (about 28 percent) were in regulated care (either in centres or family homes). About 430,000 (about 48 percent) were in informal arrangements with unregulated babysitters or other caregivers. About 200,000 (22 percent) were cared for by relatives (Cleveland and Krashinsky, 2001). Current estimates are that there are enough regulated childcare spaces in Canada for about 12 percent of children from 0 to 12 years (Friendly, Beach, and Turiano, 2002).

A daycare worker reads to preschoolers.

FIGURE 5.1   Proportion of Fathers Claiming Parental Leave

The proportion of fathers who claimed or planned to claim paid parental benefits jumped from about 3% in 2000 to 10% by 2001. This is both a statistically and socially significant increase. Although the length of time involved is not known, approximately 1 in 10 fathers take a formal leave from their job to be at home caring for a newborn. This rate moves Canada ahead of many other countries, but still leaves it considerably behind those that offer non-transferable leave to fathers — Norway, for example, where almost 80% of fathers take parental leave.

Fathers' participation in paid parental leave in selected countries

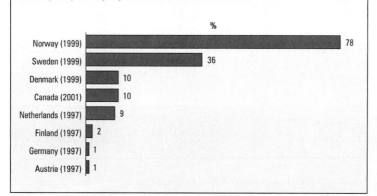

Source: Adapted from the Statistics Canada publication "Canadian Social Trends," Catalogue 11-008, Winter 2003, page 15.

The provision of childcare for children with special needs is even more inadequate. A 1998 study of childcare centres in Canada indicated that, with no legal requirement or financial incentive to do so, one-third of those studied did not include any children with special needs. Only about 12 percent included five or more children with special needs (Hope Irwin, 2001). Yet an estimated four percent of all Canadian children aged between 5 and 14 years had some form of activity limitation in 2001, according to Statistics Canada's Participation and Activity Limitation Survey. Many of their parents reported not getting the help they needed to cope with their children's condition. More than half the parents reported that the family's employment situation had been affected, with mothers bearing the major impact in seven out of 10 cases (Statistics Canada, 2003c).

Though critics challenge the failure of successive federal governments to live up to their promises regarding childcare, in one respect at least there has been some recognition at the federal level of children's need for care and parents' need to work. Effective December 31, 2000, the federal Employment Insurance Act was amended to allow eligible parents up to 35 weeks of **parental leave**. The leave can be taken by one parent or shared by both. Added to the existing maternity leave provision of up to 15 weeks, this legislation effectively provides paid leave for up to a year, at 55 percent of average insured earnings up to a maximum of $413 per week (Marshall, 2003). To be eligible, parents had to work for 600 hours during the previous 52 weeks.

One aim of this legislation, which was followed by appropriate labour code amendments in all the provinces and territories, was to allow parents to care for their babies longer, and still have secure re-entry to employment. An overview of labour market activity before and after the benefit changes indicated several positive trends. The overall proportion of new mothers receiving maternity or parental leave benefits increased from 54 percent in 2000 to 61 percent in 2001. (Those who did not receive benefits were not in the paid labour force, had not worked long enough to be eligible or had not applied for them, or were self-employed.) For mothers planning to return to work after childbirth, the most common intended return time changed from 5-6 months in 2000 to 9-12 months in 2001. Longer leaves were correlated with higher earnings. Women who took longer leaves were also less likely to have partners planning to share the leave. However, the proportion of fathers taking or planning to take parental leave increased from 3 percent in 2000 to 10 percent in 2001. This rate moves Canada ahead of many other countries—but far behind countries such as Sweden, where some 36 percent of fathers take parental leave, or Norway, with a participation rate of 78 percent. In Sweden and Norway, however, parental leave is non-transferable. In other words, if fathers fail to take up their share, that proportion is lost (Marshall, 2003)

Unpaid Work in the Home

The need for childcare while both parents are working is a major preoccupation for many Canadian families. But children need care after working hours. And this care must also be fitted around meal preparation, house cleaning, laundry and all the other activities that sustain life. This is work that must be done in all households, whether or not there are

The presence of children greatly increases the amount of caring work families need to undertake.

children present. These activities were traditionally seen as "women's work" in a world view which considered the home as the domain of women and the workplace as the domain of men. In lone-parent families, the vast majority of which are headed by women, there is little challenge to this image of domestic work. But, for couples, where there is the potential to share the work, a point of contention now for scholars is whether women's increased participation in paid work has been accompanied by a corresponding increase in men's unpaid work. At the level of the individual family, this stereotypical division of labour stands as a sturdy backdrop against which heterosexual couples must negotiate, resist, and compromise. For gay and lesbian families, the irrelevance of the old gender stereotypes means there is no default position. Negotiation becomes even more relevant, although it is conducted on different terms.

At present there is little research evidence about the way unpaid work is divided in gay and lesbian households. But what there is suggests a division of family work that is much more egalitarian than in heterosexual households (Dunne, 2000; Nelson, 1996, 2001; Patterson, 1995). For example, Nelson's study of 30 lesbian families in Alberta found childcare in the families in which babies were conceived within the relationship by donor insemination shared the same childcare tasks with equal frequency. Many said the only difference was that the biological mothers occasionally breast-fed (Nelson, 2001). In families where children had been born in prior, heterosexual relationships, the biological mothers tended to do more of the mothering tasks. In all the families, however, the division of other domestic work was equal, and based on individual abilities and tastes. Housecleaning and cooking tended to be evenly shared. And the work was not allocated along conventionally "masculine" or "feminine" lines. Nelson noted that the woman who enjoyed cooking or sewing might also be the one who kept the family cars running and built the shed in the back yard (Nelson, 1996: 111). Couples tried not to get trapped in conventional divisions of labour, as the following interview excerpt shows:

> [We are] really sensitive to roles in the house because, as far as domestic roles go, I'm more handy than Blaire is and she's more particular about cleanliness than I am, and so it's really easy for us to fall into those roles. . . Like if Blaire was hanging a mirror or something, there was a time I would have just stepped in and said, 'Here, let me do that.' . . . Because I would always step in and Blaire would never be able to hang a picture or whatever. And the same goes for things around the house, you know, if Blaire let me get away with it, she'd do the laundry all the time. So we really force each other to do what has to be done and not depend so much on roles (Nelson, 1996: 111)

Scholars have suggested that the interaction of sexual orientation and gender may work to create not only new kinds of family structures, but also new processes—including a more egalitarian division of labour (Stacey and Biblarz, 2001).

For heterosexual couples, however, the overall picture is different. In the study by Luxton and Corman of working-class steelworker couples in Hamilton, one woman, staying at home to care for children when first interviewed in 1984, was re-interviewed 10 years later, when she had been employed full-time for seven years. She commented, "It's a big change, eh, from the way things used to be. I'm working and my husband, well, when I was at home he never did anything around the house except bill paying. He still doesn't do much, but some" (Luxton and Corman, 2001: 36). This situation, for heterosexual couples, illustrates what U.S. sociologist Arlie Hochschild described as the "stalled

FIGURE 5.2   Parents Aged 25 to 44, with Children under 25

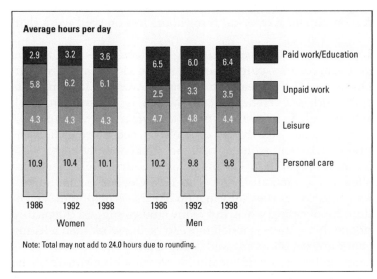

Average hours per day

Paid work/Education

Unpaid work

Leisure

Personal care

	Women			Men	
1986	1992	1998	1986	1992	1998
2.9	3.2	3.6	6.5	6.0	6.4
5.8	6.2	6.1	2.5	3.3	3.5
4.3	4.3	4.3	4.7	4.8	4.4
10.9	10.4	10.1	10.2	9.8	9.8

Note: Total may not add to 24.0 hours due to rounding.

Source: Statistics Canada (2001). Catalogue no. 11-008, *Canadian Social Trends*, Winter

revolution." Writing of the 1980s, she claimed that women had changed. But workplaces generally remained unresponsive to the needs of workers with family demands. And men were continuing to allow women to do the "**second shift**" of domestic work when they returned home from their paying jobs (Hochschild, 1989). Another sociologist, Ralph LaRossa, writing of the same period in the U.S., had a similar view of men as parents. He noted that, with increasing numbers of women (and in particular women with young children) entering the workforce, popular expectations were that fathers would be picking up much more of the childcare work. He pointed to the abundant media imagery of men as sensitive, involved fathers. But LaRossa claimed that there was a lag between the *culture* of fatherhood, as suggested in the media, and the *conduct* of fatherhood—what men as fathers were actually doing in their families. Men may have been more involved, but much of the childcare people thought they must have been doing was actually being picked up by other family members, or contracted out to paid caregivers (LaRossa, 1988).

Many studies, in Canada and elsewhere, suggest that when women enter the paid work force, they do somewhat less domestic work, and their male partners do a little more—but the gender gap persists. These findings seem to support Hochschild's claim that women work a "second shift" at home. Beaujot (2000) points out, however, that many Canadian studies along these lines predated the formal time-use studies instituted by Statistics Canada in several cycles of the General Social Survey. These studies, started in 1986 and repeated in 1992 and 1998, have shown that, although differences have persisted in the time women and men spend on unpaid work, there are corresponding differences in time spent on paid work as well. These differences are accentuated by marital status and the presence of children.

As Figure 5.2 indicates, patterns of paid and unpaid work are similar for single women and men in the 25–44 years age range. Among couples in this age range without children, women on average do slightly more unpaid work, and slightly less paid work, than men. But it is among couples with children that the clearest differences emerge. The total workday for parents has increased by almost an hour over the past decade, as both parents reduce the time they spend on personal care activities, and fathers cut back on leisure activities. But, although the total workload is similar for both mothers and fathers, the division of labour is obviously more along gendered lines. Mothers on average spend about three more hours per day on unpaid work, and three hours less on paid work than fathers (Fast et al., 2001).

These findings clearly reflect those noted above concerning gender differences in hours of paid employment. For heterosexual couples, parenthood is associated with an increase in paid employment on the part of men, and a decrease on the part of women. This suggests that one way to ensure that family work is covered, for many couples, is for women to work fewer paid hours. What happens, though, in families where both partners are working full-time? The 1992 General Social Survey showed that in dual-earner heterosexual families where both partners were working full-time, women continued to be mainly responsible for the ongoing daily chores of meal preparation, cleaning, and laundry, while men were responsible for outdoor maintenance (Marshall, 1993). The 1998 General Social Survey showed a similar pattern (Palameta, 2003). Survey information like this is helpful in sketching the broad outlines of the division of caring work. But many studies suggest the picture is much more complicated. For one thing, there is much more to caring work than a listing of chores. Preparing meals requires grocery shopping and cooking food. But it also involves remembering people's tastes and preferences, and creating a pleasant atmosphere at the dinner table (DeVault, 1991). Caring for children involves more than changing diapers or supervising homework. It also involves mental energy in worrying about health, educational or discipline problems, planning activities, and managing the schedule—activities that mothers, rather than fathers tend to take on (Daly, 2002; Walzer, 1996). Organizing and managing this "second shift" of family work, and dealing with the consequences when family members feel rushed, overlooked, or overscheduled, may constitute a "third shift" of emotional work as well (Hochschild, 1997).

In much of the foregoing, the focus has been on families with young children. These are the families in which caring work is most intensive and least discretionary, and in which the division of labour may be most contentious. This is not to suggest that caring work is not important in other kinds of families. It is also important to note the changes in people's caring responsibilities over the life course, as children grow and parents age.

One significant demographic trend of relevance here is the lengthening of the time young adults live with their parents. In 2001, 41 percent of 20- to 29-year-olds lived with their parents, compared to 27 percent in 1981. The need for more schooling, job insecurity, later marriage, and relationship dissolution, are all considered to contribute to this trend (*Canadian Social Trends*, 2003). Mitchell's (2004) study of young Canadian adults (aged 19-35) who share households with their parents explores some of the implications of this trend. Although noting earlier research documenting the "considerable reciprocity in exchanges of instrumental and emotional support during midlife coresidence" (Mitchell, 2004: 121), Mitchell found that the provision of domestic services, largely by mothers, was much more of a one-way street. She points out that extended family responsibilities, many largely borne by mothers, may also take on a different form in an era of cutbacks in social and health services. Helping an adult child through unemployment, mental health problems, or addiction becomes more critical—and more difficult.

Another kind of caring work confronting families as they age is eldercare. This too is a category of family responsibility likely to increase as the "baby boom" generation ages.

The most recent information on eldercare in Canada comes from the 1996 General Social Survey, which investigated social and community support, and collected data on the amount of time people spent caring for a friend or relative aged 65 and over with a long-term physical or health limitation. The data indicated that among these informal care-givers, 61 percent were women, whose average age was 46, and most were caring for a parent (Frederick and Fast, 1999).

It is also important to note, however, that not all seniors require help. Beaujot (2000) cites an earlier (1992) time-use survey indicating that only 9.1 percent of women, and 10.5 percent of men participated in eldercare activities on a given day. Meanwhile, scholars point out that until they are well past retirement, seniors are more likely to give family help than to receive it (Beaujot, 2000; Lindsay, 1999). This raises questions about the extent to which there really is a "sandwich generation" of adults (primarily women) caught between the dual care demands of their children and their aging parents. For Beaujot (2000: 221), the point to be made is not that there is a widespread need for elder-care, but that in the specific circumstances where there is a need, there may be "enormous personal costs" borne by caregivers.

CONNECTING PAID WORK AND FAMILY WORK

The U.S. feminist economist Heidi Hartmann, writing in the early 1980s, linked women's continuing responsibility for domestic work to their position in the paid work force. Her argument went as follows: Because women worked for low pay in a segregated work force, they were dependent on men for financial support in order to raise families. This financial dependence obligated them to compensate by taking on the bulk of the domes-tic labour, and also set up a cycle of dependence, since women with domestic burdens are less able to commit to the kinds of work that would ensure their financial independence. Hartmann's general claim was that the dual systems of patriarchy and **capitalism** ensured men's control over women's labour, both at home and at work.

This theory is no longer considered to work as an overarching explanation for the gendered division of paid and unpaid labour. For one thing, it is much too general, placing all women and all men in two mutually exclusive but internally homogeneous categories which mask important differences among women and among men. And it does not adequately account for the negotiation and decision-making of individual couples. But Hartmann's explanation may make good sense for certain segments of the labour market. For example, for the working class women of Flin Flon who participated in Meg Luxton's 1976 study, periods of high unemployment meant there were not enough jobs for the women who wanted to work, and marriage became the main survival strat-egy (Luxton, 1980). Hartmann's argument also raises some general issues that are worth exploring in an attempt to uncover reasons for the importance of gender in the division of paid and unpaid work.

Earnings is the first issue. Beaujot (2000) cites several studies in Canada and the U.S. which suggest that the greater a woman's earning power, the more domestic work her male partner contributes to the household. Greater employment opportunities for women in the last few decades have meant that not all women are financially dependent on men. But, as noted above, women do earn, on average, less than men. This may mean that, for pragmatic reasons, the man's job in any partnership where there are children may come to be privileged over the woman's, since it is the one more important to the financial security of the family. It follows, then, that the holder of the privileged job is also the one required to make fewer accommodations for family or other responsibilities. This may also explain why, in families with pre-school children, women miss more work for family or personal responsibilities than men do—an average of 4.0 days in 2000, compared to 2.1 days for men (Akyeampong, 2001).

Another example of how one job gets to be privileged comes from a study of the ways a small sample of professional men combined work and family responsibilities. One man, the father of two young children, whose wife worked part-time, commented:

> [I]f I have to work late, or whatever and the kids have something going at night, I'll be call-ing [my wife] and saying, 'I can't make it—can you do it?' Or, if she can't do it, then I'll leave and go and do it. But, I mean, my job here basically isn't 9 to 5, and I can't always be home at 5 o'clock in the evening, you know . . . I'll try to make it, let's put it that way, but if I can't then hopefully [she] can do it (Ranson, 2001: 22).

Job segregation is a second issue raised by Hartmann. The widespread occupational segregation of the labour force noted above places women and men in different kinds of work and different kinds of workplaces. Women's work at the low end of the occupa-tional ladder is often the kind of short-term, contingent work that, because it offers so few rewards and benefits, is more easily interrupted. At the higher end, traditionally female occupations such as teaching and nursing are more accustomed to dealing with workers with family responsibilities, and are more accommodating of their needs. This means that options such as part-time work or flexible schedules may be easier to negotiate for women in these occupations (Ranson, 1998).

At the same time, occupations and workplaces dominated by men tend to be much less understanding of the family responsibilities of their employees, both men and women. In part this is because such workplaces historically were the domain of workers (men) who were able to delegate their family responsibilities. Women entering these workplaces were expected to operate on the same terms. As feminist sociologist Joan Acker pointed out, in most organizations, jobs had conventionally been understood as being performed by abstract and disembodied "workers" who existed only for the job. But, in the real world of actual workers, the closest approximation to a worker like this was "the male worker whose life centers on his full-time, life-long job, while his wife or another woman takes care of his personal needs and his children" (Acker, 1990: 149). The fact that women were positioned very differently with respect to family responsibilities and did not have some-one at home to take care of the family exposed the extent to which supposedly gender-neutral working conditions and expectations were in fact highly gendered.

Unionization

Union membership is one way women and men work collectively to improve wages and working conditions. Although factors such as personal, job, and workplace characteristics also come into play, there is consistent evidence that unionized workers do earn on aver-age more than non-unionized workers (Fang and Verma, 2003; Jackson and Schellenberg,

1999; Jackson 2003). **Collective bargaining** has also brought some significant benefits related to family responsibilities. Most workers covered by major **collective agreements** have access to paid maternity leave, often up to between 76 and 100 percent of normal pay. Several unions, such as the Canadian Auto Workers and the Canadian Union of Postal Workers, have been able to negotiate funds for childcare in their collective agreements. These funds have been used to establish innovative programs, such as those designed to meet the needs of shift workers (Jackson and Schellenberg, 2001).

In 2003, some 30 percent of both women and men worked in unionized jobs (Statistics Canada, 2003c). Union membership, however, tends to be concentrated in the public sector, which accounts for about three-quarters of all members. The concentration is especially significant for women, since women's employment is already concentrated in public and social services (Jackson, 2003).

Organizations and "Work-Life Balance"

Recognition that the balance of paid work and family responsibilities might be difficult for some employees has led some organizations to institute so-called "family-friendly" policies aimed at making this balance easier. Flexible schedules, for example, were seen as one way to help people accommodate family demands—such as meeting children at the school bus at 3:30 P.M.—that could not be met with a 9-5 schedule. But access to such policies and programs has been slow, and occasionally the policies themselves have been problematic.

The economic turbulence of the 1990s, when many organizations were restructuring, generally was not a period when employers were sensitive to employees' responsibilities outside work, nor one when employees felt able to make demands. Commenting on their ten years of research in the area, Higgins and Duxbury comment that "employers' sensitivity to work-family issues continues to lag behind the emergence of these concerns as an issue for employees" (Higgins and Duxbury, 2002: 11). The authors' survey data, in 1991 and 2001, indicate that most respondents at both time points had little or no flexibility in terms of when, or where, they worked. And those who had greatest need of it—notably those with children and those with eldercare responsibilities—were less likely to have flexible arrangements available to them. Yet, in spite of their scant availability, flexible work schedules remain the most common "family-friendly" work arrangement. The 1999 Work and Employment Survey (WES) conducted by Statistics Canada indicated that about one-third of employees could avail themselves of flexible work schedules, but only about five percent could make use of **telework**, six percent had childcare services provided by the employer, and four percent had access to eldercare services (usually in the form of information and referral services). WES data also indicated that access to family-friendly arrangements was more likely for university and college graduates, and those in higher-end professional and managerial jobs (Comfort, Johnson, and Wallace, 2003). There is other evidence that such arrangements do not always work in the ways they were intended. For example, the WES showed that access to flextime was greatest among young people aged 15 to 24, not among women in their child-rearing years. And more men than women (44 percent compared to 36 percent) reported a flextime arrangement (Comfort, Johnson, and Wallace, 2003).

Another perspective on family-friendly policies merits consideration. At issue is what family-friendly policies are really intended to achieve. Usually, they are framed in gender-neutral terms, and their declared goal is to facilitate women's full participation in the workplace, while also allowing men to take on their share of family responsibilities. But some argue, in a similar vein to Acker (1990), cited above, that the main goal is to enable women to work in the same way as men, rather than questioning whether this is the best way to work. This approach sees women as the prime beneficiaries of "family-friendly" policies, and further entrenches the idea that they are *for* women, rather than for everyone. This in turn sets them up as special concessions or benefits for women (Jones and Causer, 1995; Lewis, 1997), rather than as rights to which all workers are entitled. Liff and Ward (2001) call this a "women's problems" approach to equality—one which accentuates women's "difference" and seeks to accommodate it. Several British studies of women in male-dominated occupations (Jones and Causer, 1995; Liff and Ward, 2001; Rubin, 1997) show that women are aware of the way such "special concessions" may mark them as different, and recognize the consequences of taking them up.

At the same time, failure to enact policies to help people balance work and family responsibilities continues to disadvantage women, and may explain the tendency among Canadian women to delay childbearing until their careers are established (Drolet, 2003). This tendency may apply particularly to women in professional and managerial positions. In their 2001 survey, Higgins and Duxbury found that women in technical and professional positions were less likely to have children than their male counterparts, and than women in other occupations. Their data suggest that many of the professional women in their sample did not see motherhood and career as being compatible (Higgins and Duxbury, 2002).

More recent research in this area is moving away from "work-family balance" to a broader focus on "work-life integration." This conceptual shift involves a recognition that the challenges of balancing multiple roles and associated responsibilities is not a "woman's issue," but a wider social concern (Johnson, Lero, and Rooney, 2001). Work-life conflicts involve role overload (having too much to do), spillover from work to family and other responsibilities, and spillover from family to work (Higgins and Duxbury, 2002). Men, as well as women, experience all three, though possibly in different ways.

GENDER, IDEOLOGY, AND THE DIVISION OF LABOUR

The discussion of both paid work and caring work has made it clear that they are inextricably linked. The circumstances surrounding paid work critically influence employees' family lives. And family responsibilities shape the terms and conditions of their paid employment. The linkages are reciprocal, for both women and men.

Also connecting people's work and caring activities are pervasive and often deeply held beliefs about gender. Because there are now examples in most people's experience of men's expertise in caring for children and women's accomplishments in a wide range of paid employment, few would claim that men and women are not *capable* of such activities. But there continues to be an expectation that women ultimately will be responsible for the caring work, even when they are also employed full-time, and that men ultimately will be responsible for their family's financial support, even when they are also involved in hands-on caring work. Old ideologies about the proper place of women and of men continue to cast long shadows.

Since at least the beginning of the 20th century, a particular model of motherhood (based heavily on the situation of the white, middle-class family) has been projected as universal across the English-speaking industrialized world. This model establishes one woman (the biological mother) as primarily responsible for mothering during her children's formative years, with the children constructed reciprocally as needing her constant care and attention (Glenn, 1994; Hays, 1996; Wearing, 1984). Implied in this model of motherhood are complementary expectations about men as fathers. And although, as noted earlier, there are now a host of media images of the "new father" who is involved in the emotional and practical care of his children, old expectations about men as "good providers" have not disappeared (Bernard, 1981/1995; Hood, 1986; Wilkie, 1993). Ideologies such as these act as "**master discourses**" (Kaplan, 1992), shaping not only what people actually do, but how they make sense of what they do.

The workings of these "master discourses" appear in many studies. For example, Potuchek (1997) found that the young women she surveyed expected to have careers, as did the men. But, although the women saw paid employment as an option to be weighed against later family responsibilities, the men saw it as an obligation. Men, but not women, expected to be family breadwinners. Luxton and Corman (2001) found similar gendered beliefs guiding the thinking of the working-class steelmaking families they interviewed in Hamilton, Ontario. Ranson (1998) found that women in full-time paid employment still judged their own mothering according to the image of the homemaker mother described above. One interviewee was a particularly vivid example. She said:

> I would just like to raise [my child] in the way I guess I was raised and my mom was always home with us kids. And I remember feeling so secure . . .I just think back to the fifties, the sixties, the seventies where the moms were at home, and they were sewing and cooking and, that's the type of thing that I remember and that's what I would like to be even though I'm not like that at all, I don't sew and I don't really love cooking. But that would be my perfect model (Ranson, 1998: 59)

Studies of men who are primary caregivers indicate similar ambivalence. Men's association with paid work is closely tied to understandings of masculinity. So a man who is not a breadwinner frequently feels that his masculinity is being judged and found wanting (Luxton and Corman, 2001; Ranson, 2003).

"Doing Gender"

How can the persistence of these ideologies of gender be explained? In a landmark article published in 1987, U.S. sociologists Candace West and Don Zimmerman gave an account which, along with the work of other gender scholars at the time (e.g., Berk, 1985; Connell, 1987) has significantly influenced subsequent scholarly research and theorizing. The argument West and Zimmerman put forward is that gender is not an attribute that people have, like a nose, but rather is something that people *do*. There are expectations about what is appropriate for women and for men to do, and those expectations are reproduced to the extent that individual women and men conform to them by doing what is expected. When individuals go against prevailing expectations (as, for example, when men become primary caregivers, or when women become company CEOs), they are aware of being held to account by those around them. This accountability helps explain why it sometimes is hard for people to go against the grain and break with gender stereotypes as they manage their work and family lives. But the more people do what conforms to these broad expectations about appropriate gender behaviour, the more entrenched the stereotypes become. There is evidence from many studies to suggest that the transition to parenthood in particular accentuates and entrenches differences between women and men (Fox, 2001; McMahon, 1995; Walzer, 1996). There is also a moral dimension to this gendering process. The accountability that is part of "doing gender" ties to people's beliefs about how they *should* behave, in order to be seen as caring mothers or responsible fathers (Doucet, 2001, 2004 forthcoming).

Expectations about gender operate at many levels, beginning with the individual. For example, a Canadian study exploring how working parents decide who should stay home from work with a sick child found strong parental agreement that if a child were very sick, the mother would stay home. Both mothers and fathers agreed that in such circumstances, the mother either had more resources (for example, expertise or patience), or the sick child would prefer the mother, or the mother would be unable to concentrate on work, and so might as well be home (Blain, 1993: 411).

The same study indicated that more is involved in this kind of decision-making than individual ideologies of gender. Blain found that people's choices were affected by factors such as the availability of childcare, and the degree of autonomy available to them at work. For example, the professionals and academics in her sample had considerable flexibility to adjust work schedules to accommodate the care of a sick child. But other parents were much more constrained. Blain cites the example of Lucille, a part-time cashier with no sick time benefits, and her husband Don, who had personal but not family sick-time benefits. This couple's coping strategy involved Lucille taking unpaid time off work, because her children came first "and they [her employer] know it," or Don phoning in sick in order to stay home to care for a sick child. Blain noted that this couple dreaded the onset of an illness like chickenpox, which would require a child to be out of daycare for more days than Don had available as personal sick leave (Blain, 1993: 417).

Decision-making is heavily influenced by programs, policies, and often unarticulated expectations operating at the level of the workplace, the availability of resources such as childcare in the community, and the wider social context of government policy on issues such as maternity and parental leave. Canadian sociologist Bonnie Fox's (2001) study of the way parenthood "produces" gender makes the point that this process is based on the fact that responsibility for children is gendered and privatized. Beliefs about mothers being best able to care for an infant link to, and may provide a rationale for, the shortage of non-parental childcare resources noted earlier. In the absence of any alternative, mothers perform as expected—thereby entrenching themselves as childcare experts (because they are getting all the practice), and strengthening the likelihood that they will continue to be held ultimately accountable for their children's well-being. Fox makes another important point: Women who take on primary childcare almost inevitably take on more housework too.

CONCLUSION

Seen from one angle, the division of paid work and caring work in Canadian families generally looks uneven and inequitable. In Hochschild's terms, the revolution still appears to be stalled. Women are participating in the labour force at nearly the same rate as men. Most Canadian children live in families in which both parents are in paid employment. Yet workplaces are still not doing much to accommodate the needs of workers with family responsibilities, especially those for whom work is already precarious. And men seem still not to be taking on their full share of the "second shift."

What is clear, though, is that change must be both individual and structural. Families willing to work for an equitable division of paid and unpaid work need external support, in the shape of accommodating workplaces and government policies on issues such as parental leave and the provision of quality childcare. Otherwise, family work comes to be seen as a private responsibility. When this is the case, all too often it becomes a burden assumed by women rather than men.

In Canada, the general assumptions governing family policies are that the policies should help families adapt to the demands of paid work, and that anything provided in the way of public support is just a supplement to what families do. Sociologists Pat and Hugh Armstrong suggest turning things around, and asking how paid work can be adapted to family lives, or thinking about family support as just a supplement to the public provision of services (Armstrong and Armstrong, 2002).

These different assumptions are more likely to inform policy in the Scandinavian welfare states such as Norway and Sweden, which over the years has been specifically geared to bringing about gender equity in the sharing of family responsibilities. These countries also provide some interesting examples of the way state policy can shift public perceptions and shape individual behaviour over time. For example, in Norway, flexible parental leave provisions meant that only a small proportion of fathers—between about one and four percent—voluntarily shared leave time with mothers. The policy was changed in 1993 to include a quota of four weeks which could be used only by fathers. By 1998, nearly 80 percent of eligible Norwegian fathers took parental leave while their partners returned to work. Those who participated in a research study on their experiences said that *having* to take the leave actually gave them permission to do what they wanted to do anyway. It was like "a gift they could not refuse" (Brandth and Kvande, 2001: 260).

Even without the sort of public support available to Norwegian families, there is evidence in Canada and elsewhere that families are becoming more willing to go "against the grain" of conventional expectations and stereotypes in the ways they organize their work and family lives (Dienhart, 1998; Doucet, 2004; Ranson, 2003; Risman and Johnson-Sumerford, 1998). The more commonplace such arrangements become, the more people's expectations about how things *should* be done will change as well.

Suggested Readings

Armstrong, Pat and Hugh Armstrong (2002). "Thinking it through: Women, work and caring in the new millennium." *Canadian Woman Studies* 21/22 (4/1): 44-50. This article is a thoughtful analysis of the linkages between paid and caring work, the relations which govern its performance, and the effects of a globalizing economy on the provision of care and its providers.

Atlantis, (2004). Spring/Summer: 28(2). Special issue on unpaid work

Beaujot, Roderic (2000). *Earning and Caring in Canadian Families*. Peterborough: Broadview Press. This book combines a comprehensive summary of Canadian data on earning and caring activities, with good discussion of the theoretical issues illuminated by the data.

Fox, Bonnie (2001). "The formative years: How parenthood creates gender." *Canadian Review of Sociology and Anthropology* 38(4): 373-390. This article is based on the author's study of a group of heterosexual couples as they made the transition to parenthood. It illustrates the way particular versions of mothering and fathering are negotiated and taken up by partners.

Luxton, Meg and June Corman (2001). *Getting By in Hard Times: Gendered Labour at Home and on the Job*. Toronto: University of Toronto Press. This book is about working-class steelworker families in Hamilton during a period of economic restructuring. It contains rich information based on interviews about how families manage at home and at work during tough economic times.

Nelson, Fiona (2001). "Lesbian families." In *Family Patterns, Gender Relations*." edited by Bonnie J. Fox. Don Mills: Oxford University Press. This chapter explores the ways lesbian couples organize and think about childcare and family work, and the negotiation that replaces gender stereotypes as a basis for dividing family work.

Tougas, Jocelyne (2001). "What we can learn from the Quebec experience." In *Our Children's Future: Child Care Policy in Canada*, edited by Gordon Cleveland and Michael Krashinsky. Toronto: University of Toronto Press. This is a short but interesting discussion of Quebec's childcare strategy, and the factors which contributed to making Quebec's approach so different from other jurisdictions in Canada.

Risman, Barbara and Danette Johnson-Sumerford (1998). "Doing it fairly: A study of post-gender families." *Journal of Marriage and the Family* 60: 23-40. This article describes a U.S. study of couples who divide housework and childcare equally and without regard to gender. It explores how the arrangement came about, and its effects on their relationship.

Web Resources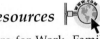

The Centre for Work, Families and Well-Being is at the University of Guelph. It offers a compendium of Canadian statistics on work, family, and well-being, as well as information on recent research projects: **www.worklifecanada.ca**

The Childcare Resource and Research Unit is at the University of Toronto, and includes Canadian and cross-national material on childcare and family leave, as well as other family-related material: **www.childcarecanada.org**

The Vanier Institute of the Family offers a "virtual library" of research information and occasional papers written by Canadian family scholars: **www.vifamily.ca**

CHAPTER SIX

Ethnic Families

Patricia Albanese

INTRODUCTION

My own family immigrated to Canada from Italy when I was five-and-a-half years old. What a life change, even at that age! For the first few months I was devastated, but not for the obvious reasons. I was one of the "chattiest" kids around, but no one, except my immediate family understood a word I said. That changed quickly enough, but even that was not without its problems. By the age of six, I became an interpreter for my monolingual parents.

I remember more than anything wanting to be like other Canadian kids. My embarrassment peaked everyday at lunch time at school, when the other kids pulled out their peanut butter and jelly sandwiches on Wonderbread© and I pulled out my veal and roasted peppers on a crusty Italian bun. Oh, the horror, as I so much wanted to be "mangia-cake." I even stormed home one day and insisted we buy square bread. My mom obliged. My next lunch had mortadella and (extra-stinky) provolone cheese on crusty bread—cut into squares! It felt like she'd never understand my woes. I know I didn't understand hers.

Today, ethnic foods are "in" and my veal and roasted pepper sandwiches are considered gourmet. The reality is that culture is in constant flux. Clearly, culture did not change fast enough for a six-year-old, but it probably appeared (and appears) to change too fast for many immigrant parents who often struggle to transmit ethnic culture to their Canadian or Canadianizing children.

I always felt Italian, but I never seemed "Italian-enough" for second-generation Italo-Canadian kids. What confused me was that I spoke Italian; many of them did not. I had lived in Italy; most of them had not. Nonetheless, I did not live in an Italian neighbourhood in Toronto, nor did I seem to speak or dress or think like they did. Furthermore, my Italian family never seemed like a "typical Italian family" as it was described in family textbooks. But I was Italian and we were an Italian family—so where did we go wrong?

Many family textbooks published in the 1970s (Boissevain, 1975; Leslie, 1976) and 1980s (Staples and Mirande, 1989) wrote about "the Italian Family," "the Mexican Family," "the Chinese family," but I am sure that as I did myself, other "ethnic" students did not always see themselves or their families reflected in the textbook profiles. In reality, ethnic groups in Canada are **heterogeneous**, and this heterogeneity stems from the diversity of experiences that depend upon the period of immigration, the nature of immigration policies during that period, the size of the immigrant group, the region from which families emigrate, the regions and neighbourhoods they immigrate to, the amount of discrimination they experience, the economic opportunities available upon their arrival, and so on.

Despite the heterogeneity that may exist within a group, these shared experiences shape the lives of ethnic families from diverse groups in patterned and predictable ways. This chapter aims to present some of the experiences of ethnic families by outlining immigration policies and patterns and discussing various manifestations of ethnic diversity and convergence throughout the life course, particularly as they are shaped by government policies and broader social currents.

DEFINING ETHNICITY AND RACE

Ethnicity

Driedger (2003) explains that when we use the term **ethnicity** we are dealing with "cultural, organizational (tribe, nation), and ideational (religion) values, attitudes and behaviour of Canadians," and that all of these have to do with "social, socio-psychological, cultural and organizational dimensions of human interaction" (p. 9). Similarly, Isajiw (1999) defined an **ethnic group** as "an involuntary, community-type group of persons who share the same distinct culture or who are descendants of those who have shared a distinct culture and who identify with their ancestors, or their culture or group" (Isajiw, 1979; Isajiw, 1999: 19). Fleras and Elliott (2002), on the other hand, provide a more critical definition. Like Isajiw (1999) and Driedger (2003), Fleras and Elliott (2002) note that ethnicity includes an explicit or implicit system of beliefs, values, loyalties, and practices, but they add that ethnicity is "a principle by which people are defined, differentiated, organized, and rewarded on the basis of commonly shared physical or cultural characteristics" (p. 268). Thus, ethnicity involves a collective awareness of shared commonalities, and a basis for distribution of recognition and rewards.

The 2001 census revealed that the Canadian population included over 90 different ethnic groups that had 15,000 members or more (see www12.statcan.ca/english/census01/products/highlight/ETO/Table1.cfm). It was also found that between 1996 and 2001, there was a 24.6% increase in the number of visible minorities living in Canada (Statistics Canada, 2001). By 2001, 13.4% of people living in Canada were visible minorities, with visible minorities making up 21.6% of British Columbia's population and 19.1% of Ontario's (Statistics Canada, 2001). This said, we cannot write about ethnic or immigrant families without also including in the introduction a definition of the term **race**.

Race

A race is commonly understood as a group of people differentiated on the basis of inherited biological traits. When we look around, racial differences seem obvious enough, but what exactly do we mean by race, and how many races actually exist? Many scientists throughout the past century or so have attempted to classify humankind into racially distinct groups, but all such attempts so far have resulted in complete failure (Montagu, 1974). That is, in order to scientifically classify individuals into racial groupings, scientists must determine what characteristics (such as hair colour and texture; facial structure and shape; position, size, shape of nose, eyes, mouth; musculature; stature; etc.) are associated with whiteness, blackness, "orientalness," etc. After extensive research, it was found that there was as much variation within a category of people as there was between categories. In other words, brown eyes, for example, were found among more than one "race." Also, how "dark" did one have to be to be considered negroid? The categories were clearly not mutually exclusive, and genetic likeness among groups was far greater than differences (Montagu, 1972). Nonetheless, the term race exists, so, how many races actually exist? Scientists identified three (mongoloid, Caucasoid, and negroid), then five, then seven, then nine, then thirty, then over 100 different races, because no matter how many categories were identified, there were still people and peoples who fell outside the existing categories.

Although it appears that race has everything to do with one's skin colour and distinct physical attributes, it is not always the case. For example, until 1941, in the Canadian census, the term race was used to refer to French-origin and English-origin Canadians, two groups that seemingly share physical characteristics. Similarly, there are cases, such as in Italy, where some Italians view southern Italians (from more economically depressed regions of Italy) as black (Ignatiev, 1995). To an unknowing observer, no physical differences separate one group from the other; nonetheless, the distinction was clear in the minds of those who made it. In this case, southern Italians were **racialized**. In other words, the label "black" carries with it more than the significance of colour, it includes a set of meanings attached to (real or imagined) cultural traits.

Although it all seems so complicated and muddled, what actually remains constant and clear in all cases is that those deemed (or self-declared) superior are classified as white(r), while the less powerful, subordinate groups are classified as black(er). As a result, races, as genetically or biologically distinct groups, are generally regarded as having no empirical validity or scientific merit. On the other hand, race is real as a social construct and remains real in its consequences.

Currently, race is defined as an arbitrary and socially constructed classification of people into categories on the basis of real or imagined physical characteristics. These socially constructed differences are manipulated to define and reinforce unequal relations. As a result, race and racialization are real in what they do to and for groups and individuals, particularly in terms of access to power, prestige, and privilege. One need only ask a Chinese migrant to Canada in the 1880s or members of Canada's **First Nations** today.

CANADA—A LAND OF IMMIGRANTS?

It has often been said that Canada is a land of immigrants, since it was claimed that all of Canada's inhabitants, even its Aboriginal peoples (a clearly problematic classification) migrated to Canada at some point in time. As a result of this way of thinking, the study of ethnic groups in Canada has been framed around a discussion of the charter groups (English and French), non-charter European "ethnics," and Canada's Aboriginal peoples (Driedger, 2003). More recently, **visible minorities** have been added to this mélange. This recent addition is a direct result of changes to Canada's immigration policies, which for the first 100 years were *openly* discriminatory in their inclusion of desirable or preferred immigrants and exclusion of undesirable/non-preferred, mostly visible minority immigrants. Before discussing immigration policies, it is imperative that we include a discussion of First Nations families in this country.

Canada's first peoples are not a homogenous group. To begin with, Canada's First Nations include **Status (Registered)** and **Non-status Indians**, **Métis** and **Inuit**, and within these groups there is considerable variation and cultural diversity. For example, today, the majority of Registered Indians in Canada reside in about 900 different communities, spanning some 5,000 kilometres (Armstrong, 2000). They are separated not only by distance but are also differentiated by history, language, and culture; as a result, each community has developed a unique way of life. Nevertheless, despite their many differences, Canada's First Nations have a number of things in common. To begin with, substantial socio-economic disparities continue to exist between First Nations communities and other Canadian communities. On-reserve Registered Indians were more than twice as likely as other Canadians to have less than a grade 9 education, employment rates were 60% lower, and average incomes were half the national average (Armstrong, 2000). Furthermore, First Nations families often share some characteristics that set them apart from other Canadian families. For example, the 1996 census revealed that First Nations families were twice as likely to be lone-parent families (26% compared to 13% among non-Aboriginal Canadians) (Armstrong, 2000). Furthermore, about 60 percent of Aboriginal people who live together are legally married, compared to about 67 percent in the general Canadian population (Frideres and Gadacz, 2001).

First Nations families are larger on average and have higher fertility rates than other Canadians. This was found to be true even among Aboriginal families who lived off reserve (McDonald, 1994). Furthermore, households are more than six times as likely to be overcrowded (31% compared to 5% for other Canadians) (Armstrong, 2000), and infant mortality rates are about twice that of all other Canadians (Bobet, 1994). Aboriginal peoples themselves acknowledge that the family is under severe stress from internal violence. The Royal Commission on Aboriginal Peoples (1996) reported that many First Nations presenters at public hearings argued that the breakdown in traditional Aboriginal families is a key factor in the social problems with which they are grappling. Many argued that the rehabilitation of their families was central to personal and community healing (Report of the Royal Commission on Aboriginal People, 1996). But the question remains, What accounted for the differences? What caused the problems in the first place?

The answer to these questions is found by looking to one of the most ignominious parts of Canada's history and the legacy of colonialism. Five hundred years of European colonization of the Americas has resulted in cultural genocide and the decimation of Aboriginal institutions and social organization. Colonization was an economic process, but also involved the implementation of social policies and regulations aimed at manipulating Aboriginal communities to serve colonial goals. Once many of the initial colonial goals were met (resource extraction, settlement, etc.), the Canadian government implemented the *Indian Act* (1876), which regulated almost every aspect of Aboriginal life, including such things as mate selection. For example, until 1985 (and the passing of *Bill C-31*), if an Indian woman married a non-Indian, she automatically lost her Indian status and was no longer considered to be an Indian, as defined by the *Indian Act*. Nor were her children considered Indian. In contrast, under the same provisions, it was possible for a non-Indian woman who married an Indian man to gain Indian status (Indian and Northern Affairs, 1997, online).

The overall goal of the *Indian Act* was to assimilate Canada's First Nations, as noted by Bettina Bradbury in Chapter 4 of this book. One of the central instruments used to do this throughout most of the 20th century was the residential school system (Menzies, 1999). With the residential school system, children were forcibly removed from their own communities and families to institutions aimed at "civilizing them into European ways," thereby solving the "Indian problem." In effect, what the schools did was "serve as vehicles for marginalizing generations of young men and women from the Canadian mainstream and from home environments" (Barmen, 1996: 273 in Menzies, 1999: 241).

Many Aboriginal families were torn apart by the initial removal of the children and were further adversely affected on their return, when as young adults they were expected to recommence "normal" family life among kin they were taught to be ashamed of. When many of these young adults formed their own families, usually in economically and socially depressed communities, they themselves experienced the removal of their children through cross-cultural foster placement and adoptions. As a result, generations of Aboriginal Canadians had their culture devalued and ridiculed, while at the same time enduring family disruptions propagated by assimilationist government policies. While the Canadian government was occupied (unsuccessfully) assimilating and (successfully) decimating First Nations families, it was busy implementing immigration policies aimed at populating its vast terrain.

IMMIGRATION POLICIES AND FAMILY LIFE

The link between Canadian family demography in general and immigration policies is concrete but not always obvious, especially today. Historically, one of the goals of immigration was to do what Canadian families themselves singlehandedly could not: populate the country. Towards the end of the nineteenth century, Canada's population grew by 460,000 to 640,000 people every 10 years (Li, 2003). Most of this growth was due to **natural increase** (the difference between births and deaths). In other words, Canada's population grew because there were more births than deaths. But, at the time there were also more people leaving Canada (**emigration**) than entering it (**immigration**). In the last decades of the nineteenth century, **net migration** (the difference between emigration and immigration) produced a population loss (McKie, 2000), while natural increase compensated for that loss. In the period between 1901 and 1911, high rates of immigration accounted for 39 percent of the population increase, but again, emigration largely reduced the full impact of this (Li, 2003). Immigration levels were low during the Great Depression and Second World War, but grew substantially in the post-War period. As a result of the baby boom, high levels of immigration, and relatively low levels of emigration, Canada's population grew. Net migration accounted for about 25 per cent of Canada's population growth from 1941 to 1981 (Li, 2003). But, by the mid-1980s, low fertility rates persisted and immigration levels began to rise, resulting in immigration playing a larger role than in the past in contributing to population growth. Li (2003) noted that between 1991 and 1996, net migration accounted for 46.8 percent of the increase in this country's total population and a 71 percent increase in Canada's total labour force (also see Statistics Canada, 2003a).

In sum, from the time of Confederation (1867), Canadian families never have been capable of maintaining population growth. Immigration exceeded the natural population increase in two decades, 1901-1911 and 1911-1921. Today, the total number of immigrants entering Canada has fallen, but immigrants continue to play a significant role in building and maintaining population growth.

The Early Years

When Canada came into existence on July 1, 1867, John A. MacDonald, "the nation-builder" and his Conservative government dreamt of a Canada extending from the Atlantic to the Pacific Ocean (at the time, Canada was made up of Ontario, Quebec, Nova Scotia, and New Brunswick), but there was a long way to go before this would be realized. One of the more important and difficult challenges was to claim and populate the West, before Canada's ambitious southern neighbour, the United States, did so. Closely linked to the government's goal was the need to promote large-scale immigration to the region. As a result, measures were taken to establish a network of emigration agents to advertise Canada to prospective immigrants. From the onset, the goal was to attract farmers, agricultural labourers, and female domestics from Great Britain, the United States, and northern Europe, in that order (Knowles, 1992). At the time, the government had its unofficial list of preferred immigrants and another, even longer list, of those considered "undesirable."

Brochure to recruit families to the West (Canadian Pacific Archives, 1923).

Although the first legislation on immigration, passed in 1869, was silent on admissible classes, this country's leaders were not. For example, it was recorded in the House of Commons that John A. MacDonald declared that "Scotch emigration being as a rule, of the very best class" should be encouraged (Knowles, 1992: 46). In this period of "open-door" immigration, doors were shut to many "undesirables."

White Families Wanted—Settling the Prairies (1896-1914)

When the supply of British and American immigrants fell short of the demand for workers and settlers, Canada began to recruit immigrants from "desirable" parts of Europe. In the Prairies, the need for settler-farmers as opposed to urban "labourers" placed a new emphasis on attracting farming families to Canada. German, Scandinavian, and Dutch migrant families arrived in large numbers, some coming northward from the United States. These were followed by families of Ukranian, Polish, Hungarian, Romanian, and Russian origin. Many of these families moved into western Canada before 1920, but after men acted as scouts or advance agents. Between 1901 and 1911 there was an increase of well over 800,000 in the Canadian population who were of origins other than British or French (Burnet with Palmer, 1988). At first, these families were not without their problems. Except for areas hit by drought, by the 1920s immigrant families that settled the West were well established and relatively prosperous (Burnet with Palmer, 1988).

The Canadian government employed a number of initiatives to recruit and maintain fit, permanent settlers to the West. For example, in order to attract Mennonites, an Anabaptist sect committed to a simple life and pacifism, the Cana-

German immigrant family, circa 1911 (National Archives Canada).

dian government offered them freedom from military service and from swearing the oath of allegiance, the promise of exercising their religious principles, and travel assistance of $30 per adult to "Mennonite families of good character" (Knowles, 1992: 50). This was in sharp contrast to the treatment of (equally necessary) migrant labourers, deemed "undesirable" for permanent settlement.

Chinese and East Indian Bachelor Communities

From the earliest period, the government made every effort to exclude non-whites from entering Canada. When visible minority migrants were needed as sources of cheap labour, the government did all it could to create transitional "bachelor" communities. Families and women were discouraged to migrate so that permanent communities would not be established. The Chinese in Canada are a long established group, despite government efforts to have it otherwise. They first arrived in the late 1850s, with the first Chinese community established at Barberville, British Columbia, during the Fraser gold rush. By the late 1880s, with the need for a large pool of cheap, unskilled labour to build the Canadian Pacific Railway, thousands of young Chinese men were brought in. From the outset, the Canadian government insisted that only single male Chinese labourers be allowed to enter the country—with the provision that they return to their homeland after working on the railroad (as **sojourners**). According to John A. MacDonald, a Chinese migrant was "a sojourner in a strange land...and he has no common interest with us...gives us his labour and is paid for it, and is valuable, the same as a threshing machine or any other agricultural implement which we may borrow from the United States or hire and return to its owner" (Knowles, 1992: 48).

Clearly, the government's aim was to have an abundance of cheap labour to work in dangerous conditions, while creating a spirit of transition in Chinese communities (Ramcharan, 1982). To deter mass migration and especially the entry of Chinese women and labourers' family members, in 1886 the Canadian government levied a head tax of $50 per migrant. The tax was raised to $100 and then $500 by 1903. Many of these "single" men left behind wives and children, with the hope of returning to China after earning money in Canada. Between 1904 and 1923, the $500 head tax, levied on all (and only) Chinese immigrants, served to limit Chinese family life in Canada, since it became difficult for even relatively affluent Chinese small business owners to bring to Canada members of their families (Wickberg, 1981). This limitation changed to outright prohibition in 1923, when the *Chinese Immigration/Exclusionary Act* forbade any new Chinese immigration. The effect was that no more than two dozen Chinese migrated to Canada between 1923 and 1947, when the Act was replaced. In the meantime, laws were passed to ensure that the Chinese communities already in Canada remained "bachelor communities." For instance, in British Columbia, laws were passed forbidding white women from working in Chinese restaurants (Wickberg, 1981).

Given these immigration restrictions, there were relatively few Chinese families in Canada before 1950, and as a result, few Canadian-born Chinese. Furthermore, those who were born in Canada did not acquire the right to vote by virtue of being citizens (Roy, 1981). With all this, by the end of the 1930s, the largely male Chinese population began to decline as elderly Chinese men died, and others, confronted with economic hardship during the Great Depression, returned to China. Different, but equally restrictive policies were imposed upon East Indian immigrants, with similar motivations and results.

Although it is difficult to determine exactly when the first East Indian immigrants arrived in Canada, by 1908 about 5,000 had entered Canada, with more than half arriving in 1907-1908. Most got jobs in the lumber industry, railway construction, or on farms on the west coast. But discrimination began in earnest. Various efforts were made to limit the number of East Indians immigrating to Canada. This included, as with the Chinese, limiting immigration to males only, by imposing an Order-in-Council whereby all immigrants of Asian origin had to be in possession of $200 (this was similar to the head tax on Chinese, which was to be paid upon entry), and were prohibited from landing as immigrants unless they came from the country of their birth by continuous passage. Since there was no direct steamship service between Indian and Canada at the time, the law basically prohibited the entry of East Indians to Canada. Due to these restrictions, only a small East Indian community was allowed to thrive, and it did so as a closed enclave.

For both Chinese and East Indian migrants, the family/kinship network was the most important institution for basic survival in the new country. In both cases, family served as a link to larger community networks. These networks came to act as housing, employment, and social agencies. Nonetheless, for these early, mostly male immigrants, having a normal family life was virtually impossible. Early Canadian law (head tax, financial requirements, etc.) prevented entire families from affording the trip to Canada. Many of these men married before leaving for Canada, but had to leave wives and children and extended families back home. Brides later joined their husbands. For most married Chinese men, it was not until after 1947 that they were finally allowed to reunite with wives (and now adult) children. Few intermarriages occurred, due to discrimination and restrictions placed on contact with "white women."

By 1921, the sex ratios of "desirable" immigrant groups resembled (but were not identical to) sex ratios of British-origin Canadians (122 men for every 100 women for Germans; 126.5 for Dutch; 145.2 for Eastern Europeans; 113.2 for British-origin). Sex ratios of "non-preferred" or undesirable groups such as Italians (204.1), Japanese (250.2), and Chinese (3,297.1 men to 1 woman!) reflected discriminatory immigration policies (Burnet with Palmer, 1988). The Chinese and South Asian populations in Canada were almost wholly male for a very long time. For example, even with the passing of time, the sex ratio imbalance among the Chinese remained immense: 3,297.1 men per woman in 1921, 3,601.6 in 1941, and 211.5 in 1961 (Burnet with Palmer, 1988).

Similarly, due to restrictive immigration policies, West Indian immigration to Canada did not exceed 3,400 between 1905 and 1955, but in this case, more women than men were admitted. From 1955 to 1960, the Department of Citizenship and Immigration allowed in about 300 West Indian domestics a year, again as a source of cheap labour in an occupation that few Canadians wanted. In the period between 1960 and 1965, this number was increased to about 1000 per year and extended to include skilled workers (Ramcharan, 1982). A number of other immigrant groups also obtained access to Canada during the post-War period.

Industrialization/Urbanization and Post-War Immigrant Families

When the 1930s economic depression and World War II were behind us, immigration to Canada increased again. Restrictions on Asian immigration were lifted (1947), and numerous other groups, including South Europeans and political immigrants from Eastern Europe, were allowed to immigrate, this time to address the economic needs of industrialized and rapidly expanding urban centres. In this period, particularly throughout the 1960s, between 80 and 90 percent of Italian, Portugese, and Greek arrivals were family-sponsored immigrants (Isajiw, 1999). Also unique during this period (between 1962 and 1967) was the fact that the government, for the first time, abolished almost all restrictions on immigration based on ethnicity. The new emphasis was on addressing the economic needs of the country. As a result, the government began to establish education, training, and skills as the main criteria for assessing and selecting unsponsored immigrants.

Post-1967—Merit Point System

The immigration regulations of 1967 introduced a new immigration system to Canada. Changes to the *Immigration Act* removed race restrictions for entry to Canada and introduced a new merit point system in Canadian immigration. "Independent" immigrants

TABLE 6.1 Toronto's Immigrants: Top Ten Source Countries (Principal Applicants and Dependants)

Country	2000			2001			2002		
	Num.	%	Rank	Num	%	Rank	Num	%	Rank
India	15,841	14.39	2	17,625	14.09	2	18,290	16.39	1
China, People's Rep. of	18,544	16.85	1	21,476	17.17	1	17,584	15.76	2
Pakistan	10,753	9.77	3	11,581	9.26	3	10,357	9.28	3
Philippines	4,034	3.66	5	6,028	4.82	4	5,260	4.71	4
Iran	3,036	2.76	7	2,977	2.38	8	4,711	4.22	5
Sri Lanka	4,237	3.85	4	4,274	3.42	6	3,711	3.33	6
United Arab Emirates	2,258	2.05	8	3,338	2.67	7	3,178	2.85	7
Korea, Republic of	3,536	3.21	6	4,684	3.74	5	2,976	2.67	8
Ukraine	2,029	1.84	11	2,313	1.85	14	2,254	2.02	9
Jamaica	2,068	1.88	10	2,337	1.87	13	2,054	1.84	10
Russia	2,149	1.95	9	2,430	1.94	12	2,014	1.80	11
Saudi Arabia	1,464	1.33	17	2,603	2.08	9	1,793	1.61	12
Romania	1,911	1.74	13	2,445	1.95	10	1,670	1.50	15
Total for Top Ten Only	**66,456**	**60.37**		**77,031**	**61.58**		**70,375**	**63.07**	
Total Other Countries	**43,613**	**39.63**		**48,083**	**38.42**		**41,205**	**36.93**	
Total	**110,069**	**100**		**125,114**	**100**		**111,580**	**100**	

Source: Citizenship and Immigration Canada (2003). *"Facts and Figures 2002 - Immigration Overview."*
http://www.cic.gc.ca/english/pub/facts2002/toronto/toronto_2.html

were granted entry to Canada based on the number of points accorded for various qualifications they possessed (education, job skills, knowledge of English or French, etc.), and not the colour of their skin or their country of origin. The removal of national origin restrictions resulted in a shift in the number of immigrants arriving from places other than Europe and the US, and, as a result, there was a significant change in the composition of Canada's population (Kallen, 2003), including a rise in the number of visible minority immigrants (see Table 6.1). Between 1967 and 1975, about 115,000 West Indians alone migrated to Canada (Ramcharan, 1982).

In the 1950s and 1960s, most immigrants came from the United States, the UK, and Europe. By 1987 only 30 percent of immigrants were from these areas. The remaining 70 percent were from Africa, the Caribbean, Asia, Latin America, and South America (Boyd, 1990). With these immigrants came other changes. Since the 1970s, a growing proportion of immigrants to Canada were women. From 1945 to the 1960s, about 40 percent of immigrants were women. By the 1970s this rose to 50 percent, and this number is increasing. For example, since 1988, the number of Chinese immigrant women from Hong Kong has exceeded that of their male counterparts (Man, 2003). Data collected by Citizenship and Immigration Canada (www.cic.gc.ca/english/pub/facts2001/1imm-07.html) show that in 1999, 2000, and 2001, the number of female immigrants, principle applicants, and dependents outnumbered the number of male immigrants. There were 93,040 males and 96,873 females in 1999, 112,298 males and 115,009 females in 2000, and 123,512 males and 126,830, in 2001 (Citizenship and Immigration Canada, 2002, online). Overall, the last few decades have seen significant shifts in the number, look, and sound of immigrants to this country. As a result, Canadian family demography also, to a certain extent, has taken on some new and interesting characteristics.

ETHNICITY THROUGH THE LIFE COURSE: FAMILY DEMOGRAPHY OF IMMIGRANTS

Today, in this country, the study of ethnic groups in general, and ethnic families in particular, has taken a new turn. We have moved away from both discourses about "the celebration of our diversity" and those that discuss ethnic families using "deficit models" and related jargon. Gone are the days when we would read about ethnic diversity as a "rich resource," and that "we can take pride in the fact that people have come or are coming here from all parts of the world, bringing with them varied outlooks, knowledge, skills and traditions, to the great benefit of all" (Burnet with Palmer, 1988: vi). Hopefully, also gone are the days when we read or write about "the Italian family," "the Chinese family," etc. to see how they "measure up" to "the Canadian family," using language equated with a deficit research model (what characteristics *they* don't have that *we* have and celebrate). There are comparisons to be made and aspects of ethnic diversity to be celebrated, but family research should and has moved beyond both, to reflect the positive and negative complexity of ethnic families' experiences, particularly as they relate to government policies and broader socio-economic conditions.

Mate Selection and Rates of Ethnic Exogamy

In 1928 Emory Bogardus pioneered a scale to measure personal attitudes towards diverse ethnic groups in the United States. He sought to determine the degree of social distance or discrimination towards various ethnic/racial groups by asking a series of questions including: Would you exclude [the group] from your country? Allow them citizenship? Accept them as neighbours? Allow members of the group to join your clubs? Become close kin by marriage? Here, willingness to (inter)marry members of a particular ethnic group was found to be one the best indicators of ethnic/racial tolerance. In the original research (1927), these questions were asked about four ethnic groups (English, Swedes, Poles, and Koreans). The study found that Americans were most accepting of English, then Swedes, then Poles, and lastly, Koreans (Isajiw, 1999). The study was replicated often over the years, with similar results each time. For example, one Toronto study done in the 1970s found, as did other studies, that racial/racialized groups were rated at the bottom of the scale—with attitudes reflecting the lowest likelihood of intermarriage (Isajiw, 1999). These studies showed that, although many would not object to having immigrants and visible minority immigrants in particular as fellow citizens, they would object to having them as kin by marriage. Attitudes and actual practice are not always the same, but some interesting patterns and trends persist.

There are surprisingly few large-scale studies of ethnic intermarriage or **exogamy** in this country. National studies on exogamy, particularly those using census data, have been difficult to do. One of the reasons is that until about 30 years ago, the Canadian government, when asking residents for ethnic origin in the census, asked only about father's ethnicity. With only a slight variation in 1971, the census asked "to what ethnic or cultural group did you or your ancestors (on the male side) belong on coming to this country?" (Halli, Trovato, and Driedger, 1990). It was only in 1981 that the census dropped "on the male side" when gathering ethnic information.

Madeline Richard (1992) conducted research on intermarriage at two points in Canadian history (1871 and 1971) and found that, overall, patterns of ethnic intermarriage, as reflected by exogamy of Canadian-and foreign-born husbands, revealed greater variation in the twentieth century than in the nineteenth century among the ethnic groups that she studied. She found that in 1971, Canadian-born husbands of Italian, Dutch, Polish, and Scandinavian origin all had a propensity for ethnic intermarriage. From this she surmised that this pattern reflected their long-term residence in Canada (Richard, 1992). But her own more recent findings do not always reflect this. That is, Kalbach (née Richard, 2000) found that Germans ("old" immigration) exhibited the highest rate of exogamy, followed by blacks/Caribbeans (relatively recent arrivals) and Italians ("middle-aged" immigration). Therefore, other factors are at play when we try to understand rates of intermarriage. In most cases, rates of intermarriage do reflect length of time in this country (period of immigration, rate of assimilation, etc.), but also the group's size, residential concentration/dispersion, age and sex distribution, and levels of discrimination faced by the group.

Kalbach's recent research indirectly reveals that discrimination and inequality, at various levels (on the basis of gender and race), indeed are at play when it comes to rates of exogamy. She found that Canadian-born husbands and wives have higher proportions of ethnic exogamy than their foreign-born counterparts, supporting the idea that length of time in Canada is a factor contributing to rates of exogamy (Kalbach, 2000). But she also found that, in general, husbands were more exogamous than wives.

Although she did not conclude so, and the findings may not be clear, inequality and discrimination do seem to play a role here. For example, husbands and wives who were equally likely to be native or foreign-born, nonetheless exhibited differences when it came to rates of exogamy. Perhaps the persistence of traditional gender ideologies and sexism are at play. Lower rates of exogamy among women may be the result of heightened social control of daughters over sons. They may also reflect the idea, like that found in older census collection methods, that men/fathers carry on the ethnic line, thereby granting men more freedom in choosing a mate (i.e., *their* children will carry *his* ethnicity).

She found also that East Indian and Chinese have the lowest rates of ethnic exogamy Kalbach, 2000). Although many East Indians and Chinese are "new arrivals," Chinese and East Indians, as groups, actually have been in this country as long as Germans and other "older" arrivals, yet rates of exogamy among these groups remain low. Clearly, race and/or racism are factors to be considered. Another detail that supports this hypothesis is the fact that, when visible minority immigrants do marry outside their ethnic group, they tend to marry members of other visible minorities. That is, Kalbach (2000) found that Chinese, East Indian, Arab, Latin/Central/South American, and black/Caribbean wives who practiced exogamy chose other visible minorities such as Filipinos, West Asians, or Indo-Pakistanis as marriage partners.

Therefore, although ethnic intermarriage seems to be on the rise (Kalbach, 2000), racial tolerance may not be keeping pace. Perhaps not to the same degree, but, similarly to what Bogardus found in the United States in 1928, many Canadians may accept members of diverse ethnic groups to their country, neighbourhoods, and clubs, but not necessarily to their beds as kin by marriage.

Cohabitation

To date there has been little written about rates of cohabitation among ethnic or foreign-born Canadian residents. The little we do know is not very specific or profound. However, one Statistics Canada report (Cat. No. 91-209-XPE) provides some insight into the topic. A multivariate statistical analysis of first-union formations in 1996 revealed that mother tongue (French, English, or other) and place of birth (Canada or outside Canada) had some effect on whether one decided to legally marry or cohabit. For example, it was found that in Quebec, those who spoke a language other than French were less likely to cohabit than those who spoke French. For the rest of Canada (excluding Quebec), those who spoke a language other than English or French were less likely to cohabit than those who spoke English or French (Dumas and Bélanger, 1997). Similarly, those who where born outside Canada were less likely than those born in Canada to cohabit in a first union. It was found that women born in Canada were almost twice as likely as immigrant women to choose cohabitation as a first union (Dumas and Bélanger, 1997).

One can only speculate, but other than individual and cultural variations in attitudes towards cohabitation, one may also have to consider immigration policies, sponsorship rules, and perceptions about sponsorship in order to understand why such variations exist. That is, although the Canadian government currently recognizes common-law unions in the immigration and sponsorship process (see http://www.cic.gc.ca/english/sponsor/index.html for rules and information on sponsoring relatives), immigrants themselves may believe that the Canadian government and immigration officials do not view their common-law unions as "legitimate" or "legal." Furthermore, the immigration and sponsorship process does require additional documentation to support the existence of the common-law union (the completion of form IMM5409—"Statutory Declaration of Common-Law Union"); therefore, legal marriage may seem to be a simpler alternative for immigrant families, resulting in lower rates of cohabitation among foreign-born residents. Similarly, a "sponsored fiancée" (a person, usually a woman, who has been sponsored to come to Canada as a fiancée) is allowed to come to Canada with the requirement that she legally marry her sponsoring fiancé within ninety days of her arrival (CLEO, 2001). In other words, in this case, common-law union is not a legal option, and this may be contributing to the lower rates.

Work and Economic Life of Immigrant Families

Once in this country, immigrants face the often difficult challenge of finding employment. In the first few decades of the twentieth century, large numbers of immigrant families settled in rapidly expanding urban areas. From the outset, many families found one income insufficient for survival. As a result, many immigrant women began working in grocery stores, bakeries, cleaning other people's houses, or taking jobs in the needle trades or food processing. They often chose jobs that allowed them to take work home, which helped them care for children, prepare meals, and bring home a paycheque (Burnet with Palmer, 1988). Thus, the dual-income family and the double burden on women that comes with it, long predate academic discussions on the topic (Armstrong and Armstrong, 1978; Hochschild, 1989).

Research conducted in the 1980s revealed that these patterns persisted late into the century. For example, foreign-born women have lower unemployment rates than Canadian-born women (Boyd, 1990). On the other hand, because many foreign-born women lacked knowledge of either official language (more so than foreign-born men), many worked in low-paying, ethnically segmented labour markets, or in menial occupations. In 1980, they were more likely than Canadian-born women to work longer hours on a weekly basis, to be employed full-time, and to have lower than average weekly earnings (Boyd, 1990). Another study found that, although immigrant women soon after their arrival join service and other occupations, they only "gradually move into professional, technical and clerical jobs as length of residence in Canada increases" (Basavarajappa and Verma, 1990: 308). This in itself is an interesting finding, because for some women this has resulted in unanticipated negative consequences at home, as I discuss in some   detail below. Overall, unemployment and underemployment are facts of life for many immigrant family members.

The Longitudinal Survey of Immigrants to Canada (LSIC) conducted by Statistics Canada and Citizenship and Immigration Canada (a survey of 12,000 recent arrival immigrants, interviewed six months after their arrival in October 2000), found that within a relatively short period of time, 44 percent of newcomers had found employment (Statistics Canada, 2003). Of those who found jobs, 8 out of 10 worked full-time. The rest

TABLE 6.2 Major Occupation Groups of Immigrants before and after Arriving in Canada, 2001

Occupation groups	Men		Women	
	Before arriving	After arriving	Before arriving	After arriving
	%			
Management occupations	12.7	4.4	8.0	2.6
Occupations in business, finance, and administration	8.1	9.8	25.3	17.9
Natural and applied sciences and related occupations	38.6	18.8	16.8	6.8
Health occupations	3.5	1.8	10.0	4.2
Occupations in social science, education, government service, and religion	7.3	4.8	17.6	6.2
Occupations in art, culture, recreation, and sport	1.8	1.0	3.8	1.8
Sales and service occupations	10.2	24.9	12.1	37.3
Trades, transport, and equipment operators and related occupations	9.9	10.4	0.7	2.7
Occupations unique to primary industry	3.6	1.8	1.3	2.6
Occupations unique to processing, manufacturing, and utilities	4.1	22.3	4.4	17.9
	Number			
Immigrants with occupations before and after arriving in Canada	39,700	43,800	22,300	28,300

Source: Statistics Canada (2002a). *Longitudinal Survey of Immigrants to Canada: Process, Progress and Prospects.* Cat. no. 89-611-XIE. (www.statcan.ca/english/freepub/89-611-XIE/tables/table5.htm)

worked part-time. At the time of the survey, close to 40 percent of newcomers were looking for work.

Of those who were employed, six out of ten did not work in the same occupational fields as they did before coming to Canada (see Table 6.2). Prior to coming to Canada, the most common occupational groups for men were natural and applied sciences (38.6%) and management (12.7%), and for women, business, finance, and administration (25.3%) and social science, education, government services, and religious occupations (17.6%). When they arrived in Canada, both men and women most often were employed in sales and service occupations—their single largest employer (24.9% of men and 37.3% of women) (Statistics Canada, 2003).

For many of the new arrivals, the most critical hurdles faced when trying to find work were lack of experience in Canada and difficulty in transferring their qualifications (Statistics Canada, 2003). As a result of these difficulties, immigrant families are among the fastest-growing groups now living in poverty, and many find themselves among the low-wage poor (those working full-year, full-time, for low wages). A Statistics Canada study by Hou and Picot (2003) revealed that low-income rates among recent immigrants (in Canada five years or less) almost doubled between 1980 and 1995, and that low-income rates rose continually for each successive cohort of immigrants over the 1980 to 2000 period (also see Burke, 1994).

Although poverty is clearly a problem for many immigrant families recently arriving in Canada, one study found that poverty itself did not have serious mental health consequences for the children growing up in these families. Beiser et al. (2002) revealed that, although foreign-born children were twice as likely as other Canadian children to live in poor families, they had lower levels of emotional and behavioural problems than their Canadian-born counterparts. Overall, the mental health effects of poverty among foreign-born children could not be explained by the disadvantages these poor families often suffer. The effect of poverty on the mental health of immigrant children was mediated by other factors, including single-parent status, ineffective parenting, parental depression, and family dysfunction. Another study found that socio-economic hardship in immigrant families necessitates collaboration among family members, and consequently results in more positive (less adverse) intergenerational relations (Kwak, 2003).

Fertility, Family Size, and Parenting

A recent Statistics Canada report on the demographic situation in Canada revealed that fertility rates among foreign-born women start to decline soon after their arrival to Canada (Statistics Canada, 2002). The fertility rate among immigrant women who arrived between 1996 and 2001 was 3.1 children per woman, which was much higher than Canada's total fertility rate of 1.5 children per woman in 2000. In contrast, women who immigrated to Canada some 10 to 15 years earlier had a fertility rate of 1.5, identical to Canada's total fertility rate. This study found that the tendency for fertility rates to converge was especially apparent among women who immigrated before the age of 15, and therefore received at least part of their schooling in Canada. Similarly, from 1996 to 2001, the total fertility rate of second-generation women was low, 1.4 births per woman, considerably lower than their first-generation immigrant mothers (Statistics Canada, 2003a). Thus, it appears that fertility rates of immigrant and second-generation women eventually come to mirror those of other women in Canada.

Between 1976 and 2001, fertility rates for Canadian-born women fell by 10 percent (from 1.64 in 1976-1981 to 1.47 in 1996-2001). Over the same period, rates for immigrant women also fell by 10 percent, from 2.03 children per woman to 1.82. The fastest decline occurred among women from southern Europe, whose rates decreased by 25 percent (from 2.17 to 1.62). On the other hand, the fertility rates of immigrant women from South Asia (2.5 children per woman in 1996-2001), Central-Western Asia and the Middle East (2.2), and Africa (2.4) remained high during the 25-year period under investigation (Statistics Canada, 2003a). Although fertility rates of Asian-born women were declining, they remained higher than those of Canadian-born women. Among Asian-born women fertility rates fell from 2.54 children per woman in the period between 1976-1981 to 1.89 between 1996 and 2001 (Statistics Canada, 2003a). So, although differences remain, some changes are apparent. But what has this meant for immigrant children?

Every culture has images and ideas about how children should be socialized and these are reflected in differences in child-rearing ideologies and practices. It is commonly believed that when immigrants move to a new country they are faced with different, sometimes conflicting, ideas on the matter. Closer analysis reveals that many similarities exist across cultures. Shimoni, Este, and Clark (2003) conducted a pilot (non-representative) study of immigrant fathers of preschool children from diverse ethnic groups (Yugoslav, South American, South Asian, and Hong Kong and mainland Chinese) to determine what internal and external factors shaped fathers' perceptions, values, goals, and hopes concerning fatherhood. They found that without exception, when asked about what values and beliefs guide their fathering, all respondents, regardless of ethnicity, mentioned honesty, integrity, and respect for others. Across all groups, fathers expressed a desire that their children grow up educated, financially secure, and having positive family relations. Overall, most fathers spoke of the opportunities that living in Canada would provide for their children, that they would not otherwise have received in their country of origin.

There were some differences found when it came to the question of the importance of preserving elements of the ethnic culture. Among the Chinese fathers interviewed (Hong Kong or mainland) there was little or no mention of the importance of preserving former traditions. Latin American fathers referred to the importance of their religion, and all South Asian fathers expressed a wish that cultural values be preserved (Shimoni, Este, and Clark, 2003). When asked about engagement in child rearing, the study found that the immigrant fathers were engaged as providers (when they could, since only 12.5% of respondents were employed full-time), guiders, mediators between the two cultures, and with recreational interaction with their children. Therefore, despite cultural differences, numerous similarities in attitudes about parenting/fatherhood were apparent. Where differences are apparent, we might do well to look to broader socio-economic factors for answers, as opposed to culture.

Before the 1990s, the traditional approach to research on immigrant offspring stressed an optimistic scenario, embedded in linear or straight-line theory (Boyd, 2000). According to this "straight-line" approach, with increasing length of time spent by immigrants in the host society, and with each generation, the descendants of immigrants would become more like "Canadian-born" Canadians. Recent models challenge the optimistic view that, with time, any disadvantages associated with immigration status would disappear. Scholars today have identified three possible outcomes for immigrant children: 1) assimilation with economic success; 2) continued emphasis on ethnic identity, resulting in integration into ethnic enclaves; or 3) the assumption of underclass identities and integration into marginal labour markets (Boyd, 2000). Boyd (2000: 144) noted that "although the 'jury is still out' on the fate of immigrant offspring of non-European ethnic origin," the experiences of growing up in Canada and earning a living in adulthood varied according to the ethnic group's experiences. Many non-European immigrant families live within well-developed ethnic economies (Myles and Hou, 2003); however, many ethnic economies have not been large enough to offer much employment for subsequent generations (Boyd, 2000).

Boyd (2000) found that the likelihood of developing an underclass identity also varies according to the group's experiences. That is, she found that "living in households or families with poor economic resources is particularly likely for immigrant offspring whose ethnic origins are Arabic, Black/Caribbean, Latin/Central/South American, Spanish (born in the Americas), Vietnamese and West Asian" (Boyd, 2000: 149). She added that "regardless of birthplace, children in some groups are more likely than those in other groups to be in households characterized by higher density, to be in lone-parent families, and to experience low economic status" (Boyd, 2000: 150).

Boyd (2000) found that although "immigrant children have lower percentages living in lone-parent families than do corresponding Canadian born children" (p. 150), there is a tendency for some immigrant youth to grow up in settings of high density and reduced economic resources. Immigrant youth from Arab, Black/Caribbean, Latin/Central/South America, Vietnam, or West Asian were, to varying degrees, more likely than other youth to experience this. Youth living in these impoverished circumstances also were more likely to leave home and school early and to experience disadvantage in the labour force (Boyd, 2000: 151), which resulted in more of them assimilating into ethnic enclaves or being absorbed into the underclass. What should be made clear here is that it was not culture, but rather economic circumstances that determined a group's or family's economic successes and failures.

On the whole, however, recent results from the first three waves of the National Longitudinal Survey of Children and Youth reveal that, on average, children of immigrants generally do at least as well as the children of Canadian-born parents when it comes to school performance (reading, writing, mathematics skills, and overall aptitude). The children of immigrant parents whose first language was either English or French had especially high outcomes, while children of other immigrants had lower performance in reading, writing, and composition, but comparable performance in math to the performance of other children (Worswich, 2001). With more years in the Canadian educational system, immigrant children's school performance improves, and by the age of 13 it becomes equal to or better than the performance of children of Canadian-born parents (Worswick, 2001). In conclusion, there are circumstances in which immigrant children and youth experience difficulties because of their immigrant status; however, much of this has to do with socio-economic factors associated with the immigration process (such as language issues and parents' employment status).

Stress and Conflict—A Focus on Domestic Violence

Immigration policies in general perpetuate and reproduce discourses of women's dependence, particularly given that, frequently, immigrant men are categorized as independent applicants and women as their dependants (Satzewich, 1993; Creese, Dyck, and McLaren, 1999). This results in and reinforces the view that immigrant men are providers, while immigrant women are unemployed/unemployable dependants. In reality, when immigrants arrive, it is not uncommon for women to find (low-paid, low-status, service sector) employment before or at the same time as their husbands. As a result, Shimoni, Este, and Clark (2003) noted that fathers/husbands who are new arrivals or refugees face multiple stressors, which include underemployment or unemployment, and the role reversal that occurs when mothers obtain work outside the home. Thus, although the immigration process reinforces the discourse of immigrant male independence, and therefore traditional patriarchal ideology, the reality often is very different. The "masculinizing" ideology in the immigration process and subsequent "demasculinizing" reality in the settlement process can result in social isolation and loss of self-respect for some fathers and husbands. This can lead to the creation of an environment conducive to increased risk of domestic violence. Although all women from all types of families are at risk of domestic violence, immigrant women in particular face barriers and dilemmas less often encountered by other women. For example, an immigrant woman in a violence relationship may be less likely than other women to report the abuse. On top of the obvious fears faced by other women, immigrant women may face language barriers, isolation (few friends or family in the country), fear that she or her children will be deported, or that her husband will be deported, if he should have a criminal record. Many women feel especially powerless during the sponsorship period. The fact is that once a woman has obtained permanent resident status she cannot lose that status or be removed from Canada *only* because she leaves an abusive partner, even if the abusive partner is her sponsor. However, sponsored fiancées may lose their status and be deported (CLEO, 2001). Women who do not have permanent resident status (including women whose sponsorship applications are in progress, refugee claimants, and live-in caregivers) and want to leave abusive relationships are indeed vulnerable and do risk deportation (CLEO, 2001). Although much more work needs to be done in this area, there are indications that immigration policies and the settlement experience (connected to male un/underemployment) do place women at increased risk of domestic violence, and the misconceptions and legal reality surrounding sponsorship regulations do seem to contribute to the likelihood that this violence will go unreported.

Immigrant Household Structure

Research dating back to the mid-1980s reveals that a slightly smaller percentage of immigrant children live in households headed by a lone parent, compared to other Canadians. In 1986, about 12 percent of immigrant children were in lone-parent families, compared to about 14 percent of all Canadian children (Burke, 1994). This pattern was found to persist into the 1990s (Beaujot, Gee, Rajulton, and Ravanera, 1995; Boyd, 2000). Although the numbers mask the wide diversity that exists within the category, those whose mother tongue was anything other than English or French were less likely to live in and head lone-parent families (Beaujot, Gee, Rajulton, and Ravanera, 1995). The same study also found that residents between the ages of 27 and 29 with a mother tongue other than English or French also were more likely to be living with their parents and less likely to be living independently, compared to other Canadians in that age group. Men with a mother tongue other than English or French were the least likely to be living alone (Beaujot, Gee, Rajulton, and Ravanera, 1995).

Overall, like other Canadians, most immigrants live in nuclear families. It should be noted, however, that the number of three-generation households, although small (representing less than 3% of all family households in 1996), rose by 39 percent in the decade between 1986 and 1996, from 150,000 to 208,000, a rate of increase more than twice that of all other family types (Che-Alford and Hamm, 2000). In-depth analysis and provincial distribution of these households reveal a strong association between the growth in three-generation households and immigration patterns. It was found that, overall, almost half (46%) of all three-generation households in this country were headed by immigrants. In British Columbia and Ontario, immigrants headed six out of every ten three-generation households (Che-Alford and Hamm, 2000). Che-Alford and Hamm (2000) noted that, among immigrants who arrived between 1986 and 1996, Asians made up 75% of three-generation household heads. Thus, although most immigrants eventually come to live in nuclear families, some immigrants, especially those coming from Asia, do retain or reconstruct three-generation (extended family) households.

Aging and Ethnicity

One often-overlooked group when it comes to understanding family demography and life cycles of ethnic groups in this country is the elderly. Although in 1999 only two men and five women entered Canada in the immigration class known as "retirees," close to five thousand more (1,822 men and 2,666 women) (principle applicants and dependents) arriving that same year were 65 years of age or older (Citizenship and Immigration, 2002, online). Of course, on top of these, there are thousands of immigrants who entered this country over the past decades who are now of retirement age or older.

Although the elderly have been a relatively easy group to overlook, this is certainly not because of any lack of interesting and important issues they face. For example, a study done in the United States found that because of work and other family obligations, members of ethnically and racially diverse families who have not used nursing homes in the past are now doing so (Kolb, 2003). Although this probably is true for any number of elderly Canadians, finding proper paid care for ethnic minority seniors is especially challenging. In addition to cultural variations in attitudes towards nursing home placement, there are numerous obstacles to finding and providing culturally appropriate care. Few of us have to think about the issue at this point in our lives, but imagine what it would be like to be removed from your own home and forced to live with people who *do not* speak the same language as you, eat the same foods, pray to the same god, look like you, or understand your history, your experiences, values, and role expectations? And all this occurs at a point in the senior's life when s/he may be least capable of dealing with this change owing to struggles with physical, emotional, and psychological health. On the other hand, working in a nursing home and trying to meet the very diverse physical, psychological, and *cultural* needs of aging individuals can be equally challenging and difficult.

Today, numerous ethnic groups have created, or supported in various ways, the creation of ethnically and culturally specific retirement residences and nursing homes. In Toronto, there are, among others, facilities for Italian, Chinese, Ukranian, and Jewish Canadians. But, clearly, these communities are somewhat larger, more affluent, and more **institutionally complete** than others, particularly compared to some recent arrivals. What happens to aging members of ethnic groups that are smaller, less affluent, or more widely dispersed across the country, that lack community viability?

In addition, some face economic hardship, particularly if some or most of their working lives were spent in other countries, and those countries do not provide pension benefits to aging émigrés. In Canada, they are eligible to receive Old Age Security payments (the maximum annual benefit in January 2003 was $453.36 per month) and Guaranteed Income Supplement (in the January 2003 the maximum monthly benefit for a single pensioner was $538.80 per month), but are not eligible for the Canada/Quebec Pension (CPP/QPP) if they were not members of Canada's labour force (Guppy, Curtis, and Grabb, 1999). The fewer the years they spent in the Canadian labour force, the lower their CPP contribution, and consequently, the lower their pension.

To be eligible for Old Age Security (OAS), citizens or legal residents of Canada have to have lived in Canada a minimum of ten years after reaching age 18. Furthermore, the amount the person receives is determined by how long s/he has lived in Canada. A person may qualify for maximum benefits (full OAS) if she has lived in Canada, after reaching age 18, for periods that total at least 40 years (Human Resources Development Canada, 2002). As a result, many immigrant seniors do not qualify for full pensions and end up living in poverty. Given the growing number of seniors in the Canadian population, there is clearly a need for more research in this area. Furthermore, having a foreign- and Canadian-born "aging population" means that there will be a need to maintain high rates of immigration to maintain population growth—and so the cycle begins again.

CONCLUSION

Like all families in Canada, ethnic and immigrant families are shaped by government policies and broader social and economic processes around them, and, like all other families, ethnic families are negotiated and reconstituted on a number of levels throughout the life course. At the same time, immigrant and ethnic families are touched by government policies (e.g., affecting Aboriginal families and seniors), immigration procedures (sponsorship and the merit points system) and settlement experiences (un/underemployment), in a number of unique ways.

Cultural variations in attitudes towards such things as cohabitation, family size, parenting practices, violence against women, and aging can be used to explain some of the diversity in ethnic family structure and experiences. On the other hand, there is considerable variation in attitudes and practices *within* any ethnic group. Would it be fair and accurate to conclude that *all* Canadians accept that cohabitation is "okay"? That spanking is an inappropriate method of disciplining children? That birth control or abortion should be used in family planning? It would be equally inaccurate to say that Italian families or Greek families or Chinese families or East Indian families or Jamaican families take certain forms or have specific experiences because of their distinct cultural values and attitudes. This chapter shows that, apart from cultural factors, government policies go a long way in shaping, constraining, and altering ethnic family patterns and experiences throughout the life course.

Suggested Readings

Emberley, Julia (2001). The Bourgeois Family, Aboriginal Women, and Colonial Governance in Canada: A Study in Feminist Historical and Cultural Materialism. *Signs* 27(1): 59-85. Among other things, this article includes interesting material on the disentitlement of Aboriginal women from political decision-making.

Fleras, Augie and Jean Leonard Elliott (2003). *Unequal Relations: An Introduction to Race and Ethnic Dynamics in Canada* (4th edition). Toronto: Prentice Hall. This book provides a critical look at minorities in Canada. It includes chapters entitled "The Politics of Race" and "Gendered Diversity."

Kalbach, Madeline A. and Warren E. Kalbach (eds.) *Perspectives on Ethnicity in Canada*. Toronto: Harcourt Canada. This book contains many interesting articles. Two in particular are especially useful in understanding ethnic family life: M. Boyd's "Ethnicity and Immigrant Offspring" and M. Kalbach's "Ethnicity and the Altar."

Knowles, Valerie (1992). *Strangers at Our Gates: Canadian Immigration and Immigration Policy, 1540-1990*. Toronto: Dundurn Press. This relatively small book contains almost everything you ever wanted to know about Canadian immigration policies.

Li, Peter (2003). *Destination Canada: Immigration Debates and Issues*. Don Mills: Oxford University Press. This book provides a critical analysis of past and contemporary immigration issues.

Lynn, Marion (ed.) (2003). *Voices: Essays on Canadian Families - 2nd Edition*. Toronto: Thomson Nelson. This edited collection contains a whole section on ethnocultural issues, with five chapters focusing on diverse ethnocultural groups in Canada.

Menzies, Robert, Robert Adamoski, and Dorothy E. Chunn (eds.) (2002). *Contesting Canadian Citizenship: Historical Readings*. Peterborough: Broadview Press. This collection includes seventeen chapters combined into sections on theories and definitions of citizenship and nationhood, issues surrounding belonging and exclusion, and the construction of boundaries of citizenship.

Report of the Royal Commission on Aboriginal People (1996). *Gathering Strength, Volume 3*. Ottawa: Canada Communications Group Publishing. Volume 3 is particularly relevant here, since it provides useful information about Aboriginal families. It is especially valuable because it includes the voices of members of Canada's First Nations communities.

Web Resources

Centre of Excellence for Research on Immigration and Settlement (CERIS) has a number of centres across the country, but its resources, including a virtual library are available online at **http://www.ceris.metropolis.net**

Citizenship and Immigration Canada has a number of very useful sources of information on its Web site. In addition to access to past and current "Facts and Figures" on immigration, one can find government policies and regulations on immigration, as well as definitions and explanations of diverse categories of immigrants. This and more can be found at **http://www.cic.gc.ca/english/sponsor/index.html**

Community Legal Education Ontario (CLEO) has a Web site (**http://www.cleo.on.ca**) which provides an abundance of useful legal information.

Indian and Northern Affairs Canada is a goldmine. At **http://www.ainc-inac.gc.ca** one can find the *Indian Act*, past and recent amendments to the Act, as well as recent statistics and reports on income, housing, family structure, etc. of First Nations peoples.

The Statistics Canada Web site at **http://www.statcan.ca** is easy to access and worthwhile to check for any number of topics. It contains summaries of studies, full articles and reports, tables, graphs, etc., and many of these are free of charge.

PART THREE

The Dynamics of Family Life

CHAPTER SEVEN

Partnering, Cohabitation, and Marriage

Sue J. Wilson

INTRODUCTION

Family life in Canada has undergone important changes over the past quarter century. The generation of Canadians now coming of age will marry later, have smaller families, and face a greater likelihood of divorce than their parents' generation did. They are also more likely to become sexually active in adolescence, to cohabit, both before first marriage and following separation or divorce, or to become a single parent. Attitudes and social expectations have changed over time as well. Canadians are now more accepting of non-marital cohabitation, childbirth outside of marriage, and homosexual relationships. There has also been a shift to greater individualism: People generally expect greater personal fulfilment from relationships and feel less strongly about long-term commitment. Despite these changes, most Canadians will have a number of "romantic" relationships and marry at least once, and most Canadian women will have a child.

In the past, family formation followed more or less predictable stages: courtship, followed by marriage, then parenthood. Completing these stages was once synonymous with gaining adult status. Now, partnering behaviour is more varied and much less predictable. Social changes including immigration, the availability of birth control, and changing attitudes, economic changes such as women's labour force participation, and technological changes have altered expectations regarding interpersonal relationships, sexuality, cohabitation, marriage, and parenthood. More Canadians live singly, and the number of non-family households increases with each census. Although family life is increasingly diverse, establishing an intimate partnership is still an important aspect of developing emotional intimacy.

In this chapter we describe ways in which people develop intimate relationships. Partnering is a key stage in individual development and a fundamental process in family formation. In Western countries this typically begins when a couple "falls" in love. Increased sexual intimacy is an important aspect of the development of emotional intimacy, and we will note the evolving nature of sexual intimacy over time. Dating too has changed. Canadians of all ages, including previously married adults, may be interested in partnering, and a variety of dating services have been devised to meet their needs. It is also increasingly common for unmarried couples to live together. For younger Canadians, cohabitation is a prelude or alternative to marriage. For older Canadians, cohabitation is a prelude or alternative to remarriage (Le Bourdais et al., 2000: 15). Regardless of age or sexual preference, people are attracted to others much like themselves in age, class, race, or ethnicity. Sociologists have used **exchange theory** to help explain this process. The chapter concludes with a brief discussion of the role of children in the development of couple intimacy and family formation.

THE DEVELOPMENT OF INTIMATE RELATIONSHIPS

Developmental psychologists such as Erikson (1959) argue that young people reach a stage of readiness for intimate relationships. Indeed, our ongoing capacity for intimacy grows with the developing sense of self. Just as the capacity for intimacy is a key psychological accomplishment, becoming a couple is an important and complex stage in the family life cycle. People who live together, regardless of sexual preference, must negotiate the economic, social, sexual, and child-rearing dimensions of their lives together. The negotiation process is made more complex by the changing roles of women and the increased likelihood that couples come from different cultural backgrounds, that they live some distance from their family of origin, and that they receive less support from the community (McGoldrick, 1999).

Social scientists find love an elusive subject. Is love a biological imperative (found in all societies throughout time) or a social development (accompanying the rise of individualism)? "Definitions of romantic love always seem incomplete and dry versions of a sometimes explosive experience, which might cause the reader to wonder if the author of the definition has ever been in love" (Beall and Sternberg, 1995: 417). Beall and Sternberg argue that love is a social construction, experienced differently over time, and within different cultures and subcultures. Consequently, what is desirable and sexually attractive varies from culture to culture, and subculture to subculture. Like attraction, the relationship between love, sex, and marriage varies over time and from culture to culture. For example, the Victorian ideal of love was closely connected to marriage, but dissociated from sexuality, particularly for women. A century later love and sexuality are perhaps more strongly related than love and marriage. In developing relationships, "it seems reasonable to view love as both 'cause' for relationship development and 'outcome' derived from an intimate relationship. As a 'cause,' feelings of love contribute to our attraction to the partner, our willingness to trust the partner, our commitment to the relationship. ... As an 'outcome,' love is the emotion that emerges from the positive and intimate interactions we have with a partner" (Anderson and Sabatelli, 1995: 126). As Cherlin (2000: 126) points out, "although most people in the developed world marry for love, they don't marry only for love."

Dion and Dion (1993) propose that romantic love is more likely to be an important basis for marriage in societies such as the United States and Canada that are individualistic. In contrast, in collectivistic societies such as Japan, India, or China, family life includes extended family and arranged marriage is more common. In these cultures, kinship networks and economic considerations are more important determinants of marriage than romantic love or intimacy. But, as Dion and Dion (1993: 59) note, the proportion of love marriages has increased in Japan over the last three decades, and might be expected to increase in China, where the one-child policy will have fostered an increased sense of individualism.

Declines in marriage and increased cohabitation, high rates of marital dissolution, small family size, and increases in living singly suggest a shift away from marriage and family as "the core of personal life" (Jamieson, 1998: 136). Although "diversity is the rule" in intimate relationships, three elements appear to be characteristic: i) networks of support, ii) increasing female-centredness, and iii) a succession of partners and patterns throughout the life-cycle (Castells, 2004: 286-7). The increased complexity of family life requires ongoing negotiation of rules and responsibilities.

Giddens (1992) has come to a similar conclusion regarding increased negotiation. He argued that the women's movement and the sexual revolution of the 1960s created the context for a transformation of intimacy, with far-reaching implications. This new kind of intimacy predicts a radical democratization of interpersonal relationships. The democratization of personal life extends to friendships and to relations with parents, children, and other kin (Giddens, 1992: 182). The transformation Giddens describes is based on a shift to more intense intimacy that Giddens called "**pure relationships**." Pure relationships involve greater equality, more intimacy, and more disclosure, but, because they have no other purpose than the satisfaction they bring, they are also more fragile. A pure relationship "refers to a situation where a social relation is entered for its own sake, for what can be derived by each person from a sustained association with another; and which is continued only in so far as it is thought by both parties to deliver enough satisfactions for each individual to stay with it" (Giddens, 1992: 58). The pure relationship is not stable. Either partner can end the relationship when it is no longer fulfilling (ibid: 137). Jamieson (1998) disagrees that the shift to pure relationships is as extensive as Giddens implies. She argues that both greater equality and greater intimacy are more evident in public discourse than in private relationships. For example, women continue to be burdened by the demands of paid and unpaid work, despite the public discourse of equality. (Gillian Ranson discusses this in Chapter 5.) Nor is disclosure necessarily tied to intimacy, as anyone who watches Oprah can attest (Jamieson, 1998: 160).

Sexuality and Intimacy

Until the 1960s, women waited to be asked out on a date. Dating presumed a double standard—or more accurately several double standards. Men were expected to plan and pay for the date. They were also expected to make sexual overtures. Women controlled how far to proceed on the sexual activity continuum. Now women are as likely to do the asking, expect to pay their share of the expenses, and may be as active as men in initiating sexual activity.

Lillian Rubin's book *Erotic Wars* (1990) analyzed the aftermath of the sexual revolution. Rubin found dramatic differences in courtship between people over forty and those under forty at the time of the study. In the older group, both men and women valued virginity in women. Casual sex was uncommon, and the notion of maintaining a good reputation a

---

Exhibit 7.1   How People Meet

Dating was once a more integral part of the courtship process, but is now more casual, and involves recreational as well as screening opportunities for men and women of all ages, literally from adolescence to old age. Dating behaviour has necessarily changed to accommodate an older age of marriage, and shifting patterns of cohabitation and divorce. Although some couples may meet in traditional face-to-face encounters, increasingly there are mediated opportunities to meet. Dating events such as speed dating provide the opportunity to meet (albeit very briefly) dozens of individuals in an evening. Typically, 50 men and 50 women buy tickets to the event, giving each individual the possibility of quickly screening before asking for or giving contact information.

Singles advertisements, computer dating services, and Internet chat rooms are perhaps less efficient than speed dating, but allow individuals to gain more information before meeting. In the case of advertisements (such as those found in newspaper personal columns), the information is minimal. Videos provide far more information and thus more extensive screening, managed by a third party. Internet dating or computer-mediated relationships (CMR) begin with an online discussion, which may become increasingly personal. "Intriguingly, unlike face-to-face relating, the importance of physical attractiveness in CMR, as a relationship determinant, is minimized by the ability to know someone through intense mutual self-disclosure and intimate sharing of private worldviews" (Merkle and Richardson, 2000: 189). Reminiscent of Giddens's (1992) prediction regarding pure relationships, Internet users say they like having the opportunity of building trust and getting to know the other person before meeting (Hardey, 2000).

What is the potential for meeting romantic partners on the Internet? Researchers disagree about the answer to this question. Although Internet conversations typically involve high levels of disclosure, Cornwell and Lundgren (2001) found that people in Internet relationships felt less involved in the relationship and tended to think of these relationships as less serious than relationships based on face-to-face interactions. Others find Internet relationships more intimate than face-to-face relationships. The anonymity of the Internet fosters greater intimacy and closeness and encourages a high level of disclosure (McKenna et al., 2002).

---

strong suppressor. Men were assumed to have far more active sexual needs than women, and so they might be forgiven for having intercourse with "loose" women. "Good girls" did not have premarital sex. Engaged couples might become sexually involved, but only once a commitment was firmly established. The younger group in Rubin's sample were much more likely to have been sexually active in adolescence, to value sexual variety, and to become involved in same-sex relationships.

At the root of changes in attitudes to sexuality documented by Lillian Rubin is the change in young women's sexual expression. Rubin found that these women exhibit few remnants of the double standard of the 1960s. Now, young women including adolescents are as likely to initiate and be involved in sexual activity as are young men. And, as Rubin found out, younger women are more apt to be involved in a wider variety of sexual activity than was typical of their parents' generation. Earlier in the chapter we referred to Giddens's notion of pure relationships. These, he argued, were relationships of sexual and emotional equality (Giddens, 1992: 2). What Giddens called plastic sexuality developed in this context. According to Giddens, plastic sexuality is sexuality freed from reproduction and male dominance. As such it could only develop in the context of women's emancipation and the availability of safe and effective contraception. Plastic sexuality is a fluid and evolving form of sexuality, which extends to both heterosexual and homosexual relationships.

Castells (2004) has proposed that we are now experiencing a sexual revolution unlike the sexual liberation of the 1960s and 1970s. The current revolution is characterized by the "de-linking of marriage, family, heterosexuality and sexual repression (or desire)"—factors that have been linked for the past two centuries (ibid, 2004: 294). Sexuality and desire are increasingly separate from marriage and family, although, as Castells (2004:

Exhibit 7.2   *Traditional Weddings*

Canadian researcher Dawn Currie (1993) found that young couples were anxious to have traditional religious weddings, but not because they were particularly religious. Couples were attracted by the traditional aspects of the marriage ceremony, despite the fact that conventional wedding ceremonies and receptions are filled with customs that are both patriarchal and sexist (See Nett, 1988). For example, fathers "give" brides away, brides wear white, a sign of virginity, and guests throw rice, a symbol of fertility. On the other hand, brides have moved away from promises to love, honour, and obey their partner.

Currie interviewed brides and grooms about their plans for what she referred to as a "modern traditional" wedding. Most had been living together before the wedding, and most brides planned to combine marriage, parenthood, and employment. Couples decided to marry because marriage symbolized to them a stronger commitment than living together. It was also important to make the commitment public, by having a large wedding and including a wide circle of friends and family.

In all cases, wedding plans were extensive and elaborate. Great attention was paid to details, although this was both time-consuming and expensive. Bridal magazines or books, and in some cases bridal consultants rather than mothers, were sources of information and help. Bridal magazines regularly publish extensive checklists describing details to be settled in advance, and those to be done on the wedding day. In all cases, couples were surprised by the expense, so some couples had to deal with the added stress of debt. Typically, women assumed most of the responsibility for planning the event. Currie's research shows that weddings remain an important part of romance for Canadians. Reference: Currie, D. (1993) "Here Comes the Bride; the Making of a 'Modern Traditional' Wedding in Western Culture." *Journal of Comparative Family Studies* 24(3): 403-421.

Couples are attracted to the traditional aspects of the marriage ceremony.

Exhibit 7.3   Honeymoons

In the nineteenth century, honeymoons were not the occasions for intimacy that they have become today. In the 1840s and 1850s, upper-class couples often were accompanied by family and friends on a wedding trip designed to fulfil social obligations. But, beginning in the 1860s, the wedding trip became a private affair, and, by the turn of the century, Niagara Falls had become a popular and affordable destination. Bulcroft and Bulcroft (1997) studied the American honeymoon as depicted in popular magazines from 1880 to 1995. From the turn of the century until the 1930s, the honeymoon was an opportunity to practise domestic roles. By the 1950s, the role of the honeymoon had changed to emphasize sexual adjustment. "Husbands were encouraged to be gentle and considerate. Brides were often cautioned that the honeymoon may not lead to sexual satisfaction, but they should keep on trying to achieve it" (Bulcroft et al.: 480). The emphasis today is on individual emotional satisfaction and achieving the ultimate romantic experience. "As the narratives imply, the risk of emotional disappointment can be alleviated by careful planning" (Bulcroft et al.: 480). The honeymoon has changed in form and function in response to changing patterns of intimacy. Nevertheless, honeymoons remain important aspects of wedding plans, and continue to highlight romance, despite the declining interest in marriage. Reference: Bulcroft, Kris and Richard Bulcroft (1997), "The Social Construction of the North American Honeymoon." *Journal of Family History* 22(4): 462-491.

---

295) argues, the effect is far from liberating. Indeed, he refers to current sexual expression as sexual poverty. Although the age of first intercourse has declined (ibid: 296), sexual frequency has also declined (Christopher and Sprecher, 2000: 1002). Sexual frequency decreases with age and begins to decline in year two of any relationship, but then increases. Cohabiting couples report more frequent sex than married couples, but they claim to be less satisfied with their sexual relationships (ibid). Although frequency of intercourse has decreased, oral sex, auto-eroticism, and masturbation have become more frequent modes of sexual expression (Castells, 2004: 296-8; Giddens, 1992: 11). These trends, coupled with increased cohabitation both before and after marriage, indicate increased sexual autonomy and an increased separation of sexuality and marriage.

THEORIES: SIMILARITIES AND DIFFERENCES BETWEEN PARTNERS

Generally, people seem to be attracted to others much like themselves. Usually couples are of the same race or ethnicity, religion, and social class, and they are about the same age. This phenomenon is referred to as **homogamy**. **Endogamy** describes the tendency to marry within one's group. In some societies there have been strong supports for racial endogamy. Racial intermarriage was strictly illegal in the United States until 1967, when the Supreme Court found a Virginia law forbidding interracial marriage unconstitutional. Interracial marriage between Blacks and whites in the United States remains relatively uncommon. In Canada, 3.1% of all married or cohabiting unions are mixed-race unions, compared to 2% in the United States (Milan and Hamm, 2004). Almost one-half million Canadians live in mixed-race unions. Among these unions, common-law relationships out-number marriages, per-haps because younger Canadians are more apt to live common-law and to live in mixed-race unions (ibid). Table 7.1 shows the numbers of visible minority couples and the proportions of these who marry within and outside their group. Japanese-

TABLE 7.1 Proportion of Mixed-Race Unions

CST	Proportion of mixed couples is highest for Japanese		
Selected visible minority groups	Total couples	Partners within the same visible minority group	Mixed unions
	Number	% of couples	
Japanese	25,100	30	70
Latin American	57,800	55	45
Black	117,800	57	43
Filipino	78,700	67	33
Southeast Asian	45,200	74	26
Arab/West Asian	73,800	76	24
Korean	24,800	82	18
Chinese	265,600	84	16
South Asian	232,000	87	13

Source: Statistics Canada Cat. no. 11-008; Milan, Anne and Brian Hamm, "Mixed Unions." *Canadian Social Trends*, Summer 2004

Canadians are far more apt to marry or live with a non-Japanese person than are individuals of any other ethnic group. Least likely to form mixed unions are Chinese or South Asians. Mixed-union relationships reflect the increased diversity in Canada, where the number of people identifying as visible minority members was over four million in 2001. They also reflect shifting norms of homogamy and endogamy.

People also tend to form intimate partnerships with others who share similar beliefs. If we assume that belief systems are the foundation of action, it may seem obvious that we will get along better with people who have similar beliefs. This may be most evident for people who share the same religion, but may also be the case for people with similar social class backgrounds. Whom and what we value are typically defined by the belief system of our families of orientation. These need not be identical to the belief system of our partner, but if there are large gaps, there will be tensions.

Differences in religion, race, or ethnicity, or large gaps in age or experience are thought to create problems in relationships. However, comparative divorce rates reveal that the difficulties supposed to beset interracial or interreligious marriages are rarely as great as people believe. In fact, differences in age and education may pose a greater problem (Heaton and Pratt, 1990). When religion is important to one or both partners, marriages between people of the same religion tend to be more satisfying than other marriages. Couples of the same denominations who attend church with similar frequency have the most successful, stable marriages. However, spouses need not hold similar beliefs to achieve marital satisfaction. It appears that religious homogamy increases marital satisfaction not because spouses hold identical spiritual beliefs, but because social and familial integration are strengthened through church attendance. In other words, marrying a person of the same religion increases social integration, which, in turn, increases marital satisfaction.

There are limits placed on similarity in mate selection. *Exogamy*, or the requirement that one marry someone outside the group, is embedded in the incest taboo, and in prohibitions against sexual relationships or marriage between members of a kin group. Exogamous prohibitions are usually embedded in law. In Canada, two people must be at least eighteen years old to marry (or have parental permission), and they may not be close relatives.

Exchange Theory

When sociologists speak of romance, they typically use the language of consumers: mate selection, marital choice, and marital satisfaction. The reason for this language is the strong assumption that partnering is an exchange relationship. The language of exchange is in sharp contrast to the literary notion of romantic love, which suggests not that we shop around for a mate, but that we wait for the one perfect mate.

Exchange theory uses a market analogy to explain attraction and commitment. The theory assumes that individuals maximize rewards and minimize costs in intimate relationships. Rewards include acceptance, approval, support, and intimacy, as well as the benefits of being associated with the other person because he/she is attractive, wealthy, or intelligent. Costs might include time and effort, opportunity costs, or annoying habits. According to exchange theory, people are initially attracted to others who are similar in physical attractiveness, wealth, power, or social position. We screen out people who are very different from us in important ways. This explains the patterning of homogamy and endogamy described above. Of course, there will be trade-offs. You might overlook the fact that someone is physically unattractive if he/she is rich, or funny, or have another quality you value. If important characteristics are not balanced, one partner will become dissatisfied and move to end the relationship. The greater one's options, the more likely he or she will be to move on. If other witty, attractive, wealthy, and intelligent people are in short supply, a person will be more likely to forgive a partner's shortcomings.

"For some fifty years, family researchers and experimental psychologists have been listing the attributes individuals desire in a 'romantic relationship' partner and have speculated on how changes in these desires across time and sub-samples have provided a barometer of social trends and demographic developments" (Goodwin, 1990: 501-502). Generally, researchers have looked at both physical and psychological preferences. In a typical study, respondents are asked to rank the things they feel are most important in a partner. For example, British sociologist Robin Goodwin (1990) asked students at the University of Kent to rank characteristics they sought in a mate. Male respondents ranked the following in order of preference: friendship, honesty, personality, attractiveness, and kindness. Female respondents ranked the following traits: friendship, honesty, companionship, love, and personality. The process of balancing attributes is not the same for men and women. Townsend and Levy (1990) interviewed hundreds of American college students, and found that female students tend to consider men who are less physically attractive equally acceptable as a mate, providing they have high social status. On the other hand, male students are less likely to find less attractive women acceptable, despite high social status.

Hatfield and Sprecher (1995) compared marital partner preferences of American, Japanese, and Russian students. Respondents were asked to rate characteristics such as "physically attractive" on a five-point scale of preference. For the sample as a whole, "internal" personality attributes such as "kind and understanding" were rated higher than "external" attributes such as money, ambition, or physical attractiveness. In all cultures, men rated physical attractiveness as more important than women did. Women in all three countries placed greater importance on intelligence, ambition, potential for success, money, status, position, kindness, and understanding, as well as expressiveness and openness. American men and women expected more in terms of marital preferences than did men and women in the more collective cultures of Russia and Japan. Japanese students were the least choosy of the three.

Wording used in singles' advertisements is another measure of characteristics people value in an intimate partner. Generally, men who use singles' advertisements appear to be interested in finding women who are, first and foremost, physically attractive. Women are most interested in financial security. For example, Smith, Waldorf, and Trembath (1990) studied personal ads from a singles' magazine. Interestingly, more than one-third of the men's, but only two percent of the women's ads stated a weight preference. Those men who had a weight preference wanted women who were thin, slim, or petite.

The tendency to trade off one attribute for another helps explain the so-called **mating gradient**—the mating of attractive young women with older, more prosperous men. Of course, as Jesse Bernard (1982) pointed out, if women consistently marry up in terms of education and earning potential, two categories of people will remain single: highly educated women and undereducated men! The most common marriages between people of different occupational levels, educational levels, and other status characteristics are those between men and attractive younger women of lower social status. This means that marriage is a more common means of upward social mobility for women than it is for men.

Typically, in first marriages, grooms are slightly older than brides. However, when people marry later in life, age differences are often greater. Older grooms tend to be quite a bit older than brides. To such a union, the younger woman brings youthful good looks and an ability to bear children; the older man usually brings a higher social position. The opposite match (that is, a bride much older than the groom) is less common. Perhaps that is because older women are less often able to bring a high social position to the relationship. For years, age discrepancy was assumed to be a relationship risk factor. Now this assumption is debated, and the conclusion is more tentative (see Berardo, Appel, and Berardo, 1993). Boyd and Li (2003) analyzed age-discrepant relationships using the 2001 Canadian census. The majority of Canadian heterosexual relationships continue to adhere to the script that men should be older, and most relationships are homogamous with respect to age. Fifty-eight percent of couples have an age range of no more than three years. Large age differences are relatively rare. Men were 10 or more years older than women in 7% of couples, and women were 10 or more years older in only 1% of couples (Boyd and Li, 2003: 30). A higher proportion of age-discrepant relationships are common law, and more of these unions are racially mixed (ibid: 31), suggesting that these couples are unconventional in several ways.

Exchange theory focuses on the long-term prospects of relationships. Of course, there may not be an unlimited supply of perfect potential mates. The marriage market describes the quantity and quality of available mates. The marriage market reflects such things as regional differences in sex ratios, or the size of ethnic or racial communities. The

FIGURE 7.1 Probability for Women of Experiencing a Marriage or a Common-Law Union as a First Union, Canada, 2001

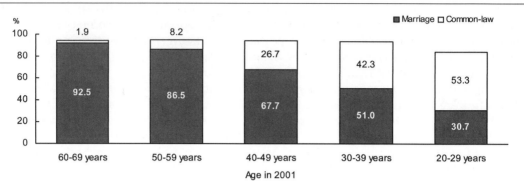

Source: Statistics Canada Cat. no. 89-576-X1E, "Changing Conjugal Life in Canada." July 2002

marriage squeeze describes the effect of an imbalanced sex ratio. In other words, it is what happens when there are too many or too few partners for the number of men and women seeking partnerships. For example, the youngest baby boomers were born in 1960. When baby-boom women were thinking about dating in 1975, there were lots of slightly older teenagers as potential partners. Male baby boomers born at the end of the boom were not so fortunate. They found far fewer younger dating partners among those slightly younger teenagers, because the birth rate had dropped dramatically. Because of these "shortages," if these young men wanted to form intimate relationships, they had to compete with older men for women closer in age, or to compete with younger men for far younger women. These men will face the same issue of shortage throughout their lives.

COHABITATION AND MARRIAGE

Although the majority of Canadians marry, the proportion of married couples in the population is declining. In 2001, 70% of families were married couples and 14% were cohabiting couples. In 1981 the percentages were 83% and 6% respectively (*The Daily*, October 22, 2002). The actual number of marriages declined by about 20,000 between 2002 and 2003. Dramatic increases in cohabitation reflect changing attitudes towards non-marital sexuality, changing views of marriage, and sexual equality. In the past, people who cohabited risked social disapproval. Indeed, unmarried people who lived together were described as living in sin! Now, cohabitation is common, and socially accepted. Cohabitation, or common-law marriage, was first measured nationally in the 1981 Canadian census. The number of cohabiting couples has increased with each census, as attitudes to cohabitation change and the average age of marriage increases. Cohabitation rates are higher in Canada than in the United States or Great Britain, lower than in Scandinavia, and roughly equal to those in France (Wu, 2000: 51). Cohabitation is far more common in Quebec than in any other province. (Rates of cohabitation are highest in the two northern territories, but the populations are relatively small.) In 2001, 30% of couples in Quebec were cohabiting (Statistics Canada, 2002b). This is approximately the same proportion as in Sweden. Furthermore, cohabiting couples in Quebec do not fit the profile of cohabiters in the other provinces, who tend to be young and childless. In Quebec, common-law unions are increasing between older couples and couples with children. Half of all common-law families with children live in Quebec.

Canadians of all ages cohabit, although cohabitation is more common among young (under 30) adults. Only 1 percent of Canadian women aged 60 to 69, compared to 52 percent of 20- to 29-year-olds lived common law as a first union (Le Bourdais et al., 2000: 15). Young people now are also more likely to continue living common law, rather than marry as the previous generation did. Figure 7.1 shows the likelihood of cohabiting by age.

Is cohabitation a prelude to marriage or an alternative to it? The fact that a majority of cohabiters have never been married and half of cohabiters marry their partner suggests that cohabitation is a premarital stage. Nevertheless, researchers have consistently found that cohabiting couples have lower commitment to the institution of marriage. Cohabiters are more likely to express the value of individual freedom within marriage (Thompson and Colella, 1992), and are less committed to the ideal of marital permanence (Axinn and Thornton, 1992). Cohabiters are also less conventional in their ideas about family life (Axinn and Thornton, 1992; Thomson and Colella, 1992) and tend to have less conventional family backgrounds. These patterns may help explain the instability of cohabiting relationships.

For individuals, the reasons for cohabiting are varied. Some may live together to save money by sharing expenses. In other cases, couples cohabit because one or both partners are legally married to someone else. They may be waiting for a divorce to be finalized, or they may not intend to divorce (for religious or other reasons). For many couples, cohabiting may simply be a practical way to maintain an intimate interpersonal relationship without the ties, commitment, and legal responsibilities of marriage.

Marriage

Where marriage is key to family continuity, the choice of mates is too important to be left to the young. In many parts of Africa, Asia, and the Middle East, families arrange marriages for their children. **Arranged marriages** preserve family resources, protect the economic well-being of the couple, and ensure family continuity from generation to generation. "It is a contract to ensure, above all, the maintenance of caste or community boundaries, the safeguarding of land, property and social status. It is an arrangement between parents on behalf of their children." (Ralston, 1997: 50) In a semi-arranged marriage, children have more say in decisions. They may be free to express preferences or to reject a person they consider unsuitable. Potential choices will be limited to people of the same race and ethnic group, the same religion and the same class, but will also consider the importance of love and compatibility. (As we saw earlier in the chapter, even in relationships in which partners choose freely, most people marry someone much like themselves.) In both arranged and semi-arranged marriages, the role of intermediary is key (Ralston, 1997).

Arranged marriages remain common in many countries throughout the world, and among some groups in Canada. In Japan, for example, 25 to 30 percent of all marriages are arranged (Applbaum, 1995). These couples typically meet through a go-between who will later arrange a family meeting if the couple wishes to move toward marriage. Arranged marriage has remained popular for some Japanese young people who might otherwise have difficulty finding desirable marriage partners. In the Canadian West, sparse population made it difficult for young people to meet and court. Nancy Millar's study of marriage customs in Western Canada found a surprisingly high number of arranged marriages between 1860 and 1945 (Millar, 1999). Children of immigrants may also enter into an arranged marriage. As an American-born daughter of Indian immigrants from Calcutta explained in Newsweek (Pal, 1999: 12), agreeing to an arranged marriage is, in part, about preserving cultural heritage and "a link to a homeland that my parents have fought to preserve." But she added, it is also simply easier. "Marrying an Indian means a lot less explaining: Why don't my parents call one another by their first names? Why do they eat with their hands? What is that red dot on my mother's forehead?" But as young people move away from the extended household for education or employment, they also move away from the family's influence.

Are second-generation immigrants as apt to marry in an arranged marriage as their parents? Canadian sociologist Helen Ralston (1997) interviewed middle-aged South Asian immigrant women about their marriages and their expectations regarding the marriages of their children. Ralston spoke to women living in Atlantic Canada, British Columbia, New Zealand, and Australia. Most women in the study had married by arrangement shortly before immigrating. As immigrant wives they were legally, socially, financially, and practically dependent on their husbands (ibid: 53), subordinated by tradition, culture, and economic dependence. Many had experienced violence in their marriages. Half of the women living in Atlantic Canada and one-third living in

FIGURE 7.2 Marriages per 1,000 Population, Canada, 1921–1998

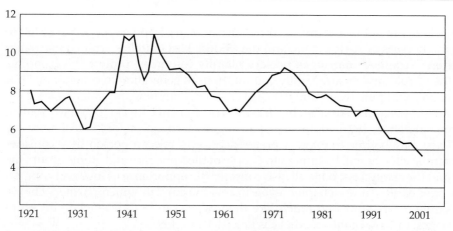

Source: Statistics Canada, *The Daily* "Marriages." November 20, 2003

British Columbia did not prefer that their children marry within the south Asian community. Mothers thought that, although it might be suitable for a son raised in Canada to marry a woman raised in India, the reverse would involve a difficult adjustment because of more egalitarian attitudes to gender relationships in Canada (ibid: 55). Women wanted their children to have greater freedom in selecting a life partner than they had experienced.

In Canada the marriage rate is decreasing and a smaller proportion of Canadians live in couple relationships. The number of marriages is declining, although it is not a steady downward trend (Statistics Canada, CANSIM, table 053-0001). Figure 7.2 shows the extent to which marriage rates have fluctuated since 1921. Rates peaked at the beginning and end of World War II, dropped in the early 1960s, rose again in the 1970s, but have followed a slow, but not necessarily steady, decline since 1971. Now, Canadians typically remain single until their late twenties. The increased age of marriage reflects the need for more formal education to find sustaining work, as well as changing values, including values regarding premarital sexuality. Of course, some people who postpone marriage simply never marry, and marriage is not a universal goal. Some people stay single because that is the way they prefer to live. Others may wish to marry, but are not legally able to.

One reason that people may postpone or avoid marriage is a concern about high rates of marriage failure. "Marriage is the only family relationship that we swear is forever and the only one that we swear is exclusive; yet it is the one relationship that is least likely to be either exclusive or forever" (McGoldrick, 1999: 231). The number of divorces has been decreasing since the late 1980s, and the age of divorce is increasing. The greatest risk of divorce is in the first four years of marriage (*The Daily*, May 4, 2004), a phenomenon referred to as the *starter marriage* (Paul, 2002). Divorce rates in Canada are lower than divorce rates in the United States or Britain, but higher than in Sweden (Ambert, 2002: 6). One of the reasons for the decrease in the divorce rate is the drop in the marriage rate. Because fewer people are getting married, fewer people are at risk of divorce. Another key to declining marriage rates is increased cohabitation.

Canadian General Social Survey data for 2001 show that common-law unions are twice as likely to end in separation as marriages are to end in divorce (Statistics Canada, 2002a). It is also the case that couples who cohabit before marriage have higher divorce rates than couples who marry without cohabiting first (Hall, 1996). This notion seems counterintuitive, since it seems more logical to assume that cohabitation allows people the opportunity to screen poor relationships (Wu, 1999). Two explanations have been offered for the greater instability of marriages that follow cohabitation. One is the **selectivity hypothesis**, which suggests that "people who choose to cohabit before marriage are a select group of individuals who share certain values and characteristics that negatively affect marital stability" (Wu, 1999: 112). Generally, cohabiters have less commitment to marriage, either to a particular marital relationship or to the institution of marriage. "The **experience hypothesis** maintains that the experience of living together itself influences the way people perceive marriage and family life and undermines the notion that marriage is a lifetime commitment." (Wu: 112). Both hypotheses have empirical support.

The decline in marriage rates has lead to much speculation about the failure of marriage and family life. Are people turning away from marriage as an institution? Does a drop in the marriage rate mean a decline in intimacy? The rise in cohabitation suggests that people still want to form intimate relationships. In 1995, over 94 percent of Canadian women aged 30 to 69 had lived in at least one marriage or common-law union (Le Bourdais, 2000: 14). The key difference may be a loss of commitment and stability. If this is the case, what are the implications for child-bearing and child rearing if fewer and fewer Canadians marry?

Children

Child-bearing, like marriage, is changing. Despite an older average age of child-bearing, smaller family size, increases in non-marital child-bearing, and the availability of artificial fertilization, the majority of children are born to married couples, and most married couples have at least one child. Fertility in Canada is now the lowest ever recorded. At 1.49, Canadian rates are lower than the United States, where fertility rates are 2.1 (*The Daily*, December 22, 2003). Over the century, fertility declined during the Great Depression, peaked during the baby boom, and has followed a slow but steady decline since 1961. Each year the fertility rate establishes a new historical low. On the other hand, the proportion of women who remain childless is about the same now as it was in the early years of the twentieth century (Milan, 2000: 7). Rates of childlessness vary over time in response to social and economic changes. For example, fertility declined and childlessness rose during the Depression. The widespread availability of birth control in the late 1960s allowed women a far greater measure of fertility control than they had ever experienced. Since more and more women have their first child at what once was thought of as middle age, it is difficult to know how many childless women in their thirties or even forties will remain childless. The child-bearing period has extended, so that births to women in their forties are no longer unusual. Indeed, there have been cases of births to women over sixty.

Heaton and Jacobson (1999) looked at persistence and change in decisions to remain childless, using American longitudinal survey data. These authors suggest that two contradictory trends appear to affect child-bearing decisions. The first is postponement of child-bearing. Significant numbers of women postpone child-bearing until age, career, or lifestyle reduce the likelihood that they will become parents. The second trend is the strong relationship between parenthood and spousal and family commitment. Despite increases in non-marital child-bearing, the strongest predictor of child-bearing is marriage. In addition, people in this study who expressed doubt about the stability of their marriages were much more likely to remain childless. According to the 1995 General Social Survey, most Canadians aged 20 to 39 want a child. As with the American study, the desire for children is greater for married adults. In Canada, it is also greater for those who attend religious services regularly (Dupuis, 1998).

Although most children are born to married couples, about one-third of Canadian children are born to unmarried women, some of whom may be cohabiting. The majority of unmarried mothers are adults, not adolescents. As the number of adolescent births declines, the number of children available for adoption decreases. An unknown number of parents seek adoption outside Canada.

A gay couple celebrate their commitment ceremony, performed by a United Church minister in their home.

GAY AND LESBIAN PARTNERING

Before 1970 the family lives of gays and lesbians were invisible. When gay liberation activists joined second-wave feminists in protest, they were both stridently anti-family (Stacey, 1996: 106). According to Stacey (1996: 143) "Self-identified queer families serve on the pioneer outpost of the postmodern family condition, confronting most directly its features of improvisation, ambiguity, diversity, contradiction, self-reflection and flux." Because disclosure remains an issue, we do not have a comprehensive understanding of gay and lesbian relationships. The research that has been done inevitably is plagued by methodological problems (Ambert, 2003; Kurdek, 2004). Because disclosure makes large representative samples difficult to obtain, studies typically are based on self-selected samples, biased in favour of young educated respondents, many of whom are active in gay and lesbian communities. Ambert points out that the proportion of gays and lesbians in the population may be smaller than the 10% estimated by Kinsey in the 1950s. The Canadian census estimated that there are 34,200 same-sex couples, of which 3000 are raising children. This means that .5% of households are same-sex couples. Fifty-five percent of same-sex couples were men (*The Daily*, Oct 22, 2002). American data suggest that between 40 and 60 percent of gay men and between 45 and 80 percent of lesbians are currently involved in romantic relationships, and up to 20 percent of these are long-term (Kurdek, 2004: 99).

Do gay and lesbian couples differ from heterosexual couples? Kurdek (1998) identified five dimensions of relationship quality: intimacy, autonomy, equality, constructive problem solving, and barriers to leaving the relationship. Kurdek reasoned that there might be differences in the ways in which same-sex marriages and cohabiting gay or lesbian relationships experienced these dimensions. His research was based on a longitudinal study of American couples who were contacted annually over a five-year period. Kurdek's findings supported the expectation of differences in experience. Partners in lesbian cohabiting relationships reported higher levels of intimacy than were reported by partners in heterosexual relationships, and both gay and lesbian partners reported higher levels of autonomy than heterosexual partners. Lesbians, but not gay couples, reported greater relationship equality, perhaps, Kurdek (1998) reasoned, because they experience inequality in other kinds of relationships. There were no discernible differences in the ways couples solved problems, but same-sex couples experienced fewer barriers to ending a relationship than did heterosexual couples. Kurdek also was able to use his data to measure relationship stability over time. Interestingly, all three types of relationships indicated declining satisfaction over time. Although there were high rates of relationship stability, gay and lesbian couples were more likely to dissolve the relationship. Kurdek suggested that this might reflect differences in social and cultural supports for married couples compared to same-sex couples.

Same-sex civil marriage has been legalized in Denmark, Sweden, and Norway, and in 2003 became legal in Ontario and British Columbia. Although many gays and lesbians reject marriage as a heterosexual, paternalistic institution and do not wish to marry, others value marriage as a way of recognizing their relationship. The federal Modernization of Benefits and Obligations Act, which was passed into legislation in June 2000, extends benefits and obligations to same-sex couples on the same basis as common-law, opposite-sex couples. The federal government, as an employer, provides pension and other benefits to unmarried couples whether they are same-sex or opposite-sex. The federal legislation acknowledges notions of equality enshrined in the Canadian Charter of Rights and Freedoms and follows legislative changes already introduced in several provinces.

In aggregate terms, we know little about the numbers of cohabiting same-sex relationships, or the numbers of gay or lesbian parents. American estimates suggest that the numbers are large. "The numbers of lesbian mothers are estimated to range from one to five million, and gay fathers from one to three million" (Patterson and Redding, 1996). The authors argue that social and legal sanctions against same-sex parents make accurate estimates impossible. Presumably, many gay and lesbian parents work hard to conceal their sexual orientation for fear of legal consequences regarding custody or visitation.

PREDICTING MARITAL HAPPINESS AND STABILITY

It would be useful if we could predict the chances of marital happiness or success, but, of course, relationships are too complex for such predictability. However, we do know that the more similar couples are, the more likely they are to say they are happy. As indicated earlier in the chapter, couples that live together before marriage face a higher likelihood of divorce than couples who do not. A Canadian study (Hall and Zhao, 1995) found that premarital cohabiters were more than twice as likely to divorce as non-cohabiters. It is also the case that couples who report having known each other for a long time prior to marriage and who had a long engagement report that they have happier marriages (Cate and Lloyd, 1988).

John Gottman and his colleagues have written extensively about the relationship factors that lead to marital breakdown. In his view there are two critical periods: the first seven years, and when the oldest child reaches fourteen (Gottman and Levenson, 2000). At both stages divorce is likely if there is a combination of continued marital dissatisfaction, thoughts about separation and divorce, and a wife-demand–husband-withdraw pattern of interaction. Divorce is more likely early in the marriage if these factors are combined with contempt, criticism, defensiveness, and stonewalling. Later divorce is predicted by an absence of positive affect in the early years of marriage, which eventually takes a toll (Gottman and Levenson, 2000). In the end, there are no easy answers to the puzzle of what makes some marriages better than others. Success in marriage, like success in most things, depends on some combination of good fortune and hard work.

Canadian sociologist Anne-Marie Ambert's (2001) book *The Effect of Children on Parents* argues that children have significant positive and negative effects on parents. In reviewing the literature on the ways children impact marital and family relations, Ambert describes ways parents underestimate the impact of newborns. According to one of Ambert's respondents: "I think I had not expected to be so tired. I thought it would be a cinch because I am young but I just wasn't prepared for all that is involved in the care of a baby even though I had read books before. My husband was even less prepared than me so you can imagine that the house is one big mess right now and I am very discouraged" (Ambert, 2001: 55). So, although couples with children are less likely to divorce than childless couples, there is no doubt that children create stress in their parents' relationships.

The decision to have a child is perhaps the most fundamental life transition. Parents do not necessarily anticipate the extent to which the demands of infants and children strain a relationship (Carter, 1999: 249). Ironically, children increase marital stability, but decrease satisfaction. For years, research evidence consistently showed that marital satisfaction declined with the birth of children, and did not begin to rise again until children leave home for school or work (Olsen, McCubbin, et al., 1983). More recent evidence suggests that marital satisfaction declines fairly steadily over the first decade of marriage, and drops more slowly thereafter (Bradbury, Fincham, and Beach, 2000: 964-5). On the other hand, most people feel strongly both that children are important to marriage, and that children are better raised by a married couple.

CONCLUSION

This chapter has examined the foundations of family formation—partnering. We have seen the complex interweave between changing attitudes and changing behaviour, and the ways these are affected by larger societal trends including immigration, economic recession, and war. We have discovered that partnering in Canada at the beginning of the twenty-first century does not necessarily lead to marriage, is not limited to a single partner, is not always heterosexual, may or may not include children, and is not necessarily permanent. Contemporary Western family arrangements are diverse and fluid. Although Giddens (1992) argues that we are experiencing a new kind of intimacy based on greater equity and greater choice, as we saw in Chapter 5, the sexual division of labour remains largely intact, and women who raise children alone are economically vulnerable. Relationships now are less stable and less predictable. Nevertheless, neither marriage nor child-bearing has gone out of fashion. Most Canadians marry eventually, and most women have a child. Romantic love, based on trust, desire, and acceptance, is assumed to be the glue that holds couples and, ultimately, families together. We expect a great deal of intimate relationships—including that they be both exclusive and lasting. In many ways these are unrealistic expectations. The emotional intensity of the initial period of being in love cannot last. Perhaps it is inevitable that disappointment, disillusionment, and divorce are so common in North America.

Generally, partnering is guided by the principle of homogamy. In other words, we typically form intimate partnerships with people much like ourselves. Homogamy applies to social characteristics, beliefs, and personality. But how does homogamy occur? Is it because the places we meet people, such as schools and workplaces, are typically homogeneous? Or, is homogamy the result of preference? Do we typically only meet similar people, or are we typically only attracted to similar people?

Some couples may have long-term relationships without marriage. Regardless of the changes in family life, marriage is still a universal, public, and formal declaration of commitment. Marriage signals the beginning of a new family unit, and as such, is the foundation of social and family life in our society.

Suggested Readings

Milan, Anne (2000). "One Hundred Years of Families," Statistics Canada (Catalogue no. 11-008) Spring: 2-13. This article provides a useful overview of the changing demographic of families.

Paul, Paula (2002). *The Starter Marriage and the Future of Matrimony.* New York: Villard. Starter marriages, according to the author, last less than five years and end childless. This highly readable book is an interesting analysis of first marriages in the United States.

Waite, Linda J. (2000). *The Ties That bind: Perspectives on Marriage and Cohabitation.* A current collection of readings providing up-to-date analysis of partnering from a demographer's point of view.

Wu, Zheng (2000). *Cohabitation: An Alternative Form of Family Living.* Toronto: Oxford. Wu has analyzed trends in cohabitation, using the Canadian census and the General Social Survey to explain the dramatic increase in cohabitation patterns in Canada.

Web Resources

Statistics Canada: **http://www.statcan.ca.** This site is very easy to access and is searchable for any number of topics. It contains summaries of studies, full articles and reports, tables, and graphs, etc., many of which are free of charge.

CHAPTER EIGHT

Childhood and Child Rearing

Glenda Wall

INTRODUCTION

Childhood is clearly related to biology, but it is also a social and historical construct. Social understandings about what children need, what is expected of children, and the place of children in the larger society vary by culture and era. Philippe Ariès underscored this fact with the publication of *Centuries of Childhood* in 1962. Ariès ignited much debate among historians with his claim that the concept of childhood did not exist in medieval Europe. In his words (1962: 128):

> In medieval society the idea of childhood did not exist; this is not to suggest that children were neglected, forsaken or despised. The idea of childhood is not to be confused with affection for children: it corresponds to an awareness of the particular nature of childhood, that particular nature which distinguishes the child from the adult, even the young adult. In medieval society this awareness was lacking. That is why, as soon as the child could live without the constant solicitude of his mother, his nanny or his cradle-rocker, he belonged to adult society.

Through the analysis of paintings and diaries, Ariès presented a picture of a society in which children simply were not conceived of as a distinct group. Rarely, Ariès pointed out, were children represented in paintings of the time, and when they were, they were depicted as miniature adults. Ariès's work has been attacked by historians critical of the limited nature of his sources and of his interpretations. All critics agreed that medieval conceptions of childhood differed substantially from current understandings, but many did not accept the contention that childhood did not exist, and went on to research and detail alternative interpretations (Jenks, 1996: 66; Orme, 2001; Heywood, 2001: 12–15).

What is clear, at the very least, is that childhood *as we currently understand it* did not exist in medieval Europe, nor in other times and places. Conceptions of children as essentially evil, essentially innocent, or as a blank slate to be shaped through socialization and learning have predominated at various times and in various degrees throughout Western history. What is clear also is that the period of dependency that characterizes childhood grew longer in Western society with the emergence of education as an institution geared toward children. As Bettina Bradbury notes in Chapter 4 of this book, children in Canada in the seventeenth and eighteenth centuries were key income earners for their families at a very young age, and thus entered adult worlds much earlier than children do today.

Children's labour continued to be important for many rural and poor families in Canada even into the twentieth century. However, by the late 19th century, the efforts of social reformers, Factory Acts limiting child labour, and legislation requiring that children attend school for longer periods of time combined to extend childhood and prolong children's dependency on parents (Bradbury, Chapter 4). This period of dependency has continued to increase over the twentieth century. It wasn't until after the Second World War that we saw the emergence of the adolescent or teenager in the Western world (Jenks, 1996: 63). A new, distinct period of extended quasi-childhood and thus longer dependency on adults resulted.

Along with the focus on social reform and education, new importance began to be placed on the family environment within which children grew. The proliferation of child-rearing advice literature which began to be disseminated to Canadian mothers during the course of the 20th century attests to this growing concern about the family environment. It also provides a good vehicle for studying changing social views of childhood and children's needs. This material does not tell us how individual parents and children actually behaved, but it does provide valuable information about how children's needs were socially understood, and the concomitant social expectations that families faced.

This chapter will examine the cultural conceptions of childhood evident in twentieth century child-rearing advice in Canada. It will also examine the social and scientific context within which this advice emerged, with a view to better understanding the roots of current taken-for-granted understandings of children and what they need. Primary socialization of children takes place within families, and thus cultural understandings of childhood have a profound effect on how family life is experienced for both parents and children. The implications that social constructions of childhood have for the experience of families, therefore, will also be explored. It must be noted that mothers have been the main target and recipient of child-rearing advice and this continues, although to a lesser degree, to this day. Mothers have also been the ones who have taken on the majority of the responsibility for children's care in the family. Therefore, much of the following exploration of child-rearing advice and practices and their implications focuses more heavily on mothers than on fathers. The final section of the chapter will examine how current conceptions of childhood in Canada interact with structural realities and social policy, and what this means for the future of childhood and the treatment of children in our society.

CHILD-REARING ADVICE THROUGHOUT THE 20TH CENTURY

Advice in the Early 20th Century

The emergence of expert child-rearing advice was linked to the growing authority of medical science in the late nineteenth and early twentieth centuries. Indeed, early child-rearing advice in Canada centred around medical concerns over high rates of infant mortality in the early part of the twentieth century. In this era before refrigeration, inoculation for many contagious diseases, and safe sewage and water systems, losing at least one baby before the age of one was a common experience for many families. Arnup (1994: 15) reports that infant mortality rates were as high as one in three babies in Montreal during the first decade of the 20th century. Arnup (1994) and Comacchio (1993) detail the subsequent war that was waged on infant mortality—a war that included government funding for certified milk depots, well-baby clinics, and a major educational campaign aimed at mothers. However, as both Comacchio (1993: 145) and Arnup (1994: 149–52) point out, this war did not include a battle against poverty or unsafe living conditions. Instead, mothers' behaviour and lack of knowledge was targeted, and a great deal of advice literature resulted.

Parenting advice at this time, then, focused heavily on ways to keep children free of germs. This included emphasizing the importance of breast-feeding, cleanliness, and proper food preparation. Mothers, however, were encouraged to rely on science not just for ways to keep their children physically healthy, but also for proper ways to discipline and socialize their children. Child-rearing experts, who came largely from the ranks medicine and psychology, promoted "scientific management" of children. This involved rigid scheduling, early toilet training, and the encouragement of solitary play. Keeping a baby on a strict four-hour feeding schedule, not picking a baby up when it cried, and beginning toilet training shortly after birth were all meant to encourage self-discipline and to avoid the establishment of bad habits in children. As is stated in the 1940 edition of *The Canadian Mother and Child* (Couture, 1940: 166): "The first principle to bear in mind in training children in good habits is regularity. This applies, as you already know, to the matter of sleep, feeding, cleanliness, and also to correct toilet habits."

What view of children is portrayed in this approach? The early influences of behaviourism certainly can be seen in the assumption that children could and should be properly trained and managed. What is interesting here is that, although children's physical and moral health was rhetorically linked in educational campaigns to the health and strength of the nation, children's emotional and psychological well-being—their happiness and personal fulfilment—was not an object of expert concern. Furthermore, as Weiss (1978) has suggested, the needs of mothers and children often overlapped in the early advice literature. Early toilet training meant fewer diapers for a busy mother to sew and wash by hand. Strict sleeping and eating schedules and the encouragement of solitary play were useful to women overburdened with work. Indeed, as Weiss (1978) notes, the point was commonly made in the literature that a child, once properly trained, was much easier for a mother to care for. This is all very different from the **child-centred advice** that characterized the post-World War II literature.

Child-Rearing Advice in the Latter Half of the 20th Century

A distinct shift in child-rearing advice began following World War II. Canadian society in general experienced dramatic cultural and structural change at this time. The return of men from overseas and the post-War economic boom allowed many families a degree of economic comfort they had not experienced before. As Coontz (1992) points out, after two world wars and a depression in the first half of the century, the cultural desire for prosperity and stability was strong. In Canada, marriage rates rose, the average age of first marriage and first birth decreased, and family size increased after World War II (Vanier Institute, 1994). The "traditional family" with male bread-winner and female homemaker became, for the first time, more than just a cultural ideal for many middle-class families.

And mothers, who had been increasingly encouraged in the first part of the century by medical science to view motherhood as a full-time occupation (Arnup, 1994), now had a greater ability to do this. The production and promotion of labour-saving devices also increased the cultural expectation that mothers had more time than ever before to spend on their children.[1]

There are other changes of note as well. Child-rearing advice at this time began to focus less on children's physical health, since refrigeration, medical advances, vaccinations for infectious diseases, and clean water supplies meant infant mortality rates were no longer the concern they once were. At the same time, new research in developmental psychology, discussed in more detail below, focused attention on the mother-child relationship and its role in children's psychological health.

It was in this context that Dr. Spock's ground-breaking advice book *Baby and Child Care* first appeared in 1946. Spock's approach fit within, and helped to define, a more child-centred and "permissive" approach to parenting. Spock's opening words to parents were: "Trust yourself. You know more than you think you do." Mothers were encouraged to relax, enjoy their babies, and trust their common sense, rather than worrying about the strict rules of scientific management. The child, in Spock's conception, was both more innocent and more psychologically vulnerable than the child of past expert advice. Weiss (1978: 40) also notes that in the post-World War II period children were depicted much more passively in terms of their ability to influence their own lives. They were rarely, at this time, described in such judgmental terms as "fussy" or "spoiled." Spock's work reflects this point of view. As well, psychologists were now describing many of the practices of scientific parenting as psychologically damaging to children. Now, too much attention to early toilet training, for instance, could result in lasting maladjustment for the child.

Several feminist historians and social scientists have examined the implications of this shift in advice, not only for children, but also for mothers (Ehrenreich and English, 1978; Weiss, 1978; Richardson, 1993; Hays, 1996). As Weiss (1978: 39–41) notes, the needs of the mother and the child no longer overlapped in the new literature. The child's needs now took the forefront, and good mothering involved anticipating and adapting to children's requirements. She also notes that the directive in the new literature to "enjoy your baby" and the implication that motherhood should be fun and fulfilling had its downside as well. The realistic difficulties of parenting tended to be glossed over in the focus on fun and fulfilment and, by implication, any lack of maternal gratification became abnormal. Finally, as children increasingly were cast as more morally neutral and psychologically vulnerable, mothers became more blameworthy when something went wrong. There were no longer bad children, only bad mothers.

THE ROLE OF DEVELOPMENTAL PSYCHOLOGY

Maternal Deprivation

Twentieth century research in developmental psychology had an enormous impact on child-rearing advice and on conceptions of childhood in popular culture as well. Many of the things that we take for granted today about children's needs stem from this research and the ways in which professionals and institutions responded to it. Particularly influential was the post-War work of John Bowlby on **maternal deprivation** and attachment (Bowlby, 1953, 1958, 1969). At the time of Bowlby's research, ethology, the study of animal instinct and behaviour and its implications for human behaviour, was enjoying a great deal of popularity. It was also a time when institutions for children in Europe and America were filled with children orphaned, injured, or separated from their parents during the war. Bowlby analyzed reports of such children, many of whom were institutionalized infants severely deprived of human contact and stimulus. Some of the infants studied, for example, had between 15 and 50 different caretakers, and were left on their own for most of the time "in cubicles enclosed on three sides so that they were rarely able to see what was going on" (Eyer, 1992: 67). Despite the fact that the infants were deprived of far more than just a mother, Bowlby identified maternal deprivation as the key factor in explaining the compromised development of these children (Eyer, 1992: 48–50). As Eyer (1992: 50) details, Bowlby went on to suggest that for normal child development to occur, young children needed a loving mother, "as an ever present companion." The absence of a mother during the early years, even if temporary, was said to have profound effects for later child development and adult personality. Having a mother who worked full-time, Bowlby suggested, was similar in its effect on child development to the death of the mother (Eyer, 1992: 50).

Attachment

Bowlby began to more fully develop his theory of attachment in the mid-1950s. He based this work not only on his own ideas about maternal deprivation, but also on animal studies such as those conducted by Harlow (1958) on socially isolated and abused infant monkeys, and by Konrad Lorenz (1952) on imprinting behaviour in newborn birds (Eyer, 1992; Hrdy, 1999: 396–401). Bowlby proposed that, like others in the animal kingdom, human infants instinctually sought a strong social bond to their mothers in order to ensure their survival. A strong attachment was necessary, he suggested, for a child's subsequent emotional, psychological, and cognitive development, and the strength of this bond was dependent on the continual presence of a warm, loving, and responsive mother.

A contemporary of Bowlby's, Mary Ainsworth, drew on Bowlby's ideas in her study of infants to develop what she called the strange situation test. It was this test that allowed a child's attachment to the mother to actually be measured, and it thus lent **attachment theory** much more scientific credibility (Hrdy, 1999: 401). The Strange Situation Test involved a mother accompanying a young child to a room with toys and a stranger. The mother left after a short while and later returned. The stranger offered comfort if the child seemed upset while the mother was gone. If the child played independently while the mother was present, protested the mother's leaving, and was comforted by her return, the child was said to be securely attached. Infants who behaved otherwise were classified as insecurely attached. Ainsworth, based on her observations of mother-infant pairs in the home, concluded that sensitive and responsive mothers were associated with infants who developed secure attachments, while insecurely attached infants had mothers that were more negative and less responsive (Eyer, 1992: 66). The Strange

Situation Test thus made it possible to measure not only attachment, but also, by implication, the quality of mothering a child received. The test, and its accompanying inferences about quality of mothering, went on to be used in hundreds of studies around the world (Eyer, 1992: 66; Hrdy, 1999: 404) .

Both the validity and reliability of the Strange Situation Test have been challenged, as has attachment theory in general (Eyer, 1992: 67–68; Belsky and Cassidy, 1994). Critics have pointed out that there may be many reasons for a child's behaviour in the strange situation test which include different inborn temperaments, different cultural child-rearing practices, or simply healthy autonomy from parents. Furthermore, researchers have pointed out that children form attachments to inanimate objects, and that seemingly secure attachments can form in abused infants as well. Attachment theory is derived from animal studies and studies of severe deprivation. Linking animal and human behaviour is highly problematic, as is the assumption that, since severe deprivation has severe consequences, then any separation from a primary caregiver will have major consequences (Bruner, 2000). And, as many researchers have pointed out, the children and monkey infants that Bowlby based his conclusions on were deprived of virtually all social contact, not just that of a mother. Subsequent studies also showed that children in daycare did not display attachment problems, and that early attachment measures did not necessarily predict a child's later behaviour, especially if child-rearing conditions changed in the interim (Eyer, 1992: 69; Bruer, 1999: 57–58).

Adherents to attachment theory, however, appear to far outnumber the sceptics. The Strange Situation Test became the foundation for hundreds of studies, and many of the assumptions associated with attachment theory continue to be taken for granted in child-rearing advice literature and government policy today. To be fair, attachment theory has changed over the years. Although mothers continue to be the main attachment figure in most studies, fathers and other caregivers are now more commonly included, and continuous and uninterrupted contact between mother and infant rarely is still seen as necessary for secure attachment to form. The ideas of Bowlby and those surrounding him, however, profoundly affected the direction taken by those dispensing child-rearing advice in the mid-twentieth century, and continue to shape and reflect ideas of proper mothering and children's needs today.

CHILDREN'S NEEDS AND CHILD REARING TODAY

Intensive Parenting

The post-World War II trend in child-rearing advice that placed mothers' needs second to children's psychological and cognitive needs intensified as the century progressed, according to many authors, Sharon Hays (1996) coined the term "**intensive mothering**" to describe social expectations that surround mothering today. The "good mother" of present, according to Hays, is constantly attentive to the development of her child's self-worth, psychological health, and intelligence. She argues that such attentiveness requires more time, emotional labour, and financial resources than ever before, and this at a time when women

---

Exhibit 8.1   *Lullaby Lessons*

Sally Jaeger sits on a floor in the basement of a downtown Toronto church. On her feet, which stick out from under her flowing, peasant skirt, are red and black striped socks. She wears two large necklaces—one of wooden farm animals, the other of plastic vegetables. Her earrings are a fork and a knife.

"Do you know why there is no spoon?" she asks. The wandering toddlers and distracted parents in front of her barely register the question. "Because the dish ran away with the spoon," she says with a big grin.

So begins today's class on *Mother Goose*. Eight times a week, for 45 minutes a session, Jaeger repeats rhymes, songs, and little stories so that parents can learn to play with their children. Indeed, they're lining up for the chance to take the classes.

It seems that after establishing their careers and carefully planning for pregnancy, today's super-prepared parents head home and find themselves at a bit of a loss. The lullabies and nursery rhymes that their parents used to soothe and distract them with have long been forgotten. Any babysitting experience is too far in the past, and grandparents aren't around.

So, along with the infant swimming lessons and toddler gymnastic classes, parents are signing up for nursery-rhyme courses. With wriggly babies in tow, moms and dads are learning songs about fleas and farm animals.

"The thought of paying to learn nursery rhymes is bizarre," said Katherine Grier, a nursery-rhyme instructor in St. John's, Nfld., but "families are spread out all over the place."

One film producer and mother of two said she originally took the class because it was the "good mummy" thing to do to introduce culture to her child as soon as possible. But she kept going because it allowed her to get beyond endless repetitions of *Old Mac-Donald* and *Pat-a-Cake*. "I found the silences can easily creep into your day and you're tired and they get longer and longer," she said. With her daughter Laura, and now her son Arthur, she sings about such mundane tasks as chopping vegetables to keep the children involved and entertained.

"People know it is important to talk to your baby and sing with your baby and read books with your baby," said one parent, a family literacy instructor at a local college, "but day after day, I found with my own child, it's difficult to find that muse, to find something to do."

Excerpted from "Lullaby Lessons" by Ijeoma Ross, *Globe and Mail* August 9, 2000: R1.

---

are experiencing unprecedented workplace demands. Why is it, she asks, that

> many professional-class women seem to find it necessary to take the kids to swimming and judo and dancing and tumbling classes, not to mention orthodontists and psychiatrists and attention-deficit specialists? Why is the human bonding that accompanies breast-feeding considered so important that elaborate contraptions are now manufactured to allow children to suckle on mothers who cannot produce milk? Why are there aerobics courses for babies, training sessions in infant massage, sibling-preparedness workshops, and designer fashions for two-year-olds? Why must a 'good' mother be careful to 'negotiate' with her child, refraining from demands for obedience to an absolute set of rules? .... Why does she find it necessary to apologize to the child if she somehow deviates from the code of appropriate mothering?

Hays suggests then, that parents, and mothers in particular, are being held more responsible than ever for their children's emotional health and cognitive development,

Mother Goose expert Sally Jaeger (foreground) leads moms, dads, and their children through a fun-filled class on lullabies and nursery rhymes. Her lessons help parents connect with their little ones.

and that the duties involved in meeting these responsibilities are expanding and intensifying. Arguably, parents are also being held more responsible than ever for their children's physical safety. Amidst increasing social fear of crime, children no longer spend the unsupervised time outdoors that they once did. An increasing number of parents now walk or drive their children to school rather than let them walk unattended (D'Amato, 2004). Parents are expected to educate themselves about the proper use of child safety seats in cars, and police conduct spot checks to ensure children are buckled in correctly. In an unprecedented case in Edmonton in 1999, parents were charged with criminal negligence causing death when their five-year-old son was accidentally hit by a cable installation van while riding his bike on the street (Mitchell, 1999). The parents, police alleged, let their son ride his bike without proper supervision. Legal experts commenting on the case stated that "even a few years ago charges in such a case would never have been considered" (Mitchell, 1999: A8).

The shifts in social understandings of children's needs that are reflected in Hays's questions above are connected to many of the recent changes in family form and functioning that are outlined in the first chapter of this book. The dual-earner family is now the norm even among families with very young children.

TABLE 8.1 Percentage Employment of Mothers, by Family Status and Age of Youngest Child, 1976–2003

	Female lone parents				Women with partners			
	Youngest child under age 3	Youngest child aged 3-5	Youngest child aged 6-15	Total with children under age 16	Youngest child under age 3	Youngest child aged 3-5	Youngest child aged 6-15	Total with children under age 16
				%				
1976	27.9	45.0	53.9	48.3	27.7	36.2	45.7	38.4
1977	31.2	46.9	54.9	49.8	29.3	37.0	46.4	39.4
1978	30.6	42.8	55.2	49.1	32.2	40.4	48.5	42.1
1979	34.6	45.8	55.6	50.6	34.8	42.8	50.3	44.1
1980	36.3	50.6	59.1	53.8	37.1	44.7	52.7	46.4
1981	32.3	51.4	61.3	54.4	40.0	46.2	55.4	48.9
1982	31.7	48.2	57.2	51.1	40.1	46.4	55.1	48.7
1983	30.8	44.2	55.1	48.8	43.1	48.5	55.1	50.0
1984	30.2	44.8	57.6	50.5	45.3	49.7	56.9	51.9
1985	34.1	46.8	58.0	51.4	47.9	52.8	59.1	54.3
1986	29.6	46.7	60.0	51.7	51.2	55.5	62.1	57.4
1987	33.3	50.6	60.1	52.9	52.0	57.2	64.4	59.1
1988	33.1	50.7	63.1	54.5	53.9	59.6	67.2	61.5
1989	30.0	50.7	65.7	55.4	55.2	60.7	69.7	63.4
1990	31.5	49.8	65.2	55.1	55.8	61.4	71.0	64.3
1991	31.5	47.9	61.9	52.2	57.2	62.4	70.3	64.6
1992	27.9	43.5	61.3	50.0	57.5	62.4	69.4	64.3
1993	25.7	44.6	59.2	48.4	58.7	62.6	70.5	65.2
1994	27.7	47.1	60.2	50.1	59.8	61.9	70.3	65.4
1995	29.1	41.9	61.1	50.2	59.8	64.4	71.7	66.6
1996	33.1	46.4	62.6	53.3	61.2	63.4	71.4	66.8
1997	35.5	50.0	64.1	55.2	62.1	65.1	72.8	68.2
1998	33.1	51.9	66.6	56.8	63.2	66.6	73.4	69.2
1999	37.6	55.3	69.4	60.9	63.1	68.4	74.4	70.0
2000	42.3	55.6	71.6	63.0	62.9	70.0	75.1	70.6
2001	46.0	60.8	73.7	66.6	63.6	68.5	75.7	71.0
2002	46.7	59.5	74.2	66.9	64.1	69.9	77.5	72.3
2003	46.9	60.7	74.8	67.9	64.9	70.2	76.9	72.3

Other changes are also related to the move of mothers into the paid workplace. There is, for one thing, a growing cultural expectation that fathers will be more involved with their children than they have been in the past. Although the actual behaviour of fathers is changing more slowly, there are indications that fathers are indeed spending more time than before, not only playing with, but also caring for their children (Silver, 2000). Although fathers are beginning to play a greater role in childcare, however, both fathers and mothers are now facing increasing levels of stress related to balancing work and family demands (Duxbury and Higgins, 2001). On the other hand, families are having fewer children, and having them later in life, which opens up the possibility of expending more parental time, energy, and money on individual children. Intensive parenting becomes more feasible when family sizes are smaller. Social expectations of intensive parenting, however, can also contribute to declining birthrates. Combined with increasing workplace demands, they may be a contributing factor to the decision taken by a growing number of women and couples to remain childless or to have fewer children.

Other theorists have noted a connection between current child-rearing advice and the increasing emphasis on individual responsibility that characterizes neo-liberalism (Wall, 2001: 603, 2004a; Nadesan, 2002). As social programs increasingly are presented in political rhetoric as unaffordable, there is growing pressure for individuals to manage both their own future success and the risks that they pose to society. Accompanying this shift in political rationality is a great deal of talk about the importance of adaptability in our rapidly changing, technological, and global economy. In this uncertain and individualistic climate, aspiring middle-class parents, some researchers argue, face increasing pressure to take all possible steps to "maximize" and perfect their children, to give them the cultural and intellectual capital to "exceed the norm" and gain a competitive edge (Beck-Gernsheim, 1996; Blum, 1999: 3; Nadesan, 2002, 411–14, 417).

This pressure is reflected in the dramatically increasing sales of educational toys throughout the 1990s (Nadesan, 2002: 412). It is also reflected in the growing popularity of preschools and private schools among the middle class, and the proliferation of structured, supervised lessons and activities for children of all ages, prompting some experts to warn of the effects of a generation of over-scheduled, pressured, and hurried children (Daly, 2000; MacDonald et al., 2003). Of course, contributing to the proliferation of structured activities is not only the concern about children's cultural opportunities, but also the social fear of crime that has made unstructured and unsupervised playtime much less common than in the past. In my own interviews with middle-class mothers, I have repeatedly heard about the difficulties parents face attempting to resist the pressure to enrol their children in an ever-widening and unmanageable array of lessons, sports, and activities (Wall, 2004b). They fear that resisting this pressure may mean not only missed opportunities for their children, but that it may be viewed by others as a lack of parental concern and involvement. Child-rearing advice literature, since the early 1990s, has participated in this intensification of parental responsibilities and duties through the incorporation of another strand of developmental psychology—what has come to be known as "new brain science."

Child-Rearing Advice and New Brain Science

Since the early 1990s there has been a proliferation of educational material aimed at convincing parents of the importance of secure attachment and ample stimulation in a child's early years (usually defined as the first three to five years of life) in order to ensure optimal brain development and future brain potential (Nadesan, 2002; Wall, 2004a). Parents are told that their behaviour affects the amount and type of synaptic connections made in their young child's brain, and that it thus will affect the ways in which their child's brain will become wired (Wall, 2004a). Once the connections are made (or not), they are told, that wiring becomes very difficult to undo. Invest in Kids, a Canadian foundation dedicated to promoting awareness of the importance of the early years for brain development, has trademarked a slogan that sums up this sentiment: "The years before five last the rest of their lives." Thus it is now not only children's personality and emotional stability that are at stake if parents fail to give their young children sufficient time, attention, and stimulation of the right type, but their brain capacity and future intellectual potential as well.

The new claims being promoted in child-rearing advice have not gone uncriticized in the scientific community. The most notable critique has been John Bruer's (1999) *The Myth of the First Three Years*. Bruer and others contend that there is actually little evidence in the field of neurology to suggest that kids would benefit from extra enrichment over what they would normally experience in everyday life, or that the years before five are as crucial as the expert advice suggests (Gopnik, Meltzoff, and Kuhl, 1999; Bruer, 1999: 57–58, 85; Bruner, 2000: 28; Wall, 2004a). These criticisms have had little effect on the enthusiasm with which the brain development claims have been promoted by both child-rearing experts and the media in general, however. Like attachment research before it, the early years discourse associated with new brain research has quickly become part of the taken-for-granted social understanding of children's needs and appropriate parenting behaviour.

The Child in the Womb

Technological advances in the 20th century that made it possible to see, monitor, and photograph the fetus have also played a part in the increasingly child-centred focus that characterizes expert child-rearing advice. As historian Barbara Duden (1993) points out, the experience of pregnancy and the ways in which society treats pregnant women have changed dramatically with the visualization of the fetus and the proliferation of fetal imagery in our society. In times before fetal imagery and modern medicine, a woman's pregnancy was often acknowledged only when she felt the movement of her fetus and made it known that she had "quickened." A modern woman, Duden notes (1993: 94) "has no comparable power to redefine her social status by making a statement about her body. In our society we are accepted as...pregnant only when we are certified as such by a professional." And our experiences of pregnancy are very different. She notes (1993: 7):

> my mother most emphatically insists that when she was carrying me she never thought of me as a fetus. And I remember a time when the fetus could be featured only in the kind of books that also showed labia majora and pubic hair. But now we are overwhelmed with fetuses....How did the unborn turn into a billboard image?

Women now, Duden (1993: 7, 50–55) contends, view themselves very much as "an ecosystem for a fetus," and the social acceptance of this interpretation has resulted in what she calls the emergence of "the public fetus." The protection of the "life" that is the fetus has become a public responsibility, and the pregnant woman has come under much more scrutiny from both experts and the public at large.

Duden is not alone in suggesting that fetal imagery and the discourse of fetal rights have resulted in the mother being viewed less in terms of a person in her own right and more as an ecosystem for a growing child (Daniels, 1993; Kaplan, 1994). The recent focus on public and expert regulation of the behaviour of pregnant women is referred to by Weir (1996) as "the remoralization of pregnancy." Certainly it is evident that throughout

Exhibit 8.2 *Welcome to the Classwomb*

What follows are excerpts from an article entitled "Welcome to the Classwomb" written by Patricia Young, and featured on p. R7 of the *Globe and Mail* on April 23, 2002. Although the article does quote one scientist who is skeptical about the claims being made about fetal learning, the majority of the article outlines the views of doctors and researchers who promote extra prenatal stimulation as a way to enhance the future intelligence of children.

Think bringing up baby starts at birth? Think again. Studies at the Prenatal University suggest there may be more to know in utero.

You have poked yourself in the belly three times this morning, gnawed on a walnut sandwich and listed to Mozart. It's a typical day for those enrolled in the curriculum of Prenatal University.

The days of lolling in amniotic fluid for nine months while awaiting birth are over for the unborn child. The womb is now a classroom.

Mothers are hunting down the best Baroque tunes to ensure that their baby will speak sooner and be smarter. Want an uber-genius child? Develop a taste for ocean-going fish and nuts and snarf down as much as you can. Omega-3 fats are the building blocks for those with loftier thoughts than we mortals. Learn the new techniques to teach math to your baby before it is born.

The latest research is showing that a baby has tremendous capacity to learn while still in utero. According to some researchers, everything from sitcom theme songs heard through our mother's belly to arguments during labour are remembered and stored away in our brains.

Ten Pre-birth tips:

1. Talk to the unborn baby.
2. Avoid baby talk. Apparently the little nippers in the womb prefer serious and direct adult talk. Save the goo-goos gas for when it is born.
3. Sing. It doesn't matter if the dog starts howling and the daffodils wilt. To your baby it will sound like La Wally.
4. Stimulate the baby's brain. Any good noises help the baby become alert.
5. But don't overstimulate. Too much loud noise will leave the baby rattled and unsettled.
6. Think good thoughts. The adage about bad thoughts poisoning your system appears to be true. Your body's chemistry changes with your moods and thoughts. Your baby is awash in your chemicals.
7. Mozart, Mozart, and more Mozart. It seems the richness and 55-70 beat of Mozart and Baroque composers can supercharge your baby's brain.
8. Poke. In the late stages of pregnancy poke your belly and see if you get the correct number of kicks back. You could be shaping a math genius. But then again, you could be creating an Enron accountant.
9. Eat up and eat well. Folic acids and omega-3 fats and a varied diet will go a long way to help you have a healthy child. Lay off the cigarettes and the booze.
10. Trust yourself. Science is just catching up with what moms have always known.

the 1980s and '90s the list of behaviours which pregnant women were expected to abide by, or refrain from, was continually growing. A good expectant mother must now carefully monitor what she eats, being sure to consume the proper number of servings from the necessary food groups and to limit her consumption of foods that might contain contaminants or other substances harmful to her developing fetus. She must take vitamin supplements, get proper exercise, avoid hazardous workplaces, and abstain from alcohol,

A father tries stimulating his unborn child by playing a little music near the mother's womb.

cigarettes, and drugs of any kind. Most of these behavioural limits extend past the birth of the baby, especially if the mother continues to have a bodily connection to her child through breast-feeding (Wall, 2001).

Understandings of pregnancy and unborn children thus both reflect and participate in the trend toward an increasingly child-centred focus in social understandings of child-rearing. It is not surprisingly, therefore, to see that intensive parenting and stimulation to enhance brain development are also extending into the pre-birth period. As the accompanying excerpts from the newspaper article entitled "Welcome to the Classwomb" illustrated above, expectant mothers now find advice on ways to give their children a competitive advantage by beginning to stimulate and educate them as early as possible.

CHILDHOOD IN CANADA TODAY AND IN THE FUTURE

What do these developments suggest about our current conceptions of childhood? Some authors propose that we are witnessing a shift in the treatment and understanding of children, moving away from a view of children as the property of adults toward a view of children as autonomous individuals, as citizens with rights (James, Jenks, and Prout, 1998: 6–7; Jenson, 2001). Certainly, there are indications that this is occurring, even though, as with other cultural changes, the actual behaviour of individuals and institutions lags behind changing social values. Children around the world now have civil rights as laid out in the United Nations Convention on the Rights of the Child. Canada was one of many countries to formally sign and ratify this convention in 1990. In January 2004 the Supreme Court of Canada placed limits on the ability of parents and teachers to use corporal punishment on children, following a lengthy public debate and legal battle over the morality and legality of spanking. Physical punishment of children is not supported by the UN Committee on the Rights of the Child and is already illegal in a number of European countries. Mistreatment of children in general is tolerated less and less, as the ever-increasing number of reports to child welfare authorities over the last two decades indicate. In Ontario between 1993 and 1998, the number of investigations conducted by child welfare authorities increased by 44% (Trocmé, Fallon, MacLaurin, and Copp, 2002).

It seems then that children in Canada are more socially valued and better treated than ever before. There are, however, other factors to take into consideration when analyzing the place of children in Canadian society today. As mentioned previously, the focus on the importance of children is taking place within the context of a political shift towards individualism and neo-liberalism. The idea behind the welfare state—that society has a collective responsibility for addressing social ills—is being eroded. Social programs in Canada experienced dramatic cutbacks and redesign in the 1990s, as the federal government scrapped the Canada Assistance Plan and cut by one-third the money available to the provinces for health, education, and social assistance. Jenson (2001), in an analysis of changes to Canadian federal social assistance programs and policies, suggests that spending is being redefined as investment rather than service provision. Furthermore, she suggests, social equality is being recast in political rhetoric as "equality of opportunity." This fits within a political rationale that focuses on individual self-enhancement and responsibility. Children, Jenson proposes, given their potential to become good or bad future citizens, are increasingly being cast as good investment opportunities.

This focus on investment in children is evident in the early years discourse as well. Consider this quote from the Ontario Early Years Study (McCain and Mustard, 1999: 2) commissioned by then-premier Mike Harris to study ways in which government policy could make use of new developments in brain research:

> The entrants to the workforce of 2025 will be born next year. From this generation will come a key factor in determining the wealth base of Ontario in 25 years....Ensuring that our future citizens are able to develop their full potential has to be a high priority for everyone. It is crucial if we are to reverse "the real brain drain."

It was on the basis of this study that the Ontario government established a large network of Early Years Centres in the province which are mandated to provide parenting education and information (Wall, 2004a). The focus on children as the key to national prosperity is reminiscent in many ways of the discourse surrounding the infant mortality campaigns early in the twentieth century. The difference is that now children's brain potential, rather than their physical health, is the determining factor (Comacchio, 1993; Arnup, 1994; Wall, 2004a).

Although governments target children as the preferred investments of the future, support for families has been eroding in other ways. Cutbacks to social assistance programs in the 1990s have left many poor families with children deeper in poverty than

FIGURE 8.1 Percentage of Children with Delayed Vocabulary, by Household Income

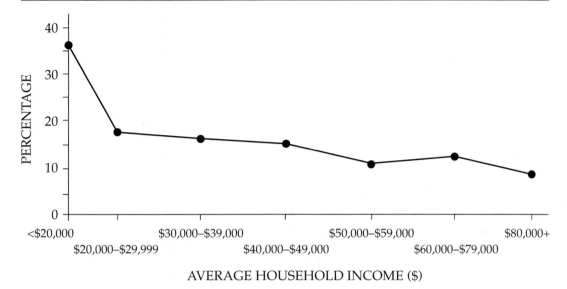

Note: Children scored less than 85 on the Peabody Picture Vocabulary Test scale, 4- to 5-year-olds only, two-parent families.

Source: Reprinted with the permission of the Canadian Council on Social Development.

ever before. After welfare cutbacks of 21% in Ontario in 1995, a single mother on welfare went from $8,488 below the poverty line to $9,852 below the poverty line (Little, 2003: 241). With the implementation of workfare in Ontario that accompanied the welfare reforms of the mid-1990s, single mothers with children aged four and up began to be treated the same as those with no dependents. They are expected to be in a workfare program or actively searching for work in order to be eligible for welfare. As Little (2003) reports, this has increased stress and limited the time and energy available for parenting in families that are already under tremendous pressure.

Funding to licensed childcare centres also suffered during the 1990s (Ontario Campaign 2000, 2000). Despite numerous political promises over the last two decades, Canada still has no national childcare program. In almost 7 of 10 families with children under six, both the mother and father now work, and 55% of single mothers are in the labour force. Yet there is space in licensed childcare centres for less than one-third of the children in these families (Vanier Institute, 2000: 87; Johnson, Lero, and Rooney, 2001: 43–44). Affordable housing also became a major issue during the 1990s, as governments opted out of the production of low-income housing. The number of households paying more than half of their income in rent increased by 43% from 1990 to 1995, and families with children are now the fastest growing population requiring emergency shelter in Canada (Campaign 2000, 2001).

Finally, despite a 1989 House of Commons resolution to eliminate child poverty by the year 2000, an average of one in five children lived below Statistics Canada's low-income cut-off during the 1990s. The number of children that experienced poverty at

FIGURE 8.2 Percentage of Children with Basic Health Problems Related to Daily Functioning, by Household Income*

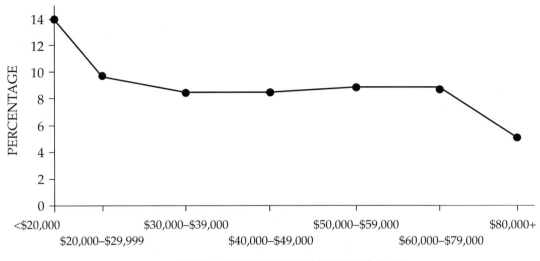

* Statistics Canada terms this as "functional health" and bases it on eight attributes: vision, hearing, speech, mobility, dexterity, cognition, emotion, and pain and discomfort

Note: Two-parent families with children aged 4 to 11 years.

Source: Reprinted with the permission of the Canadian Council on Social Development.

some point during the decade is even higher. One in three Canadian children lived below the poverty line for a least one year between 1993 and 1998 (Campaign 2000, 2001). The link between poverty, health, basic functioning, and learning ability in children has been well established, as is illustrated in the study by Ross and Roberts (1999) from which Figures 8.1 and 8.2 are drawn. There is also no doubt a link between the declining social supports available to families living in poverty in the 1990s and the fact that the number of children taken into care by child welfare authorities in Ontario rose by 60% between 1995 and 2001 (Trocmé, Fallon, Bruce, and Copp, 2002; Wall, 2004a).

There seems, then, to be a discrepancy between the social importance of child potential emphasized in current parenting advice and educational programs, and the ways in which children's needs are provided for by social policy in Canada. This discrepancy raises many questions: What happens to children whose parents cannot afford educational toys, music lessons, and sports? What happens to those young children whose parents do not have the time or resources to spend quality time with them, nor the money to provide quality child care? What happens to children who are removed from families who lack the supports or resources to care for them and are placed in overloaded foster-care systems?

The growing recognition of the importance of children and their potential has not been coupled in social policy with a strong acknowledgment of social responsibility to support families. The focus on educating parents about the importance of the early years fits, instead, within a neo-liberal model of individual responsibility. It ignores the larger structural barriers that prevent parents from providing an enriched environment for their children. There are dangers as well in the uncritical acceptance of cultural understandings of childhood that background the needs of parents. Children are raised in families, and their needs cannot easily be separated from the needs of those who care for them. As Jenson (2001: 121) suggests, "a citizenship regime that could simultaneously focus on the needs of adults and children would be a more balanced regime." Parents perform a valuable social task in raising and socializing future generations. Current child-rearing advice does implicitly acknowledge the importance of parents' roles. What official responses to this advice do not adequately do is recognize the structural difficulties that parents encounter when attempting to perform their task, nor the responsibility society has to support them in this (Wall, 2004a). It is possible to envision a conception of childhood and child-rearing that, while valuing children and their potential, would also be compatible with a recognition of the needs of parents and a social commitment to invest not only in children, but also in families.

CONCLUSION

Childhood is a biological reality, but it is also a social construction. Many of the things we take for granted today about what children need and what childhood is all about are in fact unique to our particular time and culture. Our ideas about childhood are also rooted in the authority of scientific claims that are themselves produced within, and are influenced by, a social context. These claims are not beyond question; and indeed, it is the job of sociologists to examine the social influences and implications of scientific claims. In the case of childhood, the fields of medicine and developmental psychology have had a major influence on social understandings of children and their needs, and on the direction taken by child-rearing experts.

There was a notable shift in child-rearing advice following World War II away from a focus on discipline, strict schedules, and the establishment of good habits in children toward a more permissive and child-centred approach, and a greater emphasis on children's psychological and cognitive development. This trend intensified throughout the remainder of the twentieth century, accompanied in the 1990s by a focus on maximizing children's brain development through ample and appropriate stimulation in the early years.

This chapter examined the implications of these understandings for both children and parents. Although Canadian children seem to be more valued than ever before, many experience the disadvantages associated with a withdrawal of social support to families. Part of this paradox is related to the separation of the needs of children from the needs of parents and families that is evident in both expert advice and social policy. The place of children in Canadian society in the future will be determined, in part, by the extent to which the understanding of children's needs and potential is combined with the notion of child-rearing as a social as well as individual responsibility.

Suggested Readings

Arnup, Katherine (1994). *Education for Motherhood: Advice for Mothers in Twentieth-Century Canada.* Toronto: University of Toronto Press.

Burman, Erica (1994). *Deconstructing Developmental Psychology.* London: Routledge.

Castaneda, Claudia (2002). *Figurations: Child, Bodies, Worlds.* Durham NC: Duke University Press.

Comacchio, Cynthia (1993). *Nations are Built of Babies: Saving Ontario's Mothers and Children.* Montreal: McGill-Queen's University Press.

Hwang, C. Philip, Michael Lamb, and Irving Sigel (Eds.) (1996). *Images of Childhood.* Mahwah, N.J.: Lawrence Erlbaum Associates.

James, Allison, Chris Jenks, and Alan Prout, A. (1998). *Theorizing Childhood.* New York: Teachers College Press.

Web Resources

Child and Family Canada is a public education Web site bringing together material from fifty Canadian non-profit organizations and providing a wide range of research reports, articles, and resources on children and families. **www.cfc-efc.ca**

Canadian Policy Research Networks is a private, non-profit research organization specializing in social and economic policy research. Analyses of child and family policy in Canada along with international comparisons can be found here. **www.cprn.ca**

Researchers at SUNY Stony Brook and the New York Attachment Consortium have a Web site that details current and past information and research on attachment theory. This Web site features special sections on the work of John Bowlby and Mary Ainsworth. **www.psychology.sunysb.edu/attachment/**

Endnotes

[1] Although, as many historians have pointed out, labour-saving devices increased standards of cleanliness and thus did not necessarily reduce the amount of time spent on domestic labour.

CHAPTER NINE

The Family Lives of the Middle-Aged and Elderly in Canada[1]

Susan A. McDaniel

INTRODUCTION

Families at middle and old age have not received the attention that younger families have, particularly in family sociology or family studies texts. It is younger families with children that have been of primary interest, with older people considered largely as grandparents apart from the families of direct interest (see Beaujot, 2000, for example). In recent years, this is beginning to change, as definitions and perspectives on family are broadened, and as family becomes more important in providing care and support to elders (Zukewich, 2003). New perspectives and insights about families as they age are emerging and affect the ways in which family changes through the life course are understood.

Families still tend to be categorized by either structure (for example, lone-parent families, families with children, childless couple families, same-sex families) or by their relations to the work world, such as two-career or two-earner families, or one-earner with work-at-home-spouse families. These categories are not life course or age-based, of course, and therefore tend not to focus on families as they age. Yet, analyses that enable understanding of families as they change over time are becoming increasingly important to policy (Policy Research Initiative, 2004), to ourselves as we live in families, and to societies as they age. Focusing on families in mid-life enables a dynamic perspective on families through their life courses, not visible when families are analyzed by the shapes they take.

Families in middle and older age have become the focus of social policy interest in Canada. This is because of the involvement of families in providing care and support for aging relatives and friends, as formal systems of support either shrink or do not keep pace with demand. It has been argued that eldercare, for example, is a central challenge to Canada's aging society in the 21st century (Keating et al., 1999; McDaniel, 2004; Statistics Canada, 2004). Family has become more and more politically salient, as governments in many societies, including Canada, have come increasingly to understand and to value the vital roles families play in society and in the lives of individuals, and as governments cut public supports and programs (Baker, 1995; Ward-Griffin and Marshall, 2003).

In this chapter, the focus is on families in middle and old age in Canada in the early part of the 21st century, with particular emphasis on contemporary challenges that mid-life and older families face in caregiving, social support, relationships among and across generations, and work, including work-leaving and new forms of retirement. Beginning with brief attention to the definition of middle age, middle-aged families, and the historical emergence of mid-life as a life phase in Canada, the chapter moves into discussions of the demographics of aging families, **caregiving**, social and emotional supports, and work/retirement issues. Throughout the chapter, policy issues, challenges, and concerns are highlighted, drawing on the author's experiences in policy research and policy advising. In this chapter, the terms middle age and mid-life are used interchangeably.

WHAT IS MIDDLE AGE AND WHEN DOES IT BEGIN?

What constitutes middle age or mid-life for individuals or families is far from clear. For individuals, mid-life may be thought to begin when we reach half of our average life expectancy. Estimates generated from the most recent Canadian census indicate a median age of Canadian men at 36.7 years and of women at 38.4 years (Statistics Canada, 2002a). These median ages are, for both men and women, the highest yet (Statistics Canada, 2002b). These ages may be younger than what many people would think of as mid-life. It is interesting that men are considered older slightly sooner than women, contrary to many cultural images (Abu-Laban and McDaniel, 2004). If it is considered that the average age difference between marriage/relationship partners is approximately three years (with men typically older than their spouses), then husbands would, on average, become middle-aged five years before their wives.

For families, mid-life is often determined by presumed typical life course patterns. More will be said about why and how "presumably typical life course patterns" may no longer be typical, if indeed they ever were. It is often presumed that middle age begins when the children grow up and leave home. This approach is highly problematic in Canada in the 21st century. It suggests, first, a uniformity of life course and experience which no longer exists, since family lives have become much more diverse and individuated. It may, in fact, be that uniformity of family lives never existed, except as a myth about families of the past. Second, although children still grow up, they no longer leave

The proportion of middle-aged workers in the labour force is higher than many managers estimate.

home in Canada to the same degree they once did. This produces what researchers have termed "cluttered nests" instead of the hypothesized "empty nests" that previously were thought to characterize mid-life families (Mitchell, 2002; Gee and Mitchell, 2003).

Age is a sensitive and changing social construction. Today, middle-aged men and women may appear younger than they did a generation ago, with workouts, diets and cosmetics, and sometimes some help from plastic surgeons (Abu-Laban and McDaniel, 2004). The concept of not looking one's age, particularly for women, is a reflection of the social expectations that a particular age carries with it. Does age 50 have a particular look for women or for men? Most close observers of people would probably agree that there are huge differences in appearance and attitudes between 50-year-olds, or for that matter, between people at any age. This diversity can lead to underestimations of the ages of middle-aged people. People who pretend to be younger than their real age add to the underestimation of middle age. Middle age may be an elusive concept. In research the author did with mid-life working Canadians, in large and small companies in the public and private sectors, estimates were obtained from top managers, executives, or human resources officers in various companies, of how many employees in their companies were aged 45-64. The estimates provided were considerably under what the payroll data revealed! Some of the managers were distinctly taken aback (McDaniel, 1996).

THE HISTORICAL EMERGENCE AND DIVERSITY OF MID-LIFE FAMILIES

In Canadian history, only recently have families experienced a life stage that could be termed middle age. Prior to recent times, life expectancy was so much lower that people often reached the end of their lives at ages that would be termed middle age today. Among women born in 1840, for example, last births occurred at age 40, and the women died, on average, at age 62 (Gee, 1990a). Men, typically, did not live long enough to see their last child reach adulthood. Among women who married and had children in the 19th century, most spent their entire adult lives raising dependent children. No sooner would the youngest child become an adult than the mother's life would be over. It should be emphasized, however, that not all Canadian women in the 19th century spent their adult lives raising children. As many as one-quarter of the adult female population at the turn of the twentieth century never married (Jeffreys, 1985), and many women, both married and unmarried, worked on farms or homesteads, in their homes doing paid labour such as sewing, making jams and other products for sale, or in the homes of others and early industries (Synge, 1980; Ursel, 1992; McDaniel and Lewis, 1997). Women in Canada's past, like contemporary women, often faced challenges in balancing work and family lives. Less common an experience for Canadian women in the 19th century was a period in middle age when children were grown, when they did not have the responsibility of dependent children at the same time.

Women born in 1960, on the other hand, on average, experienced their last birth at age 26. Life expectancy for these women averages 82 years (Gee, 1990a). Women in the late twentieth century had a much longer phase of their lives spent without responsibility for dependent children, a phase which some would say characterizes the mid-life family stage. The period during which adult children and parents are alive at the same time is longer than ever before in Canadian history. It has been estimated that adults in Canada today will spend more years caring for their aging parents than raising their children (Zukewich, 2003; Statistics Canada, 2004). This is indeed a profound change from the past in Canada.

Few Canadian families historically were the large extended families that many see as characteristic of our past (Ursel, 1992). As a result of lower life expectancies and preferred independent living arrangements, most families had no more than two generations: parents and their children. Of those aged 50, only 16% would have had one or more surviving parents in 1910, compared with 60% in 1991 (Gee, 1990a). Of those aged 60, only 2% had a surviving parent in 1920, compared to an estimate of almost one-quarter in 2020. In 2004, for the first time in history, Canadians have more parents than children (Statistics Canada, 2004). Clearly, there have been enormous changes in the ways in which we experience family and the ways in which we are expected to relate to multiple generations simultaneously.

Women in what would be called mid-life today were, in the early part of the 20th century, living as often as lone parents as they are today in Canada. The reasons, however, were different, with widowhood being more often the cause of lone parenthood than it is today. Lone mothers raising children on their own today are more likely to be separated, divorced, or never married. Widows in Canada's past, however, particularly those with dependent children, were as often in diminished circumstances as are single mothers today. Morton (1992) describes the precariousness of the existence of widows with children in Halifax in the 1920s and 1930s. Mother's Allowances, intended to help widows support their children, were thought to be appropriate only for widows who were "guarded in their virtue." The concern, according to Morton, was for the widow's "moral vulnerability, as sexually active women who now lived outside of marriage and male supervision" (1992: 92). Widows were thus under constant surveillance by neighbours to ensure that allowances would go only to those "who were in every respect a fit, proper, and suitable person to have the custody and care of her children" (Morton, 1992: 101). Morton describes the case of Emma Lawson, who, when her neighbours observed a man leaving her house late in the evening, had her Mother's Allowance permanently suspended. Another widow, Lillian Kennedy, lost her Allowance following an illegitimate birth (a term used until recently to describe a birth occurring to an unmarried woman).

Contrary to popular belief, Canada's past was characterized by more people, both women and men, remaining single than do today. According to recent trends, approximately 75% of young Canadians will get married at some point in their lives (Statistics Canada, 2002c). The late 1990s saw the beginning of a trend towards decreasing marriage rates (Statistics Canada, 2003a). However, early in the 21st century we are seeing an increase in the rate at which couples are choosing common-law unions (Statistics Canada, 2003b). "The 2001 GSS [General Social Survey] showed that close to 1.2 million couples were living in a common-law relationship, up 20% from 1995. In contrast, the number of married couples increased 3% from 6.2 million to 6.4 million" (Statistics Canada, 2002d).

Mid-life bachelors and spinsters, as unmarried men and women were called, were relatively common well into the 20th century in Canada. Aging bachelors were particularly common in rural areas and among some immigrant groups, most notably the Chinese, who were prohibited by Canadian immigration policy from bringing their wives or prospective wives into Canada. In Prairie towns and in British Columbia, those Chinese bachelors still alive are very old, and many have led lonely lives (Gee, 2000). Spinsters, on the other hand, tended to live largely in urban centres where they were often the most educated members of the community. The image of the grey-haired spinster with her hair in a bun, wearing sensible shoes, and as one historian puts it, "haunting libraries" may not seem appealing, yet spinsters were among the very few women who had career jobs, independent income, sometimes even pensions, opportunities to travel and write, and tended to live longer than their married sisters (Jeffreys, 1985). Mid-life did indeed exist for some never-married women in Canada's past, and it was a period of relative freedom (for some anyway), from family responsibilities particularly after the deaths of aging parents, for whom unmarried women often took responsibility.

If we think of THE traditional Canadian family, an unexpected image comes to mind. Many people, perhaps even most, let the term, "traditional family" fall from their lips quickly and without much thought. Some even see traditions beginning with the television situation comedies of the 1950s and 1960s! What is the most traditional family, in terms of contemporary cultural imagery in Canada, the family for which Canadians are known worldwide? It is certainly not the largely American television family to which the media so often hark. Rather it is the family of Marilla and Matthew Cuthbert and Anne Shirley—Lucy Maud Montgomery's *Anne of Green Gables* family—that was, and is, widely known and much beloved, even before the television series. Marilla and Matthew Cuthbert were a middle-aged brother and sister, both unmarried, who adopted Anne Shirley when they were unsuccessful in getting a boy from Children's Aid to help them on their farm. A mid-life family comprised of a brother and sister with an adopted child may be the most well known and beloved of all Canadian families, and the family that is thought of first by Canadians as a traditional family!

FAMILIES AS THEY AGE

Thinking about middle age and older families is challenging because of the tendency to specify particular age stages through which all families go. Accumulated years may be something that mid-life and older families might have in common, although it should be kept in mind that there is tremendous diversity in family life experiences at any age in Canada. Family diversity in fact may be greatest in mid-life, with some people entering relationships for the first time, others establishing second (or third, or more) relationships, still others celebrating long-lived relationships. Some may be having children for the first time, while others are grandparents, or even great-grandparents.

In addition to age similarities, there is shared history, or what is called cohort effect (McDaniel, 1997a). For example, those aged 57 in 2004 are the first of the baby boom generation, whose early twenties (university or college days) were spent listening to the Beatles and the Rolling Stones. Those aged 74 in 2004 were born around the time of the Depression, and lived their pre-teen years during World War II. The challenge in studying families by life course is to sort out what is age-related (stages we all go through) from what is cohort-related (related to the common life experiences of generations). This is important because if it is assumed that those aged 28 in 2004 will have similar life and family experiences to those aged 68 in 2004, serious problems could result. Marcil-Gratton and Legare (1992), among others, caution that the future for elderly people will not be like the past or the present. To project the future, one must not only understand the present and the past, but be precise in what can be projected and what cannot be projected on the basis of today's knowledge of the behavioural patterns of a particular generation or cohort (McDaniel, 2004). It is a mistake to presume that older people today are setting the course of family life (or anything else) for those who will be older tomorrow (McDaniel, 2000a).

The means by which families are seen and analyzed has changed dramatically in recent years, although outdated models still characterize much popular thought and most social policy, as pointed out by Baker (1990), Keating et al., (1994), and McDaniel and Tepperman (2004). As discussed in other chapters, developments in theorizing families and how families fit into society and articulate with other social institutions have taken sociological thought about families in new and exciting directions. Issues of inequities within households and families (Folbre, 1988; Keith, Wacker, and Schafer, 1992; Orloff, 1993), of power within families and how power constructs familial relations, of how social structures such as the economy impact on families, are among the new areas of consideration. There are also crucial issues of culture, ethnicity, and immigration (Driedger and Chappell, 1987; Gee, 1999). Families in the past were studied largely at the micro level, virtually independent of, and separate from, the wider society.

Among the new insights are that families do vital work for society, much of which remains hidden, unacknowledged, and gendered. A major aspect of that hidden work is the caring families do, work which becomes extremely important to middle age and older families (McDaniel, 1992; Keating et al., 1994; Zukewich, 2003). Also hidden have been many gender inequities in families, which may peak in mid- and later life. In part, these inequities have remained hidden because of the models frequently relied on to examine families. For example, Gary Becker (1981), Nobel Prize laureate, has been a proponent of a model of family that likens services produced in families, including the production of children, to commodities produced in the marketplace. There is a division of labour, a demand, and a supply, he argues. There is presumed choice (in much the same way that we make consumer choices), rational self-interest, and utility maximization. Family and household are seen as cooperative units that motivate efficient allocation of resources and serve the individual interests of family members.

Critics of Becker's model (Folbre, 1988, among others) note that family members may not have much choice in taking on the tasks required by their family. Rational self-interest may be an inappropriate model when power to choose is not equally distributed, and women often have less choice than men in assuming family responsibilities. As well, family membership does not usually require a competitive test of ability to do the job, so that requisite skills may be lacking when the job demands doing. And of course, families are not independent with respect to resource allocation and distribution (such as when they receive social assistance or pensions, the rules of which can change without notice or consultation). According to this model, mid-life families might simply refuse to add yet more responsibilities, arguing that too many demands on them are not in their self-interest, so that a grandmother cannot be looked after or an adult son or daughter who might return home while unemployed can no longer do so. Sharing is built into the very nature of families whose individual members may not be acting out of self-interest, but rather in the interest of the family overall. Questions clearly arise as to whose self-interest prevails at any given time, on what basis decisions are made when conflicts of self-interest occur, and in what ways decisions may be gender-based (McDaniel, 2000). Families are undeniably shaped by economic forces, but, unlike the presumptions of choice and rational self-interest, families more often are driven by caring and sharing. Nowhere is this more apparent than in mid-life families.

CANADIAN FAMILIES IN MIDDLE AND OLD AGE: DEMOGRAPHICS

Looking at the ways in which older Canadians live in families (McDaniel and Tepperman, 2004), we find that most of those aged 65 years and older live in small households. More older women than men live alone, for reasons that will be discussed later (Statistics Canada, 2003a). Vastly greater proportions of older men (75.2%) than women (43.1%) in their older years share their lives with a spouse (Statistics Canada, 2003a). Most older Canadians have siblings, some have large numbers of siblings, and most (59%) have regular contact with their siblings. Connidis (2001) shows that siblings are an important resource for the elderly and are often neglected in studies of social support. Most elderly Canadians (82%) also have children, and there is a surprising amount of regular contact with their adult children, with approximately one-half of all older Canadians living within 10 kilometres of at least one of their children. Even among those who live at a greater distances from their children, there is regular contact, with more contacts between mothers and adult children than fathers.

The ways in which we live in families in Canada have changed, as discussed earlier. Widowhood is now an expectable life event for most married women in Canada. Gender differences resulting from differential life expectancies for men and women begin to emerge in mid-life, as more women than men are without spouses (Dulude, 1987; Statistics Canada, 2002e). The 2001 Canadian census indicates that 35% of women aged 65 years or more live alone, compared with 16% of men of the same age (Statistics Canada, 2003c). Moreover, few senior women (35%), but most senior men (61%), live with a spouse or partner (Statistics Canada, 2003c).

These differences can mean sharply different life opportunities for men and women, with gender differences becoming particularly apparent in mid-life. For women, marriage is still as much an economic arrangement as an emotional one, linking with a man who typically earns more and who is expected, by law and policy, to support and share his assets with his wife. On his death or their divorce, a woman can quickly slide into poverty, or have her economic circumstances considerably diminished. Hayes and Anderson (1993) show how mid-life women become economically disadvantaged upon divorce. And Perkins (1993) shows how poverty as a result of family dependency recycles from mid-life into old age for women. Orloff reminds us that, given the ways in which families are gendered, many women are "one man away from poverty" (1993: 319). She adds emphasis to this point by stating, "Most men simply do not share their income with their children after the dissolution of marriage..." (Orloff, 1993: 319). Ozawa and Yoon (2002) demonstrate that, just as a woman's economic status is diminished with divorce, it improves again upon her remarriage. Thus, the situation is created that women without men, with the exception of some never-married women, are much more often economically vulnerable in their older years than are men without women.

Divorced or widowed men are considerably more likely to remarry than are divorced or widowed women (van den Hoonaard, 2002). The tendency to live common-law rather than remarrying after divorce has increased recently for both men and women (See Statistics Canada, 2003b). Expectations that one will remarry, if divorced or widowed, also decline substantially with age, from 44% among those aged 18-29 to 13% among those aged 50-64 (Statistics Canada, 2003b). The higher probability of divorced women in mid-life remaining unmarried adds to their economic vulnerability in mid-life. They do not benefit from pooled incomes of spouses. Not as much is known about the social lives of unmarried or divorced/separated elderly people, although some research exists (Strain and Payne, 1992; Connidis, 2001; van den Hoonaard, 2002).

Gee (1990b) and Hanson (1993) reveal, in different ways, how beliefs about how family and life course should unfold structure women's expectations concerning the timing of family life events. Gee finds, in research in British Columbia, that women strongly believe that there are appropriate ages by which one should get married, have children, and become grandmothers. She suggests that women measure the success of their lives by middle age, in part, on the basis of how closely they approximate the internalized ideals of family life events. Hanson (1993) adds force to this in arguing that the concept of "the biological time clock" is a social construction that creates undue anxiety in mid-life women. Based on analyses of medical data on fertility outcomes, Hanson concludes that the life courses of women are shaped more by social and medical family life course expectations than by medical facts. Her conclusion is that, in addition to the challenges mid-life women face with family changes, changing gender expectations, and caregiving, they also experience socially and medically reinforced time clocks for family life events. Mid-life women are caught in family and life course models that are not of their own making or shaping, by which they judge themselves and are held accountable by society.

As women's lives become more individuated and family lives more diverse, more mid-life women will experience life events in unusual sequence and possibly, because they are not expected, with increased stress. Two examples follow from the author's research on families and work in mid-life (McDaniel, 1996). A woman, married and childless for 17 years, who has already experienced the stresses of caregiving to a father in his eighties, has twins at age 40, thanks to the success of *in vitro* fertilization. She now faces the worsening health problems of her aging father, plus the demands of new and first-time mothering of twins, at a time in her life when the demands of her career have never been greater. A second example is a 40-year-old mother of two, aged one and three, whose elderly parents and parents-in-law are not able to help in any way with the children, despite living in the same community. They tend not to be supportive of her challenges in raising her children and, at the same time, continuing her career. As well, this woman is in a particularly stressful occupation that is vulnerable to government cutbacks that have characterized the public sector in the 1990s.

In mid-life families, women are differentially responsible for meal preparation (81%), meal clean-up (70%), and housecleaning/laundry (79%), according to the 1998 General

Social Survey (Statistics Canada, 2004). This was found as well in the 1996 General Social Survey (Keating et al., 1999). Men, on the other hand, tend to be responsible for house maintenance and outside work (about 75% of men do this). No more recent national data on division of household labour exist. Gender division of household work tends to peak in mid-life, and decrease after that (Keith, Wacker, and Schafer, 1992; McDaniel, 1994). The author has found, using a representative sample of those age 45 and over in Alberta, that it is women in mid-life who take most of the responsibility for organizing day-to-day family life (about 57% report doing this). A largely unexamined aspect of mid-life women's responsibilities in families involves keeping in touch with relatives, or "kin-keeping," as Rosenthal terms it (1985). In Alberta, 61.3% of women aged 45 and over take this responsibility (McDaniel, 1996). This varies with ethnic group (Kobayashi, 1999; Gee and Mitchell, 2003).

CAREGIVING FAMILIES: THE MID-LIFE FAMILY CRUNCH

Although there is much more to mid-life families than caregiving, attention is devoted particularly to caregiving here for two reasons: It is an area of strong policy interest in Canada, and it is an area which has preoccupied research on families in mid- and later life (Keating et al., 1994; McDaniel and Gee, 1993). This is revealing of the presumptions about what families are for, to borrow the title of an article by Daatland (1990). It is presumed that families, largely mid-life families, will do, or should do, caregiving to aging relatives, a presumption that has not been much questioned, as is pointed out by Keating and   colleagues (1994) in their close examination of what a caregiving family actually is. They conclude by challenging the equivalency of a caregiving family with a kin-based family, as well as simplistic views of family caregiving that they argue are used to pressure families into providing even more care (Keating et al., 1994: 285).

A national study (Keating et al., 1999), the only one of its kind thus far, looks at the contexts for caregiving overall. They find that most Canadians of all ages receive regular help with day-to-day activities from others (meals prepared for us, clothes washed for us, our houses cleaned, etc.). This is part of what living in families entails. Care, when provided to those with long-term health problems, is most likely for those aged 85 and over. This finding is supported in more recent studies and by the 2001 Census of Canada (Zukewich, 2003; Statistics Canada, 2004a, 2004b). Eldercare was found by Keating et al. to be most commonly provided by women (61%), usually wives, daughters, or daughters-in-law, but a substantial proportion of men (39%) were found to provide eldercare as well (Keating et al., 1999:34–35). However, men and women caregivers to the elderly provide different kinds of care.

Women tend to provide more hours of care, and devote themselves more to the traditionally feminine tasks of homemaking, personal care, and emotional support. Men predominate in instrumental tasks such as home maintenance and repair. In their analysis of time-use data from the 1998 Canadian General Social Survey, Michelson and Tepperman (2003: 596) found that most of the informal caregivers in the sample were women (roughly two-thirds).

TABLE 9.1 Providing Unpaid Care to Seniors by Hours Spent per Week, 1996 and 2001 Censuses of Canada, Men and Women (100,000)

Hours Spent		1996	2001
0	M	9.5	9.8
	F	9.3	9.7
<5	M	1.1	1.2
	F	1.4	1.6
5-9	M	.2	.3
	F	.5	.6
10+	M	.2	.2
	F	.4	.4
Overall	M	11.0	11.6
	F	11.6	12.2

Source: Statistics Canada. 2004b. 2001 Census of Canada. Ottawa: Statistics Canada. Catalogue no. 97F0013XCB01004 www.statcan.ca Hours spent providing unpaid care to seniors. Retrieved June 10, 2004.

The 2001 census of Canada, as shown in Table 9.1, enables comparison with the 1996 census on the numbers of hours spent by men and women in providing unpaid care to seniors. Time spent in care to seniors has increased for both men and women. It is found, consistent with Keating et al.'s smaller earlier study (1999), that women indeed spent more hours on average providing care to seniors than did men (Statistics Canada, 2004b). The overall difference in hours spent by men as compared to women remained the same from 1996 to 2001. The sex difference between those who provided no care at all narrowed in this period, and the numbers providing no care at all increased. The greatest increase in time spent caring for seniors occurred among women who spent less than five hours a week caring, and women who spent five to nine hours a week. The census provides no data on the kinds of care provided.

In recent decades, what has become known as the "**Sandwich Generation**"—women in the middle of the demands of multiple generations—has been spotlighted (Seaward, 1999). The extent of the demands placed on women in mid-life by both older and younger relatives, whether or not they actually live together in the same household, has been well documented (Neysmith, 1989; McDaniel, 1997b; Abu-Laban and McDaniel, 2004). Based on the 1998 Canadian General Social Survey, Michelson and Tepperman (2003: 596) determined that about half of caregivers are between 35 and 54 years of age and that caregivers have an average age of 51 years. Women in mid-life are the caregivers of choice for older relatives, and see themselves as taking on the caring, not necessarily out of choice, but because they believe that there is no one else to take on the responsibility (Aronson, 1992; McDaniel, 2004). Women are the ones most likely to detect a relative's need for care as a result of their closer ties to kin. And, in many ethnic groups, it is women who are expected to provide the care to elders, while men provide the instrumental support

(Mitchell, Wister, and Gee, 2002; Gee, 2000). Having care provided to you in old age by mid-life family members, typically daughters and daughters-in-law, is simply part of the pact of family for many.

As we have found, women are called upon differentially to provide emotional support to elderly relatives. Men of all ages tend to rely much more heavily on their spouses for help and support if they feel depressed. Women, on the other hand, note a wider circle of people, including family and non-family, upon whom they would call if help were needed (Connidis, 2001; McDaniel, 1994). Both men and women tend to rely on women more for emotional support.

When asked, hypothetically, to whom the respondent would turn if they were upset with their spouse, men, particularly those over age 65, stated in a national survey in Canada, that they would have no one to whom they could turn. Women of the same age mentioned daughters, friends, siblings, and other relatives to whom they could turn, although many of them also mentioned that they would have no one, particularly the oldest women (McDaniel, 1994). Older men are less connected to family in general and the supports it can offer in times of emotional need than are women. Important, for the purposes of this chapter, is confirmation that women, largely mid-life women, are central not only as caregivers but as emotional resources to both men and women in times of need (Keating et al., 1999). This involves women in widespread "**compulsory altruism**."

Middle-aged families and the women who most often do the caregiving and welfare work in families are generally taken for granted (Orloff, 1993: 312), and are pressured by rhetoric or social policy shifts to do more and more (Keating et al., 1994; Wiles, 2003). This means that providers of family care face challenges and tensions that remain largely hidden in families and households. Caring for elders, largely done by women in mid-life, is not without consequences, sometimes serious consequences (Keating et al., 1999). There are differences in patterns of consequences for women and men who provide family care. Caregiving stresses for men are more often related to working while providing care or to achievement characteristics such as education. For women, the pattern of predictors of stress and its consequences more often relates to the degree and intensity of caregiving provided (Keating et al., 1999).

Women tend to experience more strain and less support in providing this care than do men who caregive. The same pattern occurs in caring for children; women receive less support and help than men do. Women tend to be more torn by competing family demands than men, and women are simultaneously more vulnerable both in the labour market and in families. Both increase women's stress levels. Brubaker and Brubaker (1992) suggest that caregiving stresses might best be seen in the context of family interactions, with consideration to the fact that not all families are happy families, even prior to caregiving crises. They emphasize that caregiving interacts with retirement for women, sometimes further diminishing women's security in the older years. This is echoed as well by Perkins (1993), to which we shall return.

Caring work, to a degree, constructs women's lives in families as dependent, and, in the wider world, as secondary workers. Reitsma-Street (1991) finds, through an examination of the lives of delinquent girls and their self-perceptions, that girls tend to be "policed" to care, coerced into caring for others to the neglect of themselves, and expected to bear the costs associated with caring. Resisting the ways in which girls are expected to care is resisting the very definition of femininity in our society, suggests Reitsma-Street. Being labelled unfeminine is being labelled uncaring, selfish, aggressive, competitive with boys rather than supportive of them, and deviant. For delinquent girls, learning to be good (i.e., non-delinquent) is learning to be caring.

The compulsion for women to care continues well into adulthood. It is the means by which mid-life families—a euphemism for women—take on more and more social responsibility. They may care for youth having difficulty finding jobs or maintaining families on their own. Some may return to the mid-life family "nest." Women care for older people who have fewer options for professional care or institutional living with cutbacks to these programs. And they care for mid-life peers (spouses, siblings, friends, etc.) who are suffering job insecurity. Keating et al. (1999), Michelson and Tepperman (2003), and Statistics Canada (2004a; 2004b) confirm that, in Canada, women predominate in caregiving to elders. American research reflects the same trend (Navaie-Waliser, Spriggs, and Feldman, 2002; Navaie-Waliser et al., 2002). McDaniel and McKinnon (1993) as well as Michelson and Tepperman (2003) find, with different data, that it is women, most often mid-life women, who are called upon differentially to do the "caring for" older relatives, regardless of the cost to themselves and the disruption to their own lives and employment prospects. A study of women aged 45 and over in Alberta who have ever had a child (including an adopted child) finds that 60.0% of women in middle-age considered quitting their jobs because of family responsibilities (McDaniel, 1996). Tensions are high indeed for women in mid-life.

Women, particularly mid-life women, may work extra hard at family caring when times get tough in the economy, as well as work harder in the workplace to prevent economic problems from besieging their families. The gendered dimensions of family caring and its implications for full participation in society are only beginning to be examined (Orloff, 1993; Phipps, Burton, and Osberg, 2001; Navaie-Waliser, Spriggs, and Feldman, 2002). In analysis of data from the 1990 General Social Survey, Phipps and colleagues (2001) find that, due to the gendered structure of work within dual-earner households, women face a time inequality. Women are therefore more time-stressed and less satisfied with leisure time than are men. Much more research is needed on the ways in which families in mid-life work out competing demands on their time and resources.

Mid-life women often complain that they may not be best suited to provide caregiving to older relatives, but that there is little (or no) alternative. Findings, again from the author's own research, reveal compellingly that people in mid-life often do not see family care as their own preferred option when they become old and frail. Instead, they would prefer professional home care or institutional care (McDaniel, 1999). Similar findings are reported in a study in Oslo, Norway (Daatland, 1990). Two themes recur in responses to the question of preference for care when old and frail. The first is the familiar, "I don't want to be a burden to my family." The second is a concern likely to increase in degree and volume as more of the baby boom generation enters mid-life: that professional care is preferred to amateur care, whenever possible. Yet the demand persists for family members to care out of concern and consideration for others, against their own rational self-interest. The pay is certainly poor, in material terms at least, and the hours long and tedious. Caregivers note, however, that they receive rewards beyond the monetary.

Policies, both public and private, and the roles of mid-life families in caregiving are being given a second look in these early years of the 21st century (McDaniel and Gee,

1993; Keating et al., 1999; Hirst, 2001). On the one hand, caregiving is being examined as work that is very beneficial to society, even though it is as often unpaid (Brubaker and Brubaker, 1992; Orloff, 1993). On the other hand, economic constraints on the public purse have created greater needs for caregiving, since more people need care and are not getting what they need from the formal system (McDaniel and Chappell, 1999; Statistics Canada, 2004). Thus, caregiving has been thrust onto the stage of public policy as one of the fundamental social policy challenges facing Western societies in the early 21st century (Liebig, 1993; Conference Board of Canada, 1999).

SOCIAL POLICIES, ENTITLEMENT, AND GENDER IN MID-LIFE FAMILIES

Social policies developed for caregiving in Canada have focused almost completely on the person in need of care, with almost no attention to the caregiver. Sometimes, the criteria for eligibility encourage families to live apart rather than together (Gee and McDaniel, 1992). The material cost is so salient in discussions about programs that it is at times forgotten that caregiving is costly in human terms to all who do it, regardless of income level (Zukewich, 2003). **Caregiver "burnout"**—the accumulated stress that can occur in situations where one is on call 24 hours a day, every day, facing demanding eldercare—can result (Keating et al., 1999). If the primary caregiver is overstressed and ill or disabled, then two people are in need of health care. No one benefits, least of all the taxpayer (Franklin and Rossi, 2001).

Social policies work in such a way as to reproduce the familial model of women's dependency. Women, for example, more often make claims on social programs as a result of family breakdown than of unemployment. The state (governments) then becomes the substitute "breadwinner" for the family. Women on social assistance are often treated, according to Fraser (1987), as irresponsible semi-adults in need of constant monitoring and justification of what they do with their money. This is, of course, sharply reminiscent of the widows in Halifax in the 1920s, mentioned earlier. Often the monitoring retains a moral tone as well in this new century, so that a woman on social assistance is expected to be "faithful" to the state and not have a man, or men, in her life. Should there be evidence of a man in her life—the infamous search for the men's shoes under the bed by social workers—then that man is expected to support her and her children. An individual man's support then is substituted for by state support at times of dire need. Gender structures of familial and patriarchal dependency are thereby reinforced, and gender inequalities in families and in society made normative.

As Orloff (1993) and others (McDaniel, 2000a) have pointed out, threats to universality in public programs such as family allowances, pensions, and now even health care, differentially disadvantage women. This is because women have not had and continue not to have equal access to opportunities in the labour market and to be disadvantaged by their family status and gender. And this disadvantage peaks in mid-life for women. Thus, women's claims on public programs as workers tend to be much more tenuous than those of men for multiple reasons, including women's more discontinuous career paths, lesser access to workplace benefits programs, and lower incomes. Women's claims on programs as family members—e.g., single mothers with dependent children, displaced homemakers, divorced pensioners, etc.—also become tenuous in terms of public questioning of the legitimacy of these familial entitlements (McDaniel, 1993b; Orloff, 1993: 308). The presumption seems to be that women and men are equally able to take full advantage of the opportunities offered by the labour market, a presumption that simply is not borne out by the facts of women's and men's continued income and labour market patterns. Orloff argues that

> one must take into account the very real gender differences in productive and reproductive labor and access to civil and political rights and how these differences influence the ways in which men and women struggle for and claim benefits from the state as citizens
>
> Orloff, 1993: 309.

In mid-life, these gendered aspects of policy entitlements come into fuller play, as men's and women's different experiences in the labour market and in families accumulate. Men tend to accumulate advantages in *both* the labour market (promotions, job security, job benefits) *and* families (family men are seen as stable, motivated, more secure risks, while the opposite is true for family women) (McDaniel, 2004). Women in families in mid-life may have their labour market participation further compromised by being encouraged or pressured into taking early retirement, often without access to private pensions, because their husbands are retiring.

As well, the particular demands of aging relatives, as has been seen, fall differentially on women in mid-life, adding even more to the family demands placed on them and compromising further, as has also been seen, their labour market opportunities. Most, if not all, of these inequities remain invisible in the public policy sector, which contrary to these realities, tends to be moving more, rather than less, in the direction of denying the existence of gender inequities, and basing program entitlements more firmly on need (usually closely tied to labour market success/failure) and less on entitlement by family membership or citizenship. Thus, gender inequities in mid-life families are being exacerbated.

WORK, WORK-LEAVING, AND RETIREMENT FOR MID-LIFE AND OLDER FAMILIES

Work is a central concern of mid-life families, more so today than perhaps ever before. The widespread assumption that, in recent years, the workplace has become more gender neutral, or certainly less gender unequal, has accompanied the view that, with age, gender inequities in the labour market tend to decrease or disappear. Realities belie these perceptions. Strong evidence is emerging that the gender division of labour in the workplace not only is *not* declining in Canada, but, in fact, that it may be being consolidated and even growing (Boyd, Mulvihill, and Myles, 1991; Statistics Canada, 1999). These tendencies not only add to the traditional gender division of labour at work, but, very importantly, reinforce women's economic dependency in families (Boyd, Mulvihill, and Myles, 1991). This is a result of women's greater need for family support (spousal or other) as their labour market status becomes more tentative. The shift to part-time employment as a means to enable women to combine family and work adds to women's reduced status in *both* work and family (Duffy and Pupo, 1992; Orloff, 1993).

In the massive restructuring of the Canadian economy in recent years, the pattern of job loss (which is not the same thing as unemployment), is very much age-structured. Findings from the author's research have shown that a significant proportion (one-half to two-thirds) of the 3/4 million workers *displaced* from their jobs in the 1990s are, in fact, in mid-life (between the ages of 45 and 64), what industry refers to as either early retirement or attrition (McDaniel, 2003). It may be neither. Many people in mid-life have found themselves without work, without pensions or real opportunities for future full-time, secure work with benefits. Mid-life workers tend to remain unemployed for considerably longer periods than younger workers. The dynamics of transitions into and out of the paid workforce by mid-life workers are only now beginning to be examined, with the implications for women barely touched (McDaniel, 1996; Policy Research Initiative, 2004). Indications from a qualitative study by the author of unemployed middle-managers are that women face transitions out of work with more stable attitudes than do men (McDaniel, 2003). One mid-life unemployed woman who was a middle manager said that, in her view, the transition from employment to unemployment "was done better by us [women] than by them [men]." Men, much more often than women, expressed deep concerns about their family identities as breadwinners being compromised with job loss. Retirement can pose similar crises in identity for men (McDaniel, 2003). Mid-life women, on the other hand, when faced with losing employment, tended to report that they would take any job anywhere in order to support their families.

A great amount of uncertainty is being felt by mid-life people about their futures, as is evident in Table 9.2. Women report feeling particularly unprepared for retirement.

TABLE 9.2 The Quandaries of Those in Mid-Life in Canada in 2002

Who are they?
6 million people aged 45-59, including a significant proportion of baby boomers

Retirement?
About 12% do not know when, or if, they will retire
An additional 18% said that they did not intend ever to retire

When to retire?

Before age 60:	22%
60-64:	22%
At 65:	23%
After 65:	3%

Prepared?
1/3 said no—inadequate financial arrangements
33% of women said financial preparations were inadequate compared to 29% of men

Source: Statistics Canada (2003). "General Social Survey: Social Support and Aging." *The Daily* 2 September 2003. www.statcan.ca/Daily/English/030902/do30902a.htm

At the point when mid-life families are under the most intense family demands, they often face the greatest threat of job loss or economic insecurity, and are struggling to plan for retirement (Policy Research Initiative, 2004; Statistics Canada, 2003c). This means that the already intense demands on women for emotional as well as other kinds of support become even more intense. It also means that mid-life family members who have done everything according to social expectations, may be hard hit indeed by economic restructuring. One respondent in the author's research, a displaced worker in his 40's, reported that he never dreamed that he, of all people, would be out of work (McDaniel, 2003). He had previously worked in a technical occupation, one supposedly in high demand, had been very good at it, and had been with the same employer since he graduated from school. He felt that he was under much more stress as a result of his job loss than someone who had lower expectations and lesser skills. Analysis of how these situations in the workplace play out in mid-life families is continuing, but there can be little doubt that the impacts are being felt.

There is also a growing recognition of the need for employers to be sensitive to the family responsibilities that mid-life employees face. Among those retiring by choice in Canada in 2002, 7% did so to care for a family member (Policy Research Initiative, 2004: 18). Among those retirees who would have stayed employed, 9.7% retired to provide care. Some U. S. companies have started to provide caregiver benefits (Franklin and Rossi, 2001). The most common form of benefit offered by American companies is also, not surprisingly, the most inexpensive; that is, the provision of information and referral services to caregivers (Seaward, 1999). The Conference Board of Canada (1999) notes that one in four working Canadians provide care or support to someone in their household, with a

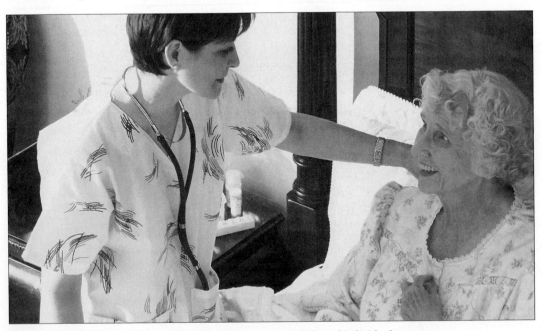

Caregiving arrangements for the elderly are often the responsibility of individual women.

full 25% providing time-consuming personal care, with significant direct costs associated with absenteeism from work caused by the demands of caring.

The conjunction of these factors in mid-life families has a number of implications. First, there are aspects of gender justice whereby women are thought to be equal and society acts as if this were true, while socio-economic changes work *against* women's equality both in families and in the wider society. These issues are explored in depth by Kirp, Yudof, and Franks (1986) and Orloff (1993), among others. Individual women in mid-life families become the elastic cuffs between perceptions and economic realities: They pick up the bits and pieces not covered by the paid labour market, as women always have in families.

There is a need for attention to the relation of family to work among those in mid-life, an area which has received scant attention. Some see a clash of two major demographic trends: the growth in the old elderly population (the so called **"frail elderly"**), and increases in the numbers and proportions of women who work outside the home. Yet this clash, if it exists, is being ignored by both employers and policy-makers. Those who recognize the problem tend to define it as a "women's issue," requiring better adaption to the new realities by mid-life women in families. Individual women, in the absence of workplace policies, are bearing the caregiving load for both young and old. About 6% of women say that they would have continued in paid work, but left instead because of the demands of caregiving and the lack of suitable options (Policy Research Initiative, 2004: 19). "Relying on unpaid caregivers becomes a primary way to control costs, yet it is done under the guise of protecting women's presumed care-giving nature" (Seccombe, 1992: 179). This works doubly to assist the public purse: capitalizing on women's "volunteer" labour, and at the same time, reducing the eligibility of the older relative for professional care by making family care the first recourse. Seccombe compellingly argues that workplace and community care policies presume traditional concepts of family, of femininity, and of limited government involvement in matters that are familial. Neysmith (1989) makes a similar argument.

CONCLUSION

From this overview of the family lives of the middle-aged and elderly, it is clear that much more attention should be given to the rapidly changing situations of Canadian families in these age groups. The challenges faced by mid-life families are many. They are coping with the increased demands of caregiving, with challenges in balancing family and work, and with increased dependency of younger relatives who are finding it more difficult to establish their own households and incomes. All this means that families in middle age, and even elderly families, face more demands. Much more needs to be known about how different kinds of families—single-parent families, blended families, families with older generations in other countries, those living common-law over the long term, and gay/lesbian families—live in mid-life and the older years. What are the stresses and rewards they experience? What supports do they have or need to have? How different are the experiences of various family types across the life course? How many different family types do people experience over their lives? These questions, and many others, remain largely unanswered thus far by social science research.

The template of the past is being rapidly dissolved, and nowhere are the changes more visible than among those in mid-life in the 2000s. This is an age group that has transformed every social institution with which it has had contact, from families of the 1950s and 1960s, to schools and universities in the late 1960s and 1970s, to music, to the very concepts of middle age. It is not surprising then that new ways to live in families in mid-life are emerging, bringing further changes in the ways that families in middle age and later relate to social policy, to the workplace, to other families, and to each other. Those changes are becoming apparent, such as the growth in age-restricted housing complexes that prohibit those under age 18 or 45 or 55, or in the immensely popular recreational vehicle market, where early retirees become perpetual migrants without any permanent home. At the same time as the responsibilities of and for family members are being familized, more families in middle life seem to be fleeing, either geographically or with the assistance of structural barriers such as age-restricted housing, from a family-centred old-age.

Relations between policy and families, and employers and families have emerged from presumptions about what families are or should be, what they do or should do for society, and the power of these expectations to shape individual experiences of family. We need to know more about families as they age, about how they live and change with time, and about what new challenges they face in an aging society.

Suggested Readings

Keating, Norah, Janet Fast, Judith Frederick, Kelly Cranswick, and Cathryn Perrier (1999). *Eldercare in Canada: Context, Content and Consequences*. Ottawa: Statistics Canada. Catalogue no. 89-570-XPE.

Kemp, Candace and Margaret Denton (2003). "The Allocation of Responsibility for Later Life: Canadian Reflections on the Roles of Individuals, Government and Families." *Ageing and Society* 23(6): 737–760.

McDaniel, Susan A. (1999). "Untangling Love and Domination: Challenges of Home Care for the Elderly in a Reconstructing Canada." *Journal of Canadian Studies* 34(3): 191–213.

Michelson, William and Lorne Tepperman (2003). "Focus on Home: What Time-Use Data Can Tell About Caregiving to Adults." *Journal of Social Issues* 59(3): 591–610.

Mitchell, Barbara A., Andrew V. Wister, and Ellen M.Gee (2002). "There's no place like home: An analysis of young adults' mature coresidency in Canada." *International Journal of Aging and Human Development* 54(1): 1–28.

Tate, Robert, Leedine Lah, and Edward Cuddy (2003). "Definition of successful aging by elderly Canadian males: The Manitoba follow-up study." *The Gerontologist* 43(5): 735–744.

van den Hoonaard, Deborah K. (2002). "Attitudes of Older Widows and Widowers in New Brunswick, Canada Towards New Partnerships." *Ageing International* 27(4): 79–92.

Zukewich, Nancy (2003). "Unpaid Informal Caregiving." *Canadian Social Trends* 70(Fall): 14–18. Statistics Canada catalogue no. 11-008.

Web Resources

A wealth of information for older persons, their families, and people interested in aging.
www.aoa.dhhs.gov

The sites sponsored by the Association of Retired Persons (ARP), the Andrus Foundation, and the National Center on Women and Aging feature cutting-edge, high quality, and timely research studies concerning monetary issues related to aging and families.
   www.aarp.org
   www.nhcoa.org/andrus_foundation.html
   www.heller.brandeis.edu/national
Modern Maturity is an accessible magazine for seniors, with many useful articles related to families.
   www.aarp.org/mmaturity.home.html
The Statistics Canada Web site provides all recent publicly available Statistics Canada data, including census tables from various surveys on family, and on aging. **www.statcan.ca**

Endnotes

[1] The author appreciates suggestions from Maureen Baker, readers of the 4th edition as well as the anonymous reviewers. Kara Granzow's help is appreciated.

PART FOUR

Families, Laws, and Policies

CHAPTER TEN

Divorce and Repartnering

Zheng Wu and Christoph Schimmele

INTRODUCTION

In her groundbreaking treatise detailing the malaise of 1950s suburban life, Betty Friedan (1963), an American feminist author and co-founder of the National Organization for Women, offers a compelling argument that traditional marriage amounted to a "comfortable concentration camp" for millions of middle-class housewives. Although controversial, Friedan's book reached a large audience, and embodied the thoughts and feelings of women across North America by cogently expressing their mass disillusionment with being confined to domestic roles. Indeed, the women of Friedan's generation were expected to achieve personal fulfilment through being housewives and mothers, and the institution of marriage was more or less premised upon this oppressive social norm. The virtual absence of women's access to fair divorce laws paralleled their social subordination and restricted opportunities outside the household. As detailed below, the enactment of "no-fault" divorce legislation thus represented a watershed for equal opportunity, and these widespread legislative reforms cannot be understood without reference to the broad social changes that unfolded in North America after World War II.

Today, divorce, remarriage, and **blended families** are normal life experiences in most advanced industrial societies. But the divorce and remarriage rates in Canada and numerous other advanced industrial countries only began to move rapidly toward their current levels after 1965. This acute, cross-national intensification of divorce and repartnering prompted a surge of scholarly research and public concern, and many people now consider the divorce and repartnering rates a barometer for the general meaning and purpose of marital and family relationships. Sociologists, family counsellors, divorce lawyers, and policy-makers recognize that divorce is a multi-stage process of family disruption and reorientation, not simply a discrete event, and comprises marital conflict, separation, legal dissolution, post-divorce adjustment and problems, and the formation of diverse family relationships and households. The present chapter provides a précis of divorce and remarriage research. Our focal topics cover the historical reasons for widespread divorce, the main interpretations and consequences of divorce, and the post-divorce repartnering process.

HISTORICAL PERSPECTIVE

Roderick Phillips (1988), a well-noted historical expert on divorce, points out that most Britons and Canadians could not dissolve their marital unions through a legal process prior to the 19th century because of inconsistent marriage regulations and inaccessible divorce legislation. Before 1753, the English state ineffectively regulated the formation of marriages, and thus legal divorce was practically impossible. The passage of Lord Chancellor Hardwicke's Marriage Act (1753) in England, which Canada eventually adopted, created the first uniform legal code regulating the formation of marriage, obviously a necessary precondition for divorce legislation. Until 1857, English law contained no provisions for divorce except through a private Act of Parliament. This method of divorce involved a lengthy, complicated, and expensive procedure, making legal divorce a privilege of the upper classes, and of men in particular. For example, a husband could obtain a divorce by proving simple adultery, but a woman had to prove her husband guilty of aggravated adultery involving bigamy, incest, sodomy, or rape. Given these limitations, divorces by a private Act of Parliament were rarely granted, numbering between 3–53 per annum from 1700–1857.

In 1857, the first English divorce legislation was enacted, transferring control over divorce from Parliament to a newly established Court for Divorce and Matrimonial Causes. The grounds for divorce remained highly conservative, but the new legislation made divorce a much less complicated and expensive process, thus providing the middle classes legal recourse for terminating troubled marriages. The secularization of divorce proved to be especially beneficial for women. Freed from the chauvinism of the Ecclesiastical Courts—only four women obtained a parliamentary divorce from 1670–1857—the new legislation was a significant social reform, even though women petitioning for divorce still had to prove their husbands guilty of aggravated adultery. However, despite this double standard and other social and economic restrictions, the 1857 reform represents an important turning point in women's legal access to divorce. To illustrate: English women obtained 42 percent of all legal divorces granted between 1859 and 1909. By comparison, women obtained a mere one percent of the legal divorces granted through Parliament between 1670 and 1857. As Phillips outlines, the English legislation was globally influential because it became the model for divorce reform throughout the British Empire.

By present expectations, the low divorce rate in the Victorian era—an annual average of between 3–39 divorces were granted in Canada from 1871 to 1910—seems incomprehensible, and reflected women's oppression under common law (Pike, 1975). Marriage was "civil death" for women living in the Victorian period, stripping wives of their property rights, a good measure of systemic gender disparities (Chambers, 1997). In 1860, the Chief Justice of Ontario reinforced the "broad wisdom" of the common law, proclaiming that marriage involved an "absolute gift in law" of the bride's property to the groom (Backhouse, 1988). A woman's "legal identity was obliterated at marriage and she was entirely under the power and control of her husband" (Chambers, 1997: 3). A married woman "could not hold, use, or dispose of property, whether land, money, chattels, or wages earned by her own labour" (ibid). Although various married women's property acts reformed substantially the common law by the 20th century, and represented crucial victories for women, this legislation was not drafted to give married women economic independence, but to protect married women's property from misuse by husbands and to provide relief to abandoned wives (Arnup, 2001).

Married women's loss of property rights epitomized the meaning of marriage. The common-law doctrine of coverture, or marital unity, was framed by the attitude that married women were subordinate to their husbands. In 1803, Sir William Blackstone summarized the dominant perception of what marriage represented: "By marriage the husband and wife are one person in law: that is, the very being or legal existence of the woman is suspended during the marriage, or at least incorporated and consolidated into that of the husband: under whose wing, protection, and cover she performs everything." Marriage was more or less an economic contract based on inflexible gender-specific duties and expectations, and individual economic security was ensured primarily via the family economy. Such practical considerations guided the choice of first spouse and the timing of remarriage (Phillips, 1988). Before the 20th century, economic interdependence was a strong disincentive to divorce for either spouse, but especially for women. Even if a divorced woman could find employment, she would receive barely a subsistence wage, implying that divorced mothers could not earn enough to financially support their children. The prospect of economic hardship prevented large numbers of wives from leaving troubled marriages.

Canadian legal standards and social attitudes regarding divorce remained highly restrictive before World War II (Pike, 1975). Charting Canadian divorce behaviour from 1900–39, James Snell (1991) argues that negative attitudes toward divorce within the public culture were based on an idealized image of what marriage represented for the state and society. E. A. Lancaster, a Conservative MP, captured the public sentiment toward marital breakdown in 1905, remarking that the "whole social fabric of the country would go to pieces" if divorce legislation were liberalized. According to this perspective, marriage was a cornerstone of national social and economic welfare. Many public policies were formulated to reward individuals for living inside the idealized family and to police those considering alternatives, especially divorce. Canadian policy-makers considered divorce a threat to the social and economic order because it graphically illustrated how the day-to-day realities of marriages often contradicted the idealized family (Snell, 1991). In this respect, restrictive divorce legislation was a mechanism for reinforcing the marriage-centred family paradigm structured around Christian morals and patriarchical authority.

THE DIVORCE REVOLUTION

Until national reforms, conservative divorce legislation suppressed the Canadian divorce rate. In 1925, the first time women could petition for divorce on the grounds of simple adultery, far less than one percent of marriages ended through legal dissolution (Sev'er, 1992). The 1968 divorce rate was almost 10 times higher than the 1925 rate. The first federal Divorce Act was enacted in 1968, marking the threshold of the divorce revolution.

Around 55 of every 1000 marriages were legally dissolved in 1968. The following year around 124 of every 1000 marriages ended in divorce, a 225 percent increase. The divorce rate continued to grow rapidly throughout following decades. By 1980, close to 260 of every 1000 marriages ended in divorce. The liberalization of divorce laws was indisputably a necessary condition for this pattern of growth to obtain, but was not a sufficient condition for mass divorce. Liberal divorce legislation *enabled* the divorce revolution, but the massive increase in the divorce rate after 1968 represented a built-up demand for divorce. The divorce spike of 1969 suggests that many married people wanted to get divorced well before 1968 but could not because of the conservative legislation.

The new legislation was the state's response to *public demand* for liberal access to divorce. The increase in public demand for divorce corresponds to a transformation of the meaning of marriage and the family. Even though most Canadians are married or expect eventually to be married, only a small portion believe that marriage constitutes a permanent, life-long arrangement. The radical shift in attitudes toward marriage emerged from a broad pattern of social and economic transition. Eighteenth century philosophies on freedom of choice and rational thought provided the intellectual foundation for these changes. However, the widespread movement toward individual autonomy did not occur until these liberal ideals intersected with the economic boom after World War II. Post-War demographic change signalled the disintegration of traditional attitudes (Phillips, 1988). Pressured by new attitudes, policy-makers in most advanced industrial countries substantially revised or reformed divorce legislation between 1960 and 1980, thus making legal divorce accessible to the masses. As outlined below, the attitudes behind the second demographic transition are rooted in several interrelated social and economic changes.

Ideational Change. Many 18th century philosophers considered traditional values and institutions a source of inequality because they suppressed individual freedom. Early feminist movements invoked philosophies from the French Revolution to challenge patriarchical dominance, arguing that the common law violated women's natural right of freedom. Mary Wollstonecraft (1759–97), a pioneer of feminism, insisted that marriage was a social contract, or partnership, between husband and wife. According to Wollstonecraft, good marriages and social progress required equal rights for women. Thus, marriages based on husbands' ownership of wives were unstable, and poor environments for educating children to be good citizens. Although English common law remained conservative well after Wollstonecraft's death, across the Atlantic the refusal of English rule sparked a broader social distaste for external control over individual liberty. As the American Revolution embraced anti-authoritarian ideals, many Americans started to view marriage as a private and *dissolvable* social contract between individuals (Basch, 1999). Indeed, many states passed divorce legislation during this period. Moreover, the libertarian culture embodied by the American Revolution is a plausible reason why Americans historically have divorced in greater numbers than Europeans and Canadians.

Women's Rights. Flowing from 19th century liberalism, the Suffrage Movement (first-wave feminism) was a watershed for women's rights. The struggle for voting rights was the central dimension of Women's Suffrage movements, but these campaigns questioned women's subjugation within civil society in numerous other respects. The Suffragettes fought for enfranchisement because voting represented the gateway to full political participation. But these women also campaigned for fair access to education, more skilled labour market opportunities, better working conditions, equal wages for equal work, and common-law reforms. Although difficult to measure, the Suffrage Movement certainly contributed to the reform of divorce legislation. Although enfranchisement did not fundamentally alter the androcentric power structure within the state, women's suffrage signified a broad change in normative attitudes on women's "appropriate" role in the social order. Winning the right to vote and stand for political office gave women the chance to participate in activities outside the domestic sphere, particularly in the labour market. In this respect, enfranchisement provided women with career alternatives to wifehood and motherhood. These improved socio-economic opportunities would eventually give women financial independence from men, a crucial factor behind mass divorce.

Socio-economic Change. Karl Marx believed that the ideas of the ruling class are the ideas that govern society in every epoch. This notion suggests a reciprocal relationship between the organization of economic production and normative behaviour. According to this logic, an economy structured around family-based production and consumption will generate norms and values that support marriage and discourage divorce. Until recently, the traditional family constituted a family economy founded on mutual dependence between husbands and wives, formed through gender-specific responsibilities and expectations and school-age children's labour inputs. Various 19th century policies illustrated the national importance of the family economy by enforcing the breadwinner versus homemaker mentality (Phillips, 1988). However, the post-War economic boom (1946–72) redefined the meaning of marriage by weakening the economic constraints on divorce. Across North America, employment, advanced education, and economic production grew at unparalleled rates, propelling vast numbers of Canadians into the middle classes. Moreover, the new affluence encouraged government management of national economies (Keynesianism), and most advanced industrial countries developed welfare programs to underwrite national economic security (Bumsted, 1992). The Canadian divorce rate doubled from 1945 to 1965, in part because of improved socio-economic mobility.

Women's Employment. Talcott Parsons (1959) argued that a gender division of labour is crucial for marital stability, and therefore believed that labour force participation among married women could trigger divorce. Gary Becker's (1977, 1981) *New Home Economics* extrapolated this argument from an economic perspective. Becker hypothesized that the primary gain from marriage comes from the social exchange necessitated by mutual economic dependence between marital partners. Put differently, a woman's incentive to get married (or remain married) progressively declines as her financial independence increases. Opponents of the *New Home Economics* contend that women's paid employment does not actually destabilize marriages, but simply makes divorce a financially viable option for women in bad marriages (Schoen, 2002). Well before these theorists, historians publishing in the early 20th century recognized that women's access to paid labour opened the door to marital separation (Cherlin, 1992). Millions of women replaced men's labour during wartime, particularly in the industrial sector, but the turning point arrived with the post-War economic boom, which greatly expanded educational and labour market opportunities for women. Women's labour market participation was additionally facilitated by equal opportunity legislation and necessitated by the deterioration of the family wage (Sayer and Bianchi, 2000). In brief, the divorce rate increased as women joined the paid labour force in greater numbers because financial autonomy empowered women to abandon *failed* marriages. This implies that 19th century divorce rates were comparatively low because of women's financial dependence, not because marriages were better.

As Inglehart (1977) observes, advanced industrial societies generally shifted from prioritizing economic security and material goals toward a value system emphasizing the need for belonging, self-esteem, and self-realization. A re-evaluation of the relevance of institutional arrangements followed this value change. "As emotional gratification became the [essential criterion] of marriage," writes Furstenberg (1990: 380), "divorce became an indispensable element in the institution of matrimony, permitting couples to rectify poor choices." Liberal attitudes toward various family issues concretized from the 1960s onward (Thornton and Young-DeMarco, 2001). Today, people's attitudes still harbour a strong commitment to marriage and the family, but the meaning of marriage is different nevertheless. Informed by libertarian ideals, most people believe that marriage is a *voluntary* institution, and thus overwhelmingly reject the traditional notion that divorce is rarely, if ever, justifiable. The cultural emphasis on individual rights influenced the enactment of **no-fault divorce** legislation in most advanced industrial societies (Fine and Fine, 1994). The introduction of no-fault divorce legislation, as detailed below, triggered the divorce revolution.

MICRO-LEVEL DIFFERENCES IN DIVORCE

The previous sections examined the structural (macro-level forces) reasons for the divorce revolution. Although these macro-level factors provide the universal opportunity for divorce, the individual responses to these forces are not uniform across social groups. Recent theory and research identify several individual-level characteristics associated with the probability of divorce. This section outlines these differences.

Children. In Canada, the risk of marital disruption is greatest during the first several years of marriage, peaking around the four to five year mark, and then begins to subside (Duchesne et al., 1999). One reason marital instability decreases over time is that marriages based on high quality relationships survive longer durations whereas poor unions quickly dissolve (Morgan, Lye, and Condran, 1988). Other reasons for marital stability can emerge over time, and these effectively counteract problems that could otherwise cause divorce. Parenthood is a major reason for marital stability. Children represent *marriage-specific* capital because the value of investments into parenthood depreciates after divorce and is not easily transferable to another marriage (Becker, 1981). Children improve marital stability because parents want to protect their human capital investments in their children. Further, as Emile Durkheim (1984) argued, the gender-based allocation of childcare responsibilities increases sex-role specialization within marriage, and this constitutes a condition of mutual dependence (marital solidarity) between parents, a robust deterrent against divorce. As Lillard and Waite spell out: "To the extent that children increase the real or psychic costs of divorce or create a long-lasting bond between parents, couples that have ever had children will have more stable marriages than childless couples" (1991: 934). Note, however, that even though children improve marital stability, this does not occur by boosting marital satisfaction. A married couple with children can be unhappier than a married couple without children, but still have a more "stable" marriage because investments in their children counteract personal reasons for divorce.

The child's gender and age are important moderating factors in parenthood's intensification of marital stability. Sons and daughters may foster an additional level of gender differentiation in child-rearing expectations and duties (Morgan et al., 1988). Fathers are expected to be role models for their sons, teaching them behaviours specific to the male gender. Likewise, mothers are expected to be role models for their daughters. These child-rearing norms suggest that, since fathers spend considerably more time socializing their sons than their daughters, this deeper relationship might build a comparatively strong father-son bond. Given maternal preference in child custody arrangements, a boy-child discourages divorce more so than a girl-child because separation jeopardizes the father-son relationship. Preschool children especially discourage marital disruption because young children require more intense care than older children (Waite and Lillard, 1991). Sex-role specialization among parents is most complete when children are young because mothers engage in domestic roles to the greatest extent when their children are young. Children's dependence on full-time parental care decreases as schooling and friendships substitute for parental time.

Socio-economic Status. The relationship between socio-economic status and divorce is gender-specific. Among husbands, high socio-economic status is generally associated with a lower risk of marital disruption. Becker (1981) argues that the mate selection process and marital behaviour resemble trading in the marketplace. According to this logic, a man and women agree to marriage because both parties benefit from trading one another's specialized skills. Husbands specialize in paid labour and wives specialize in domestic production and reproduction. Husbands trade their market earnings for the domestic services their wives provide. Both spouses gain from marriage because sex-role specialization produces a household economy based on comparative advantage (or welfare maximization) and mutual economic dependence. The gender division of labour, then, discourages marital disruption. A husband's wage-earning potential matters because the gender division of labour is incomplete unless his income covers all the financial needs of the household. The collapse of the family wage is a significant factor in mass divorce because this economic shift shattered the traditional division of labour by pushing wives into the labour market. Women's benefits from marriage decrease when they are wage-earners faced with an unfair household division of labour (Frisco and Williams, 2003). As noted above, women's economic independence is a primary reason for the divorce revolution.

Premarital Cohabitation. Spouses who cohabited before marriage have a higher risk of divorce than spouses who did not cohabit before marriage (Balakrishnan et al., 1987). This finding seems counterintuitive because, as a "trial" marriage, cohabitation presumably should screen out the poor matches, selecting mostly couples with durable relationships into marriage. The basic explanation for this counterintuitive finding gravitates around the non-traditional attitudes prevalent among cohabitors. Most pre-marital cohabitors choose non-marital unions to begin with because they perceive themselves as poor risks for stable relationships (Thomson and Colella, 1992). Cohabitors also define marriage in comparatively unconventional terms, perceiving marriage in more individualistic terms than in couple, altruistic, or religious terms. The transient nature of cohabitational relationships can undermine the notion that intimate relationships are necessarily lasting and permanent (Wu, 2000). These attitudes suggest that premarital cohabitation selects individuals with a higher tendency to resort to divorce when marital problems impinge upon their personal needs, happiness, and expectations.

Heterogamy. Heterogamous marriages are less stable than marriages between spouses with similar personal characteristics, attitudes, and social backgrounds. Marriages in which the spouses are markedly different in age, educational attainment, occupational status, religion, or ethnic status are at higher risk of marital disruption (Janssen and De Graaf, 2000). Heterogamy in age, education, and religion are the most serious causes of marital instability. The reason why these marriages are relatively more unstable is associated with the fragile bases of consensus and commonality within these unions. Most men marry women who are two to three years younger than themselves. Couples who significantly contravene this age convention tend to have unstable marriages (Tzeng, 1992). This age effect is greatest when the wife is substantially older than her husband because this difference alters the traditional marital power structure. Wide differences in educational attainment also increase the risk of divorce because education reflects an individual's values, attitudes, and social background. Large social differences alienate spouses from one another and generate marital conflict. For example, a woman with an education far beneath her husband's may feel estranged from his social network. Social conventions reinforce homogenous marriages, especially in regards to religion, ethnicity, and social class, and couples that seriously violate these norms tend to be stigmatized, which destabilizes their marriages. On the other hand, people with homogenous social backgrounds share an interconnection through shared religious and ethnic communities that solidify the marital bond (Udry, 1974).

CANADIAN DIVORCE LAW

In 1968, the Canadian government implemented the Divorce Act, legislation that made the procedures and grounds for divorce uniform across Canada. Critically outlined in papers prepared for the Law Reform Commission of Canada (1975), the 1968 legislation established two principles for legal marital dissolution.

1. *The "Fault" Principle*. This provision for divorce codified traditional grounds for divorce. Section 3 of the 1968 Divorce Act lists the various matrimonial offences considered grounds for divorce. These grounds, which petitioners for divorce had to prove their spouse committed, included adultery, sodomy, bestiality, rape, or homosexual act; going through a form of marriage with another person; and intolerable physical or mental cruelty.

2.   *Marital Breakdown*. Section 4 of the 1968 Divorce Act provides supplementary grounds for divorce based on the following circumstances: the imprisonment of the petitioner's spouse; gross addiction of the petitioner's spouse to drugs or alcohol for at least three years; disappearance of the petitioner's spouse for three years or more; non-consummation of the marriage; living separately for three years for reasons other than the petitioner's desertion of his/her spouse; living separate for five years by the petitioner deserting his/her spouse.

In 1975, the Law Reform Commission challenged these grounds for divorce, and posed the question whether the legislation should be reformed to amend the fault grounds (Section 3) and introduce divorce by consent and unilateral demand. These legal scholars concluded that Section 3 should be repealed because judicial interpretation of matrimonial offences can dismiss divorce petitions on unreasonable grounds. For example, the Commission referred to a case in which a female petitioner was refused a divorce on the grounds of cruelty because of insufficient evidence proving that the cruelty was intolerable. In addition, a member of the Commission argued that divorce by consent, which was practised before the Church enforced dogma on the indissolubility of marriage, made common sense. The Commission agreed that the family was the basis of the social order, but insisted that couples should be able to terminate irreconcilable marriages through a non-acrimonious process. Pointing out that 90 percent of divorces are uncontested, the Commission observed that official recognition of the no-fault principle would give the courts more time to focus on more significant issues, such as **child custody**, maintenance, and property division.

The Commission also criticized the Divorce Act for not providing coherent guidelines for maintenance, and offered several principles for legislative reform. The Commission insisted on gender-neutrality before the law, and remarked that marriage per se does not create the right to maintenance. However, recognizing gender inequalities within marriages, the Commission argued that the right to maintenance should follow the internal arrangements of the marital union. Hence, to determine the right to maintenance, the courts had to consider factors such as the financial needs and responsibilities created through sex-role specialization in a given marital union, child custody arrangements upon divorce, a spouse's physical or mental ability to maintain himself or herself, and a spouse's ability to obtain paid employment. The Commission suggested that the amount of maintenance should be awarded on the basis of financial need and the gender-division of labour that characterized the marriage. Finally, the Commission raised special concerns about children's welfare after divorce, and argued that the courts should refuse a divorce unless the parents made appropriate arrangements for their children's economic, social, and emotional well-being.

The Divorce Act, 1985, responded to the numerous criticisms of the original legislation made by legal scholars and special interest groups. The new legislation overhauled the previous Divorce Act according to three principles (Richardson, 2001). First, the new legislation replaced the fault grounds with evidence of marital breakdown. The revamped criteria for marital breakdown included separation for one year, adultery, and physical or mental cruelty. By including the latter two categories, the new legislation is not purely no-fault divorce, but these circumstances have weak influence on maintenance and child custody settlements. Second, the 1985 legislation made maintenance a gender-neutral issue by abolishing alimony. Women are no longer automatically entitled to support because of their marital status, and men gained the right to request maintenance under the law. But the 1985 legislation is also gender-sensitive in acknowledging that married women often face comparatively greater economic disadvantage upon divorce. The third change concerned child custody awards. Abandoning the maternal preference standpoint, which insisted that mothers are best suited to raise young children, the new legislation considers the child's best interests in custody awards.

Furthermore, the 1985 legislation adopted the principle of divorce by mutual consent, making the road to legal dissolution less complicated and confrontational. As Richardson (2001) observes, individuals can now obtain an uncontested divorce without petitioning before the court, which reduces the emotional stress and financial expense of court hearings. Today, most couples are encouraged to reach divorce settlements through arbitration rather than the courts. However, very few divorcing couples use free mediation services instead of hiring lawyers to work out divorce settlements. Legal divorce is often a messy affair, coloured by animosity built up during marital breakdown. To address this problem, the Special Joint Committee on Child Custody and Access was struck in 1997 to develop recommendations to resolve bitter fights over child custody and **access**. The Committee's recommendations focused on the rights and welfare of children and recognized that the parent-child relationship does not terminate with divorce. Collectively, the recommendations sought to establish guidelines to ensure fair parental access to children after divorce, to eliminate maternal bias in parenting decisions, and to encourage shared parenting.

The enactment of no-fault divorce legislation is sociologically important because liberal divorce laws validate the new meaning of marriage. But we must emphasize that legislative change is not the direct *causal factor* behind mass divorce. Rather, the new legislation removed formal social controls on marital behaviour, thus giving people the opportunity to terminate marriages that failed for other reasons. Previously, fault-based divorce legislation reinforced social and moral norms regarding the sanctity and permanence of marital unions (Nakonezny, Shull, and Rodgers, 1995). Under these conditions, a person could obtain a divorce only by proving his/her spouse guilty of seriously inappropriate marital behaviour, such as adultery or long-term desertion. According to fault-based divorce legislation, the guilty spouse was required to provide an appropriate economic settlement to the innocent spouse. In most instances, settlements under fault law contained a gender bias, making the husband provide **alimony** and **child support** and giving the wife child custody. Overall, fault-based grounds for divorce upheld marriage by policing behaviour contrary to traditional norms.

By contrast, no-fault divorce legislation does not require a petitioner to prove his/her spouse guilty of a marital offence (Weitzman, 1985). No-fault divorce legislation recognizes that contemporary marriages are social contracts formed primarily for individual emotional gratification, and that any serious dysfunction between married couples is sufficient grounds for divorce. No-fault divorce does not require the mutual consent of both spouses, but can be obtained through unilateral demand. Furthermore, no-fault divorce removes the financial burden from the "guilty" spouse, and instead rules that the distribution of marital wealth, maintenance, and child support should reflect post-divorce financial needs. Finally, no-fault divorce legislation was enacted to "improve the social-psychological and communication climate of divorce" by suppressing the adversarial nature of divorce proceedings so prevalent under fault-based petitions (Nakonezny et al., 1995: 478).

INTERPRETING DIVORCE

Reforms to divorce legislation historically have postdated social–structural changes in the meaning of marriage and the family. Over the past two centuries, North American families have moved from extended kinship networks to nuclear households to diverse family households. The shift to an industrial economy changed the value of children, bringing a period marked by low fertility and large human capital investments in children within bourgeois families (Lesthaeghe, 1995). Before that, fertility was high because the family economy depended upon children's labour. Advanced market capitalism and urbanization changed the structure of families. Within the confines of the bourgeois, nuclear family, children were valued for non-economic reasons. In *The Making of the Modern Family*, Edward Shorter (1975) observes that the development of the nuclear family—i.e., the withdrawal of father, mother, and children from extended kinship networks—followed the replacement of instrumental needs by sentimental concerns in the meaning and organization of the family. This family model dominated North American society until the 1950s.

Figure 10.1 gives a snapshot of Canadian divorce trends between 1968 and 2000. Note the jump in the 1986 divorce rate, representing how accessible legislation "uncorked" public demand for ending bad marriages. In 2000, over 70,000 Canadian couples divorced (Statistics Canada, 2002a). About 38 percent of Canadian marriages are expected to terminate through divorce by the 30th wedding anniversary. Furthermore, as Table 10.1 illustrates, divorce begets divorce, and growing up alongside the divorce revolution has

TABLE 10.1   Cumulative Percentage of Marital Disruption by Marriage Cohort

| Year | All | Marriage Cohort | | | | |
		<1960	1960-69	1970-79	1980-89	1990+
1	.8	.3	.3	.9	1.0	1.2
2	2.0	.9	1.2	2.2	2.4	4.9
3	3.7	1.2	2.2	3.4	4.5	13.0
4	5.6	1.6	3.5	5.3	5.9	24.7
5	7.9	1.6	5.0	7.5	8.1	—
10	19.6	3.5	11.6	17.1	33.3	—
15	29.7	6.9	19.3	25.6	—	—
20	38.5	10.5	25.3	42.9	—	—

Source. Statistics Canada, 1995 General Social Survey. *N* = 5,313. Authors' calculations.

FIGURE 10.1 Total Divorce Rate: Canada, 1969–2000

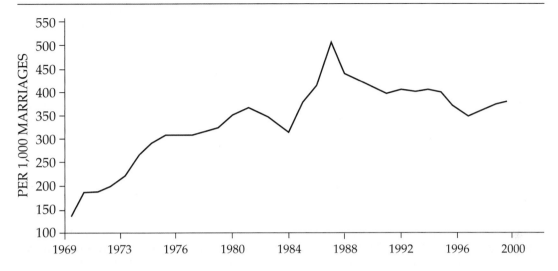

Note: The total divorce rate is defined as the number of divorces by the 30th wedding anniversary per 1,000 marriages.

Source: Dumas, J. and Péron, Y. (1992). "Marriage and Conjugal Life in Canada." Catalogue no. 91-534E, Ottawa: Statistics Canada, p.47. Duchesne, D. et al. (1999). *Vital Statistics Compendium 1996*. Catalogue no. 84-214-XPE, Ottawa: Statistics Canada, p.17. Statistics Canada. *The Daily*, May 18, 1999; July 11, 2002.

"normalized" divorce for younger marriage cohorts. For example, fewer than two percent of marriages formed before 1960 ended in divorce within four years. On the other hand, nearly 25 percent of marriages formed after 1990 ended in divorce within this time frame. In 2003, 1.5 million Canadians, or roughly 5 percent of the general population, reported being currently divorced. About 15 percent of Canadians reported ever being divorced. According to 2001 census data, almost 25 percent of Canadian families with children at home are lone-parent families, and 80 percent of these are headed by single mothers.

Mass divorce is a central issue in the "family in crisis" debate. The conservative reaction to the divorce revolution suggests that marital breakdown represents a negative pattern of family decline. David Popenoe (1988, 1993), a leading proponent of this thesis, argues that families are weakening throughout advanced industrial societies. Popenoe believes that family decline is occurring in the sense that families are becoming less functional environments for raising children, and are now more concerned with self-fulfillment and egalitarian ideals than with altruistic values. Not surprisingly, Popenoe considers divorce a human tragedy, and associates the concurrent growth of single-mother households (fatherlessness) with various social problems, including substance abuse, juvenile delinquency, teenage pregnancy, child poverty, and rising crime rates. An important component of Popenoe's thesis is the influence of mother's paid employment on the putative "decline of the family." In Popenoe's words: "At the same time that our society has disclaimed the role of wives in the traditional nuclear family, it has also heavily discarded the basic structure of that family type—two natural parents who stay together for life" (1993: 531).

In a debate with Popenoe, Judith Stacey (1993: 545) writes that his version of "the family is a positivist, empirical institution amenable to a structural-functional definition." Contrary to Popenoe, Stacey insists that the family is *not* an institution, but rather an ideological construct, and rhetoric on traditional family values has raised the spectre of "family decline" to de-legitimize alternatives to unbroken, heterosexual nuclear families. Even though Popenoe recognizes this problem, conservative interpretations of divorce are often motivated by ideological values that portray female-headed households (and women's independence in general) in negative terms. In other words, these interpretations implicitly *blame women* for the divorce revolution, whether they intend to or not. Stacey agrees with Popenoe's argument that women's economic independence and social autonomy are central to the collapse of the "Ozzie and Harriet" family model, but notes that "these developments expose the inequity and coercion that always lay at the vortex of the supposedly voluntary companionate marriage of the 'traditional nuclear family'" (546).

As Betty Friedan elegantly captured in *The Feminist Mystique*, the 1950s family model placed expectations and constraints on women that drove thousands of middle-class wives into a malaise often requiring professional therapy and long-term prescriptions for anti-depressants. Millions of middle-class American women were taught

> how to catch a man and keep him, how to breastfeed children and handle their toilet training, how to cope with sibling rivalry and adolescent rebellion; how to buy a dishwasher, bake bread, cook gourmet snails, and build a swimming pool with their own hands; how to dress, look, and act more feminine and make marriage more exciting; how to keep their husbands from dying young and their sons from growing into delinquents. They were taught to pity the neurotic, unfeminine, unhappy women who wanted to be poets or physicists or presidents. They learned that truly feminine women do not want careers, higher education, political rights—the independence and opportunities the old-fashioned feminists fought for (1963: 15).

Quite simply, divorce was more or less unthinkable for the women of this generation. Hence, from a feminist perspective, the core problem of conservative interpretations of the divorce revolution flows from a complete ignorance of the high costs women paid for marital stability throughout the "golden age" of marriage and the family. As this chapter outlines, the divorce rate over the past century is a rough measure of women's status within civil society.

Most feminists question the usage of the 1950s family as a baseline model for gauging the present situation, particularly the ahistorical assumption that alternatives to the heterosexual nuclear family threaten the social order (Stacey, 1993). Arnup writes that "families have changed in size, membership, and function throughout history," and these transitions usually have fuelled debates about the future of the family (2001: 2). Indeed, the decline of marriage is a crisis only in comparison to the marriage rate prevalent from 1940–60 (Cherlin, 1992). The men and women born between 1920 and 1945 were peculiar in that this generation married more frequently and at younger ages than any other cohort in recorded history. Although the outcomes of divorce, as discussed in the following section, are hardly inconsequential, divorce itself does not cause social problems. Since nobody plans on divorce, marital breakdown can be likened to anomie because there are no social rules for the way the divorce process should happen. According to this logic, divorce is troublesome because of weak social supports and norms governing family needs, behaviour, and relationships following marital breakdown.

DIVORCE OUTCOMES

Most interpretations of the divorce revolution are characterized by specific understandings of the various economic, psychosocial, and emotional consequences of marital dissolution. Divorce is obviously a stressful life experience that involves adjusting to difficult circumstances. The main issues for adults concern decline of economic welfare, decreased social support, single-parenting, and child custody rights. For children, post-divorce problems gravitate around the decline in parental support and contact, contin-

What are the consequences for children raised in single-parent families?

ued tension between parents, and economic hardship. However, feminist scholars remark that divorce is not the cause of the many social problems conservative-minded people associate with broken homes. In fact, divorce is often an effective solution to dysfunctional family environments, and the actual problems are poverty and inadequately funded public programs and services (Amato, 2000). This section reviews divorce outcomes in terms of economic welfare, child custody and access, and post-divorce child-parent relationships.

Economic Consequences

The fundamental misjudgment within no-fault divorce legislation is that the orientation toward gender neutrality glosses over social structural disparities between husbands and wives (Weitzman, 1995). The legislation presumes incorrectly that men and women have equal opportunities in the labour force, essentially ignoring the gender division of labour during the marriage, the gender-burden of childcare, and other barriers to post-divorce economic recovery. Prior research consistently demonstrates that women without husbands, and especially single-mothers, have substantially lower economic status and a much higher risk of living below the poverty line than married women and divorced men because of these disadvantages (Holden and Smock, 1991). Moreover, since maternal custody is the normal living arrangement, most children experience a large drop in their economic welfare after divorce. As Richardson aptly points out, "as long as women remain the primary caregivers of children, are responsible for most of the domestic labour, and are paid less than men, basing family law on assumptions of equality between men and women will only lead to greater inequality following marriage breakdown" (2001: 227).

Although most women experience acute family income decline after separation or divorce, the effect is steeper for those exiting wealthier households. Women exiting households in the upper one-third of family income distribution experience roughly a 50–70 percent decline in household income (Weiss, 1984; Weitzman, 1985). By comparison, women exiting lower income households experience a 20–30 percent decline in household income. One estimate indicates that mothers and children face a 35–45 percent drop in needs-adjusted income after separation (Bartfeld, 2000). Men experience much lower, if any, household income losses upon separation. Estimates range between 7–10 percent, with several studies indicating that men's incomes rebound to pre-separation levels within two years (Holden and Smock, 1991). Some evidence shows that men's household income even *improves* after separation, even with spousal and child support payments. Although much controversy surrounds how much women's household income declines after separation (e.g., see Peterson's 1996 critique of Weitzman's well-publicized estimates), the bottom line is that a sizable proportion of divorced women face economic hardship.

For most women, post-divorce economic problems are long-term. Even though women's paid labour time increases sharply after separation, in most cases their financial difficulties persist for five or more years after marital separation, with no or only moderate improvement in income-to-needs ratio (Holden and Smock, 1991). As a result, women's repartnering decisions are particularly sensitive to their post-divorce socio-economic status (De Graaf and Kalmijn, 2003). Some women may be "pushed" into **repartnering** if a new union promises to restore their household income to pre-divorce levels (Sweeney, 1997). Supporting this assumption, the available evidence indicates that remarriage is the primary method through which divorced women re-establish economic welfare, especially for mothers with young children (Morrison and Ritualo, 2000). Although less beneficial than remarriage in absolute dollars, nonmarital cohabitation also provides economic returns large enough to replenish pre-divorce family household income status. However, when not leading to marriage, cohabitation does not sustain children's economic recovery over time.

Child custody arrangements underpin the economic problems that most single-parent households experience. Childcare responsibilities significantly diminish the time a custodial mother can allocate to paid labour. These duties include planning and preparing meals, shopping for food and clothing, bathing and dressing children, supervising children, bringing children to and from school and extra-curricular activities, helping with homework, arranging medical appointments, caring for sick children, planning social events, and so forth. These duties frequently intrude on the regular nine-to-five workday, which means that single mothers require accessible daycare and flexible work hours. However, professional daycare services are prohibitively expensive for most single mothers, and few employers provide a work schedule flexible enough for these women to integrate full-time employment with childcare (Holden and Smock, 1991). Consequently, the primary jobs available to divorced mothers are usually low-paid, non-professional positions.

Even though the distribution of childcare duties is heavily skewed, most orders for child support payments are inadequate to cover even basic household expenses, which is another fallacy of "gender-neutral" legislation. Canadian research indicates that 60 percent of households headed by divorced mothers have incomes below the poverty line (Richardson, 2001). Initial investigations into this situation estimated that formal child support obligations were so insufficient that 97 percent of single-mother households would fall below the poverty line if they depended on child support income alone (Chambers, 1979). In January 1997, the Canadian government implemented new child support guidelines in response to the problem of inconsistent and inadequate court-ordered child support awards. The new guidelines (these are not requirements) reduced the need for litigation by establishing a basic standard of child support based on the non-custodial parent's income and number of dependent children (Barham, Devlin, and LaCasse, 2000).

A critique of these guidelines uncovers two fundamental shortcomings (Barham et al., 2000). First, the guidelines fail to guarantee economic equity for all Canadian families, because the child support awards are calculated without considering the custodial parent's socio-economic status. Basing child support awards strictly on the non-custodial parent's income can leave children vulnerable to economic hardship in circumstances in which the custodial parent does not have sufficient labour market opportunities. Second, the income-based calculations overlook the non-custodial parent's net assets such as savings, investments, and home ownership. Net assets determine a non-custodial parent's overall ability to pay child support, and this wealth could be equitably distributed to cushion the post-divorce economic decline of single mothers and children. The authors recognize that the guidelines provide reasonable child support in some instances, but conclude that they are inadequate for sustaining children's pre-divorce economic well-being and equalizing the standard of living between custodial and non-custodial households.

Another serious issue custodial parents face is non-payment of child support. Recent estimates indicate that the national default rate (including late payment, partial payment, and full default) ranges somewhere between 50–75 percent—in only 43 percent of cases is child support paid regularly— and 30 percent of non-custodial parents made no payments for six or more months (Richardson, 2001). Although the federal government has implemented measures to prevent default, such as automatic income deductions, the present child support legislation remains an ineffective mechanism for preventing post-divorce economic hardship.

Child Custody and Access

Child custody and access are probably the most complicated and stressful issues of the divorce process, considering the meaning children have for parents. Historically, child custody assignments in Canada followed the patriarchal traditions that structured marital unions and divorce legislation. The 19th century British common law routinely awarded custody to fathers on the principle that "the father, regardless of his character and behaviour, had an absolute right to entire and untrammelled control over his children" (Stone, 1990: 170). An unkind father could even block a mother's visitation and communication privileges. Historians speculate that this unfair child custody and access legislation discouraged many women from seeking a divorce. However, most separations and divorces involved child custody negotiations and settlements that ended up being rather different from the patriarchical nature of the common law (Stone, 1990). Fathers often rejected child custody to avoid the responsibilities and financial expense of child-care. Other fathers surrendered child custody because of the growing sentiment suggesting that motherhood represented professional childcare.

The Child Custody Bill (1839), or Lord Talfourd's Act, officially broke the absolute paternal right to child custody (Boyd, 1989). Lord Talfourd's Act gave mothers the right to petition for custody of children under seven years old. This legislative change followed the belief that maternal nurturing was pertinent to young children's social development. All subsequent legislation gradually reoriented custody awards from the father's absolute rights toward maternal bias. But this process of legislative change was not a benign recognition of maternal custody rights. Boyd (1989: 130–31) writes that "increased maternal rights can be traced to the increasing split between home and workplace linked to industrialization and urbanization, the emergence of the middle class, and the growing tendency to view childhood and adolescence as distinct developmental periods which required time, nourishment, and moulding by mothers." Her argument implies that, similar to changes in divorce legislation, legal acknowledgement of maternal rights were shaped by shifting gender ideologies and socio-economic revolution.

The Victorian period cast women primarily as homemakers and mothers (the domestic sphere), and men's greater involvement in business, commerce, and industry (the public sphere) compelled them to allocate more supervision of domestic matters to their wives (Backhouse, 1981). In essence, women's child custody rights increased only after social structural changes triggered by industrialization confined middle- and upper-class women to the domestic sphere (Millar and Goldenberg, 1998). The notion that mothers are better suited to parenting than fathers (the **tender years doctrine**) guided Canadian child custody awards between 1920 and 1986. The reverse of this maternal bias, of course, was that women were considered ill-suited for public life (Boyd, 1989). On this principle, maternal preference could be discarded for women who aspired to be anything other than mothers. For example, in a review of Canadian custody awards (1980–87), Boyd (1987) discovered that many working mothers lost child custody because the judges considered their lifestyles incompatible with creating a stable, nurturing home for children.

The 1985 Divorce Act replaced the tender years doctrine with a supposedly gender-neutral "best interests of the child" doctrine (Millar and Goldenberg, 1998). Single-parent custody and joint-parent custody are the normal legal categories governing post-divorce child custody, visitation rights, and parental decision-making. Custody refers to rights over care, upbringing, and other parental responsibilities associated with legal guardianship. Recognizing that parent-child relationships continue after divorce, the reformed legislation was intended to foster the active involvement of both parents with their children after divorce. Hence, the 1985 legislation regularly grants non-custodial parents generous access privileges. But non-custodial parents lose their authority to participate in decisions regarding child welfare and development (Payne, 1986). The Act's broad and imprecise definition of "custody" effectively deprives non-custodial parents of the rights and responsibilities they possessed before divorce, excluding them from all major decisions concerning the child's upbringing. Although permitting **joint custody**, the language of the legislation appears to favour sole custody, providing that the custodial parent is willing to provide maximum access privileges to the non-custodial parent.

The 1985 legislation contains provisions to promote the best interests of the child in all judicial decisions regarding child custody and access. Access is guided by the principle that a child should have as much contact with the non-custodial parent as is consistent with his/her best interests. Other terms of access include the non-custodial parent's right to information about his/her child's health status, welfare, education, and whereabouts. Since 1986, the gender gap in child custody awards increased, despite the abolition of the tender years doctrine. From 1990–95, mothers received sole custody awards more than six times as often as fathers, compared to five times more often from 1978–84 (Millar and Goldenberg, 1998). One possible reason for this gender bias in the pattern of child custody awards is that fathers leave child custody uncontested because they want to avoid childcare responsibilities. According to a feminist perspective, rather than being motivated by parental responsibility and concerns, a primary reason some Canadian fathers threaten to challenge for custody is to pressure their ex-partners into lowering their divorce settlement demands.

Millar and Goldenberg (1998) observe that there is insufficient evidence to support these claims, and instead focus on gender-specific capital that may weigh in favour of women under the best interests of the child doctrine. These authors hypothesize that women's predominant role as "primary parents" endows them with more parenting skills than fathers, and thus most women are better equipped to serve the best interests of the child. Some feminists argue that the principle of gender equality in child custody legislation is misguided because it undervalues women's parenting skills, and simply assumes that fathers can take on primary parenting responsibilities whether or not they regularly preformed childcare duties during the marriage. Boyd argues that "legal provisions which presume a norm of shared parenting before it has become a social reality may reinforce unequal power relations between men and women rather than encourage their demise" (1989: 148). Even though this concern is noteworthy, maternal preference still characterizes the gender pattern of judicial child custody awards. Moreover, Millar and Goldenberg's conclusions do not support the hypothesis that women's superior parenting skills account for the current maternal bias in these awards.

Overall, the new legislation did not radically change the pattern of child custody, because most divorcing spouses reinforce maternal bias through their own needs, preferences, and beliefs (Richardson, 2001). So, how do custody arrangements affect father-child relationships and child welfare? Many children born in recent decades will experience living in a single-mother household sometime during childhood or adolescence (Bumpass and Sweet, 1989). As many studies indicate, the amount and quality of contact between non-custodial parents and their children gradually erodes after divorce (Amato, 1993). Also, children in single-parent households receive less parental supervision than children in two-parent households. Household composition influences the life course of children because the family is the primary unit of socialization (Demo and Acock, 1988). Socialization, a teaching and learning process, refers to parent-to-child transmission of basic life skills including language and behavioural norms, but also parent-specific values, such as cultural habits, religious ideas, and personal attitudes—in all, socialization involves the formation of personalities.

According to structural functionalists (e.g., Talcott Parsons), the heterosexual nuclear family is crucial for normal child development. These households are responsible for children's economic maintenance, social support, emotional validation, and socialization. How divorced parents fulfil the same functions is a central question of divorce research (Seltzer, 1994). Divorce is problematic because the absence of a parent, usually the father, means that children lose the regular presence of a role model, teacher, and provider. Seltzer (1994) notes that a father's parenting role is defined by co-residence, and thus non-custodial fathers often disengage from their children during the divorce process. The "emphasis on parenthood as socially defined is consistent with the finding that children living with stepfathers are much more likely to say that their stepfather is a member of their family than they are to include their non-resident biological father as a family member" (Seltzer, 1994: 237). The normative vacuum surrounding the expectations and responsibilities of non-custodial parents further complicates post-divorce parent-child relationships and interactions (Seltzer, 1991). Divorced fathers may hesitate to remain active parents because they are uncertain how their ex-wives and children will respond to their attempts at maintaining contact.

For children, divorce represents a dilution of parental resources. A stable family environment is unquestionably a major component in a child's development and welfare. Hence, losing a parent to divorce is a disruptive event affecting cognitive functioning, self-esteem, and behaviour. On average, and regardless of socio-economic and ethnic background, the children of divorce have higher anxiety and depression rates, exhibit greater deviant behaviour, and perform worse in school than children from intact families (McLanahan and Sandefur, 1994). Adjusting to divorce is more difficult for younger children and boys. However, critics of structural-functional theories of child development argue that departures from the nuclear family do not inherently produce negative consequences (Demo and Acock, 1988). Children's negative reactions to divorce are often short-lived or mitigated by other factors. For example, when both parents share the instrumental and social parenting responsibilities, children adjust to post-divorce life better than when single-mothers carry the burden alone (Seltzer, 1991). But, in most instances, mothers end up providing most of their children's economic, emotional, and social needs, and even provide more childcare in joint-custody arrangements (Seltzer, 1994).

Having an involved non-custodial parent suppresses the negative effects of divorce on children. Unfortunately, most fathers tend to withdraw from their children's lives to distance themselves from their ex-wives, or because they begin devoting more parenting time to children from remarriages (Seltzer, 1994). On the other hand, mothers are often unwilling to relinquish control over parenting decisions, further discouraging fathers from staying involved. Custodial mothers more or less arrange access privileges, and may use this managerial position to limit contact time. Even when mothers want fathers to be more involved, they usually want fathers to parent on their terms without interfering in child-rearing decisions. A mother may discourage a father's involvement because she fears that his greater economic resources will override her autonomy in decisions concerning the child's welfare and development. And "without the formal and emotional benefits of paternity, divorced fathers have few incentives to stay involved with their children" (Seltzer, 1994: 260).

Divorce is the outcome of a relationship that has deteriorated beyond repair, and inter-parental conflict rarely terminates with legal marital dissolution. This can negatively affect children, because access rights are the battleground for some continuing inter-parental conflicts. Power struggles over parenting decisions and bitterness stemming from **marital breakdown** make shared parenting unrealistic in most instances (Richardson, 2001). Although the 1985 Divorce Act was intended to promote "the best interests of the child," no legislation can totally resolve the emotional and social fallout from marital breakdown. A potential way to promote active father involvement is to offer couples extended public conciliation and mediation services after divorce in order to provide them with a neutral atmosphere in which to resolve their interpersonal differences, grievances, and conflicts. Other options include providing single mothers public daycare, job training programs, and enhanced financial support. By easing the post-divorce economic disparities between men and women, mothers may feel less anxious about including fathers in parenting decisions.

REPARTNERING

Throughout North America, the most travelled pathway into remarriage before World War II was widowhood, because few people divorced. Since the 1960s, following the rapid growth in North American **divorce rates**, a larger proportion of people have re-entered the marriage market than ever before. About one-third of Canadian marriages have at least one previously divorced or widowed spouse (Wu, 1994). Although some conservative-minded people interpret rising divorce rates as a sign that the institution of

A blended family at work.

marriage is weakening, increases in remarriage rates have almost matched these upward divorce trends. Between two-thirds and three-quarters of divorced Canadians eventually will remarry (Statistics Canada, 1988). These statistics indicate that the divorce rate represents a growing intolerance of particular *unhappy* marriages and a growing public acceptance of divorce, rather than widespread disillusionment with and rejection of marital unions per se, since marriage remains the hegemonic organizing principle of Canadian family life (Bumpass, Sweet, and Castro-Martin, 1990).

Peter Uhlenberg remarks that, even though remarriage is an important life course adjustment, "remarriage is marriage, and the cultural meaning of marriage is relevant in determining the motivation to remarry" (1989: 74). Sociologists and demographers define remarriage as a tri-stage process that involves marital disruption, different individual-level chances of repartnering, and the transition into reconstituted families (Uhlenberg and Chew, 1986). In the first stage, an individual is exposed to the possibility of remarriage after experiencing divorce or partner death. The second stage is determined by the individual's desire or need for remarriage and ability to attract eligible partners in the marriage market. The final stage is an extended process of recovering from marital disruption and adjusting to the challenges of remarried life.

As Table 10.2 shows, about 4 percent of Canadian women and 6 percent of Canadian men form a remarriage within 3 years of marital dissolution. After 5 years, these proportions rise to 7 percent for women and 12 percent for men. After 10 years, these proportions reach 14 and 20 percent for women and men, respectively. Age at marital dissolution, duration of the marriage, the presence of children, socio-economic status, and gender all factor into the probability of remarriage.

Age at divorce affects an individual's pool of eligible partners in the marriage market (Bumpass et al., 1990). The marriage market, in accordance with the sex-ratio hypothesis, consists of all eligible partners (Guttentag and Secord, 1983). But the number of eligible

TABLE 10.2   Cumulative Percentage of Repartnering after Marital Disruption

	Women			Men		
Year	Remarried	Cohabited	Total	Remarried	Cohabited	Total
1	.7	9.5	10.2	.6	14.9	15.5
2	2.7	17.3	20.0	2.7	23.5	26.3
3	4.2	22.1	26.3	6.3	31.0	37.3
4	5.6	25.9	31.4	10.1	35.8	45.9
5	7.2	28.8	36.0	11.8	38.6	50.5
10	13.5	39.1	52.5	20.4	49.2	69.6
15	16.4	45.4	61.8	23.4	54.3	77.7
20	19.2	49.4	68.6	26.6	55.5	82.1

Source. Statistics Canada, 1995 General Social Survey. $N = 1,674$. Authors' calculations.

FIGURE 10.2 Remarriage Rate: Canada, 1955–1989

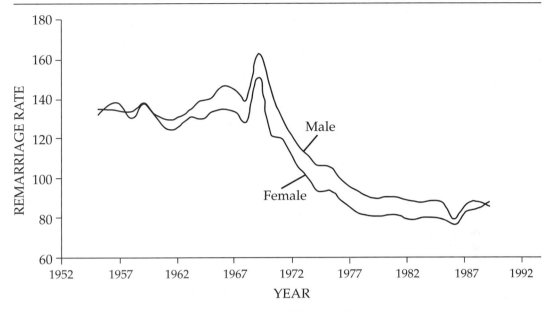

Note: Remarriage rate is defined as the number of marriages per 1,000 previously married population.

Source: Dumas, J. and Péron, Y. (1992). *Marriage and Conjugal Life in Canada*. Catalogue no. 91-534E, Ottawa: Statistics Canada, p.47.

partners does not include all *available* adults. The sex–age structure within a given population and norms within a given community impose macro-level constraints on opportunities in the marriage market. According to this hypothesis, a low sex-ratio scenario (an oversupply of women) confines women's chances of remarriage through the deficit of available male partners. Also, the social definition of acceptable partners is grounds for an additional subtraction from the gross marriage market. For example, women tend to marry men who are older and have equivalent or better socio-economic backgrounds to themselves. Therefore, sex-ratio disadvantages and socio-cultural norms reduce the marriage market for divorced women, and thus lower their repartnering chances.

Prior fertility is another repartnering differential. Through childcare duties and issues, the parental relationship continues after divorce and remarriage. This relationship diverts human capital away from second unions, a putative liability for a divorced person's attractiveness on the marriage market (Becker et al., 1977). Given maternal preference in child custody, post-marital living arrangements favour men's remarriage chances, because the custodial parent's chances are impeded by childcare responsibilities (Stewart, Manning, and Smock, 2003). Younger co-resident children squeeze the time mothers have for finding new partners and investing in new marriages (Lampard and Peggs, 1999). A gender pattern in remarriage may also surface through psychosocial differences in the ways parenting responsibilities are perceived by potential new partners. A recent study shows that children enhance the chances of repartnering for men who appear to be "good fathers," defined by their level of involvement with non-resident children, because this increases their attractiveness to women (Stewart et al., 2003). On the other hand, eligible male partners may hesitate to partner with divorced mothers because of their parental connection with their ex-husbands and the perceived step-parenting burden.

Gender-specific effects on repartnering also occur through socio-economic status. As noted above, economic hardship may "push" some divorced women into remarriage. According to British evidence, divorced men from "non-manual" social classes remarry faster than divorced men from "manual" social classes (Haskey, 1987). Presumably, this is because men from the "non-manual" classes have good marriage market status, at least in terms of the number of available partners, considering that most women marry men from equivalent or better socio-economic backgrounds than themselves. An opposite effect obtains for women, suggesting that post-marital financial hardship "pushes" women with poor socio-economic prospects into remarriage, whereas the timing of remarriage among women from "non-manual" social classes is comparatively slow. According to rational choice theory (the New Home Economics), women's participation in paid labour lowers the benefits of marriage, and this may explain why women with good socio-economic prospects have comparatively lower chances of remarriage.

Cohabitation

Canadian remarriage rates have been declining since the 1990s (the Vanier Institute of the Family, 2000). However, the decline in remarriage is somewhat superficial, because non-marital **cohabitation**, or common-law marriage, among divorced Canadians increased dramatically during this period (Cherlin and Furstenberg, 1994). Cohabitation is the preferred second union choice among divorced Canadians, and around 22 percent of divorced women and 31 percent of divorced men report having formed a cohabitational relationship three years after marital disruption. In other words, the cohabitation rate is five times higher than the remarriage rate during the first three years following marital disruption. The overall repartnering rate following marital disruption, which combines cohabitation and remarriage, is high. Table 10.2 shows that, by the twentieth year of marital disruption, 69 percent of women and 82 percent of men have repartnered. These statistics demonstrate that although marriage (remarriage) rates have declined and divorce rates have increased, divorced Canadians have not abandoned intimate co-residential relationships altogether.

For some family observers, cohabitation is a greater threat than divorce to the continued predominance of marriage because, unlike divorce, cohabitation is a functional substitute for marriage (Wu, 2000). The rapid increase in cohabitation is attributable to diverse social forces, namely the changes in social norms and attitudes towards sexual behaviour outside marriage, the rise of ideologies emphasizing individual autonomy and the importance of self-fulfillment, socio-economic change, and changing gender ideologies (Lesthaeghe and Surkyn, 1988). As with divorce, the improvement in women's educational attainment, labour force participation, and wage rates plays a pivotal role in the popularity of nonmarital cohabitation. Remember that the New Home Economics suggests that men and women marry only if both spouses benefit from a reciprocal trading relationship within the marital union (Becker, 1981). In these terms, recent changes in the marketplace have reduced the benefits of marriage. These changes unleashed non-marital cohabitation because this type of union offers an alternative lifestyle to traditional families based on a comparatively rigid division of labour that constrains women's labour market opportunities.

Stepfamilies

Diverse family histories and kinship networks, fractured family loyalties, and prior children are the primary characteristics that separate remarriages from first marriages. A stepfamily refers to a marital or cohabitational family with children from a previous relationship. A "blended" stepfamily refers to families containing stepsiblings or half-siblings. In Canada, stepfamilies account for 12 percent of two-parent households (Statistics Canada, 2002b). Of all stepfamilies, 40 percent are "blended" families, 50 percent are "her-children-only" families, and 10 percent are "his-children-only" families. Of all "blended" stepfamilies, 80 percent include children born into the current union. Adjusting to stepfamily life is a challenge for both adults and children (Coleman and Ganong, 1990). The adjustment process is complicated by unshared family histories, the residual presence of former spouses and extended family members, and several other sources of interpersonal tension among remarried family members. One investigation estimates that remarried families need an average of seven years to fully complete the adjustment process (Papernow, 1988).

Patricia Papernow (1993) details three developmental phases that stepfamilies experience while adjusting to the reconstituted family environment. In the early phase, the remarried family is fractured along biological lines and by differences in parental roles and attitudes. Biological parents and step-parents enter the remarriage under the belief that the reconstituted family will resolve the suffering and problems that divorce created. This fantasy is short-lived, and numerous interpersonal conflicts tarnish the initial immersion into remarried family life. For example, the step-parent commonly becomes an "outsider" within the remarriage through subtle exclusion from the previously established relationship and emotional union between the biological parent and child. And children may resent their step-parents because they perceive remarriage as losing another parent, seeing the new spouse as competition for their biological parent's attention and affection. These feelings of alienation and resentment can retard the development of the spousal relationship. Many remarriages begin on unstable ground because of these challenges to emotional security within the new family environment. To move on, the family members must become aware of their reasons for feeling emotionally insecure. Achieving awareness takes one to four years, depending on personal attitudes and family complexity.

The middle phase of the adjustment process occurs when old boundaries of family unity begin to dissolve, and new bases of family identity and stability begin to surface. Family conflicts are vocalized during this period, as family members openly confront their interpersonal differences, express their individual needs and preferences, and negotiate agreements about family functioning. During this phase, families decide on common household rules and expectations, the allocation of personal attention, and step-parenting rights and obligations. Stepfamilies need two to three years to fully complete this phase. The final phase of adjustment is complete when stepfamilies achieve what Papernow calls *structural solidification*. Agreements on family needs and expectations made during the middle phase improve family functioning and cohesiveness. By the later phase, remarried family members have resolved most of their interpersonal conflicts, have a shared history, and have well-defined statuses and roles. Although less cohesive than biological families, mature stepfamilies have reliable, nurturing, and supportive family relationships. Most stepfamilies complete the final phase of the adjustment process in one to two years.

Cherlin and Furstenberg (1994) argue that parenthood and kinship are *achieved* statuses within stepfamilies, whereas these are *ascribed* statuses in unbroken families. Simply put, parental roles and definitions of kinship are clearly assigned within unbroken families, but stepfamilies have comparatively few norms to guide parenting behaviour and define family relationships. For example, how do children define their mother's new spouse when they already have a father? Or, how does the new spouse interact with his stepchildren when they have a biological father? These questions are not automatically resolved. Step-parenthood is an achieved status because the step-parent's role is determined over time through repeated social interactions and the accumulation of shared family history. In any case, the way in which step-parents and stepchildren bond depends on several factors, including the child's age, the child's contact with the non-custodial biological parent, the child's personality, and the quality of the remarriage. To illustrate: A supportive step-parent may become a surrogate parent for a young co-residential child, especially if the biological parent is uninvolved. Alternatively, a step-parent may be no more than a distant relative to an older non-resident child.

Given the day-to-day challenges of stepfamily building, it should come as no surprise that remarriages are more unstable than first marriages. According to Cherlin (1978), remarriage is an "incomplete institution" because there are no standard solutions for the various problems and confusions within reconstituted family life. "People in first marriages rarely stop to notice that a full set of kinship terms exists, that the law regulates their relationships, or that custom dictates much of their behaviour toward spouses and children" (Cherlin, 1978: 646). The terms father and mother specify roles and expectations, whereas the terms stepfather or stepmother do not define the step-parent-stepchild relationship. Unlike father or mother, the terminological meaning of stepfather and stepmother are diffuse simply because step-parenting is not an ascribed obligation. An absence of behavioural norms, then, presents a source of interpersonal confusion regarding appropriate roles, and also leaves stepfamilies without effective guidelines for resolving interpersonal differences and providing new bases for order and security. Although many stepfamilies work through these difficulties, stepfamily building and organization are different from forming "traditional" families because the circumstances surrounding divorce and remarriage disrupt conventional patterns of family unity.

CONCLUSION

Since the 19th century, a broad pattern of social, economic, and legislative change has redefined the meaning of marriage and the family. The introduction of liberal divorce legislation uncorked public demand for divorce built up by socio-economic change, new attitudes toward marriage and the family, and women's rights. Many people are concerned that divorce embodies the destruction of the tradition family. In a sense, these people are correct, particularly if we focus on the negative aspects of divorce, such as economic hardship and fatherlessness, and the emergence of alternatives to married life. But such opinions neglect an essential anthropological and sociological fact: Family change has been an integral dimension of human societies throughout recorded history. Indeed, the family is a mirror of the broader social world, reflecting the conditions and norms of communities within a given historical period. In this respect, the rapid increase in divorce falls within a widespread social phenomenon that includes the Civil Rights movement, the Anti-war Movement, and the Women's Movement. All historical transformations in the meaning of marriage and the family have followed social structural changes, especially the development of new modes of production, such as the transition from agrarian to industrial societies, and renegotiations of gender ideologies.

The "decline of the family" thesis is misleading because it makes individual interests and symptomatic events (e.g., divorce, cohabitation) the main culprits of the so-called crisis. Moreover, this perspective is *ahistorical* because it makes an a priori presumption that the heterosexual nuclear family is the natural order of things, and it is *ideological* because it assumes that family structures that deviate from this norm represent a horrible threat to society. Social problems have indeed followed divorce, but divorce per se is not the root of these hardships. Since divorce is an unexpected and negative event, there are no social rules or conventions governing the way divorced families should behave, nor are there conventions for the way divorced and blended families fit into society. Divorced fathers are unsure of how to remain involved with non-custodial children. Employers have not adapted to the flexible schedules single mothers require. And the relationship between step-parents and stepchildren is undefined. All of these situations present the most significant challenges associated with the divorce and repartnering processes.

Part of the reason some people are so concerned is that divorce is a stark reminder of how much things have changed—rapid social transformation often inspires nostalgia for "the ways things were." Some conservative reactions against divorce—such as the movement to repeal no-fault legislation—cannot be abstracted from traditional religious dogma or deeply sexist attitudes. Bemoaning the "decline of the family" forgets that historical patterns of marital stability were enforced by patriarchical gender relationships. From this perspective, what is troublesome is the prevalence of conservative attitudes toward family change, since these norms block legislative and policy changes that could cushion the problems that divorced and blended families currently experience.

Suggested Readings

Amato, Paul R. (2000). "The Consequences of Divorce for Adults and Children." *Journal of Marriage and the Family* 62: 1269–1287. A recent overview of 1990s divorce research focusing on how individuals from divorced families compare to individuals from intact families in terms of various measures of welfare.

Ambert, Anne-Marie (2001). *Families in the New Millennium.* Boston, MA: Allyn and Bacon. This volume is a recent, in-depth account of diverse research and theories on families and family change, and focuses on common themes such as social disparities, gender ideologies, and public policy. The volume contains a chapter on divorce and remarriage.

Coleman, Marilyn, Lawrence G. Ganong, and Mark Fine (2000). "Reinvestigating Remarriage: Another Decade of Progress." *Journal of Marriage and the Family* 62: 1288–1307. This article provides a comprehensive review of remarriage and stepfamily research published in the 1990s. The article reviews and critiques the main research trends, methodologies, and theories generated during this decade.

Cherlin, Andrew (1992). *Marriage, Divorce, Remarriage*. Cambridge, MA: Harvard University Press. This volume is written in accessible language and terminology, and gives a solid overview of the reasons why current patterns of marriage, divorce, and remarriage differ from those that prevailed during the "golden age" of marriage.

Sev'er, Aysan (1992). *Women and Divorce in Canada: A Sociological Analysis*. Toronto, Canada: Canadian Scholars' Press. One of the few sociological examinations of Canadian divorce, this volume provides a feminist interpretation of divorce patterns and implications, and gives a condensed overview of historical conditions and sources of change.

Web Resources

The Vanier Institute of the Family (**www.vifamily.ca**) is a comprehensive and continually updated Web site focusing on families in Canadian society. The Web site contains a virtual library that includes over one hundred articles on divorce and remarriage written by experts in these fields.

The National Council on Family Relations (**www.ncfr.org**) provides a forum for family researchers and policy-makers to share and transmit knowledge about family issues, and publishes the prestigious *Journal of Marriage and Family and Family Relations*. The Web site provides detailed information on the Council's various activities and publications, which include an exceptionally diverse collection of scholarly articles on divorce and remarriage.

CHAPTER ELEVEN

Patterns of Family Violence

Walter S. DeKeseredy

INTRODUCTION

Like their neighbours south of the border, when Canadians are not worried about the economy, terrorist attacks, or deadly viruses (e.g., SARS), they worry about violent crimes committed by strangers on the streets or in other public places (Glassner, 1999). Canadians' intense fear of "stranger danger," however, is not well-founded. Of course, small proportions of them are robbed, mugged, or murdered by unknown predatory offenders, and their pain and suffering should not be trivialized. Still, what sociologists Richard Gelles and Murray Straus stated close to 20 years ago still holds true in Canada today: "You are more likely to be physically assaulted, beaten, and killed in your own home at the hands of a loved one than anyplace else, or by anyone else in society" (1998: 18). Many people find this hard to believe because they were socialized to view the family primarily as a source of love and as a safe refuge from the pains inflicted by the outside world (Duffy and Momirov, 1997). Others do not see violence in the family as a social problem because they have never indirectly or directly experienced it. Unfortunately, few families are conflict-free, and many are plagued by harms that few of us could imagine. In fact, it is estimated that almost one million Canadian women are beaten or sexually assaulted by male intimates annually, and several hundred children are sexually abused (Harrison, 1997).

Violence in the family "could happen to anyone" (LaViolette and Barnett, 2000). The main objective of this chapter is to describe the sociological patterns of four major examples of "not the way to love" (Fitzpatrick and Halliday, 1992): wife abuse, child abuse, sibling violence, and elder abuse. Empirical and theoretical work on these "intimate intrusions" is reviewed, and progressive prevention strategies are also briefly discussed (Stanko, 1985). However, it is first necessary to examine how social scientists define violence in the family.

DEFINITION OF VIOLENCE IN THE FAMILY[1]

A review of the extant social scientific literature on violence in domestic settings clearly reveals that defining violence in the family is the subject of much debate. Of central concern here are controversies that focus on the breadth of definitions (broad versus narrow) and language (e.g., family violence vs. violence against women and children).

The Breadth of Definitions

There is considerable disagreement about what injurious acts should be included in a definition of violence in domestic/household settings. For example, many North American survey researchers, policy-makers, journalists, and members of the general public focus only on physical abuse (e.g., beatings and kicks) or sexual assaults involving forced penetration. Psychological, verbal, spiritual, and economic abuse are deleted from their formulations because grouping these types of assaults with physically injurious behaviours is seen as muddying "the water so much that it might be impossible to determines what causes abuse" (Gelles and Cornell, 1985: 23).

Others oppose broad definitions for different reasons. Consider Fekete (1994: 60), who asserts that the Canadian national survey on woman abuse in dating (CNS),[2] a large-scale study that used a broad definition, was ideologically driven and specifically designed to "show that different heterosexual interactions are all variants of the same tree." *Globe and Mail* columnist Margaret Wente makes a similar point in her critique of Statistics Canada's (1993) national Violence Against Women Survey (VAWS).[3] According to her, this study "painted a false picture of the world because it failed to make any distinction between the transient and insignificant conflicts of everyday life and truly violent behaviour as it is commonly understood by most people" (1994: A2).

Ironically, some feminist critiques of surveys such as the CNS are similar. For example, Fox (1993) states that "by combining what is debatably abusive with what *everyone* [italics added] agrees to be seriously abusive," the CNS research team trivialized the latter. Although several studies have identified women who see psychological abuse as equally (if not more) harmful as physically and sexually violent behaviours (Walker, 1979; Kirkwood, 1993; Straus and Sweet, 1992; Schwartz, 2000), Fox (1993) views psychological or emotional victimization as "soft-core abuse." There also are feminists who define psychological assaults as early warning signs of physical and sexual attacks rather than as abusive in and of themselves (e.g., K. Kelly, 1994).

On the other hand, a growing number of researchers and government agencies contend that intimate violence is multidimensional in nature and that research should recognize that

Protesters in Quebec demonstrate after a man was charged with killing his wife at a women's shelter.

many family members' lives rest on a "continuum of unsafety" (Stanko, 1990). Again, psychological or emotional abuse can be more painful than physical and sexual violence, and some women simultaneously experience different types of abuse. For example, while writing this chapter in January 2004, I was in the process of conducting an exploratory study of separation/divorce sexual assault in rural Ohio.[4] Of the 20 women interviewed at that time, only 20 percent experienced just one type of non-sexual abuse (e.g., physical, economic, psychological, etc.). Mary is one of my respondents, and below is what happened to her during the process of leaving her violent male partner:

> He had taken my car for about a day and I was you know, by the time he finally returned it and everything, I was taking him home, back to his mom's house and he tried to wreck the car. It was snowing; real bad weather and he tried to wreck the car and everything. I got angry with him and I think I slapped him. He said something and I said, "It is over. It is completely over." You know and he just, he just started punching me in the face and just clawing my face and punching my face and everything.

The major definitional debates reviewed above are not trivial and seriously affect how data are gathered (Trainor, 2002a), as well as the quality and quantity of social support services for people who experience violence in domestic/household settings. It is to a more in-depth discussion of narrow definitions that I now turn.

Narrow Definitions

Many Canadians assert that we should only use legal definitions of physical and sexual assault. Some politicians and government agencies agree. For example, Member of Parliament Roger Gallaway claims that studies such as the CNS "are distorted even further by a broadening of the concept of 'abuse'" (cited in Farrell, 2002: 2). Note, too, that the definition of violence against spouses used in Statistics Canada's 1999 General Social Survey (GSS) was informed by the Canadian Criminal Code (Jiwani, 2000; Pottie Bunge, 2000a; Trainor, 2002a), which is why it found only eight percent of 14,269 women reported at least one incident of intimate partner violence committed by a current or ex-spouse between 1994 and 1999 (Statistics Canada, 2002). Furthermore, the 1999 GSS found that only three percent of women with a current partner or ex-spouse were victimized in the year before the survey (Trainor, Lambert, and Dauvergne, 2002).

Compare these figures with those generated by other studies described in Table 11.1 that used a modified version of either the Conflict Tactics Scale (CTS) or the revised Conflict Tactics Scale (CTS-2) to measure wife abuse.[5] Except for Statistics Canada's (1993) VAWS, all these studies generated much higher incidence rates (the percentage of women who were physically abused in the past year), because they were not presented to respondents as crime surveys, as was the case with the 1999 GSS. Crime surveys create a set of "demand characteristics," and unless respondents clearly label acts as criminal in their own mind, they tend not to report them (Koss, 1996; Straus, 1998; Schwartz, 2000). If people do not think of their spouse's violence as "criminal," they may not report it in such a survey. In fact, close to 83 percent of marital violence incidents are not reported in contexts in which the research emphasis is on criminal assault and victimization (Mihalic and Elliot, 1997).

TABLE 11.1 North American Wife Abuse Surveys

	Description of Surveys				Abuse Rates			
Survey	Survey Location & Date	Sample Description	Interview Mode	Measure of Abuse	Abuse Past Year (%)	Severe Abuse Past Year (%)	Abuse Ever (%)	Severe Abuse Ever (%)
Straus et al. (1981)	U.S. National 1975	2,143 married or cohabiting men and women	Face-to-face	CTS (aggregate)[1]	12.1	3.8	—	—
Schulman (1979)	Kentucky 1979	1,793 presently or formerly married and cohabiting men and women	Phone	CTS[2]	10.0	4.1	21.0	8.7
Straus & Gelles (1986)	U.S. National 1985	3,520 presently or formerly married or cohabiting men and women	Phone	CTS (aggregate)	11.3	3.0	—	—
Brinkerhoff & Lupri (1988)	Calgary 1981	526 men and women	Face-to-face and self-administered questionnaire	CTS (men only)[3]	24.5	10.8	—	—
Kennedy & Dutton (1989)	Alberta 1987	1,045 men and women	Face-to-face and phone	CTS (aggregate)	11.2	2.3	—	—
Lupri (1990)	Canada National 1986	1,530 married or cohabiting men and women	Face-to-face and mail questionnaire	CTS (men only)	17.8	10.1	—	—
Smith (1986)	Toronto 1985	315 women aged 18-55	Phone	CTS/open questions and 1 supplementary question	10.8	—	18.1	7.3
Smith (1987)	Toronto 1987	604 presently or formerly married or cohabiting women	Phone	CTS & 3 supplementary questions	14.4[4]	5.1	36.4[5]	11.3
Statistics Canada (1993)	Canada National 1993	12,300 women 18 years of age and older	Phone	CTS[6]	3.0	—	29.0	—

[1]Men as aggressors and women as victims from different couples.
[2]Women as victims.
[3]Men as aggressors.
[4]Past year rates based on CTS alone.
[5]Abuse-ever rates based on CTS (25.0, 7.8) plus supplementary questions.
[6]Includes a sexual assault item.

Low rates of violence such as those uncovered by Statistics Canada constitute a major problem for at least three reasons. First, many policy-makers listen only to large numbers (Smith, 1994). Unfortunately, if government officials are led to believe by some survey researchers using narrow definitions that violence against women is not a statistically significant issue, they are unlikely to devote sufficient resources to prevent and control one of Canada's most pressing social problems (Jiwani, 2000).

Second, narrow definitions tend to create a "hierarchy of abuse based on seriousness" (L. Kelly, 1987). Just because the law does not define an abusive incident as serious does not mean that legal definitions coincide with women's real-life feelings and experiences. For example, in 33 American states, men who rape their wives are exempt from prosecution in some situations (Bergen, 1999; Rogness, 2003), even though marital rape causes major pain and suffering.[6] Consider the harm done to one of my rural Ohio respondents while she was under the influence of a potent drug given to her by a man she left:

> I agreed to meet with him to discuss visitation and child support for our daughter and I wanted to go to a public place after everything he had done because it wasn't just sexual, it was mental, physical. And I showed up there. I had a couple of friends who were sitting throughout keeping an eye on me. Ordered the drink, got up to use the bathroom, drank my drink and that was pretty much the last thing I remembered until the next morning when I woke up with a killer headache and my daughter crying in her crib. That's what woke me up. I looked over. He was in bed next to me. I was actually—I had strangulation marks around my neck. I had marks around my wrists and an open wound on my face and he had obviously had sex. You know a woman can tell that thing. And, I asked him straight up what happened and he goes, "Ah, well you got drunk." And I said, "How do I get drunk on one drink?" I've been drinking since, you know, you know. I don't make it a normal habit, but one drink is not enough to put someone in that kind of situation.

Below is another example of a terrifying event that typically is excluded from narrow definitions. For this California woman, what her husband did on Christmas Eve was worse than being beaten, although the law did not define her as a battered wife. Her "atrocity tale" is part of a divorce petition she submitted several years ago (Goffman, 1961):

> Her husband arrived home late, drunk and angry, and upon entering the house and seeing the little tree, all fixed up, he became so angry that the took the tree and tore it to pieces, took all the little gifts and presents off of the tree and mutilated and destroyed them.... Not being satisfied with this, and while cursing and defaming the plaintiff, he took all of the table linens and mattresses and sheets and quilts off the bed, took them to the kitchen and dumped them on the floor, gathered up all the food there was in the house and spilled these on the floor, put the cooking utensils on the floor and then took the stove pipe and dumped soot over the bed linen and food and everything he had put on the floor and then turned water all over this mess, then broke and tore up all the furniture (Peterson del Mar, 1996: 124).

Narrow definitions not only trivialize many abused women's subjective experiences, they also restrain them from seeking social support. If a survivor's husband's brutal conduct does not coincide with what researchers, criminal justice officials, politicians, or the general public refer to as abuse or violence, she may be left in a "twilight zone" where she knows that she has been abused but cannot define or categorize it in a way that would help her (Duffy and Momirov, 1997). As stated by one of my rural Ohio interviewees who was harmed by separation/divorce sexual assault, "I don't sit around and share. I keep it to myself.... I'm not one to sit around and talk about what's happened."

Third, narrow definitions exacerbate the problem of under-reporting (Smith, 1994; DeKeseredy, Rogness, and Schwartz, 2004). As stated before, if people are asked questions based on narrow, legal criteria, researchers will elicit data underestimating the amount of abuse experienced by their respondents (Schwartz, 2000). Consequently, the scientific credibility of an entire survey is "put into jeopardy, for one cannot know if those women who disclosed having been abused are representative of all victims in the sample" (Smith, 1994: 110).

Broad Definitions

Definitions of violence in the family and other social problems constitute a primal social scientific act or decision (Ellis, 1987). Again, many researchers who study male-to-female violence in intimate relationships use definitions that include a much broader range of physically abusive behaviours than those officially designated as criminal. The empirical implications of such a decision are significant and more accurately reflect the terrifying experiences of many women who suffer in silence behind closed doors (DeKeseredy, Rogness, and Schwartz, 2004). Even so, many feminist researchers contend that we should develop and operationalize even broader definitions because violence takes many varied forms (Lupri, Grandin, and Brinkerhoff, 1994; DeKeseredy and Schwartz, 2001).

These scholars call for definitions that include physical and sexual violence, as well as psychological, verbal, economic, and spiritual violence. They also argue that the latter four behaviours are just as or more threatening than physically and/or sexually violent acts (Duffy and Momirov, 1997; DeKeseredy and Schwartz, 2001). Consider the voice of an abused woman interviewed by MacLeod (1987: 12):

> The thing that's most hurting for me is the way he makes me feel so dirty, so filthy. He treats me like a dog, worse even. He tells me I'm ugly and worthless. He spits on me. It's not enough to hit me and kick me. He spits on me. Sometimes I think the hitting is better than being made to feel so low.

Many feminist researchers do not deny totally the value of narrow definitions of violence, but they see the limitations of such an approach at the same time. Dobash and Dobash (1998: 4) for example, argue that:

> A more "narrow" or circumscribed definition of violence, with each type examined in its own right and statistics gathered accordingly, may sometimes have the advantage of increasing clarity about the nature and context of a specific form of violence, but may simultaneously lose the prospect of generalizing across a much wider spectrum of violence(s).

Similarly, British feminists Kelly and Radford (1998) argue that an attempt to isolate certain specific illegal acts of abuse may, in fact, be useful and important for certain analytical tasks. Yet it is essential to keep in mind the differences between analytical and experiential boundaries. For example, one may ignore rape for the time being and instead study wife beating. However, it is impossible to make such a differentiation completely, since rape is an integral component of wife beating, as described in Exhibit 11.1. Like

---

Exhibit 11.1   A Canadian Example of Both Physical and Sexual Violence during Separation/Divorce

---

One of Ann's attempts to leave resulted in her being taken for a ride to a remote nature conservation area, some hours' drive north of Toronto. Rob's stated goal was reconciliation. Ann had gone along with his offer because she took it to be genuine. The ride was not smooth, because Ann did not immediately give in to Rob's reconciliation request. This was quite unlike Ann. Previously she would have readily given in to whatever Rob wanted. Ann was generally obedient, but on that hot and humid summer day, she did not immediately comply. Ann complained and asked Rob to treat her better. For her resistance, Rob's revenge was quite merciless. He stopped the van in the middle of the road, dragged Ann out into the bush, and violently raped her. The brush was sticky, and they were in the middle of the wilderness.

The rape was only the beginning of hours of torture that Rob inflicted on Ann. He ripped off all her clothes, jumped into his van, and started to drive away. Ann chased the van, totally exposed while he drove ahead, watching her anguish from the rearview mirror. Ann ran for seven miles. "It was a marshy area, the road was full of slithery things; he knew that I was deadly afraid of slithery things! I was hysterical." When Ann collapsed from her ordeal of the rape, coupled with her fear of the bush land and heat exhaustion, Rob picked up her nude body, drove back into the city, and dumped her on the front lawn of her parents' home.

Source: Sev'er (2002: 99–100)

---

many other women who want to leave, are trying to leave, or who have left abusive or extremely possessive marital/cohabiting partners, Ann was both physically and sexually abused by a man who was "fanatically determined" not to let her go (Russell, 1990).

Similarly, child abuse is often "multidimensional in nature" (DeKeseredy and Hinch, 1991). For example, a woman who participated in my separation/divorce sexual assault told me that shortly before she left her partner she walked into the bedroom and found him "masturbating in front of my children to *Penthouse*...."[7] Then she said that a few months after they split up:

> He came back...for a so-called emergency visitation and he was able to take my daughter away from me for eight hours even though, the DNA had never been proven. And when my daughter finally came back, she had severe diaper rash, smelled like cigarettes and alcohol, and had bruises right, right on her thighs and on her wrists.

Researchers use different types of broad definitions, depending on their field of interest. For example, Linda MacLeod and I primarily study woman abuse, and we argue the following broad definition of this problem should be used:

> Woman abuse is the misuse of power by a husband, intimate partner (whether male or female), ex-husband, or ex-partner against a woman, resulting in a loss of dignity, control, and safety as well as a feeling of powerlessness and entrapment experienced by the woman who is the direct victim of ongoing or repeated physical, psychological, economic, sexual, verbal, and/or spiritual abuse. Woman abuse also includes persistent threats or forcing women to witness violence against their children, other relatives, friends, pets,

and/or cherished possessions by their husbands, partners, ex-husbands, or ex-partners (DeKeseredy and MacLeod, 1997: 5).

Duffy and Momirov (1997: 54) provide an example of a broad definition of child abuse:

[C]hild abuse is defined as acts of commission or omission, usually by those entrusted with the care and nurturing of the child, which function to deny the child the reasonable opportunity to develop his or her potential as a human being.

In sum, many non-violent, highly injurious behaviours are just as worthy of in-depth empirical, theoretical, and political attention as those that cause physical harm. Furthermore, physical abuse, sexual abuse, and psychological abuse are not mutually exclusive. Indeed, psychological abuse almost always accompanies physical assaults in intimate relationships (Okun, 1986; Gelles and Straus, 1988; DeKeseredy and Joseph, 2004).

Language[8]

What name should we give the problems examined in this chapter? Many readers are likely to respond to this question by saying, "That's a silly question! You are addressing violence in the family. So use the term family violence." Others contend that this name or the term "domestic violence" is necessary because it differentiates between violence in the family and violence involving friends, acquaintances, co-workers, and strangers (DeKeseredy and MacLeod, 1997). Then there are government agencies and community groups who also favour the label domestic or family violence because they claim that it is more inclusive (Denham and Gillespie, 1999). "Family violence" and "domestic violence" are gender-neutral terms, which suggest that violence results from ordinary, everyday social interactions in the family that have gone wrong, and that women are as responsible for the problem as men (Ellis, 1987; DeKeseredy and Hinch, 1991). So do terms such as "spousal violence," "marital violence," and "conjugal violence." These names situate violence in the home, but do not specify that women are more often the people abused and that men are more often the abusers (Duffy and Momirov, 1997; Sev'er, 2002). In reality, women and children are much more likely to be assaulted in families than are men.

This is why almost all feminist scholars use the terms "woman abuse," "wife beating," "woman battering," or "violence against women and children." For them, violence at home is gendered and a "tactic of coercive control" used to maintain male power and domination over wives and children (Yllo, 1993; Jasinski, 2001). For example, Smith's (1990) Toronto survey of wife beating shows that men who espouse the ideology of familial patriarchy are more likely to beat their wives than are men who do not adhere to this ideology. Similarly, DeKeseredy and Kelly (1993a) found that Canadian male undergraduates who physically, sexually, and psychologically abuse their dating partners are more likely to espouse this ideology than are those who are not abusive. Familial patriarchal ideology is a discourse which supports the abuse of women who violate the ideals of male power and control over women in intimate relationships (Smith, 1990; DeKeseredy and Schwartz, 1993).

Familial patriarchy also influences men to abuse women during and/or after separation/divorce. Consider that 80 percent of the rural Ohio women I interviewed so far stated that the males who sexually assaulted them feel that "men should be in charge at home." Note how one of my respondent's partner treated her until she finally left him:

> His favourite thing was, "If you are going to be at work, you're going to be here cooking and cleaning, doing laundry. And if I ever catch you sitting on your ass, I'm going to beat the fuck out of you, you know."

Another woman told me:

> I was probably beat five days out of the week and he would take off because I got to work at three and he'd be back from his job like at four. He'd take off and go to the bars. He would either take the starter off my car, or take the battery out of my car, or yank the phone out of the wall and then he would come home and beat me because he thought I was screwing around on him.

Most non-feminists use gender-neutral terms and justify their approach by referring to Conflict Tactic Scale data showing that women are as violent as men in intimate, heterosexual relationships. Statistics Canada's (2002) 1999 GSS uncovered such data and found that eight percent of 14,269 women and seven percent of 11,607 men reported at least one incident of intimate partner violence committed by a current or former spouse between 1994 and 1999. These results have been seized upon by some journalists and many fathers' rights groups to support claims that women are as violent as men and that Canada is seeing a resurgence of what Steinmetz (1977–78) referred to as the "battered husband syndrome" (Jiwani, 2000). For example, Earl Silverman, program coordinator for the Calgary-based advocacy group, Family of Men Support Society, told the *Globe and Mail* that Statistics Canada's (2002) findings show "that there has been a severe bias against men in the past not considering them as victims" and "[t]o try to deny the other side of the coin reduces the credibility of the first side" (Foss, 2002: 8).

Do 1999 GSS data actually show that men and women are equally violent? Many researchers, myself included,[9] contend that these results are deceptive for several reasons. First, the GSS provides only raw counts of violent acts committed, and thus misses the fact that much of male and female violence is used for different reasons (Jiwani, 2000). As demonstrated by studies that added context, meaning, and motive measures to the CTS, a common cause of women's violence in intimate relationships is self-defence, whereas men typically use violence to control their partners (Saunders, 1986; Ellis and Stuckless, 1996; DeKeseredy, Saunders, Schwartz, and Alvi, 1997). As Ellis asserts in his critique of the 1999 GSS, "Ignoring context, meaning and motive is misinforming... And not separating different types of violence is misleading" (cited in Foss, 2002: 2).

Of course, some women strike some men, sometimes with the intent to injure. Still, relying on simple counts of behaviours does not mitigate and change the meaning of the conclusion that women overwhelmingly are the predominant victims of intimate adult violence for several reasons. For example, the CTS alone cannot accurately determine gender variations in intimate violence because of the following:

- Males are more likely to under-report their violence (Edleson and Brygger, 1996).
- The CTS measures only conflict-instigated violence and ignores male violence used to control women or violence that may not stem from any single identifiable cause (e.g., dispute, difference, or spat) (DeKeseredy and Schwartz, 1998b).

- The CTS excludes some major types of abusive behaviour, such as forced isolation (Jiwani, 2000).

These criticisms are dismissed by supporters of gender-neutral definitions, including Canadian politicians who were members of the 1998 Special Joint Committee on Child Custody and Access (SJC) (Pearson and Gallaway, 1998). The SJC devoted considerable attention to a document submitted by fathers' rights activist Ferrel Christensen (2002) claiming that Canadian feminist survey researchers engage in "prostituted science and scholarship," and that violence in intimate relationships is sexually symmetrical. Obviously, Christensen and others with similar views influenced the SJC, because it concluded that "because of the existence of violence against men, the Committee would not recommend that family law or divorce legislation employ a gender-specific definition of family violence" (Pearson and Gallaway, 1998: 81).

Consider, too, that prior to coming to the above conclusion, the SJC had access to CNS data showing that only a distinct minority of female undergraduates reported that they had initiated a physical attack since leaving high school, and that much of the violence reported by women was in self-defence or fighting back (DeKeseredy, Saunders, Schwartz, and Alvi, 1997). I even publicly presented these findings to the SJC, but these and similar results uncovered by other researchers (e.g., Saunders, 1986) were ignored, as they typically are by conservative politicians, the mainstream media, and prominent critics of feminist research on intimate violence (e.g., Pearson, 1997; Mills, 2003).

Summary

Defining the types of violence described in this chapter generates heated debates that will not be resolved in the near future, if ever. This is because wife beating, child abuse, elder abuse, and other types of violence in the family are highly politicized areas of inquiry. Furthermore, definitions of these issues are used as political weapons in social struggles (Ellis, 1987; DeKeseredy and Schwartz, 2003). For example, those who use broad definitions argue that child abuse, wife beating, and so on are widespread social problems (Duffy and Momirov, 1997). From their standpoint, governments should spend a considerable amount of money on prevention and control initiatives (Denham and Gillespie, 1999). On the other hand, proponents of narrow definitions view violence in the family as a relatively rare problem and assert that government resources should not be diverted from "more serious problems" such as terrorism and war to deal with it (Ellis, 1987; Sev'er, 2002).

Again, many academics, members of the general public, and politicians view violence behind closed doors in gender-neutral terms. Sharply opposed to this view are people like me, who contend that violence in the family is a function of gender, power, and control (Yllo, 1993; Sev'er, 2002). I also argue that such violence is multidimensional in nature. Nevertheless, due in part to space limitations and in part to the shortage of Canadian research on some other behaviours that are considered violent or abusive (e.g., separation/divorce sexual assault), only physical assaults that do not result in death will be primarily addressed in the following sections.

This is not to say, however, that homicide in family/household settings is a trivial issue. In fact, spousal homicides account for a sizeable portion of all murders in Canada.

In fact, in 2000, 17 percent of *all* victims of solved homicides and 52 percent of the victims of all family homicides were killed by their legal or common-law partners (Pottie Bunge and Sauve, 2002). Such murders are generally related to jealousy or a woman's attempt to end a relationship (Russell, 2001), and in Canada, between 1991 and 2000, murder victimization rates were the highest among separated women (37.4 wives per million separated couples) (Pottie Bunge and Sauve, 2002). As Polk (2003: 134) reminds us, "[T]ime and time again the phrase 'if I can't have you, no one will' echoes through the data" on homicide in the context of sexual intimacy. Consider what one of my rural Ohio interviewees went through and still fears:

> And I mean the one night he'd come home and pull a double barrel and cock both barrels and said he was going to kill me. And it was like, wait a minute here. You know, it was two o'clock in the morning. I was sound asleep and I got up at four and go to work. But he'd always keep pressuring me, "If you leave me, I'll find you, I'll kill you. If you leave me, I'll find you, I'll kill you."

Unfortunately, this scenario and what happened to O. J. Simpson's ex-wife Nicole is "not unusual" (Gardner, 1994: A9).

"LIVING IN A HOUSE OF HORRORS": WIFE ABUSE[10]

Although patriarchal practices and discourses are endemic in Canada, every major social institution, such as the family, the workplace, and the military, has been affected by laws and other means of eliminating sexism (Renzetti and Curran, 1995; DeKeseredy and Schwartz, 2003). Consider what happened in the late 1980s and early 1990s. Public awareness and outrage emerged over wife beating and other forms of woman abuse (Denham and Gillespie, 1999). And, due in large part to more than two decades of practical struggles waged by feminists to get politicians to define male-to-female violence as a major social problem (Levan, 1996), the mass murder of 14 women at Universite de Montreal's Ecole Polytechnique, and alarming wife abuse survey data generated by sociologists (e.g., Smith, 1987), between 1988 and 1996 the Canadian federal government committed $176 million to various initiatives on violence in the family, especially wife abuse (Denham and Gillespie, 1999). The research described in this section is a product of these major achievements (McKenna and Larkin, 2002a).

The Extent of Wife Abuse

Data presented in Table 11. 1 show that wives and female cohabiting partners are just as, if not more, likely to be beaten in Canada than in the U.S. For example, based on both national U.S. male and female responses to the CTS, Straus and Gelles (1986) found an 11.3 percent annual incidence rate. This figure is slightly lower than the 1975 rate (12.1%) reported by Straus, Gelles, and Steinmetz (1981). In sharp contrast to these figures, Table 11.1 shows three Canadian studies that report higher CTS rates. Canadian CTS figures, including those generated by Statistics Canada (1993, 2002), are also higher than that (1.9%) recently elicited in the U.S. by Tjaden and Thoennes' (1998) National Violence

Against Women Survey. However, the similar or higher Canadian CTS rates may be a function of sampling differences and other methodological factors.

Wife abuse cuts across all socio-economic categories (Menard, 2001), but some Canadian women are at higher risk than others. For example, the 1999 GSS found that Aboriginal women reported a five-year prevalence rate (12.6%) of violence committed by a current or former partner that is three times that (3.5%) reported by non-Aboriginal women (Trainor and Mihorean, 2001). The difference is even larger for a one-year period (8.1% vs. 1.6%) (Brownridge, 2003).

Economically disadvantaged women are also at higher risk of being physically assaulted by their spouses. In fact, poverty and unemployment are powerful determinants of various types of woman abuse (Raphael, 2001a; DeKeseredy, Alvi, and Schwartz, 2004). Consider the plight of women living in Canadian public housing estates. These are key arenas where gendered power relations are played out (Raphael, 2001b; DeKeseredy, Alvi, Schwartz, and Tomaszewski, 2003). Others assert that the influence of "hard drugs" (e.g., crack cocaine) into these contexts has exacerbated the degradation and abuse of women who live in what Venkatesh (2000) refers to as "cities-within-cities." Furthermore, joblessness, unbalanced gender ratios, poverty, and men's attempts to resist women's struggles for gender equity all have enhanced cultural support for woman abuse in public housing communities (Bourgois, 1995; DeKeseredy and Schwartz, 2002).

The Quality of Neighbourhood Life Survey (QNLS) supports the above assertions. Conducted by several colleagues and me, it was administered in six public housing estates in an urban centre in Eastern Ontario (see DeKeseredy, Alvi, Schwartz, and Perry, 1999; DeKeseredy, Alvi, Schwartz, and Tomaszewski, 2003). The majority of the women in our sample live in "severely distressed households" (Kasarda, 1992), which simultaneously exhibit five characteristics: low income, less than high school education, poor work history, single parenthood, and dependency on government assistance.

Using a modified version of Straus, Hamby, Boney-McCoy, and Sugarman's (1996) CTS-2, we found that 19.3 percent of the female respondents were, in the year before the study, victimized by intimate partner violence (DeKeseredy, Alvi, Schwartz, and Perry, 1999). This rate is higher than all of the annual rates presented in Table 11.1. Thus, as in the U.S., women in public housing estates, living under conditions of concentrated urban disadvantage, seem to suffer from violence from intimates at a greater rate than other women (Renzetti and Maier, 2002), even though relatively few of them are living in traditional marital relationships (Holzman and Piper, 1998). We also found that cohabiting and separated/divorced female public housing residents reported higher rates of violence than their married counterparts (DeKeseredy, Schwartz, and Alvi, 2004).

Theories of Wife Abuse

Contrary to popular belief, most wife beaters are not "sick" or mentally ill (Sev'er, 2002). In fact, it is estimated that less than 10 percent of all incidents of intimate violence are caused by psychological disorders (Gelles and Straus, 1998). This is one of the main reasons why sociological theories are used more than psychological perspectives. Space limitations preclude an exhaustive summary of all sociological theories of wife abuse.[11] Instead, described below is an integrated sociological theory that combines macro- and micro-level factors. Developed by Martin Schwartz and me (see DeKeseredy and Schwartz, 2002), this perspective was constructed partly in response to Jasinski's (2001: 17) assertion that "Acknowledging the existence of multiple risk factors is an important step in understanding the dynamics of violence against women." In fact, today, more and more leading experts in the field are calling for theory integration in explaining male-to-female victimization.

Economic Exclusion/Male Peer Support Model[12]

Again, some women are at higher risk of being beaten by their marital/cohabiting partners than are other women. Why do female public housing residents experience more violent threats to their health and well-being than women in the general population? Certainly, although it is important to know the extent of wife abuse and other forms of woman abuse in public housing in order to develop useful social support services for victims, we also need to identify the major sources of this problem in order to develop effective prevention and control strategies. Moreover, as Raphael (2001a: 454) reminds us, although this field is in its infancy, the empirical work done so far "makes it clear that economic variables need to be better incorporated into the current theoretical mix than they have been heretofore."

Economic exclusion and the role of patriarchal male peer support are major components of the theoretical model described in Figure 11.1, which is a modified version of Sernau's (2001: 24) Web of Exclusion Model. Heavily informed by sociological perspectives offered by Sernau, Schwartz, and me (see DeKeseredy and Schwartz, 1993 and by Wilson (1996) and Young (1999), this model argues that recent major economic transformations in North America (e.g., the shift from a manufacturing to a service-based economy) displace working-class men and women, who often end up in public housing and other "clusters of poverty" (Sernau, 2001). Unable to economically support their families and live up to their culturally defined role as "bread winner," socially and economically excluded men experience high levels of life events stress because "their normal paths for personal power and prestige have been cut off" (Raphael, 2001b: 703). Such stress prompts them to seek social support from men with similar problems (DeKeseredy, Alvi, and Schwartz, 2004). Such support may help men resolve intimate relationship problems or facilitate the management of their stress, "but there are no guarantees that such a resolution is free of cost" (Vaux, 1985: 102). As demonstrated by studies of woman abuse in courtship (e.g., DeKeseredy, 1988a; Schwartz and DeKeseredy, 1997), male peer support may alleviate dating life events stress, but it can also have negative consequences for the health and safety of women. For example, I found that for men with high levels of such stress, social ties with abusive peers were strongly related to woman abuse in Canadian college dating (see DeKeseredy, 1988b). Similarly, patriarchal male peer support in public housing promotes wife beating, sexual assault, and other highly injurious "macho activities" (Raphael, 2001b; Websdale, 2001).

The economic exclusion/male peer support model fills several gaps in the theoretical literature on wife beating, but it is not a predictive model. Furthermore, like any social scientific perspective, it can be improved. For example, consistent with integrated male peer support theories of woman abuse on campus (e.g., Godenzi, Schwartz, and DeKeseredy, 2001), Figure 11.1 does not specifically address whether members of patriarchal male peer

FIGURE 11.1 The Economic Exclusion/Male Peer Support Model

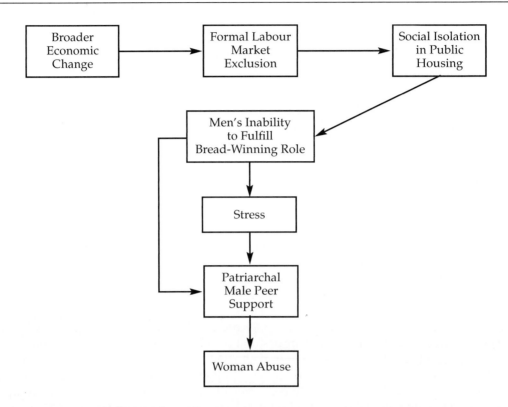

groups are intentionally recruited into these alliances or whether they gravitate to such groups as a way of selectively attempting to sustain or receive support for their earlier acquired values and behaviour. The model also does not specify that men may interact with and be influenced by peers who live away from public housing. Another point to consider is that, as with every other male peer support model, racial/ethnic variations in male peer support dynamics remain to be examined. Hopefully, future theoretical work on the relationship between economic factors, male peer support, and woman abuse in North American public housing will address these and other shortcomings.

"SPARE THE ROD AND SPOIL THE CHILD": CHILD ABUSE

In 1998, when I was living in Ottawa, Ontario, I had a conversation with a mature under-graduate student about violence in the family. She said to me, "Sometimes, if they get out of hand, I slap and spank my children. Do you think I am abusive?" *I think so, but many Canadians disagree with me.* In fact, there is little consensus on the meaning of

---

Exhibit 11.2　*Child Abuse or Normal Discipline?*

Three-year-old Jimmy was playing with his puppy near a pond in his backyard. He tried to make his puppy drink from the pond by roughly holding his face to the water. Jimmy's father saw him forcing the puppy to drink and yelled at him to stop. After Jimmy did not respond, his father pulled Jimmy away from the dog and began holding his head under water to "teach him a lesson" about the appropriate way to treat his dog.

Angela's baby, Maria, had colic from the day she was born. This meant that from 4:00 in the afternoon until 8:00 P.M., everyday, Maria would cry inconsolably. No matter what Angela did, nothing would help Maria to stop crying. One evening, after Maria had been crying for three straight hours, Angela began shaking Maria out of frustration. The shaking caused Maria to cry more loudly, which, in turn, caused Angela to shake the five month-old more vigorously. Angela shook Maria until she lost consciousness.

Ryan and his brother Matthew were playing with their Power Rangers when they got into a disagreement. Both boys began hitting each other and calling one another names. Alice, the mother of the boys, came running into the room and pulled the boys apart. She then took each boy, pulled down his trousers, put him over her knee, and spanked him several times.

Source: Barnett, Miller-Perrin, and Perrin (1997: 42–43)

---

physical child abuse (Alvi, DeKeseredy, and Ellis, 2000). Some people contend that any form of physical punishment is abuse, while others assert that physical punishment should be regarded as abuse only if it harms or threatens a child's physical or mental health. What do you think? How would you define each of the three situations described in Exhibit 11.2?

Most readers would define the first two vignettes in Exhibit 11.2 as abusive, while the third would be seen as appropriate discipline. For example, Straus (1991) found that a very large number of Americans sees nothing wrong with what the mother of Ryan and Matthew (see Exhibit 11.2) did to them. In fact, in North America, spanking "is the norm rather than the exception" (Flynn, 1998). But doesn't spanking hurt, and don't people who spank children condone the use of violence to resolve conflicts or to "get one's way" (Barnett, Miller-Perrin, and Perrin, 1997)? Isn't spanking associated with other forms of violence in the family, such as sibling violence? Although research shows that the answer to this question is "yes" (Straus, 1994; Payne and Gainey, 2002), many Canadians view spanking as legitimate behaviour and strongly defend the "right" of parents to raise their children as they see fit (Alvi, DeKeseredy, and Ellis, 2000; Kornblum and Julian, 2004). As described in Exhibit 11.3, this is due in part to the fact that spanking is legal in Canada except under certain conditions. Note, too, that spanking is the most universal type of physical violence (Tower, 2002), but that it is illegal in some other countries such as Sweden.

Here, any type of intentional parent-to-child physical violence is defined as abuse, because almost all violent behaviours result in some degree of pain and suffering. The rates of child abuse described below are guided by this definition.

Exhibit 11.3   Canadian Spanking Laws

A Supreme Court of Canada ruling handed down on January 30, 2004 upholds the "spanking laws" in Canada, but for the first time, the high court has issued guidelines that say spanking teenagers or children under age two, hitting a child in the head, or using objects such as belts or rulers are actions that go too far.

In a deeply split 6-3 decision, the court ruled...the so-called "spanking" defence in Canadian law does not protect or excuse "outbursts of violence against a child motivated by anger or animated by frustration."

Still, parents, their stand-in caregivers, and teachers may use reasonable force if it is for "educative or corrective purposes," Chief Justice Beverley McLachlin wrote for the majority.

"The reality is," wrote McLachlin, that without such a defence, Canada's "broad assault law would criminalize force falling far short of what we think as corporal punishment, like placing an unwilling child in a chair for a five-minute 'time-out.'"

Source: CanadianLawSite.Com (2004: 3).

The Extent of Child Abuse

How many Canadian children are physically victimized by their parents? It is impossible to accurately answer this question because:

- Only the most extreme cases come to the attention of the professional community.
- Many people do not disclose incidents because of fear of reprisal, shame, and the failure to recognize that parent-to-child violence is abuse.
- There are no Canadian national representative sample survey data.

For these and other reasons, national representative sample surveys similar to those conducted in the U.S. are necessary. To a certain extent, Health Canada addressed this concern by funding the Canadian Incidence Study of Reported Child Abuse and Neglect (CIS), which provides data on children reported to and investigated by child welfare services from October to December 1998 (Trocme et al., 2001). Below are some of the major results of the CIS, derived from 51 sites in all Canadian provinces and territories:

- Most (69%) of the substantiated reports of physical abuse (34%) involved inappropriate punishment,[13] while 31 percent were other forms of physical abuse (e.g., intentionally burning a child).
- Shaken Baby Syndrome accounted for one percent of substantiated reports.
- Most investigations of parents involved biological mothers (61%) and biological fathers (38%).
- Forty-one percent of the investigations involving biological mothers and 45 percent of those involving biological fathers were substantiated.
- Fifty-three percent of the investigations involved boys and 43 percent involved girls.

Despite enhancing a social scientific understanding of child abuse in Canada, the above and other data generated by the CIS are unreliable because they were not gathered from members of the general public. Again, many cases never come to the attention of the professional community. MacMillan and her colleagues (1997) conducted the Ontario Health Supplement Study (OHSS), designed to address this problem. They surveyed 9,953 Ontario residents aged 15 years and older and found that 31.2 percent of the males and 21.1 percent of the females reported physical abuse while growing up. Also, natural fathers were the persons most commonly identified as engaging in physical abuse, a finding that challenges gender-neutral definitions discussed earlier.

To the best of my knowledge, the OHSS is the largest Canadian general population survey of its kind, and the rates uncovered would have been higher if the research team had asked questions about spanking and slapping. Nevertheless, their findings are similar to prevalence rates reported in many other countries using similar definitions of child abuse (Cole, 1997; Cawson, Wattam, Brooker, and Kelly, 2000). Still, it is difficult to determine whether Canadian parents are more or less violent than their U.S. counterparts because different measures, samples, and time periods were used in the two national U.S. surveys on violence in the family.

Both surveys used renditions of the CTS to measure parent-to-child violence, and the first one, conducted in 1976 by Straus, Gelles, and Steinmetz (1981), found that:

- Three percent of the parents interviewed said that they kicked, bit, or punched their referent child in 1975, and about eight percent of the respondents reported having committed these acts at least once while their child was growing up.

- Slightly more than 10 parents in 1,000 reported having beaten their child at least once a year, and slightly more than 40 parents in 1,000 said that they have ever beaten their child.

- Approximately 30 children in 1,000 were threatened with a weapon while growing up, while roughly one in 1,000 children had a parent who shot or tried to shoot or stab him or her.

- Responses to the "child abuse index" (i.e., violent acts that could result in injury) show that 3.6 percent of the parents surveyed reported an abusive act of violence.

Administered in 1985, Straus and Gelles's (1986) National Family Violence Resurvey generated the following data:

- Approximately 75 percent of the parents in the sample reported at least one violent act.

- About two percent of parents engaged in one act of abusive violence (e.g., a high probability of injuring a child).

- Nearly 1.5 million children are seriously injured each year.

- Each year, 6.9 million children are "abused" (includes being hit with an object).

Child abuse increases the risk of crime outside the family (Alvi, 2000; Payne and Gainey, 2002). In fact, many North American adult and adolescent female offenders have a history of physical and sexual abuse, as well as neglect (DeKeseredy, 2000b; Chesney-Lind and Pasko, 2004). Furthermore, the background of many women in Canadian federal correctional facilities "underscores the important links between women's childhood victimization and their later criminal careers" (Chesney-Lind, 1997: 27). Consider Widom's (1989) U.S. study, which shows that abused or neglected girls were twice as likely as other girls in the study to have an adult criminal record. Abused boys, too, are at very high risk of becoming adult criminal offenders (Kruttschnitt and Dornfeld, 1991; Weeks and Widom, 1998). Thus, it appears that if we could prevent child abuse and neglect, we could reduce adult crime (Currie, 1998).

Theories of Child Abuse

There are a number of risk factors associated with child abuse, but one of the most consistent findings is that people who grew up in violent homes abuse their children. To explain this problem, many researchers, practitioners, and members of the general public use a "commonly stated" perspective on violence in the family: social learning theory (Duffy and Momirov, 1997; Payne and Gainey, 2002).

"Violence Begets Violence": Social Learning Theory

According to social learning theory, physical punishment and growing up in a household where parents physically assault each other trains people to abuse their children (Barnett, Miller-Perrin, and Perrin, 1997). The following case of an abusive mother is an example of this learning process:

> When I was a child, my step-father beat me. He beat me often enough to prompt me to swear that when I had kids I wouldn't lay a hand on them.
>
> It didn't work that way. The first couple of years everything went fine, then Bob (her husband) started making frequent and lengthy trips out of town. After he was gone a few days, I started taking it out on the kids.
>
> When Bob would ask me why the kids were black and blue, I would pass it off by saying they fell while playing or bumped into the door (Straus, Gelles, and Steinmetz, 1981: 107–8).

Social learning theorists argue that not only do people learn techniques of being violent, but they also learn the social and moral justifications for child abuse (Barnett, Miller-Perrin, and Perrin, 1997). For example, many parents claim that hitting children is "necessary, normal, and good" (Straus, Gelles, and Steinmetz, 1981). External sources also teach people to hit their children and to justify their actions. Consider what this affiliate of the Vancouver-based Focus on the Family said about spanking: "We recommend it. If parents don't realize that a defiant child will soon be running the household and soon become a problem to teachers and even police and others, then we're missing something important here" (cited in Alvi, DeKeseredy, and Ellis, 2000: 160). The social learning perspective also asserts that children who are abused and/or those who observed their parents hitting each other learn that "love and violence go together" (Straus and Smith, 1990).

There is some support for social learning theory, but as Straus, Gelles, and Steinmetz (1981: 122) remind us, it is wrong to "put the whole burden of violence on what is learned in the family." For example, many people raised in non-violent homes abuse their children. On the other hand, many people who directly experienced child abuse or watched their fathers beat their mothers never assault their marital partners or children (Jasinski, 2001). Indiana Congressman Dan Burton is one major example of someone who managed to "break the cycle of violence" in his family (Payne and Gainey, 2002). Below he describes some of his painful childhood experiences:

> Mother wasn't the only object of his violence. She told me about a time when I was six months old. My parents took me to the movies, and I started crying as babies do. He took me out to the lobby. Later my mother saw that I was black and blue from my shoulder to my ankles. Another beating, I remember vividly, took place when I was ten.... Dad gave me a lot of groceries to get and ordered me to a little store a few blocks away. It was snowing like crazy when I started back to the motel with the groceries. The bags got wet and broke, spilling the groceries everywhere.... When I got back, my father beat the hell out of me. I was terrified of him (Burton, 1994: 92).

Power, a factor ignored by social learning theory, is one of the most important determinants of child abuse. Some researchers claim that fathers assault their children "because they have power," while mothers do so "because they have little power" (Cole, 1988: 523; Duffy and Momirov, 1997). From a feminist standpoint, father-to-child abuse is rooted in men's historical right to own, control, and discipline their wives and children. Furthermore, even today, despite the ongoing efforts of the women's movement, most wives, regardless of whether they work outside the home, do the bulk of child rearing, cleaning, and other domestic duties (Alvi, DeKeseredy, and Ellis, 2000; Baker, 2001). This results in overwork, alienation, and frustration (Payne and Gainey, 2002). Consequently, some women express their misery and suffering by hitting their children, who are the "only available victims with less power than them" (Duffy and Momirov, 1997: 149).

"A NORMAL PART OF GROWING UP": SIBLING VIOLENCE

The growing amount of media, public, and professional attention given to both wife abuse and child abuse has led many North Americans to believe that violence against wives and children are the most common forms of violence in the family (Barnett, Miller-Perrin, and Perrin, 1997). However, national U.S. survey data (e.g., Straus, Gelles, and Steinmetz, 1981) show that sibling violence occurs more frequently than husband-to-wife assaults and parent-to-child violence. Sibling violence is also the most common and overlooked form of violence experienced by family members in the U.S. (Payne and Gainey, 2002). If you have one or more brothers and/or sisters, does the following incident sound familiar to you?

> I can't remember a time when my brother didn't taunt me, usually trying to get me to respond so he would be justified in hitting me. Usually he would be saying I was a crybaby or a sissy or stupid or ugly and that no one would like me, want to be around me, or whatever. Sometimes he would accuse me of doing something, and if I denied it, he would call me a liar. I usually felt overwhelmingly helpless because nothing I said or did would stop him. If no one else was around, he would start beating on me, after which he would stop and go away (cited in Barnett, Miller-Perrin, and Perrin, 1997: 50).

Chances are, too, that even if you haven't engaged in or been the target of sibling violence, you have witnessed this behaviour. Consider what happened to my daughter and me in December 2001 while we were visiting one of my cousins in Detroit. She needed

---

Exhibit 11.4   Sibling Violence and Excuses

How many of the following excuses have you heard to justify one sibling's acts toward another?

- Don't worry about; it's just normal sibling rivalry.
- They were just playing doctor.
- Kids will be kids.

- He really didn't mean to hurt his sister. He loves her.
- It's just normal childhood curiosity.
- Kids are always calling each other names.
- I told him not to hit her again.
- They will grow out of it.

Source: Wallace (1996: 100)

---

groceries and asked me to watch her four young children while she went shopping. As soon as she left, one of her two boys started insulting one of his two sisters and grabbed her underwear. She then punched him and he responded by dragging her to the bathroom to give her a "swirly." In other words, he was going to put her head in the toilet. His other sister and I physically restrained the boy, but he managed to punch her in the nose and it started bleeding. Fortunately, his mother came home five minutes later and the violence stopped because her children were worried that they were going to be spanked. My daughter and I were in a state of shock, but my cousin told us, "Don't worry. This happens all the time. You know what kids are like." As described in Exhibit 11.4, this is just one of several excuses parents use to justify sibling violence.

Definition of Sibling Violence

Sibling violence includes many highly injurious physical, sexual, and psychological behaviours. Still, only non-lethal physical assaults will be discussed here due to the shortage of theoretical and empirical work on other abusive acts. Thus, sibling violence is defined here as any form of intentional physical violence inflicted by one child in a family unit on another.[14] Children do not have to be related by birth in order for their physically injurious acts to be considered violent. There are many cases in which children from different marriages or cohabiting relationships end up in the same household and physically hurt one another (DeKeseredy and Ellis, 1997).

Why Is Sibling Violence Overlooked?

According to Gelles and Cornell (1990: 85), Wiehe (1997), and Payne and Gainey (2002), sibling violence is overlooked for the following reasons, some of which were briefly discussed before:

- Siblings hitting one another is so common that few people regard these behaviours as violent.

- Most parents consider sibling conflict an inevitable part of growing up and rarely discourage their children from engaging in violent behaviour with siblings. In fact,

Sibling violence is often overlooked in studies of family violence.

most parents ignore violence and only intervene when "minor" events are seen as escalating into major conflicts.

- Sibling rivalry is defined as a "normal" part of sibling relations, and many parents believe that such rivalry provides a good training ground for the successful management of aggressive behaviour in the "real world."
- Social norms encourage expressions of aggressive behaviour among siblings and thus hinder the recognition of sibling violence as deviant and worthy of serious concern.

Some social scientists also contribute to the belief that sibling violence is acceptable behaviour. Bank and Kahn (1982), for example, state that there are five "positive" aspects of sibling aggression:

- Aggression can be reassuring when parents are emotionally or physically unavailable.
- It forces children into a social "laboratory" where they can learn how to manage and resolve disputes, and aggression fosters the development of competence, morality, courage, and creativity.
- Sibling aggression teaches children skills that can be used in other relationships, such as the ability to deflect aggression and to defeat another without humiliation.

- Sibling aggression promotes feelings of loyalty.
- Sibling aggression enables children to "displace" their aggression onto a more appropriate target.

If you ask survivors of sibling violence if they agree with the above assertions, "a resounding 'NO' would be heard" across Canada (Wiehe, 1997: 2). I'm sure you would get the same response in the U.S. and other countries. Consider the damaging long-term effects of sibling violence described by one of Wiehe's adult respondents:

> I am afraid that everyone is going to abuse me in some way. I don't trust anyone. I feel in everything people say or do that they want to hurt me. I always take the blame for any mistake made or I feel that everyone is blaming me (1997: 141).

Other negative consequences of sibling violence include sexual dysfunction, interpersonal relationship problems, drug abuse, repeat victimization, and anger toward offenders (Wiehe, 1997; Payne and Gainey, 2002).

The Extent of Sibling Violence

To the best of my knowledge, only two Canadian sociological studies have examined sibling violence. The first, conducted by Desmond Ellis and me (see Ellis and DeKeseredy, 1994), was exploratory, and focused primarily on the prevalence of sibling violence. The second, conducted by Bly (1994), examined the risk markers associated with this harm.

Ellis and I administered questionnaires to a non-random sample of 215 undergraduate students and conducted face-to-face interviews with 34 learning-disabled children aged between six and eleven. Rather than define sibling violence for our respondents, we asked them to describe what happened when they "got into fights," "had problems getting along with their brothers and sisters," "did or had done to them things they did not like," and "hurt their feelings or hurt their bodies" (e.g., bruises, bumps, and cuts). Approximately 48 percent of the university students reported that they had been physically hurt by their siblings, and 100 percent of the learning-disabled children reported having been physically victimized.

This study should not be compared with the following U.S. findings because different measures, samples, and definitions were used:

- Seventy-two percent of Steinmetz's (1977) undergraduate student respondents reported experiencing sibling violence.
- The first National Family Violence Survey found that more than 8 out of 10 parents surveyed who had two or more children between the ages of 3 and 17 reported that there was one incident of sibling violence in the year before the survey. This translates into more than 36 million individual acts of sibling violence in one year (Straus, Gelles, and Steinmetz, 1981).
- Between 63 and 68 percent of the adolescent siblings in Steinmetz's (1982) sample of families used physical violence to resolve conflicts with their brothers or sisters.
- Eighty-eight percent of the males and 94 percent of the females in Roscoe, Goodwin, and Kennedy's (1987) sample of 244 junior high school students stated that they

were victims of sibling violence in the year before the study. Similarly, 85 percent of the males and 96 percent of the females stated that they were perpetrators of sibling violence during the same time period.

Despite the methodological differences between U.S. and Canadian studies, it is fair to conclude that sibling violence is a major North American social problem. The statistics reported here are alarming, and even higher ones would be obtained using a superior research design proposed elsewhere (see DeKeseredy and Ellis, 1997). Moreover, Canadian prevalence rates obtained by Desmond Ellis and me are significantly higher than the estimates of male-to-female violence in adult, heterosexual relationships generated by the CNS (see DeKeseredy and Kelly, 1993b) and the 1999 GSS (Statistics Canada, 2002). Therefore, it is reasonable to assume that, as in the U.S., sibling violence is the most common form of violence in the family.

Theories of Sibling Violence

Seven years ago, Duffy and Momirov (1997) stated that there is no "well-developed theory" of sibling violence. Unfortunately, this observation still holds true today. In fact, most contributions to the social scientific study of sibling violence are *atheoretical*. The few attempts to account for the reasons siblings physically hurt one another use the widely popular and most commonly cited explanation: social learning theory.

Some social learning theorists (e.g., Straus, Gelles, and Steinmetz, 1981) state that children exposed to marital violence and who are physically assaulted by their parents learn that violence is a legitimate way of resolving disputes with their siblings. There is some support for this theory, but U.S. national survey data do not reveal a causal relationship between sibling violence and other forms of violence in the family (Hotaling, Straus, and Lincoln, 1990). In fact, many children who have been exposed to wife-beating and other types of violence at home do not physically harm others (Gelles, 1998). Therefore, many other variables, such as those identified by Bly's (1994) Canadian qualitative study of 21 children between the ages of 7and 15, should be taken into account in further attempts to develop and test theories of sibling violence.

Some examples of key risk factors that warrant attention in future theoretical work are: learning difficulties; physical handicaps; size and strength; a low proportion of parental interactions signifying warmth; marital separation; inconsistent discipline; poor monitoring of children's behaviour; poverty; father's criminal record; mixed sibling groups; low self-esteem; and gender role socialization (Bly, 1994; DeKeseredy and Ellis, 1997; Duffy and Momirov, 1997; Wiehe, 1997; Payne and Gainey, 2002).

A richer understanding of sibling violence requires the development of a multifactor interactional theory. No individual risk factor identified here and in other sources fully explains sibling violence or any other type of violence in the family (Barnett, Miller-Perrin, and Perrin, 1997). Thus, researchers should construct and test theories that focus on how individual, social psychological, and broader cultural and social factors interact with one another to contribute to sibling violence (DeKeseredy and Ellis, 1997). The preventive and protective factors associated with these variables should also be taken into account (Barnett, Miller-Perrin, and Perrin, 1997).

THE DARK SIDE OF THE GOLDEN YEARS: ELDER ABUSE

Elderly family members have been abused for generations (Duff and Momirov, 1997). Nevertheless, prior to the 1980s, this problem received little social scientific attention in North America (Fisher, Zink, Rinto, Regan, Pabst, and Gothelf, 2003). Today, elder abuse is defined as a major type of intimate violence, and recent interest in this harm is the product of at least four factors. First, there is a rapidly growing number of North Americans aged 60 years or older (Dauvergne, 2002; Grossman and Lundy, 2003). Second, since people are living much longer than their ancestors, more middle-aged children than ever before are required to look after their elderly parents (Kornblum and Julian, 2004). Third, higher proportions of the elderly vote in elections than do members of other age groups (Alvi, DeKeseredy, and Ellis, 2000). Thus, they have considerable political power, which influences politicians to address their concerns (Duffy and Momirov, 1997). The fourth factor that contributed to the recognition of elder abuse as a social problem is the growing professional interest in the criminal victimization of the elderly (Fisher, Zink, Rinto, Regan, Pabst, and Gothelf, 2003).

The Extent of Elder Abuse

Two factors make it extremely difficult, if not impossible, to determine the exact extent of elder abuse in North America. First, unlike young family members, senior victims typically are disconnected from many social networks, such as workplaces, schools, and recreational centres (Vinton, 2001). Thus, the elderly are often referred to as "hidden victims." For example, if a battered child attends her mathematics class with bruises and cuts, her parents' abusive conduct is likely to be recognized by a teacher. On the other hand, a physically abused elderly person may be confined to his or her home with no one but the abuser observing (Payne and Gainey, 2002). Typically, a third party reports elder abuse (Duffy and Momirov, 1997).

The precise measurement of elder abuse is also hindered by victims' reluctance to report violent events (Payne and Gainey, 2002). The elderly's unwillingness to disclose abuse is a function of one or more of the following factors:

- Victims may fear being blamed for their victimization or fear retaliation from their abuser. Some victims even blame themselves for the violence perpetrated against them (Vinton, 2001).

- Victims may accept or tolerate physical assaults as preferable to perceived dangers or life-events stress associated with alternative living arrangements (e.g., a nursing home) (Payne and Gainey, 2002).

- Victims may not know where in their community they can turn for help, or the social support resources in their community may be inadequate (Duffy and Momirov, 1997).

- Victims who suffer from psychological disorders, such as dementia, may not be able to recall abusive events or may not even be aware that they were harmed (Okleford, Barnes-Holmes, Morichelli, Morjaria, Scocchera, Furniss, Sdogati, and Barnes-Holmes, 2003).

- Some victims may be more concerned about the welfare of their abusers than their own (Duffy and Momirov, 1997).

Despite these problems, several North American researchers have tried to obtain reliable representative sample survey data on the extent of elder abuse. In Canada, the 1999 GSS found that very few seniors (1%) reported being victimized by physical or sexual violence (Dauvergne, 2002). Podnieks's (1990) national telephone survey of elder abuse elicited an even lower rate (0.5%). These results likely are the products of several methodological problems. For example, the 1999 GSS was presented as a crime survey. As stated earlier in this chapter, unless respondents clearly label acts of violence as criminal in their own minds, they tend not to report them (Mihalic & Ellioit, 1997). Another point to consider is that Podnieks's study excluded violent acts committed by children and other family members who live in separate residences. People do not have to live with loved ones to physically assault them; data generated by dating violence and separation/divorce woman abuse studies strongly support this assertion. Also absent from Podnieks's data set are reports of violent acts committed by more than one co-resident child.

In sum, although the sampling procedures used in the studies reviewed here are superior to those used in previous Canadian studies,[15] the findings do not provide reliable data on the prevalence of violence against elderly family members. If Canadian researchers do not develop better measures of elder abuse and attempt to overcome the above and other methodological shortcomings identified by Kozma and Stones (1995), among others, many battered senior citizens will remain hidden "behind closed doors" (Straus, Gelles, and Steinmetz, 1981).

U.S. surveys also have generated low rates of elder abuse. For example, the National Crime Victimization Survey found that across a nine-year period (1993–2001), females aged 55 or older were assaulted by an intimate partner at a rate of 0.44 per 1,000 (Rennison and Rand, 2003). Moreover, Pillemer and Finkelhor (1988) found that of their approximately 2,000 elderly Boston-area respondents who lived alone, 3.2 percent reported having been victimized. Physical and verbal abuse accounted for most of these incidents, and almost two-thirds of the victims were abused by their spouses. Pillemer and Finkelhor (1988) also found that less than one-fourth of the victims were abused by their children, and that the most likely victim is a woman aged 80 or older. These results are similar to Podnieks's, but cannot be compared to those uncovered by the 1999 GSS because, according to Pottie Bunge (2000b: 27), "there were too few cases of physical and sexual violence against older persons reported to the GSS to permit detailed analysis by personal characteristics of victims."

Theories of Elder Abuse

No single theory of elder abuse dominates the sociological literature, and it is highly unlikely that a single perspective would ever be able to explain the complex nature of violence against elderly family members (Fattah and Sacco, 1989). However, an important theme in the sociological literature is dependency (Duffy and Momirov, 1997; Payne and Gainey, 2002).

Dependency and Elder Abuse

Two conflicting theories relate dependency to elder abuse. The first contends that family members experience considerable stress when a physically or mentally disabled person becomes dependent on them for financial, emotional, and physical care (Steinmetz and Amsden, 1983; Quinn and Tomita, 1986; Lachs and Pillemer, 1995). The lack of resources to cope with such stress engenders frustration, which often leads caregivers to victimize elderly dependents (Tindale et al., 1994; Pittaway, Westhues, and Peressini, 1995). This dependency perspective argues also that, since caregivers have much more power than dependent elders do, they have little to lose by being abusive (Phillips, 1986).

This dependency theory lacks strong empirical support (Payne and Gainey, 2002). Moreover, Pillemer (1985) asserts that if the power difference between elders and caregivers is as extreme as some scholars argue, there is little need to be violent. Instead, he argues that the abusive relative's dependency results in violence, and he offers a competing vision of dependency theory. Based on his analysis of studies that are methodologically superior to those that inform the first dependency account, Pillemer (1985) argues that children are dependent on their elderly parents for housing, money, etc., and that it is wrong to view abusive offspring as more powerful than their parents. In fact, being financially dependent on victims seems to be one of the most common forms of dependency contributing to abuse (Payne and Gainey, 2002). Pillemer further asserts that this type of dependence—not that of the elderly victim—generates stress that results in abuse. The relationship continues, not because the elderly victims fear reprisal, but because they feel a sense of responsibility or commitment to their abusive children (Duffy and Momirov, 1997).

Pillemer's (1985) dependency theory has several limitations. For example, in their critique of his account and other dependency theories, Fattah and Sacco (1989) argue that stress alone cannot explain elder abuse. They and Duffy and Momirov (1997) call for a more precise clarification of the nature of the relationship between stress and caregiver's violence. Fattah and Sacco state also that it is unclear whether stress is a cause of violence or a consequence of the guilt and anxiety generated by violence. More research, then, is needed to make more conclusive statements about the role of stress and dependency (Duffy and Momirov, 1997).

CONCLUSION

Many Canadian families are not as safe and loving as many people think. It should be noted also that in addition to physically assaulting their sons, daughters, wives or cohabiting partners, parents, and siblings, many family members engage in other forms of abuse such as psychological mistreatment, homicide, and sexual assault. In fact, violence behind closed doors is multidimensional in nature.

The good news, though, is that violence in domestic/household settings is increasingly demanding the attention of Canadian social scientists and policy-makers. For example, academic and government researchers are developing a substantial body of knowledge on the violent behaviours addressed in this chapter. They also have tried to demystify some injurious common myths about these social problems, such as the following:

- Violence in the family is rare.
- Only poor people are violent.
- Abused children (or children who witness abuse) always become abusive parents or spouses.
- Battered women "ask for it."
- Alcohol and drugs are the real causes of violence in the family.
- Violence and love cannot coexist.
- Women who claim date rape are "lying," "deserve what they got," or were "asking for it" (Barnett, Miller-Perrin, and Perrin, 1997: 13–15).

Still, several improvements are necessary in future research, such as gathering Canadian representative sample survey data on child abuse and sibling violence, as well as more in-depth research on the violent experiences of different ethnic and cultural groups. Nevertheless, research alone does little, if anything, to prevent violence in the family. Hence, practitioners assert that we should devote most of our time, energy, and other resources to the development of prevention strategies. Space limitations preclude a detailed discussion of effective solutions to "private violence" (Renzetti and Maier, 2002). In fact, one could write (and several people have written) entire books on curbing one or more variants of violence in the family. Guided by my own research and policy work done by colleagues in other countries (e.g., U.S. and Sweden), I recommend that the following steps immediately be taken:

- Eliminate norms that encourage and legitimate violence in our society and families. For example, spanking any child, regardless of his or her age, should be outlawed as it is in Sweden. Media violence (e.g., computer games), which glorifies and legitimates violence, also should be eliminated (Gelles and Cornell, 1990; Barnett, Miller-Perrin, and Perrin, 1997).
- Create and implement ways of reducing violence-provoking stress created by society, such as poverty, gender inequality, and unemployment. Some strategies that help achieve this goal are adequate housing, quality education, and job-creation initiatives (Wilson, 1996; Raphael, 2001b; DeKeseredy, Alvi, Schwartz, and Tomaszewski, 2003).
- Integrate families into a network of kin and community. The reduction of isolation can help alleviate stress and other problems that lead to violence in the family, and enhance informal processes of social control (Barnett, Miller-Perrin, and Perrin, 1997; DeKeseredy, Alvi, Renzetti, and Schwartz, 2004).
- End the cycle of violence in the family. Physical punishment of children is perhaps the most effective way of teaching violence. Eliminating it would also be an important step in crime prevention (DeKeseredy, 2000b).
- Encourage men to speak out against violence in the family and to confront those who abuse their loved ones (Thorne-Finch, 1992; DeKeseredy, Schwartz, and Alvi, 2002).

There are, of course, many more initiatives that could be listed here and have been by others. The key is for people from all walks of life to work closely together to promote the creation and maintenance of peaceful families. Unfortunately, in light of growing joblessness, massive cuts to social services, and other economic factors, "[t]he struggle to keep people focused on pushing for the necessary structural change is going to be more difficult" (Denham and Gillespie, 1999: 47). Nevertheless, if Canadians do not stay focused and use the above and other strategies, many family members will continue to suffer in silence.

Suggested Readings

Duffy, A. and J. Momirov (1997). *Family Violence: A Canadian Introduction.* Toronto: Lorimer. To the best of my knowledge, this is still the only Canadian book that offers a comprehensive sociological understanding of the types of violence addressed in this chapter. Other topics are also covered, such as parent abuse and adolescent abuse.

McKenna, M. J. and J. Larkin (Eds.) (2002b). *Violence Against Women: New Canadian Perspectives.* Toronto: Inanna. This collection of articles provides students, researchers, practitioners, and policy analysts with a rich overview of key issues surrounding violence against women in Canada.

Payne, B. K., and R. R. Gainey (2002). *Family Violence and Criminal Justice: A Life Course Approach.* Cincinnati: Anderson. This book offers a comprehensive review of major conceptual, theoretical, and political issues surrounding violence in American families.

Renzetti, C. M., J. L. Edleson, and R. Kennedy Bergen (Eds.) (2001). *Sourcebook on Violence Against Women.* Thousand Oaks, CA: Sage. This widely read and cited book is essential reading for anyone seeking an in-depth social scientific understanding of different types of violence against women, including rape, wife beating, and sexual harassment. Considerable attention also is given to prevention and intervention strategies.

Trainor, C. (Ed.) (2002b). *Family Violence in Canada: A Statistical Profile 2002.* Ottawa: Statistics Canada. People seeking more information on recent data gathered by Statistics Canada will find this a useful resource.

Web Resources

Centre for Research on Violence Against Women and Children. This international site is dedicated to the Montreal massacre of 1989. Links include sites in Canada, the United Kingdom, and the United States. Many people view this site as an excellent source of information on violence against women and children: **http://www.uwo.ca/violence/**

Minnesota Higher Education Center Against Violence and Abuse. This site provides rich information on various types of violence in American families: **http://www.mincava.umn.edu**

National Clearinghouse on Family Violence. Considered to be one of the best electronic resources on violence behind closed doors, this site includes numerous publications on child abuse, wife beating, elder abuse, and other forms of intimate violence: **http://www.hc-sc.gc.ca/nc-cn**

Violence Against Women: Special Issues and Activism. A page including many links to sites on violence against women, particularly rape and domestic violence:
http://www.soc.umn.edu/~overall/women.htm

Abuse of Older Adults: A Fact Sheet from the Department of Justice Canada. This site is an excellent resource for people who need brief but important information on elder abuse in Canada: **http://canada.justice.gc.ca/ens/ps/fm/adultsfs.html**

Endnotes

1   This section includes revised sections of work published previously by DeKeseredy (2000a) and DeKeseredy and Schwartz (2001).

2   See DeKeseredy and Schwartz (1998a) and Pollard (1993) for more in-depth information on the Canadian national survey and the data generated by it.

3   See Johnson (1996) for more information on the VAWS and the results of this study.

4   See DeKeseredy and Joseph (2004) for more information on this study.

5   The CTS was developed originally in the 1970s by Straus (1979) to study violence within families. Applied to violence in marital/cohabiting relationships, this measure and the recently developed CTS-2 (Straus, Hamby, Boney-McCoy, and Sugarman, 1996) solicit information from men and women about the various tactics they used to resolve conflicts in their relationships. Most versions of the CTS consist of at least 18 items that measure three different ways of handling interpersonal conflict in intimate relationships: reasoning, verbal aggression (referred to by some researchers as psychological abuse), and physical violence. The CTS has been criticized on several grounds, including its inability to measure the contexts, meanings, and motives of violence (DeKeseredy and Schwartz, 1998b).

6   In these states, a husband is exempt from prosecution if his partner is vulnerable or cannot consent because she is psychologically impaired, unconscious, or asleep (Mahoney and Williams, 1998). This can include administering substances that inhibit a woman's ability to resist unwanted sex. Furthermore, in some states, such as Ohio, it is legal to rape a spouse with objects other than the penis, such as bottles or gun barrels (Schwartz, 2002; Rogness, 2003).

7   Penthouse is a widely read pornographic magazine.

8   This section includes sections of an article published previously by DeKeseredy and Schwartz (2003).

9   See DeKeseredy and Schwartz (2003) for an in-depth critique of the 1999 GSS.

10 The phrase "house of horrors" is included in the title of Sev'er's (2002) book on women who left abusive male partners.

11 See Jasinski (2001) for an in-depth review of sociological theories of woman abuse.

12 This section includes sections of an article published previously by DeKeseredy and Schwartz (2002).

13 For example, hitting a child with a hand or object that caused physical harm or that put the child at considerable risk of being physically harmed.

14 This is a slightly modified version of Wallace's (1999) definition of sibling violence.

15 See Kozak, Elmslie, and Verson (1995) for a critical review of these studies.

CHAPTER TWELVE

Families, the State, and Family Policies

Maureen Baker

STATE INTERVENTION AND FAMILY DISCOURSE

Governments and social agencies have seen "the family" as a major social institution and the basic unit of economic, physical, and emotional support. Historically, Canadian governments respected family autonomy and privacy unless children were flagrantly neglected or abused, discipline problems came to the attention of school authorities or the police, or families were visibly impoverished or malnourished. Nevertheless, the state has been involved in family life for over a hundred years (Ursel, 1992), requiring the registration of marriages, births, and deaths, as well as legalizing marriage ceremonies and divorce procedures. The state has required the payment of taxes and emergency military service by young men, but has also provided income security and social services for those in need. By the **state**, we are referring to federal and provincial legislatures and government departments that develop laws and policy as well as agencies mandated to enforce these policies, such as social service agencies and correctional services. **Welfare states** refer to government-sponsored social services and income support programs designed to improve the social and economic well-being of families and individuals.

Researchers and theorists studying the development of welfare states have shown that nations differ in the way they think about social provision, the kinds of programs they create, and the way these programs are delivered. Different countries have been categorized by the generosity of their benefits and the philosophy underlying their social programs. Canada has been viewed as a **liberal welfare state** because most of its benefits are based on individual and family responsibility for economic and social well-being (Esping-Andersen, 1990, 1996; O'Connor, Orloff, and Shaver, 1999). Parents are held responsible for the care and support of their children, both within marriage and after divorce, and spouses are expected to assist each other during marriage. When social benefits are provided, they are relatively ungenerous, well below minimum wages and even below accepted poverty levels. In contrast, **social democratic** nations focus more on the collective responsibility for children's well-being, and place more importance on redistributing income and promoting gender equity. **Corporatist welfare states** depend on unions and corporations joining with governments to provide social insurance programs financed through employer and employee contributions (Esping-Andersen, 1990).

Within Canada, state involvement varies dramatically by province. The federal government has retained jurisdiction over some income support programs (old age security, Canada Pension Plan, Employment Insurance), federal tax concessions for families, maternity/parental benefits, and divorce law. The provinces have acquired jurisdiction over marriage law, maternity leave provisions, child protection, schooling, childcare services, the delivery of health services, and social assistance. They also control the division of matrimonial property upon separation of spouses and laws pertaining to the implementation of child custody, access, child support, and spousal support (Guest, 1997; McGilly, 1998). In addition, provinces such as Ontario allow municipalities to create and administer childcare provisions and income support for some categories of welfare recipients. In general, divided jurisdiction has allowed inconsistencies to develop between federal, provincial, and municipal policies, and also has made it difficult to create national family policies in matters of provincial jurisdiction (Baker, 1995).

State involvement in families also varies by gender. Feminist scholars have argued that women's access to social provision within liberal welfare states has been shaped by assumptions about their family roles and relationships (Sainsbury, 1993; Leira, 2002). As low-income wives and widows, women have been seen as "deserving" of public support and also have been eligible for income support through their husband's work-related entitlements. As lone mothers, women have been offered minimal benefits and close scrutiny concerning their maternal behaviour and "morals," to ensure that they are truly eligible and not defrauding the system (Swift, 1995; Little, 1998). In contrast, men typically have received state benefits as earners rather than fathers. Work-related benefits are often financed through social insurance contributions, and involve less investigation into their personal lives and higher payments (Sainsbury, 1993, 1996). Increasingly, Canadian women also are eligible for work-related benefits (such as Employment Insurance, Worker's Compensation, and Canada Pension Plan), but their benefit levels tend to be lower than men's because they are wage-related, and women tend to earn lower wages and make lower contributions.

State involvement has also varied over the decades, because social policies and social programs were created in an incremental fashion by different governments with varying political agendas. Historically, state involvement has been more intrusive for low-income families, especially certain cultural groups. Social workers have been permitted to investigate the personal circumstances and living conditions of welfare recipients, even though such investigations would be considered an infringement of privacy for higher-income families. The state has always been most interventionist for visible minorities such as First Nations' families. Children were forcibly removed from their families in the early 20th century, placed in residential schools, or adopted by white families (Baker, 1995: 183). Although this level of intrusion is no longer acceptable, the people involved continue to suffer from the legacy of these policies.

All social and economic policies impact on family life, but the term **family policy** usually focuses on the pursuit and attainment of collective goals and values in addressing problems of families in relation to society (Zimmerman, 1992). In this chapter, family policies will be defined as the implicit and explicit ideas about the state's obligation to families, as well as the individual's responsibility to other family members. These ideas are implemented through income security programs, marriage and divorce laws, services related to maternity and child welfare, and programs dealing with the integration of paid work and family life.

Family policies are not always based on informed knowledge about how people actually live or why they live this way. Instead, they are sometimes based on policy-makers' preconceived notions about the importance of family in society, women's role in families, parents' responsibilities toward their children, and reasons behind the need for government assistance (Baker, 1990a). These ideologies and values permeate our culture, yet change over time with economic, political, and social trends. For the most part, male politicians created Canada's family-related social programs from the 1940s to the 1970s, when society substantially differed from the present. Although most programs have been amended since then, many still overstate the homogeneity, or uniform nature of families, implying that most people live in nuclear family units consisting of breadwinner/father and homemaker/mother and are legally married and living with their two or three children. As we have illustrated throughout the book, this is no longer the way most Canadians live.

Most researchers and social service workers, regardless of their political views, now agree that some aspects of family life should *not* be considered "private" or inconsequential to the state. Parents must be required and helped to nurture and support their children. The physical and emotional safety of women, children, and the elderly needs to be protected within the home. Laws are required to prevent siblings from reproducing or fathers from raping their daughters. In addition, parents with dependent children (especially mothers) often require help to resolve the inevitable and growing conflict between the need to earn a living and the need to raise children.

A number of policy issues already have been discussed in previous chapters of this book, such as childcare in Chapter Five, divorce and support issues in Chapter Ten, and violence against women and children in Chapter Eleven. In this chapter, I will focus on marriage law, maternity/parental leave and benefits, provincial social assistance programs, and federal child benefits. For each section, I will attempt to provide some historical chronology and also to place Canadian policies within a cross-national context to illustrate the range of policy options.

GENDERED PRACTICES IN THE PATRIARCHAL FAMILY

For over a century, political economists have argued that the development of the state and the processes of urbanization and industrialization shape family life (Engels, 1884; Bradbury, 1993). When European settlers first came to Canada, these processes were widespread in Britain and France, and the patriarchal family headed by the husband/father was already the accepted structure. The early settlers brought their European marriage customs and legal traditions with them, and foisted them upon the indigenous peoples, who typically lived in extended families with their own distinct customs and practices. In Quebec, French **civil law** was established as the legal system, while the rest of Canada adopted English **common law**. Under both systems, husbands and fathers held legal authority over their wives and children, and wives retained the legal status of a minor child. In addition to having no political rights, wives could not sell or acquire property, but had to depend on their husbands to control it on their behalf.

The Married Women's Property Act, first passed in England in 1870, was introduced gradually to the Canadian provinces after 1872 (Dranoff, 1977: 48). This legal change was seen as a milestone by reformers because it allowed married women to retain and control their own wages, income, or property. This was particularly important for middle- or upper-class women who inherited property. However, it was also important for wives who earned an income taking in boarders, caring for neighbours' children, selling eggs, cleaning houses, doing laundry for other families, teaching music lessons at home, or working in local factories. In the late nineteenth century, women's groups fought for greater legal control within their families. They also demanded access to universities, entrance into the professions, the right to participate in politics, and protection from dangerous or unhealthy working conditions (Baker, 1993: 116).

The construct of the patriarchal family was used in the long fight over women's rights to deny women both political and legal rights. Opponents argued that "the family" was the basic unit of society and men as "family heads" voted and controlled property on behalf of their wives. Giving married women the vote was tantamount to giving each family two votes. Women's rights advocates fought this patriarchal view for many decades before it became more equitable after the 1870s. Yet some of the battles are still

The father was the official head of the household in "traditional" Canadian families until the 1960s.

being fought, such as disputes over access to childcare, reproductive rights, the division of matrimonial property, spousal support, and child support after divorce (Baker, 2001).

Prior to the twentieth century, the husband was granted custody of the children in the rare case of marital separation and custody dispute. The right to maternal custody was granted in England in 1839, but the Canadian provinces did not allow mothers equal rights with fathers in guardianship or custody of their children until after 1917. British Columbia was the first province to pass such legislation, but Quebec did not amend its *Civil Code* until 1964 (Dranoff, 1977: 39).

Until the 1960s, the marital roles of men and women in Canada differed by law and custom, but were seen as **complementary**. As part of the wedding ceremony, a bride promised to "love, honour, and obey" her husband, indicating that he was officially the head of the household. A groom promised to "love, honour, and cherish" his wife. He was obligated to support her for life, but also had the right to make certain family decisions, such as where they would live and at what standard of living. A wife was expected to live wherever her husband lived, to be sexually available to him when he wished, to maintain the household, and to care for their children. In return, she was entitled to dower rights, or the right to one-third of his property should the marriage dissolve, in recognition of these services. During the marriage, the husband was expected to provide her with "the necessities of life," but *he* decided what was necessary (Dranoff, 1977: 25, 26).

Since the 1970s, marriage and divorce laws have gradually been reformed, both in Canada and other countries, to view marriage as a heterosexual partnership between equals. In some places, marriage laws include both heterosexual and gay/lesbian couples. Both partners are now expected to support their children and each other. The provinces establish the minimum age of marriage and determine which relationships are **incestuous**, or too close to allow marriage and procreation. Increasingly, children are gaining the right to protection against neglect or mistreatment by their parents, and older children are permitted some input into custody decisions in the event of parental divorce. The family no longer is perceived to be immune from legal intervention in the way it used to be. Children are no longer considered to be the property of parents, to be treated any way they want, and wives are not required to be obedient or always sexually available to their husbands. Although the family used to be viewed as a legal unit represented by the husband/father, individual family members have acquired more legal rights.

Despite these changes, not everyone is impressed with the direction of the change. Conservatives often feel that "the family" and the sanctity of marriage are given little protection and that laws that focus on individual rights actually discourage legal marriage and child-bearing. Furthermore, conservatives have particularly criticized divorce reform, the enforcement of child support, greater acceptance of same-sex relationships, and recent legal efforts to permit gay and lesbian marriages. At the same time, reformers on the political left as well as gays/lesbians and feminists contend that some families, especially those led by lone mothers, have been impoverished by reforms that give joint custody to both parents or assume that mothers are self-supporting. Furthermore, they argue that same-sex couples continue to have their family life disregarded or disrespected by the state.

Numerous amendments have been made in family and divorce laws in the past two decades, but some family policies have been restructured more than others. In Chapters

One and Five, we noted that labour market changes and higher employment rates for mothers have generated greater need for wage protection during pregnancy and childbirth, leave for family responsibilities, and childcare for employed parents. In the next section, we examine some of these issues.

PROVINCIAL SOCIAL ASSISTANCE AND SOCIAL SERVICE PROGRAMS

Social assistance and social services are designed and administered by the provincial, territorial, and municipal governments with financial assistance from the federal government. Social assistance programs, which serve as a social safety net and are known as "welfare," provide income support payments to the long-term unemployed and the "unemployable," usually between the ages of 18 and 65. Welfare payments have been based on a needs test, which compares the budgetary requirements of an applicant and any dependants with the assets and income of the household (NCW, 2003). Social services include child welfare programs and interventions for violent or **at-risk families**.

With Confederation in 1867, the provinces were assigned responsibility for their public assistance programs, but the provinces passed many of these costs on to the municipalities and private charities (Baker and Tippin, 1999: 78). In 1913, the municipalities paid about 53 percent of public welfare costs (excluding "relief" or unemployment benefits), the provinces paid about 30 percent, and the federal government paid about 17 percent (Ursel, 1992: 170). Benefits were minimal and highly stigmatized, based on a liberal notion of the welfare state, that the state should not interfere in family life unless absolutely necessary. By the 1930s, the division of expenditures was nearly equal among the three levels of government, but the responsibility for funding social programs gradually shifted to cost-sharing arrangements between the federal and provincial governments (ibid).

Over these years, the provinces had pressured the federal government for more financial assistance, as the cost of social service rose with higher unemployment and marriage breakdown. In 1966, the **Canada Assistance Plan** (CAP) was signed, in which the federal government agreed to pay 50 percent of provincial welfare costs that coincided with federal guidelines. Provinces were required to base social assistance solely on financial need, and could not ask beneficiaries to perform community service or work for their benefit. The provinces were also required to provide an appeal procedure (Baker and Tippin, 1999: 79). CAP was designed to meet the cost of basic requirements of a single person or family when all other financial resources had been exhausted. Most provinces created a single, unified program, but Ontario, Manitoba, and Nova Scotia retained a two-tiered system in which long-term benefits (such as for sole-support parents) are paid by the province, while municipalities pay short-term and emergency aid (in these cases, there is a residence requirement). The establishment of CAP allowed all provinces to expand their child welfare programs and to raise benefit levels for impoverished individuals and families (Baker, 1995). Childcare subsidies for low-income families were also funded through the Canada Assistance Plan, but childcare advocates continued to argue for more spaces and higher subsidies (Friendly, 1994).

Throughout the 1970s and 1980s, social assistance income grew at an average of 27 percent, but the per capita income of Canadians increased by only 20 percent over the same period (Dooley, 1995). This led to public perceptions that welfare recipients were relatively well off. Yet, in 1990, a lone mother solely dependent on government transfers had a cash income equal to only three-quarters of the poverty line (ibid). In 1990, the federal government began to curb CAP transfer payments to the "richest" provinces, causing the provincial governments to tighten eligibility. Provincial governments responded to rising costs and federal cutbacks by reducing eligibility for welfare. Alberta and Ontario, with conservative governments, actually cut benefits from the mid-1980s to the mid-1990s (Evans, 1996; Shragge, 1997).

Most provinces had also tightened their child support enforcement procedures throughout the 1980s and early 1990s, focusing on "making fathers pay" and catching "dead-beat dads," non-resident fathers who defaulted on their payments. The discourse surrounding these reforms involved both "enforcing parental responsibilities" and "reducing child poverty." These phrases became mantras that replaced full discussion about why some people have low incomes, why some parents fail to support their children, and what is the best solution to family poverty. It is worth noting that none of the Canadian enforcement schemes allows mothers on social assistance to keep any of the child support money paid by the father, unlike comparable programs in Australia and the United Kingdom (Baker and Tippin, 1999: 80). This means that, although the provincial government saves welfare expenditures, women and children on social benefits are no better off when fathers pay, and child poverty is not reduced.

Throughout the 1990s, a number of provinces, including Ontario and Alberta, introduced "workfare" programs that attempted to move benefit recipients into paid work as quickly as possible. These employability initiatives, unlike earlier programs based on the **male breadwinner family**, tend to assume that all beneficiaries are autonomous wage earners capable of self-support, who make rational economic choices to maximize their income. Although these programs have been portrayed as opportunities for dependants to exit from welfare and poverty, the reality for low-income mothers is that paid work marginalizes their unpaid domestic work, yet does not always improve their take-home income. Furthermore, these programs can be expensive for governments because they involve skills training and childcare services when clients are mothers with young children. New social programs which assume that paid work is the best way to exit from poverty often are based on misleading assumptions that need to be re-examined, especially when the clients are low-income mothers (Shragge, 1997; Baker and Tippin, 1999).

Welfare rates have always varied by province, and fall below poverty lines or low-income cut-offs in all jurisdictions. For example, couples on social assistance with two children would receive 49 percent of poverty line income if they lived in Quebec in 2002, but up to 65 percent in Prince Edward Island. Welfare incomes for couples with two children varied from 20 percent in Ontario to 33 percent in Prince Edward Island, as a percentage of average provincial income (National Council of Welfare, 2003). The lack of welfare generosity in some provinces relates to a broad range of incomes, high unemployment rates, low economic growth, and a lower per capita tax base, but also to a more punitive philosophy about why people need assistance and what role the state should play in personal life. Controversies continue about how to fund welfare costs, how to help those in need without dampening work incentives and encouraging "dependency," how much income recipients really need, and how to ensure that they do not abuse the system (Baker and Tippin, 1999: 80).

In 1996, CAP ended as a 30-year agreement, and the federal government replaced it with block grants to the provinces for social assistance, tertiary education, and health and medical services. The new program, called the Canada Health and Social Transfer (CHST), enabled the provinces to redefine the principles behind social assistance, to initiate welfare-to-work programs, and to keep their social assistance rates as low as possible (Baker and Tippin, 1999: 86, 87). At the same time, the federal government has continued to restructure federal child benefits, making them more visible as a means of social support for Canadian families. The federal government has also extended parental benefits, as we discuss in the next section.

MATERNITY/PARENTAL LEAVE AND BENEFITS

Before the 1930s, women left their jobs when they married and stayed home to raise their children while their husbands earned the major income for the family. In later decades, women waited until they became pregnant before leaving paid work, and by the 1960s they returned to work when all their children entered primary school. Increasingly, taking time off for child rearing is becoming untenable with labour market restructuring, job competition, and the need for more than one household income. Consequently, most Canadians now agree that employed women should have the right to paid leave during pregnancy, and that their jobs should be held open for them until they can return to work after giving birth.

Qualifying for maternity leave and cash benefits are two separate processes in Canada. Leave from employment is governed by provincial employment standards legislation, except for employees working under federal jurisdiction. By the end of the 1970s, all provinces had passed laws entitling women employees to at least 17 weeks of unpaid maternity leave. Since the 1990s, most provinces have expanded the number of weeks of unpaid leave, and extended it to biological fathers and adoptive parents. The laws relating to maternity leave used to exclude most casual or temporary workers by requiring continuous employment for a specified length of time that varied by jurisdiction. Now, employees are no longer required to work for any specific length of time in some provinces before becoming eligible for parental leave (Baker, 1995: 161).

When the federal *Unemployment Insurance Act* was amended in 1971, wage replacement benefits were first introduced on a national level for employees absent from work for pregnancy and childbirth. Unemployment Insurance (UI), which was established as a social insurance program in 1940, was designed to provide income protection for workers suffering from temporary interruptions from employment income, but who were available for work. Originally, many categories of workers were excluded from UI, such as white-collar employees, seasonal workers, and pregnant women (Cuneo, 1979). Coverage was gradually expanded, and eligible workers may now obtain regular unemployment benefits, sickness benefits, maternity, or parental benefits. Adoption benefits were added in 1984 and parental benefits in 1990. Parental benefits were created after a court challenge using the *Canadian Charter of Rights and Freedoms* successfully argued that biological fathers should have the same rights as adoptive fathers (Baker, 1995).

In 1996, UI was changed to "Employment Insurance," and eligibility was based on hours rather than weeks of work. Now, eligible pregnant workers can receive up to 15 weeks of maternity benefits, and adoptive and biological parents are entitled to 35 weeks of parental benefits. New mothers often combine maternity and parental benefits, receiving government support for up to 50 weeks (HRDC, 2003). The value of maternity, adoption, and parental benefits depends on previous earnings, but the maximum is now 55 percent of eligible earnings, down from the original 60 percent. However, some unionized and professional employees have their benefit level "topped up" by their employers to as high as 100 percent of previous earnings (Baker and Tippin, 1999: 95-6).

Canada's system of maternity/parental leave and benefits compares favourably with systems in the United States, New Zealand, Australia, and the United Kingdom. Since 1993, the US federal government has required employers with more than 50 employees to provide *unpaid* leave. A minority of states provide paid maternity benefits through state or employer disability and sickness programs, but most women are ineligible because only some states require such programs, and smaller firms, where most women work, do not offer them (Baker, 1997a). The Australian government does not require all employers to pay maternity or parental benefits to their employees, although many unionized firms pay such benefits (Baker and Tippin, 1999). New Zealand recently introduced 12 weeks of parental benefits at a flat rate for employees working for the same employer for a year. In some European countries, such as France, Germany, the Netherlands, and Sweden, the wage replacement rate for maternity or parental benefits varies from 80 percent to 100 percent of previous wages (up to a maximum), sometimes for extended periods (Jenson and Sineau, 2001; Daly and Rake, 2003). Furthermore, several countries (such as France and Sweden) offer the option of working part-time and receiving partial benefits, with a guarantee of returning to full-time work when the children enter elementary school or, in Sweden, reach the age of twelve. In comparison to these European countries, Canada's system of maternity/parental leave and benefits seems ungenerous.

Once children are born, they are quite costly to rear to adulthood. Parents who are unable to find paid work or adequate childcare must rely on family support or turn to state income support programs. In the next section, we will examine the development of federal programs for children.

FEDERAL CHILD AND FAMILY BENEFITS

Federal income support for Canadian families dates back to 1918, when income tax concessions were first provided for taxpayers with dependants. These were designed to encourage marriage and child-bearing, but also to acknowledge that employees with dependants had greater financial responsibilities than unmarried individuals without children. In 1945 the Canadian government began to pay a monthly family allowance to all mothers with dependent children at home, as did other liberal welfare states such as the United Kingdom and Australia (Baker, 1995). These tax concessions and the Family Allowance became known in Canada as "child and family benefits." Over the years, child benefits (as well as old age pensions and unemployment benefits) were expanded and reformed with different governments and new ideas about the federal government's role in assisting families in need. Generally, Liberal governments expanded these benefits throughout the 1960s and 1970s, creating both child tax deductions (which especially assisted middle-income earners) and child tax credits (designed to help the poor). Nevertheless, Canadian child benefits still remained relatively ungenerous compared to those of social democratic nations such as Sweden and Denmark (Baker, 1995; Gauthier, 1996; Hunsley, 1997; Korpi, 2000).

Child benefits became a focus of restructuring after the Conservative (Mulroney) government came to power in 1984 (Kitchen, 1997). The government and many taxpayers claimed that the universal Family Allowance (FA) was no longer affordable or needed by many families. Instead, they argued that scarce government resources should be targeted to the poor to reduce "**child poverty**." Discussions of poverty focused almost exclusively on child poverty, since children were always seen as the deserving poor, whereas adults drawing social benefits were often suspected of defrauding the welfare system.

The Conservatives were determined to cut social expenditures, but these reforms also coincided with the surge of mothers entering the labour force. Women's groups and the child welfare lobby argued that the universal Family Allowance should be retained, because it gave the clear message that government and society valued child rearing and that reproduction was important to the nation as well as to individuals and families (Kitchen, 1990). Furthermore, they argued that the FA was the only family income over which some mothers had complete control because it was delivered to the mother, whereas tax deductions typically went to the father (as the higher earner). Researchers and advocacy groups for the poor noted that a monthly allowance was more advantageous to low-income families than an annual tax benefit. Furthermore, they argued that if child benefits were to be reformed, the child tax deduction should be converted to a refundable tax credit and paid in instalments to make it more advantageous to low-income families (Battle, 1992).

After 1984, parliamentary committees discussed the reform of family benefits for several years, but, eventually, the Mulroney Conservative government reduced the value of the child tax deduction (established in 1918), and then changed it to a credit in 1988 when other taxes were reformed. Furthermore, they lowered the threshold income of the refundable child tax credit that was established by the Liberals in the 1970s to assist low-income families with children. Finally, in December 1992, the government rolled the three child benefits[1] into one benefit: the Child Tax Benefit (CTB). This benefit was targeted to middle- and lower-income families rather than being paid to all families with children. Since 1993, Canada has not offered a universal benefit for families with dependent children, unlike many European countries. However, several other liberal welfare states also abolished universal family allowances around the same time. Australia targeted their family allowance in 1987, but added a supplement for low-income families, which Canada did not do. New Zealand targeted the family allowance in 1991, but the United Kingdom retained its universal allowance, despite the Thatcher government's attempts to target it to low-income families (Baker and Tippin, 1999: 205).

In 1993, the Canadian Child Tax Benefit began to be administered by the taxation department rather than the department in charge of social services, reflecting the growing influence of economic rationalism within the federal government (Baker and Tippin, 1999: 89). This benefit initially provided about $85 a month to the mother or guardian, about the same amount that was received under the previous system of family allowance and tax benefits. Yet the new benefit was targeted to middle- and low-income families, initially with a supplement for the "working poor" worth $500 a year. Kitchen (1997: 66) noted that the introduction of this supplement reflected the growing unease that some families were better off on welfare than working in a low-wage job. Nevertheless, she argued that the supplement for "working parents" has no place in a child benefit program because it originates in Victorian morality and the ideology that the poor do not want to work. However, another reason for not increasing child benefits for welfare recipients was the federal government's concern that the provinces could simply lower their social assistance rates to compensate.

In 1989, the Canadian Parliament resolved to eliminate child poverty by the year 2000, yet poverty rates increased during and after the 1990-91 recession. Furthermore, the percentage of children in low-income families increased from 15.3 percent in 1989 to 21.0 percent in 1995 (Battle, 1997). Between 1986 and 2002, the welfare incomes of single-parent families with one child were eroded in most Canadian provinces (NCW, 2003: 60).

In 1996, the federal government announced changes to child benefits, again designed to "reduce child poverty," to "provide work incentives" to low-wage parents, and "to take children off welfare." Beginning in July 1997, the working income supplement (WIS) was increased and restructured to take into consideration the number of children in the family. In July 1998, the enriched WIS payment and the Child Tax Benefit were combined to form one new payment: the Canada Child Tax Benefit (CCTB). The CCTB provides more money for the first child than for subsequent children, and offers maximum benefits to low-income families who are not receiving provincial social assistance. Families who do not claim the childcare expenses deduction receive an additional amount for each child under seven, as they did under the previous version of the benefit. However, the working income supplement and the additional amount for larger families became less visible under the new system (National Council of Welfare, 1997: 6).

Critics argue that the "new" money for the CCTB was the same money cut from federal transfers to the provinces for social assistance just before and at the time that the Canada Health and Social Transfer replaced the Canada Assistance Plan. Furthermore, this payment was not based on the financial needs of children, but rather on the working status of their parents, since the provinces could deduct the enriched WIS component from social assistance benefits. This reinforces the old dichotomy between the "deserving" and "undeserving" poor, and the newer emphasis on paid employment. In addition, people earning less than $10,000 (or more than $22,397) cannot claim the maximum supplement, which means that many part-time or low-wage workers are penalized (Kitchen, 1997; Pulkingham and Ternowetsky, 1997; NCW, 2003). Furthermore, although the government said that it was "taking children off welfare," it is difficult to see how the poverty of children can be removed from the poverty of their parents.

The Canadian government does not consider the income tax deduction for childcare expenses ($7,000 per preschool child and $4,000 for children aged 7 to 16) as a "child benefit," but rather as an employment expense. If we view this deduction as a child benefit, then the Canadian government is providing more generous benefits to high-income families than to middle- and low-income families (Kitchen, 1997). Furthermore, the Liberal government spent less money on direct income support for families with children in 1996 than the Conservatives did in 1985, when the Mulroney government began restructuring child and family benefits (ibid). The federal government's retreat from cost sharing since 1996 further reduced public resources for childcare and child welfare services (Doherty, Friendly, and Oloman, 1998).

Quebec has always retained its own child benefits, and for this reason they are worth noting. Since 1974, the Quebec government supplemented the federal family allowance, and since the late 1980s, also paid parents an allowance for preschool children and an allowance for newborn children (HRDC, 1994). This benefit for newborns was particularly controversial because it paid much more money for the third child than for the first and second child in a family. Furthermore, it was introduced with pronatalist and Québecois nationalist discourse by the Bourassa Liberal government (Baker, 1994). When the federal government abolished the family allowance in December 1992, Quebec retained its own family allowances.

In 1996, the Parti Québecois government announced a new family policy package. Part of this included a childcare program that would cost parents only $5.00 per day, whether or not they were in paid work. This program was phased in from 1997 until 2001, when the government increased the number of spaces, the wages of educators, and its childcare budget. Quebec became the only province in Canada to develop a universal system of childcare for preschool children (CRRU, 2003). In October 1997, the Quebec government also integrated provincial social assistance and family allowances into one targeted family allowance, based on family income, number of children, and the number of parents in the family (Quebec Government, 1997). The cash payment for newborns, which did not increase the francophone population, was quietly withdrawn, despite the fact that it was introduced with a flourish in 1988 (Baker and Tippin, 1999: 92). In April 2003, the Parti Québecois lost the election to the Liberals. In May 2003, the Liberals announced their intention to slow the expansion of the childcare program, increase parental fees, and encourage for-profit childcare (CRRU, 2003). After considerable public protest, the new government released a consultation paper in August 2003 with several proposals to alter the childcare system. The debates continue.

After 1997, the federal government increased the amount of money allocated for the Canada Child Tax Benefit; yet many families continue to live in poverty. The Child Poverty Action Group (1998) argued that Canadian public policy condemns women to poverty as either mothers or workers, and that the absence of strong family policies remains a major barrier to the social and economic equality of women. They argued that the federal government needs to play a leadership role to ensure adequate and consistent standards of living for all children, women, and families across Canada. The CCTB, they noted, offers some promise, partly because it involves greater co-ordination between federal and provincial governments. Yet they criticized this initiative as being too narrowly focused on welfare reform and low-wage work, and for offering no long-term commitment to resolve child poverty.

Recent changes in both provincial social assistance and federal child benefits place greater pressure on parents to alter their balance between paid work and caregiving, since paid work and full citizenship rights are being increasingly linked. The federal government

TABLE 12.1 The Establishment and Reform of Social Benefits in Canada

Family Tax Benefits 1918-1993	Tax deductions for taxpayers with dependants started with first Income Tax Act; tax credits were added in 1972
Mothers/Widows Pensions 1920+	Developed around 1920, but date varies by province
Old Age Pension 1926, 1951	Established in 1926 as a pension for those with low incomes Converted to a universal pension in 1951
Family Allowance 1945-1993	Paid to all mothers for each child (replaced by the Child Tax Benefit in 1993)
(Un)Employment Insurance 1940	Established as a federal social insurance program Maternity benefits added in 1971 Adoption benefits added in 1984 Parental benefits added in 1990 Renamed Employment Insurance in 1996
Medicare 1966	Public insurance was established for hospital and diagnostic services in 1958 and for visits to physicians in 1966. Together these programs are called "Medicare."
Canada/Quebec Pension Plan 1966	Financed by contributions from employees, employers, and government; pays survivors benefits and disability benefits
Canada Assistance Plan 1966-96	A cost-sharing arrangement in which the federal government agreed to match provincial expenditures on social assistance and social services if they met federal guidelines. Replaced by Canada Health and Social Transfer (CHST) in 1996.
Childcare Expenses Deduction 1971	This income tax deduction is still available for the lower earner in a two-parent family or for lone parents (up to $7,000 can be deducted from taxable income for each preschool child)
Spouses Allowance 1975	Established as an income-tested pension for spouses aged 60-64 of old age pensioners, mainly women
Child Tax Benefit 1993-1998	The former Family Allowance and tax deductions and credits for children were rolled into this targeted tax benefit for lower- and middle-income families in 1993. Replaced by the Canada Child Tax Benefit in 1998.
Resolution to end "child poverty" 1989	An all-party agreement in Parliament
Canada Child Tax Benefit 1998	The Child Tax Benefit and the Working Income Supplement were rolled together to form this benefit.

Sources: Derived from a number of books and reports, such as Ursel (1992), Guest (1997), Baker and Tippin (1999), and NCW (2003).

also increased child benefits at the same time that it cut transfer payments to the provinces, permitting provincial governments to restrict entitlement to social services and income support. Furthermore, the amount of money that the federal government allocated to resolve child poverty has been too little to counteract labour market trends and government policies that promote unemployment and underemployment. Table 12.1 summarizes the development of family-related policies in Canada.

COMPARING THE GENEROSITY OF FAMILY POLICIES

Why do some states expect family members to assist one another with minimal public support, while others provide expensive social benefits and services? For decades, researchers have tried to understand the uneven development of welfare states, although most have focused on benefits related to work rather than family. Researchers have argued that a number of factors influence the generosity of family benefits, but they tend to focus on the strength of advocacy groups and their relationships to the government (Baker, 1995; Gauthier, 1996; Sainsbury, 1996; Baker and Tippin, 1999; O'Connor, Orloff, and Shaver, 1999). Explanations for both the development and restructuring of Canadian family policies will be considered within a comparative perspective.

States that have initiated generous programs for families with children tend to have a history of left wing or social democratic governments and a central government that includes various interest groups in decision-making, especially trade unions and feminist groups. Unlike many European countries, Canada has never voted into power a social democratic government in Ottawa. Instead, elections have alternated between moderate Liberal and Conservative governments that have emphasized business interests rather than a more equitable redistribution of income or improvements in social well-being. These governments have tended to create stronger alliances with business communities than with social reform groups. Unlike countries such as Sweden, Canada has never adopted a legal structure that required the voices of labour or women to be heard in policy decisions. Instead, policy-makers rely on votes, petitions to members of Parliament, and submissions to parliamentary committees, but politicians are under no legal obligation to create policies that include these opinions (Baker, 1995).

Social policy-making in Canada arises from at least two levels of government and has been permeated with jurisdictional disputes. If the federal government wants to create a national social program, federal negotiators must obtain a consensus from the provinces and territories, as well as from First Nations peoples. This is time-consuming and politically difficult, but may be considered worth the effort for reasons of national unity. Canadians across the country have different vested interests, and the federal government must always balance these opposing views in order to remain in power. Consequently, making major changes to social programs at the federal level is difficult and risky, especially as the population grows more heterogeneous and decision-making becomes more decentralized. When each province and territory creates its own family policy, inconsistencies become widespread, and without national standards, entitlement can become inequitable across the country and family benefits can easily be eroded.

States with more generous family programs have often experienced demographic and social changes such as declining fertility, an aging population, or a high percentage of mothers in the labour force, accompanied by strong advocacy groups arguing for family policy reform to counteract these forces (Baker, 1995; Pampel and Adams, 1992; Wennemo, 1992, 1994). Compared to Europe, Canada has experienced moderate fertility and only recently has become concerned about an aging population. Canada has always relied on immigration to augment the birth rate and maintain population growth, as well as to settle the land and provide workers with the required skills. In addition, urbanization and industrialization occurred later in Canada than in Europe, which delayed women's entrance into the labour force and postponed the decline of birth rates.

Canada also experienced a baby boom after the Second World War, not equalled in Europe, that kept the Canadian population relatively young (Beaujot, 2000). Conservative and patriarchal family values accompanied by relatively high birth rates continued until the early 1960s, especially in Quebec, giving Canada a younger population that was less concerned with financing future pension programs than in most European nations. Even now, seniors form only 12 percent of the Canadian population, compared to 15 to 17 percent in some European countries (Statistics Canada, 1998: 72, 74). In recent years, however, the decline of birth rates, population aging, increasing cultural and racial heterogeneity, the rise in mothers' labour force participation, and the need for childcare services have changed family life and societal needs, leading to new political lobby groups pressing for reform.

ADVOCACY FOR FAMILY REFORM

Advocacy for Canadian family reform has come from a variety of sources, but especially from women's groups. At the beginning of the 20th century, groups such as the National Council of Women and the Women's Christian Temperance Union lobbied for family and social reform. These groups have been called "maternal feminists" because they supported the gendered family and elevated women's role as mothers and homemakers. Nevertheless, they fought hard for public policy initiatives such as the reduction of infant and maternal mortality rates, alcohol abuse in the home, child prostitution, and pornography (Pupo, 1988).

Since the 1970s, numerous groups have organized to improve women's access to legalized abortion, employment equity, a fairer division of matrimonial assets, and greater family support. The National Action Committee on the Status of Women (NAC), established in 1972 (Heitlinger, 1993: 82), became a strong voice for women's employment benefits, reproductive rights, improved pensions, and numerous other issues, speaking for women's groups across the country. In addition, Women's Legal Action and Education Fund (LEAF) has been instrumental in fighting legal cases involving women's interests. Yet, at the same time, a strong lobby from western-based conservative groups continues to promote "family values," focusing on a 1950s-style family with a gendered division of labour (Baker and Phipps, 1997).

Gay and lesbian groups and individuals have argued that definitions of family should be expanded to include the caring relationships of same-sex couples, that legal marriage should be an option for all couples, and that state and employer benefits should be extended to all spouses and families. In addition, organizations fighting child poverty, such as the Child Poverty Action League and Campaign 2000, and welfare organizations, such as the Canadian Council on Social Development and National Council of Welfare, place pressure on governments to reform family policies and programs. Childcare advocacy groups also have worked hard to improve accessibility, regulation, and affordability of childcare services (Friendly, 1994; Freiler and Cerny, 1998).

In some European countries, such as France and Sweden, declining fertility and population aging have led to considerable concern about financing future social programs. Advocacy groups in those countries argued successfully that more social support for child rearing and the integration of work/family would raise labour market productivity, improve equity for women, and ensure future pension contributions. Declining fertility was also an important political issue in Quebec in the 1980s and 1990s, when governments introduced a wide range of programs designed to support families, including additional parental leave, more childcare services, housing grants for young families, and cash birth incentives. Declining fertility alone, however, was not enough to inspire Quebec advocacy groups or to make the government change its policies. Nationalist concerns about Quebec's relative power within the Canadian federation enhanced the argument about the potential problems of declining fertility (Baker, 1994).

A gay couple marries outside B.C. Supreme Court

The public demand for divorce and the subsequent poverty of lone mothers and their children generated the need for family law reform, including child custody provisions, more equitable division of matrimonial property, and better enforcement mechanisms for child support. In addition, more employed mothers increased the demand for leave for family responsibilities, affordable and high quality childcare, and equal pay for comparable work.

A major focal point for advocacy has been the issue of "child poverty." International comparisons have indicated that poverty rates of families with children are much higher in Canada than in most industrialized countries (except the United States and Mexico), as Table 12.2 indicates (OECD, 2003). Furthermore, Canadians remain poor longer than most Europeans as a result of tax and transfer programs that are less effective in redistributing income. Canada's own parliamentary committees have recognized that allowing children to live in poverty could be costly in the future. In 1989, Prime Minister Mulroney spoke at the United Nations about the country's commitment to eradicate child poverty by the year 2000, and Parliament passed a resolution to that effect in the same year. Advocacy groups such as Campaign 2000 continue to monitor the government's progress and reach conclusions similar to UNICEF. The 2002 "Report Card" of Campaign 2000 indicates that 14.5 percent of all children in Canada lived in poverty in 1989; the figure rose to 21.0 percent in 1996 before falling to 16.5 percent in 2000. Furthermore, the depth of poverty (or how far family income falls below the poverty line) has increased for two-parent families with children (Campaign 2000, 2003).

Over the years, Canadian families have become more heterogeneous. Cultural diversity resulting from high immigration rates has led to considerable debate over family membership, what family practices are acceptable in Canada, what role the government should play in family life, and what kinds of social programs are necessary and desirable. For example, increasing cultural diversity has required the immigration department to clarify the definition of "family" and "dependant," and has encouraged health practitioners and policy-makers to consider the legality of practices such as female

TABLE 12.2 Child Poverty Rates* by Household Type in Selected Countries

Country	Children Living in Lone-Parent Families	Children Living in Other Families
Sweden	6.7	1.5
Denmark	13.8	3.6
France	26.1	6.4
Germany	51.2	6.2
Australia	35.6	8.8
Canada	51.6	10.4
UK	45.6	13.3
USA	55.4	15.8
Mexico	27.6	26.1

*Living in households with incomes of 50% or less of the national median.

Source: UNICEF (2000). *A League Table of Child Poverty in Rich Nations*. Florence: UNICEF: 10.

circumcision. Lifestyle diversity is also placing greater pressure on governments to permit legal marriage among same-sex couples, and to offer them access to the benefits that are available to heterosexual spouses and families. In addition, the population now contains many more lone-parent families who struggle to combine earning and caring, and more stepfamilies bringing together children from different parents. When lobby groups publicly disagree with one another or ask for different policy changes, governments can more easily disregard their views and say that public opinion is "divided" or "too diverse" for policy formulation.

Conservative lobby groups (such as the Fraser Institute in Vancouver) contend that the cost of social programs has been increasing over past decades, is now "out of control," and that politicians must reduce public expenditures. Recent governments have responded more to this kind of claim than to others by tightening eligibility for social programs, as more taxpayers continue to question whether they are receiving value for their tax dollars. Without comparing social spending and levels of taxation with other countries, Canadians nevertheless believe that their social programs are too costly and that taxes should be lower. In comparison to the United States, of course, Canadian income tax rates and social spending look high, although they are not particularly high by European standards (Baker, 1995; Korpi, 2000; OECD, 2001). The perception that Canadians are spending too much on social programs has inhibited the development of family programs and encouraged greater public acceptance of cutbacks. Conservative governments have tended to consult economists and financial experts rather than sociologists, social service providers, and researchers with social democratic views. This suggests that the philosophy of the government in power, as well as its alliances, contacts, and advisors, remains critically important to the development of family policy.

CONCLUSION

The government of Canada has never developed explicit family policies, in part because it lacks the jurisdiction to intervene in many areas of family life. In addition, there is little consensus about how to create more explicit and cohesive family policies. In fact, two broad opinions are prevalent among the lobby groups pressuring government. One contends that family structure and practices reflect pressures and changes in the broader society as well as personal preferences. Therefore, governments cannot easily modify them through legislation or regulations. Nevertheless, parents make an important contribution to society by raising children, and deserve ongoing state support to combine paid work with childcare and to raise children under difficult circumstances. The contrasting view is that "the family" is deteriorating and declining as the major institution in society. The state has an obligation to fight against unhealthy influences and the intrusion and growing social acceptance of alternative lifestyles. One way of doing this is to tighten welfare rules, ensure that the family remains a legal and heterosexual unit, and strictly enforce parental and spousal obligations.

In recent years, governments have tried to strengthen families, but have found that new policies are difficult to create, costly to enforce, and often create unintended results. Any new initiative is fraught with controversy and opposition from various lobby groups. Interest groups from the political left and those who applaud new family forms are suspicious of the call for "a family policy" because they fear it could represent a conservative agenda opposing greater equality for women and "families of choice." Groups on the political right often argue that new programs are too expensive and reward the "undeserving" poor. Creating social policies and programs that integrate these two opposing viewpoints has been challenging, both in Canada and in other countries.

Suggested Readings

Baker, Maureen (1995). *Canadian Family Policies: Cross-National Comparisons.* Toronto: University of Toronto Press.

Baker, Maureen and David Tippin (1999). *Poverty, Social Assistance and the Employability of Mothers: Restructuring Welfare States.* Toronto: University of Toronto Press.

Gauthier, Anne Hélène (1996). *The State and the Family: A Comparative Analysis of Family Policies in Industrialized Countries.* Oxford: Clarendon Press.

Hunsley, Terrance (1997). *Lone Parent Incomes and Social Policy Outcomes: Canada in International Perspective.* Queen's University: School of Policy Studies.

Lewis, Jane (2003). *Should We Worry About Family Change?* Toronto: University of Toronto Press.

Kamerman, Sheila B. and Alfred J. Kahn (eds.) (1997). *Family Change and Family Policies in Great Britain, Canada, New Zealand and the United States.* Oxford: Clarendon Press.

Web Resources

The Caledon Institute of Social Policy is a centre-left "think tank" based in Ottawa, which produces discussion papers on a variety of social policy issues impacting on families: **www.caledoninst.org**

The Canadian Council on Social Development is a voluntary organization that was developed in the 1920s to provide research, public education, and political lobbying for progressive social changes: **www.ccsd.ca**

Campaign 2000, which was created in 1989 to monitor "child poverty" in Canada, publishes an annual "report card": **www.campaign2000.ca**

The Childcare Resource and Research Unit at the University of Toronto includes Canadian and cross-national research and other material on childcare issues: **www.childcarecanada.org**

Endnotes

[1] The child tax deduction, the refundable child tax credit, and the non-refundable child tax credit.

PART FIVE

The Future of Family Life

CHAPTER THIRTEEN

The Future of Family Life

Maureen Baker

THE CHANGING FOCUS OF FAMILY RESEARCH

Over the years, research topics within family sociology have varied, reflecting the concerns of academics, the educated public, governments, and the media. In choosing research topics, social researchers are influenced by policy controversies, media reactions, demographic and economic trends, issues raised by social movements such as feminism and gay rights, personal circumstances, and research funding decisions. Throughout this book, various contributors have noted some of the changes since the beginnings of family sociology, but I will quickly review some of them here.

Meg Luxton noted in Chapter Two that family studies as an academic discipline in English-speaking universities began both in Europe and North America. Most of the founders of the sociology of the family were educated males of European origin, who created generalized theories to explain how social and economic changes influenced family life and tried to identify universal family patterns. By today's standards, some of these ideas represented a European male perspective of family life, but they were also influenced by national, cultural, and class backgrounds. Yet these ideas shaped the discipline and addressed important theoretical concerns. In fact, many of the issues they addressed continue to be relevant today.

Family sociology had several beginnings. One involved European men who empirically studied or theorized about European families. The pioneer of empirical family research is usually identified as Frederic Le Play (1806–1882), who studied the rural European "stem family," or extended family, consisting of parents and one married son who would eventually inherit the family property. Le Play began family sociology by lamenting the rise of the nuclear family (which he called the "unstable family"), the demise of patriarchal authority, and the decline of hierarchy. Nevertheless, he helped grant legitimacy to the study of family structure and social history (Gilding, 1997: 46).

Friedrich Engels (1820–1895) was one of the first European scholars to document British family life and to theorize about how transformations in the economy, urbanization, and industrialization impacted on family relations. He was especially concerned with how changes in the economic basis of society from feudalism to capitalism moved production outside the household and into the factory. The movement of production outside the home encouraged a family structure that was more patriarchal than previously, with husbands earning wages and serving as the family's intermediary to the community and state. Family research using a political economy perspective has continued until the present, emphasizing the importance of money, power, and social class in family practices, attitudes, and lifestyle.

European anthropologists such as Bronislaw Malinowski (1884–1942) and Alfred Radcliffe-Brown (1881–1955) also studied family life and culture by travelling to various parts of the world, including the South Pacific and Australia. They tried to identify universal behaviours and social structures, including family systems, and to explain the ways in which specific practices were integrated into the entire culture. Later, the American Margaret Mead (1901–1978) was one of the first female anthropologists to carry out field research among South Pacific cultures and to focus primarily on gender, family, and sexuality. The ideas of these researchers were widely debated among academics and educated   citizens at the time.

Although North American researchers have been studying family life since the 1890s, most of their research prior to the 1920s involved ethnographic observation or was closer to social work than to social science. Another stream of American family sociology originated from research on social interaction, small groups, and the family as a **social institution**. Throughout the 1950s and 1960s, the American sociologist Talcott Parsons (1902–1979) and his collaborator Robert Bales researched and theorized about the American family from a structural-functionalist perspective. American researchers also investigated romantic love, personal attraction, marital satisfaction, and social patterns in sexual behaviour, largely based on large-scale surveys. The famous Kinsey studies of male sexuality, published in 1948, revealed a widespread disregard for sexual exclusivity, monogamy, and premarital chastity, despite lip service to these norms. As a result of these findings, other researchers were encouraged to investigate young people's attitudes and practices concerning dating behaviour and premarital sex (Baker, 2001).

During the 1950s, which was typified by rising marriage rates, high fertility, and the suburbanization of North American cities, family researchers began to investigate marital satisfaction and happiness, and continued their interest in patterns of mate selection. When the work of Sigmund Freud was translated into English and became available to North American readers, research into early childhood development and maternal behaviour became popular. The English child psychologist John Bowlby also synthesized earlier studies on the importance of mothering and began his controversial work on maternal deprivation, as Glenda Wall discusses in Chapter 8. This kind of research continued into the 1950s, and explored bonding between mother and infant in non-humans as well as humans. These research findings reinforced the expectation that mothers would give priority to child rearing and homemaking because they concluded that children needed considerable love and stimulation early in their lives. At the time, people thought that only mothers could provide these for young children.

Until the 1950s and 1960s, few Canadian studies dealt specifically with family life, largely because sociology was not taught as a separate discipline in Canadian universities until the 1950s or later. Discussion and analysis of Canadian families were found within community studies such as *Crestwood Heights*, a study of a Toronto community by Seeley et al. (1956), rather than within separate family projects. In French Canada, family research focused on rural and religious traditions (Garigue, 1962), but studies of social mobility and urbanization also made reference to family life as one factor influencing patterns of mobility (Elkin, 1964: 68).

Many American studies in the 1950s and 1960s investigated the impact of mothers' employment on children's behaviour, as the proportion of "working mothers" increased. Researchers found correlations between employed mothers and juvenile delinquents, but later realized that the relationship between these variables was mediated by family income and community poverty. Researchers also continued their studies in the social work tradition of "problem families," those affected by poverty, absent fathers, alcohol, or disabilities. For sociologists such as Talcott Parsons and Robert Bales (1955), the ideal family was implicitly portrayed as a two-parent, one-earner family, with father as earner and mother as care provider and homemaker, and with two or three children. All other family forms were seen as "deviant," as Meg Luxton noted in Chapter Two.

As more women entered paid work, sociologists started talking about the **dual-career family**. Later it was acknowledged that the two-earner family was a more appropriate concept, because most people worked at jobs to earn a living, rather than at careers that involved lifetime planning and progress through the ranks. In Chapter Three, Margrit Eichler notes that research of this era retained a white middle-class bias, since researchers focused on professional rather than working-class couples. The fact that working-class wives had always earned money and contributed to the household was overlooked, and researchers saw the two-income family as revolutionary and likely to be detrimental both to children and marriage.

By the 1970s, several new themes became important. The concept of **open marriage**, in which partners operated as separate individuals and explored their "full potential" was advocated by some (O'Neill and O'Neill, 1972). Possible alternatives to the nuclear family, such as communal living or a series of non-legal intimate relationships, were discussed, and concern was expressed about the **death of the family** as an institution (Cooper, 1971). The changing role of women and its implications for family life also became the subjects of considerable debate and research, but few researchers discussed families as heterosexual and gendered units. The egalitarian family was viewed as the new emerging form, despite the lack of evidence that equality actually existed between spouses.

Several studies in the mid-1970s destroyed the myth of the egalitarian family. American decision-making studies from the 1960s had concluded that both husbands and wives shared family decision-making (Blood and Wolfe, 1960), but later studies found having more personal resources (such as higher income and higher status) enabled people to control important decisions such as where the family lived and at what living standard (Gillespie, 1971; Kandel and Lesser, 1972). Canadian time-budget studies also showed that the husbands of employed wives did about six minutes more housework per day than the husbands of housewives (Meissner et al. 1975; Clark and Harvey, 1976), dispelling myths of equality in domestic work. At the same time, Canadian legal decisions reinforced the inherent inequalities of family roles, which were supposed to be separate but equal.

Throughout the 1970s, marriage breakdown became more open and prevalent in Canada and other industrialized countries, leading to higher divorce rates, more one-parent households, disputes about the division of matrimonial property and child custody, and higher rates of poverty for lone mothers and their children. Research began to focus on these issues, as well as domestic labour, family violence, and childcare, as they became controversial topics in the media.

By the 1980s, "the family" was seen less as a haven from a heartless world and more as a complex institution involving both satisfaction and grief. Governments sponsored studies of child abuse and wife battering, as well as policy research on the division of matrimonial property after divorce, child custody, and child support. This research tended to reinforce the negative side of family life. At the same time, feminist scholars revived the sociology and history of domestic life by adding female viewpoints and discussing the various experiences of women and children in different social circumstances (Parr, 1982, 1990; Fox, 1980; Luxton, 1980; Eichler, 1983, 1988; Mandell and Duffy, 1988).

Throughout the 1990s, many of the assumptions of **liberal feminism** were incorporated into family research. Families were less likely to be described as egalitarian, cohesive, stable, and co-operating, and family experiences were acknowledged as different for males and females, as well as for people from different races, cultures, ages, and social classes. Furthermore, more family analysis used a historical perspective and focused on the impact of changing ideas about intimacy and sexuality (Giddens, 1992). Younger researchers studied families using different theoretical perspectives, including various feminist perspectives and post-modern theory, rather than relying on the structural- functional or the systems approach. The interpretations and meanings of marriage, child rearing, divorce, and remarriage were analyzed from the viewpoint of various family members. Researchers also began to compare government discourse and "public stories" about families with the gendered realities, to see if they were as egalitarian or as intimate as people claimed. Many concluded that power relations, social inequality, and gendered practices continue to constrain the choices and lifestyles of men and women (Bittman and Pixley, 1997; Jamieson, 1998; Baker, 2001).

Compared to previous decades, social researchers and theorists now present a more analytical and critical picture of family life and family policy. Current researchers are less likely to see families as units and to assume that one member can relate the experiences of all others, as Eichler notes in Chapter Three. More researchers recognize that husbands, wives, and children often have different experiences within the same households, and that laws and social policies sometimes have different consequences for men and women (Baker and Tippin, 1999; O'Connor, Orloff, and Shaver, 1999). For example, family law reform appears to have exacerbated poverty for some lone mothers by eliminating alimony and awarding temporary support to ex-wives on the assumption that they will become self-supporting. Researchers are also examining how medically assisted conception affects family life (Eichler, 1996; Daniels and Haimes, 1998).

Early family researchers tended to base their studies on a simplistic or monolithic model of "the family," which often meant white, middle class, heterosexual couples and their children, as discussed in Chapter Three. However, researchers now acknowledge that family experiences differ by gender, social class, ethnic and cultural group, and sexual orientation. Nevertheless, public discourses about families are created and perpetuated by politicians, bureaucrats, and the media and insinuate their way into social policies and programs. These ways of thinking and talking about families may subtly encourage people to accept without question an image of family life that no longer exists or that is culturally inappropriate.

Family interaction is complex and difficult to study because people may be reluctant to discuss delicate personal matters with social researchers or government representatives in order to maintain their privacy. When people are questioned or observed, they sometimes tell researchers what they think they want to hear or alter their behaviour to appear more socially acceptable. In addition, some people cannot easily express their feelings, and sometimes do not understand their own behaviour. Over the years, researchers have struggled to discover how people really behave at home, or what they actually think or feel, while retaining ethical research practices that do not alter behaviour or harm participants.

In Chapter One, we examined trends in family demography and cross-cultural variations in family patterns. In subsequent chapters, we discussed historical trends and cultural patterns, research and theories on various issues affecting family life, and the impact of social policies on family well-being. We have seen how family life has been modified with industrialization, urbanization, technological changes, increasing immigration, more flexible labour market requirements, and changing ideas about personal and sexual behaviour. We have also noted that some of these same changes have influenced legal reform and public discourse about family life. Now let us examine how the past and present may influence future family patterns.

THE FUTURE OF FAMILY LIFE

Dating, Cohabitation, and Marriage

At the end of the 19th century, a higher percentage of the Canadian population was unmarried or widowed, as noted by Bettina Bradbury in Chapter Four and Susan McDaniel in Chapter Nine. The Great Depression of the 1930s, two world wars, and major political and social upheavals shaped people's daily lives, influenced their opportunities, and transformed their circumstances and attitudes towards relationships and intimacy. From the 1950s to the 1970s, marriage rates increased, with more opportunities to meet new partners, higher living standards, and easier divorce and remarriage possibilities (Beaujor, 2000).

Now, about 95 percent of Canadians marry at some point in their lives (McDaniel and Tepperman, 2000), but compared to the 1970s, more people now are living alone, are separating or divorcing, and are cohabiting with opposite-sex or same-sex partners. Furthermore, a growing number of children live with cohabiting but unmarried parents, experience parental divorce, and spend a portion of their lives in a lone-parent household or with step-parents, as Wu and Schimmele noted in Chapter Ten. Children and young people are now growing accustomed to impermanence in both intimate relationships and paid work. However, we need to keep in mind that family life was often unstable early in the 20th century, although this instability usually arose from the death of a parent.

In the 21st century, young people are delaying marriage and child-bearing while they continue their schooling and establish some financial security. Liberal sexual practices and more effective birth control methods also contribute to delayed marriage. Legal marriage has become less important for a satisfying sexual life, but also less important for physical and emotional well-being and financial support, although two incomes can certainly purchase a better standard of living than one. Greater employment opportunities for women, apartment and condominium developments, household labour-saving devices, and attitudes promoting independence have made single living more feasible and desirable for people of all age categories. People can now work full-time and maintain a household by purchasing services or using labour-saving devices. Although this reduces the need for another person in the home, it is expensive and does not diminish people's desire for companionship and intimacy. Yet, a full social and sexual life is increasingly possible outside legal marriage and even outside cohabitation, as Sue Wilson discussed in Chapter Seven.

In the future, an increasing percentage of the population will live outside marriage. This trend will be perpetuated by the necessity to acquire a college or university education in order to find meaningful work, the need to repay student loans and acquire some job security before "settling down," and the growing concern about commitment in a world of high divorce rates. As more people remain or become single, the gap between family lifestyles and single lifestyles will also become more conspicuous. Compared to married people, single people tend to spend less time at home and more time socializing with friends, attending movies or other paid entertainment, travelling, eating in restaurants, or pursuing their hobbies away from home. Housing patterns will need to be made more conducive to one-person households, but at the same time, some immigrant groups will require larger homes for their extended families.

"Dating" will continue to become more egalitarian and non-marital sex more prevalent and socially acceptable. This pattern will be prevalent among older people as well as younger ones. New patterns will evolve to help people meet partners, including specialized clubs, personal advertising in newspapers, Internet dating, and commercial introduction agencies. As the Canadian population becomes more culturally diverse, intimate relationships between different racial, ethnic, and religious groups will become more prevalent. Most people, however, will continue to choose partners from their own racial, cultural, and social backgrounds, because these relationships seem more comfortable and are often based on shared understandings.

Although patterns of sexuality became more liberal during the 1960s and 1970s, a more conservative approach developed during the 1980s and 1990s. The fear of sexually transmitted diseases is a major contributing factor to this trend, especially since the AIDS virus is now apparent in the population. In addition, some women felt that the "sexual revolution" of the 1960s and 1970s did not lead to greater freedom, better relationships, or more happiness, and consequently became more cautious about sexual practices.

The double standard of sexual behaviour for men and women continues, since men retain more opportunity to date widely and to enjoy recreational sex with fewer negative consequences than women. Single women who date a number of men still tend to pay a price in terms of sexual harassment, assumptions of availability from friends or colleagues, or unwanted pregnancies (McDaniel and Tepperman, 2000: 58). As in the past, women who experience a variety of partners continue to receive a "reputation," which may be less damaging than in the past, but nevertheless influences future relationships. There is little evidence that the double standard of sexual attitudes and behaviour will disappear in the near future, although it may slowly diminish.

Despite the increase in cohabitation and marriage dissolution, the desire for commitment and permanence in relationships appears to continue. Young people still aspire to fulfilling and lasting relationships, partly because the media promote the romantic ideal, but also in an effort to counter uncertainties in parental marriages, the job market, and the future of the entire planet. Although adolescents understand intellectually that divorce rates have been increasing, many remain optimistic about their own future relationships (Baker, 1985; Looker and Thiessen, 1999).

Unmarried people of all ages increasingly expect to live alone, with a partner or friends, but not with parents, siblings, or other relatives. Whether or not single people establish a household separate from their families continues to depend on their own wishes, but also on their cultural background, social class, and financial circumstances. Parents from some cultural groups expect their young people to live at home before marriage and to share a household with parents after marriage, as Patrizia Albanese has shown in Chapter Six. Other young people may prefer to live alone, but cannot afford to rent an apartment without a permanent job or a stable income. Those who have not completed high school or college will increasingly be disadvantaged in both the labour market and the housing market, and may consequently see their personal independence delayed.

In the future, more employed people will change jobs or careers several times throughout their lives, while others will work in temporary jobs with little security, low pay, and few benefits (Torjman and Battle, 1999). Labour market trends will also require more people to work independently with minimal supervision, to create workspace at home, and to purchase computers and fax machines for **teleworking**. People often depend on their workplace for social contact, and those who work at home will need to create new opportunities for social interaction. Lack of job security and income may encourage others to share accommodation, cohabit, marry, or repartner in order to afford a home or to support their children.

For all age groups, the single life and living alone have become more feasible and acceptable, especially now that being unmarried no longer implies celibacy. Consequently, the social importance of legal marriage as a rite of passage to adult status will continue to subside, and marriage rates will fall as the legal distinction between cohabitation and marriage declines. Although more couples are living together without going through a wedding ceremony, most of these couples will eventually marry, especially if they decide to produce children. This pattern of cohabitation until childbirth (and even afterwards) has been apparent in Scandinavian countries for years, and it appears that Canadians (and especially Quebeckers) are moving in the same direction.

Young people with divorced parents, as well as older divorced adults, will demonstrate continued reluctance to enter into legal marriage without some previous knowledge of what it is like to live with their partner. Living together will become an acceptable "courtship pattern" or preliminary stage to marriage. In addition, opposition to gendered marital roles and traditional expectations will continue to grow, especially among educated women, and cohabitation will become an alternative to legal marriage for more people.

In the past, cohabiting couples tended to be people who questioned traditional practices. As cohabitation becomes more prevalent, this correlation will diminish and cohabitation will become more conventional, as it is in Sweden and Denmark (OECD, 2001). Yet, there will always be people who for religious or other reasons do not believe that living together without legal marriage (or obtaining a divorce) is morally right. Although cohabitation may give potential marital partners a more realistic notion of what they are getting into, it has not ensured future marital stability. Couples who live together before legal marriage have experienced higher divorce rates than those who never lived common-law (Wu, 2000; Beck-Gernsheim, 2002). Consequently, widespread cohabitation will encourage rather than prevent marriage instability in the future. Furthermore, as more people question gendered practices within marriage and more people openly proclaim their sexual preference, greater variety will become apparent in living arrangements, marriage contracts, wedding ceremonies, and personal lifestyles.

A small but increasing percentage of married or cohabiting couples live apart for temporary periods in order to obtain post-secondary education, find work, or pursue a more challenging career opportunity. Commuting couples may acquire two homes, and may maintain their own set of friends, bank accounts, cars, and household responsibilities. Working men, such as sales representatives, sailors, members of the armed forces, or migrant workers have always spent weeks and months apart from their wives and families in order to make a living. But now, a growing minority of middle-class couples are maintaining two careers by accepting positions in different locations. Commuter marriages are relatively rare, but are becoming more prevalent among dual-career couples with two high-income jobs. They may offer greater personal independence within the security of a couple relationship, as well as better career options, but these arrangements are expensive, emotionally difficult, time-consuming, and require high career commitment from both partners. Consequently, most couples will reject this option, especially if they have young children.

As more couples delay marriage and conception, more will adopt a lifestyle that focuses on work, career development, leisure pursuits, and travel, rather than home ownership, child-bearing and child rearing. Many will become accustomed to a child-free lifestyle and decide to continue with it permanently. If this choice becomes prevalent, policy-makers are sure to express more concern about declining birth rates and an aging population. In addition, more child-free marriages could lead to higher divorce rates, since separation and divorce are much simpler without concerns over child custody, care, and support.

Despite the instability of many relationships, legal marriage remains popular for the vast majority of the Canadian population and will continue to do so in the future. Even those who eventually divorce often say that they derived considerable satisfaction from their marriage during some time period. Most young people still expect to marry and to remain with the same partner throughout their lives. This suggests that Canadian marriages are changing, becoming more voluntary and somewhat less permanent, but that there is no indication that the desire for intimacy and children is becoming devalued. In fact, many people continue to raise their expectations of intimate relationships and marriage, which suggests that high rates of separation, but also re-partnering, will continue in the future.

Gendered Households in the Future

The Canadian labour force has changed substantially in recent years, as more partnered women and mothers accept full-time employment. Within families, however, fewer changes are apparent in the gendered division of labour, as Gillian Ranson shows in Chapter Five. Nevertheless, the impact of **women's double workload** and their demands for equality will eventually be felt in families as well as in the larger society. In some families, disputes over housework and childcare may promote or aggravate marital conflict and lead to separation and divorce. In others, the additional pressures may lead to hiring help, although more women may expect their husband and older children to share housework and childcare. Although most married women under 50 are now in the labour force, wives retain most of the responsibility for childcare and routine household chores. Younger husbands married to full-time employees, especially women earning higher incomes, are most likely to share childcare and housework (Marshall, 1993).

Despite minor modifications to the gendered division of labour at home, the transition to shared housework will not be easy for some couples. Few full-time employees of either sex choose willingly to spend their evenings or weekends cleaning toilets or vacuuming. Furthermore, some adults have never taken the time to learn certain domestic skills and may be reluctant to begin, especially men from certain cultural groups. Similarly, some wives do not bother to learn how to operate the power lawnmower or fix the car. In order to attain an equal division of labour, parents and educators will need to teach children to care for others, to perform a variety of household tasks, and to expect gender equality in their future homes. Yet children tend to learn from parental models rather than from verbal advice given by adults. Without egalitarian role models, many children will receive the clear message, regardless of what they are told, that housework and childcare are still "women's work," even when women work full-time.

What message do children learn about sharing household tasks when more high- and middle-income families rely on cleaning services to take care of housework?

In the future, more households will hire cleaners for a few hours each week, but this will remain an option for higher-income families. Furthermore, domestic cleaning is likely to remain an occupation dominated by women and immigrants with low education and/or poor language skills, because pay and prestige are low. New labour-saving devices will undoubtedly be invented as well, although these will require higher family incomes to purchase. As labour-saving devices become more commonplace in Canadian homes, more hours of work will be needed to afford them.

Increasingly, children and husbands in dual-earner families will be expected to perform more household tasks, causing greater conflict within families. It is unlikely, however, that many men will want to become homemakers in the future for the same reasons that women are rejecting this job—it is unpaid and retains low status. Yet, feminist researchers have concluded that employment equity cannot be achieved without equality in the home (Freiler and Cerny, 1998; Doherty, Friendly, and Oloman, 1998). Attitudes about sharing domestic work seem to have changed faster than behaviour. When explicitly asked, young couples say that they are in favour of equality in marriage, yet time-budget studies indicate that women continue to do most of the housework, childcare, and "emotional work" in Canada and other countries. Furthermore, this gendered division of labour tends to increase after the birth of each child (Bittman and Pixley, 1997).

In the past three decades, Canadian women have acquired greater access to paid work and are now better able to support themselves on their own earnings. Having their own money may give wives more bargaining power in their marriage and permit them to leave unhappy relationships if they wish. Yet wives still earn considerably less than their husbands. Furthermore, breadwinning wives are not treated by their husbands or families with the same deference or given the same authority as breadwinning husbands (Potuchek, 1997). Furthermore, women more often are offered and accept jobs that replicate the homemaker/mother role, such as nurse, teacher, cleaning woman, babysitter, or secretary. These jobs usually come with relatively low pay and little upward mobility. Consequently, over time, the gap between the job status of husbands and wives tends to grow, since married men are more likely than married women to be promoted.

Only recently have women made inroads into "non-traditional" jobs, including professions such as medicine and law. Although a few women have entered skilled labour jobs, technical and scientific jobs have remained dominated by men (Statistics Canada, 2001: 254). Furthermore, men have not entered female-dominated jobs such as daycare worker, nurse, elementary school teacher, or secretary in any significant numbers for the same reasons they have not voluntarily accepted full responsibility for household chores. Traditionally "female" positions tend to be perceived as lower status and receive lower pay than many positions dominated by men. Furthermore, some of the employment gains by women have been cancelled out by layoffs, transformations in the labour force, and the polarization of "good jobs" and "bad jobs" (Torjman and Battle, 1999).

In the future, men may find themselves spending more time in the household, with more responsibility for cooking, cleaning, and childcare. High rates of unemployment, more opportunities for teleworking and self-employment, increased rates of joint custody, and expanded parental leave and benefits may encourage this pattern. In contrast, more wives will be employed full-time and experience a "time crunch," requiring other people to accept more responsibility for cooking, shopping, and caring for children. These might be men, but could also be older children, female relatives, or female employees.

Family obligations affect employees' willingness to work hard, to work overtime, and to accept more responsibility on the job. Changes in men's family obligations and more women in higher-level jobs may force employers to be more cognizant of the family responsibilities of all employees. As well, the increased numbers of women in the labour force might encourage employers and employees to become more accepting of women working in non-traditional fields. However, changes in the gendered division of labour within the workplace will come about slowly because concerns about productivity, efficiency, profit-making, and tradition remain more important in a capitalist society than justice and equity. In addition, relations will change as the result of conflicts among employees, union/management negotiations, court challenges, and demands by advocacy groups for new legislation and better enforcement of existing laws.

Within families, equalizing gender roles will take time and will require difficult negotiations between spouses (Luxton, Rosenberg, and Arat-Koc, 1990; Dempsey, 1997). Although some couples will adapt with a minimum of conflict, others will quarrel, separate, and seek new relationships that place fewer demands on them. Yet subsequent generations of young people likely will be more accepting of gender equality within marriage and within workplaces.

Child-Bearing and Adoption in the Future

Family size has continued to decline throughout this century, as women bear fewer children, more unmarried people live on their own, and more partners separate and divorce. Most demographers project that low birth rates will continue in the near future because children are increasingly costly in urban environments, and combining work and family life is complicated when both parents are employed. Consequently, one-parent families, small families with one or two children, and childless couples will become more prevalent in the future. More couples will probably opt for a child-free lifestyle, given the high financial costs and the personal sacrifices required to raise children.

At the same time, medically assisted conception will enable more low-fertility couples to reproduce. Already, some couples are postponing child-bearing until an age at which conception is more difficult and the risks of fetal deformities higher. Clearly, reproductive technologies have the capacity to revolutionize family life, separating social and biological parenthood, and changing generational lines (Eichler, 1996). However, only a small minority of people currently use reproductive technologies, and governments likely will outlaw certain services or exempt others from public medical insurance. Although more single women and lesbian couples are using assisted conception, most of the future growth in fertility services probably will come from heterosexual couples trying to create nuclear families.

At the same time, more couples who want to adopt will be encouraged to turn to inter-country adoptions, since fewer Canadian infants will be available. Unplanned births to adolescents and young women have declined since the 1970s, with improved contraception and access to legal abortion. Furthermore, unmarried mothers are raising their own children with social assistance and their own earnings. There is no indication that the decline in the availability of Canadian infants for adoption will change in the foreseeable future or that a significant percentage of Canadians will choose to adopt older children. In fact, the goals of **family preservation** in child welfare agencies, combined with the factors above, will compel more people to turn to Third World countries for infant adoption.

Although parliamentary reports have reiterated that children are our greatest "future resource," little has been done in North America, compared to some European countries, to assist couples in combining work and family life (Jenson and Sineau, 2001). In Canada, parental benefits under Employment Insurance have been extended to nearly a year, and some provinces (such as Quebec) have expanded low-cost childcare services. Numerous policy discussions have taken place about assisting parents to raise children and earn a living, but policy options tend to be punitive rather than enabling. Governments could require employers to provide more flexible work hours, shared work with pro-rated benefits, more generous maternity and parental leave and benefits, and leave to care for sick children or for other family responsibilities. Initially, these changes would cost employers and governments more money, but absenteeism and lost productivity resulting from work/family conflicts already cost governments and employers a considerable amount (Duxbury and Higgins, 2003).

Politicians and policy-makers are often concerned that declining birth rates eventually will lead to an older population requiring higher government expenditures on old age pensions and medical care. They argue that more retired people in the population will reduce the tax base and become a drain on social programs. Older people are less likely to be employed and to pay income taxes, and are also less likely to purchase goods and services and pay the goods and services tax (GST). A disproportionate amount of government money has been spent on health care and pensions for elderly people in comparison to services for children. If governments want to encourage people to have more children, however, they will have to create a more conducive social and employment environment. They cannot realistically expect that cash grants at birth, small tax credits for dependent children, or tax deductions for childcare expenses will encourage many couples to have larger families. After all, children are expensive and time-consuming for parents, and most employers currently offer few concessions for employees with family responsibilities.

Extended hours for shopping and business, automated teller machines, and the development of fast food have helped employed parents to manage their personal lives more effectively. Governments and employers could further assist working parents by providing more childcare spaces in neighbourhoods or in the workplace. Parents would then be relieved of the burden of transporting their children to and from care services that are neither close to home nor work. Governments also could increase tax incentives for families with dependent children or adults with special needs. They could create more equity between parents and individuals without children by providing more generous family benefits. Furthermore, governments and social agencies could provide greater assistance to individuals or couples who want to adopt children from another jurisdiction, and for couples who require fertility treatment.

In times of economic recession or cutbacks, many of these reforms are unlikely to be introduced, because governments are preoccupied with spending cuts and deficit reduction, and these reforms would entail such politically difficult alternatives as tax increases or a shift in government priorities. Furthermore, many employers are more concerned with restructuring and staying in business than with assisting employees to combine work and family life. Unions are also busy maintaining their membership and attempting to retain full-time jobs. However, the development of new state programs to help families become possible when elections are imminent, government coffers contain surpluses, or when a minority government rules. In addition, a shortage of skilled women workers might encourage employers to become more concerned about issues related to work-family balance.

Canadian social programs have undergone many changes since the 1960s, yet families with dependent children (especially one-parent families) have not benefited as much as have elderly people. The development of the Old Age Pension, Guaranteed Income Supplement, and Registered Retirement Savings Plans, along with inflation in the housing market, has improved the economic status of elderly people. However, most child benefits (except the tax deductions for childcare) have remained relatively low in value, and federal child benefits are now delivered as a tax benefit targeted to middle- and lower-income families. In the past few years, more federal money has been invested in these benefits, although this may not compensate for the cuts to transfer payments throughout the 1990s (Leblanc, 2000).

Canada continues to experience much higher rates of poverty among families with children than many industrialized countries, especially those in northern Europe. Numerous studies have indicated that child and family poverty is related to unemployment, low minimum wages and state income support relative to living costs, the loss of full-time permanent jobs to part-time and temporary positions, inequities in the labour force (such as job segregation and lower pay for female workers), and lack of affordable childcare services. Intervention in the labour market designed to improve or maintain family income has not been a political priority for Canadian governments. Instead, they have focused on making parents work harder and longer hours for wages that have not kept up with the rising cost of living, and occasionally supplementing family income with modest levels of income support.

The Future of Families in Mid-Life and Later Life

In popular discourse, mid-life has been associated with crises and menopause, yet research reveals that these portrayals are not very realistic (Poole and Feldman, 1999). Increasingly, both men and women remain in the labour force during middle age, and their occupational lives may be just starting to solidify and prosper during their forties and fifties. In addition, family income is often at its highest point since marriage, and parents may find that their children are now more self-sufficient and require less supervision. Mid-life couples may enjoy a higher standard of living, with more time and money set aside for leisure activities or paid work.

Mid-life often means renewed energy for women (Gee and Kimball, 1987: 49). With freedom from time-consuming child-rearing tasks, women can return to school or re-enter the labour force, although an increasing number of Canadian women are remaining in the labour market throughout their adult lives, except for brief periods for maternity or retraining. In the past, many women's lives were shaped by marriage, childbirth, child

Middle age for women today may mean the enjoyment of career success, not a mid-life crisis over the end of one's childbearing years.

rearing, and housework. When they reached middle age and passed through menopause, the end of fertility was thought to cause a mid-life crisis because so much of their social value was related to child-bearing, sexuality, and physical attractiveness. Yet many middle-age women welcome menopause because the relentless fear of pregnancy is over and child-rearing tasks are reduced. Furthermore, more women are now advancing in the labour market, as Susan McDaniel noted, and by mid-life can derive considerable satisfaction from their occupational success.

By mid-life, some men are also reaching high occupational ranks and income, deriving considerable satisfaction from their work. As their wives become more established in the labour force and children leave home, men's financial responsibilities may lessen. Other men may be tired of the occupation they have pursued for twenty years or more, or feel frustrated that they were unable to achieve their occupational goals. Still others may be forced into early retirement or laid off, exacerbating the financial insecurity that marked their entire lives. Clearly, educational attainment, occupational status, and income (or **social class**) influence the experiences of men and women in mid-life.

By mid-life, some men realize that they have devoted so much time to their jobs that they have neglected family relationships as well as close friendships with other men. Others may enjoy male companions, but tend not to create close personal relationships as women do. Middle-aged and older men consequently spend more of their leisure time alone than women do or in the company of work buddies who are merely acquaintances rather than intimate friends (Connidis, 1989a; Poole and Feldman, 1999). There is little indication that this will change substantially in the near future.

Couples who have been married for years may continue to enjoy a satisfying relationship with many shared experiences and memories. Those who have been recently remarried may be just beginning a new life full of hope. Some men may even be starting families with their new partners. Regardless of whether middle-aged parents live in one- or two-parent families, whether they have been married for years or recently developed new relationships, they may be watching their children mature into adults with growing satisfaction or concern.

Although Canadians are having fewer children and completing child-bearing at younger ages, children tend to remain dependent on parents longer than during the 1970s and early 1980s. Now, the process of acquiring an "empty nest" is becoming more gradual for parents, and the transition to the post-parental stage is being prolonged once again, as it used to be before the Second World War. More young people over 18 lived with their parents while attending college or university in 1990s than in the early 1980s (Boyd and Pryor, 1990). Although this prolonged dependency could lead to more companionate relationships between parents and their adult children in the future, it could also encourage adolescent rebellion and family tensions.

More young adults will delay establishing their own households as educational requirements for employment continue to be inflated, wages remain low, the cost of housing grows, and employment security becomes more elusive. Parents will be expected to help their adult children finance their education, since part-time jobs seldom provide sufficient income for living expenses and post-secondary education. Now, there is less certainty about full-time employment after graduation and many graduates will return home until they find work that is secure enough to pay for their own living expenses. However, not all parents will be able to afford this, and young people from lower-income families will continue to leave home earlier. Lifetime education and job retraining will become more necessary in the future.

The trend for women to delay parenting until they are over 30, which is apparent among a growing minority of Canadians, also will delay the post-parental stage of family life. Some parents will be in their sixties when their children leave home. The trend toward delayed first births, which is most noticeable among middle-class educated women and couples, will not only postpone child launching, but also delay the future age of retirement. With continuing child rearing and educational expenses, fewer parents will be able to afford early retirement.

As more women become self-supporting in mid-life, their personal and marital satisfaction may rise. Those residing with a partner will be better able to enjoy a higher standard of living. Employment may bring considerable personal development as well as new social contacts. At the same time, those who are also mothers may enter a period of decreased responsibility for their children and home, and may be able to find more time for themselves and their friends.

With two incomes, couples in unhappy relationships will be better able to separate, divorce, and begin a new life. After marital separation, however, the income of most women falls compared to that of their partner. Neither child custody arrangements nor women's relative incomes have changed much in recent years, and custodial mothers and other divorced women will continue to live on lower incomes than their male counterparts. Furthermore, women's continuing caring responsibilities for children and older parents, as well as the unfavourable sex ratio, will discourage their remarriage. Although financial insecurity may encourage cohabitation, women appear to be less eager than men to remarry because many experienced unequal power relations in their previous relationships and shouldered more of the burdens of housework, childcare, and emotional work.

Growing financial pressures and the need for two incomes may keep some couples living together regardless of the quality of their relationship, yet more middle-aged people in the coming decades will leave unhappy marriages. Many will establish satisfying lives in new relationships, either within or outside legal marriage. Remarriage will probably remain popular for those seeking financial and legal security. With increasing rates of joint custody and remarriage, the boundaries of blended families will become even more blurred as greater numbers of children live in the households containing their biological parents, step-parents, and stepsiblings.

Studies of the children of divorced parents indicate that these young people tend to leave home at an earlier age. As the percentage of children from divorced families rises, we may see more young people leaving home earlier and forfeiting higher education in their effort to establish their own household away from the complications of blended families. Yet, high accommodation costs and inability to support themselves may prevent some from leaving home even when they want to do so. This inability to leave home could augment parent/adolescent conflict and reduce the quality of family life.

With rising life expectancies, mid-life could also mean prolonged responsibility towards aging parents and parents-in-law, as Susan McDaniel discusses in Chapter Nine. Furthermore, the tendency for women to serve as primary caregivers for both children and elderly relatives likely will continue in the future. As more middle-aged women remain in the labour force and therefore are unavailable to provide personal care for elderly relatives, they will become managers of care rather than caregivers (Connidis, 1989b). In other words, women will negotiate with state services and private care providers on behalf of their elderly parents. As birth rates decline, however, fewer adult children will be available to protect the interests of elderly parents in the future. This suggests that more community services will be required to care for frail elderly adults.

The greater prosperity of many two-income families over the past two decades, as well as early retirement incentives, have allowed some older couples to travel, to spend more money on entertainment, or to choose early retirement. At the same time, the downsizing and restructuring of many firms, combined with competition from younger workers, may force more middle-aged and older employees to leave their positions before they are ready psychologically or financially. Some will establish their own businesses, but this kind of occupational gamble is most feasible when children have left home and a spouse earns a steady income. Higher disposable incomes and more generous early retirement programs may encourage others to retire in their fifties and spend more time on leisure activities. However, as the trend to non-standard employment continues, there is no evidence that more employees in the future will acquire employment-based pension plans.

Instead, we are more likely to see a greater gap between older people who are dependent on minimal government pensions and those who enjoy a combination of government pensions, employer-sponsored pensions, and private retirement savings.

Most couples bear children, who eventually produce grandchildren. Relationships between grandparents and their grandchildren may become more salient in the future as life expectancies rise and these relationships have longer to develop. Yet the trend toward delayed childbirth will mean that some children will be quite young when their grandparents die, as the years between generations lengthen.

The Impact of Immigration and Cultural Differences on Family Life

Throughout Canada's history, population growth has been sustained largely through immigration, initially from Europe and the United States, but now increasingly from Asia, Africa, Central America, and the Caribbean. Canada has always used foreign workers and immigrants to fill gaps in the labour force, and many of these workers initially arrive as single people or without their spouse and family. In addition, Canada accepts refugees from war-torn countries or those whose lives are in danger. Many refugees and immigrants who arrive in Canada remain there, while others move on to another country (especially the United States) or eventually return home when the trouble subsides. Patrizia Albanese has shown us in Chapter Six that we cannot assume that immigrants bring with them all the cultural values of their homeland. Many migrate because they are searching for a new lifestyle, while others may simply find that some of their cultural practices are not feasible to retain. In other cases, childhood patterns of socialization and cultural values relating to dating, marriage, and child-bearing are modified, especially by the generation born in Canada. These young people may choose to drop some of their parent's values and practices, while retaining others.

Many immigrants and refugees come to Canada on their own, without other family members. Although some maintain close telephone and e-mail contact with relatives overseas, others may not be able to return, communicate, or visit without endangering the lives of their relatives or friends. Some refugees do not see their spouse, parents, and other family members until the war is over, until they can obtain landed immigrant status and sponsor their relatives to come as immigrants, or until they can save enough money to visit.

Immigration laws have influenced the origin and composition of immigrant families in this country. Initially, the laws gave preference to British and western European families, but encouraged some "visible minorities" to leave their families behind while they worked or studied temporarily in Canada. After the 1960s, immigration laws permitted immigrants from more countries. Family members were welcomed during the prosperous years of the 1960s and 1970s through the "family class" category, and later, preference was given to immigrants with specific job skills or investments that contribute to job creation and economic productivity. Increasingly, new immigrants to Canada have higher education, professional and managerial backgrounds, and greater wealth. However, restrictions are still placed on the sponsorship of relatives, especially members of the extended family, elderly parents, and those with disabilities or health problems. In the future, government cutbacks will require immigrant families to accept greater financial responsibility for any relatives they sponsor.

Cultural diversity has encouraged new ideas about what families should be and do, about the role of government in family life, and what kinds of social programs are necessary and desirable. For example, increasing cultural diversity has required the immigration department to clarify the definition of "family" and "dependant," but this has not varied much from traditional policy-related definitions. Cultural practices such as female circumcision, the wearing of the *hijab*, and preference for male children have challenged Canadian practices, traditions, and laws. In some cases, immigrant and indigenous attempts to retain their own culture or to change Canadian society have been resisted by the descendents of the original English or French settlers. Generally, cultural practices that differ substantially from the dominant model of family have not been embraced. Nevertheless, some efforts have been made to permit "heritage languages" to be taught within the school curriculum, to promote culturally specific family services, and to encourage First Nations to develop their own childcare and child welfare services.

Increased cultural diversity during periods of high unemployment and economic recession has given rise to public concern that immigration targets are too high and refugee laws too lax. In the near future, we may see lower immigration targets, stricter refugee screening, and more emphasis on admitting skilled, educated, and wealthy immigrants. At the same time, more government resources will be allocated to helping existing immigrants integrate and to develop campaigns against racial and cultural prejudice and discrimination. Cultural diversity is already visible in Canadian schools, universities, workplaces, and public spaces. There is little evidence, however, that state social programs will substantially change to embrace the growing cultural diversity.

Nevertheless, more young people now consider skin colour or cultural background to be unimportant in choosing their friends or intimate partners. Many discover that they have as much in common with fellow students or work mates from different cultures as with people from their own culture who have different levels of education or income, or who work in different types of jobs.

CONCLUSION

Conservatives have predicted the decline or death of the family since the beginning of written history, and have argued that young people and their sexual behaviour were out of control. Contrary to this view, the contributors to this book have aptly demonstrated that family life has never been stable, but has always been influenced by changes in the economy, the labour market, social policies, technology, and popular culture. Our predictions of the future have focused on the implications of labour market changes on work and family life, but also on the importance of technological change and new ideas. This includes the role of higher education and hard economic times in delaying marriage and child-bearing, the high cost of child rearing within two-income families, the impact of women's paid work on marital dynamics, and the influence of economic opportunities on lifestyle and retirement. Yet, we have also emphasized that social class, gender, and cultural differences mediate the impact of these changes.

As job opportunities for women expanded in the 1970s, the new economic realities required reform both in labour law and family law. Women's experiences in higher education, the labour force, and in their marriages gave added impetus to feminist discourse. It is not surprising that feminist ideas have influenced social science research and theory, especially the sociology of the family. At the same time, more gay and lesbian couples contend that gendered practices within families, compulsory heterosexuality, and Canadian laws have marginalized their intimate relationships, which deserve greater respect and recognition.

Family sociology is moving away from an emphasis on white, middle-class experience and is beginning to examine the cultural diversity of family life, as immigration from Third World countries increases and surpasses immigration from Europe, and as cultural groups in Canada solidify their identities. Children's experiences in families continue to be influenced by their social class origins and family structure, but cultural and lifestyle diversity is challenging our assumptions about what it means to grow up in a family in Canada. Diversity will continue to influence family life and will necessarily become more significant in family research in the future.

None of these changes implies, however, that the desire for meaningful and lasting intimate relationships is declining. On the contrary, motivations to develop and maintain a satisfying marriage and family life remain high. In fact, a larger percentage of Canadians have experienced marriage, either legal or common-law, in the past three decades than at any other time in Canadian history. A growing belief is apparent that marriage and family life should be personally satisfying rather than only based on duty, family obligation, the perpetuation of family name, or economic survival. Furthermore, more people believe that neither the state nor organized religion should become involved in their intimate relationships. This emphasis on choice, love, and personal satisfaction in Canadian family life will continue well into the future.

Suggested Readings

Beck-Gernsheim, Elisabeth (2002). *Reinventing the Family: In Search of New Lifestyles*. Cambridge: Polity Press. Beck-Gernsheim discusses the choices people make to expand their personal opportunities and relationships, and to avoid the increasing tensions between the demands of family and employment.

Giddens, Anthony (1992). *The Transformation of Intimacy: Sexuality, Love and Eroticism in Modern Societies*. Cambridge: Polity Press. Giddens argues in this controversial book that the separation of sex from reproduction holds the possibility of democratizing relations between men and women.

Smart, Carol and Bren Heale (1999). *Family Fragments?* Cambridge: Polity Press. This book draws on a British qualitative study of separating parents, and examines the diverse and fluid patterns of parenthood that are negotiated and renegotiated after separation.

Wu, Zheng (2000). *Cohabitation: An Alternative Form of Family Living*. Toronto: Oxford University Press. Based on Canadian data, this book examines the social, legal, and policy implications of the remarkable demographic shift represented by cohabitation.

Web Resources

The Centre for Research on Families and Relationships involves collaborative research from several universities in Scotland : **www.crfr.ac.uk**

Glossary

Access is the legal arrangement for contact between non-custodial parents and their offspring following separation or divorce.

Ageist bias views children and the aged as only passive members of families.

Alimony was spousal support awarded to divorced women before the enactment of no-fault divorce legislation.

Androcentricity is the adoption of a male viewpoint or perspective.

Anticipatory socialization involves preparation for a future role by watching and imitating someone else performing that role.

Arranged marriage is one in which the partner is selected by elder family members, but the young people may have the right to veto the choice.

At-risk families refer to those who have a high probability of going hungry, having inadequate accommodation, or being abused or neglected by parents or other relatives.

Attachment theory, developed by John Bowlby in the 1950s, emphasized the importance of a strong and secure emotional attachment of infants to their mothers in order for normal development to occur.

Bilateral descent is lineage traced through the families of both the bride and groom.

Bill C-31 was the Canadian legislation in 1985 eliminating the section of the *Indian Act* that caused women to lose their Indian status when they married non-Indian men.

Blended family is a stepfamily formed through post-marital cohabitation or remarriage that includes stepsiblings, half-siblings, or both.

Boundary maintenance involves the clarification of the limits to roles or group membership.

Canada Assistance Plan (CAP) was the federal-provincial cost-sharing program in place from 1966 to 1996 to cover the cost of social assistance and social services.

Capitalism is the economic system in which the production and distribution of goods and services depend on private capital and profit-making.

Cap on CAP refers to the 1990 reduction of federal contributions to the Canada Assistance Plan in the three "fiscally strongest" provinces.

Caregiver burn-out is the accumulated stress from providing 24-hour care to a dependent family member or close friend.

Caregiving means providing help or support to someone else, including personal care such as with bathing and dressing, and/or emotional care such as listening and offering support.

Census family is a term used by Statistics Canada to refer to a husband and wife living with or without never-married children, or a lone parent living with never-married children.

Child-centred advice refers to expert child-rearing advice that emerged after World War II, treating children's needs as all-important and defining mothers' rights and responsibilities in terms of these needs.

Child custody involves the guardianship of a child and the authority to make decisions about the child's welfare and upbringing.

Child poverty refers to the percentage of children living with impoverished parents; the concept is designed to enhance sympathy for the plight of blameless children.

Child support refers to the privately arranged or court-ordered financial support non-custodial parents must pay to support their offspring.

Child Support Guidelines advise Canadian judges of the appropriate amount of child support given the income of the non-custodial parent and the number of children.

Civil law, which is used in Quebec and many European countries, is based largely on written statutes rather than previous court cases or custom (like common law).

Civil unions are marriages approved by the state, but not necessarily by the church.

Cohabitation (or common-law marriage) is an intimate union between a (heterosexual) couple who share a household and live together in marriage-like circumstances.

Collective agreement covers wages or salaries, benefits, and other working conditions negotiated by an organized group of workers.

Collective bargaining is the process by which employment agreements are negotiated between employees and employers

Common law refers to the body of general, largely unwritten legal conventions based on prior judicial rulings and traditional customs.

Common-law relationship refers to cohabitation without legal marriage.

Complementary needs theory of mate selection states that people marry those whom they think will complement their psychological needs.

Complementary roles involve separate spheres for men and women in marriage.

Compulsory altruism refers to the sense of compulsion to give or to care out of duty or the belief that no one else will do it.

Conflict perspective emphasizes power differentials and conflicts of interest between groups or organizations.

Conflict Tactic Scale is used in survey research to measure different ways of handling conflict in family or intimate relationships.

Conservative bias fails to understand the significance of fundamental family changes and ignores the unpleasant aspects of family life.

Contingent workforce consists of employees who do not have full-time, permanent jobs, but work in non-standard employment as needed by employers.

Contract work lasts for a specified time period dictated by the employer's contract.

Corporatist welfare states offer social security based on social insurance programs funded by employers, employees, and government, with higher benefits for those with higher incomes.

Custom of Paris was the legal code that became the basis of civil law in Lower Canada and was modified in 1866 to create Quebec's Civil Code. It set the rules for marriage and family, property, and much of commercial law.

Death of the family was a slogan that meant that the family as we know it has changed forever.

Developmental approach assumes that children pass through stages of cognitive, motor, and psychological development, and that particular tasks or concepts must be adequately learned before a child passes through the next stage of development.

Divorce rate is the annual number of divorces per 1000 marriages (or per 1000 population) within a specific jurisdiction, such as a country or province.

Double standard involves evaluating identical situations and behaviours differentially for men or women.

Dual-career families have adults with occupations involving advancement through the ranks as they gain more experience and expertise.

Economic family is used by Statistics Canada to refer to related people sharing a household.

Emigration is the movement or migration of people out of a region or country.

Employment status refers to a person's relationship to the paid labour force as an unemployed person, or a part- or full-time employee.

Endogamy refers to marriage within one's group, which may be a race, ethnicity, religion, caste, or socioeconomic status.

Ethnic enclaves refer to business and job opportunities established within communities that are usually owned, operated, or controlled by members of the same ethnic group.

Ethnic exogamy occurs when an individual marries a person of an ethnic origin different from his or her own; as opposed to ethnic intramarriage or endogamy, which occurs when an individual marries a person of the same ethnic or cultural origin as her/himself.

Ethnic group consists of people who share ancestral origins, customs, and beliefs, and who are separated from others by way of social boundaries.

Ethnicity is a process of shared awareness of ancestral differences and group belonging which is used as a basis for differential distribution of recognition, rewards, and relationships.

Eugenics movement was a 19th century social movement to improve the quality of the human race, especially through selective breeding.

Exchange theory uses a market analogy to explain attraction and commitment, assuming that individuals maximize rewards and minimize costs in intimate relationships.

Exogamy is marriage outside the group.

Experience hypothesis suggests that marriages following cohabitation are more likely to end in divorce because the experience of cohabitation negatively influences the perception of marriage.

Extended family involves several generations, or siblings and their spouses and children, who share a household and resources.

Factory Acts were passed by the Canadian provinces during the 1880s to regulate working conditions, introduce safety measures, curtail child labour, and restrict female employment.

Family economy refers to the waged and unwaged contributions of all family members to ensuring the survival of the household.

Family life cycle approach sees the family as an ever-changing unit in which relationships and interaction vary with psychosexual development and with social events such as marriage, birth, divorce, or retirement.

Family policy involves the pursuit and attainment of collective goals and values in addressing problems of families in relation to the state.

Family preservation is a principle governing child welfare that relies on the extended family and social support to keep children living with family members rather than placing them in foster homes or institutions.

Family values include beliefs and attitudes that emphasize the (patriarchal) nuclear family as the basic unit of society and the importance of raising children.

Family violence is an act committed by one family member against another intended to be emotionally or physically threatening or harmful.

Family wage was one wage sufficient to support the entire family, hence avoiding the paid labour of young children, daughters, or wives.

Family wage economy refers to waged work needed to support the entire household.

Fathers' rights movement is based on the assumption that fathers have lost legal rights from family law reform.

Feminist perspective focuses on women's viewpoints and experiences, as well as how social structures and cultural understandings impact on women.

Feminist theories of wife abuse emphasize male attempts to control their partners within a society that condones violence and perpetuates patriarchal authority.

Feminization of poverty refers to the trend for more poor people to be female or for more poor families to be female-led.

Filles du roi were the 700 poor and orphaned young women sent from Paris to become brides to male settlers in Quebec from 1663 and 1673.

First default principle means that the state will intervene in the enforcement of child support only after the first time payment is not made.

First Nations refers to both Status and Non-status "Indians" in Canada.

Flexible work fulfils specific and usually short-term needs of an employer.

Frail elderly are older people who near the end of their lives experience poor or failing health.

Functionalism - See Structural-Functional perspective.

Gay marriage involves two male partners.

Gender refers to the social or cultural meanings attached to being male or female in a particular society.

Gender insensitivity ignores sex or gender when it is a socially important variable.

Gender neutral means that something could pertain equally to male or female.

Gender relations are the ways that males and females interact in a society, considering their different socialization and life experiences.

Gendered society encourages males and females to develop different skills and interests, and to work at different jobs.

Globalization refers to the world scale of economic and other activity made possible by the spread of information and telecommunications technology.

Heterogeneous means diverse or different in structure.

Heterosexism is a bias which assumes that everyone is heterosexual or that homosexuality is abnormal or insignificant.

Homogamy refers to the similarities in the age, social class, race, and ethnicity of couples.

Homophobia is the fear or disapproval of homosexuals or homosexuality.

Household refers to related or unrelated people who share a dwelling.

Householdism confuses family and household, treating the family as the smallest unit of analysis when in fact the household is the more important unit in the particular circumstance.

Ideologies of gender are beliefs about appropriate behaviour and roles for women and men that often are linked to specific political and social agendas.

Ideology is a set of ideas that reflects the interests and beliefs of a social group or society, and forms the basis of social or political action.

Immigration refers to the movement of people into another society or country.

Incest refers to inappropriate sexual activity between related persons.

Indian is a term used by the Canadian government to describe all the Aboriginal peoples who are not Inuit or Metis.

Indian Act is Canadian federal legislation, first passed in 1876, that sets out certain government obligations and regulates the management of Indian reserve lands. The Act has been amended several times.

Indian status refers to legal designation as an "Indian" as defined by the *Indian Act*.

Industrialization is the process by which manufacturing industries become dominant in a country's economy.

Institutional completeness is the degree to which an ethnic group or community develops its own institutions and formal organizations, such as places of worship, publications, and welfare organizations.

Intensive mothering is a term that suggests that "good" mothering involves much more time, emotional involvement, and financial expenditure than in the past.

Interactionist theory - See Symbolic interaction perspective.

Intimate feminicide refers to the killing of females by male partners or former partners.

Inuit refers to the Aboriginal people in northern Canada who live in Nunavut, the Northwest Territories, Northern Quebec, and Labrador.

In vitro fertilization involves the union of sperm and egg outside a human being, typically in a test tube.

Joint custody is the legal situation where both parents share authority over decisions regarding child welfare and upbringing after divorce.

Kin-keeper refers to the person who maintains the family as a group socially and organizes family celebrations and rituals.

Labour force participation refers to engagement in formal paid employment.

Lesbian marriage is between two women partners.

Liberal feminism is the ideology that women should have rights and opportunities equal to men in education, employment, and politics.

Liberal welfare states base social security largely on need and target benefits to low income and problem families.

Lone-parent family is a household comprised of one parent living with his or her never-married children.

Macro-level theory explains human behaviour by focusing on how societal structures (such as the law, education, or political systems) influence people's lives.

Male breadwinner family is a two-parent family with father as principal earner and mother as care provider.

Male peer support involves attachments to male friends that sometimes encourage abuse against women.

Marginal economy refers to jobs that are temporary and low-paying.

Marital breakdown is the legal grounds for divorce based on circumstances that impair marital functioning, such as spousal desertion or long-term separation.

Marriage market uses an economic analogy to describe the availability of potential marriage partners and how they are valued in a particular culture or period.

Marriage squeeze refers to the numerical imbalance between men and women that prevents some from finding partners.

Married Women's Property Acts modified marriage rules in the 19th century to allow wives to keep their own property separate from that of their husbands and to enable wives to become the legal owners of their own wages, earnings, savings, or inheritance.

Marxist theories of family suggest that family forms are specific to a certain period of history and will change as economies evolve from capitalism to socialism.

Master discourses refer to shared ways of thinking and speaking about a subject.

Maternal deprivation is a psychological theory popularized by John Bowlby in the 1950s which linked severe developmental and psychological problems in children to lack of loving care by a mother or mother-substitute.

Maternal feminism was the 19th century social movement which viewed men and women as different but equal, and argued that women should have more say in public life in order to humanize public policy.

Maternity leave is the official time away from paid employment taken by a mother for childbirth or adoption.

Mating gradient refers to the mating of attractive young women with older, more prosperous men.

Matriarchy is a system that gives women more authority than men.

Matrifocal family is one that is focused around the mother.

Matrilineal descent traces relatives through the mother's side of the family.

Matrilocal residence means that the groom comes to live with the bride's family or in her community.

Matrimonial fault is an act considered to violate the marriage contract and therefore to be a justification for divorce.

Means-tested benefit bases entitlement to social benefits on financial assets, property, and income.

Métis people have both Aboriginal and European ancestry, and a unique culture drawing upon their diverse origins.

Micro-level theory suggests that human behaviour can be explained by focusing on interpersonal relations rather than the structures of society.

Microstructural bias disproportionately emphasizes psychological or interpersonal variables to the neglect of macrostructural (political or economic) variables.

Mid-life or middle age can be the mid-point in life expectancy, but more often it is seen as the life stage between raising children or the early stage of one's career, and old age.

Migration refers to geographic mobility between one locale and another.

Modified extended family refers to relatives who maintain frequent and close contact with one another but live in separate households.

Monogamy is a system of marriage in which each adult is allowed only one spouse at a time.

Monolithic bias assumes that all families are similar and overemphasizes uniformity of experience and structure at the expense of diversity.

Motherwork refers to unpaid housework and childcare done by mothers, which was formerly not considered as "work" by most social scientists.

Multi-generational households are those in which children, parents, and grandparents live together.

Natural increase is population growth resulting from more births than deaths.

Neo-liberalism is a political rationality that supports the restructuring of societies to better meet the demands of a global market economy, emphasizing competition, individual self-enhancement, and personal responsibility for problems.

Neo-local residence means that the bride and groom live in a separate location from their birth families.

Net migration is the difference between immigration and emigration for a given area and time period.

No-fault divorce is the legal provision for marital dissolution through a non-acrimonious process, as opposed to fault-based divorce that involves proving a spouse guilty of a matrimonial offence or fault.

Non-standard employment is part-time, temporary, or outside formal business hours.

Non-Status Indian is not registered under the *Indian Act* because ancestors were never registered or status was lost under former provisions of the *Act*.

Nuclear family refers to husband, wife, and their children sharing the same household and co-operating economically.

Occupational segregation by gender means that men and women do different types of paid work.

Open marriage is a relationship in which marriage partners operate as separate individuals in order to explore their full potential.

Paradoxical gynocentricity ignores men in discussions of family, household, or procreation.

Parental leave refers to the official time away from paid employment that may be taken by either the mother or father at childbirth or adoption.

Patriarchy is a social or family system giving men more authority than women.

Patrilineal descent means that lineage or family relationships are traced through the male side of the family.

Patrilocal residence means that the bride moves into or near her husband's family home.

Personal resource theory suggests that the person with more resources, such as higher education or income, good looks, or youth, has more bargaining power in an intimate relationship.

Political economy perspective emphasizes the links between economic changes, the work people do, policy decisions, and personal life.

Polyandry is a system of marriage in which women are allowed more than one husband at a time.

Polygamy is a system of marriage in which adults are allowed more than one spouse at a time.

Polygyny is a system of marriage in which men are allowed more than one wife at a time.

Power of the purse is a theory that the person who earns more of the money controls the relationship or has greater decision-making power.

Private/public dichotomy refers to the distinction between family matters and work or public life, which used to be viewed as distinct and synonymous with the roles of women and men.

Psychoanalytic theories of socialization stress the importance of early childhood experiences and subconscious emotions in shaping personality.

Pure relationships are intimate and egalitarian relationships that are sustained only as long as they are satisfying to both parties.

Quiet Revolution refers to the secularization of Quebec during the late 1960s and 1970s, which was accompanied by sharply declining birth rates.

Race is an arbitrary and socially constructed classification of people into categories based on real or imagined physical characteristics.

Racialization is a process of attributing racial meanings to people or their behaviour.

Racist bias assumes that the family form typical of the dominant group is superior to other family forms, ignoring racist practices.

Radical feminist theories focus on gender differences and men's power that controls and oppresses women.

Reference group are the people looked to for ideas of acceptable behaviour and for the development of self-image.

Repartnering is the transition into cohabitation or remarriage after divorce, but can also refer to union formation after a cohabiting couple separates.

Reserve labour force refers to those workers drawn upon when employers need additional but temporary employees.

Residential school system provided boarding school education for First Nations' children, but also encouraged them to downplay their cultural background and to integrate into the larger Canadian society.

Restructuring refers to organizational changes to increase efficiency and save costs, usually involving layoffs.

Role is a pattern of behaviour governed by social expectations, rights, and duties associated with a specific position in a social situation (such as a husband in a family).

Role model is a person whose behaviour is patterned by others.

Same-sex marriage refers to gay and lesbian marriage.

Sandwich generation refers to family members, usually women, in the middle of the demands of multiple generations.

Second shift is the household work remaining to be done at the end of a day's paid work.

Secularization refers to the process of becoming less constrained by religious writings or authorities, or the separation of church and state.

Selectivity hypothesis suggests that people who choose to cohabit share values and characteristics detrimental to marital stability.

Serial monogamy means marriage to one partner at a time, but several over a lifetime.

Service sector is the part of the economy that provides services rather than goods.

Severely distressed households refer to those characterized by low income, low education, poor work history, single parenthood, and reliance on government benefits.

Sexist bias refers to unquestioning assumptions about how gender influences attitudes or behaviour, including androcentricity, paradoxical gynocentricity, gender insensitivity, house-holdism, and double standards (separately defined in this glossary).

Sexual division of labour refers to the ways that particular types of work are associated with males or females.

Shared parenting means that both parents share in the physical care and decision-making regarding the child during marriage or after divorce, regardless of who has legal custody.

Social class is a category of people who believe that they share a similar social and economic position.

Social construction of reality means that the meanings and justifications of behaviour are created through social interaction and cultural understandings.

Social democratic welfare states attempt to prevent poverty and inequality by providing state services and income support for everyone, regardless of family income.

Social exchange theory uses economic analogies from cost-benefit analysis to explain marriage and family relations, which are assumed to involve a process of negotiation and the assessment of time/emotional investments.

Social institution is an established set of roles, norms, and relationships organized around some central activity or social need.

Social insurance pools the risk of unemployment, disability, or sickness among employers, employees/citizens, and the state, and is financed through contributions from all three groups.

Social learning theory is the view that development occurs when children process social and cultural information from their environment by observing others, interpreting what they see, and then acting.

Social mobility is movement between levels of society or social classes.

Social status is a hierarchical position in society equated with rank or prestige.

Socialist-feminist theories focus on the relationship between women's work within the family and in the labour force, the patterns of capitalist investment and profit, and the organization of paid work.

Socialization refers to the complex learning process through which individuals develop their personality and acquire the knowledge, skills, and motivation necessary for participation in social life.

Sojourners are temporary migrant labourers.

Sponsorship period is the legislated time that new immigrants are financially dependent on the citizens who sponsored their arrival in a country.

State refers to the government as well as public agencies that support and enforce its policies.

Status Indian is an indigenous person registered under the Canadian *Indian Act*.

Stranger danger refers to assaults on people in public places by strangers.

Structural-functional perspective focuses on how social structure influences individual behaviour, and assumes that behaviour is governed by rules, laws, and expectations which maintain the structure of society.

Subsistence labour involves families producing food and goods for their own consumption.

Survey research gathers quantitative data from a large sample through questionnaires.

Symbolic interaction perspective assumes that people create their own social reality by defining and interpreting the symbolic meanings of those responding to them.

Systems theory sees the family as a system of interactions and relationships in which the behaviour of one member influences all others and behavioural patterns recur.

Task-oriented or instrumental leader is a person whose primary concern is to get things done, such as earning a living or finding accommodation.

Teleworking involves working (often at home) through telecommunication or computer links to the main workplace.

Tender years doctrine is the philosophy that mothers should receive custody of young children after divorce because proper child development requires maternal love and nurturing.

Two-parent family consists of two parents raising their own biological or adopted children.

Victimization studies ask participants if they have ever been the victim of violence or of certain illegal acts.

Visible minorities are racial or cultural groups who can be identified as members of a minority group by their skin colour, facial features, or manner of speaking.

Welfare state refers to laws and social programs designed to protect citizens in times of unemployment, illness, old age, or insufficient income.

"What" definition of the family focuses on the services and support provided by various members.

"Who" definition of the family focuses on group membership or family structure.

Women's double day or double workload means working for pay during the day and coming home to unpaid housework and childcare in the evenings.

Working class is the category of people who earn their income from wage labour.

References

Abu-Laban, Sharon and Susan A. McDaniel (2004). "Aging Women and the Standards of Beauty." In *Feminist Issues: Race, Class and Sexuality* (4th edition), edited by Nancy Mandell. Toronto: Prentice-Hall.

Acker, J. (1990). "Hierarchies, jobs, bodies: a theory of gendered organizations." *Gender and Society* 4: 139-158.

Adair, Vivienne and Christine Rogan (1998). "Infertility and Parenting: The Story So Far." In *The Family in Aotearoa/New Zealand*, edited by V. Adair and R. Dixon. Auckland: Addison Wesley Longman.

Akyeampong, E. (2001). "Fact-sheet on work absences." *Perspectives* (Catalogue no. 75-001-XPE), Winter: 47-49.

Albury, Rebecca M. (1999). *The Politics of Reproduction: Beyond the Slogans.* Sydney: Allen and Unwin.

Alvi, S. (2000). *Youth and the Canadian Criminal Justice System.* Cincinnati: Anderson.

Alvi, S., W. S. DeKeseredy and D. Ellis (2000). *Contemporary Social Problems in North American Society.* Toronto: Addison Wesley Longman.

Amato, P. R. (1993). "Children's Adjustment to Divorce: Theories, Hypothesis, and Empirical Support." *Journal of Marriage and the Family* 55: 23-38.

___, (2000). "The Consequences of Divorce for Adults and Children." *Journal of Marriage and the Family* 62: 1269-1287.

Ambert, Anne-Marie (1997). *Parents, Children and Adolescents. Interactive Relationships and Development Context.* New York: Hayworth Press.

___, (2001). *The Effect of Children on Parents.* New York: Hawthorne.

___, (2002). *Divorce: Facts, and Consequences.* Ottawa: The Vanier Institute of the Family.

___, (2003). *Same-Sex Couples and Same-Sex-Parent Families: Relationships, Parenting, and Issues of Marriage.* Ottawa: The Vanier Institute of the Family.

Anderson, Bonnie and Judith P. Zinsser (1991). *A History of Their Own. Women in Europe from Pre-History to the Present.* New York: Harper and Row.

Anderson, Karen (1991). *Chain Her By One Foot. The Subjugation of Women in 17th-Century New France.* New York: Routledge.

Anderson, Perry (1998). *The Origins of Postmodernity.* London: Verso.

Anderson, S. and R. Sabatelli (1995). *Family Interaction.* Toronto: Allyn and Bacon.

Applbaum, Kalman (1995). "Marriage with the Proper Stranger: Arranged Marriage in Metropolitan Japan." *Ethnology* 34 (Winter): 37-51.

Arat-Koc, Sedef (1989). "Importing Housewives: Non-Citizen Domestic Workers and the Crisis of the Domestic Sphere in Canada." *Studies in Political Economy* 28: 33-58.

Ariès, P. (1962). *Centuries of Childhood: A Social History of Family Life.* New York: Vintage Books.

Armstrong, Pat and Hugh Armstrong (1978). *The Double Ghetto: Canadian Women and Their Segregated Work*. Toronto: McClelland and Stewart.

___, (1994). *The Double Ghetto: Canadian Women and their Segregated Work* (3rd edition). Toronto: McClelland and Stewart.

___, (2002). "Thinking it through: Women, work and caring in the new millennium." *Canadian Woman Studies* 21/22 (4/1): 44-50.

Armstrong, Robin (2000). "Mapping the Conditions of First Nations Communities." In *Canadian Social Trends*, Volume 3. Toronto: Thompson Educational: 28-32.

Arnup, K. (1994). *Education for Motherhood: Advice for Mothers in Twentieth-Century Canada*. Toronto: University of Toronto Press.

___, (2001). *Close Personal Relationships Between Adults: 100 Years of Marriage in Canada*. Ottawa, Canada: Law Commission of Canada.

Aronson, Jane (1992). "Women's Sense of Responsibility for the Care of Older People: 'But Who Else is Going to Do It?'" *Gender and Society* 6(1):8-29.

Axinn, W. and A. Thornton (1992). "The Relationship between Cohabitation and Divorce: Selectivity or Causal Inference?" *Demography* 29: 357-74.

Backhouse, C. B. (1981). "Shifting Patterns in Nineteenth Century Custody Law." In *Essays in the History of Canadian Law*, edited by D, H. Flaherty. Toronto, Canada: University of Toronto Press: 212-248.

___, (1988). "Married Women's Property Law in Nineteenth-Century Canada." *Law and History Review* 6: 211-257.

___, (1991). *Petticoats and Prejudice. Women and Law in Nineteenth Century Canada*. Toronto: Women's Press.

___, (1992). "Married Women's Property Law in Nineteenth-Century Canada." In *Canadian Family History: Selected Readings*, edited by Bettina Bradbury. Toronto: Copp-Clark Pitman.

Bailey, Martha (2000). "Domestic Partnerships." In *Special Issue of Canadian Journal of Family Law* 17(1), edited by Martha Bailey.

Baillargeon, Denyse (1999). *Making Do. Women, Family and Home in Montreal during the Great Depression*. Waterloo: Wilfred Laurier University Press.

Baird, P. (1997). "Individual interests, societal interests, and reproductive technologies." *Perspectives in Biology and Medicine* 40(3): 440-52.

Bakan, Abigail and Daiva Stasiulis (1994). "Foreign Domestic Worker Policy in Canada and the Social Boundaries of Modern Citizenship." *Science and Society* 58(1): 7-33.

Baker, Maureen (1985). *"What Will Tomorrow Bring?..." A Study of the Aspirations of Adolescent Women*. Ottawa: Canadian Advisory Council on the Status of Women.

___, (1990a). "The Perpetuation of Misleading Family Models in Social Policy: Implications for Women." *Canadian Review of Social Work* (Summer): 169-182.

___, (1993). *Families in Canadian Society* (2nd edition). Toronto: McGraw-Hill Ryerson.

___, (1994). *Canada's Changing Families: Challenges to Public Policy*. Ottawa: Vanier Institute of the Family.

___, (1994b). "Family and Population Policy in Quebec: Implications for Women." *Canadian Journal of Women and the Law* 7(1): 116-132.

___, (1995). *Canadian Family Policies: Cross-National Comparisons*. Toronto: University of Toronto Press.

___, (1997a). "Advocacy, Political Alliances and the Implementation of Family Policies." In *Child and Family Policy: Struggles, Strategies and Options*, edited by Jane Pulkingham and Gordon Ternowetsky. Toronto: Fernwood Publishing.

___, (2001). *Families, Labour and Love: Family Diversity in a Changing World*. Sydney: Allen and Unwin and Vancouver: UBC Press.

___, (2001). "Paid and Unpaid Work: How Do Families Divide Their Labour?" In *Families: Changing Trends in Canada* (4th edition). Whitby, ON: McGraw-Hill Ryerson: 96-115.

Baker, Maureen and Shelley Phipps (1997). "Family Change and Family Policy: Canada." In *Family Change and Family Policies in Britain, Canada, New Zealand and the U.S.*, edited by Sheila Kamerman and Alfred Kahn. Oxford, UK: Oxford University Press.

Baker, Maureen and David Tippin (1999). *Poverty, Social Assistance and the Employability of Mothers: Restructuring Welfare States*. Toronto: University of Toronto Press.

Balakrishnan, T. R., K. V. Rao, E. Lapierre-Adamcyk, and K. J. Kròtki (1987). "A Hazard Model Analysis of the Covariates of Marriage Dissolution in Canada." *Demography* 24: 395-406.

Bank, S. P. and M. D. Kahn (1982). *The Sibling Bond*. New York: Basic Books.

Barham, V., R. A. Devlin, and C. LaCasse (2000). "Are the New Child-Support Guidelines 'Adequate' or 'Reasonable'?" *Canadian Public Policy* 26: 1-15.

Barker, John (2003). "Dowry." In *International Encyclopedia of Marriage and Family* (2nd edition), edited by James J. Ponting Jr. New York: Macmillan Reference USA and Thomson Gale: 495-6.

Barnett, O. W., C. L. Miller-Perrin, and R. D. Perrin (1997). *Family Violence Across the Lifespan: An Introduction*. Thousand Oaks, CA: Sage.

Bartfeld, J. (2000). "Child Support and the Post-Divorce Economic Well-Being of Mothers, Fathers, and Children." *Demography* 37: 203-213.

Basavarajappa, K. G. and Ravi B. P. Verma (1990). "Occupational Composition of Immigrant Women." In *Ethnic Demography: Canadian Immigrants and Cultural Variations*, edited by Shiva S. Halli, Frank Trovato, and Leo Driedger. Ottawa: Carlton University Press: 297-314.

Basch, N. (1999). *Framing American Divorce: From the Revolutionary Generation to the Victorians*. Berkeley, CA: University of California Press.

Baskerville, Peter and Eric W. Sager (1999). *Unwilling Idlers: The Urban Unemployed and Their Families in Late Victorian Canada*. Toronto: University of Toronto Press.

Battle, Ken (1992). "White Paper Whitewash: The New Child Benefit." *Perception* 16(2,3): 34-40.

Beall, Anne and Robert Sternberg (1995). "The Social Construction of Love." *Journal of Personal Relationships* 12(3): 417-438.

Beaujot, Roderic (2000). *Earning and Caring in Canadian Families*. Peterborough, Ontario: Broadview.

___, (2004). *Delayed Life Transitions: Trends and Implications*. Ottawa: Vanier Institute of the Family.

Beaujot, Roderic, Ellen M. Gee, Fernando Rajulton, and Zenaida R. Ravanera. (1995). *Family Over the Life Course*. Ottawa: Statistics Canada.

Beck, Ullrich and Elisabeth Beck-Gernsheim (1995). *The Normal Chaos of Love*. Cambridge: Polity Press.

Becker, G. (1981). *A Treatise on the Family*. Cambridge, MA: Harvard University Press.

Becker, G., E. M. Landes, and R. T. Michael (1977). "An Economic Analysis of Marital Instability." *Journal of Political Economy* 85: 1141-1187.

Beck-Gernsheim, E. (1996). "Life as a planning project." In *Risk, environment and modernity: Towards a new ecology*, edited by S. Lash, B. Szerszynski, and B. Wynne. London: Sage.

___, (2002). *Reinventing the Family: In Search of New Lifestyles*. Oxford: Polity Press.

Beiser, Morton, Feng Hou, Ilene Hyman, and Michel Tousignant (2002). "Poverty, Family Process, and the Mental Health of Immigrant Children in Canada." *American Journal of Public Health* 92(2): 220-229.

Bélanger, Alain (1999). *Report on the Demographic Situation in Canada 1998-1999*. Ottawa: Minister of Industry.

Bélanger, Alain, Carrière, Yves, and Gilbert Stéphane (2001). *Report of the Demographic Situation in Canada 2000*. Statistics Canada (Catalogue no. 91-209-XPE) June. Ottawa: Ministry of Industry.

Bélanger, Alain, and Jean Dumas (1998). *Report of the Demographic Situation in Canada 1997*. Ottawa: Ministry of Industry.

Belsky, J. and J. Cassidy (1994). "Attachment: Theory and Evidence." In *Development Through Life: A Handbook for Clinicians*, edited by M. Rutter and D. Hay. Oxford: Blackwell Scientific Publications

Bergen, R. K. (1999). "Marital Rape." [Online]. Available: http://www.vaw.umn.edu/finaldocuments/Vawnet/mrape.html

Bergert, Ann M. (2000). "The Experience of Women in Unsuccessful Infertility Treatment: What Do Patients Need When Medical Intervention Fails?" *Social Work in Health Care* 30(4): 45-69.

Berk, S. F. (1985). *The Gender Factory: The Apportionment of Work in American Households*. New York: Plenum.

Bernard, J. (1981/1995). "The good-provider role: its rise and fall." In *Men's Lives* (3rd edition), edited by M.S. Kimmel and M.A. Messner. Boston: Allyn and Bacon.

Bittman, Michael and Jocelyn Pixley (1997). *The Double Life of the Family. Myth, Hope & Experience*. Sydney: Allen and Unwin.

Blain, J. (1993). "'I can't come in today, the baby has chickenpox!' Gender and class processes in how parents in the labour force deal with the problem of sick children." *Canadian Journal of Sociology* 18(4): 405-429.

Blood, Robert O. and D. M. Wolfe (1960). *Husbands and Wives*. New York: The Free Press.

Blum, L. (1999). *At the Breast: Ideologies of Breastfeeding and Motherhood in the Contemporary United States*. Boston: Beacon Press.

Bly, R. M. (1994). *Sibling Violence: Prevalence, Risk Markers and Protective Factors*. Toronto: LaMarsh Research Centre on Violence and Conflict Resolution, York University.

Bobet, Ellen (1994). "Indian Mortality," In *Canadian Social Trends*, Volume 2. Toronto: Thompson Educational: 57-60.

Boissevain, Jeremy (1975). "Family, Kinship and Marriage Among Italians of Montreal," In *Marriage, Family and Society*, edited by S. Parvez Wakil. Toronto: Butterworths: 287-294.

Bourgeault, Ron (1983). "The Indian, the Metis and the Fur Trade: Class, Sexism, and Racism in the Transition from `Communism' to Capitalism." *Studies in Political Economy* 12(Fall): 45-80.

Bourgois, P. (1995). *In Search of Respect: Selling Crack in El Barrio*. New York: Cambridge University Press.

Bowlby, J. (1953). "Some Pathological Processes Set in Train by Early Mother-Child Separation." *Journal of Mental Science* 99: 265-272.

___, (1958). "The Nature of the Child's Tie to His Mother." *International Journal of Psycho-Analysis* 39: 350-373.

___, (1969). *Attachment*. New York: Basic Books.

Boyd, Monica (1990). "Immigrant Women: Language and Socio-economic Inequalities and Policy Issues," In *Ethnic Demography: Canadian Immigrants and Cultural Variations*, edited by Shiva S. Halli, Frank Trovato, and Leo Driedger. Ottawa: Carlton University Press: 275-296.

___, (2000). "Ethnicity and Immigrant Offspring." In *Perspectives on Ethnicity in Canada*, edited by Madeline A. Kalbach and Warren E. Kalbach. Toronto: Harcourt Canada: 137-154.

Boyd, Monica and Anne Li (2003) "May-December: Canadians in age-discrepant relationships." *Canadian Social Trends* (Autumn): 29-33.

Boyd, Monica, Mary Ann Mulvihill, and John Myles (1991). "Gender, Power and Postindustrialism." *Canadian Review of Sociology and Anthropology* 28(4):407-436.

Boyd, Monica and Edward Pryor (1990). "Young Adults Living in Their Parents' Home." In *Canadian Social Trends*, edited by C. McKie and K. Thompson. Toronto: Thompson Educational Press: 188-191.

Boyd, S. B. (1987). "Child Custody and Working Mothers." In *Equality and Judicial Neutrality*, edited by S. Martin and K. E. Mahoney. Calgary, Canada: Carswell.

___, (1989). "From Gender Specificity to Gender Neutrality? Ideologies in Canadian Child Custody Law." In *Child Custody and the Politics of Gender*, edited by C. Smart and S. Sevenhuijsen. London, England: Routledge: 126-157.

___, (2003). *Child Custody, Law, and Women's Work*. Toronto: Oxford University Press.

Boydston, Jeanne (1990). *Home and Work. Housework, Wages, and the Ideology of Labor in the Early Republic*. New York: Oxford University Press.

Bradbury, Bettina (1992). "Gender at Work at Home: Family Decisions, the Labour market and Girls' Contributions to the Family Economy." In *Canadian Family History*, edited by Bradbury. Toronto: Copp-Clark Pitman.

___, (1993). *Working Families. Age, Gender and Daily Survival in Industrializing Montreal*. Toronto: McClelland and Stewart.

___, (2000). "Single Parenthood in the Past: Canadian Census Categories, 1891-1951 and the 'Normal' Family." *Historical Methods Newsletter* 33(4) Fall.

Bradbury, Bettina, Peter Gossage, Evelyn Kolish, and Alan Stewart (1993). "Property and Marriage: The Law and Practice in early Nineteenth Century Montreal." *Histoire sociale/ Social History* XXVI (May): 9-39.

Bradbury, Thomas, Frank Fincham, and Steven Beach (2000). "Research on the Nature and Determinants of Marital Satisfaction: A Decade in Review." *Journal of Marriage and the Family* 62(4) Nov.: 964-980.

Bradshaw, Jonathon et al. (1996). T*he Employment of Lone Parents: A Comparison of Policy in 20 Countries*. London: Family Policy Studies Centre and Joseph Rowntree Foundation.

Brandth, B. and E. Kvande (2001). "Flexible work and flexible fathers." *Work, Employment and Society*, 15(2): 251-267.

Brinkerhoff, M. and E. Lupri (1988). "Interspousal Violence." *The Canadian Journal of Sociology* 13: 407-434.

Bristow, Peggy et al. (1994). "We're Rooted Here and They Can't Pull Us Up." *Essays in African Canadian Women's History*. Toronto: University of Toronto Press.

Brody, Hugh (1975). *The People's Land. Eskimos and Whites in the Eastern Arctic*. Great Britain: Penguin Books.

___, (1987). *Living Arctic. Hunters of the Canadian North*. Vancouver: Douglas and McIntyre.

Brown, Jennifer (1980). *Strangers in Blood: Fur Trade Families in Indian Country*. Vancouver: University of British Columbia.

Brown, Judith (1988). "Iroquois Women: an Ethnohistoric Note." In *Family Bonds and Gender Divisions*, edited by Bonnie Fox. Toronto: Scholars' Press: 83-98.

Brownlie, Robin Jarvis (2003). *A Fatherly Eye. Indian Agents, Government Power, and Aboriginal Resistance in Ontario, 1918-1939*. Toronto: University of Toronto Press.

Brownridge, D. A. (2003). "Male Partner Violence Against Aboriginal Women in Canada: An Empirical Analysis." *Journal of Interpersonal Violence* 18: 65-83.

Brubacher, Ellie and Timothy H. Brubacher (1992). "The Context of Retired Women as Caregivers." In *Families and Retirement*, edited by Maximiliane Szinovacz, David J. Ekerdt and Barbara H. Vinick. Newbury Park, California: Sage: 222-235.

Bruer, J. T. (1999). *The Myth of the First Three Years*. New York: Free Press.

Bruner, J. (2000). "Tot Thought." *New York Review of Books* XLVII (4): 27 - 30.

Bulcroft, Kris and Richard Bulcroft (1997). "The Social Construction of the North American Honeymoon." *Journal of Family History* 22(4): 462-491.

Bullen, John (1992). "Hidden Workers: Child Labour and the Family Economy in Late Nineteenth-Century Urban Ontario," In *Canadian Family History*, edited by Bettina Bradbury. Toronto: Copp-Clark: Pittman.

Bumpass, L. L. and J. A. Sweet (1989). "Children's Experience in Single-Parent Families: Implications of Cohabitation and Marital Transition." *Family Planning Perspectives* 21: 256-260.

Bumpass, L. L., J. A. Sweet, and T. Castro-Martin (1990). "Changing Patterns of Remarriage." *Journal of Marriage and the Family* 52: 747-56.

Bumsted, J. M. (1992). *The Peoples of Canada: A Post-Confederation History*. Toronto: Oxford University Press.

Burgess, Joanne (1986). "Work, Family and Community: Montreal Leather Craftsmen, 1790-1831." Doctorate, University of Quebec at Montreal, History.

Burke, Mary Anne (1994). "Canada's Immigrant Children." In *Canadian Social Trends*, Volume 2. Toronto: Thompson Educational: 35-40.

Burley, David G. (1994). *A Particular Condition of life. Self-Employment and Social Mobility in Mid-Victorian Brantford, Ontario*. Montreal and Kingston: McGill-Queen's University Press.

Burton, D. (1994). "When Violence Hits Home: A Congressman's Searing Memories of His Abusive Father." *People Weekly* (April 4): 91-95.

Cameron, Jan (1990). *Why Have Children? A New Zealand Case Study*. Christchurch: Canterbury University Press.

Campaign 2000 (2001). "Family Security in Insecure Times: Tackling Canada's Social Deficit." *November 2001 Bulletin*.

Campaign 2000 (2003). *Report Card 2002*. (www.campaign2000.ca).

CanadianLawSite.Com (2004). "Canadian Family Violence Laws." [Online]. Available: http://www.canadianlawsite.com/family-violence-laws.htm.

Canadian Social Trends (2003). "Update on families." (Catalogue no. 11-008), Summer: 11-13.

Carter, Sarah (1990). *Lost Harvests. Prairie Indian Reserve Farmers and Government Policy*. Montreal and Kingston: McGill-Queen's University Press.

___, (1999). *Aboriginal People and Colonizers of Western Canada to 1900*. Toronto: University of Toronto Press.

Castells, Manuel (2000). "Materials for an exploratory theory of the network society." *British Journal of Sociology* 51(1): 5-24.

___, (2004). *The Power of Identity* (2nd edition). Malden MA: Blackwell Publisher.

Cate, R. M. and S. A. Lloyd (1988). "Courtship." In *Handbook of Personal Relationships*, edited by S. Duck. New York: John Wiley: 409-427.

Cawson, P., C. Wattam, S. Brooker, and G. Kelly (2000). *Child Maltreatment in the United Kingdom: A Study of the Prevalence of Child Abuse and Neglect*. London: National Society for the Prevention of Cruelty to Children.

Chambers, D. L. (1979). *Making Fathers Pay: The Enforcement of Child Support*. Chicago, IL: University of Chicago Press.

Chambers, L. (1997). *Married Women and Property Law in Victorian Ontario*. Toronto: University of Toronto Press.

Chaykowski, Richard P. and Lisa M Powell (1999). "Women and the Labour Market: Recent Trends and Policy Issues." *Canadian Public Policy* XXV Supplement, (November): S1-S25.

Cheal, David (1996). "Stories About Step-families." In *Growing Up In Canada: National Longitudinal Survey of Children and Youth*. Ottawa: Human Resources Development Canada and Statistics Canada: 93-101.

Che-Alford, Janet and Brian Hamm (1999). "Under One Roof: Three Generations Living Together." *Canadian Social Trends* (Catalogue no. 11-008), Summer 53: 6-9.

Cherlin, A. (1978). "Remarriage as an Incomplete Institution." *American Journal of Sociology* 84: 634-650.

___, (1992). *Marriage, Divorce, Remarriage*. Cambridge, MA: Harvard University Press.

Cherlin, Andrew J. (1997). "A Reply to Glenn. What's Most Important in a Family Textbook?" In *Family Relations* 46 (3): 209-211.

Cherlin, A. J. and F. F. Furstenberg (1994). "Stepfamilies in the United States: A Reconsideration." *Annual Review of Sociology* 20: 359-381.

Chesney-Lind, M. (1997). *The Female Offender: Girls, Women, and Crime*. Thousand Oaks, CA: Sage.

Chesney-Lind, M. and L. Pasko (2004). *The Female Offender: Girls, Women, and Crime* (2nd edition). Thousand Oaks, CA: Sage.

Christensen, F. (2000). *Prostituted Science and Scholarship: A Submission to the Special Senate-Commons Committee on Custody and Access*. [Online]. Available: http://www.fathers.bc.ca/prostituted_science.htm.

Christopher, F. Scott and Susan Sprecher (2000). "Sexuality in Marriage, Dating and Other Relationships: A Decade Review." *Journal of Marriage and the Family* 6(4) Nov.: 999-1017.

Chunn, Dorothy E. (1992). *From Punishment to Doing Good. Family Courts and Socialized Justice in Ontario, 1880-1940*. Toronto: University of Toronto Press.

Citizenship and Immigration Canada. (2002). "Immigration Overview, Immigration by Age and Sex." [Online]. www.cic.gc.ca/english/pub/facts2001/1imm-07.html.

___, (2003). "Facts and Figures 2002 - Immigration Overview." [Online] http://www.cic.gc.ca/english/pub/facts2002/toronto/toronto_2.html

Clark, Susan and Andrew Harvey (1976). "The Sexual Division of Labour: The Use of Time." *Atlantis* 2 (1): 46-66.

CLEO (Community Legal Education Ontario) (2001). "Immigration and Refugee Fact Sheet: Immigrant Women and Domestic Violence." Toronto: CLEO.

Cleveland, G. and M. Krashinsky (2001). Introduction. In *Our Children's Future: Child Care Policy in Canada*, edited by G. Cleveland and M. Krashinsky. Toronto: University of Toronto Press.

Cliche, Marie Aimée (1991). "Unwed Mothers, Families and Society during the French Regime." In *Canadian Family History*, edited by Bettina Bradbury. Toronto: Copp-Clark Pittman.

Cohen, Marjorie (1988). *Women's Work: Markets and Economic Development in Nineteenth-Century Ontario*. Toronto: University of Toronto Press.

Cole, S. G. (1998). "Child Battery." In *Family Bonds and Gender Divisions*, edited by B. Fox. Toronto: Canadian Scholars' Press.

Cole, T. B. (1997). "Editor's Note." *Journal of the American Medical Association* July 9.

Coleman, M. and G. Ganong (1990). "Remarriage and Stepfamily Research in the 80s: New Interest in an Old Family Form." *Journal of Marriage and the Family* 52: 925-940.

Collective Clio, The (1987). *Quebec Women. A History*. Toronto: Women's Press.

Comacchio, C. (1993). *Nations Are Built of Babies: Saving Ontario's Mothers and Children 1900-1940*. Montreal: McGill-Queen's University Press.

___, (1999). *The Intimate Bonds of Family: Domesticity in Canada, 1850-1940*. Toronto: University of Toronto Press.

Comfort, D., K. Johnson and D. Wallace. (2003). *Part-time Work and Family-friendly Practices in Canadian Workplaces*. Ottawa: Ministry of Industry.

Coney, Sandra and Anne Else (1999). *Protecting Our Future. The Case for Greater Regulation of Assisted Reproductive Technology*. Auckland: Women's Health Action Trust with the NZ Law Foundation.

Conference Board of Canada (1999). "Elder Care Taking Its Toll on Canadian Workers." *News Release* November 10.

Connell, R. W. (1987). *Gender and Power*. Cambridge: Polity Press.

Connidis, Ingrid Arnet (1989). *Family Ties and Aging*. Toronto: Butterworths.

___, (1989a). "Contact Between Siblings in Later Life." *Canadian Journal of Sociology* 14(4): 429-442.

___, (2001). *Family Ties and Aging*. Thousand Oaks, California: Sage.

Conrad, Margaret, Alvin Finkel, and Cornelius Jaenen (1993). *History of the Canadian Peoples. Beginnings to 1867*. Toronto: Copp-Clark Pitman.

Cook, Ramsay and Wendy Mitchinson (1976). *Their Proper Sphere. Woman's Place in Canadian Society*. Toronto: Oxford University Press.

Coontz, Stephanie (1988). *The Social Origins of Private Life. A History of American Families, 1600-1900*. New York: Verso.

___, (1992). *The Way We Never Were: American Families and the Nostalgia Trap*. New York: Basic Books.

Cooper, David (1971). *The Death of the Family*. London: Penguin Books.

Cornwell, B and Lundgren D. C. (2001). "Love on the Internet: Involvement and Misrepresentation in Romantic Relationships in Cyberspace vs. Realspace." *Computers in Human Behavior* 17(2) March: 197-211.

Cossman, Brenda (1997). "Family Inside/Out." In *Feminism and Families: Critical Policies and Changing Practices*, edited by Meg Luxton. Halifax: Fernwood: 124-141.

Council on Families in America (1995). *Marriage in America. A Report to the Nation*. New York: Institute for American Values.

Couture, M. D. (1940). *The Canadian Mother and Child*. Ottawa: King's Printer.

Creese, Gillian, Isabel Lowe Dyck and Arlene Tigar McLaren (1999). "Reconstituting the Family: Negotiating Immigration and Settlement." *Vancouver RIIM Centre of Excellence Working Paper Series*: No. 99-10.

Crompton, S. and M. Vickers (2000). "One hundred years of labour force." *Canadian Social Trends* (Catalogue no.11-008), Summer: 2-13.

CRRU (2003). The Childcare Resource and Research Unit, University of Toronto. Website www.chilcarecanada.org

Cuneo, Carl (1979). "State, Class and Reserve Labour: The Case of the 1941 Unemployment Insurance Act." *Canadian Review of Sociology and Anthropology* 16(2): 147-170.

Currie, Dawn (1993). "Here Comes the Bride; the Making of a 'Modern Traditional' Wedding in 'Western Culture.'" *Journal of Comparative Family Studies* 24(3): 403-421.

Currie, E. (1998). *Crime and Punishment in America*. New York: Metropolitan Books.

Daatland, Svein Olav (1990). "'What are Families for?' On Family Solidarity and Preferences for Help." *Aging and Society* 10:1-15.

Daenzer, Patricia (1993). *Regulating Class Privilege. Immigrant Servants in Canada, 1940s-1990s*. Toronto: Canadian Scholars' Press.

Daly, K. (2000). *It Keeps Getting Faster: Changing Patterns of Time in Families*. Ottawa: Vanier Institute of the Family.

___, (2002). "Time, gender and the negotiation of family schedules." *Symbolic Interaction* 25(3): 323-342.

Daly, Kerry and Michael Sobol (1993). Adoption in Canada, Final Report. May. Ottawa: Health and Welfare Canada.

Daly, Mary and Katherine Rake (2003). *Gender and the Welfare State*. Cambridge: Polity Press.

D'Amato, L. (2004). "Our Kids Stay Indoors...and Out of Shape." *Kitchener-Waterloo Record* Feb 7: A1.

Daniels, C. R. (1993). *At Women's Expense: State Power and the Politics of Fetal Rights*. Cambridge: Harvard University Press.

Daniels, K. and E. Haimes (1998). *Donor Insemination: International Social Science Perspectives*, edited by K. Daniels and E. Haimes. Cambridge: University of Cambridge Press.

Daniluk, J. (2001). "Reconstructing their Lives: A longitudinal, qualitative analysis of the transition to biological childlessness for infertile couples." *Journal of Counselling and Development* 79: 439-449.

Das Gupta, Tania (1995). "Families of Native People, Immigrants, and People of Colour." In *Canadian Families-Diversity, Conflict and Change*, edited by N. Mandell and A. Duffy. Toronto: Harcourt Brace: 141-174.

Davidoff, Leonore and Catherine Hall (1987). *Family Fortunes. Men and Women of the English Middle Class, 1780-1850*. Chicago: University of Chicago Press.

Dauvergne, M. (2002). "Family Violence Against Older Adults." In *Family Violence in Canada: A Statistical Profile 2002*, edited by C. Trainor. Ottawa: Statistics Canada: 26-33.

Davies, Lorraine and Patricia Jane Carrier (1999). "The Importance of Power Relations for the Division of Household Labour." *Canadian Journal of Sociology* 24(1): 35-51.

Davis, Angela (1981). *Women, Race and Class*. New York: Random House.

De Graaf, P. M. and M. Kalmijn (2003). "Alternative Routes in the Remarriage Market: Competing Risk Analyses of Union Formation after Divorce." *Social Forces* 81: 1459-1498.

Dehli, Kari (1996). "Between 'Market' and 'State'? Engendering Education Change in the 1990s." *Discourse studies in the cultural politics of education* 17(3): 363-376

DeKeseredy, W. S. (1988a). "Woman Abuse in Dating Relationships: The Relevance of Social Support Theory." *Journal of Family Violence* 1: 1-13.

___, (1988b). *Woman Abuse in Dating Relationships: The Role of Male Peer Support*. Toronto: Canadian Scholars' Press.

___, (2000a). "Current Controversies on Defining Nonlethal Violence Against Women in Heterosexual Relationships: Empirical Implications." *Violence Against Women* 6: 728-746.

___, (2000b). *Women, Crime and the Canadian Criminal Justice System*. Cincinnati: Anderson.

DeKeseredy, W. S., S. Alvi, C. M. Renzetti, and M. D. Schwartz (2004). "Reducing Private Violence Against Women in Public Housing: Can Second Generation CPTED Make a Difference?" *The CPTED Journal* (in press).

DeKeseredy, W. S., S. Alvi, and M. D. Schwartz (2004). "Curbing Woman Abuse and Poverty: Is 'Wedfare' the Cure?" *Violence Against Women* (in press).

DeKeseredy, W. S., S. Alvi, M. D. Schwartz, and B. Perry (1999). "Violence Against and the Harassment of Women in Canadian Public Housing." *Canadian Review of Sociology and Anthropology* 36: 499-516.

DeKeseredy, W. S., S. Alvi, M. D. Schwartz, and E. A. Tomaszewski (2003). *Under Siege: Poverty and Crime in a Public Housing Community*. Lanham, MD: Lexington Books.

DeKeseredy, W. S. and D. Ellis (1997). "Sibling Violence: A Review of the Canadian Sociological Research and Suggestions for Further Empirical Research." *Humanity and Society* 21: 397-411.

DeKeseredy, W. S. and R. Hinch (1991). *Woman Abuse: Sociological Perspectives*. Toronto: Thompson Educational.

DeKeseredy, W. S. and C. Joseph (2004). "Understanding Separation/Divorce Sexual Assault in Rural Communities: The Contribution of an Exploratory Study." Paper presented at the National Institute of Justice Conference on Criminal Justice Research and Evaluation, Washington, D.C., July.

DeKeseredy, W. S. and K. Kelly (1993a). "Woman Abuse in University and College Dating Relationships: The Contribution of the Ideology of Familial Patriarchy." *Journal of Human Justice* 4: 25-52.

___, (1993b). "The Incidence and Prevalence of Woman Abuse in Canadian University and College Dating Relationships." *Canadian Journal of Sociology* 18: 137-159.

DeKeseredy, W. S. and L. MacLeod (1997). *Woman Abuse: A Sociological Story*. Toronto: Harcourt Brace.

DeKeseredy, W. S., M. M. Rogness, and M. D. Schwartz (2004). "Separation/Divorce Sexual Assault: The Current State of Social Scientific Knowledge." *Aggression and Violent Behavior: A Review Journal* (in press).

DeKeseredy, W., D. Saunders, M. D. Schwartz, and S. Alvi (1997). "The Meanings and Motives for Women's Use of Violence in Canadian College Dating Relationships: Results from a National Survey." *Sociological Spectrum* 17: 199-222.

___, (2000). "The Role of Profeminist Men in Dealing with Woman Abuse on the Canadian College Campus." *Violence Against Women* 6: 918-935.

DeKeseredy, W. S. and M. D. Schwartz (1998a). *Woman Abuse on Campus: Results from the Canadian National Survey*. Thousand Oaks, CA: Sage.

___, (1998b). "Measuring the Extent of Woman Abuse in Intimate Heterosexual Relationships: A Critique of the Conflict Tactics Scales." U.S. Department of Justice Violence Against Women Grants Office Electronic Resources [Online]. Available: http://www.vaw.umn.edu/research.asp.

___, (1993). "Male Peer Support and Woman Abuse: An Expansion of DeKeseredy's Model." *Sociological Spectrum* 13: 394-414.

___, (2001). "Definitional Issues." In *Sourcebook on Violence Against Women*, edited by C.M. Renzetti, J.L. Edleson and R.K. Bergen. Thousand Oaks, CA: Sage: 23-34.

___, (2002). "Theorizing Public Housing Woman Abuse as a Function of Economic Exclusion and Male Peer Support." *Women's Health and Urban Life* 1: 26-45.

___, (2003). "Backlash and Whiplash: A Critique of Statistics Canada's 1999 General Social Survey on Victimization." *Online Journal of Justice Studies 2003*.

Demo, D. H. and A. C. Acock (1988). "The Impact of Divorce on Children." *Journal of Marriage and the Family* 50: 619-648.

Demos, John (1995). *The Unredeemed Captive. A Family Story from Early America*. New York: Vintage Books.

Dempsey, Ken (1997). *Inequalities in Work and Marriage: Australia and Beyond*. Melbourne: Oxford University Press.

Denham, D. and J. Gillespie (1999). *Two Steps Forward... One Step Back*. Ottawa: Health Canada.

DeVault, M. (1991). *Feeding the Family*. Chicago: University of Chicago Press.

Dickason, Olive Patricia (1992). *Canada's First Nations. A History of Founding Peoples from Earliest Times*. Toronto: McClelland and Stewart.

Dienhart, A. (1998). *Reshaping Fatherhood: The Social Construction of Shared Parenting*. Thousand Oaks: Sage.

Dion, Karen and Kenneth Dion (1993). "Individualistic and Collectivistic Perspectives on Gender and the Cultural Context of Love and Intimacy." *Journal of Social Issues* 49(3): 53-69.

Dobash, R. E and R. P. Dobash (1998). "Cross-Border Encounters: Challenges and Opportunities." In *Rethinking Violence Against Women*, edited by R. E. Dobash and R. P. Dobash. Thousand Oaks, CA: Sage: 1-22.

Dodd, Diane (1983). "The Birth Control Movement on Trial, 1936-1937," *Histoire sociale/Social History* 32.

Doherty, Gillian, Martha Friendly, and Mab Oloman (1998). *Women's Support, Women's Work: Child Care in an Era of Deficit Reduction, Devolution, Downsizing and Deregulation*. Ottawa: Status of Women Canada.

Donchin, A. (1996). "Feminist Critiques of New Fertility Technologies: Implications for Social Policy." *Journal of Medicine and Philosophy* 21: 475-98.

Dooley, Martin (1995). "Lone-Mother Families and Social Assistance Policy in Canada." In *Family Matters: New Policies for Divorce, Lone Mothers, and Child Poverty*, edited by M. Dooley et al. Toronto: CD Howe Institute: 35-104.

Doucet, A. (2001). "'You see the need perhaps more clearly than I do': Exploring gendered processes of domestic responsibility." *Journal of Family Issues* 22(3): 328-357.

___, (2004). "Fathers and the responsibility for children: a puzzle and a tension." *Atlantis: A Women's Studies Journal* 28(2).

Dranoff, Linda Silver (1977). *Women in Canadian Law*. Toronto: Fitzhenry and Whiteside.

Driedger, Leo (2003). *Race and Ethnicity: Finding Identities and Equalities* (2nd edition). Don Mills: Oxford University Press.

Driedger, Leo and Neena Chappell (1987). *Aging and Ethnicity: Toward an Interface*. Toronto: Butterworths.

Drolet, M. (2003). "Motherhood and paycheques." *Canadian Social Trends* (Catalogue no. 11-008), Spring: 19-21.

Drolet, M. and R. Morissette (2002). "Better jobs in the new economy?" *Perspectives* (Catalogue no. 75-001-XPE), Autumn: 47-55.

Dua, Enakshi (1999). "Beyond Diversity Exploring the Ways in Which the Discourse of Race Has Shaped the Institution of the Nuclear Family." In *Scratching the Surface: Canadian anti-racist feminist thought*, edited by Enakshi Dua and Angela Robertson. Toronto: Women's Press: 237-260.

Dubinsky, Karen (1993). *Improper Advances. Rape and Heterosexual Conflict in Ontario, 1880-1929*. Chicago: University of Chicago Press.

Duchesne, D., F. Nault, H. Gilmour, and R. Wilkins (1999). *Vital Statistics Compendium, 1996*. Ottawa, Canada: Statistics Canada.

Duden, B. (1993). *Disembodying women: Perspectives on pregnancy and the unborn*. Cambridge: Harvard University Press.

Duffy, A., N. Mandell, and N. Pupo (1989). *Few Choices: Women, Work and Family*. Toronto: Garamond Press.

Duffy, A. and J. Momirov (1997). *Family Violence: A Canadian Introduction*. Toronto: Lorimer.

Duffy, Ann and Norene Pupo (1992). *Part-Time Paradox: Connecting Gender, Work and Family*. Toronto: McClelland and Stewart.

Dulude, Louise (1987). "Getting Old: Men in Couples and Women Alone," In *Women and Men: Interdisciplinary Readings*, edited by G. H. Nemiroff. Toronto: Fitzhenry and Whiteside.

Dumas, Jean (1994). *Report on the Demographic Situation in Canada 1993*. Ottawa: Statistics Canada (catalogue 91-209E), March.

Dumas, Jean and Alain Bélanger (1997). *Report on the Demographic Situation in Canada 1996*. (Catalogue no. 91-209-XPE). Ottawa: Statistics Canada.

Dunne, G. (2000). "Opting into motherhood: Lesbians blurring the boundaries and transforming the meaning of parenthood and kinship." *Gender and Society* (14): 11-35.

Dupuis, Dave (1998). "What Influences People's Plans to have Children?" *Canadian Social Trends*, Statistics Canada (Catalogue No. 11-008), Spring: 2-5.

Durkheim, E. (1984) [1893]. *The Division of Labour in Society*. New York: The Free Press.

___, (2003). *Work-Family Conflict in Canada in the New Millennium. A Status Report*. Ottawa: Health Canada.

Edleson, J. L. and M. Brygger (1996). "Gender Differences in Reporting of Battering Incidents." *Family Relations* 35: 377-382.

Ehrenreich, B. and D. English (1978). *For Her Own Good: 150 Years of the Expert's Advice to Women*. Garden City, NY: Anchor Press/Doubleday.

Eichler, Margrit (1988). *Families in Canada Today* (2nd edition). Toronto: Gage Educational (1st edition 1983).

___, (1996). "The Impact of New Reproductive and Genetic Technologies on Families." In *Families: Changing Trends in Canada* (3rd edition), edited by M. Baker. Toronto: McGraw-Hill Ryerson: 104-118.

___, (1996). "The Production of Technologically-Mediated Families," In *Journal of Comparative Family Studies* 25(2): 281-308.

___, (1997a). *Family Shifts: Families, Policies, and Gender Equality*. Toronto: Oxford University Press.

___, (1997b). "Feminist Methodology." *Current Sociology* 45(2): 9-36.

Elizabeth, Vivienne (2000). "Cohabitation, Marriage, and the Unruly Consequences of 'Difference.'" *Gender and Society* 14(1), February: 87-100.

Elkin, Frederick (1964). *The Family in Canada*. Ottawa: The Vanier Institute of the Family.

Elliott, J., M. Richards, and H. Warwick (1993). The Consequences of Divorce for the Health and Well-Being of Adults and Children. Final Report for Health Promotion Trust (2). Centre for Family Research, Cambridge, UK.

Ellis, D. (1987). *The Wrong Stuff: An Introduction to the Sociological Study of Deviance*. Toronto: Collier Macmillan.

Ellis, D. and W. S. DeKeseredy (1994). *Pre-Test Report on the Frequency, Severity and Patterning of Sibling Violence in Canadian Families: Causes and Consequences*. Report prepared for the Family Violence Prevention Division, Health Canada. Ottawa: Health Canada.

Ellis, D. and N. Stuckless (1996). *Mediating and Negotiating Marital Conflicts*. Thousand Oaks, CA: Sage.

Engels, Frederick [1884] (1972). *The Origin of the Family, Private Property and the State*. New York: Pathfinder.

Erikson, E. (1959). *Identity and the Life Cycle*. New York: International Universities Press.

Esping-Andersen, Gøsta (1990). *The Three Worlds of Welfare Capitalism*. Cambridge: Polity Press.

Evans, Patricia (1996). "Single Mothers and Ontario's Welfare Policy: Restructuring the Debate." In *Women in Canadian Public Policy*, edited by Janine Brodie. Toronto: Harcourt Brace: 151-171.

Exley, Catherine and Gayle Letherby (2001). "Managing a Disrupted Lifecourse: Issues of Identity and Emotional Work." *Health* 5(1): 112-132.

Eyer, D. (1992). Mother-Infant Bonding: A Scientific Fiction. New Haven: Yale University Press.

Fang, T., Anil Verma (2002). Union wage premium. *Perspectives* (Catalogue no. 75-001-XPE), Winter: 17-23.

Farrell, J. (2000). "Brochure Spread Anti-Male Bias: Panel." *Calgary Herald* June 19 [Online]. Available: http://www/mesacanada.com/brochure.htn

Fast, J., J. Frederick, N. Zukewich, and S. Franke (2001). "The time of our lives . . ." *Canadian Social Trends* (Catalogue no. 11-008), Winter: 20-23.

Fattah, E. A. and V. F. Sacco (1989). *Crime and Victimization of the Elderly*. New York: Springer-Verlag.

Fekete, J. (1994). *Moral Panic: Biopolitics Rising*. Montreal: Robert Davies.

Ferri, E. (1984). *Step Children: A National Study*. Windsor, UK: NFER-Nelson.

Fine, M. A. and D. R. Fine (1994). "An Examination and Evaluation of Recent Changes in Divorce Laws in Five Western Countries: The Critical Role of Values." *Journal of Marriage and the Family* 56: 249-263.

Finkel, Alvin, Margaret Conrad, and Veronica Strong-Boag (1993). *History of the Canadian Peoples. 1867 to the Present*. Toronto: Copp-Clark Pitman.

Fisher, B. S., T. M. Zink, B. A. Rinto, S. L. Regan, S. R. Pabst, and E. J. Gothelf (2003). "Guest Editors' Introduction." *Violence Against Women* 9: 1409-1416.

Fitzpatrick, D. and C. Halliday (1992). *Not the Way to Love: Violence Against Young Women in Dating Relationships*. Amherst, Nova Scotia: Cumberland County Transition House Association.

Fleishing, Usher (2003). "Bride-Price." In *International Encyclopedia of Marriage and Family*. (2nd edition), edited by James J. Ponting Jr. New York: Macmillan Reference USA and Thomson Gale: 175-6

Fleras, Augie and Jean Leonard Elliott (2002). *Engaging Diversity: Multiculturalism in Canada*. Toronto: Nelson Thomson Learning.

___, (2003). *Unequal Relations: An Introduction to Race and Ethnic Dynamics in Canada* (4th edition). Toronto: Prentice Hall.

Flynn, C. P. (1998). "To Spank or Not To Spank: The Effect of Situation and Age of Child on Support for Corporal Punishment." *Journal of Family Violence* 13: 21-37.

Folbre, Nancy (1988). "The Black Four of Hearts: Towards a New Paradigm of Household Economics." In *A Home Divided: Women, Income and the Third World*, edited by D. Dwyer and J. Bruce Stanford. California: Stanford University Press: 248-289.

Forestell, Nancy M. (1999). "The Miner's Wife: Working-Class Femininity in a Masculine Context, 1920-1950." In *Gendered Pasts: Historical Essays in Femininity and Masculinity in Canada*, edited by Kathryn McPherson, Cecelia Morgan and Nancy M. Forestell. Toronto: Oxford University Press.

Foss, K. (2002). "Men as Likely to Face Abuse from Partner, Statscan Says." *The Globe and Mail* June 27: A8.

Fox, Bonnie (1980). *Hidden in the Household: Women and Their Domestic Labour Under Capitalism*, edited by Bonnie Fox. Toronto: Women's Press.

___, (1993). "On Violent Men and Female Victims: A Comment on DeKeseredy and Kelly." *Canadian Journal of Sociology* 18: 320-324.

___, (1993). "The Rise and Fall of the Breadwinner-Homemaker Family," In *Family Patterns. Gender Relations*, edited by Bonnie Fox. Toronto: Oxford University Press.

___, (2001). "The formative years: how parenthood creates gender." *Canadian Review of Sociology and Anthropology* 38(4): 373-390.

Fox, Bonnie and Meg Luxton (2000)."Conceptualizing Family.'" In *Family Patterns, Gender Relations* (2nd edition), edited by Bonnie Fox. Toronto: Oxford University Press.

Franklin, Mary Beth and Josephine Rossi (2001). "On the Job Aid for Caregivers." *Kiplinger's Personal Finance* 55(8): 82-83.

Fraser, Nancy (1987). "Women, Welfare and the Politics of Need Interpretation." *Hypatia* 2(1):103-121.

Frederick, J. and J. Fast (1999). "Eldercare in Canada: Who does how much?" *Canadian Social Trends* (Catalogue no. 11-008), Autumn: 26-30.

Freiler, Christa and Judy Cerny (1998). *Benefiting Canada's Children: Perspectives on Gender and Social Responsibility*. Ottawa: Status of Women Canada.

Frideres, James S. and René R. Gadacz (2001). *Aboriginal Peoples in Canada: Contemporary Conflicts* (6th edition). Toronto: Prentice Hall.

Friedan, B. (1963). *The Feminine Mystique*. New York: Dell.

Friendly, Martha (1994). *Child Care Policy in Canada. Putting the Pieces Together*. Don Mills: Addison Wesley.

Friendly, M. (2003). Early childhood education and care: an issue for all Canadians. Paper presented at the Canadian Social Welfare Policy Conference, Ottawa, June 2003.

Friendly, M., J. Beach, and M. Turiano (2002). *Early Childhood Education and Care in Canada 2001*. Toronto: Childcare Resource and Research Unit, University of Toronto.

Frisco, M. and K. Williams (2003). "Perceived Housework Equality, Marital Happiness, and Divorce in Dual-Earner Households." *Journal of Family Issues* 24: 51-73.

Furstenberg, F. F. (1990). "Divorce and the American Family." *Annual Review of Sociology* 16: 379-403.

Gaffield, Chad (1990). "The Social and Economic Origins of Contemporary Families." In *Families: Changing Trends in Canada* (2nd edition), edited by Maureen Baker. Toronto: McGraw-Hill Ryerson: 23-40.

Gagan, David (1981). *Hopeful Travellers. Families, Land, and Social Change in Mid-Victorian Peel County, Canada West*. Toronto: University of Toronto Press.

Gardner, S. (1994). "Real Domestic Tragedy Continues." *Social Psychology Quarterly* 46: 271-285.

Garigue, Philippe (1962). *La Vie familiale des Canadiens Français*. Montréal: Presses de l'Université de Montréal.

Gauthier, Anne Hélène (1996). *The State and the Family: A Comparative Analysis of Family Polices in Industrialized Countries*. Oxford: Clarendon Press.

Gauvreau, Danielle (1991). *Québec. Une ville et sa population au temps de la Nouvelle France*. Québec: Presses de l'Université du Québec.

Gee, Ellen M. (1990a). "Demographic Change and Intergenerational Relations in Canadian Families and Social Policy Implications." *Canadian Public Policy* 26(2): 191-199.

___, (1990b). "Preferred Timing of Women's Life Events: A Canadian Study." *International Journal of Aging and Human Development* 31(4): 279-294.

___, (1999). "Ethnic Identity among Chinese Canadian Elders." *Canadian Journal on Aging* 18: 415-429.

___, (2000). "Living arrangements and quality of life among Chinese Canadian Elders." *Social Indicators Research* 51(3): 309-329.

Gee, Ellen M. and Meredith M. Kimball (1987). *Women and Aging*. Toronto: Butterworths.

Gee, Ellen M. and Susan A. McDaniel (1992). "Social Policy for an Aging Canada." *Journal of Canadian Studies* 27(3): 139-152.

Gee, Ellen M. and Barbara A. Mitchell (2003). "One roof: Intergenerational exchanges and interdependence in multi-generational families." In *Voices: Essays on Canadian Families* (2nd edition), edited by M. Lynn. Toronto: Nelson Thomson Learning.

Gelles, R. J. (1998). "The Youngest Victims: Violence Toward Children." In *Issues in Intimate Violence*, edited by R.K. Bergen. Thousand Oaks, CA: Sage: 5-24.

Gelles, R. J. and C. P. Cornell (1985). *Intimate Violence in Families*. Beverly Hills: Sage.

___, (1990). *Intimate Violence in Families* (2nd edition). Newbury Park: Sage.

Gelles, R. J. and M. A. Straus (1988). *Intimate Violence: The Causes and Consequences of Abuse in the American Family*. New York: Simon and Schuster.

Gérin-Lajoie, Marie (1902). *A Treatise on Everyday Law*. Montreal: John Lovell and Son.

Giddens, Anthony (1992). *The Transformation of Intimacy: Sexuality, Love and Eroticism in Modern Societies*. Cambridge: Polity Press and Stanford, CA: Stanford University Press.

Gilding, Michael (1997). *Australian Families: A Comparative Perspective*. Melbourne: Longman.

Gillespie, Dair (1971). "Who Has the Power? The Marital Struggle." *Journal of Marriage and the Family* 33: 445-458.

Glassner, B. (1999). *The Culture of Fear*. New York: Basic Books.

Glenn, E. N. (1994). Social constructions of mothering: a thematic overview. In *Mothering: Ideology, Experience and Agency*, edited by E. N. Glenn, G. Chang and L. R. Forcey. New York: Routledge.

Glenn, Norval B. (1997). "A Response to Cherlin, Scanzoni, and Skolnik. Further Discussion of Balance, Accuracy, Fairness, Coverage, and Bias in Family Textbooks." In *Family Relations* 46(3): 223-226.

The Globe and Mail (2000). "Short of marriage." (Editorial) *The Globe and Mail* March 24.

Godenzi, A., M. D. Schwartz and W. S. DeKeseredy (2001). "Toward a Gendered Social Bond/Male Peer Support Theory of University Woman Abuse." *Critical Criminology* 10: 1-16.

Goffman, E. (1961). *Asylums: Essays on the Social Situation of Mental Patients and Other Inmates*. New York: Anchor.

Goldthorpe, J. E. (1987). *Family Life in Western Societies. A Historical Sociology of Family Relationships in Britain and North America*. Cambridge: Cambridge University Press.

González-López, Maria José (2002). "A Portrait of Western Families: New Modes of Intimate Relationships and the Timing of Life Events." In *Analysing Families: Morality and Rationality in Policy and Practice*, edited by A. Carling, S. Duncan and R. Edwards. London: Routledge: 21-48.

Goode, William J. (1964). *The Family*. Englewood Cliffs, New Jersey: Prentice-Hall.

Goodwin, R. (1990). "Sex Differences Among Partner Preferences: Are the Sexes Really Very Similar?" *Sex Roles* 23(9/10): 501-513.

Gopnik, A., A. N. Meltzoff, and P. K. Kuhl (1999). *The Scientist in the Crib*. New York: William Morrow.

Gottman, John and Robert Levenson (2000). "The Timing of Divorce: Predicting When a Couple Will Divorce over a 14 Year Period." *Journal of Marriage and the Family* 69(3), August: 737-745.

Grossman, S. F. and M. Lundy (2003). "Use of Domestic Violence Services Across Race and Ethnicity by Women Aged 55 and Older: The Illinois Experience." *Violence Against Women* 9: 1442-1452.

Guest, Dennis (1997). *The Emergence of Social Security in Canada* (3rd edition). Vancouver: University of British Columbia Press.

Guppy, Neil, James Curtis, and Edward Grabb (1999). "Age-Based Inequalities in Canadian Society," In *Social Inequality in Canada: Patterns, Problems, Policies* (3rd edition), edited by James Curtis, Edward Grabb and Neil Guppy. Toronto: Prentice Hall: 246-257.

Guttentag, M. and P. C. Secord (1983). *Too Many Women? The Sex Ratio Question*. Beverly Hills, CA: Sage Publications.

Hall, David (1996). "Marriage as a Pure Relationship: Exploring the Link Between Premarital Cohabitation and Divorce in Canada." *Journal of Comparative Family Studies* 27(1): 1-13.

Hall, D. R. and J. Z. Zhao (1995). "Cohabitation and Divorce in Canada: Testing the Selectivity Hypothesis." *Journal of Marriage and the Family* 57 (May): 421-427.

Hamel, Therese (1984). "Obligation scolaire et travail des enfants au Québec: 1900-1950." *Revue d'histoire de l'Amérique française* 38(1): 39-58.

Hamilton, Roberta and Michele Barrett (1986). *The Politics of Diversity*, edited by R. Hamilton and M. Barrett. London: Verso.

Hanson, Barbara Gail (1993). "The Myth of the Biological Time Clock?" Presented at the American Sociological Association meetings, 1992.

Hardy, Michael (2002). Life beyond the Screen: Embodiment and Identity through the Internet. *Sociological Review* 50(4) Nov.: 570-585.

Harlow, H. (1958). "The Nature of Love." *American Psychologist* 15: 673-85.

Harrison, D. (1997). "Foreword." In *Family Violence: A Canadian Introduction*, edited by A. Duffy and J. Momirov. Toronto: Lorimer: vii-ix.

Hartmann, H. (1976). "Capitalism, patriarchy and job segregation by sex." *Signs* 1(3): 137-169.

Harvey, David (1990). *Condition of Postmodernity*. Oxford: Oxford University Press,

Haskey, J. (1987). "Social Class Differentials in Remarriage after Divorce: Results from a Forward Linkage Study." *Population Trends* 47: 34-42.

Hatfield, Elaine and Susan Sprecher (1995). "Men's and Women's Preferences in Marital Partners in the United States, Russia and Japan." *Journal of Cross-Cultural Psychology* 26(6): 728-751.

Hayes, Christopher L. and Deborah Anderson (1993). "Psychological and Economic Adjustment of Mid-Life Women After Divorce." *Journal of Women and Aging* 4(4): 83-99.

Hays, S. (1996). *The Cultural Contradictions of Motherhood*. New Haven: Yale University Press.

Heaton, Tim and Cardell Jacobson (1999). "Persistence and Change in Decisions to Remain Childless." *Journal of Marriage and the Family* 61(2) May: 531-40.

Heaton, T. and E. Pratt (1990). "The Effects of Religious Homogamy on Marital Satisfaction and Stability." *Journal of Family Issues* 11: 191-207.

Heitlinger, Alena (1993). *Women's Equality, Demography, and Public Policy. A Comparative Perspective*. London: Macmillan.

Hendrick, S. and C. Hendrick.(1992). *Romantic Love*. Sage: Newbury Park.

Heywood, C. (2001). *A History of Childhood*. Cambridge: Polity Press.

Higgins, C. and L. Duxbury (2002). The 2001 National Work-Life Conflict Study: Report One. Retrieved Feb. 17, 2004.

Highway, Tomson (1999). *Kiss of the Fur Queen*. Toronto: Doubleday.

Hirst, Michael (2001). "Trends in Informal Care in Great Britain in the 1990s." *Health and Social Care in the Community* 9(6): 348-357.

Hobson, Barbara (2002). *Making Men into Fathers. Men, Masculinities and the Social Politics of Fatherhood,* edited by B. Hobson. Cambridge: Cambridge University Press.

Hochschild, Arlie (1989). *The Second Shift.* New York: Avon Books.

___, (1997). *The Time Bind: When Work Becomes Home and Home Becomes Work.* New York: Metropolitan Books.

Holden, K. C. and P. J. Smock (1991). "The Economic Costs of Marital Dissolution: Why Do Women Bear a Disproportionate Cost?" *Annual Review of Sociology* 17: 51-78.

Holzman, H. R. and L. Piper (1998). "Measuring Crime in Public Housing: Methodological Issues and Research Strategies." *Journal of Quantitative Criminology* 14: 331-351.

Hood, J. (1986). "The provider role: its meaning and measurement." *Journal of Marriage and the Family* 48: 349-359.

Hope Irwin, S. (2002). "Child care inclusion in Canada: advances at risk." *Transition* 32(1): 7-9.

Hotaling, G.T., M.A. Straus, and A.J. Lincoln (1990). "Intrafamily Violence and Crime and Violence Outside the Family." In *Physical Violence in American Families: Risk Factors and Adaptions to Violence in 8,145 Families,* edited by M.A. Straus and R.J. Gelles. New Brunswick, NJ: Transaction: 431-472.

Hou, Feng and Garnett Picot (2003). *The Rise in Low Income Rates Among Immigrants in Canada.* (Catalogue no. 11F0019MIE20003198). Ottawa: Statistics Canada.

HRDC (2003). Human Resources Development Canada Web site (www.hrdc-drhc.gc.ca/ae-ei), Employment Insurance. (Cat. no. 11F0019MIE20003198), October. Ottawa: Statistics Canada.

Hrdy, S. B. (1999). *Mother Nature: A History of Mothers, Infants, and Natural Selection.* New York: Pantheon Books.

Hufton, Olwen (1975). "Women and the Family Economy in Eighteenth Century France." In *French Historical Studies* IX(1), Spring:1-22.

Human Resources Development Canada. (2002). "Old Age Security: Basic Pension." [Online]. www.hrdc-drhc.gc.ca/isp/pub/over/overviewpub4_e.shtml.

Hunsley, Terrance (1997). *Lone Parent Incomes and Social Policy Outcomes. Canada in International Perspective.* Kingston, Ontario: School of Policy Studies, Queen's University.

Hurl, Lorna F. (1988). "Overcoming the Inevitable: Restricting Child Factory Labour in Late Nineteenth Century Ontario." *Labour/Le Travail* 21.

Hurley, Mary C. (2003). Sexual Orientation and Legal Rights. Ottawa: Library of Parliament, Parliamentary Research Branch, 92-1E, rev. Sept. 2. Available on the Web at http://www.parl.gc.ca/information/library/PRBpubs/921-e.htm.

Iacovetta, Franca (1992). *Such Hardworking People. Italian Immigrants in Post-War Toronto.* Montreal and Kingston: McGill-Queen's University Press.

Ignatiev, N. (1995). *How the Irish Became White.* New York: Routledge.

Indian and Northern Affairs (1997). Bill C-31: Legislation Amending the Indian Act. Government of Canada. On line. www.ainc-inac.gc.ca/pr/leg/index_e.html.

Inglehart, R. (1977). *The Silent Revolution: Changing Values and Political Styles Among Western Publics.* Princeton, NJ: Princeton University Press.

Isajiw, Wsevolod W. (1979). "Definitions of Ethnicity." *Occasional Papers in Ethnic and Immigration Studies.* Toronto: Multicultural History Society of Ontario.

___, (1999). Understanding Diversity: Ethnicity and Race in the Canadian Context. Toronto: Thompson Educational.

Jackson, A. (2003). "Is work working for women?" Canadian Labour Congress. Research Paper #22. Retrieved Feb. 2, 2004. www.clc-ctc.ca.

Jackson, A. and G. Schellenberg (1999). "Unions, collective bargaining and labour market outcomes for Canadian working women: past gains and future challenges." In *Women and Work,* edited by R. Chayakowski and Lowell. Kingston: John Deutsch Institute for the Study of Economic Policy, Queen's University.

James, A., C. Jenks, and A. Prout (1998). *Theorizing Childhood*. New York: Teachers College Press.

Jameson, Frederick (1991). Postmodernism or The Cultural Logic of Late Capitalism. Durham: Duke University Press.

Jamieson, Lynn (1998). *Intimacy: Personal Relationships in Modern Societies*. Cambridge: Polity Press.

Janssen, J. P.G. and P. D. De Graaf (2000). "Heterogamy and Divorce: Lack of Similarity in Preferences or a Lack of Social Support?" *Mens en Maatschappij* 73: 298-319.

Jasinski, J. L. (2001). "Theoretical Explanations for Violence Against Women." In *Sourcebook on Violence Against Women*, edited by C.M. Renzetti, J.L. Edleson and R.K. Bergen. Thousand Oaks, CA: Sage: 5-23.

Jean, Dominique (1992). "Family Allowances and Family Autonomy: Quebec Families Family History Encounter the Welfare State, 1945-1955," In *Canadian Family History*, edited by B. Bradbury. Toronto: Copp-Clark Pittman.

Jeffrys, Sheila (1985). "Spinsterhood and Celibacy." In *The Spinster and Her Enemies: Feminism and Sexuality, 1880-1950*, edited by Sheila Jeffreys. London: Routledge and Kegan Paul.

Jenks, C. (1996). *Childhood*. New York: Routledge.

Jenson, J. (2001). "Canada's Shifting Citizenship Regime: Investing in Children." In *The Dynamics of Decentralization*, edited by T. C. Salmon and M. Keating. Montreal: McGill-Queen's University Press.

Jenson, Jane and Mariette Sineau (2001). *Who Cares? Women's Work, Childcare, and Welfare State Design*. Toronto: University of Toronto Press.

Jiwani, J. (2000). "The 1999 General Social Survey on Spousal Violence: An Analysis" [Online]. Available: http://www.casac.ca/survey99.htm.

Johnson, H. (1996). *Dangerous Domains: Violence Against Women in Canada*. Toronto: Nelson.

Johnson, K. L., D. S. Lero, and J. A. Rooney (2001). *Work-Life Compendium 2001: 150 Canadian Statistics on Work, Family, and Well-Being*. Guelph ON: Centre for Families, Work and Well-Being, University of Guelph.

Johnston, Patrick (1983). *Native Children and the Child Welfare System*. Toronto: Canadian Council on Social Development in association with James Lorimer.

Jones, C. and G. Causer (1995). "'Men don't have families: equality and motherhood in technical employment." *Gender, Work and Organization* 2: 51-62.

Kalbach, Madeline A. (2000). "Ethnicity and the Altar.' In *Perspectives on Ethnicity in Canada*, edited by Madeline Kalback and Warren Kalbach. Toronto: Harcourt Canada: 111-120.

Kalbach, Warren and Wayne W. McVey (1979). *The Demographic Basis of Canadian Society* (2nd edition). Toronto: McGraw-Hill Ryerson. (1st edition 1971).

Kallen, Evelyn (2003). *Ethnicity and Human Rights in Canada* (3rd edition). Toronto: Oxford University Press.

Kandel, Denise and Gerald S. Lesser (1972). "Marital Decision-Making in America and Danish Urban Families." *Journal of Marriage and the Family* 34 (February): 134-138.

Kaplan, E. A. (1992). *Motherhood and Representation*. London: Routledge.

___, (1994). "Look who's talking, indeed: Fetal images in recent North American culture." In *Mothering: Ideology, Experience, and Agency*, edited by E. N. Glenn, G. Chang and L. R. Forcey. New York: Routledge.

Kasarda, J. D. (1992). "The Severely Distressed in Economically Transforming Cities." In *Drugs, Crime, and Social Isolation*, edited by A.V. Harrell and G.E. Peterson. Washington, D.C.: Urban Institute Press: 45-97.

Katz, Michael (1975). *The People of Hamilton, Canada West. Family and Class in a Mid-Nineteenth-Century City*. Cambridge, Mass: Harvard University Press.

Keating, Norah, Janet Fast, Judith Frederick, Kelly Cranswick, and Cathryn Perrier (1999). *Eldercare in Canada: Context, Content and Consequences*. Ottawa: Statistics Canada. (Catalogue no. 89-570-XPE).

Keating, Norah, Karen Kerr, Sharon Warren, Michael Grace, and Dana Wertenberger (1994). "Who's the Family in Family Caregiving?" *Canadian Journal on Aging* 13(2): 268-287.

Keith, Pat M., Robbyn R. Wacker, and Robert B. Schafer (1992). "Equity in Older Families." In *Families and Retirement*, edited by Maximiliane Szinovacz, David J. Ekerdt, and Barbara H. Vinick. Newbury Park, California: Sage: 189-201.

Kelly, K. (1994). "The Politics of Data." *Canadian Journal of Sociology* 19: 81-85.

Kelly, L. (1988). *Surviving Sexual Violence*. Minneapolis: University of Minnesota Press.

Kelly, L. and J. Radford (1998). "Sexual Violence Against Women and Girls: An Approach to an International Overview." In *Rethinking Violence Against Women*, edited by R. E. Dobash and R. P. Dobash. Thousand Oaks, CA: Sage: 53-76.

Kemeny, A. (2002). "Driven to excel: a portrait of Canada's workaholics." *Canadian Social Trends* (Spring): 2-7.

Kennedy, L. W. and D. G. Dutton (1989). "The Incidence of Wife Assault in Alberta." *Canadian Journal of Behavioural Science* 21: 40-54.

Kirkwood, C. (1993). *Leaving Abusive Partners*. Newbury Park, CA: Sage.

Kirp, D. L., M. G. Yudof, and M. S. Franks (1986). *Gender Justice*. Chicago: University of Chicago Press.

Kitchen, Brigitte (1990). "Employment Strategies for Women and the Sexual Division of Labour." In *Unemployment and Welfare*, edited By G. Riches and G. Ternowetsky. Toronto: Garamond: 141-160.

___, (1997). "The New Child Benefit. Much Ado About Nothing." *Canadian Review of Social Policy* 39(Spring): 65-74.

Knowles, Valerie (1992). *Strangers at Our Gates: Canadian Immigration and Immigration Policy, 1540-1990*. Toronto: Dundurn Press.

Kobayashi, Karen M. (1999). "Bunka No Tanjyo (Emergent Culture): Continuity and Change in Older Nisei (Second Generation) Parent-Adult Sansei (Third Generation) Child Relationships in Japanese Canadian Families." Unpublished Ph.D. Dissertation, Sociology, Simon Fraser University.

Kolb, Patricia J. (2003). *Caring for our Elders: Multicultural Experiences with Nursing Home Placement*. New York: Columbia University Press.

Korinek, Valerie J. (2000). *Roughing It in the Suburbs: Reading Chatelaine Magazine in the Fifties and Sixties*. Toronto, University of Toronto Press.

Kornblum, W. and J. Julian (2004). *Social Problems* (11th edition). Upper Saddle River, NJ: Pearson.

Korpi, Walter (2000). "Faces of Inequality: Gender, Class, and Patterns of Inequalities in Different Types of Welfare States." *Social Politics* 7(2): 127-191.

Koss, M. (1996). "The Measurement of Rape Victimization in Crime Surveys." *Criminal Justice and Behavior* 23: 55-69.

Kozak, J. F., T. Elmslie, and J. Verdon (1995). "Epidemiology of the Abuse and Neglect of Seniors: A Review of the National and International Research Literature." In *Abuse and Neglect of Older Canadians: Strategies for Change*, edited by M.J. MacLean. Toronto: Thompson Educational: 129-142.

Kozma, A. and M. J. Stones (1995). "Issues in the Measurement of Elder Abuse." In *Abuse and Neglect of Older Canadians: Strategies for Change*, edited by M.J. MacLean. Toronto: Thompson Educational: 117-128.

Krashinsky, M. (2001). "'Are we there yet?': The evolving face of child care policy in Canada." *Transition* 31(4): 3-5.

Kruttschnitt, C. and M. Dornfeld (1991). "Childhood Victimization, Race, and Violent Crime." *Criminal Justice and Behavior* 18: 448-463.

Kurdek, Lawrence A. (1998). "Relationship outcomes and their predictors: Longitudinal evidence from heterosexual married, gay cohabiting and lesbian cohabiting relationships." *Journal of Marriage and the Family*, 60(3), August: 553.

___, (2004). "Gay Men and Lesbians." In *Handbook of Contemporary Families*, edited by Marilyn Coleman and Lawrence Ganong. Thousand Oaks: Sage: 96-115.

Kwak, Kyunghwa (2003). "Adolescents and Their Parents: A Review of Intergenerational Family Relations for Immigrant and Non-Immigrant Families." *Human Development* 46: 115-136.

Lacelle, Claudette (1987). *Urban Domestic Servants in 19th-Century Canada*. Ottawa: Parks Canada.

Lachapelle, R., and J. Henripin (1982). *The Demolinguistic Situation in Canada: Past Trends and Future Prospects*. Montreal: The Institute for Research on Public Policy.

Lachs, M. and K. Pillemer (1995). "Abuse and Neglect of Elderly Persons." *New England Journal of Medicine* 332: 437-443.

Lampard, R. and K. Peggs (1999). "Repartnering: The Relevance of Parenthood and Gender to Cohabitation and Remarriage among the Formerly Married." *British Journal of Sociology* 50: 443-465.

Landry, Yves (1992). *Les Filles du Roi au XVIIe Siècle: Orphelines en France, Pionnières au Canada*. Montréal: Leméac.

LaRossa, R. (1995). "Fatherhood and social change." In *Men's Lives*, edited by M. S. Kimmel and M.A. Messner. New York: Macmillan.

Laslett, Peter (1971). *The World We Have Lost*. London: University Paperbacks.

LaViolette, A. D. and O. W. Barnett (2000). *It Could Happen to Anyone: Why Battered Women Stay* (2nd edition). Thousand Oaks, CA: Sage.

Law Reform Commission of Canada (1975). *Studies on Divorce*. Ottawa, Canada: Information Canada.

Leblanc, Daniel (2000). "Ottawa Boosts Child Benefit by $2.5-Billion." *The Globe and Mail* 29 February (Internet).

Le Bourdais, Céline, and Nicole Marcil-Gratton (1994). "Quebec's Pro-Active Approach to Family Policy: 'Thinking and Acting Family.'" In *Canada's Changing Families: Challenges to Public Policy*, edited by M. Baker. Ottawa: Vanier Institute of the Family.

Le Bourdais, Celine, Ghyslaine Neill, and Pierre Turcotte (2000). "The Changing Face of Conjugal Relationships." *Canadian Social Trends*, Statistics Canada (Catalogue no. 11-008), Spring: 14-17.

Leira, Arnlaug (2002). *Working Parents and the Welfare State. Family change and Family Policy in Scandinavia*. Cambridge: Cambridge University Press.

Leslie, Gerald R., and Sheila K. Korman (1989). *The Family in Social Context* (7th edition). New York: Oxford University Press.

Lesthaeghe, R. (1995). "The Second Demographic Transition in Western Countries: An Interpretation." In *Gender and Family Change in Industrialized Countries*, edited by K. Oppenheim Mason and A. Jensen. Oxford, England: Oxford University Press: 17-62.

Lesthaeghe, R. and J. Surkyn (1988). "Cultural Dynamics and Economic Theories of Fertility Change." *Population and Development Review* 14: 1-45.

Levan, A. (1996). "Violence Against Women. In *Women and Canadian Public Policy*, edited by J. Brodie. Toronto: Harcourt Brace: 319-354.

Lewin, Ellen (1996)."'Why in the World Would You Want to do That?': Claiming Community in Lesbian Commitment." In *Inventing Lesbian Cultures in America*, edited by Ellen Lewin. Boston: Beacon Press: 105-130.

Lewis, Jane (2003). *Should We Worry About Family Change?* Toronto: University of Toronto Press.

Lewis, S. (1997). "'Family-friendly' employment policies: a route to changing organizational culture or playing about at the margins?" *Gender, Work and Organization* 4: 13-23.

Li, Peter (2003). *Destination Canada: Immigration Debates and Issues*. Don Mills: Oxford University Press.

Liebig, Phoebe S. (1993). "Factors Affecting the Development of Employer-Sponsored Eldercare Programs: Implications for Employed Caregivers." *Journal of Women and Aging* 5(1): 59-78.

Liff, S. and K. Ward (2001). "Distorted views through the glass ceiling: the construction of women's understandings of promotion and senior management positions." *Gender, Work and Organization* 8: 19-36.

Lindsay, Colin (1992). *Lone-Parent Families in Canada*. (Catalogue no. 89-522E) Ottawa: Minister of Industry, Science and Technology. December.

___, (1999), "Seniors: A diverse group aging well." *Canadian Social Trends* (Catalogue no. 11-008), Spring: 24-26.

Little, Margaret H. (1998). *No Car, No Radio, No Liquor Permit: The Moral Regulation of Single Mothers in Ontario, 1920-1997*. Toronto: Oxford University Press.

___, (2003). "The Leaner, Meaner Welfare Machine: The Ontario Conservative Government's Ideological and Material Attack on Single Mothers." In *Making Normal: Social Regulation in Canada*, edited by D. Brock. Toronto: Nelson Thompson.

Loewen, Royden K. (1993). *Family, Church and Market: A Mennonite Community in the Old and the New Worlds, 1850-1930*. Toronto: University of Toronto Press.

Looker, E. Dianne, and Victor Thiessen (1999). "Images of Work: Women's Work, Men's Work, Housework" *Canadian Journal of Sociology* 24(2): 225-254.

Lorenz, K. (1952). *King Solomon's Ring*. London: Methuen.

Lunman, Kim (2004). "Martin health plan gets 48% support." *The Globe and Mail* Feb. 2: A4.

Lupri, E. (1990). "Male Violence in the Home." *Canadian Social Trends* 14: 19-21.

Lupri, E., E. Grandin, and M.B. Brinkerhoff (1994). "Socioeconomic Status and Male Violence in the Canadian Home: A Re-examination." *Canadian Journal of Sociology* 19: 47-73.

Lux, Maureen (2001). *Medicine That Walks: Disease, Medicine and Canadian Plains People, 1880-1940*. Toronto: University of Toronto Press.

Luxton, M. (1980). *More Than a Labour of Love: Three Generations of Women's Work in the Home*. Toronto: Women's Press

___, (Forthcoming). "Feminist Political Economy and Social Reproduction." In *Rethinking Social Reproduction: Current Debates in Feminist Political Economy*, edited by Kate Bezanson and Meg Luxton.

Luxton, M. and J. Corman (2001). *Getting By in Hard Times: Gendered Labour at Home and on the Job*. Toronto: University of Toronto Press.

___, (2001). *Getting By in Hard Times: Restructuring Gender and Class in Hamilton, Ontario 1980-1996*. Toronto: University of Toronto Press.

Luxton, M., Harriet Rosenberg, and Sedef Arat-Koc (1990). *Through the Kitchen Window: The Politics of Home and Family* (2nd edition). Toronto: Garamond Press.

MacDonald, G., C. Alphonso, I. Peritz, and A. Willis (2003). "School Craze." *Globe and Mail* Feb 8: F1 – F2.

MacLeod, L. (1987). *Battered But Not Beaten: Preventing Wife Battering in Canada*. Ottawa: Advisory Council on the Status of Women.

MacMillan, H. L., J. E. Fleming, N. Trocme, M. H. Boyle, M. Wong, Y. A. Racine, W. R. Beardslee, and D. Offord (1997). "Prevalence of Child Physical and Sexual Abuse in the Community: Results from the Ontario Health Supplement." *Journal of the American Medical Association Abstracts* 9 (July).

Man, Guida (1996). "The Experience of Middle-Class Women in Recent Hong Kong Chinese Immigrant Families in Canada" In *Voices: Essays on Canadian Families*, edited by Marion Lynn. Toronto: Nelson: 271-300.

____, (2003). "The Experience of Middle-Class Women in Recent Hong Kong Chinese Immigrant Families." In *Voices: Essays on Canadian Families* (2nd edition), edited by Marion Lynn. Toronto: Nelson Thomson.

Mandel, Ernest (1978). *Late Capitalism*. London: Verso.

Mandell, Nancy and Ann Duffy (1988). *Reconstructing the Canadian Family: Feminist Perspectives*. Toronto: Butterworths.

Marcil-Gratton, Nicole (1999). "Growing Up With Mom and Dad? Canadian Children Experience Shifting Family Structures." *Transition* 29(1), September: 4-7.

Marcil-Gratton, N. and J. Legare (1992). "Will Reduced Fertility Lead to Greater Isolation in Old Age for Tomorrow's Elderly?" *Canadian Journal on Aging* 11(1): 54-71.

Maroney, Heather Jon and Meg Luxton (1997)."Canadian Feminist Political Economy" In *Understanding Canada Building on the New Canadian Political Economy*, edited by Wallace Clement. Montreal and Kingston: McGill-Queens: 85-117.

Marshall, Dominique (1998). *Aux origines de l'État Providence: familles québecoises, obligation scolaire et allocations familiales, 1940-1955*. Montréal: Presses de l'Université de Montréal.

Marshall, Katherine (1993). "Employed Parents and the Division of Housework." *Perspectives on Labour and Income Statistics Canada* (Catalogue no. 75-001E), Autumn: 23-30.

____, (2001). "Part-time by choice." *Perspectives* (Catalogue no. 75-001-XPE), Spring: 20-27.

____, (2003). "Benefiting from extended parental leave." *Perspectives On Labour and Income* (Summer): 15-21.

McCain, M. and J. F. Mustard (1999). *Early Years Study: Final Report*. Toronto: Publications Ontario.

McCarthy, Martha A. (1999)."Supporting Same Sex Families." Paper delivered at the Domestic Partnerships Conference, Queen's University, Kingston, October.

McDaniel, Susan A, (1992). "Caring and Sharing: Demographic Aging, Family and the State." In *The Remainder of Their Days: Impact of Public Policy on Older Families*, edited by Jon Hendricks and Carolyn Rosenthal. New York: Garland: 121-144.

____, (1993). "Where the Contradictions Meet: Women and Family Security in Canada in the 1990's." *National Forum on Family Security*. Ottawa: Canadian Council on Social Development.

____, (1994). *Family and Friends 1990: General Society Survey Analysis Series*. Ottawa: Statistics Canada (Catalogue no. 11-612E, No. 9).

____, (1996). "Family/Work Challenges Among Older Working Canadians, In *Voices: Essays on Canadian Families*, edited by Marion Lynn. Toronto: Nelson: 195-214

____, (1997a). "Serial Employment and Skinny Government: Reforming Caring and Sharing among Generations." *Canadian Journal on Aging* 16(3): 465-484.

____, (1997b). "Health Care Policy in an Aging Canada: The Alberta 'Experiment.'" *Journal of Aging Studies* 11(3): 211-227.

____, (1999). "Untangling Love and Domination: Challenges of Home Care for the Elderly in a Reconstructing Canada." *Journal of Canadian Studies* 34(3): 191-213.

____, (2000). "'What Did You Ever Do For Me?': Intergenerational Linkages in a Reconstructing Canada." In *The Overselling of Population Aging: Apocalyptic Demography and Inter-generational Challenges*, edited by Ellen M. Gee and Gloria Gutman. Toronto: Oxford University Press: 129-152.

____, (2003). "Hidden in the Household: Now it's Men in Mid-Life." *Ageing International* 28(4): 326-344.

____, (2004). "Generationing Gender: Justice and the Division of Welfare." *Journal of Aging Studies* Special Issue: "New Directions in Feminist Gerontology." 18(1): 27-44.

McDaniel, Susan A., and Neena Chappell (1999). "Health Care in Regression: Contradictions, Tensions and Implications for Canadian Seniors." *Canadian Public Policy/Analyse de Politiques* XXV(2): 100-110.

McDaniel, Susan A., and Ellen M. Gee (1993). "Social Policies Regarding Caregiving to Elders: Canadian Contradictions." *Journal of Aging and Social Policy* 5(1 & 2): 57-72.

McDaniel, Susan A., and Robert Lewis (1997). "Did They or Didn't They: Intergenerational Supports in Canada's Past and A Case Study of Brigus, Newfoundland, 1920-1949." In *Family Matters: Papers in Post-Confederation Canadian Family History*, edited by Lori Chambers and Edgar-Andre Montigny. Toronto: Canadian Scholars Press.

McDaniel, Susan A., and Allison McKinnon (1993). "Gender Differences in Informal Support and Coping Among Elders: Findings from Canada's 1985 and 1990 General Social Surveys." *Journal of Women and Aging* 5(2): 79-98.

McDaniel, Susan A., and Lorne Tepperman (2000). *Close Relations: An Introduction to the Sociology of the Families*. Scarborough, Ontario: Prentice Hall, Allyn and Bacon.

McDaniel, Susan A., and Lorne Tepperman (2004). *Close Relations: An Introduction to Sociology of Families* (2nd edition). Scarborough, Ontario: Prentice Hall, Allyn and Bacon.

McDonald, Ryan J. (1994). "Canada's Off-Reserve Aboriginal Population." In *Canadian Social Trends, Volume 2*. Toronto: Thompson Educational: 51-56.

McFetters, Ann (2004). "Bush backs ban on gay marriage." *Post-Gazette National Bureau* at www.post-gazette.com/pg/04056/277246.stm.

McGilly, Frank (1998). *Canada's Public Social Services. Understanding Income and Health Programs* (2nd edition). Toronto: Oxford University Press.

McGoldrick, M. (1999). "Becoming a Couple." In *The Expanded Family Life Cycle* (3rd edition), edited by B. Carter and M. McGolderick. New York: Allyn and Bacon: 231-248.

McKenna, Catelyn, Amie Green, and Marcie Gleason (2002). "Relationship Formation on the Internet: What's the Big Attraction?" *Journal of Social Issues* 58(1): 9-31.

McKenna, K. M. J., and J. Larkin (2002a). "Introduction." In *Violence Against Women: New Canadian Perspectives*, edited by J. Larkin and K.M.J. McKenna. Toronto: Inanna Publications: 9-20.

___, (2002b). *Violence Against Women: New Canadian Perspectives*, edited by K.M.J. McKenna and J. Larkin. Toronto: Inanna Publications: 9-20.

McKie, Craig (2000). "A History of Emigration from Canada." In *Canadian Social Trends, Volume 3*. Toronto: Thompson Educational: 11-14.

McLanahan, S. S. and G. Sandefur (1994). *Growing Up with a Single Parent: What Hurts, What Helps*. Cambridge, MA: Harvard University Press.

McLaren, Angus and Arlene Tigar McLaren (1997). *The Bedroom and the State. The Changing Practices and Politics of Contraception and Abortion in Canada, 1880-1997*. Toronto: Oxford University Press.

McLean, Lorna (1991). "Single Again: Widow's Work in the Urban Family Economy, Ottawa, 1871." *Ontario History* 83(2).

McMahon, M. (1995). *Engendering Motherhood: Identity and Self-Transformation in Women's Lives*. New York: The Guilford Press.

McNair, Ruth, Deborah Dempsey, Sarah Wise, and Amaryll Perlesz (2002). "Lesbian Parenting: Issues, Strengths and Challenges." *Family Matters* 63(Spring/Summer): 40-49.

McPherson, Kathryn, Cecelia Morgan, and Nancy M. Forestell (1999). *Gendered Pasts:Historical Essays in Femininity and Masculinity in Canada*. Toronto: Oxford University Press.

Mead, Margaret (1935). *Sex and Temperament in Three Primitive Societies*. New York: Dell.

Meissner, Martin, Elizabeth W. Humphreys, Scott M. Meis, and William J. Scheu (1975). "No Exit for Wives: Sexual Division of Labour and the Cumulation of Household Demands." *Canadian Review of Sociology and Anthropology* 12(Part 1): 424-439.

Menard, A. (2001). "Domestic Violence and Housing: Key Policy and Program Challenges." *Violence Against Women* 7: 707-721.

Menzies, Charles R. (1999). "First Nations, Inequality, and the Legacy of Colonialism." In *Social Inequality in Canada: Patterns, Problems, Policies*, (3rd edition), edited by James Curtis, Edward Grabb, and Neil Guppy. Toronto: Prentice Hall: 236-244.

Michaels, M. W. (1996). "Other Mothers: Toward an Ethic of Postmaternal Practice." *Hypatia* 11(2): 49-70.

Michelson, William and Lorne Tepperman (2003). "Focus on Home: What Time-Use Data Can Tell About Caregiving to Adults." *Journal of Social Issues* 59(3): 591-610.

Mihalic, S. and Elliot, D. (1997). "If Violence is Domestic, Does it Really Count?" *Journal of Family Violence* 12: 293-311.

Milan, Anne (2000). "One Hundred Years of Families," *Canadian Social Trends*, Statistics Canada (Catalogue no. 11-008), Spring: 2-13.

___, (2003). "Would You Live Common-law?" *Canadian Social Trends* (Autumn): 2-6.

Milan, Anne and Brian Hamm (2004). "Mixed Unions." *Canadian Social Trends* (Summer): 2-6.

Millar, Jane and Karen Rowlingson (2001). *Lone Parents, Employment and Social Policy: Cross-National Comparisons*, edited by J. Millar and R. Rowlingson. Bristol: Policy Press.

Millar, Nancy (1999). *Once Upon a Wedding*. Calgary: Bayeaux Arts.

Millar, P. and S. Goldenberg (1998). "Explaining Child Custody Determinations in Canada." *Canadian Journal of Law and Society* 13: 209-225.

Mills, L. (2003). *Insult to Injury: Rethinking Our Responses to Intimate Abuse*. Princeton, NJ: Princeton University Press.

Mitchell, A. (1999). "Criminal Charges in Son's Cycling Death Creating Controversy." *The Globe and Mail* Sept. 25: A8.

Mitchell, B. A. (2002). "'Mature' adult children living with parents: Patterns, predictors and issues for aging families." *Gerontology Research Centre News* 20(2): 3-4.

___, (2004). "Home, but not alone: Socio-cultural and economic aspects of Canadian young adults sharing parental households." *Atlantis* 28(2): 115-125.

Mitchell, Barbara A., Andrew V. Wister, and Ellen M.Gee (2002). "There's no place like home: An analysis of young adults' mature coresidency in Canada." *International Journal of Aging and Human Development* 54(1): 1-28.

Mitchinson, Wendy (1991). *The Nature of Their Bodies: Women and Their Doctors in Victorian Canada*. Toronto: University of Toronto Press.

___, (2002). *Giving Birth in Canada, 1900-1950*. Toronto: University of Toronto Press.

Montagu, Ashley (1972). *Statement on Race* (3rd edition). London: Oxford.

___, (1974). *Man's Most Dangerous Myth: The Fallacy of Race* (5th edition). London: Oxford.

Moogk, Peter N. (1983). "In the Darkness of a Basement: Craftsmen's Associations in Early French Canada." In *Economy and Society during the French Regime to 1759*, edited by Michael S. Cross and Gregory S. Kealey. Toronto: McClelland and Stewart.

Moore, Oliver (2003). "Bush wants to 'codify' heterosexual unions." *The Globe and Mail* July 31. www.theglobeandmail.com

Morgan, S. P., D. N. Lye and G. A. Condran (1988). "Sons, Daughters, and the Risk of Marital Disruption." *American Journal of Sociology* 94: 110-129.

Morrison, D. R. and A. Ritualo (2000). "Routes to Children's Economic Recovery after Divorce: Are Cohabitation and Remarriage Equivalent?" *American Sociological Review* 65: 560-580.

Morissette, R. (2002). "On the edge: financially vulnerable families." *Canadian Social Trends* (Catalogue no. 11-008), Winter: 13-17.

Morton, Suzanne (1992b). "The June Bride as the Working-Class Bride: Getting Married in a Halifax Working-Class Neighbourhood in the 1920s." In *Canadian Family History*, edited by B. Bradbury. Toronto: Copp-Clark Pittmam.

___, (1992). "Women on their Own: Single Mothers in Working Class Halifax." *Acadiensis* XIX(2): 90-107.

Murdock, George (1949). *Social Stucture*. New York: Macmillan.

Myles, John and F. Hou (2003). "Neighbourhood Attainment and Residential Segregation among Toronto's Visible Minorities" (Catalogue no. 11F0019MIE - no. 206). *Analytical Studies Branch Research Paper Series*. Ottawa: Statistics Canada.

Nadesan, M. H. (2002). "Engineering the Entrepreneurial Infant: Brain Science, Infant Development Toys, and Governmentalit." *Cultural Studies* 16(3): 401 - 432.

Nakonezny, P. A., R. D. Shull, and J. L. Rodgers (1995). "The Effect of No-Fault Divorce Law on the Divorce Rate Across the 50 States and Its Relation to Income, Education, and Religiosity." *Journal of Marriage and the Family* 57: 477-488.

Nanda, Serena (1991). "Arranging a Marriage in India." In Philip R. DeVita, ed. *The Naked Anthropologist: Tales From Around the World* (Belmont, California: Wadsworth)

* FURTHER REFLECTIONS ON ARRANGED MARRIAGE

The previous essay was written from the point of view of a family seeking a daughter-in-law. Arranged marriage looks somewhat different from the point of view of the bride and her family. Arranged marriage continues to be preferred, even among the more educated, Westernized sections of the Indian population. Many young women from these families still go along, more or less willingly, with the practice, and also with the specific choices of their families. Young women do get excited about the prospects of their marriage, but there is also ambivalence and increasing uncertainty, as the bride contemplates leaving the comfort and familiarity of her own home, where as a "temporary guest" she has often been indulged, to live among strangers. Even in the best situation, she will now come under the close scrutiny of her husband's family. How she dresses, how she behaves, how she gets along with others, where she goes, how she spends her time, her domestic abilities—all of this and much more—will be observed and commented on by a whole new set of relations. Her interaction with her family of birth will be monitored and curtailed considerably. Not only will she leave their home, but with increasing geographic mobility, she may also live very far from them, perhaps even on another continent. Too much expression of her fondness for her own family, or her desire to visit them, may be interpreted as an inability to adjust to her new family, and may become a source of conflict. In an arranged marriage, the burden of adjustment is clearly heavier for a woman than for a man. And that is in the best of situations.

In less happy circumstances, the bride may be a target of resentment and hostility from her husband's family, particularly her mother-in-law or her husband's unmarried sisters, for whom she is now a source of competition for the affection, loyalty, and economic resources of a son or brother. If she is psychologically or even physically abused, her options are limited, as returning to her parents' home or getting a divorce is still very stigmatized. For most Indians, marriage and motherhood are still considered the only suitable roles for a woman, even for those who have careers, and few women can comfortably contemplate remaining unmarried. Most families still consider "marrying off" their daughters as a compelling religious duty and social necessity. This increases a bride's sense of obligation to make the marriage a success, at whatever cost to her own personal happiness.

The vulnerability of a new bride may also be intensified by the issue of dowry that, although illegal, has become a more pressing issue in the consumer conscious society of contemporary urban India. In many cases, where a groom's family is not satisfied with the amount of dowry a bride brings to her marriage, the young bride will be harassed constantly to get her parents to give more. In extreme cases, the bride may even be murdered, and the murder disguised as an accident or a suicide. This also offers the husband's family an opportunity to arrange another match for him, thus bringing in another dowry. This phenomenon, called dowry death, calls attention not just to the "evils of dowry" but also to larger issues of the powerlessness of women as well.

National Council of Welfare (1997). *Welfare Incomes 1995*. Ottawa: Minister of Supply and Services Canada.

___, (2003). *Welfare Incomes 2002*. Ottawa: Minister of Public Works and Government Services Canada.

Navaie-Waliser, Maryam, Aubrey Spriggs, and Penny H. Feldman (2002). "Informal Caregiving: Differential Experiences by Gender." *Medical Care* 40(12): 1249-1260.

Nelson, F. (1996). *Lesbian Motherhood*. Toronto: University of Toronto Press.

___, (2001). "Lesbian families." In *Family Patterns, Gender Relations* (2nd edition), edited by Bonnie J. Fox. Don Mills ON: Oxford University Press.

Nett, Emily M. (1981). "Canadian Families in Social-Historical Perspective." *Canadian Journal of Sociology* 6(3), Summer: 239-260.

___, (1988). *Canadian Families. Past and Present*. Toronto: Butterworths.

Neylan, Susan (2002). *The Heavens are Changing: Nineteenth-Century Protestant Missions and Tsimshian Christianity*. Montreal and Kingston: McGill-Queen's University Press.

Neysmith, Sheila (1989). "Closing the Gap between Health Care Policy and the Home-Care Needs of Tomorrow's Elderly." *Canadian Journal of Community Mental Health* 8(2): 141 150.

Noel, Françoise (2003). *Family Life and Sociability in Upper and Lower Canada, 1780-1870*. Montreal and Kingston: McGill-Queen's University Press.

Noel, Jan (1991). "New France: Les femmes favorisées?" In *Rethinking Canada. The Promise of Women's History*, edited by Veronica Strong-Boag and Anita Clair Fellman. Toronto: Copp-Clark Pitman.

Ockleford, E., Y. Barnes-Holmes, R. Morichelli, A. Morjaria, F. Scocchera, F. Furniss, C. Sdogati and D. Barnes-Holmes (2003). "Mistreatment of Older Women in Three European Countries: Estimated Prevalence and Service Responses." *Violence Against Women* 9: 1453-1464.

O'Connor, Julia S., Ann Shola Orloff, and Sheila Shaver (1999). *States, Markets, Families: Gender Liberalism and Social Policy in Australia, Canada, Great Britain and the United States*. Cambridge: Cambridge University Press.

OECD (Organisation for Economic Co-operation and Development) (2001). *Society at a Glance*. Paris: OECD.

___, (2001). *The New Economy Beyond the Hype: The OECD Growth Project*. Paris: OECD.

Okun, L. (1986). *Woman Abuse: Facts Replacing Myths*. Albany: State University of New York Press.

Olsen, David H. and Hamilton McCubbin (1983). *Families: What Makes Them Work?* Beverly Hills: Sage

O'Neill, Nena and George O'Neill (1972). *Open Marriage. A New Life Style for Couples*. New York: Avon Books.

Ontario Campaign 2000. (2000). *Child Poverty in Ontario: Report Card 2000*.

Orloff, Ann Shola (1993). "Gender and the Social Rights of Citizenship: The Comparative Analysis of Gender Relations and Welfare States." *American Sociological Review* 58(3): 303-328.

Orm, N. (2001). *Medieval Children*. New Haven: Yale University Press.

Ozawa, Martha N. and Hong-Sik Yoon (2002). "The Economic Benefit of Remarriage: Gender and Income Class." *Journal of Divorce and Remarriage* 36(3/4): 21 - 40.

Pal, Salmali (1999). "Looking for My Prince Charming." *Newsweek* 133(11): 12.

Palameta, B. (2003). "Who pays for domestic help?" *Perspectives* (Catalogue no. 75-001-XPE), Autumn: 39-42.

Paletta, Anna (1992). "Today's Extended Families." *Canadian Social Trends* 27(Winter): 26-28.

Palmer, Donald (1997). *Structuralism and Poststructuralism for Beginners*. New York: Writers and Readers.

Pampel, Fred C. and Paul Adams (1992). "The Effects of Demographic Change and Political Structure on Family Allowance Expenditures." *Social Service Review* 66(4), December: 524-546.

Papernow, P. (1988). "Stepparent Role Development: From Outsider to Intimate." In *Relative Strangers: Studies of Stepfamily Processes*, edited by W. R. Beer. Totowa, NJ: Rowan and Littlefield: 54-82.

___, (1993). *Becoming a Stepfamily: Patterns of Development in Remarried Families*. San Francisco, CA: Jossey-Bass.

Parr, Joy (1982). *Childhood and Family in Canadian History*, edited by Joy Parr. Toronto: McClelland and Stewart.

___, (1990). *The Gender of Breadwinners. Women, Men and Change in Two Industrial Towns, 1880-1950*. Toronto: University of Toronto Press.

Parsons, T. (1955). "The American family: its relations to personality and to the social structure." In *Family, Socialization and Interaction Process*, edited by T. Parsons and R. Bales. Glencoe: The Free Press.

Parsons, Talcott and Robert F. Bales (1955). *Family Socialization and Interaction Process*. New York: The Free Press.

Patterson, C. (1995). "Families of the lesbian baby boom: parents' division of labour and children's adjustment." *Developmental Psychology* 31: 115-123.

Patterson, Charlotte and Richard Redding (1996). "Lesbian and Gay Families with Children: Implications of Social Science Research for Policy." *Journal of Social Issues* 52(3): 29-50.

Payne, B. K. and R. R. Gainey (2002). *Family Violence and Criminal Justice: A Life-Course Approach*. Cincinnati: Anderson.

Payne, J. D. (1986). *Payne's Commentaries on the Divorce Act, 1985*. Don Mills, Canada: Richard De Boo.

Pearn, John (1997). "Gatekeeping and Assisted Reproductive Technology: The ethical rights and responsibilities of doctors." *Medical Journal Australia* 167(September 15): 318-320.

Pearson, L. and R. Gallaway (1998). *For The Sake of the Children: Report of the Special Joint Committee on Child Custody and Access*. Ottawa: Public Works and Government Services Canada.

Pearson, P. (1997). *When She Was Bad: Violent Women and the Myth of Innocence*. Toronto: Random House.

Perkins, Kathleen (1993). "Recycling Poverty: From the Workplace into Retirement." *Journal of Women and Aging* 5(1):5-24.

Perry, Adele. 2000. *On the Edge of Empire: Gender, Race, and the Making of British Columbia, 1849-1971*. Toronto: University of Toronto Press.

Peterson del Mar, D. (1996). *What Trouble I Have Seen: A History of Violence Against Wives*. Cambridge, MA: Harvard University Press.

Peterson, R. R. (1996). "A Re-Evaluation of the Economic Consequences of Divorce." *American Sociological Review* 61: 528-536.

Phillips, R. (1988). *Putting Asunder: A History of Divorce in Western Society*. Cambridge, England: Cambridge University Press.

Phipps, Shelly, Peter Burton, and Lars Osberg (2001). "Time as a Source of Inequality Within Marriage: Are Husbands More Satisfied With Time for Themselves Than Wives?" *Feminist Economics* 7(2): 1-21.

Picchio, Antonella (1992). *Social Reproduction: the political economy of the labour market*. Cambridge: Cambridge University Press.

Pierson, Ruth Roach (1990). "Gender and the Unemployment Debates in Canada, 1934-1940." *Labour/Le Travail* 25(Spring): 77-103.

Pike, R. M. (1975). "Legal Access to Divorce and the Incidence of Divorce in Canada: A Sociohistorical Perspective." *Canadian Review of Sociology and Anthropology* 12: 115-133.

Pillemer, K. A. (1985). "The Dangers of Dependency: New Findings on Domestic Violence Against the Elderly." *Social Problems* 33: 146-158.

Pillemer, K. A. and D. Finkelhor (1988). "Prevalence of Elder Abuse: A Random Sample Survey." *The Gerontologist* 28: 51-57.

Pittaway, E. D., A. Weshues, and T. Peressini (1995). "Risk Factors for Abuse and Neglect Among Older Adults." *Canadian Journal on Aging* 14: 20-44.

Podnieks, E. (1990). *National Survey on Abuse of the Elderly*. Toronto: Ryerson Polytechnical Institute.

Policy Research Initiative, Government of Canada. (2004). Population Aging and Life Flexibility: The Pivotal Role of Increased Choice in the Retirement Decision. Discussion Paper. Ottawa: Policy Research Initiative.

Polk, K. (2003). Masculinities, femininities and homicide: Competing explanations for male violence. In *Controversies in Critical Criminology*, edited by M.D. Schwartz and S.E. Hatty. Cincinnati: Anderson: 133-146.

Pollard, J. (1993). *Male-Female Dating Relationships in Canadian Universities and Colleges: Sample Design, Arrangements for Data Collection and Data Reduction*. Toronto: Institute for Social Research, York University.

Poole, Marilyn and Susan Feldman (1999). *A Certain Age. Women Growing Older*, edited by M. Poole and S. Feldman. Sydney: Allen and Unwin.

Popenoe, D. (1988). *Disturbing the Nest: Family Change and Decline in Modern Societies*. New York: de Gruyter.

___, (1993). "American Family Decline, 1960-1990: A Review and Appraisal." *Journal of Marriage and the Family* 55: 527-555.

___, (1994). "The Family Condition of America. Cultural Change and Public Policy." In *Values and Public Policy*, edited by Henry J. Aaron, Thomas E. Mann and Timothy Taylor. Washington, D.C.: Brookings Institution: 81-112.

Porter, Ann (1993). "Women and Income Security in the Post-War Period: The Case of Unemployment Insurance." *Labour/Le Travail* 31(Spring): 111-144.

Pottie Bunge, V. (2000a). "Spousal violence." In *Family Violence in Canada: A Statistical Profile 2000*, edited by V. Pottie Bunge and D. Locke. Ottawa: Statistics Canada: 11-19.

___, (2000b). "Abuse of Older Adults by Family Members." In *Family Violence in Canada: A Statistical Profile 2000*, edited by V. Pottie Bunge and D. Locke. Ottawa: Statistics Canada: 27-30.

Pottie Bunge, V. and J. Sauve (2002). "Declines in Spousal Homicide." In *Family Violence in Canada: A Statistical Profile 2002*, edited by C. Trainor. Ottawa: Statistics Canada: 9-12.

Potuchek, J. L. (1997). *Who Supports the Family: Gender and Breadwinning in Dual-Earner Marriages* Stanford, California: Stanford University Press.

Prentice, Alison et al. (1988). *Canadian Women. A History*. Toronto: Harcourt Brace Jovanovich.

Pryor, Jan and Bryan Rodgers (2001). *Children in Changing Families. Life After Parental Separation*. Oxford: Blackwell Publishers.

Pulkingham, Jane and Gordon Ternowetsky (1997). "The Changing Context of Child and Family Policies." In *Child and Family Policies. Struggles, Strategies and Options*, edited by J. Pulkingham and G. Ternowetsky. Halifax: Fernwood: 14-39.

Pupo, Norene (1988). "Preserving Patriarchy: Women, the Family and the State." In *Reconstructing the Canadian Family: Feminist Perspectives*, edited by N. Mandell and A. Duffy. Toronto: Butterworths: 207-237.

Queen, Stuart A., Robert W. Habenstein, and J. S. Quadagno (1985). *The Family in Various Cultures* (5th edition). New York: Harper and Row.

Quinn, M. J. and S. K. Tomita (1986). *Elder Abuse and Neglect: Causes, Diagnosis and Intervention Strategies*. New York: Springer.

Ralston, Helen (1997). "Arranged, 'Semi-Arranged' and 'Love' Marriages Among South Asian Immigrant Women in the Diaspora and their Non-Migrant Sisters in India and Fiji." *International Journal of Sociology of the Family* 27(2): 43-68.

Ram, Bali (1990). *New Trends in the Family. Demographic Facts and Figures*. Statistics Canada (Catalogue no. 91-535E). Ottawa: Minister of Supply and Services Canada, March.

___, (1994). "Family Formation" In *Perspectives on Canada's Populations. An Introduction to Concepts and Issues*, edited by Frank Trovato and Carl F. Grindstaff. Toronto: Oxford University Press.

Ramcharan, Subhas (1982). *Racism: Nonwhites in Canada*. Toronto: Butterworths.

Ramu, G. N. and Nicholas Tavuchis (1986). "The Valuation of Children and Parenthood Among the Voluntarily Childless and Parental Couples in Canada." *Journal of Comparative Family Studies* XVII (1): 99-115.

Ranson, G. (1998). "Paid work, family work and the discourse of the 'full-time mother'." *Journal of the Association for Research on Mothering* 1(1): 57-66.

___, (2001). "Men at work: change—or no change?—in the era of the 'new father'." *Men and Masculinities* 4(1): 3-26.

___, (2003). "Different paths, different parents? An exploration of the discursive framing of mothering and fathering in 'non-traditional' Canadian families." Paper presented at the Annual meeting, Canadian Sociology and Anthropology Association, Dalhousie University, Halifax.

Raphael, J. (2001a). "Domestic Violence as a Welfare-to-Work Barrier: Research and Theoretical issues." In *Sourcebook on Violence Against Women*, edited by C.M. Renzetti, J.L. Edleson and R. Kennedy Bergen. Thousand Oaks, CA: Sage: 443-456.

___, (2001b). "Public Housing and Domestic Violence." *Violence Against Women* 7: 699-706.

Rebick, Judy (2000). *Imagine Democracy*. Toronto: Stoddart

Reitsma-Street, Marge (1991). "Girls Learn to Care; Girls Policed to Care," In *Women's Caring: Feminist Perspectives on Social Welfare*, edited by Carol Baines, Patricia Evans and Sheila Neysmith. Toronto: McClelland and Stewart.

Rennison, C. and M. Rand (2003). "Nonlethal Intimate Partner Violence Against Women: A Comparison of Three Age Cohorts." *Violence Against Women* 9: 1409-1416.

Renzetti, C. M. and D. Curran (1995). *Women, Men and Society*. Boston: Allyn and Bacon.

Renzetti, C. M., J. L. Edleson, and R. Kennedy Bergen (2001). *Sourcebook on Violence Against Women*, edited by C. M. Renzetti, J. L. Edleson and R. K. Bergen. Thousand Oaks, CA: Sage.

Renzetti, C. M. and S. L. Maier (2002). "Private Crime in Public Housing: Fear of Crime and Violent Victimization Among Women Public Housing Residents." *Women's Health and Urban Life* 1: 46-65.

Report of the Royal Commission on Aboriginal Peoples (1996). Vol. 3, "Gathering Strength." Ottawa: Minister of Supply and Services: 9-106.

Reskin, B. and Patricia Roos (1991). *Job Queues, Gender Queues: Explaining Women's Inroads into Male Occupations*. Philadelphia: Temple University Press.

"Responses to Special Section on Family Textbooks (July 1997)," (various authors) (1998.) *Family Relations* 47(1): 5-6.

Richard, Madeline A. (1992). *Ethnic Groups and Marital Choices: Ethnic History and Marital Assimilation in Canada, 1871 and 1971*. Vancouver: UBC Press.

Richardson, C. J. (2001). "Divorce and Remarriage." In *Families: Changing Trends in Canada* (4th edition.), edited by M. Baker. Toronto: McGraw-Hill Ryerson: 208-237.

Richardson, D. (1993). *Women, Motherhood, and Childrearing*. New York: St. Martin's Press.

Riley, Denyse (1988). "Am I that Name?" *Feminism and the Category of 'Women' in History*. Minneapolis: University of Minnesota Press.

Risman, B. and D. Johnson-Sumerford (1998). "Doing it fairly: a study of post-gender families." *Journal of Marriage and the Family* 60 (February): 23-40.

Rogness, M. M. (2003). Toward an Integrated Male Peer Support Model of Marital/Cohabiting Rape in the United States. M.A. Thesis, Department of Sociology, Ohio University.

Roscoe, B., M. P. Goodwin and D. Kennedy (1987). "Sibling Violence and Agonistic Interactions Experienced by Early Adolescents." *Journal of Family Violence* 2: 121-137.

Rosenfeld, Mark (1988). "'It was a Hard Life': Class and Gender in the Work and Family Rhythms of a Railway Town." In *Canadian Family History*, edited by B. Bradbury. Toronto: Copp-Clark Pittman.

Rosenthal, Carolyn (1985). "Kinkeeping in the Familial Division of Labor," *Journal of Marriage and the Family* 47: 965-974.

Ross, D. P. and P. Roberts (1999) *Income and Child Well-Being: A New Perspective on the Poverty Debate.* Ottawa: Canadian Council on Social Development.

Roy, Patricia E. (1981). "Citizens Without Voices: East Asians in British Columbia, 1872-1947." In *Ethnicity, Power and Politics in Canada*, edited by Jorgen Dahlie and Tissa Fernando. Toronto: Mathuen: 151-171.

Rubin, J. (1997). "Gender, equality and the culture of organizational assessment." *Gender, Work and Organization* 4(1): 24-34.

Rubin, L. (1990). *Erotic Wars*. New York: Farrar, Straus and Giroux.

Russell, D. E. H. (1990). *Rape in Marriage*. New York: Macmillan.

___, (2001). "Defining Femicide and Related Concepts." In *Femicide in Global Perspective*, edited by D.E.H. Russell and R.A. Harmes. New York: Teachers College Press: 12-28.

Rutherford, Myra. (2002). *Women and the White Man's God: Gender and Race in the Canadian Mission Field*. Vancouver: UBC Press.

Sainsbury, Diane (1993). "Dual Welfare and Sex Segregation of Access to Social Benefits: Income Maintenance Policies in the U.K., the U.S., the Netherlands and Sweden." *Journal of Social Policy* 22(1): 69-98.

Sangster, Joan (2000). *Regulating Girls and Women: Sexuality, Family and the Law, Ontario, 1920-1960*. Oxford University Press.

Satzewich, V. (1993). "Migrant and Immigrant Families in Canada: State Coercion and Legal Control in the Formation of Ethnic Families." *Journal of Comparative Family Studies* 24: 315-338.

Saunders, D. (1986). "When Battered Women Use Violence: Husband Abuse or Self-Defense?" *Violence and Victims* 1: 47-60.

Sayer, L. C. and S. M. Bianchi (2000). "Women's Economic Independence and the Probability of Divorce." *Journal of Family Issues* 21: 906-943.

Scanzoni, John (1997). "A Reply to Glenn. Fashioning Families and Policies for the Future—Not the Past." *Family Relations* 46(3): 213-217.

Schoen, R., N. M. Astone, K. Rothert, N. J. Standish, and Y. J. Kim (2002). "Women's Employment and Marital Happiness, and Divorce." *Social Forces* 81: 643-662.

Schulman, M.A. (1979). *A Survey of Spousal Violence Against Women in Kentucky*. Washington, D.C.: Law Enforcement Assistance Administration.

Schwartz, M. D. (2000). "Methodological Issues in the Use of Survey Data for Measuring and Characterizing Violence Against Women." *Violence Against Women* 6: 815-838.

___, (2002). *Marital Rape*. Unpublished Manuscript, Ohio University.

Schwartz, M. D. and W. S. DeKeseredy (1997). *Sexual Assault on the College Campus: The Role of Male Peer Support*. Thousand Oaks, CA: Sage.

Seaward, Marty R. (1999). "The Sandwich Generation Copes with Elder Care." *Benefits Quarterly* 15(2): 41-48.

Seccombe, Karen (1992). "Employment, the Family, and Employer-Based Policies," In *Gender, Families and Elder Care*, edited by Jeffrey W. Dwyer and Raymond T. Coward. Newbury Park, CA: Sage.

Seccombe, Wally (1991). *A Millennium of Family Change: Feudalism to Capitalism*. London: Verso.

___, (1993). *Weathering the Storm Working Class Families from the Industrial Revolution to the Fertility Decline*. London:Verso.

Seeley, J., A. Sim, and E. Loosely (1956). *Crestwood Heights*. Toronto: University of Toronto Press.

Seltzer, J. A. (1991). "Relationships Between Fathers and Children Who Live Apart: The Father's Role After Separation." *Journal of Marriage and the Family* 53: 79-102.

___, (1994). "Consequences of Marital Dissolution for Children." *Annual Review of Sociology* 20: 235-266.

Sernau, S. (2001). *Worlds Apart: Social Inequalities in a New Century*. Thousand Oaks, CA: Pine Forge Press.

Sev'er, A. (1992). *Women and Divorce in Canada: A Sociological Analysis*. Toronto, Canada: Canadian Scholars' Press.

___, (2002). *Fleeing the House of Horrors: Women Who Have Left Abusive Partners*. Toronto: University of Toronto Press.

Shimoni, R., David Este, and Dawne E. Clark (2003). "Paternal Engagement in Immigrant and Refugee Families." *Journal of Comparative Family Studies* 34(4): 555-568.

Shorter, E. (1975). *The Making of the Modern Family*. New York: Basic Books.

Shragge, Eric (1997). *Workfare: Ideology for a New Under-Class*. Toronto: Garamonde.

Silver, C. (2000). "Being There: The Time Dual-Earner Couples Spend With Their Children." *Canadian Social Trends* (Summer): 26 - 29.

Silvera, Makeda (1989). *Silenced*. (2nd edition). Toronto: Sister Vision Press.

Silverman, Eliane Leslau (1984). *The Last Best West. Women on the Alberta Frontier, 1880-1930*. Montreal: Eden Press.

Skolnik, Arlene (1997). "A Response to Glenn. The Battle of the Textbooks: Bringing in the Culture War." *Family Relations* 46(3): 219-222.

Smart, Carol and Bren Neale (1999). *Family Fragments?* Cambridge: Polity Press.

Smith, Elizabeth (1980). *'A Woman with a Purpose': The Diaries of Elizabeth Smith, 1872-1884*, edited, with an Introduction by Veronica Strong-Boag. Toronto: University of Toronto Press.

Smith, J. E., V. A. Waldorf, and D. L. Trembath (1990). "Single White Male Looking for Thin, Very Attractive..." *Sex Roles* 23(11/12): 675-685.

Smith, M. D. (1986). "Effects of Question Format on the Reporting of Woman Abuse: A Telephone Survey Experiment." *Victimology* 11: 430-438.

___, (1987). "The Incidence and Prevalence of Woman Abuse in Toronto." *Violence and Victims* 2: 173-187.

___, (1990). "Patriarchal Ideology and Wife Beating: A Test of a Feminist Hypothesis." *Violence and Victims* 5: 257-273.

___, (1994). "Enhancing the Quality of Survey Data on Violence Against Women: A Feminist Approach." *Gender and Society* 8: 109-127.

Smith, Raymond T. (1996). *The Matrifocal Family: Power, Pluralism and Politics*. New York: Routledge.

Snell, James (1988). "Marital Cruelty: Women and the Nova Scotia Divorce Court, 1900-1930." *Acadiensis* 18(1).

___, (1991). *In the Shadow of the Law: Divorce in Canada, 1900-1939*. Toronto: University of Toronto Press.

Spock, B. (1945). *Baby and Child Care*. New York: Pocket Books.

Stacey, Judith (1990). *Brave New Families: Stories of Domestic Upheaval in Late Twentieth Century America*. USA: Basic Books.

___, (1996). *In the Name of the Family*. Boston: Beacon.

Stacey, J. and T. Biblarz. (2001). "(How) does the sexual orientation of parents matter?" *American Sociological Review* 66(2): 159-185.

Stanko, E. A. (1985). *Intimate Intrusions: Women's Experiences of Male Violence*. London: Routledge.

___, (1990). *Everyday Violence: How Women and Men Experience Sexual and Physical Danger*. London: Pandora.

Staples, Robert and Alfredo Mirande (1989). "Racial and Cultural Variations Among American Families." In *Family in Transition* (6th edition.), edited by A. Skolnick and J. Skolnick. Glenview, Il.:Scott, Foresman and Company: 480-503.

Statistics Canada (1988). *Marrying and Divorcing: A Status Report.* Ottawa: Statistics Canada.

___, (1993). *Violence Against Women Survey.* Ottawa: Statistics Canada.

___, (1997). "1996 Census: Marital Status, common-law unions and families." *The Daily* October 14.

___, (1998). *Characteristics of Dual-Earner Families 1996.* Ottawa: Ministry of Industry.

___, (1999). "Marriages." *The Daily* October 28.

___, (1999). "Survey of Labour and Income Dynamics: The Wage Gap between Men and Women." *The Daily* December 20.

___, (2000). "*Women in Canada 2000: A Gender-based Statistical Report.*" Ottawa: Industry Canada.

___, (2001). *Canada Year Book 2001.* Ottawa: Minister of Industry.

___, (2001). "Ethnocultural Portrait of Canada." *2001 Census of Population.* Ottawa: Statistics Canada. http://www.statcan.ca

___, (2002). Family violence: Impacts and consequences of spousal violence. *The Daily* June 26. [Online]. Available: http://www.statcan.ca/Daily/English/020626/d020626a.htm.

___, (2002). *Report on the Demographic Situation in Canada* (Catalogue no. 91-209XPE). Ottawa: Statistics Canada.

___, (2002). "2001 Census: marital status, common-law status, family dwellings and households." *The Daily* October 22.

___, (2002a). "Divorces." *The Daily* (December 2): 9-11.

___, (2002a). Table 051-0001: Estimates of Population by Age Group and Sex, Canada, Provinces and Territories, Annual. E-stat [on line retrieval system]. Statistics Canada Census.

___, (2002a). *Longitudinal Survey of Immigrants to Canada: Process, Progress and Prospects* (Catalogue no. 89-611-XIE). www.statcan.ca/english/freepub/89-611-XIE/tables/table5.htm.

___, (2002a). *Canadian Social Trends* (Catalogue no. 11-008) Winter: 29. Ottawa, Canada.

___, (2002a, b, c, d). *Changing Conjugal Life in Canada* (Catalogue no. 89-576-XIE). Ottawa, Canada.

___, (2002b). *Profile Of Canadian Families and Households: Diversification Continues* (Catalogue no. 96F0030XIE2001003).

___, (2002b). "Median age reaches all time high." *Census 2001, Analysis Series, Age and Sex Profile.* Retrieved August 8, 2003. http://www.statcan.ca

___, (2002c). "Proportion of 'traditional' families continues to decline." *Census 2001, Analysis Series, Canadian Families and Households.* Retrieved August 8, 2003. http://www.statcan.ca

___, (2002e). "More seniors living with a spouse, more living alone and fewer living in health care institutions." *Census 2001, Analysis Series, Canadian Families and Households.* Retrieved August 8, 2003. http://www.statcan.ca

___, (2003b). "Canada's Demographic Situation: Fertility of Immigrant Women." *The Daily* December 22.

___, (2003). *Census of Canada 2001.* Ottawa: Ministry of Industry, Science and Technology. http://www.statcan.ca

___, (2003). *Highlights of the Longitudinal Survey of Immigrants to Canada, 2000-2001* (Catalogue no. 89-611-XIE). Ottawa: Statistics Canada.

___, (2003a). "Average Time Spent on Activities, by Sex." Canadian Statistics (online), www.statcan.ca.

___, (2003a). Participation and Activity Limitation Survey: Children with Disabilities. *The Daily* July 29.

___, (2003a). *Annual Demographic Statistics 2002.* (Catalogue no. 91-213-XPB). Ottawa: Statistics Canada

___, (2003b). "The People; Marriage." *The Canada E-Book.*   Retrieved August 8, 2003. http://www.statcan.ca

___, (2003b, c). *Canadian Social Trends* (Catalogue no. 11-008), (Spring). Ottawa: Statistics Canada.

___, (2003b). *Update on families. Canadian Social Trends* (Catalogue no. 11-008). (Summer): 11-13.

___, (2003c). *Women in Canada: Work chapter updates* (Catalogue no. 89F0133XIE). Ottawa: Ministry of Industry.

___, (2003c). " Marriages." *The Daily* June 2. Ottawa: Statistics Canada.

___, (2003c). "General Social Survey: Social Support and Aging." *The Daily* September 2. www.-statcan.ca/Daily/English/030902/d030902a.htm

___, (2004). "Divorces," *The Daily* May 4.

___, (2004a). "Caring for Seniors." *Canada e-book* (From General Social Survey 1998). Retrieved January 21, 2004. http://www.statcan.ca

___, (2004b). *2001* "Hours spent providing unpaid care to seniors." *Census of Canada* (Catalogue no. 97F0013XCB01004). Ottawa: Statistics Canada.   Retrieved June 10 2004. www.statcan.ca

Status of Women (1990). *Canada Nairobi Forward-Looking Strategies for the Advancement of Women: Issues and the Canadian Situation.* Ottawa: Status of Women Canada.

Steinmetz, S. K. (1997). "The Use of Force for Resolving Family Conflict: The Training Ground for Abuse." *The Family Coordinator* 26: 19-26.

___, (1977-78). "The Battered Husband Syndrome." *Victimology* 3-4: 499-509.

___, (1982). "A Cross-Cultural Comparison of Sibling Violence." *International Journal of Family Psychiatry* 2: 337-351.

Steinmetz, S. K. and D. J. Amsden (1983). "Dependent Elders, Family Stress and Abuse." In *Family Relationships in Late Life,* edited by T. H. Brubaker. Beverly Hills: Sage.

Stewart, S. D., W. D. Manning, and P. J. Smock (2003). "Union Formation among Men in the U.S.: Does Having Prior Children Matter?" *Journal of Marriage and the Family* 65: 90-104.

Stone, L. (1990). *Road to Divorce: England, 1530-1987.* Oxford: Oxford University Press.

Strain, Laurel and B. J. Payne (1992). "Social Networks and Patterns of Social Interaction Among Ever-Single and Separated/Divorced Elderly Canadians." *Canadian Journal on Aging* 11(1): 31-53.

Strange, Carolyn (1988). "From Modern Babylon to a City Upon a Hill: The Toronto Social Survey of 1915 and the Search for Sexual Order in the City." In *Patterns of the Past. Interpreting Ontario's History,* edited by Roger Hall, William Westfall and Laurel Sefton McDowell. Toronto: University of Toronto Press.

Straus, M. A. (1979). "Measuring Intrafamily Conflict and Violence: The Conflict Tactics (CT) Scales." *Journal of Marriage and the Family* 41: 75-88.

___, (1994). *Beating the Devil Out of Them: Corporal Punishment in American Families.* New York: Lexington Books.

___, (1998). "The Controversy Over Domestic Violence by Women: A Methodological, Theoretical, and Sociology of Science Analysis." Paper presented at the Claremont Symposium on Applied Social Psychology on Violence in Intimate Relationships. Claremont, CA, February.

Straus, M. A. and R. J. Gelles (1986). "Societal Change and Change in Family Violence from 1975 to 1985 as Revealed by Two National Surveys." *Journal of Marriage and the Family* 48: 465-479.

Straus, M. A., R. J. Gelles, and S. K. Steinmetz (1981). *Behind Closed Doors: Violence in the American Family.* New York: Anchor.

Straus, M.A., S. L. Hamby, S. Boney-McCoy, and D. B. Sugarman (1996). "The Revised Conflict Tactics Scales (CTS2): Development and Preliminary Psychometric Data." *Journal of Family Issues* 17: 283-316.

Straus, M. A. and C. Smith (1990). "Family Patterns and Child Abuse." In *Physical Violence in American Families: Risk Factors and Adaptions to Violence in 8,145 Families,* edited by M. A. Straus and R. J. Gelles. New Brunswick, NJ: Transaction: 245-262.

Straus, M. A. and S. Sweet (1992). "Verbal/Symbolic Aggression in Couples: Incidence Rates and Relationships to Personal Characteristics." *Journal of Marriage and the Family* 54: 346-357.

Strong-Boag, Veronica (1979). "Wages for Housework: Mothers' Allowances and the Beginnings of Social Security in Canada." *Journal of Canadian Studies* 14: 24-34.

Sullivan, Maureen (1996). "Rozzie and Harriet: Gender and Family Patterns of Lesbian Coparents." *Gender and Society* 10(6): 747-768.

Sutherland, Neil (1976). *Children in English-Canadian Society. Framing the Twentieth-Century Consensus.* Toronto: University of Toronto Press.

___, (1990). "'We always had things to do': The Paid and Unpaid Work of Anglophone Children between 1920 and the 1960s." *Labour/Le Travail* 25(Spring).

Sweeney, M. M. (1997). "Remarriage of Men and Women after Divorce: The Role of Socioeconomic Prospects." *Journal of Family Issues* 18: 479-502.

Swift, Karen J. (1995). *Manufacturing 'Bad Mothers': A Critical Perspective on Child Neglect.* Toronto: University of Toronto Press.

Synge, Jane (1980). "Work and Family Support Patterns of the Aged in the Early Twentieth Century." In *Aging in Canada: Social Perspectives*, edited by Victor W. Marshall. Don Mills, Ontario: Fitzhenry and Whiteside.

Thobani, Sunera (1999). "Closing the Nation's Ranks: Canadian Immigration Policy in the 21st Century," In *Reclaiming the Future. Women's Strategies for the 21st Century*, edited by Somer Brodribb. Charlottetown: Gynergy Books: 75-96.

Thomas, Derrick (2001). "Evolving Family Living Arrangements of Canada's Immigrants." *Canadian Social Trends* (Summer): 16-22.

Thomson, E. and U. Colella (1992). "Cohabitation and Marital Stability: Quality or Commitment?" *Journal of Marriage and the Family* 54(1): 259-67.

Thorne-Finch, R. (1992). *Ending the Silence: The Origins and Treatment of Male Violence Against Women.* Toronto: University of Toronto Press.

Thornton, A. and L. Young-DeMarco (2001). "Four Decades of Trends in Attitudes Toward Family Issues in the United States: The 1960s Through the 1990s." *Journal of Marriage and the Family* 63: 1009-1037.

Thornton, Patricia A and Sherry Olson (1991). "Family Contexts of Fertility and Infant Survival in Nineteenth-Century Montreal." *Journal of Family History* 16(4).

Tindale, J. A., J. E. Norris, R. Berman and S. Kulack (1994). *Intergenerational Conflict and the Prevention of Abuse Against Older Persons.* Ottawa: Family Violence Prevention Division, Health Canada.

Tjaden, P. and N. Thoennes (1998). *Stalking in America: Findings from the National Violence Against Women Survey.* Washington, D.C.: National Institute of Justice and Centers for Disease Control and Prevention, Department of Justice.

Torjman, Sherri and Ken Battle (1999). *Good Work. Getting it and Keeping it.* Ottawa: Caledon Institute of Social Policy.

The Toronto Star (2000). "Gay couples win historic fight" (by Valerie Lawton) February 12.

Tougas, J. (2001a). "What we can learn from the Quebec experience." In *Our Children's Future: Child Care Policy in Canada*, edited by G. Cleveland and M. Krashinsky. Toronto: University of Toronto Press.

___, (2001b). "Quebec's child care model: making family a priority." *Transition* 31(4): 13.

Tower, C. C. (2002). *Understanding Child Abuse and Neglect.* Boston: Allyn and Bacon.

Trainor, C. (2002a). "Highlights." In *Family Violence in Canada: A Statistical Profile 2002*, edited by C. Trainor. Ottawa: Statistics Canada: 1.

___, (2002b). *Family Violence in Canada: A Statistical Profile 2002*, edited by C. Trainor. Ottawa: Statistics Canada.

Trainor, C., M. Lambert and M. Dauvergne (2002). "Spousal Violence." In *Family Violence in Canada: A Statistical Profile 2002*, edited by C. Trainor. Ottawa: Statistics Canada: 6-9.

Trainor, C. and K. Mihorean (2001). *Family Violence in Canada: A Statistical Profile 2001*. Ottawa: Statistics Canada.

Trigger, Bruce (1976). *The Children of Aataentsic*. Montreal and Kingston: McGill-Queen's University Press.

Trocmé, N., B. Fallon, B. MacLaurin and B. Copp (2002). *The Changing Face of Child Welfare Investigations in Ontario*. Ottawa: Centre of Excellence for Child Welfare.

Trocme, N., B. MacLaurin, B. Fallon, J. Daciuk, D. Billingsley, M. Tourigny, M. Mayer, J. Wright, K. Barter, G. Burford, J. Hornick, R. Sullivan and B. McKenzie (2001). *Canadian Incidence Study of Reported Child Abuse and Neglect: Final Report*. Ottawa: Public Works and Government Services of Canada.

Tzeng, M. (1992). "The Effects of Socioeconomic Heterogamy and Changes on Marital Dissolution for First Marriages." *Journal of Marriage and the Family* 54: 609-619.

Udry, J. R. (1974). *Social Context of Marriage* (3rd edition). Philadelphia: J. B. Lippincott.

Uhlenberg, P. (1989). "Remarriage: A Life-Cycle Perspective." In *Later Phases of the Family Cycle*, edited by C. Höln and R. Mackensen. Oxford, England: Clarendon Press: 66-82.

Uhlenberg, P. and K. S. Y. Chew (1986). "The Changing Place of Remarriage in the Life Course." In *Current Perspectives on Aging and the Life Cycle*, edited by Z. S. Blau. Greenwich, CT: JAI Press: 23-52.

UNICEF (2000). *A League Table of Child Poverty in Rich Nations*. Florence: UNICEF (Innocenti Research Centre).

United Nations (2000). *The World's Women 2000*. New York: United Nations.

Ursel, Jane (1992). *Private Lives, Public Policy. 100 Years of State Intervention in the Family*. Toronto: Women's Press.

Valverde, Mariana (1991). *The Age of Light, Soap, and Water. Moral Reform in English Canada, 1885-1925*. Toronto: McClelland and Stewart.

van den Hoonaard, Deborah K. (2002). "Attitudes of Older Widows and Widowers in New Brunswick, Canada Towards New Partnerships." *Ageing International* 27(4): 79-92.

Vanier Institute of the Family (1994). *Profiling Canada's Families*. Ottawa: Vanier Institute of the Family.

___, (2000). *Profiling Canada's Families II*. Ottawa, Canada: Vanier Institute of the Family. http://www.vifamily.ca/library/profiling2/profiling2.html.

Van Kirk, Sylvia (1980). *"Many Tender Ties": Women in Fur-Trade Society, 1670-1870*. Winnipeg: Watson and Dwyer.

Vaux, A. (1985). "Variations in Social Support Associated with Gender, Ethnicity, and Age." *Journal of Social Issues* 41: 89-110.

Veevers, Jean (1980). *Childless By Choice*. Toronto: Butterworths.

Venkatesh, S. (2000). *American Project: The Rise and Fall of a Modern Ghetto*. Cambridge: Harvard University Press.

Vinton, L. (2003). "A Model Collaborative Project Toward Making Domestic Violence Centers Elder Ready." *Violence Against Women* 9: 1504-1513.

Vosko, L., N. Zukewich, and C. Cranford (2003). "Precarious jobs: a new typology of employment." *Perspectives* (Catalogue no. 75-001-XPE), Winter: 39-49.

Walker, L. (1979). *The Battered Woman*. New York: Harper and Row.

Wall, G. (2001). "Moral Constructions of Motherhood in Breastfeeding Discourse." *Gender and Society* 15(4): 592 - 610.

___, (2004a). "Is Your Child's Brain Potential Maximized?: Mothering in an Age of New Brain Research." *Atlantis*: 28(2): 41 - 50.

___, (2004b). "Maternal Encounters with Cultural Imperatives Surrounding Child Development." Paper presented at the 2004 Qualitative Analysis Conference, Carleton University, Ottawa.

Wallace, H. (1996). *Family Violence: Legal, Medical, and Social Perspectives*. Boston: Allyn and Bacon.

___, (1999). *Family Violence: Legal, Medical, and Social Perspectives* (2nd edition). Boston: Allyn and Bacon.

Walzer, S. (1996). "Thinking about the baby: gender and divisions of infant care." *Social Problems* 43(2): 219-234.

Ward, Peter (1990). Courtship, Love, and Marriage in Nineteenth-Century English Canada Montreal and Kingston: McGill-Queen's University Press.

Ward-Griffin, Catherine, and Victor W. Marshall (2003). "Reconceptualizing the relationship between 'public' and 'private' eldercare." *Journal of Aging Studies* 17(2): 189 - 208.

Waring, Marilyn (1990). *If Women Counted*. San Francisco: Harper.

Watson, M. (2001). "Embedding the 'new economy' in Europe: a study in the institutional specificities of knowledge-based growth." *Economy and Society* 30(4): 504-523.

Wayne, Michael (1995). "The Black Population of Canada West on the Eve of the American Civil War: A Reassessment Based on the Manuscript Census of 1861." *Histoire sociale/Social History* XVIII: 56.

Wearing, B. (1984). *The Ideology of Motherhood*. Sydney: Allen and Unwin.

Websdale, N. (2001). *Policing the Poor: From Slave Plantation to Public Housing*. Boston: Northeastern University Press.

Weedon, Chris (1999). *Feminism, Theory and the Politics of Difference*. Oxford: Blackwell.

Weeks, Jeffrey (2002). "Elective Families: Lesbian and Gay Life Experiments." In *Analysing Families*, edited by A. Carling, S. Duncan and R. Edwards. London: Routledge: 218-228.

Weeks, R. and C. S. Widom (1998). "Self-Reports of Early Childhood Victimization Among Incarcerated Males." *Journal of Interpersonal Violence* 13: 346-361.

Weir, L. (1996). "Recent developments in the government of pregnancy." *Economy and Society* 25(3): 372-392.

Weiss, N. (1978). "The Mother-child Dyad Revisited: Perceptions of Mothers and Children in Twentieth Century Child-rearing Manuals." *Journal of Social Issues* 34(2): 29-45.

Weiss, R. (1984). "The Impact of Marital Dissolution on Income and Consumption in Single-Parent Households." *Journal of Marriage and the Family* 46: 115-127.

Weitzman, L. J. (1985). *The Divorce Revolution: The Unexpected Social and Economic Consequences for Women and Children in America*. New York: Free Press.

Wennemo, Irene (1992). "The Development of Family Policy." *Acta Sociologica* 35: 201-217.

___, (1994). *Sharing the Cost of Children*. Stockholm: Swedish Institute for Social Research.

Wente, M. (1994). "Why the Statscan Tale Needs Debunking." *The Globe and Mail* December 3: A2.

West, C. and D. Zimmerman (1987). "Doing gender." *Gender and Society* 1(2): 125-151.

Wickberg, Edgar (1981). "Chinese Organizations and the Canadian Political Process: Two Case Studies," In *Ethnicity, Power and Politics in Canada*, edited by Jorgen Dahlie and Tissa Fernando. Toronto: Mathuen: 172-176.

Widom, C. S. (1989). "Child Abuse, Neglect and Violent Criminal Behavior." *Criminology* 27: 252-271.

Wiehe, V. R. (1997). *Sibling Abuse: Hidden Physical, Emotional and Sexual Trauma* (2nd edition). Thousand Oaks, CA: Sage.

Wiles, Janine (2003). "Informal Caregivers' Experiences of Formal Support in a Changing Context." *Health and Social Care in the Community* 11(3): 189-207.

Wilkie, J. (1993). "Changes in U.S. men's attitudes toward the family provider role." *Gender and Society* 7: 261-279.

Wilson, W. J. (1996). *When Work Disappears: The World of the New Urban Poor*. New York: Knopf.

Worswick, Christopher (2001). "School Performance of the Children of Immigrants in Canada, 1994-1998." (Cat. no. 11F0019MIE, No. 78). *Analytical Studies Branch Research Paper Series*. Ottawa: Statistics Canada

Wu, Zheng (1994). "Remarriage in Canada: A Social Exchange Perspective." *Journal of Divorce and Remarriage* 21: 191-224.

___, (1999) "Premarital Cohabitation and the Timing of First Marriage," *Canadian Review of Sociology and Anthropology* 36(1): 109-127.

___, (2000). *Cohabitation: An Alternative Form of Family Living*. Toronto: Oxford University Press.

Yeatman, Anna (1994). "The Epistemological Politics of Postmodern Feminist Theorizing." In *Postmodern Revisioning of the Political*. New York: Routledge.

Yllo, K. (1993). "Through a Feminist Lens: Gender, Power and Violence." In *Current Controversies on Family Violence*, edited by R.J. Gelles and D.R. Loseke. Newbury Park, CA: Sage: 47-62.

Young, Brian (1981). *George-Etienne Cartier. Montreal Bourgeois*. Kingston and Montreal: McGill-Queen's University Press.

Young, J. (1999). *The Exclusive Society*. London: Sage.

Zimmerman, Shirley L. (1992). *Family Policies and Family Well-Being. The Role of Political Culture*. Newbury Park, California: Sage.

Zukewich, Nancy (2003). "Unpaid Informal Caregiving." Statistics Canada (Catalogue no. 11-008). *Canadian Social Trends* 70(Fall): 14-18.

Photo Credits

Page 10, CP Picture Archive/John Kenney

Page 24, © Rubberball/Rubberball Productions

Page 30, CP Picture Archive/Fred Chartrand

Page 44, CP Picture Archive/Fred Chartrand

Page 55, © Mark Richards/PhotoEdit/Picture-Quest

Page 58, Superstock

Page 73, Photographer unknown/National Archives of Canada/PA-185530

Page 87, Unidentified artist/National Archives of Canada/C-108134

Page 107, CP Picture Archive/Aaron Harris

Page 109, © Digital Vision/Digital Vision

Page 126, Canadian Pacific Railway Archives BR.196

Page 127, William James Topley/National Archives of Canada/PA-010264

Page 149, © Plush Studios/Brand X Pictures

Page 159, CP Picture Archive/Logan Wallace

Page 170, © Deborah Baic, 2000

Page 175, © Annie-Griffiths-Belt/CORBIS/MAGMA

Page 182, © Digital Vision/Digital Vision

Page 196, Superstock

Page 215, Digital Imagery © copyright 2000 PhotoDisc, Inc.

Page 221, © Buccina Studios/Getty Images

Page 230, CP Picture Archive/Christinne Muschi

Page 249, © Laura Dwight/CORBIS

Page 261, Notman Photographic Archives, McCord Museum of Canadian History, Montreal

Page 273, CP/Richard Lam

Page 287, © Dick Luria 1994

Page 292, © Jacobs Stock Photography/Getty Images

Index

Aboriginal, 124–125
Aboriginal peoples, 44, 45–46, 60
    assimilation, 76
    childcare, 75
    division of labour by sex, 74–75
    education, 74, 88, 259
    European diseases, 76
    Europeans, first contact between, 72–76
    exploitation, 73
    homogeneous perspective, 74
    Indian Act, 76
    inter-racial unions, 73
    marriage, 75
    missionaries and, 73
    residential schools, 88, 259
    settlers, impact of, 124–125
    woman abuse, 240
abortions, 19
abuse. *See* child abuse; family violence; woman abuse
access, 211
    defined, 211–212
    detailed arrangements, 211
    "liberal," 211
    "reasonable," 211
adoption
    future of, 289–291
    same-sex couples, 61
    step-adoptions, 61
adoption rates, 19
advocacy for family reform, 273–275
African-Americans, 81
ageist bias, 58, 63
alimony, 93, 210–211, 282
American Revolution, 205
androcentricity, 58
Anne of Green Gables, 185
Aries, Philip, 163
arranged marriages, 8–11, 146, 155–156
artisanal families, 83–84
at-risk families, 263
attachment theory, 167–168

attrition (job), 195
authority system, 11

baby boom, 14, 93, 158, 185
bachelors, 184–185
Bales, Robert, 280, 281
Barrett, Michelle, 30
battered husband syndrome, 237
Becker, Gary, 186–187, 206
Berger, Brigitte, 29–30
Berger, Peter, 29–30
best interests of the child, 34
biases
    ageist bias, 58, 63
    androcentricity, 58
    application, example of, 61–63
    conservative bias, 56–58, 63
    double standards, 59
    gender insensitivity, 59
    heterosexist bias, 60–61, 62
    householdism, 59
    microstructural bias, 59–60, 62
    monolithic bias, 55–56, 62
    paradoxical gynocentricity, 58
    racist bias, 60, 63
    sexist bias, 58–59, 63
bigamy, 7
bilateral descent pattern, 11, 12
biological theories, earlier, 3
birth control, 148
    historical perspective, 79
Black women, oppression in U.S., 49
blended families, 25–26, 225–226
boundary maintaining, 41
Bowlby, John, 280
Boyd, Susan, 211
brain science, 172
bride price, 10

Campaign 2000, 273, 274
Canada Assistance Plan, 106–107, 176, 263, 266, 268
Canada Child Tax Benefit, 267, 268, 269
Canada Health and Social Transfer, 106, 266, 268

Canadian Charter of Rights and Freedoms, 266
Canadian Council on Social Development, 273
Canadian Incidence Study of Reported Child Abuse and Neglect, 244
Canadian national survey on woman abuse in dating, 230–234
capitalism, 113
capitalist liberal democracies, 36–37
caregiving, 182
caregiving families, 189–193
"census family," 5
Centuries of Childhood (Aries), 163
charter groups, 123–125
Cheal, David, 47, 49
Cherlin, Andrew, 226
child abuse, 229
    broad definition, 236
    extent of, 244–246
    multidimensional nature of, 235
    physical punishment as, 242–244, 246–247
    power, and, 247
    risk of crime, increase in, 245
    serious social problem, 244
    social learning theory, 246–247
    societal concerns about, 242–243
    theories of, 246–247
child custody, 216
    access. *See* access
    best interests of the child, 218
    bitterness of disputes, 211
    case law, 217
    disputes over, 34
    "friendly parent" presumption, 211
    joint legal, 211, 217–219
    maternal, right to, 262
    prior to twentieth century, 262
    shared parenting, 211, 218
    sole legal, 211

spousal violence, importance of, 211
tender years doctrine, 218
Child Custody Bill, 218
child labour, 85–86, 164
child poverty, 176–178, 267, 268, 274
Child Poverty Action Group, 269
Child Poverty Action League, 273
child-centred advice, 165
childbearing
    attitude data, 158
    changing patterns, 158
    future of, 289–291
    postponement of, 283
childcare, 3, 106–108, 269
    aboriginal peoples, 75
    children with special needs, 108
    culture of parents, compatibility with, 108
    divorce, 207
    employed parents, for, 107–109
    expense of, and limit on family size, 15
    family daycare providers, wages of, 107
    family size, and, 15
    funding, 106–107, 177
    income tax deduction, 106, 268
    inequitable provision, 107
    licensed, rarity of, 107
    low-income families, 106
    parental concerns, 106–109
    political importance of, 107–108
    Quebec, in, 106
    regulated, rarity of, 107
    subsidies, 106, 263
    women's responsibility for, 111
childhood, 163
    future trends, 175–179
childlessness, 23
children
    abuse of. *See* child abuse
    contribution to housework, 111
    costs of raising, 105–109
    custody, 34
    during industrialization era, 85–86, 88–89
    education, 88–89
    immigrants, of, 136–138
    poverty, 268, 274

remarriages, and, 225–226
socialization. *See* socialization
Chinese head tax, 128
Civil Code, 260, 262
civil law, 260
civil union, 61
"classwomb," 174
cluttered nest, 56
co-residence, 32
cohabitation, 13, 18–19, 146, 224
    alternative to marriage, as, 154–155
    breakdown, 208
    dissolution rates, 18
    future of, 283–286
    immigrants, 133
    increasing rates of, 208
    prelude to marriage, as, 154–155
cohort effect, 185–187
collective agreements, 115
collective bargaining, 115
Collins, Patricia Hill, 49
common law, 76, 78–79, 205, 260
    custody, 217
common-law couples, 99
common-law relationship, 13
    See also cohabitation
common-sense assumptions, 31
commuter marriages, 286
compulsory altruism, 191
Conflict Tactic Scale, 231, 237–240
conjugal violence, 236
conservative bias, 56–58, 63
conservative views, 261
contingent workforce, 103
contract work, 103
corporatist welfare state, 258–260
Council of Families in America, 62–63
Crestwood Heights (Seeley, Sim, and Loosely), 39, 280
Criminal Code, 231
crude birth rates, 14
cultural history of Canadian families
    Aboriginal peoples and Europeans, 72–76
    English Canadians, 76–80
    French Canadians, 76–80
    immigrants in Canada, 80–83
    middle-class families, 89–91
cultural variations
    arranged versus free-choice marriage, 8–11

authority system, 11
births outside marriage, rise in, 24–25
blended families, 25–26
bride price, 10
cohabitation versus legal marriage, 18–19
descent, patterns of, 11–12
dowry, 8–10
family trends, 12
fertility, decline in, 14–16
    impact of, 295–296
inheritance, 12
life expectancy, rising, 13–14
lone-parent families, increase in, 23–25
monogamy versus polygamy, 7–8
mothers in labour force, 17–18
nuclear versus extended families, 6–7
separation and divorce rates, 21–23
culture, 121
custody, 34, 216
    See also child custody
    common law, 217
Custom of Paris, 76, 77–78
cycles of violence, 42

Darwin, Charles, 35
dating, 146–147
    future of, 283–286
    video, 148
    violence, 230–234
Day, David, 211
dead-beat dads, 264
death of the family, 281
demographics, 187–189
dependency theory of elder abuse, 253–254
descent, patterns of, 11–12
developmental approaches, 42
division of labour
    changes in, 110–114
    children's contribution, 111
    divorce, and, 116–118
    dual-earner households, 116–118
    future of, 286–289
    implications of uneven division, 116–118
    inequitable, 111–112
    "marital power relations," and, 116–118

role reversal, 116–118
second shift, 111
time-use/time-budget studies, 111
women's responsibility for unpaid work, 111
divorce, 13, 34, 93, 202
access. *See* access
among immigrants, 138–139
before 1968, 93
Canada, in, 209–212
child custody. *See* child custody
child support. *See* support
childcare, 207
children, 208
cohabitation, 208
dissolvable social contract, 205
economic consequences of, 215–217
employment, 206
factors, 23
free choice versus arranged marriages, 8
grounds for, 203
historical perspective, 203–204
law reform in Canada, 21, 22, 209–212
legislative changes, 209–218
liberalization of divorce law, 203
"marriage breakdown" as grounds for, 21
marriage breakdown, relationship to, 203
mediation, encouragement of, 210
mid-life families, 187–188
no-fault, 207
outcomes, 215–221
patterns and processes, 211–215
poverty, 187–188, 215–217
rates of, 21–23, 211–215
spousal support. *See* support
uncontested, 210
unsatisfactory division of household labour, 116–118
women's income, and, 23
Divorce Act, 204
Divorce Act, 1968, 209, 211
Divorce Act, 1985, 209, 210, 221
divorce rate, 221
doctrine of coverture, 204
domestic labour. *See also* division of

labour
industrialization, effects of, 87–88
paid domestic workers, 45
time-use/time-budget studies, 111
unpaid, 46, 116–118
value of, 46
women's responsibility for, 111
domestic violence, 236
immigrants, 138
double standard, 59, 93, 147–148, 203, 284
dower, 77
dowry, 8–10
dual-career couples, 286
dual-earner families
cultural perspective, 104–105
division of labour in, 116–118
emergence of, 281
greater prosperity of, 295
"non-standard jobs," 100–101
societal changes, and, 104
wives' higher incomes, effect of, 102–104

early retirement, 195
economic abuse, 230
"economic family," 5
education, 164
Aboriginal peoples, 74, 259
kindergartens, 105
system, development of, 88
egalitarian family, myth of, 281
Eichler, Margrit, 30
elder abuse, 229
awareness of, increased, 252
dependency and, 253–254
extent of, 252–253
theories of, 253–254
eldercare, 113, 189, 190
elderly people, 189–193
emigration, 125
employment and divorce, 206
Employment Insurance, 108, 265
employment status, 104
empty nest, 56, 293
endogamy, 150
Engels, Frederick, 36, 43, 279
Erotic Wars (Rubin), 147
ethnic group, 122
ethnic intermarriage, 130–131
ethnicity. *See also* immigrants
definitions of, 122–125

general findings on ethnic families, 131–141
eugenicist, 79
exchange theory, 42, 146, 152–154
exogamy, 130–131, 152
experience hypothesis, 157
extended families, 6–7, 139–140, 146, 184, 279
First Nations, 6
extended family, 4, 31
extended kin group, 31

Factory Acts, 85–86, 164
familial ideology, 44–46
families
aging, 185–187
Becker model of, 186–187
boundaries of, 72
categorization, 181–187
changing, 26–28
definitions of, 4–5, 52–55
economic unit, 4–5
ethnic. *See* ethnicity; immigrants
farming, 83–84
functions, 4–5
labour market, 34
legal intervention, immunity from, 261
legal term, as, 32
legality, 4–5
meanings of, 31–32, 71
normative regulation, 32
shifting patterns of, 32–34
social unit, 4–5
structure, 4–5
trends in, 26–28
"what" definition, 52–53
"who" definition, 52–53
Family Allowances, 95, 266–267
family daycare providers, wages of, 107
family economies
apprenticeship, 84
artisanal families, 83–84
Factory Acts, 85–86
family wage economy, 83
farming families, 83–84
industrialization, 84–89
family economy, 83
family formation, mid-century patterns, 146
family life cycle, 56, 146
family money, 102–104
family policies

federal child/family benefits, 266–271
generosity, comparison of, 271–272
jurisdictional disputes, 272
maternity leave/benefits, 265–266
meaning of, 259–260
parental leave/benefits, 265–266
preconceived notions, and, 260
reform, advocacy for, 272–275
social assistance programs, 263–265
social service programs, 263–265
spending on, 275
working income supplement, 268
family preservation, 290
Family Shifts: Families, Policies, and Gender Equality (Eichler), 30
family trends, 12
family values, 52
family violence, 41, 236
breadth of definitions, 230–234
broad definitions, 234–236
child abuse. *See* child abuse
Conflict Tactics Scale, 231
conservative bias, and, 57–58
dating violence, 230–234
definitions, 229–239
elder abuse, 252–254
gender-neutral terms, 237–238
homicide, 239
legal definition, 230
multidimensional nature of, 235
narrow definitions, 231–234
nineteenth century, 93
sibling violence, 247–251
stepfamilies, 226
terminology, 236–239
versus "stranger danger," 229
wife beating. *See* woman abuse
women's motives for, 238–239
family wage, 88, 105
family wage economy, 83
farming families, 83–84
federal child/family benefits, 266–271
Federation nationale Saint Jean-Bap-

tiste, 91
feminist theories, 42, 43–47
domestic responsibilities and labour force opportunities, 116–118
economic consequences of divorce, 215
familial ideology, 44–46
nuclear families, 44
radical, 46–47
social reproduction, labour of, 46
socialist feminists, 46
structural-functionalism, criticism of, 45
fertility, 14, 158, 273
adoption rates, 19–20
age-specific rate, 15
birth control, 15
childcare effects, 17
compulsory education, effect of, 15
crude rate, 14
family planning, 15
First Nations, 16
immigrants, 15, 136
medically assisted, 20–21
remarriage, 222
test-tube babies, 20–21
total rate, 15
wage labour effect, 15, 17
fertility, decline in, 14–16
fetal rights, 173
filles du roi, 77
First Nations, 123
extended families, 6
fertility, 16
First Nations' families. *See* Aboriginal peoples
first wave feminism, 90–91
flexible work, 101
frail elderly, 197
Fraser Institute, 275
French Canadians. *See also* historical perspective
family size, 15–16, 79–80
fertility, 79–80
French Revolution, 205
Freud, Sigmund, 37, 280
Friedan, Betty, 202, 214
future of family life
adoption, 289–291
childbearing, 289–291
cohabitation, 283–286

cultural differences, impact of, 295–296
dating, 283–286
gender roles, 286–289
immigration, impact of, 295–296
marriage, 283–286
mid-life families, 291–295
older families, 291–295

Gairdner, William, 30, 36
gay and lesbian, 94, 272
marriage, 13, 52
gender gap in earnings, 104
gender insensitivity, 59
gender roles, 286–289
General Social Survey, 46, 103, 111–112, 157–158, 189, 190, 230, 237
genetic theories, 3
globalization, 101
good enough mothering, 48
"good family," 52
government policies. *See* state intervention
grandchildren, 295
Great Depression, 86, 93, 158

head tax, 81, 128
Health Canada, 244
heterogamy, 207
heterogeneous, 121
heterosexist bias, 60–61, 62
historical perspective
Aboriginal peoples. *See* Aboriginal peoples
birth control, 79
Common Law, 76, 78–79
conservative view of family, 79
Custom of Paris, 76, 77–78
family, importance of, 77
filles du roi, 77
large families and poverty, 79
marriages, 92
married women outside Quebec, 78
Quebec Act of 1774, 78
homogamy, 150
homophobia, 60
homosexuality. *See also* lesbian and gay
heterosexist bias, 60–61

illegality of, 33
legal rights, 33
honeymoons, 150
"household," 5
householdism, 59

ideal mate, concept of, 150–152
ideational change, 205
ideology, 44
   gender, 100
immediate family, 32
immigrant women
   citizenship rights, 44
   domestic labour, 45
   lower birthrates, 15–16
   workforce, in, 134–136
immigrants. *See also* ethnicity
   African-Americans, 81
   arranged marriage, 155–156
   children, independence of,
   136–138
   children, marriage of, 137–138
   Chinese head tax, 81
   cohabitation, 133
   colour, of, 60
   conflict, 138–139
   customs, criticism of, 82
   discrimination against, 81
   domestic violence, 138
   empty residences in daytime,
   134–136
   extended family, reduction of,
   139–140
   family size, 136
   family solidarity, maintenance
   of, 138–139
   fertility, 15, 136
   gender roles, changes in, 136
   high cost of living, 134–136
   "last best west," 82
   mate selection, 132
   mothers, isolation of, 82
   moving back to country of origin, 139
   new families, formation of,
   137–138
   nuclear family, 139
   racism against, 81
   stress, 138–139
   women in workforce, 134–136
immigration, 96, 125
   Chinese bachelor community,
   128
   First Nations peoples, decline

   of, 124–125
   impact of, 295–296
   Italian immigration, case,
   130–131
   Jewish immigration, case,
   128–130
   merit system, 130–131
   multinational European,
   125–128
   "point system," 130–131
   post-World War II, 130–131
   pre-World War I, 128–130
   pre-World War II, 125–128
   recent trends, 130–131
   residential segregation,
   129–130
   social segregation, 129–130
   Upper Canada, settlement of,
   125
in vitro fertilization (IVF), 57, 188
incest taboo, 152
incestuous, 262
income support programs, 259
India, arranged marriages in, 9
Indian Acts, 76, 124–125
industrialization, 84–89, 100
infant mortality rates, 164–166
inheritance, 12
intensive parenting, 168–172
International Wages for Housework
   Campaign (1985), 46
intimacy
   changing patterns, 146
   dating, 146
   honeymoons, 150
   lesbian and gay partnering,
   159
   sexuality, and, 147–150
   singles advertisements, 148
   video dating, 148
intimate intrusions, 229
Inuit, 124–125
Invest in Kids, 172
Irish famine, 81
Iroquois Confederacy, 12
Italian immigration, case, 130–131

Jameson, Frederick, 48
Jewish immigration, case, 128–130
job retraining, 293
joint custody, 219
   See also child custody

Kennedy, Lillian, 184

kin group, 31
kin membership, 12
Kinsey studies of male sexuality,
   208
kinship, 32
kinship group, 75, 146

labour force/market, 25
   families, 34
   mothers in, 17–18
   "non-standard jobs," 100–101
   service positions, 100–101
   service sector, expansion of,
   18
   trends, 100–103
   women, increased participation
   of, 101–103
Laing, R. D., 41
Law Reform Commission of
   Canada, 209
law reform in Canada, 21, 22,
   209–212
Lawson, Emma, 184
Le Play, Frederic, 279
lesbian and gay partnering
   discrimination, 29
   family, definition of, 5
   intimacy, 159
   legal rights, 29
   relationship quality, 159–160
liberal feminism, 282
Liberal government (federal), 29
liberal welfare state, 258–260
life expectancy
   rising, 13–14
   women, 184
lifetime education, 293
lineage, 31
   Aboriginal people, 75
living apart together, 14
lone-parent families
   government support for, 95
   increase in, 23–25
   participation in work force,
   108
   post-War 40s and 50s, 93–94
   poverty rates, 25
   remarriage rates, 25
Lord Talfourd's Act, 218
love, 146
love match, 9
Lubbock, John, 36
lullaby lessons, 169
Macdonald, John A., 76, 128

maintenance, 210
male peer support model of wife
    abuse, 240–242
male-breadwinning family, 264
Malinowski, Bronislav, 38, 280
marital breakdown, 221
marital happiness and stability,
    160–161
marital norms, 226
marital violence, 236
marriage, 13, 24–25, 155
    Aboriginal peoples, 75
    arranged marriages, 8–11, 146
    Canada, rate in, 157
    children, and, 158
    contract, as, 23
    decrease in rate of, 150
    dissolution rates, 18
    divorce and, 157
    early colonial period, in, 92
    endogamy, 150
    exchange theory, 152–154
    exogamy, 152
    first, 158
    free-choice marriage, 8–11
    future of, 283–286
    gay and lesbian, 13
    homogamy, 150
    honeymoons, 150
    ideal mate, concept of,
        150–152
    immigrants, children of,
        137–138
    increased conflict within, 23
    marital happiness and stability,
        160–161
    New France, in, 92
    open, 281
    partner preferences, 150–152
    partners, similarities and dif-
        ferences between, 150–152
    patterns of, changing, 157
    postponement of, 283
    rate, 13
    remarriage. *See* remarriage
    romance and companionship,
        89
    same-sex. *See* lesbian and gay
    sex, stress on, 92
    social practices, changing, 33
    starter, 157
    versus cohabitation, 18–19
    wedding traditions, 149

marriage breakdown, 21, 203, 221,
    281
    See also divorce
marriage broker, 8
marriage market, 8, 153, 222
marriage squeeze, 154
Married Women's Property Act
    (1884), 78, 91, 261
Martin, Clara Brett, 78
Marx, Karl, 36, 43, 206
Marxist theories, 42–43
master discourses, 117
mate selection. *See* marriage
maternal deprivation, 166–167
maternal feminists, 272
maternal instincts, 3
maternalists, 90–91
maternity leave/benefits, 108,
    265–266
mating gradient, 153
matriarchal systems, 11
matriarchy, 11
matrifocal, 11
matrilocal system, 12
matrilocality, 11
matrimonial fault, 21
McIntosh, Mary, 30
Mead, George Herbert, 40
Mead, Margaret, 11, 280
men
    dating, 146
    erosion of authority, 18
    "fading father" stereotype, 218
    parental benefits, 108–109
    responsibilities, future, 288
Métis, 124–125
microstructural bias, 59–60, 62
mid-life families
    aging, 185–187
    "biological time clock," concept
        of, 188
    caregiver "burnout," 193
    caregiving responsibilities,
        189–193
    "cluttered nests," 183
    cohort effect, 185–187
    demographics, 187–189
    diversity of, 184–187
    divorce, 187–188
    "empty nests," 183
    entitlement, 193–194
    future of, 291–295
    gender, 193–194
    gender differences, 187–189

historical emergence of,
    184–185
    middle-age, meaning of,
        183–184
    retirement, 194–197
    social policies, 181–183,
        193–194
    women's responsibilities in,
        188–189
    work, 194–197
    work-leaving, 194–197
middle-class women, 89–91
    first wave feminism, 90–91
    labour during world wars, 91
    maternalists, 90–91
    separate spheres, 90
    size, limit on, 89
    social reform movements, 90
    "two-phase work cycle,"
        100–101
    university education, 91
    women's work, role of, 90
mixed-race unions, 150
Modernization of Benefits and Obli-
    gations Act, 160
modified extended family, 6
monogamy, 7–8
monolithic bias, 55–56, 62
Morgan, Lewis Henry, 36
Mormons, 7
Moslem law, 7
mothers
    labour force, in, 17–18
    maternity benefits, 108
    parental benefits, 108–109
    part-time work, 104–105
    work/family conflicts,
        104–105
Mothers' Allowances, 95, 184–185
Mulroney, Brian, 274
multi-family household, 6
multi-generational households, 99
multiple intimate sexual groups, 34
Murdock, George, 7–8, 38

National Action Committee on the
    Status of Women, 272
National Council of Women, 91,
    272
National Family Violence Resurvey,
    245
National Family Violence Survey,
    250

National Longitudinal Survey of
Children and Youth, 218
National Organization of Women,
202
National Violence Against Women
Survey, 239–240
natural family, 30
natural sex differences, 3
neolocal system, 12
net migration, 125
New Economy, 101
New Home Economics (Becker), 206
non-standard employment, 103
non-status Indians, 124–125
normative regulation, 32
nuclear families, 4, 6–7, 30, 31, 37,
214, 279
feminist theories, 44
immigrants, 139
structural-functionalism, 38,
40

occupational segregation by gender,
103
Old Age Pensions, 96
older families
aging, 185–187
demographics, 187–189
future of, 291–295
retirement, 194–197
social policy interest in,
181–183
work, 194–197
work-leaving, 194–197
Oneida Community, 7
Ontario Early Years Study, 176
Ontario Health Supplement Study,
245
open marriage, 281
Organization of Economic Co-operation and Development, 25
*Origin of the Family, Private Property
and the State* (Engels), 43
"out-of-wedlock," 19, 33
Owentites, 36

paid work, 99
average earnings, 108
blue-collar occupations, 101
children, costs of raising,
105–109
"family friendly policies,"
115–116
family money, 102–104

gendered expectations and
constraints, 108
labour force trends, 100–103
lone-parent families, 108
parental benefits, 108–109
patterns of, 116–118
"pink collar" jobs, 101
professionals, 101
shared earnings, 102–104
"two-phase work cycle,"
100–101
work/family conflicts,
104–108
Palmer, Dorothea, 79
paradoxical gynocentricity, 58
parental leave/benefits, 108–109,
265–266
parents and parenting of grandchildren, 295
Parsons, Talcott, 39, 40, 105, 206,
220, 280, 281
partnering, 145
paternity, 7
patriarchal systems, 11, 60, 260
patriarchal theory, 35–37
patriarchy, 11, 113
patrilineal descent, 11, 12
patrilocal system, 12
Penman Company, 85
physical abuse, 230
physical punishment, 176
plastic sexuality, 149
policies. *See* family policies
political activists, 37
polyandry, 7
polygamous relations, 34
polygamy, 7, 34
polygyny, 7
Post-War Baby Boom, 14
post-War 40s and 50s
baby boom, 93
early marriage, 93–94
Family Allowances, 95
immigration, 130–131
lone-parent families, 93–94
Old Age Pensions, 96
unmarried women in, 93–94
welfare state, development of,
95–96
postmodernism, 47–49
poststructuralist theory, 47–49
poverty, 92, 176–178, 264
Canadian history, in, 79
child, 268, 274

divorce, 187–188, 215–217
high rates in Canada, 290–291
international comparisons,
274
lone-parent families, 25
rate, 25
wife abuse, and, 240
pre-World War I and immigration,
128–130
pre-World War II and immigration,
125–128
precarious employment, 103–104
premarital sexual relations, 148
"primary family," 35
primary parent, 219
pro-capitalistic framework, 36–37
problem families, 56
"procreative family," 36
provincial social assistance/social
service programs, 263–265
psychological abuse, 230
pure relationships, 147–148

Quality of Neighbourhood Life Survey, 240
quasi-childhood, 164
quasi-family members, 53
Quebec
birth rates, 15–16
child benefits, 268
fertility, declining, 273
married women's names, 12
patterns, 155
Quiet Revolution, 16, 80
separation of bed and board,
93
Quebec Act of 1774, 78
Quebec charter groups, 123–125
Quiet Revolution, 16, 80

race, 122
racial endogamy, 150
racial intermarriage, 150
racialized, 123
racism, 81
families and, 45
racist bias, 60, 63
Radcliffe-Brown, Alfred, 280
radical feminist theory, 47
religious weddings, 149
remarriage, 13, 202
age gap between spouses, 26
blended families, 25–26
children, presence of, 225–226

fertility, 222
lone parents, 25
marriage breakdown, risk of, 221–223
prevalence of, 221
stabilizing influence of, 26
repartnering, 202, 216, 221
See also remarriage
reproductive technologies, 57
fatherhood after, 64–65
motherhood after, 65–66
research on family
beginnings of, 279
current, 282
development of, 280–281
liberal feminist assumptions, 282
pioneer of, 279
sociological theories. *See* socio-logical theories
residential school system, 60
residential segregation, 129–130
restructure, 101
retirement, 195–196
revenge of the cradle, 79
rituals, 41
roles, 41
Roman Catholic Church, 36
romantic love, 92, 146
Royal Family, 31
Rubin, Lillian, 147

same-sex couples, 4, 61
See also lesbian and gay
same-sex marriage, 13, 61
Sandwich Generation, 190
Schlesinger, Benjamin, 39
scholarship, bias in. *See* biases
school attendance, 164
Seccombe, Wally, 45
second shift, 111
second wave feminism, 90
Sedgewick, Rev. Robert, 90
selectivity hypothesis, 157
separate spheres, 90
separation. *See* divorce
serial monogamy, 7
service sector, 100
expansion of, 18
sexism, 43
sexist bias, 58–59, 63
sexual assaults, 230
sexual attitudes, 149–150
sexual behaviour, 33, 284
sexual division of labour, 71

sexual frequency, 150
sexual mingling, 36
sexual poverty, 150
sexuality, 147–150
Shaken Baby Syndrome, 244
shared earnings, 102–104
shared parenting, 211, 218
shifting patterns of family, 32–34
Shortt, Elizabeth Smith, 91
sibling violence, 229
definition of, 248
extent of, 250–251
frequency of, 247–248
overlooked, 248–250
risk factors, 251
social learning theory, 251
theories of, 251
Simpson, Nicole, 239
Simpson, O. J., 239
single-parent families. *See* lone-par-ent families
singles advertisements, 148
slapping, 245
social assistance programs, 263–265
social change, and structural func-tionalism, 39
social class, 292
social control, 95
social democratic, 258–260
social institution, 280
social learning theory, 246–247, 252
social policies, 193–194
See also family policies
social reform movements, 90
social reproduction, labour of, 46
social segregation, 129–130
social service programs, 263–265
socialist feminists, 46
socialization, 32
children with special needs, 108
sociological theories
developmental approaches, 42
exchange theory, 42
feminist theories, 42, 43–47
Freudian analysis, 37
history and development of, 34–37
liberal, 37–42
Marxist theories, 42–43
patriarchal theory, 35–36
postmodernism, 47–49
poststructuralist theory, 47–49
structural-functionalism the-ory, 37–40

symbolic interactionism, 40–41
systems theory, 41–42
soft-core abuse, 230
sojourners, 128
spanking, 242–244, 245
Special Joint Committee on Child Custody and Access, 211, 238
Spencer, Herbert, 36
spinsters, 184–185
spiritual abuse, 230
spousal abuse. *See* woman abuse
spousal support, 34
spousal violence, 236
Stacey, Judith, 48
state, 258–260
state intervention, 258–260
See also family policies
gender, variations by, 259
gendered practices, 260
income support programs, 259
political agendas, and, 259
visible minorities, and, 259
state policies. *See* family policies
Statistics Canada
definition of family, 5
divorce rates, 211–215
ethnic data, collection of, 124
monolithic bias, and, 56
multi-family households, 6
two-parent family assumption, 56
unpaid domestic labour, 46, 116–118
Web site, 188
women in work force, 115–116
status Indians, 124–125
Status of Women Canada, 211
stem family, 279
See also extended families
stepfamilies. *See* blended families
Strange Situation Test, 167–168
structural-functionalism theory, 37–40
subsistence labour, 101
Suffrage Movement, 205–206
support, 23, 93, 210, 282
child support, 215–217
enforcement of, 263
spousal support, 34
surnames, 12
sweatshops, 86
Sweden, legal marriage rate in, 17
symbolic interactionism, 40–41
systems theory, 41–42

Tchambuli of New Guinea, 11
teleworking, 285
temperance, 92
temporary maternity leaves, 102
The Anti-Social Family (Barrett and McIntosh), 30
The Family Among the Australian Aborigines (Malinowski), 38
The Feminist Mystique (Friedan), 214
The War Against the Family (Gairdner), 30
The War over the Family (Berger and Berger), 29–30
Third United Nations World Conference on Women, 46
three-generation household, 6
time crunch, 288
"traditional family," 71, 165, 185
   arguments for, 29–30
   lesbian and gay family relationships, and, 29
treaties, 76
trial marriage, 208
two-parent families, 56
Tylor, E. B., 36

unemployment, 92
Unemployment Insurance Act, 108, 265
unemployment rate, 25
unionization, 114
United Nations, 46
United Nations Convention on the Rights of the Child, 176
universal human grouping, 38
unpaid work
   childcare, 111
   domestic labour. *See* division of labour; domestic labour
   "emotional work," 111
   "kin keeping," 111
   research on, 111
   time-use/time-budget studies, 111
   women's responsibility for, 111
unstable family, 279
Upper Canada, settlement of, 125
urbanization, 84–89
Vanier Institute of the Family, 104
variations in family life, 4
verbal abuse, 230
video dating, 148
Violence Against Women Survey, 230

violence begets violence, 246
violence in families. *See* family violence

wages, 96
Web of Exclusion Model, 241
wedding traditions, 149
welfare. *See* provincial social assistance/social service programs
welfare rates, 264
welfare state, 95–96, 119, 258–260
Wente, Margaret, 230
Westermark, E., 36
Whitton, Charlotte, 91
widowhood, 184, 187
wife beating, 236
Wollstonecraft, Mary, 205
woman abuse, 236
   Aboriginal peoples, 240
   extent of, 239–241
   intimate femicide, 239
   male peer support model, 241–242
   poverty, and, 240
   public awareness of, 240
   rape, 234–235
   terminology, 238–239
   theories of, 240–242
   trivialization of, 240
woman battering, 236
women, 48
   Aboriginal, 74–75
   abuse of. *See* woman abuse
   average earnings, 108
   caregiving responsibilities, 189–193
   childhood victimization and later crime, 246
   colour, of, 45
   dating, 147–150
   eldercare, 190
   emotional support, 191–193
   equal rights for, 91
   Factory Acts, effect of, 86
   high earnings, and, 102
   income and divorce, 23
   increased participation in labour force, 101–103
   labour force, in, 17–18
   life expectancy, 184
   middle-class. *See* middle-class women
   mothers, as. *See* mothers
   motives for violence, 238–239

"non-traditional" jobs, and, 288
responsibilities in middle-aged families, 188–189
Sandwich Generation, 190
self-defence, 238
social policy, claims on, 194
spousal support, 34
subordination of, 33, 35
voting rights, 91
Women's Christian Temperance Union, 272
women's double workload, 286
Women's Legal Action and Education Fund (LEAF), 272
women's rights, 205
work, 194
   See also paid work; unpaid work
work/family conflicts, 104–108, 289
workaholics, 103
working class, 35
   expansion of, 84–89
working income supplement, 268
workplace policies, absence of, 195
World Ethnographic Sample (Murdock), 7